Advanced Textbooks in Economics

Series Editors: C. J. Bliss *and* M.D. Intriligator

Currently Available:

PRICING AND PRICE REGULATION

ADVANCED TEXTBOOKS IN ECONOMICS

VOLUME 34

Editors:

C. J. BLISS

M. D. INTRILIGATOR

Advisory Editors:

W. A. BROCK

D. W. JORGENSON

A. P. KIRMAN

J.-J. LAFFONT

J.-F. RICHARD

ELSEVIER
Amsterdam – Lausanne – New York – Oxford – Shannon – Tokyo

PRICING AND PRICE REGULATION

An Economic Theory for Public Enterprises and Public Utilities

---

DIETER BÖS

Institute of Economics
University of Bonn
Germany

1994

ELSEVIER
Amsterdam – Lausanne – New York – Oxford – Shannon – Tokyo

ELSEVIER SCIENCE B.V.
Sara Burgerhartstraat 25
P.O. Box 211, 1000 AE Amsterdam, The Netherlands

Library of Congress Cataloging-in-Publication Data

Bös, Dieter.
    Pricing and price regulation : an economic theory for public
enterprises and public utilities / Dieter Bös. -- [3rd ed.]
        p.   cm. -- (Advanced textbooks in economics ; v. 34)
    Includes bibliographical references and index.
    ISBN 0-444-88478-5 (acid-free paper)
    1. Pricing. 2. Price regulation. 3. Government business
enterprises--Prices. 4. Public utilities--Prices.   I. Title.
II. Series.
HF5416.5.B67   1994
338.5'26--dc20   94-36208
                                                            CIP

                              HF
                              5416.5
                              .B67
                              1994

First edition 1986: 'Public Enterprise Economics'
Second, revised edition 1989
Third, completely revised edition 1994: published under the title 'Pricing and Price Regulation'

ISBN: 0 444 88478 5

This book is printed on acid-free paper.

Printed in The Netherlands

INTRODUCTION TO THE SERIES

The aim of the series is to cover topics in economics, mathematical economics and econometrics, at a level suitable for graduate students or final year undergraduates specializing in economics. There is at any time much material that has become well established in journal papers and discussion series which still awaits a clear, self-contained treatment that can easily be mastered by students without considerable preparation or extra reading. Leading specialists will be invited to contribute volumes to fill such gaps. Primary emphasis will be placed on clarity, comprehensive coverage of sensibly defined areas, and insight into fundamentals, but original ideas will be not be excluded. Certain volumes will therefore add to existing knowledge, while others will serve as a means of communicating both known and new ideas in a way that will inspire and attract students not already familiar with the subject matter concerned.

The Editors

An Overview of the Contents of this Book

Part One   The Basic Pricing Model

Presents a full-information general equilibrium model of an economy where one sector applies special pricing rules which do not follow from unconstrained profit maximization; the model is based on Boiteux (1956) and has been developed further by Hagen (1979) and Bös (in this book since its first edition 1986).

Part Two   Pricing Policies for Welfare Maximization

Thoroughly discusses the welfare-economic benchmark rules, for instance marginal-cost pricing, Ramsey and Feldstein pricing. Also deals with optimal pricing in the presence of rationed labor markets, with peak-load pricing and with the problem of optimal quality of the goods provided.

Part Three   Pricing Policies for Political and Bureaucratic Aims

Analyzes the pricing policies of vote-seeking politicians, empire-building bureaucrats, output-maximizing and energy-saving public utilities.

Part Four   Price Regulation

Explains why rate-of-return regulation has recently been replaced by price-cap regulation. Also explains why many simple rules, like yardstick regulation, fail to achieve optimal prices, which shows that it is quite complicated to induce managers truthfully to reveal their private information. How this can be properly done is shown in various principal-agent models on regulation with uncertain costs, uncertain demand and with soft budget constraints.

What is New in this Book?

This book builds upon the second edition of my book on 'Public Enterprise Economics'.[1] However, it is more than a mere third edition, hence the new title. The most noticeable innovation is the inclusion of the new theories on regulation under asymmetric information, on soft budget constraints and on mixed markets, which are treated in the new part four of the book. Since the book should not become too voluminous, I decided to drop the empirical part on London Transport (part four of the second edition of 'Public Enterprise Economics'). After all, by publishing this empirical application in the first and in the second edition, I have made my point that the theoretical approaches can be applied in practice.

However, writing the new part four was not the only major change. I also revised all the chapters I had published before and rewrote parts of them completely. Compared with the second edition of 'Public Enterprise Economics', about fifty percent of the text has been newly written.[2] Of the previous references 85 have been dropped and replaced by 225 new ones, mainly from the eighties and nineties.

New passages of the book, which should be of particular interest for the reader, provide answers to the following questions:

- what is the background of the new wave of privatization in Western economies and in transition economies? (pp. 18–34)

- what is the present state of the debate on the efficiency of public enterprises compared with private firms? (pp. 50–7)

- when does Ramsey-pricing lead to general equilibrium and to Pareto optimality? (pp. 135–7)

- which prices should be charged for publicly provided intermediate goods? (pp. 156–66)

---

[1] Advanced Textbooks in Economics, Vol. 23, Amsterdam: North-Holland 1989.

[2] I gratefully acknowledge helpful comments on earlier drafts of the new passages of this book by Giacomo Corneo, Monique Ebell, Maurice Garner, Gábor Gyárfás, Kåre Hagen, Nico Hansen, Eckhard Janeba, Günther Lang, Christoph Lülfesmann, Kristina Kostial, Lorenz Nett, Wolfgang Peters, Ray Rees, Peter Ruys, Georg Tillmann. The usual disclaimer holds. I am also indebted to Lydia Danner for faultlessly preparing the camera-ready manuscript and to Michael Ackermann for drawing the figures. The Special Research Unit 303 at the University of Bonn provided financial support.

- can welfare-optimal prices be achieved by simple rules? (pp. 249–68)

- to what extent can yardstick competition be used to regulate public utilities? (pp. 259–63)

- is price-cap regulation better than rate-of-return regulation? (pp. 269–88)

- how should a regulator proceed who is not perfectly informed about cost- or demand-side characteristics of the regulated firm? (pp. 289–340)

- how do soft budget constraints affect managerial effort and government control of regulated firms? (pp. 341–52)

- what are the optimal non-linear prices for the products of regulated firms? (pp. 353–67)

- is it possible to achieve X-efficiency by compensating the manager according to a performance-related or profit-related linear incentive pay? (pp. 371–81)

- does competition from private firms really spur public enterprises? (pp. 389–99)

- how far have the privatization activities of the past decade reduced the public-enterprise sector in various European countries? (pp. 400–3)

Bonn, July 1994   Dieter Bös

Technical Note

Formulas are indicated by a number which refers to the order in which they appear within one chapter. When reference is made, say to equation (25), it is always the equation of the same chapter. References to formulas of other chapters are made by using two numbers, the first referring to the chapter and the second to the order within the chapter. Equation (8–2) is thus the second equation of chapter 8.

Contents

Part Two   Normative Theory
Pricing Policies for Welfare Maximization

A   *Basic Rules*

B   *Intermediate Goods*

C   *Adjustment to Rationed Markets*

1
Introduction

In this book we are dealing with an economy where one sector applies special pricing rules which do not follow from unconstrained profit maximization. This sector is embedded in a market economy of the US or Western European type. The special pricing rules are determined by the interplay of state institutions and representatives of an enterprise. The prices could either refer to goods produced by a public enterprise or by a regulated private enterprise. In both cases there is a mixture of political and economic determinants of the enterprises' activities as compared to the mainly commercial determinants of the activities of private unregulated enterprises. In several European countries, although privatization may have reduced the extent to which prices are politically determined, the privatizing politicians intentionally did not eliminate the political hold on the utilities entirely.[1]

If state institutions are fully informed, they can monitor the enterprise perfectly. Therefore the management of the enterprise can be forced to operate in the direct interest of the state institution. In other words, *pricing* can be entrusted to the board of the enterprise because of the perfect control exerted by the state institution. This book presents a general economic theory which covers all of the various possible cases of such pricing decisions. This theory has its roots in the French literature on government planning in a market economy; in particular in Boiteux's seminal approach.

If, on the other hand, state institutions are not fully informed, perfect control of the management is impossible. Only indirectly can the management be induced to act in the interest of the monitoring state institution. Typically, the management will not comply fully, even if most cleverly designed incentive incomes are paid. This is the subject of many recently developed theories of *price regulation*. This book presents the regulator's decisions in the framework of a similarly general economic theory as applied to the full-information setting. This is an obvious choice of modelling because it makes it possible to draw on the well-developed results of pricing under full information when dealing with price regulation under asymmetric information.

To avoid clumsy terminology, I shall often speak of 'public enterprise' where the text can equally well be understood to be dealing with a regulated

---

[1] 'Public enterprise' and 'public utility' are defined in an overlapping way. There are many public utilities which are public enterprises, in particular in Europe. However, in the US and the UK public utilities typically are privately-owned regulated enterprises.

public utility which is privately owned.[2] This will particularly be the case in the 'pricing' parts of the book (chapters 2–23) because the underlying French planning theory concentrated on publicly owned firms. In the 'price-regulation' part (chapters 24–34) I shall typically speak of a 'regulated firm' or 'public utility'. Both terms are meant to encompass both publicly and privately owned firms.

1.1 Normative and Positive Theory

1.1.1 The Objectives

It is the government which is the driving force behind the special pricing rules treated in this book. Now, *government usually does not aim to maximize profits*. This negative assertion allows for different positive statements regarding the government's objectives:

(i) Government ought to maximize welfare. This statement is the basis of a *normative economic theory of pricing and price regulation*. 'Normative' means that the application of the respective pricing rules can be justified by some higher-order value judgments as formally expressed by social welfare functions. As 'ought' implies 'can', normative pricing rules are empirically applicable. There are many examples where welfare-maximizing pricing has actually been applied.[3] On the other hand, it must be admitted that there are many cases where prescriptions of the welfare kind failed in practice.[4] However, even if practical applications might have failed on several occasions, normative theory of pricing and price regulation is extremely important because it presents those *benchmark models* needed for a critical evaluation of public or regulated firms' day-to-day operations. After presenting the basic pricing model in part I of the book, we will turn to a detailed treatment of pricing policies for welfare maximization, deriving the most important normative pricing principles in part II.[5] The normative theory of price regulation is included in part IV of the book.

It may be noted that in the full-information setting of part II the government's ability fully to control the firm makes it unnecessary to deal with managerial objectives which differ from the government's. This is different in

---

[2] The dichotomy of a public firm and the private sector in such a case is replaced by the dichotomy of a privately-owned regulated utility and the unregulated private sector and all formulations in the text must be read accordingly.

[3] See, for example, Quoilin (1976) on Electricité de France.

[4] See, for instance, the NEDO-report (1976) on British nationalized enterprises.

[5] In the first and in the second edition of this book the empirical applicability of normative theory was illustrated in a special part of the book, using London Transport data. In the present edition these empirical chapters have been dropped.

the asymmetric-information setting of part IV, where the manager has some private information which he uses to pursue his own objective, for instance maximization of his personal income, thus forcing the welfare-maximizing regulator into a sort of compromise between welfare and managerial utility.

(ii) Government has particular political or bureaucratic objectives. Such objectives are the basis of a *positive theory of pricing and price regulation*. 'Positive' means that the respective objective functions are meant as an actual description of economic reality: politicians try to win votes, bureaucrats attempt to build their own empires, or to maximize output, to give only a few examples. Price setting rules of the positive type cannot be justified by means of higher-order value judgments. But they are, of course, a good basis for an analytical investigation of prices which have actually been charged by public or regulated firms. The theory of positive pricing rules will be presented in part III of the book,[6] the positive theory of price regulation is included in part IV of the book.[7]

Once again, in the full-information setting of part III, managerial objectives which differ from the government's are irrelevant because the government controls everything. If, say, a public enterprise maximizes output, then this is the government's objective, even if it was the management which invented the concept and persuaded the government. In other words: in the full-information models there is always only one objective and this objective is the government's. This is different in the asymmetric-information setting of part IV: since perfect control is impossible, we always have to consider both the objective of the government regulator and the deviating objective of the management.

1.1.2 Incentives and Information

The traditional theory, as presented in parts II and III of this book,[8] assumes that there is only one objective which matters for the decisions of the public enterprise. Two alternative explanations lend themselves to make this strong assumption plausible:

- first, the various actors engaged in public-sector pricing and investment are assumed to be interested in the same objective:[9] the government officials

---

[6] The reader who is interested in the empirical applicability of positive pricing rules, may once again be referred to the first and the second edition of this book.

[7] See chapter 33 below.

[8] With the basic outline of the model presented in chapters 3 and 4 below.

[9] This idea could be taken as a justification for the civil-servant status of employees in public enterprises (where it is still found). According to this hypothesis, civil servants are willing to accept a higher degree of social responsibility than regular private-law employees.

who monitor the enterprise, the senior management of the enterprise, the accountants, the secretaries, all feel as if they belong to a community which adheres to the same objective, say welfare or some other social objective.

• second, the government officials are fully informed about everything in the firm and hence succeed in forcing all other actors into following the governmental instructions.

Both justifications have been challenged by the recent theories on regulation which will be treated in part IV of the book. First, these theories take it for granted that each of the various actors, whose interplay is responsible for pricing and investment, follows its own objective: government representatives may be interested in welfare, or in votes, bureaucratic regulators in large budgets, managers of the enterprise in receiving a high income for low effort. Second, the officials who regulate a firm with respect to prices, quality, market entry etc., are assumed to be imperfectly informed about particular circumstances which determine costs or demand. Moreover, they are not able to observe managerial effort or, at least not able to verify the managerial effort level before a court. The managers in the firm, however, are perfectly informed about all cost or demand characteristics and, of course, about their own effort. Because of this informational advantage of the managers, the regulator cannot directly force them to exert that level of effort which would be optimal from the regulator's point of view. The managers will rather use their advantage to ensure themselves a higher income and to exert less effort than would be the case if the government regulator were fully informed. The best the regulator can do is to pay an incentive-compatible income to the manager: treat the manager as if you would have to ask him to tell you the truth about the hidden information.[10] The incentive-compatible income, therefore, includes both a payment for the managerial effort and an information rent.

It should be mentioned that the full-information models of parts II and III of the book remain very important in spite of their shortcomings on the information and incentive side. They still are ideal for use as benchmark models with which to compare the asymmetric-information models of part IV of the book. Pricing rules of part IV look like pricing rules of part II or III, however, they include some correction terms which take account of the regulator's imperfect information. This similarity of pricing rules is mainly caused by the similarity of constraints facing public enterprises (public utilities) in *all* parts of the book. The requirement of market clearing, the technology, budgetary constraints, matter in quite the same way in full-information models as in asymmetric-information models.

---

[10] This formulation refers to the so-called revelation principle, for details see section 28.1.

1.1.3 The Constraints

(i) Constraints I: Markets

Public enterprises and public utilities supply private goods, i.e. goods which customers buy in different quantities.[11] These goods are sold at the market and, accordingly, the firm has to consider the demand side of the market and has to cope with actual or potential competitors on the supply side.

Public monopolies are often obliged to cover all *demand* at a given price, even if a deficit results. Such a strict constraint would, of course, never be imposed on private enterprises which are usually assumed to stop production if losses occur in the long run. On the other hand we should not forget the many cases of consumers left unserved by public monopolies, as they were in the past by the telephone administrations in Britain, Germany, and France due to capital restrictions imposed by governments. In Britain the quality of the services of British Rail and the London Underground is being impaired by similar restrictions. The acceptance of excess peak demand in electricity, transportation or telephone services may even be welfare optimal.[12]

Competition on the *supply* side is often eliminated if a public monopoly is sheltered against potential market entrants. Such sheltering may be justified on welfare grounds if the monopoly behaves appropriately. Otherwise, barriers to entry should be abolished to force the monopoly into entry-resistant policies which can be shown to be welfare optimal under certain assumptions (Baumol–Bailey–Willig, 1977). On the other hand, there are many public enterprises in oligopolistic competition with private ones or even in nearly perfect competition. Examples are nationalized and private automobile companies or the small communal breweries in Germany which compete with the many private ones. In these cases, the market forces must be explicitly taken into account by the enterprise and, therefore, by any model of pricing and price regulation.

When buying their inputs, on the other hand, public enterprises and public utilities typically have to compete for blue and white collar staff with private firms whereas they may be monopsonistic with respect to capital inputs, e.g. if state railways buy locomotives.

(ii) Constraints II: Production

In our theoretical approaches we will postulate efficient production by all firms which are explicitly considered in the models. This implies the absence

---

[11] Typical public goods like defense or the legal system are not supplied by enterprises; see below subsection 1.2.2 (i).

[12] See chapter 15.

of production slack, that is, the enterprises operate along the production-possibility frontier. There are only a few exceptions where we shall explicitly deal with production slack:

- in chapter 2 we shall consider several theories on production slack and several empirical approaches comparing the efficiency of production in public and private enterprises;
- in chapters 5 and 6 we will show that increasing production slack may even be welfare-improving under certain assumptions of the enterprise's feasible policies.

(iii)   Constraints III: Profits

Enterprises, which are owned or regulated by the government, generally are not expected to fully exploit their monopoly power. This holds in particular for public utilities, where quite often prices that exactly cover costs are taken as an indicator of public-spirited motives. Hence, the explicit consideration of a profit constraint is characteristic when it comes to government's determination of special pricing principles. Various forms of profit constraints have been used in theory and practice, from the direct prescription of a maximum difference between revenue and costs, to the imposition of a maximum rate of return or explicit price caps.

There are major differences between publicly and privately owned firms when it comes to profit constraints. First, a regulator must not enforce prices which are so low that they result in bankruptcy of a privately owned firm. Hence, cost-covering prices are the lowest which can be imposed on the firm. In public enterprises, even long-run deficits are possible and have been upheld by government subsidies in many cases. Second, profits of privately owned utilities go to the private owners. If the utilities are publicly owned, their profits are government revenues which can be used for public expenditures, for the reduction of the tax burden or of public debt. Deficits, on the other hand, have to be paid from taxpayers' money or from increased public debt. Hence, the shadow price of public funds matters when the government imposes a particular profit constraint on a public enterprise.

Private unregulated firms, to draw a comparison, are typically expected to maximize profits. Only in exceptional cases, as a temporary relief, does government intervene in the case of private enterprises' deficits. Chrysler in the United States and AEG in Germany are good examples from the early eighties.

(iv)   Constraints IV: Managerial Participation and Incentive Compatibility

The traditional public-enterprise models describe a command economy, where some fully-informed institution decides on prices and inputs. The readiness of the management of the enterprise actually to implement this command optimum is not challenged in these models and, consequently, it does not seem necessary explicitly to consider the question of how to ensure the management's participation in the practical realization of the optimum. Meanwhile, industrial-organization-type modelling has accentuated the interplay of the various actors whose decisions jointly lead to particular prices and investments. In models of this type it becomes important explicitly to consider the managerial-participation constraint, what income a manager must be offered to attract him to join the firm or, alternatively, what income he must be paid to guarantee he does not leave the firm. Participation constraints are meaningful both in full-information benchmark models and in asymmetric-information models.

In contrast, incentive-compatibility constraints are only necessary in asymmetric-information models. While the exact formulation of an incentive-compatibility constraint is difficult and will be left until chapter 28 below, a simple example might clarify the meaning of incentive compatibility. Assume that a welfare-maximizing government (regulator) knows that there exist more efficient and less efficient firms, but when coming to regulate a particular firm it does not know the exact efficiency type of this firm. Hence the manager could cheat by pretending to run a low-efficiency firm whence the output is due to his very high effort, whereas in fact he runs a high-efficiency firm and only exerts a low level of effort. Since both the efficiency type of the firm and the exerted effort are unobservable to the regulator, he could not detect such a lie. To avoid being cheated, the regulator must pay a compensation to the manager which induces him to exert just that level of effort which is welfare optimal for his type of efficiency.

*

There may exist many further constraints on public-enterprise policy, for instance the obligation not to dismiss as many workers as economically optimal or not to increase prices until after the next election. A good contemporary example might be the European Commission's rules[13] on public procurement of such manufactures as telecommunications equipment that authorize the public utilities (mostly public enterprises) to pay a premium for equipment of Community origin.

Such provisions seem to be typical for public enterprises. Sometimes private firms have to cope with similar types of troublesome government intervention. In public enterprises, however, the government will more often intervene directly, whereas in private enterprises indirect instruments of subsidization and moral suasion will prevail.

---

[13] Remember how these rules have incensed the USA.

1.2   The Institutional Setting

1.2.1   Range of Activity

Public enterprises can be found in almost every sphere of economic activity.[14]
However, looking across countries, there are particular areas where public enterprises are more likely to be found than in others. These areas are closely
associated with supplying *essential goods and services*, either to industries or
directly to consumers. 'Essential' means that they cannot be cut off without
danger of total or partial collapse of an economy. Starting from an allocative
point of view, we stress the importance of these goods and services as part
of the *infrastructure* for producers and consumers. Starting from a distributional point of view, we would have to stress their importance for providing
consumers with the *necessities of life*.

Essential goods and services are almost the same in all industrialized
countries. Hence, it is possible to present a fairly general basic catalogue of
candidates for public enterprises. How many of these become public enterprises differs from country to country, as do the institutional arrangements
which are used to attain the goals mentioned above (ranging from the establishment of public enterprises to the regulation of private enterprises).

The basic catalogue is as follows:

(i)   *Public utilities*, i.e. energy, communication and transportation.
Examples include:

- electricity, gas, water,
- telecommunications, postal services,
- radio, TV,
- airlines, railroads, urban public transport, toll bridges,
- stockyards, refuse collection.

The prices of public utilities are subject to government intervention in most
Western countries. In Europe they tend to be public enterprises; some of them
recently have become private regulated firms, in particular in the UK. In the
United States, they are usually either regulated enterprises (both public and
private) or public enterprises.

(ii)   *Basic goods industries*, producing coal, oil, atomic energy and steel.
Nationalized enterprises in these branches can be found in most Western European countries. The percentages of nationalized enterprises in these branches
do, however, vary from country to country, Austria, France, Italy and Spain
being the countries with the highest percentages.

---

[14] The following are some examples, presented in alphabetic order: automobiles (Renault), beer (State Hofbräuhaus in Munich), books (government printing offices), china
(Royal Prussian china manufacture in Berlin), cigarettes (public monopolies in France and
in Austria) etc.

(iii) *Finance*. Saving-banks are often established as local public enterprises, whence their interest rates are public prices. In most European countries there are at least some publicly owned banks, and in some countries – Austria, Italy, France – more extensive nationalization has taken place.[15] Public insurance companies are extensively regulated in most countries, from rates to terms of policies and the calculation of risks and reserves.

(iv) *Education and health*. Here we refer to tuition and fees at publicly owned schools and universities and the pricing of publicly owned hospitals.

1.2.2 More Precise Definitions[16]

The responsibility for pricing and investment is shared between the enterprise and the government. Acting for the enterprise is its management which in many parts of this book will be called the 'board' of the enterprise. Acting for the government are appropriate government agencies, appointed by federal, state or local governments, or other appropriate public authorities.[17]

Because of this responsibility sharing, the position of any public enterprise can only be described adequately by

- characterizing the enterprise itself,
- characterizing the relevant government agency, and
- characterizing the ways government influences the enterprise.

(i) Characterization of the Enterprise

The enterprise is typically characterized as some autonomous entity which produces or distributes goods or services, and sells them either to producers or consumers at a price which may or may not cover costs.[18] This is a technological view of an enterprise, as is usual in microeconomics. This approach is

---

[15] It is debatable whether the central banks are public enterprises. It is normal for central banks not to figure prominently as public enterprises, yet they are accepted as such in Britain, France, Germany and other European countries. The Federal Reserve Bank in the United States typically is not regarded as public enterprise.

[16] Aharoni (1986) provides a good institutional overview of public enterprises. A survey of public enterprises in nine European countries is given in Parris, Pestieau and Saynor (1987). For a similar institutional overview of US regulated industries see the new edition of the classic book by Kahn (1988), and Weiss–Klass (1986) which is an interesting collection of case studies.

[17] For example social insurance institutions: if such an institution owns a hospital or a clinic, the relevant 'government agency' of our public-pricing models is appointed by this institution.

[18] This definition excludes cases like defense, public administration or the legal system where publicly produced goods or services are not sold to producers or consumers. It includes, however, cases of sale at zero prices. (Local public transportation is, for the purposes of this study, regarded as an enterprise, even if zero tariffs are applied.)

acceptable as far as the traditional theory of public enterprises is concerned. When it comes to the regulation of public utilities, it becomes very important to characterize the enterprise not only by its technology, but also by its internal decision structures as the industrial-organization literature does.[19]

There is not much organizational diversity as far as private regulated firms are concerned: they are typically organized as limited-liability companies. In contrast, public enterprises have quite diverse legal or corporate forms, such as departmental agencies, public corporations, or state companies.[20]

Departmental agencies do not have a separate legal personality. A substantial proportion of their total staff are civil servants and their revenue account is incorporated into the government's budget, albeit, usually, in highly summarized form. They are, however, typically relieved of some elements of the normal system of governmental control and accountability. (The PTT in Austria and the Vattenfallsverket in Sweden offer examples.)

Public corporations are institutions of public law with a separate legal personality, usually created by a specific law or decree which defines the corporation's powers and duties (and also the powers and duties of the government and of any other institutions, such as consumers' consultative councils, concerned with the oversight of the corporation). Their characteristic mode of financing is by loans or allotments of capital (such as 'dotations' in France) and not by the issue of shares or stock. Such corporations are numerous in France, in Italy (where the enti di gestioni belong to this type of public enterprise) and in the USA. In Germany, this type of public enterprise is unusual.

State companies are private-law institutions, etablished under the ordinary company law, which are directly or indirectly controlled by government by virtue of its ownership of the shares, whether wholly or in part. What minimum proportion of the total share issue is regarded as conferring sufficient control for the company to be deemed a state company varies from country

---

[19] The question of how to define a firm has recently been intensively discussed in the IO-literature, see for instance Holmström–Tirole (1989), Hart–Moore (1990), and Moore (1992). In his IO-textbook Tirole (1988: 15–34) gives a good overview. He distinguishes between:

(i) the technological view. It concentrates on the properties of the production function; for the organization and size of a firm, economies of scale and scope are relevant.

(ii) the contractual view. It considers the essence of the firm to be the long-run arrangement between its units; particularly well-known is Williamson's approach focusing on the hazards of idiosyncratic exchange and on asset specificity.

(iii) the incomplete-contracting view. It 'looks at the firm as a particular way of specifying what is to be done in the event of contingencies not foreseen in a contract.' (Tirole, 1988: 16.) Ownership of machines and employment contracts determine the distribution of power within the firms.

[20] For details see Hanson (1965); Garner (1983).

to country and across international classifications. In the eyes of the European Economic Commission, over 50 percent would normally be considered necessary. This type of public enterprise is found almost worldwide and abundantly – for example, Air France, Deutsche Bahn (German Rail), the Empresa Nacional de Electricidad in Spain, and the 'nationalized industries' in Austria.

(ii)   Characterization of the Institutions of Control and Regulation

The institutions which control public enterprises vary widely: parliament, courts, ministries, special bodies or particular courts of auditing being solely or jointly responsible according to the law of the country concerned. One may question the merits of parliament and of the courts as controlling agencies of public enterprises, because parliamentary control might accentuate political aspects too much, and the courts' control might accentuate political aspects too little.

The institutions which regulate privately-owned public utilities typically do not vary so widely. Regulation is entrusted either to ministers or to special regulatory bodies like OFTEL or OFGAS in the UK. Special regulatory bodies, in such a case, are set up when privatizing the utilities to keep the firms apart from policial influences. The newly established principal-agent relationship between the minister who has to supervise a regulatory body and the regulator who is the head of this body, deserves particular attention.

(iii)   Characterization of the Ways in which Control or Regulation may Influence an Enterprise

The appropriate authorities may exercise control or regulation

• directly, by making entrepreneurial decisions, for instance on prices, on investment programs, on employment, on managerial incomes, or on external financing;
• directly, by imposing constraints on the enterprise, like profit constraints which prevent the enterprise from exploiting a monopoly position by high prices, or employment constraints which prevent the enterprise from dismissing as many employees as it would like to;
• indirectly, ex ante, by appointing the enterprise's board (in the case of partial ownership by appointing enough members of the board to ensure effective control);
• indirectly, ex post, by financial and managerial auditing; or
• indirectly, ex post, by criticisms and inquiry as well as by adjudication in disputes with third parties, e.g. consumers.

This book concentrates on the particular problems of direct control and regulation. We do not intend to give any theoretical explanations of appointments to enterprises' staffs or of auditing. If a separate regulatory body is set up, the appointment of the regulator is an important political decision whose explicit treatment also is beyond the scope of this book.

1.2.3   Institutional Diversity Versus Theoretical Abstraction

Various institutions may engage in exercising control or regulation, and the instruments used may differ from country to country. To present a general theory we must abstract from institutional detail. We will therefore characterize the institutional background by one 'board' (management) and one 'government' (regulator), ignoring specific details.

In the full-information setting of the traditional public-enterprise models, the board may be thought of as the management of a single public enterprise or group of related public enterprises, or as the composite management of the total public-enterprise sector. Typically, our economic models fit all these interpretations. For convenience, however, we will always speak of *the* public enterprise, public production or public supply. The government may be interpreted accordingly as the sponsoring department of a single public enterprise or group of public enterprises, or as the representative government agency of the public sector. Again for convenience, we will only speak of *the* government.

In the asymmetric-information setting of regulatory policy such a generalization typically cannot be applied. Private information of the manager is typically firm-specific and therefore incentive compatibility can only refer to the manager's revealing the truth about some firm-specific characteristics of costs or demand. Simultaneous regulation of more than one firm is only meaningful if these firms are very similar, ideally identical. Then the regulator can use information from manager A to regulate manager B and vice versa (for instance by applying yardstick regulation).[21]

1.3   Socialization of Commodities

A commodity is defined as socialized if every consumer is given equal access to the consumption of the good or service regardless of his income or wealth. Such a socialization has been suggested, and often applied, for medical treatment, for primary and secondary education, in European countries also for universities and opera houses. The means by which socialization is performed vary widely. Common features are low price or zero price policy and a supply of sufficient quantities.

Institutionally, the government may establish public production and meet demand at very low or zero prices. Examples are museums, schools, and universities in Europe. Alternatively, production may remain in private hands,

---

[21]   See below section 24.2.4.

but the government purchases the goods and reallocates the supply to consumers. It is equally possible that consumers themselves purchase the commodities, the government paying subsidies either to the private producers or to the consumers. The financial means for the necessary subsidization come from general or special taxation.[22]

Socialization gives equal access. However, the actual consumption will typically vary among consumers (Wilson–Katz, 1983). Therefore, socialized commodities should not be treated as public goods in the Samuelson sense (as in Usher, 1977). In any model it is sufficient to allow the public enterprise to be run at a high deficit[23] in order to achieve prices which are low enough to allow the poor to buy the same quantity as the rich if they want to. In limiting cases, therefore, the prices must be zero. The obligation to meet all demand at these prices is part of the market-clearing conditions of our model.

We should, however, understand the rationale of Usher's (1977) treatment of socialized commodities as public goods in the Samuelson sense. There is a public-good component included in the provision of health care or education, at zero or low prices. Such commodities have been socialized following an egalitarian objective: equal education, equal medical care for everybody are postulates which imply

- a public-good component, because equality seems desirable from a normative point of view;
- a redistributional objective, such as to avoid worse medical treatment or worse education for the poor;
- a merit-want[24] component, so as to achieve certain consumed quantities notwithstanding differing individual preferences.

However, we should not confuse the above ethical concept with the reality of public enterprises. In practice people are given the right to buy different quantities of higher education or health care at particular prices. Hence, any realistic model must treat these socialized commodities as private goods.[25] Such an analysis does not make any difference for our definition of socialization as long as everybody is given equal access.

There is yet another way of allowing for variation in the consumption of goods which are characterized by some public-good properties: we can treat

---

[22] In many European countries there exists a system of governmental health insurance: every income earner has to pay a special tax, the 'health insurance contribution' and the total tax yield is devoted to the subsidization of health care. Acquiring particular health care services costs nothing or a small lump-sum fee only.

[23] In our model the revenue-cost constraint Π° must be chosen sufficiently low.

[24] This term is due to Musgrave (1959) and characterizes cases where the decision of the politician intentionally deviates from the preferences of the consumers.

[25] Drèze and Marchand (1976) take a different view.

the 'public-good' components as particular quality levels which are equal for every consumer and influence the quantity demanded by each individual. By way of examples, schools or hospital services can then be treated as publicly supplied private goods, where the individually varying demand depends on the quality level, prices and individual income.[26] In my view, the above treatment is empirically much more realistic than the assumption of schools or hospital services being public goods, consumed to the same extent by everybody.

The distinction between the consumption of different quantities and the consumption of equal quality levels allows us to avoid the analysis of 'public-good pricing' in this book. We do not consider models which introduce the consumption of equal quantities as a constraint. The most typical examples of pure public goods in the Samuelson sense, namely national defense and the legal system, are not supplied by public *enterprises*. Socialized goods which are supplied by public enterprises can be treated adequately by expressing the public-good component by a quality parameter, giving any consumer the possibility to consume any quantity he wants to.

1.4   Nationalization of Enterprises

Nationalization of an enterprise involves the compulsory transfer of the enterprise from private to public ownership, generally with full compensation.[27] As for the reasons for nationalization measures, Reid and Allen (1970) point out that 'most of the nationalized industries were not taken into public ownership primarily for economic reasons, though there has often been an attempt to include an economic rationale in the decision to nationalize a particular industry'. Let us therefore begin with the most important non-economic reasons, namely the ideological ones.

1.4.1   Ideology

Large-scale nationalization changes the distribution of power within a society. Decisions on prices, investment and technology are taken out of the domain of private entrepreneurs and shifted to people who should be responsible to the public. Thus, large-scale nationalization leads to a new balance between private and public economic power; according to some socialist ideologists to a 'shift in power away from private capital in favour of labour' (Holland, 1978). It fits into this line of reasoning that a powerful motive for nationalization appears to have been resentment – the resentment of the employees against exploitation (in particular that of railwaymen, coalminers, and shipbuilders)

---

[26] See below chapters 16 and 22.

[27] We skip the intricate problems of computing the corporate value as a basis of full (or partial) compensation.

and of citizens and tradespeople against exploitation by monopolistic suppliers (in particular by public utilities).

Recently the international distribution of power has been stressed, favoring nationalization as a means of countering large-scale private enterprise, most of which are multinational (Attali, 1978; Holland, 1975, 1978). Regaining national control over the economy was an influential argument for the French nationalization activities in 1982 (Charzat, 1981). This argument restores the literal meaning of nationalization as an instrument to make the economy 'national'.

Socialist authors, moreover, sometimes regard nationalization as an instrument for achieving 'genuine' industrial democracy. The keyword is 'self-government'; and, as J. Delors (1978) puts it, 'at the base of the pyramid, in the enterprise, the essential self-government function should be assigned to workers and management to extend the idea of community life'. The basis of such ideas seems to be a sort of mystical belief that nationalization might substitute co-operation for conflict and competition, a belief which has a long tradition in the socialist discussions of nationalization.[28] However, even proponents of these ideas know the difficulties in actually bringing about such fundamental changes in the functioning of enterprises and stress the danger of enterprises becoming politically oriented and bureaucratically dominated.[29]

The above outline of the mainstream of socialist discussions indicates that they belong to 'revisionist' approaches, using the traditional socialist terminology. Nationalization is not primarily regarded as a way to achieve an ideologically desired public ownership of the means of production in a step-by-step process. '(The) public enterprise might itself appear socialist in character, but is not. For the French Left today, a formula of nationalization and state intervention not only is not socialist but could be a trap for socialists. Public ownership and state intervention may be necessary means for socialist ends, but are not socialist in themselves' (Attali, 1978: 36–7).

1.4.2 Economic Reasoning

In contemporary Western-type economies both the existence and the establishment of nationalized enterprises have been justified by attempts to show their particular allocational, distributional and stabilization superiority over private enterprises.

---

[28] See for instance the survey of the history of the discussion of nationalization in the British Labour Party in Tivey (1966).

[29] Moreover, there are many alternative means of democratization within privately owned enterprises as the recent discussions on codetermination of employees and shareholders show. For further references see Nutzinger–Backhaus (1988).

(i)   The best-known *allocational* argument justifies public utilities by their being natural monopolies. Such monopolies are characterized by a subadditive cost function and by sustainability (Baumol, 1977): it is cheaper to produce goods by a monopoly than by many firms, and potential market entrants can be held off without predatory measures. In such cases, unregulated private enterprises would exploit the market. Establishing public enterprises should ensure economically or politically desired prices and at the same time guarantee the reliability of supply.

Another allocational argument favors the entrance of public enterprises into competitive markets to maintain or restore decentralization of political and economic control. The public enterprises are conceived as centers of largely independent decision-making authorities oriented towards welfare optimization instead of profit maximization. Such ideas influenced the French nationalization activities in 1982 and the Labour Party Green Paper (1973).[30]

(ii)   The basic *distributional* argument in favor of nationalization stresses the more equal distribution of incomes or wealth which may be brought about by switching from private to public ownership. Most proponents of such an argument overlook the distinction between nationalization, which implies 'full compensation' of the former private owners, and confiscation, which implies no compensation. In case of 'full compensation', ideally the act of nationalization itself would have no influence whatever on the distribution of incomes or wealth. Only in the long run could the replacement of private entrepreneurial managers with salaried bureaucratic managers and of shareholders with rentiers who receive fixed interest income have definite effects on income distribution, arguments which can be traced back to Pigou (1937: 26–7).

The Pigovian arguments hold if all private enterprises are nationalized in a complete transition from capitalism to socialism. If only part of the economy is nationalized, the arguments are only valid if the entrepreneurs are compensated by bonds, the sale of which explicitly is forbidden. Otherwise, the compensated entrepreneurs may even be happy to get rid of their stagnating enterprises,[31] gaining the chance to reinvest the compensation payments in growing industries.

Any discussion on distributional effects of nationalization is, moreover, blurred by differing concepts concerning the computation of 'full' compensation. During the French nationalizations in the early eighties, for example, the first bill of the government (1981) chose a form of computing compensation

---

[30]   The Green Paper proposed the nationalization of 20 to 25 of the 100 leading manufacturing enterprises, in order to give the government an established position in the market using capitalistic market mechanisms to fight capitalistic (and foreign) market exploitation.

[31]   In Germany after World War II Herr Flick was forced to sell his steel industry and coal mining shares whereafter he successfully entered Mercedes and other growing corporations.

payments which afterwards was declared unconstitutional by the Constitutional Council. A second and final nationalization bill (1982) had to choose a new formula. However, the fairness of the 1982-formula afterwards was challenged by Langohr and Viallet (1986) who estimated that the former holders of the nationalized portfolios received a government-legislated takeover premium of about 20 percent over the value of the nationalized portfolio if it had not been nationalized.

Distributional effects of nationalization are not restricted to the shift in ownership and the compensation. Contrary to private firms, public enterprises are often instructed to reduce the prices of goods which are mainly demanded by lower income earners, thereby influencing the personal distribution of real incomes.

It should be noted, finally, that the overall distributional impact of nationalized industries needs more explicit study. As Littlechild (1979) observes, 'the pattern and cost of income redistribution consequent upon nationalisation is neither well known to, or explicitly approved by, society as a whole'.

(iii) Let us now turn to the *stabilization* objectives of nationalization. The long-standing planning tradition in some European market economies, first of all France and the Netherlands, leads to a heavy accentuation of public enterprises' role in the planning procedure. The French socialist author Attali (1978) concludes that planning can only be performed successfully in case of '... control by the state of at least 50 percent of investment. That is the reason why in our Common Programme in France, we propose to nationalize nine of the main private enterprise groups,...'. In 1967, Tinbergen, in his textbook on economic policy, argued that 'the existence of a public sector of some size is a favourable basis for anti-cyclic policies in the field of investment'.

Moreover, anti-cyclic variation of public labor inputs, and of public prices, have often been proposed. In long recessions, however, these policies can be highly disadvantageous, maintaining economic structures instead of allowing the necessary changes to occur – in the European steel industry there have been many situations where these problems have arisen since 1970.

With respect to *monetary policy*, it has been argued that the money supply can be controlled better if a larger part of the financial sector is nationalized. Proponents of the nationalization of banks usually stress the international financial connections which impede control of the national money supply and, thereby, of national economic policy.

1.4.3 Other Reasons

History cannot be treated exhaustively by reasoning in terms of two categories only. Hence, it should be mentioned that nationalization may be enacted for many other reasons, which are neither ideological nor economic.

Consider, for example, the historical explanation of the great 1946/47 Austrian nationalization.[32] At the end of World War II, a great part of Austrian industry was owned by Germans. The German management of those enterprises left Austria during the chaotic weeks of mid-1945 and the provisional Austrian government appointed administrations to keep the enterprises running (or to get them running again). However, the subsequent nationalization acts were not only based on this actual occupation of property which was derelict, at least economically. In Potsdam in 1945, Austria's occupying powers had claimed ownership of German property. Fearing that the occupying powers would confiscate the enterprises, the Austrian parliament unanimously decided to nationalize them. It must be noted that the Austrian parliament, when making that decision, had *an absolute conservative majority*.[33]

1.5 Privatization in Market-Oriented Economies[34]

The eighties and early nineties brought a wave of privatizations, in particular in the United Kingdom.[35] Taking an average of three criteria (employment, gross value added, gross fixed-capital formation), the public enterprise sector in the UK was reduced from just over 16 percent (1982) to 4.5 percent (1991) of the economy.[36] Other market-oriented countries also privatized public firms, although typically on a much smaller scale. In the US, where the state has always owned fewer enterprises than in European countries, a deregulation policy aimed at objectives similar to those of the UK privatization movement. The UK privatizations are of particular interest because they not only included competitive industrial firms, but also public utilities like telecommunications, gas, and electricity, which in Europe had always been considered to be central areas of public-enterprise activity.

Privatization is the partial or total transfer of an enterprise from public to private ownership.[37] As such, it is the precise reverse of nationalization. Neither procedure is embarked upon primarily for economic reasons, though

---

[32] For details see Smekal (1963), Koren (1964).

[33] The reader may be interested to learn the rest of the (hi)story. The Western occupying powers accepted the Austrian decision. The Russians did not accept it, but executed the Potsdam treaty by establishing USIA and SMV as two particular groups of enterprises under Russian leadership. The affected enterprises in the Russian zone of occupation were not given to Austria until the state treaty of 1955. At that time they employed some 50.000 employees, nearly half as many as the other nationalized enterprises.

[34] In this section 1.5, the paragraphs 2–8 are taken from Bös (1991a: 2–5).

[35] A good overview of early UK privatizations is given in Ramanadham (1988) and Vickers and Yarrow (1988). For more recent literature see Foster (1992) and Yarrow (1993).

[36] The reader may be referred to Appendix 1, pp. 400–3, for an international comparison. See also Stevens (1992).

[37] The word 'privatization' has many different meanings. In this section we concentrate

there has often been an attempt to include an economic rationale in the de-cision. However, as this is a book written by an economist, it deals with economic theories of privatization. This does not mean that I am unaware of ideological, purely political, or other arguments in favor of privatization: indeed, some short remarks on political and ideological reasons for privati-zation will help start this section. Then, however, I will turn quickly to the economic reasoning.

Needless to say, it is impossible to have a clear-cut dichotomization be-tween political and ideological reasoning on the one hand and economic rea-soning on the other. Hence, I label an argument as 'political and ideological' if, in my opinion, the argument mainly emphasizes the consequences of priva-tization in the political process and its ideological desirability from the point of view of some political party's platform. Therefore, I consider a reduc-tion of trade-union power primarily as a shift in political power. This does not mean, however, that one can ignore the serious economic, in particular distributional, consequences which may result from such a political move.

1.5.1   Political and Ideological Reasoning

(i)   People's Capitalism

Conservatives regard privatization as a means of democratization because of the resulting more widespread ownership of shares. The 'man in the street' is given the opportunity to own parts of industries of national importance. Power in the economy is reallocated by replacing the government's sole owner-ship with broad-based private ownership. Moreover, distributional objectives may be attained by selling ownership rights to *many* private individuals, in-stead of only to a few institutional shareholders. Furthermore, a subsequent left-wing government cannot easily renationalize a firm if many shares are held by lower-income earners and employees of the firm.

Therefore, the firms to be privatized in Western economies are typically reorganized as joint-stock companies and the shares are sold to the public. Persons of modest means are attracted to these stocks through appropriate government incentives. The typical incentive is the sale of shares at a price well below the attainable market price, as was done in Austria, Germany, and – more recently – the UK (Yarrow, 1986).

With respect to the practical success of a policy of 'people's capitalism', we face ambiguous evidence. Some early privatization activities in Great Britain faced the problem that the small investors sold their shares shortly

---

on one particular concept only: the transfer from public to private ownership. Other forms of privatization, like contracting out, debureaucratization, promotion of competition by market processes, 'cold privatization', etc., are not considered.

after purchasing them in order to enjoy a quick profit. 'Within one month of flotation, the number of shareholders in Amersham had fallen from 62,000 to 10,000; within one year of flotation, the number had fallen from 150,000 to 26,000 in Cable and Wireless (first tranche) and from 158,000 to 27,000 in British Aerospace' (Yarrow, 1986: 357).[38] The resale of shares such as British Telecom, British Gas, and the Trustee Savings Bank has not occurred so quickly. First, the government learned from its earlier mistakes. New shareholders were given loyalty bonuses (vouchers to set against phone or gas bills, one-for-ten bonuses) if they held onto their investment for some time, usually three years. Second, the early privatization activities reached primarily sophisticated speculative shareholders whereas subsequent privatizations reached a broader public. Purchase of shares was made as easy as possible, whereas resale requires a broker.

It remains to be seen how successful the British policy will be in the long run. In early 1989 British Telecom still had 1.2 million 'small' shareholders out of 2.3 million who had bought shares in 1984.[39] British Gas started with 4.5 million shareholders in December 1986 and had 2.5 million shareholders in April 1990.[40] In both cases nearly 50 percent of the shareholders sold their shares within a time span of 4–5 years after privatization. The West-German experience of the early 1960s showed that in the long run the lower-income shareholders did not retain their shares; now the shares are held by 'groups and persons which in any case hold part of their wealth in the form of shares' (von Loesch, 1983: 20). Austrian experience has been similar: 'It is easier to find shares for the people than people for the shares' (J. Bös, 1956: 1).

The French policy of people's shares was successful from the very beginning: 13 months after privatization 78 percent of the buyers were still holding their shares of St Gobain; 11 months after privatization 76 percent still had their shares of Paribas (Ministère de l'Economie, des Finances et de la Privatisation, 1988). The disturbance in the stock exchange in late 1987 led to a French discussion on how to insure lower-income shareholders against possible losses. One of the various possibilities mentioned was the interesting proposal to couple the sale of shares with a resale option.

(ii)   Reducing the Trade-Unions' Influence

The trade-unions' influence will typically be reduced by privatization. By way of an example, it has been argued that the privatization of the British electricity industry among other things aimed at breaking the power of the miners'

---

[38] See also Mayer and Meadowcroft (1985: 50–2).
[39] See the annual reports of British Telecom.
[40] See Pint (1990) and the annual reports of British Gas.

union because the government correctly anticipated that privatized electricity generation companies would increase the use of gas in power stations and also increase imports of coal, thus reducing the size of the British coal industry and, consequently, reducing the importance of the miners' union.[41] Similarly, the first wave of privatization in West Germany some thirty years ago was intended to reduce union power. The present strength of German trade unions, which are adamantly opposed to privatization and exert a strong influence on political parties, is a major impediment to any privatization in West Germany (von Loesch, 1983; Vogelsang, 1988). The German trade unions' opposition to privatization results mainly from the fear that employees in public firms might lose their privileges. These firms' employees may have to face wage reduction in case of privatization (Windisch, 1987: 23). Even worse problems arise in the German railway and postal systems where many employees have civil-servant status which provides job security and generous pension plans (Vogelsang, 1988).

1.5.2 Economic Reasoning

It would be too simple to explain privatization or deregulation policies by the sole reference to Mrs. Thatcher and Mr. Reagan. After all, they had to be elected and reelected, thus their policies reflected the opinions of the majority of voters. These opinions have also been shaped by the economists' profession. In the eighties the opinions of many public economists began intensively to deviate from the Musgravian view which had long been prevalent. The allocation of resources became the field of central interest. Tax theory concentrated nearly exclusively on how to reduce the disincentives from taxation. Theories of public enterprises similarly began to concentrate on the question of how a regulating government could give the best incentives for efficient production in the firm. Internal subsidization was increasingly considered undesirable, as was any form of pricing with redistributive features. Furthermore, stabilization by public enterprises fell into disapproval. Monetary policy of the Friedman type was recommended as more appropriate for the achievement of the desired stable growth of an economy. This view on allocation, distribution, and stabilization dismissed many of those arguments in favor of public enterprises which we mentioned in the preceding section on nationalization, in particular the desirability of distributional and stabilization policies of public firms.

The allocative justification of public enterprises was also questioned in the eighties. The recent fall into disfavor of internal subsidization has led to

---

[41] For the fierce criticims which the electricity regulator had to face because of his role in the recent coal crisis see McGowan (1993: 85).

careful reconsideration of the internal organization of firms which claimed to be natural monopolies.[42] It became clear that typically only parts of production exhibit those economies of scale which actually make them natural monopolies. Consequently, public utilities may be disintegrated either vertically or horizontally, with possible privatization and market entry in those parts where no natural-monopoly properties prevail. *Vertical disintegration* refers to utilities like telecommunications, electricity and gas, where it is only the distributive grid which has the properties of a natural monopoly. With respect to these grids, economies of scale are still predominant, maybe even increasing in recent decades. The reader might think of the new investments which have become necessary for the tracks of fast trains in Europe. The classical example of *horizontal disintegration* is the PTT system which in several European states was split into various firms, some of them sooner or later to be privatized and opened to market entry in their core activities (like the PTT bank services or telecommunications), some of them to remain public, but still to be exposed to market entry with respect to specific activities (like express mail or parcel services). – It may be noted that the protagonists of disintegration may have intentionally overlooked particular disadvantages of disintegration. After all, in case of vertical disintegration they practically ignored the informational and transactional disadvantages of separating upstream and downstream firms;[43] in case of horizontal disintegration they practically ignored economies of scope.

*

After presenting the background ideas which favored the recent wave of privatizations, let us present the remaining scope of public enterprises. For this purpose we begin with the economic arguments for nationalized enterprises, which we mentioned in the previous section: there are still many enterprises which are run as public firms because they are natural monopolies, there are still many governments who want to achieve distributional aims by public-sector pricing or use public firms as instruments of short-run job preservation. Moreover, public enterprises exist, and will continue to exist all over the world, for reasons of ideology, government power, trade-union power, or even political inertia (some governments may simply prefer not to engage in too much privatization). Hence, public-enterprise economics in many coun-

---

[42] Technical progress can destroy natural monopolies. If a reliable and cheap technology for cellular telephones becomes available, local telephone calls could be a very competitive market. For a strong opinion on the extent to which technical progress erodes the natural monopoly in telecommunications see Liston (1993: 37).

[43] For a detailed presentation of these and many more arguments on vertical integration see the handbook paper by Perry (1989).

tries remains an important part of government's economic activities and hence an important field of research for applied economists.

1.5.3   Public Ownership Versus Public Regulation

If government privatizes some enterprise, the implication is that it wants to rely on the market for the achievement of a welfare optimum. If perfectly competitive firms are privatized, this aim can be achieved without any further price regulation of the privatized firms. In the practice of privatization there are cases which come near to this theoretical ideal. A hotel, formerly owned by a nationalized railway company, and now sold to a private owner, competes with other hotels and the market mechanism fully replaces regulatory activities.

A totally different situation arises if a natural monopoly is privatized. Market forces will not prevent a privatized monopoly from using all allowed means to keep its monopolistic position and exploiting it in order to maximize profit. If the government is not willing to accept such a result it can *either* refuse to privatize the monopoly, *or* regulate the privatized monopoly with respect to prices, quantities, rate of return etc.

In between we find many nationalized enterprises which are neither natural monopolies, nor perfectly competitive enterprises. They typically exhibit a high degree of market power, due to legal measures, technology, capital requirements, innovations, product differentiation (goodwill) etc. If such enterprises are to be privatized for the sake of efficiency in production, the government has to abolish all legal measures preventing market entry.[44] But even then, technology, capital requirements etc., might act as barriers to entry, making further intervention necessary.

However, if regulation is inevitable, why should the government privatize at all? Why should a regulated privatized enterprise be preferable to a public enterprise? Somebody who knows public utilities from his professional business as public official or as manager would answer these questions in the following way: first, privatization would be coupled with dismissing bureaucratic government officials. A new generation of regulators would be put to work which is better informed about costs, prices, and operational efficiency

---

[44] In addition to not privatizing the monopoly or regulating the privatized monopoly, the government has a third option – forcing the monopolist to accept competitors' traffic on its system (as was done to British Telecom and is being done to British Rail). A government is entitled to impose these obligations where the assets affected are public but, had they been privately owned, such an imposition could have been considered as partial expropriation. It is thus not only 'all legal measures preventing market entry' that have to be abolished in some cases but also some of the rights of property.

than was government when the enterprises were public.[45] Second, privatization would be coupled with dismissing inefficient firm managers and employees
and it would be the new staff which would be responsible for better economic
performance. According to the two above arguments, privatization would improve productive efficiency of public utilities because of the spirit, know-how
and agility of the new men and women who are responsible for the privatized
utility both on the firm's side and on the regulator's side. Unfortunately, the
neoclassical tradition in public economics and industrial organization cher-
ishes the paradigm of the anonymity of economic actors. Hence, any theory
which explains increases in productive efficiency by referring to new managers
or regulators will be met with an unfavorable reception. Fortunately, on the
other hand, even if it is assumed that privatization does not replace any government's and firm's representatives, the principal-agent literature has to offer
many valuable insights into the comparison of public firms and private regulated ones. Recent contributions concentrate on problems of moral hazard
and adverse selection. Some basic themes of this literature will be presented
in what follows.

Let us begin with *moral hazard* problems which arise if the relevant economic actors are equally badly informed when the decision on privatization
and regulation is made. Consider a two-person setting: the government as
seller and a private agent who will serve as the 'owner-manager' of the firm. In
this case, both allocative and productive efficiency can be achieved by 'selling
the store to the agent' and stipulating a Loeb–Magat (1979) mechanism: the
government commits itself to pay the total consumer surplus to the private
owner-manager in exchange for a lump sum which the private contractor pays
to the government. In this setting, the private firm maximizes the sum of
consumer and producer surplus and hence the first best is achieved. Unfortunately, this nice theoretical idea typically will not be applied in practice.
First, the assumption of symmetric imperfect information may often fail to
hold, whence the owner-manager will not sign a contract at a moment when

---

[45] This seems to be the case in the UK. The regulators are not hampered as officials
were by the Morrisonian doctrine which inhibited them from enquiring at all closely into
such 'day to day' matters as costs and efficiency. In some other countries this change in the
informational status of regulators might be a less important consequence of privatization.
It can, for instance, be doubted whether a new generation of regulators in France would
be better informed than past and present administrations: this is because the French government has several direct channels of information as to what is going on within its major
public enterprises through civil servants on the supervisory boards, civil servants attending
meetings of the boards and committees with access to the enterprises' strategic documents
(the 'commissaires du gouvernement'), and other civil servants located within the enterprises with access to all papers and the duty of reporting to the Ministry of Finance (the
'controleurs d'etat'). A broadly similar system exists in Belgium.

he is badly informed, but only at some later point of time when he has an informational advantage which forces the regulator to pay an information rent. Second, the Loeb–Magat mechanism presupposes that the private agent is willing to accept all the risk, which often will not be the case.[46] Third, privatized public utilities typically are too large to be run by an owner-manager, whence efficiency will not be achieved by the Loeb–Magat mechanism unless the private owner passes over to the manager the sum of consumer and producer surplus. Fourth, the Loeb–Magat mechanism is complicated to explain to any politician, because consumer surplus in the many-product case is a pretty difficult concept.[47]

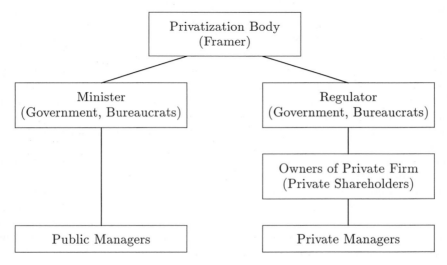

Figure 1
Source: simplified version of a figure of Shapiro and Willig (1990: 60)

More interesting than the case of symmetric imperfect information are the *adverse-selection* cases, where information asymmetries exist at the moment of contracting. They create an incentive problem which can only be solved by allowing the better informed economic agent to earn an information rent. Consider the institutional setting illustrated in figure 1. A govern-

---

[46] Risk neutrality of both regulator and owner-manager is sufficient for a Loeb–Magat contract to be signed by both parties.

[47] For the complexity of consumer surplus see, for instance, Bös (1989: 50–61). For an elaboration of the fourth point made in the text see Bös (1991a: 115–6).

ment privatization body, interested in welfare maximization, decides whether it is better to have a public firm (left-hand side of the figure) or a regulated privatized firm (right-hand side). The privatization body does not interfere with the firm's activities, it neither gives incentives to the public officials who monitor the firm, nor to the managers who run the firm, nor to the private owners in the case of privatization. Its only activity lies in 'framing', that is in making the decision whether or not to privatize according to the welfare consequences of the two compared cases.

In both cases, the firm is monitored by public officials who serve as ministers responsible for a public firm or as regulators of a privatized firm. We shall speak of 'government' if the officials are interested in welfare maximization; we shall speak of 'bureaucrats' if they want to maximize their budgets.

The firm is run by a manager who draws utility from his income and suffers disutility from his effort.[48] The actually applied effort is hidden action, it is only known to the manager. It cannot be observed by the public official or can at least not be verified before a court. Moreover, nobody is able to calculate this effort from other observations: at the contract date there is some hidden information and only the combined result from this hidden information and the manager's hidden action can be observed by persons other than the manager.[49] By way of an example, let the production costs depend on the quantities produced, on the manager's effort, and also on the manager's ability whose actual value is private information of the manager. The manager will be inclined to exploit his informational advantage to get more income or to reduce his effort level. To enhance his performance, therefore, the manager must be offered a contract which gives him an incentive to approach allocative and productive efficiency as nearly as possible. Moreover, the manager must be offered compensation for his effort which makes the job attractive, i.e. the utility he attains when working in the firm must exceed some reservation level. We assume that this level is identical in the two cases compared: the manager does not attribute a special value to working in a public instead of a private firm or vice versa.

Since we want to concentrate on the consequences which adverse selection exerts on the framer's decision to privatize or not, we also assume that the economic environment is the same for the public and for the privatized firm. There are no differences in the technology, in the demand functions etc.

After setting the stage, we can now proceed to the comparison between the public and the private regulated firm. We begin with the case of *welfare-*

---

[48] Chapter 28 below gives an extensive treatment of the principal-agent relations which are only very briefly sketched in this paragraph.

[49] Once again, the assumption of observability can be replaced by the assumption of verifiability before a court.

maximizing government officials who monitor the public firm ('minister') and the privatized firm ('regulator'). As a benchmark case we assume fully informed officials. In this case there is no difference between the case of a public and a regulated privatized enterprise. In both cases, the government officials are able to enforce the first best; welfare-optimal prices p^* and welfare-optimal effort e^* prevail. Regardless of ownership, the government officials achieve the same welfare optimum. In the regulated privatized firm the private owners will be left without any profit. The managers will always be forced down to their reservation utilities. The government officials will appropriate all rents. In this setting the privatization body is always indifferent between the case of a public and a regulated privatized enterprise.

This result changes if there is asymmetric information. It is plausible to assume that the managers have private information in both the public and the privatized firm. This private information will refer to parameters which influence costs or demand, and, of course, to the manager's own effort.[50] The government officials in both public and private firms typically will not be fully informed about these parameters and about the manager's effort. To get the relevant information, they have to ask the manager and give him the right incentives to tell the truth. To give these incentives is costly. In other words, the manager earns an information rent. Now consider a public enterprise. Let the minister consider a positive shadow price of public funds. Therefore, he faces a trade-off between the manager's information rent on the one hand and both allocative and X-efficiency on the other hand. Hence he will compromise on efficiency; in particular he will accept an effort level $e^{pub} < e^*$. In the privatized firm, conversely, there is a double information barrier.[51] First, the regulator has to sign an incentive contract with the private owners. Second, the private owners also are imperfectly informed and have to extract private information from the managers by an adequate revelation mechanism. Therefore both allocative and X-inefficiency are increased as compared with the public firm:[52] the produced quantity is lower, and so is the managerial

---

[50] In chapters 28–33 we present detailed analyses of various cases of informational advantages of managers.

[51] It can be doubted that the shareholders of a regulated privatized firm have any actual influence on the regulatory system. However, for reasons of commercial law, they cause an information barrier: the regulator cannot directly offer a contract to the manager because this manager is directly responsible to the board of his firm which represents the shareholders. An exception would be the case of an owner-manager; however, privatization of public utilities typically does not lead to situations where owner and manager coincide, because in most cases it is large-scale enterprises which are privatized in Western economies.

[52] Laffont–Tirole (1991: 85) compare the multiprincipal distortion of the private regulated firm with the classic double marginalization on two complementary goods sold by non-cooperative monopolists.

effort, $e^{priv} < e^{pub} < e^*$. – Accordingly, the welfare-maximizing privatization body will opt for the public firm.[53]

However, this decision is decisively driven by the assumption that both minister and regulator maximize welfare. Typically, this will not be the case. Let us, therefore, for the sake of argument assume that both minister and regulator have the same multiple objective: they want to maximize a weighted average of welfare and output instead of welfare alone. In this multiple objective the maximization of output would require prices which are as low as possible, preferably zero tariffs. The simultaneous consideration of welfare, comprising consumer and producer surplus, requires higher prices, although they still would possibly lead to a deficit of the enterprise. This multiple objective allows the treatment of various types of 'bureaucratic' ministers or regulators depending on the weight which is attached to the output objective. Apart from the introduction of 'bureaucrats', the organizational structure and the informational setting of both the public and privatized firm are the same as in the preceding paragraphs. Therefore, once again, the regulator of the privatized firm faces one more information barrier than the minister who is responsible for the public enterprise. Due to the consideration of bureaucrats instead of pure welfare maximizers, however, this additional information barrier now has both negative and positive consequences. Negative is the reduction of managerial effort as explained in the preceding paragraph. Positive is the taming of the bureaucrat. The additional information barrier restrains the bureaucratic regulator when he pursues his private agenda.[54] Hence he will have to accept lower output after privatization. If prior to privatization the regulator's output-maximizing attitude had been very strong, this lower output will be nearer to the welfare-optimal output than was the case in the public enterprise. The privatization body, which still is a welfare maximizer,

---

[53] This holds unless the model is enriched by further assumptions on particular weaknesses of public enterprises. Laffont–Tirole (1991), for instance, assume that investments and the benefits from investments are not verifiable. However, once investments in public firms are sunk, the government which has the residual rights of control over the public firm can 'expropriate' the managers by using the investments for purposes not originally intended. It may, for instance, tell the public managers to use the returns from their investments to employ excess labor. Anticipating such government behavior, public managers refrain from investing, in contrast to the private regulated firm. – It can well be doubted whether this is a realistic setting. In practice, it takes a great deal to discourage managements in public enterprises from investing and the diversion of the enterprises' surpluses into welfare purposes would not stop investment. After all, such diversion is an implicit purpose of public enterprise.

[54] Shapiro–Willig (1990) present this argument. For purely didactical purposes they assume that the bureaucrat is perfectly informed about the public firm (no information rent to the manager!).

evaluates the negative and the positive consequences of privatization and if the positive consequences predominate, it will decide in favor of privatization.[55]

1.6   Privatization in Post-Communist Economies

1.6.1   Economies in Transition

In dramatic peaceful revolutions in the late eighties, the communist regimes in most of the former Comecon countries collapsed. Politically these revolutions resulted from the lack of freedom, economically from the inability of these regimes to respond to consumers' expectations which had become more pronounced with the increased growth of personal incomes and which the centrally planned and overly bureaucratic communist economies were too inflexible and unwilling to cope with. Only after the fall of most communist governments did this inflexibility become fully known in non-communist countries. The former communist states had lived on their basic endowments, investing too little in infrastructure, housing, and environmental protection.

The transition to democratic societies implies the transition to decentralized market-oriented economies. The first stage of any such transition is a sort of shock because too much has to be done at once. Typically price liberalization is one of the first moves, often resulting in hyperinflation (Poland) or at least in fairly high inflation.[56] This, unfortunately, calls for a contractionary macro-economic policy at a time when the government would like to take an expansionary course. The process of moving toward market economies also loses momentum because of the many obstacles facing the operations of any private enterprises – be they privatized or newly established. Policies to cope with these obstacles include:

- improvement of infrastructure, in particular with respect to telecommunication;
- improvement of the public administration;
- establishing a system of commercial law (to cover company law, contract law, bankruptcy and liquidation law, and negligence and civil injury law);
- setting up an appropriate system of taxation;
- establishing a market-economic banking system with an independent central bank, private commercial banks and insurance companies;
- establishing a stock exchange;

---

[55] Other interesting papers on the comparison of public and privatized regulated utilities are Pint (1991) and Schmidt (1991).

[56] East Germany was, of course, an exception because it immediately gained access to a stable and convertible currency. For details on the East-German transition see Sinn and Sinn (1992) and Bös (1991b, 1992).

- resolving the firms' uncertainties about liability for environmental damages; in the case of privatization also dealing with uncertainties about property rights or liability for former firms' debts;
  - training of managers to promote entrepreneurial spirit;
  - retraining of employees to stimulate occupational changes.

Privatization of state-owned enterprises is necessary as part of the transition to a market economy. Three sectors of state-owned enterprises can be distinguished which are privatized at different speeds:

(i)   small enterprises – shops, restaurants, hotels, pharmacies, bookshops, cinemas – can be privatized quickly.[57] Even if ownership rights are unclear, the small firms can be leased to private managers with considerable success. These firms are typically labor-intensive, hence the lack of available capital does not damage their prospects too severely. They operate in a competitive environment, competing both with other privatized and newly established firms. Further government regulation is therefore unnecessary and the privatization process leads to a successful expansion of private entrepreneurial activities.

(ii)   key-sector enterprises are much more difficult to privatize and it is these enterprises on which most activities of the governments concentrate – banks, industry, wharfs, transportation, mining, energy, R&D, newspapers, printing-offices, etc. Since the process of privatization of these sectors is most controversial, it will be treated in a separate subsection to follow below (subsection 1.6.2).

(iii)   public utilities like electricity, gas, railways etc. typically are not considered as candidates for privatization. In most cases they are run-down and need considerable restructuring before being able to operate at a level comparable to the established market-oriented economies. That governments in former communist countries find privatization of public utilities too far-reaching, in part is regrettable since the expansion of some urgently needed infrastructure could be speeded up by privatization. Telecommunications would be the best candidate for privatization, some foreign telephone company taking over in restructuring the enterprise.[58] After all, the government can insist on regulating prices. The above argument can be extended: why should not private companies be allowed to build highways which are toll-financed? (The latter project, unfortunately, was explicitly rejected for East Germany.)

The privatizations in post-communist economies differ decisively from the privatizations in market-oriented economies. Since prior to the 'velvet

---

[57] Unnecessary centralizations, i.e. chains, can easily be broken up in these cases.

[58] Hungary sold 30 percent of Matav, the national telephone company, to a consortium led by Deutsche Telekom, and there are plans also to sell off the rest of the company.

revolution' in Czechoslovakia as much as 97 percent of output came from the state sector,[59] privatization is part of a *complete* transition of the economy, not only a reshuffling of the ownership structure of some minor segment of economic activity. When privatization begins in such a country, there is no market sector which surrounds and nurtures the private venture, quite different from privatizations in market-oriented economies where the formerly state-owned enterprises become part of a well-established network of private business. The situation is of course less complicated in a country like Hungary where already in 1984 only 65 percent of output came from the public sector.[60] Hence it can well be understood why Czechoslovakia started a *big-bang policy* of privatization, whereas Hungary has become a particular exponent of a *gradualistic policy*.

1.6.2 Key-Sector Enterprises Searching for Efficient Capitalistic Organizational Forms

The typical situation of a reform politician in a post-communist country is as follows. He wants to achieve rapid privatization of as many firms as possible in order to secure the irreversibility of the transition to market economies. Given the difficulties facing such a policy, the reformers apparently aim at a sort of squaring of the circle.

First, there is not enough purchasing power in post-communist states to sell all key-sector enterprises within a short period of time. Even high savings rates are not sufficient to allow the full stock of industrial property to be bought at short notice.[61] Moreover, much of the legendary monetary overhang was destroyed in the inflationary process which followed price liberalization. Institutional purchasing power, in particular from private banks and insurance companies, is also lacking.

Second, the value of the key-sector firms is unknown and often quite difficult to determine. Hence it takes much time to evaluate whether some firm is viable in a market economy or not. Since most of the data referring to viability come from the managers of the firms which are to be evaluated, moral hazard is prevalent. Sometimes, however, the managers and employees of these firms give wrong information not because of moral hazard, but simply because they do not understand modern accounting procedures.

---

[59] The figure refers to 1986. See Milanovic (1989).

[60] Milanovic (1989).

[61] For some data see Estrin (1991). The point has even been made for Germany although Western German potential investors have much more purchasing power, and Germany can more easily attract foreign capital than the post-communist states. See Sinn and Sinn (1992: 84–5, 118–24).

Third, the property rights may be unclear. There has been severe opposition to the idea that the communist 'people's property' now has become state property, which can be sold by the government to whomever it considers appropriate. In many cases workers or managers claimed ownership of their firms. Best known are the debates in Poland and the 'spontaneous privatizations' in Hungary (many of which have since been reversed by the government). Typically, the property-rights problem has been solved in favor of the government's right of disposal.[62]

Fourth, many institutional prerequisites of conventional privatization processes are missing or still not properly functioning, like a well-established stock exchange.

Fifth, much of the specialized human capital is missing which is needed for sophisticated privatizations: qualified underwriters, chartered accountants, and lawyers specialized in modern business law.

According to the above-mentioned obstacles to privatization, proposals failed which recommended the sale of shares of all key-sector firms at the stock exchange.[63] General auctions or bilateral negotiations between a government trust and potential investors must be considered superior to the stock-market approach, although their implementation will typically be part of a gradualistic policy, like Hungary's.[64] The only exception was East Germany where a big-bang policy could be implemented by bilateral negotiations because there were so many potential West German investors, endowed with sufficient purchasing power.[65] Unfortunately, all the other economies in transition lack such a big brother and therefore have to resort to other policies of privatization if rapidity is required. Management buy-outs is one of these policies. If key-sector firms are handed over to the managers in charge of the firm, this is a quick privatization, does not require much purchasing power (or none at all), and there is no need for an explicit evaluation of the firm. Unfortunately,

---

[62] In East Germany, restitution-in-kind could be claimed by those who had owned the firm prior to nationalization by the German Democratic Republic. For details see Sinn and Sinn (1992: 87–96) with a very nice example of conflicting property claims on p. 92. Restitution-in-kind can be replaced by monetary compensation of former owners if this is preferable for the transition to the market economy.

[63] In the former Czechoslovakian Republic, a participation in Skoda was sold to Volkswagen after fierce competition between Renault and Volkswagen. In an early stage Poland wanted to implement the British system. However, after selling seven enterprises in the British way at the end of 1990, the government recognized that this sort of sales would take too much time to be recommendable for the total transition of the Polish industry from planned to market economic structures. See Estrin (1991), Sachs (1991), Cieslik (1993).

[64] See, for instance, Báger (1993), Dervis–Condon (1992), Estrin (1991), Hare–Révész (1992).

[65] See, for instance, Bös (1991b, 1992), Sinn and Sinn (1992).

even if the former managers are fully able to run the privatized firm, there is one major disadvantage of such a management buy-out: the privatization process does not bestow the firm with any new capital which, however, is badly needed for restructuring the firm. Hence, management buy-outs often have to be supported by government for quite some time which is undesirable. Moreover, the general public will complain that some persons get property of firms as a sort of windfall profit while most others do not.

Therefore, mass privatizations have been suggested for economies in transition.[66] The basic idea is that the publicly owned firms should not be sold to private bidders, but that they should be given away to the adult population either free of charge or at a very low price.[67] The general population receives shares or vouchers which at some later time can be exchanged for shares. If a *direct-ownership program* is intended, the publicly-owned firms must be converted to joint-stock companies and the general population be entitled to the property rights of the firms (directly via shares or indirectly via vouchers). But if all the entitlements are given to the general population, there will be no effective management control, at least not in the short run. Because of this, typically, only a smaller percentage of shares is given to the population; the remaining entitlements can be auctioned off to private investors in such a way as to achieve effective management control. Alternatively, such control may be achieved by giving part of the entitlements to financial intermediaries or banks or by withholding a government participation in the privatized firms. If an *indirect-ownership program* is planned, the ownership of the firms is transferred – free of charge – from the government to financial intermediaries, and the entitlements in the intermediaries are distributed to the general public. The intermediaries control the firms, and they themselves should be controlled either by the government or by competition among themselves.[68] – In practice, the former Czechoslovakia was the first country to apply a scheme of mass privatization successfully.[69] In 1991/1992 nearly 1500 enterprises were put into an auction process. Three quarters of all eligible citizens (8.6m) bought voucher booklets which entitled them to bid, either directly or indirectly via some investment privatization fund. In a complicated auction process of five consecutive rounds equilibrium prices of shares in terms of vouchers were determined – certainly the largest real-life experiment of a tatonnement process.

---

[66] The rest of this paragraph in part is taken from Bös (1992: 5–6).

[67] For a good overview see Borensztein and Kumar (1991), and Bolton and Roland (1992).

[68] For detailed proposals see Lipton and Sachs (1990b), Frydman and Rapaczynski (1991) and Blanchard and others (1991).

[69] For details see Bouin (1992,1993), Bös (1993).

1.6.3   The Remaining Scope of Public Enterprises in Transition Economies

As already mentioned, typically there is no imminent privatization of public utilities in post-communist states. However, their environment changes through the privatization of industrial firms, banks etc., thus putting the public utilities in precisely that position which is treated in this book.

Public key-sector firms will also continue to play an important role for many years to come. When the vouchers have been exchanged for shares, some firms will remain in public property, either directly as government-owned or indirectly as owned by one of the financial intermediaries. In this way, the government will be left with the responsibility for non-viable firms. The government will not be willing to liquidate all these firms immediately because this would imply a major increase in unemployment.[70]

The fear of unemployment in any case is the major constraint of the speed of post-communist privatizations. The restructuring of privatized firms will let employees go because the overmanning in former socialist countries will have to come to an end. Therefore post-communist governments will refrain from selling all key-sector enterprises too quickly in spite of their interest in a rapid transition to market-oriented structures. The more political unrest increases in a country, the lower the speed of privatization.

During a considerable transition period, therefore, state-owned key-sector enterprises in a market-oriented environment will be of particular importance in post-communist states.

---

[70] For Germany see Bös (1992) and Bös–Kayser (1992).

PART ONE

THE BASIC PRICING MODEL

2
Special Pricing Rules:
Objectives and Constraints

This chapter serves a twofold purpose. First, it is a general introduction into public-enterprise and public-utility theory, dealing with problems of welfare, markets, technology and budget constraints in a general way which is basic for all of the following chapters of the book. Second, it is a special introduction into the 'pricing' parts of the book, hence it mainly concentrates on a full-information approach[1] and not on special problems of asymmetric information.

The basic pricing model in a full-information setting consists of the following components:

- maximization of either welfare or political and bureaucratic objectives

subject to

- market-clearing conditions (or market-disequilibrium conditions),
- the enterprise's technology, and
- a revenue-cost constraint.

A detailed characterization of the above objectives and constraints will be given in the following sections.[2]

2.1 Objectives I: Normative Theory

2.1.1 Commodity Versus Budget Space

We start from methodological individualism and, accordingly, let welfare depend on individual consumers' utilities. The government may attach different

---

[1] The 'pricing' parts of the book deal with a full-information general-equilibrium approach which has its early roots in the French planning tradition (Boiteux, 1956). This type of modelling was developed with particular reference to public enterprises, hence in the following we shall typically speak of 'public enterprises' although most of our text can equally well be applied to regulated private enterprises.

[2] Managerial incentive compatibility is not treated in this chapter, because here we do not concentrate on asymmetric information. Moreover, managerial participation is not treated here, as is usual in models of the Boiteux tradition. (Introducing a participation constraint in a full-information model makes economic sense, but does not lead to further economic insight.) For details on both incentive-compatibility and participation constraints see chapter 28 below which presents an explicit introduction into regulation; it is a counterpart to, and extension of, chapter 2.

weights to the individual utilities – a combination of government's and individuals' valuations seems to be characteristic for Western-type economic
systems.

We characterize the consumers by the strictly increasing and concave
utility functions $u^h(x^h)$ where $h = 1, \ldots, H$. Their consumption plans are
$x^h = (x_o^h, \ldots, x_n^h)$ where positive quantities are net demand, negative quantities net supply. $x_o^h \leq 0$ is consumer h's labor supply. The consumption
plans are assumed to refer to private goods, as defined by the aggregation
rule $\Sigma_h x_i^h = x_i, i \in I$, $I = \{o, \ldots, n\}$. These private goods can be provided
publicly or privately.

Starting from the above individual utility functions would enable us to
define welfare over the 'commodity space' by a welfare function[3]

$$W = W(u^1, \ldots, u^H); \quad \frac{\partial W}{\partial u^h} \geq 0; \quad h = 1, \ldots, H. \tag{1}$$

In maximizing such a welfare function, we typically would expect the
relevant board to use individual consumption quantities of public supply as
(indirect) policy instruments. The resulting marginal conditions would then
be transformed, taking into account the individual consumer optima.[4]

The reader will have realized that this seemingly direct approach to the
topic leads to an indirect treatment of the problem: we would prefer to optimize with respect to prices instead of individual (!) quantities. Therefore we
will define welfare over the 'budget space', starting from a welfare function

$$W = W(v^1, \ldots, v^H); \quad \frac{\partial W}{\partial v^h} \geq 0; \quad h = 1, \ldots, H \tag{2}$$

where v^h are the indirect utility functions exhibiting the dependence of the
individual optimum utility on prices and on lump-sum income:

$$v^h(p, r^h) := \max_{x^h} u^h(x^h) \quad s.t. \quad \sum_{i=o}^{n} p_i x_i^h = r^h; \quad h = 1, \ldots, H. \tag{3}$$

p is a vector of prices $(p_o, \ldots, p_n)$, with $p_o = 1$, that is, labor is chosen
as the numeraire. r^h are given lump-sum incomes, being positive, nil, or negative. Any consumer's labor income x_o^h is an endogenous result of this utility

---

[3] For the axiomatic justification of welfare functions see the seminal book of Sen (1970);
furthermore see Hammond (1977), Roberts (1980a,b), Seidl (1983).

[4] E.g. replacing $\partial u^h / \partial x_i^h$ with $\mu^h p_i$ where μ^h is the individual marginal utility of lump-
sum income r^h.

maximization. The non-labor incomes r^h, however, are exogenously given to the consumer when he maximizes his utility. Therefore we call them lump-sum incomes. Several benchmark models, however, consider public-sector pricing under the assumption that the income distribution is optimal. In those models, the consumers' lump-sum incomes are instruments of the authority which decides on public-sector pricing. Although they are endogenous for this authority, they remain exogenously given for any individual consumer.

If the welfare function is defined over the budget space, we deal in terms of indirect utility functions $v^h(p, r^h)$ and Marshallian demand functions $x_i^h(p, r^h)$. This not only makes the analytical treatment easier,[5] it also permits a more general analysis.[6] Therefore the analysis in this book will be carried out in the 'budget space', using welfare functions of type (2).

2.1.2 Allocation Versus Distribution

When defining the social welfare function we imposed a basic Paretian value judgment by postulating

$$\Lambda^h := \partial W / \partial v^h \geq 0; \quad h = 1, \ldots, H. \tag{4}$$

Welfare never increases if somebody's utility decreases. This postulate is strengthened by the assumption that W must be strictly increasing in at least one utility level.

The Paretian character of a welfare function with $\Lambda^h \geq 0$ can be seen more explicitly if, instead of choosing a social welfare function, the following alternative problem is considered

$$\max v^1(p, r^1) \quad s.t. \quad v^h(p, r^h) = v^{ho}; \quad h = 2, \ldots, H, \tag{5}$$

subject to the market-clearing conditions, the public sector's technology and its revenue-cost constraint. The individual utility levels v^{ho} are exogenously given. In any optimum following (5) there exist Lagrangean multipliers $\widetilde{\Lambda}^h$ which relate to the utility constraints ($\widetilde{\Lambda}^1 := 1$).

Optimal prices and quantities will usually differ if we follow (5) instead of maximizing (2) subject to the same constraints. However, after eliminating Λ^h and $\widetilde{\Lambda}^h$ respectively, the marginal conditions on which all our analyses will

---

[5] Optimization with respect to prices leads directly to the expressions $\partial x_i / \partial p_k$ which can be easily interpreted.

[6] Georgescu-Roegen (1968–69) has shown that corner solutions in the commodity space can be investigated directly in such an analysis. Moreover, individual indifference curves in the commodity space need not be differentiable, only differentiability in the budget space is necessary. See Chipman–Moore (1976: 70–1).

center are identical in both cases and thus both approaches lead to the *same structure*[7] *of pricing*. Hence, readers who are concerned by the restrictive characteristics of a social welfare function of type (2) may interpret the results as if they were derived using approach (5).

The reader may note that the Lagrangean multipliers $\widetilde{\Lambda}^h$ are always endogenously determined if an optimization according to (5) is performed. The board, however, may influence the values $\widetilde{\Lambda}^h$ by exogenously fixing the individual utility levels v^{ho}. This is where distributional value judgments can be introduced into such an approach. A similar way of reasoning holds for the constrained optimization of a welfare function (2). From a general point of view the social valuation of individual utility, Λ^h, is *endogenously* determined as a result of performing the optimization.

The welfare function, however, does not only imply a Paretian welfare judgment. By choosing the particular functional form of $W(v^1, \ldots, v^H)$ the board can also express any kind of distributional value judgment.
The best-known examples are:

(i)   the utilitarian welfare function

$$W = \sum_h v^h. \tag{6}$$

This simple summation of individual utilities has often been criticized because it treats individual utilities as equal, and not those variables on which utility depends. Hence, maximizing that sum would favor those who are efficient 'utility producers', which does not necessarily imply those egalitarian results one might expect from the board's distributional value judgments. A rich man who gets much pleasure from increased income has to be favored as compared to a poor man who gains less from a comparable increase in income. Only if additional assumptions are introduced, for instance identical individual utility functions with decreasing individual marginal utility of income, do egalitarian results necessarily occur.[8]

(ii)   the Rawlsian welfare function

$$W = \min_h (v^1, \ldots, v^H). \tag{7}$$

In this case only the utility of the worst-off individual counts, and all other individuals are neglected. It may be noted that Rawls himself presents this

---

[7] The *level* of prices will usually be different.

[8] Additional problems arise if individual abilities rather than incomes, are taken as exogenous starting points. See Sadka (1976b).

idea as only one part of his general criterion of distributive justice. In mathematical economics, however, Rawls' views are often reduced to the case of maximizing welfare function (7).

(iii) intermediate cases: of course, there are many possible distributional value judgments between the limiting cases of the utilitarian and the Rawlsian welfare functions. The best-known specification of these intermediate cases is as follows:[9]

$$W = \left[\sum_h (v^h)^\nu \right]^{1/\nu} ; \quad \nu \le 1. \tag{8}$$

The parameter ν measures the inequality aversion. $\nu = 1$ is the utilitarian case; $\nu \to -\infty$ leads to the Rawlsian case. ν between these values allows us to deal with varying inequality aversions of the relevant board.[10]

For reasons of differentiability it is often convenient to restrict the analysis to social welfare functions which are strictly increasing in all individual utilities, $\partial W / \partial v^h > 0$. The Rawlsian case can be approximated by assuming a very high degree of inequality aversion of the politician, for instance, assuming $\nu = -50$ if simulation analyses are to be performed and welfare is specified according to equation (8).

Before ending this subsection on allocation versus distribution we should mention the particular problem of social versus individual valuations of incomes and utility. If $W(v^1, \dots, v^H)$ is differentiated with respect to any individual income, we obtain $(\partial W / \partial v^h) \cdot (\partial v^h / \partial r^h)$, where $\partial W / \partial v^h$ is the *social* valuation of individual utility and $\partial v^h / \partial r^h$ is the *individual* marginal utility of lump-sum income. Hence, in general we should avoid economic interpretations of the whole expression, for instance by assuming 'the social marginal utility of lump-sum income, $\partial W / \partial r^h$, to decrease with increasing income'. If such an interpretation is chosen, it means that the politician happens to have chosen the welfare function W in such a way that at the optimum countervailing effects of individual utility functions are just offset to guarantee that $(\partial W / \partial v^h) \cdot (\partial v^h / \partial r^h)$ is positive, but decreasing with income. The reader should be aware of the complexity of this assumption.

2.2 Objectives II: Positive Theory

There are many possible objective functions which can be adopted in a positive pricing theory. Different objective functions might be used to represent vote-maximizing politicians, budget-maximizing bureaucrats, and revenue- or

---

[9] See, for instance, Feldstein (1973). A similar specification is used in Atkinson–Stiglitz (1980: 339–40).

[10] For $\nu=0$, W is equivalent to a log-linear function of the v^h's.

output-maximizing boards of public enterprises. As a general notation for objective functions we use

$$\Phi(p, z) \tag{9}$$

where p is the vector of prices and z is a vector of 'netputs' (outputs minus inputs) of the public enterprise. We assume all these objective functions to be twice continuously differentiable in all prices and netputs. Detailed definitions of the various types of positive-theory objectives will be given in chapter 4 below.

The above notation defines the different functions over the budget *and* the commodity space, which is a convenient approach for models which take both prices and public netputs as instrument variables. In most cases, however, the particular objectives will depend on either prices or netputs. If, for example, government wants to minimize a price index, the objective function will typically be specified by means of the usual Laspeyres index formula which includes only prices as variables. If, on the other hand, output is to be maximized, the output quantities are the only variables of the objective function.

In most cases positive theory intentionally avoids explicit consideration of utility functions, referring only to *variables which are directly observable*, such as outputs, labor inputs, output prices or wages paid. Some objective functions in positive theory, however, are defined by explicit reference to individual utility functions

$$\Phi(\cdot) = \Phi(v^1(p), \ldots, v^H(p)). \tag{10}$$

The best known example is the maximization of votes according to the neoclassical tradition of the economic theory of democracy. In deciding among different political proposals, the voter will choose the alternative that yields the highest utility and the policymaker, subsequently, will choose that policy which attracts most votes.

Another type of objective function in positive theory describes the result of collective bargaining by explicitly referring to the utility functions of those organizations which participate in the bargaining:

$$\Phi(p, z) = \Phi(U^1(p, z), \ldots, U^K(p, z)) \tag{11}$$

where $U^1, \ldots, U^K$ denote the utility functions of the relevant organizations. The best example is the description of a public enterprise under strong influence of a trade union, where U^1 is the enterprise's and U^2 the trade union's utility (Gravelle, 1984; Rees, 1984b).

Last but not least, positive theory can cope with satisficing, instead of optimizing, behavior. In this book we will treat one example where prices are determined by particular accounting axioms based only on knowledge of cost functions. Prices, according to that approach, are not derived from a maximization problem, but are designed for the purpose of sharing the costs incurred among the customers.

2.3   Constraints I: Markets

We now come to the integration of a public enterprise into the general framework of a market economy. We assume an economy with J private unregulated enterprises, $j = 1, \ldots, J$ and one public enterprise. Their production plans are $y^j = (y_o^j, \ldots, y_n^j)$ and $z = (z_o, \ldots, z_n)$. Positive quantities denote net output, negative quantities net input. This 'netput' concept is an improvement upon any approach which deals with final goods only. Products of public enterprises are very often intermediate goods. Transportation services, gas and electricity provide good examples, however, we could also refer to coal and steel if produced by nationalized enterprises.

The reader should note that the private netputs, y^j, enter our model only through the market clearing or non-clearing constraints. Hence, these market constraints are the decisive link between public and private enterprises. They determine the integration of the public enterprise into the private economy.

The number of private firms, J, is held fixed in our models, which means that the *explicit* consideration of market entry by further private competitors of the public enterprise is excluded. Potential market entry, however, can be treated *implicitly* by assuming that the public enterprise cannot raise profits higher than the costs of entry of potential rivals.[11]

2.3.1   Equilibrium of Supply and Demand

The basic model presented in part I of this book assumes that supply and demand are in equilibrium. This restriction is sometimes relaxed in order to investigate particular problems.

In the basic model we have the market-clearing conditions[12]

$$\sum_h x_i^h - z_i - \sum_j y_i^j = 0; \qquad i = o, \ldots, n. \tag{12}$$

Any firm's output is used either for consumption or as an input for its own or other firms' production. Consumers supply labor to the private and

---

[11] See section 25.1 below. For an explicit treatment of market entry see chapter 34.

[12] For the moment it is convenient to suppress all functional dependencies of the different quantities supplied or demanded.

to the public sector; they buy commodities from private firms and from the public sector. Such a market equilibrium is financially feasible. The net profits of private firms and of the public sector are equal to the sum of lump-sum payments as can be seen easily by multiplying (12) by p_i for every i and adding up to obtain

$$\sum_h \sum_i p_i x_i^h - \sum_i p_i z_i - \sum_i \sum_j p_i y_i^j = 0 \qquad (13)$$

which leads to

$$\sum_h r^h - \Pi - \sum_j \pi^j = 0 \qquad (14)$$

where Π is the deficit or profit of the public enterprise under consideration, and π^j is the profit of firm j. Thus our model implies a total redistribution of private profits to consumers and the public sector. If, however, private and public 'profits' lead to an aggregate deficit, consumers are forced to finance it by lump-sum taxes.

2.3.2 Disequilibria of Supply and Demand

Disequilibrium analysis of public enterprises is characterized by typical institutional and politically generated constraints. The most important cases are as follows:

Rationed supply – Public utilities are often obliged to cover demand at given prices, a requirement which can be written as a disequilibrium constraint for $z_i > 0$

$$z_i \geq \sum_h x_i^h - \sum_j y_i^j; \qquad i = 1, \ldots, n. \qquad (15)$$

Transportation, gas and electricity provide good examples. There are many cases where the above constraint may be fulfilled as an equality. A relevant example is where public utilities are not only obliged to cover demand but also to sell their products at comparatively low (welfare-maximizing) prices. Assuming that demand responds normally to price and that a high deficit is allowed, the above constraint can be fulfilled as an equality. As long as excess supply exists, prices can be reduced in order to increase welfare which will imply an increase in demand until the market is cleared.

On the other hand, disequilibria according to (15) may arise and can be important in practice. Examples are branch lines of European railways which the enterprises are not allowed to close although demand is low, or services which they are obliged to run although it is not worthwhile financially. These examples suggest the practical importance of the inequality constraint (15). Before leaving the case of excess supply it should be noted that the examples above constitute a buyers' market without the typical properties of such a market. According to the usual terminology,[13] a buyers' market exists if supply is rationed. In the public utility field, however, lack of competition on the supply side prevents demand from exploiting its stronger market position.

Rationed demand – For distributional or allocational reasons public outputs, $z_i > 0$, might be priced very low. To limit the cost of such a policy, the government may be willing to accept that demand be rationed

$$z_i \le \sum_h x_i^h - \sum_j y_i^j; \qquad i = 1, \ldots, n. \tag{16}$$

The German universities provide an example of selling services at zero prices and rationing demand by a sophisticated system of 'numerus clausus'. According to the usual terminology, the German universities should be viewed as providing their services in a sellers' market. However, the rationing system is built up in such a way that supply cannot exploit its market position.

Mixed cases – Interesting mixed cases occur if demand for publicly supplied goods fluctuates over time, as in the case of demand for energy or transportation services. Covering peak demand would be too expensive. Rationing demand at all times would not be desirable either. A compromise would be to require public output, $z_i > 0$, to cover the off-peak (or the minimal) demand

$$z_i \ge \left[\sum_h x_i^h - \sum_j y_i^j \right]^{min} ; \qquad i = 1, \ldots, n \tag{17}$$

and to tolerate excess demand in periods of higher demand.

Rationed labor markets – Unemployment is an important example of disequilibrium in the market for production factors and should be taken into account in public-enterprise policy. An individual's labor supply can be treated as rationed according to[14]

$$x_o^h \ge \overline{x}_o^h(L) \tag{18}$$

---

[13] See, for instance, Malinvaud (1977).
[14] To understand why $\ge$ is correct, remember $x_o^h \le 0$.

where $\overline{x}_o^h(L)$ is an exogenously given rationing function, depending on total employment L. This function may even set a consumer's labor supply equal to zero.

2.4   Constraints II: Production

2.4.1   The Production Side of our Model

The technology of *private firms* is not explicitly modelled. We assume, however, that the board in the public enterprise has information on the net supply functions $y_i^j(p)$ of private firms. This does not imply any particular knowledge of the decision rules used by private firms. In our model the private sector is exogenous and the public enterprise has to accept its behavior and adjust to it, as is usual in a 'second best' approach. We assume that private supply functions $y^j(p)$ always exist.[15]

The *public enterprise* is assumed to produce efficiently[16] according to a production function

$$g(z) = 0. \tag{19}$$

By not imposing further restrictions on $g(z) = 0$ we allow for decreasing, constant or increasing returns to scale.

Special considerations are necessary if a public enterprise is a sales organization, buying privately produced goods and reselling them to consumers or to private firms, at a higher or at a lower price.[17] A priori we could expect the netputs of the distributed goods to be zero since they are both bought and resold. The production function would then depend on the labor and capital inputs which are necessary for the distribution of the goods, but since the distributed netputs are zero we would arrive at complicated corner solutions in our models. However, such a modelling of, say, a public warehouse company, would be simply wrong. If we consider a particular period of time, there are some quantities bought and others (re)sold, but inventories also are

---

[15] If a private firm j is a monopoly, then p_j does not enter as an argument in $y^j(p)$, since the quantity y_j and the price p_j are determined simultaneously.

[16] To produce efficiently in second-best economies is welfare optimal under comparatively weak assumptions.

[17] The brandy monopolies in Austria, Germany and Switzerland buy alcohol from private producers and sell it to resellers at higher prices (Austria, Switzerland) or at lower prices (present situation in Germany). Agricultural sales organizations usually resell products at lower prices, so as to subsidize agricultural branches and/or consumers. (In France the relevant organizations, like ONIC and others, have been restructured recently to correspond to the EU rules.) Government marketing boards are particularly often to be found in developing countries; for a recent empirical investigation on the maize price policies in Zimbabwe see Buccola–Sukume (1993).

held, which prevents the netputs from being zero. As the holding of inventories is often one of the main tasks of such sales organizations, particularly in the agricultural sector, the problem of zero netputs can be ignored in what follows.

Defining public enterprise's technology in the above manner implies several serious assumptions regarding efficiency. In the following subsections we will discuss these assumptions, distinguishing between X- and allocative efficiency.

2.4.2 X-Inefficiency

(i)   The Leibenstein Approach

Excluding production slack by starting from $g(z) = 0$ instead of $g(z) \leq 0$ implies that the enterprise only produces along the production possibility frontier. Points like A, B or C in figure 2 are considered in our model, points like D or E are excluded. The latter points are 'X-inefficient' according to the terminology due to Leibenstein (1966, 1969, 1976).[18]

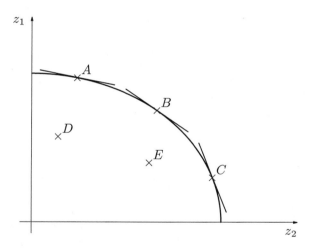

Figure 2

Let the amount of factor inputs be given. Then, X-inefficiency exists if factor inputs can be adjusted so as to increase the production of some good without reducing the production of any other good.

---

[18] For a recent comprehensive book on X-inefficiency see Frantz (1988).

Explaining such an inefficiency calls for models of the decision processes within the relevant enterprise. We have to consider any single individual within the firm, from part-time blue-collar workers to the managers. Any individual chooses that level of labor effort which maximizes his utility. This labor effort generally will not coincide with that which maximizes the firm's profits or minimizes its costs. The owners of the firm often will not be able to solve the complicated underlying principal-agent problems.

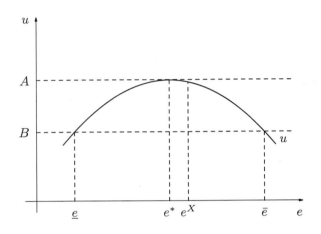

Figure 3

The main reason for X-inefficiency is the existence of inert areas in individual decisions regarding the supply of labor effort. Consider an individual whose labor supply can be described by two variables: x_o, working time, and e, which is a one-dimensional indicator of effort.[19] Let us assume for the moment that labor income $p_o x_o$ is independent of effort, e. The individually optimal effort e^* in general will differ from e^X, which would be optimal with respect to X-efficient production of the firm. It seems plausible to assume e^X to be near to e^* as the management recruits employees who are expected to meet the requirements of the various jobs. e^X may exceed e^* (figure 3).[20]

In maximizing utility the individual will consider the costs of changing effort. Changes in effort occur if the utility increase exceeds these costs.

---

[19] The index h can be dropped, because this simplification cannot lead to any misunderstanding.

[20] This figure is taken from Leibenstein (1969: 608).

Hence, individual effort may deviate from the optimum e^* without any action of the individual induced by this deviation: he or she is trapped in an inert area. In figure 3 the costs of changing effort are assumed to be constant and to amount to AB, leading to an inert area $[\underline{e}, \bar{e}]$.

As we assume e^X to be near to e^*, the X-efficient effort will be located within the inert area. The probability of X-inefficiency of a firm will be greater, the larger the individual inert areas. As X-inefficiency is defined at firm level, we have to aggregate these individual decisions. For an exact theoretical modelling at firm level we would need assumptions on the distribution of the individual deviations between e^* and e^X.

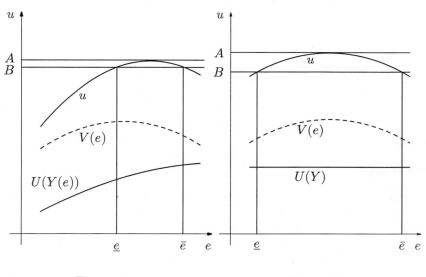

Figure 4a   Figure 4b

Although Leibenstein formulated his theory for private enterprises, it is of particular applicability for public enterprises. In terms of the above theory of inert areas we could expect X-inefficiency in private enterprises to be less important than in public enterprises, because private enterprises will link incomes with effort more often and in private enterprises the costs of changing effort will typically be lower than in public enterprises due to their bureaucratic structures. Figure 4 shows a simple comparison between a private and a public enterprise taking into account the above considerations. Following Leibenstein (1976) we assume a separable utility function $u = U(Y) + V(e)$ where $U(Y)$ denotes utility from income and $V(e)$ utility from effort. In the private economy $Y = Y(e)$ is an increasing function of e, in the public firm

Y is constant with respect to e.[21] Note that the size of the inert area of the public-firm employee is independent of the level of income Y.

(ii)   More Recent Approaches to the Behavior of Firms in the Space of Inefficient Input-Output Combinations[22]

Neoclassical economists tend to think along neoclassical frontiers. They simply do not explain movements which happen somewhere below these frontiers.[23] We do not know which incentives exactly matter within the inefficient space unless we choose some functional description of the behavior of inefficient agents within the inefficient space. However, such theories very often imply assumptions which are rather ad hoc. Two typical examples are the following.

When a public enterprise is privatized, the government will want to predict how the efficiency of the firm changes if the extent of privatization increases. Such a prediction requires a production function $g(z, \Theta)$ where z is the vector of inputs and outputs and Θ is the percentage of shares which is privately owned: we have a public firm if $\Theta = 0$ percent and a fully privatized firm if $\Theta = 100$ percent.[24] $g(z, \Theta)$ defines a particular production possibility frontier for every extent of privatization. For increasing Θ this production function is shifted until it is either impossible to increase efficiency by further increasing the extent of privatization, or until 100 percent of the firm has been sold to private owners. Then we reach a production possibility frontier $G(z)$ which does not depend on Θ any longer and is the envelope of the production functions $g(z, \Theta)$. This is an attempt to model the behavior within the space of inefficient input-output combinations. A similar procedure has been applied by Gravelle (1982a) who postulates a production function $g(z, e)$, where e is the effort of the managers. Here the production function is shifted depending on higher or lower effort of the managers.

Another approach to model the behavior in the inefficient space has been chosen in Bös (1991a: 149–76). Here it is the trade unions who are responsible for inefficiency. We postulate there is a production function $z = f(\ell^*, \kappa)$ which functionally connects the one output of the model with the capital input κ and the optimal amount of labor ℓ^* which is necessary for any combination of capital and output. The trade unions have an objective function which depends on the wages and on some inefficient over-employment $\ell - \ell^*$, where

---

[21] Obviously the same tendency holds if the public firm links income with effort, but to a lesser extent than the private firm.

[22] This subsection is taken from Bös (1988).

[23] Exceptions are Smith (1983) and Peters (1985). See also section 5.4 below.

[24] See Bös (1991a: 227–30).

ℓ is the actually used labor force. In the firm the representatives of the trade unions and the managers compromise over the actual number employed. Hence we also have an ad hoc theory to model the inefficient behavior of the firm.

(iii)   Principal-Agent Approaches Comparing the Efficiency of Public and Private Enterprises[25]

The ideas of the preceding subsection directly lead us to the next problem. It is not only the incentives within the firm whose modelling is still insufficient from a more advanced theoretical point of view. If we explicitly try to consider the principal-agent relation between the firm and some regulating authority, it is the lack of information which becomes of decisive importance. In this book the chapters 28 – 33 are explicitly devoted to that topic. Here I only want to stress that the principal-agent approaches face similar problems to the modelling of inefficiency mentioned above. Consider, for instance, Baron and Myerson's (1982) approach of regulation of a firm under unknown costs. The cost function of that model is $C(z, \theta)$ where θ is a parameter which is exactly known to the firm, whereas the government only knows the distribution of θ. We have a specification of a cost function where some additional parameter is introduced ad hoc into the cost function to cope with the problems of information and incentive structures. So it is the same basic problem of modelling which we find in these approaches on regulation as well as in my models on privatization and in other papers on public-enterprise economics which try to deal explicitly with the incentives of managers within some inefficient space of input-output combinations.

Modelling the incentives of the firm given some imperfect information of the government or some other regulating authority has become one of the main concerns in the recent theory of public and regulated private enterprises. This recent theory implies that it is not ownership *as such* which makes the difference between a public firm and a regulated private firm. Ownership *as such* matters for the distributions of incomes and wealth and these distributions are only in the background of theoretical modelling. In the spotlight of recent theories we find the incentives and the particular distribution of information which result from the distribution of ownership and from regulatory constraints. It is the difference in incentives and information, not in ownership, which constitutes the difference between public firms and private regulated firms according to most state of the art models.

Let us briefly deal with some recent studies in the field. De Fraja (1993a) compares a public and a private principal, both of whom face a manager who

---

[25] The first two paragraphs are taken from Bös (1988).

prefers higher income and lower effort. Low effort means large slack, that is, high X-inefficiency. In contrast to the manager, the principal is imperfectly informed. He cannot observe slack (effort) and also cannot observe some external factor which influences the profit of the firm. What is the best outcome the principal can achieve given his lack of information? The principal has two ways of rewarding the manager: by increasing his income or by allowing more slack. The public principal is more likely than the private principal to use the salary instrument, whereas the private principal is more likely to use the slack instrument – the result is higher X-inefficiency in the private firm. The main reason is as follows. Less slack always implies lower costs which imply lower prices. Hence, part of the benefit of the reduction in inefficiency always accrues to the consumers in form of a lower price. This is directly welfare-improving, the government therefore internalizes this effect of less slack. For private shareholders this benefit is lost. Hence they are less interested in reducing slack. Moreover, if the manager's income positively enters into the welfare function,[26] the government does not care so much about higher salaries in its firm, but is willing to pay more to achieve less slack. For a profit-maximizing private principal, however, the manager's income always reduces his profit, hence he is less willing to trade more managerial income against less slack. This is a second reason for lower X-inefficiency in the public firm in De Fraja's model.[27]

De Fraja's result, however, depends crucially on his special assumptions. Take, for instance, Pint's (1991) comparison of the principal-agent problems of a public and a regulated private enterprise. Here the public principal's objective includes the payroll as a further argument (in addition to consumer and producer surplus) and as a consequence the public enterprise is biased toward labor as a factor of production. Moreover, for good states of the world the public firm offers a steeper compensation profile (higher information rents) because of its tendency to prefer a higher output. However, the resulting higher managerial compensations in good states consist of a constant monetary income[28] and of fringe benefits ('perks') which increase if the state of the world improves. Higher perks in public enterprises seem to fit well into the general public's impression of inefficiencies in public firms. According to Pint's study it cannot generally be concluded whether X-inefficiency is higher

---

[26] For a discussion of this problem see section 28.2 below.

[27] In De Fraja's (1993a) model there are two states of the world: a low-cost and a high-cost state. His result can only be proved for the low-cost state. However, the underlying rationale is very general, hence one could think of many more situations where his result should hold.

[28] This is a case of 'bunching': in spite of differences in the states of the world, the same monetary income is paid.

in public or in private regulated enterprises. The above-mentioned inefficiencies of the public firm must be compared with the inefficiencies of the private regulated firm, for instance its bias toward capital as a factor of production. Which type of firm is more efficient depends on the case in question. This statement is in concordance with those models which deal with the question of whether privatization under regulation is welfare-superior to leaving the firm in public ownership.[29]

(iv)   Empirical Studies – Their Arguments on Comparative Efficiency of Public and Private Firms

Whether X-inefficiency is more important in public than in private enterprises has recently been tested in many empirical studies which compare the efficiency of private and public production. The studies deal with refuse collection, electricity utilities, fire protection, health care, airlines, and other cases in which the same good is supplied by public and private enterprises.[30] The evidence of these studies is mixed but, as a personal view after reading many papers on the topic, I would tentatively summarize the literature by saying that in 50 percent of all the comparisons the private firms do better, in 25 percent the public firms do better and 25 percent must be left undecided because indicator A ranks the public firm above the private firm, but indicator B ranks them the other way around.

From the general point of view which characterizes this book, the countless details of the individual case studies are less interesting than their general line of thought. Hence, in the following I shall present a synopsis of the most common arguments used in empirical efficiency comparisons between public and private firms.

First, public inefficiencies are often denoted as the price of achieving particular *macroeconomic objectives* such as reducing unemployment, or redistributing income. This suggests that the purely accounting view adopted in most empirical studies ignores the difference between the one-dimensional efficiency orientation of private firms and the multi-dimensional political, micro- and macroeconomic context in which a public enterprise works.[31]

---

[29] These models have been treated in subsection 1.5.3 above. They combine both allocative inefficieny and X-inefficiency, whereas in the present section we are interested only in X-inefficiency.

[30] The reader can refer to the surveys of these empirical studies by Borcherding–Pommerehne–Schneider (1982), Millward–Parker (1983), Boyd (1986), Mueller (1989: 261–6), Boardman–Vining (1989), and Vining–Boardman (1992).

[31] See, however, De Borger (1993). In his econometric study of the Belgian Railroads he concluded that surprisingly low efficiency losses resulted from politically caused excess labor inputs coupled with too low energy inputs.

The above-mentioned concentration on macroeconomic objectives could well lead us to the many political arguments which have been put forward to justify public enterprises' inefficiencies. As a recent trend of the empirical literature, however, some direct analogies between public- and private-sector arrangements have been drawn which support the hypothesis of *equal* efficiency of public and private enterprises. Unfortuntely, most of these analogies are superficial. Presenting the analogies in italics, and our objections against them in roman type, we may argue as follows:

- *political competition is as effective in achieving efficiency as market competition;*[32] this argument overlooks that political competition aims at different objectives than market competition, in extreme cases at pure rent-seeking;[33] the reduction of X-inefficiency often will not be too high on the political agenda. Market competition may drive a private firm into bankruptcy; political competition may often lead to increases in the subsidization of public firms with ensuing increases in X-inefficiency.[34]

- *the threat of privatization or of contracting-out of parts of the production is as effective in achieving efficiency as the threats of the takeover market for private firms;* this argument overlooks that the efficiency-increasing consequences of takeovers or of takeover threats have by no means been proved in the relevant literature.[35]

- *the internal labor market among bureaucrats is as effective in achieving efficiency as the labor market for private managers;*[36] however, one should accentuate that working competition for public jobs is not necessarily oriented at the goal of reducing X-inefficiency;[37] competing Niskanen bureaucrats might achieve their objectives better by increasing X-inefficiency.

A different explanation accentuates the greater pressure toward efficiency that is due to *ownership rights*. Private ownership entitles individual shareholders to residual rights, that is to everything which has not been decided upon by contract. In the case of public enterprises, the residual rights remain with the state, in other words, with government bureaucrats. Whereas private shareholders are interested in X-efficiency, bureaucrats are rent seekers who lack that interest. Shareholders may discipline the managers of private enterprises by (the threat of) transferring equities; managers themselves may own equities, which provides a further incentive for them to encourage efficiency.

---

[32] See Wintrobe (1987), Mueller (1989: 214), Peltzman (1990: 61).

[33] Cfr. Tollison (1982).

[34] Oum–Yu (1993) in a cross-section time-series analysis of railways in 19 OECD countries prove that X-inefficiency depends decisively on the extent of subsidization.

[35] For a brief survey see Bös (1991a: 58–60).

[36] Wintrobe (1987: 443).

[37] Cfr. Vining–Boardman (1992: 213).

Most popular, however, is the hypothesis that it is not ownership, but *competition in the product market* which matters. According to this hypothesis, the X-inefficiency of public production is due to a lack of competition in the markets for its outputs. Hence, public enterprises will not be forced to choose the optimum size of the firm,[38] nor will they be induced to produce at minimum costs unless they risk losing customers, that is to say, the more elastic the demand the greater the incentive to operate at minimum cost. Recent empirical studies have shown that the efficiency of a public enterprise can be increased substantially by establishing or increasing competition. A good example is given by Caves and Christensen (1980) using the case of the Canadian railways. Even if the market structure in such a case is duopolistic and not perfectly competitive, the pressure from another firm in the market will promote the efficiency of the public firm if the monitoring authority prevents collusion between the duopolists.

Less often to be found in the empirical literature is the argument that *asymmetric information* leads to inefficiency. Some authors[39] emphasize that in both private and public firms there is asymmetric information and, consequently, ask why private firms should be more efficient if principal-agent relations characterize both private and public firms. These authors point out that it is well-known that the market for private corporate control is far from perfect and that there may be effective political monitoring of public enterprises. However, although it is correct that asymmetric information causes inefficiencies in private firms, this does not necessarily imply equal efficiency of private and public firms. Vining–Boardman (1992: 206–9) compare empirical studies of owner-controlled and principal-agent controlled private firms. The owner-controlled firms do better. Public firms, however, are never owner-controlled. Hence, even if the efficiency losses were equal in all types of firms with principal-agent relationships, there is still a superiority of private ownership because of the special setting of an owner-controlled firm which has no equivalent in the public sector.

Arguments which are perhaps weaker stress public enterprises' higher extent of *bureaucratization* and *risk avoidance*. It is correct that appointment and dismissal of public employees follows more bureaucratic lines as compared with private management. However, a comparison of public and private firms of similar size and market position reveals similar patterns of bureaucratic organisation. Nevertheless, attitudes toward risk are assumed to differ: public employees are said to shun riskier investments and partic-

---

[38] This means inefficiency with respect to a long-run production possibility frontier. Spann (1977) mentions that public enterprises often are forced to operate at a scale that is predetermined by the given size of a political unit.

[39] See for instance Whitehead (1988: 7–8).

ularly innovative activities, and to prefer to pass unnoticed and to assume that errors of commission are more easily recognized than those of omission (Borcherding, 1980). Some empirical studies confirm this hypothesis, the best known of which compares Australian private and crown banks (Davies, 1981). The counterargument to this view is that if people do not commit their own resources, we would expect them to run risks. There are many examples where the management of public enterprises discounts risks by not evaluating them properly, to the point of brushing them aside as not being serious.

(v)   The Empirical Estimation of a Public Firm's Technology[40]

Let us start from a typical empirical case study on public firms. By way of an example, we have data on the place miles of the different nationalized railway companies, and on the man hours that were used as inputs to produce those place miles. Given data of different years and different railway companies, we face a cloud of empirical input-output combinations as illustrated in figure 5. From the point of view of the usual neoclassical theory, we would say that at least some of those points are inefficient.

Given the empirical evidence, we could apply the more traditional approach of estimating an *'average' stochastic production function*. We could then use this function to explain the determinants of inefficiencies in the past and to predict future input-output combinations if we want to. However, this is measurement of inefficiency without a theory of inefficiency. We can only say that, given a particular system of inefficient behavior, we expect a particular input-output combination to occur in some country in some year. We cannot give any advice to any firm on how to move in the direction of a neoclassical production possibility frontier because we do not know where this frontier is. Moreover, we do not have a theory of the best incentives an inefficiently working firm must be given in order to produce more efficiently. Note that this is a sort of paradox: somebody who behaves inefficiently will also use incentive schemes in an inefficient way.

Recently, a growing number of analysts has begun to estimate *'frontier' production functions*. When applied to public firms different performance approaches have been chosen.[41] Perelman and Pestieau (1988, 1994) estimate a translog function which approximates the inefficient points and then draw a parallel function through that realization which has achieved the best combination of input and output (figure 5a).[42] Tulkens (1986a,b, 1990) thinks

---

[40] Parts of this subsection are taken from Bös (1988).

[41] For a good overview over the various techniques which have been used in the frontier approach, see the contributions in Gulledge–Lovell (1992) and in Griliches–Mairesse (1993).

[42] See also the studies by Gathon–Pestieau (1991, 1992).

it better to declare as efficient all the observations having the property that no other observation exhibits more output with the same input; this 'undomination' criterion yields for the frontier a sort of step function (figure 5b). Färe and Grosskopf (1987) have decided that a sort of linearization would be the best procedure to postulate a production possibility frontier (figure 5c).[43] All these three approaches estimate empirical production possibility frontiers only, 'best practice' functions. They do not estimate production possibility frontiers in the sense of neoclassical theory.

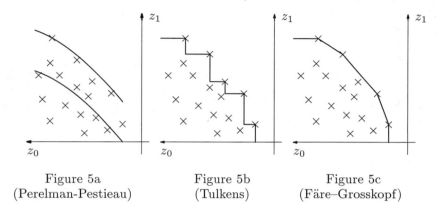

Figure 5a   Figure 5b   Figure 5c
(Perelman-Pestieau)   (Tulkens)   (Färe–Grosskopf)

Which of the three different approaches toward such a 'best practice' function is preferable? One could argue that Perelman–Pestieau's approach suffers, first, from taking one realization only as the basis of the best practice function and suffers, second, from choosing exactly that curvature which the empirical estimate of the inefficient data has led to. Maybe the neoclassical production possibility frontier follows a totally different curvature. Maybe the optimal point which is decisive for finding the best practice function is not representative for the technology at all. In the case of Färe–Grosskopf's procedure one could argue that connecting two points by a straight line may imply the loss of a lot of information and may convexify technologies which in fact should not be convexified because they are not convex by the nature of the production process. So in fact I admit that I favor Tulkens' approach because it avoids an a priori functional specification, does not overaccentuate the importance of one single observation, and does not convexify possibly non-convex parts of the technology.

---

[43] See also Färe–Grosskopf–Nelson (1990) and Oum–Yu (1993). Färe–Grosskopf–Yaisawarng–Li–Wang (1990) use an input-based Malmquist productivity index to estimate productivity growth in Illinois electric utilities.

2.4.3   Allocative Efficiency

A state of the world is allocatively efficient if no shift to any other state of
the world leads to welfare improvement. Recall figure 2. Points A, B, C
can be allocatively efficient; points D and E are not only X-inefficient but
also allocatively inefficient. Defining the technology by $g(z) = 0$ reduces the
analysis to points like A, B, or C. The binding technology frontier $g(z) = 0$
instead of $g(z) \leq 0$ becomes a necessary condition for allocative efficiency. As
figure 2 illustrates, our analysis reduces to comparing points like A, B, or C.
Such points are characterized by the different price ratios by which they are
supported.

   At this point of our analysis we must deal with the challenging argument
that welfare cannot be increased substantially by changing relative prices (that
is by switching from point A to B or C in figure 2). This argument is due to
Harberger (1954). He estimated the welfare losses of non-competitive pricing
in the US manufacturing industry to be lower than 0.1 percent of the gross
national product. Some further studies confirmed this finding.[44]

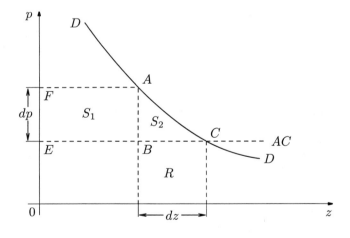

Figure 6

   The theoretical basis of these estimates is very simple and can be shown
by a diagram, as Harberger did. DD is the market demand function and AC
represents constant average costs. z is the output of the particular good. The

---

[44]   See Schwartzman (1960), Worcester (1973), Wahlroos (1984/5).

competitive equilibrium is point C; the equilibrium price $0E$. The monopolist increases his price to $0F$ which leads to lower demand (point A).

The increased price reduces consumer surplus by S_1 and S_2. However S_1 represents an increase of producer surplus and therefore is not a loss for the society, whereas S_2 is a deadweight loss. R represents resources released by the monopoly. R is not a welfare loss *if* we assume full employment, which means that the resources are simply shifted to other branches of production. Thus, according to Harberger, only S_2 is a welfare loss. If the demand function is linearly approximated between A and C, this loss can be measured by the 'little triangle' ABC as

$$\Delta = \frac{dp \cdot dz}{2}. \tag{20}$$

There is an interesting reformulation of the welfare loss in (20), due to Mueller and Cowling (1981).[45] The assumption of constant costs which equal competitive prices implies that a monopoly's profit is

$$\pi = z_m dp. \tag{21}$$

The index m refers to the monopoly and $dp = p_m - c$ as in figure 6. A profit-maximizing monopolist facing linear demand and constant costs produces one-half of the competitive output. Hence

$$dz = z_m. \tag{22}$$

If we substitute (21) and (22) into (20), we obtain

$$\Delta = \pi/2. \tag{23}$$

The welfare loss is equal to half of the monopoly profit.[46] Therefore, any empirical result which follows from the above Harberger assumptions and leads to low welfare losses from monopoly also implies that the monopoly profits are low. 'If empirically observed losses are small, the implication is not that allocative efficiency is unimportant but that real economies are competitive.' (Kay, 1983: 317).

---

[45] See also Kay's (1983) general-equilibrium formulation of the welfare-loss problem.

[46] If another setting as Harberger's is chosen, even in zero-profit equilibria substantial monopoly losses may result; see, for instance Yarrow (1985) for the case of monopolistic competition of the Cournot-Nash type, i.e. quantity setting. A typical example of his analysis (pp. 521–3) is as follows: in monopolistic competition there is an excessive number of firms of suboptimal scale and since every firm offers its own brand, too much product differentiation results, which leads to welfare losses in spite of zero profits of the firms.

For his empirical evaluation of monopoly welfare losses, Harberger added the 'little triangles' Δ over all goods and divided by gross national product. This leads to the following equation

$$L = \frac{1}{2} \cdot \sum_i \left(\frac{dp_i}{p_i} \right)^2 \cdot \mid \epsilon_{ii} \mid \cdot w_i \qquad (24)$$

where w_i is the revenue of good i as a percentage of the gross national product. By calculating L Harberger obtained his provocative result of negligible monopoly welfare losses. Because of the ideological significance of the question, this result has been discussed vigorously. Quite a few contributions contradict Harberger's hypothesis regarding the quantitative importance of allocative inefficiency.[47] The main points of criticism of the Harberger approach are:

(i)   The estimation of equilibrium prices for the purpose of comparison, as performed by Harberger, is dubious. He starts from empirical estimations of sales and of rates of profit on capital of the manufacturing industry. Assuming average costs to be constant in the long run, he defines any deviation from the 'normal' (= average) rate of profit on capital as a misallocation. The equilibrium prices, then, are given by cost, defined to include these normal profits. This means an underestimation of dp because the average rate of profit takes into account all monopoly profits.

(ii)   The price elasticity of demand and the price change dp are fixed independently of each other. If, however, the monopolists in question actually have maximized their profits, the identity of marginal revenue and marginal costs implies $(p_i - C_i)/p_i = -1/\epsilon_{ii}$ where C_i can be equated with the estimation of the competitive price level. Estimating elasticities in this manner typically leads to values that exceed those calculated by Harberger. This again results in an underestimation bias by Harberger.[48] Of course, this is correct only if the firms investigated maximized their profits, which is questionable for some oligopolistic markets.[49]

(iii)   Harberger assumed a single demand elasticity for the monopolistic sector $(\epsilon = -1)$[50] and computed dp-values for whole industries, not for single firms. As Bergson (1973) stressed, the welfare losses accrue for every particular product and as disaggregated elasticities typically exceed aggregated ones,

---

[47]   Best known are the studies by Bergson (1973) and Cowling–Mueller (1978). More recent contributions include Jenny–Weber (1983) and Olson–Bumpass (1984).

[48]   See Kamerschen (1966), Cowling–Mueller (1978).

[49]   See Scherer–Ross (1990: 664–5), Masson–Shaanan (1984).

[50]   Although monopolistic profit maxima are only well-defined for $\epsilon_{ii} < -1$.

this is a further reason for supposing that Harberger underestimated welfare losses due to monopolies.

(iv)   The costs of the acquisition of monopoly power also are neglected by Harberger.[51] Empirical studies typically consider this point by adding advertising expenditures to the monopoly profits and by taking S_2 and S_1 as welfare losses: all monopoly profits are redefined as costs and thus as welfare losses of monopolistic market structure.[52]

(v)   Harberger dealt with all goods as if they were final goods. If some of the goods are intermediate goods, the welfare loss is increased because the relevant 'competitive prices' of the final goods have to be lowered[53] due to potentially cheaper inputs. This means that there are additional welfare losses at the final good stage *and* welfare losses at the intermediate good stage.[54]

(vi)   Of course, the assumption of full employment, which allows us to neglect the rectangle R, may be questioned as well, thus raising the issue of the merits of the partial equilibrium approach of Harberger's analysis.

Taking into account these points, Cowling and Mueller (1978) computed monopoly welfare losses for the UK at between 3 percent and 7 percent of the Gross Corporate Product of the firms in their sample. For the USA the figures were 3 percent to 14 percent. If Bergson's (1973) 'simulation' analyses are reduced to the empirically significant values of elasticities (that is, substitution elasticities between -4 and -8), his computations reveal welfare losses between 0.6 percent and 15 percent of Gross Domestic Product.[55]

The above investigations suggest that the quantitative importance of allocative efficiency is considerably larger than believed by the Chicago school and their adherents. Thus, there are good reasons for viewing the problems of allocative efficiency as the center of an economic theory of public enterprise.

---

[51] Posner (1975) following Tullock (1967). See also the interchange between Littlechild (1981) and Cowling–Mueller (1981).

[52] This is quite interesting from the ideological point of view. According to Harberger S_1 means redistribution only and thus monopoly is distributionally important but at the same time allocationally unimportant. According to Posner S_1 means additional costs and not profits and thus monopoly is distributionally unimportant but at the same time allocationally important.

[53] Harberger's strange estimation of 'competitive prices' (see point (i) above) may under certain circumstances lead to results that point in the opposite direction (Scherer–Ross, 1990: 666).

[54] For this argument see Foster (1976) and Scherer–Ross (1990: 665–6).

[55] On the other hand Scherer–Ross (1990: 667), ignoring points (iii) and (iv) in the text above, still believe that monopoly welfare losses are rather small, namely between 0.5 percent and 2 percent of US Gross National Product, where estimates nearer to the lower bound 'inspire more confidence'.

2.4.4   *Efficiency and Cost Minimization*[56]

The technology frontier $g(z) = 0$ is defined on quantities of netputs, and does not depend on prices. Costs, on the other hand, by definition depend on input prices. Therefore it is impossible to describe problems of cost minimization by using the technology frontier only. Cost functions are defined in such a way that efficiency is necessary but not sufficient for cost minimization.

The inclusion of prices is not the only decisive distinction between the technology frontier and the cost function. The technology can be defined over netput quantities, the cost function can be defined only if inputs and outputs are separated. Therefore, for the following analysis we distinguish labor input $z_o < 0$, other inputs $z_k^- \leq 0$ and outputs $z_k^+ \geq 0$.

The minimum cost of efficient production is derived from the optimization approach

$$\underset{z_o, z_k^-}{\text{minimize}} \, \mathcal{F} = -p_o z_o - \sum_{k \neq 0} p_k^- z_k^-$$

$$\text{subject to}$$

$$g(z_o, z^-, z^+) = 0 \qquad (\lambda) \tag{25}$$

where λ is the Lagrangean multiplier of the technology constraint. The resulting marginal conditions

$$-p_o = \lambda(\partial g/\partial z_o)$$
$$-p_k^- = \lambda(\partial g/\partial z_k^-) \tag{26}$$

can be solved to obtain factor demands as functions of outputs and factor prices. These can be used to obtain the cost function

$$C = -p_o z_o^*(z^+, p_o, p^-) - \sum_{k \neq 0} p_k z_k^{-*}(z^+, p_o, p^-). \tag{27}$$

Marginal costs, along this cost function, are defined as

$$C_i := \frac{\partial C}{\partial z_i^+} = -p_o \frac{\partial z_o^*}{\partial z_i^+} - \sum_{k \neq 0} p_k \frac{\partial z_k^{-*}}{\partial z_i^+}. \tag{28}$$

As this definition of a cost function presupposes the validity of the marginal conditions (26), we can substitute into (28) to obtain

---

[56] This subsection follows Peters (1988).

$$C_i = \lambda \left(\frac{\partial g}{\partial z_o} \cdot \frac{\partial z_o}{\partial z_i^+} + \sum_{k \neq 0} \frac{\partial g}{\partial z_k^-} \frac{\partial z_k^-}{\partial z_i^+} \right). \tag{29}$$

From the technology

$$g(z_o(z^+, p_o, p^-), z^-(z^+, p_o, p^-), z^+) = 0, \tag{30}$$

we obtain for efficient output changes

$$\frac{\partial g}{\partial z_o} \frac{\partial z_o}{\partial z_i^+} + \sum_{k \neq 0} \frac{\partial g}{\partial z_k^-} \cdot \frac{\partial z_k^-}{\partial z_i^+} + \frac{\partial g}{\partial z_i^+} = 0. \tag{31}$$

This can be substituted into (29):

$$C_i = -\lambda \frac{\partial g}{\partial z_i^+}. \tag{32}$$

From (26) we have that $-\lambda = p_o/(\partial g/\partial z_o)$ and therefore marginal costs are given by

$$C_i = p_o \frac{\partial g/\partial z_i^+}{\partial g/\partial z_o} = \frac{\partial g/\partial z_i^+}{\partial g/\partial z_o} \tag{33}$$

because of $p_o = 1$. Equation (33) is valid if and only if costs have been minimized, implying the marginal rates of input substitution must be equal to input prices, as follows from (26), considering $p_o = 1$

$$p_k^- = \frac{\partial g/\partial z_k^-}{\partial g/\partial z_o}. \tag{34}$$

If condition (34) is not fulfilled, there is no equality between C_i and the marginal rate of transformation $(\partial g/\partial z_i^+)/(\partial g/\partial z_o)$. This result is very important because in the Boiteux model, to be described in chapter 3, the above marginal rate of transformation is taken as a proxy for marginal costs. We denote this proxy by c_i, to distinguish it clearly from C_i,

$$c_i := \frac{\partial g/\partial z_i^+}{\partial g/\partial z_o}. \tag{35}$$

As a definition, equation (35) is always valid. c_i and C_i coincide if the public enterprise operates at minimum cost, applying (34).[57] If, however,

---

[57] Cfr. Boiteux (1956, 1971: 234–9).

the public enterprise does not adapt factor inputs to given factor prices in a cost-minimizing way, we obtain

$$\frac{\partial g/\partial z_i^+}{\partial g/\partial z_o} \neq C_i. \tag{36}$$

The same deviation of c_i from C_i prevails if the public enterprise sets input prices which are not equal to the respective marginal rates of factor substitution.

2.4.5 Long-Run Versus Short-Run Investigations

Until now we have not dealt explicitly with the time horizon for which $g(z)$ is assumed to hold. This time horizon matters for the resulting pricing structures. The longer the horizon the more factors of production are variable. In the long-run *every* factor of production is variable.

Let $g(z)$ be taken to hold for such a long-run time horizon. Then the dual approach to technology, looking at the monetary costs of the efficient production inputs, leads to *long-run cost functions*. By definition these functions imply the efficient combination of variable inputs, capital stocks and those other inputs whose variation requires time. In other words, the size of the firm is always efficient.

The alternative approach defines $g(z)$ to hold for a short interval of time only. Then some factors of production must be accepted as fixed, and the dual approach leads to *short-run cost functions*.

According to the time horizon chosen, long-run and short-run total, marginal and average costs will typically differ. They will coincide only if, for some given output vector $z^+ > 0$, the short-run cost function is applied to a firm which happens to be of optimal size with respect to z^+.

Whether $g(z)$ should be applied in the long-run sense or in the short-run sense, is easy to see. If the optimal capacity can be chosen freely, it is always preferable to choose $g(z)$ in the long-run sense. The reason is simple: for any given vector of outputs, long-run total costs can never exceed short-run total costs, the short-run minimization problem being just a constrained version of the long-run minimization problem (Varian, 1992: 70).

Consider a vector of capital inputs κ which are fixed in the short run, but variable in the long run. Without restriction of generality we suppress all inputs which are variable both in the short and in the long run. The short-run cost function is as follows

$$C = C(z^+, \kappa). \tag{37}$$

The long-run cost function, on the other hand, equals

$$C = C(z^+, \kappa(z^+)) \tag{38}$$

where $\kappa(z^+)$ is the cost-minimizing demand for capital inputs. Let $\tilde{z}$ be some vector of output levels. Then $\tilde{\kappa} = \kappa(\tilde{z})$ is the associated long-run demand for capital inputs. Hence long-run marginal cost is

$$\frac{\partial C(\tilde{z}, \kappa(\tilde{z}))}{\partial z_i} = \frac{\partial C(\tilde{z}, \tilde{\kappa})}{\partial z_i} + \sum_b \frac{\partial C(\tilde{z}, \tilde{\kappa})}{\partial \kappa_b} \cdot \frac{\partial \kappa_b}{\partial z_i} \tag{39}$$

for all outputs as indexed by i. Since $\tilde{\kappa}$ is the cost-minimizing choice of the capital inputs, given $\tilde{z}$, we must have

$$\frac{\partial C(\tilde{z}, \tilde{\kappa})}{\partial \kappa_b} = 0 \tag{40}$$

for all capital inputs as indexed by b. Hence, long-run costs at $\tilde{z}$ are equal to short-run marginal costs at $(\tilde{z}, \tilde{\kappa})$. This theoretical identity of long-run and short-run marginal costs is at variance with the opinion of many empirical studies that long-run marginal costs are always higher than short-run marginal costs because the former include operating costs *and* capacity costs, the latter only operating costs. As this is the source of many misunderstandings, we should confront this practitioners' view with the theoreticians'.

We start from the annual reports of an enterprise where the production costs of the last year are published, subdivided into different cost components

$$C(t) = C^1(t) + C^2(t) + \ldots + C^N(t) \tag{41}$$

where t refers to the year under consideration. Best known is the subdivision of costs into

- operating costs, C^{OP}, which are regarded as directly dependent on the output quantities,[58] and
- capacity costs, C^{CAP}, which are regarded as directly dependent on the required plant capacity.

The salary of a London bus driver is part of the operating costs, the investment in building a new underground station is part of the capacity costs. Ex post, of course, in the annual report, costs can always be split as follows

---

[58] To simplify the analysis we assume that there are no fixed operating costs, that is, we exclude the costs of maintenance of a given capacity, which accrue even if no output is produced.

$$C(t) = C^{CAP}(t) + C^{OP}(t). \tag{42}$$

However, if we look at the changes of capacity and of operating costs which took place in some period t, there are the following two alternatives:

(i)   The enterprise changed its capacity within the time interval that is relevant for our measurement ($C^{CAP}(t) \neq 0$). Both capacity and operating inputs contributed to the total costs, they were combined in an optimal or suboptimal way to produce output. Hence we have no empirical figures on how high operating costs would have been if capacity had remained constant. Therefore, any empirical investigation must consider both parts of the costs simultaneously. $C(t)$ is an approximation to the long-run costs.

(ii)   The enterprise did not change its capacity within the relevant time interval ($C^{CAP}(t) = 0$). Total costs in period t consisted of operating costs only. $C^{OP}(t)$ is an approximation to the short-run costs.

By means of empirical analysis it is impossible to investigate long-run and short-run costs simultaneously because the only conceivable situations are (i) *or* (ii). Therefore it is wrong to pick up operating costs alone, calling them 'short-run costs', in cases in which both components of costs changed. It would be equally wrong to measure short-run costs by out-of-pocket costs which are only a part of total costs and of operating costs. They can only be an approximation to short-run costs if all other parts of costs remained unchanged within the relevant period.

Usually, the cost estimations are based on a time interval which is comparatively long (for instance one year). Thus we can assume that in most cases capacity will have changed within this interval. Accordingly, public regulators will not be informed about their short-run costs, and it will be operational to instruct public enterprises to apply long-run cost functions in their pricing rules.[59]

In actual empirical analyses a further problem arises. Typically, the enterprise in question will not combine capacity and operating costs in that cost-minimizing way which has been postulated by microeconomic theory. Hence, whatever we do, we will only obtain approximations to the theoretical concepts.

---

[59]   This may have been one of the reasons why the British White Paper (1967) instructed nationalized industries to apply long-run marginal-cost pricing. However, this White Paper failed, as clearly revealed in NEDO (1976), and was replaced with a new White Paper (1978) which intentionally avoided any explicit pricing rules. But the White Paper (1978) has not been very influential, which perhaps might have been expected because of the inconsistencies of the 1978-paper as for instance discussed in Heald (1980).

2.5 Constraints III: Profits and Deficits

2.5.1 The General Concept[60]

Let the public or regulated firm be restricted by a *revenue-cost constraint*

$$\sum_{i=o}^{n} p_i z_i = \Pi \qquad \Pi \gtrless 0. \tag{43}$$

$\Pi = 0$ implies break-even pricing; $\Pi < 0$ determines a deficit; $\Pi > 0$ requires profits. Of course, there exist lower and upper bounds for Π. The lowest Π that can be found in practice will correspond to zero prices of the outputs.[61] The highest possible Π corresponds to profit-maximizing behavior of the enterprise.

Assuming a binding constraint for all cases of Π implies a particular view of the objective of public-sector pricing which may not be familar to the American reader. Let us distinguish two cases using the example of a welfare-maximizing public enterprise:

- Π exceeds or equals the unconstrained welfare-optimal revenue-cost difference. Then an inequality constraint $\Sigma p_i z_i \geq \Pi$ would be binding and without loss of generality we can assume a priori an equality constraint as is done in (43).
- Π falls below this critical value. In this case, an inequality constraint $\Sigma p_i z_i \geq \Pi$ is not binding. However, it may well be possible that, for distributional or other reasons, the politician wants some institutions to follow a policy that leads to such a low Π. Museums or universities or schools provide examples where it makes sense not to choose zero prices but to fix a Π that is below the unconstrained welfare-optimal value. If, because of their budgetary constraints, the German states (Länder) had to introduce school fees or university fees, they would certainly choose fees below the unconstrained welfare optimal ones. And these cases can be treated appropriately by assuming an equality constraint as in (43).

In a most general formulation the revenue-cost constraint may depend on particular prices, netputs and a vector ρ of other variables:

---

[60] Since Boiteux-type models only deal with 'hard budget constraints', we forgo for the moment any treatment of soft budget constraints. The interested reader may be referred to chapter 31 below.

[61] Negative prices are quite unusual, although they may occur in special cases. By way of an example, for many students the university education in Germany is supplied at a negative two-part tariff: the educational services of the university have a marginal price of zero and additionally a government subsidy for living expenses is granted to students whose parents earn a low income (BAFÖG). The latter can be interpreted as a negative 'basic fee'.

$$\Pi = \Pi(p, z, \rho). \tag{44}$$

This general formulation of a revenue-cost constraint implies a mixture of endogenous and exogenous determination of the enterprise's deficit. Whereas p and z are endogenous, the values of ρ are exogenously given and the firm has to adjust to them. Once again, this is typical of a second-best approach. The fixing of ρ may be due to ideological motives regarding the desired size of the public-utility sector, to political fears of losing votes because of high public-utility deficits or to economic motives, that is, opportunity costs of public-utility deficits as compared with alternative uses of resources in the unregulated private sector.

A good example for the interaction of exogenous and endogenous factors in a revenue-cost constraint is rate-of-return regulation. In its binding form the appropriate constraint is defined as

$$\text{profit} = (\text{rate of return} - \text{interest rate}) \text{ x capital input.} \tag{45}$$

Here the rate of return is exogenously given for the firm and so is the interest rate, since rate-of-return regulation of an enterprise never implies a simultaneous adjustment of interest rates. The capital input is endogenous.

The following subsection presents some further examples of the general revenue-cost constraint (44).

2.5.2   *Matching Grants and Cost-Plus Constraints*[62]

Regulatory boards often advise enterprises to set prices in such a way that a particular percentage of costs is covered. Consider the following revenue-cost constraint

$$R := \sum_{i=o}^{n} p_i z_i^+ = -s \sum_{i=o}^{n} p_i z_i^- =: sC; \quad s > 0 \tag{46}$$

where R is revenue and C is total costs.[63]

It has often been overlooked that there are many forms of regulatory control based on some variant of this constraint. *Consider first the case of* $0 < s < 1$, where an enterprise is instructed to cover a percentage s of its costs by selling its products, whereas the deficit $(1-s)C$ is financed from elsewhere. Such a regulation is typically imposed on enterprises facing stagnating or declining demand, or on enterprises which are required to sell their products

---

[62] This subsection is taken from Bös–Tillmann (1983).
[63] It can be seen easily that (46) is a special case of (44).

at low prices because of 'merit-goods' considerations. In both cases it makes sense to define the constraint as an equality: the stagnating industry must recover at least sC from revenues and most probably will not be able to recover more; the merit industry should not recover more than sC, but the deficit must not exceed $(1 - s)C$ either.

Different institutional models are available for interpreting particular problems of constraint (46) in the case of $0 < s < 1$. The 'matching-grant' aspect, to use a fiscal-federalist term,[64] stresses the particular incentive structures of the underlying principal-agent relationship: what percentage of costs should an enterprise be allowed to best achieve the principal's objectives, taking into account the expected reactions of the agent? The 'mixed-bureau' aspect, to use a term of Niskanen (1971), considers the enterprise as a bureaucratic entity administering a budget which is financed partly by selling its output and partly by a grant-sponsoring authority.

Second, let us consider the case of $s = 1$, the break-even enterprise. Constraint (46) immediately lends itself to an interpretation of the enterprise's behavior when it follows a full-cost pricing principle, where total costs can be distributed among the different outputs according to the regulated enterprise's objectives. Moreover, we can interpret the constraint (46) as the simplest form of an adjustment clause,[65] as it allows the enterprise simply to react to cost increases by price increases without explicitly asking for a regulatory hearing.

The third interesting case is $s > 1$, the 'mark-up on cost' or 'cost-plus' regulation, one of the better-known procedures of price regulation (see for instance Bailey–Malone, 1970; Bailey, 1973). Although symmetric in its treatment of inputs, such a regulation has been criticized mostly because it may imply incentives for firms to waste resources (depending on the firms' objectives and on the elasticities of demand).

There are many modifications of the basic formula (46) which are mostly designed to deal with different unwanted incentive or disincentive effects of such a constraint. These refinements cannot be treated here in detail.

2.5.3 Fully Endogenized Deficits and Profits

It is no coincidence that the typical examples of the general type of revenue-cost constraint (44) have been taken from price regulation. Here the mixture of exogenous and endogenous factors makes much sense: the regulator sets the exogenous factors and the regulated firm the endogenous ones.

---

[64] Under particular institutional conditions $(1-s)C$ may even be a matching grant in the strict fiscal-federalist terminology; namely if a federal or state government gives a grant of $(1-s)C$ to a particular local public utility.

[65] See Schmalensee (1979: 121).

What happens, however, if we analyze the 'pricing' case, that is, the full-information planning model, where ultimately the government is able to control every variable and the firm is a 100 percent controlled puppet of the government? If ultimately there is only one agent, namely the government which decides on everything, then who is the outside person who imposes any exogenous deficit or profit on a firm?

The ideal way out of this dilemma is to make profit or deficit totally endogenous, thereby explicitly considering the shadow costs of public funds. The underlying assumptions are the following. The financing of deficits of a public enterprise or public utility[66] leads to reduced private consumption and private investment. Reducing private investment leads to reduced future consumption. If the rate of return on private investments exceeds the social rate of time preference that is used to discount future consumption, the social evaluation of a unit of reduced investment will exceed that of a unit of reduced consumption. This case of higher opportunity costs (higher shadow prices) of reduced investment is the usual one in practice and turns out to be a typical second-best constraint of public-enterprise or public-utility pricing.

If the production of a public enterprise or utility leads to a deficit, the opportunity costs of such a deficit will depend on the ratio of reduced investment to reduced consumption. This ratio, in turn, will depend on the share of tax or debt financing and on the incidence on consumption and investment of these methods of financing.

The consequences of different kinds of financing on the pricing policy can best be shown if, in a simple model, we start from the assumption that social costs are proportional to the deficit: social costs $= s\Sigma p_i z_i > 0$. The multiplier $s < 0$ depends on the method of financing the deficit (which affects the extent of the reduction of private investment).

The above considerations should be taken into account when fully endogenizing profit or deficit of the firm in question. Accordingly, the government would not consider an explicit revenue-cost constraint, but would maximize the sum of consumer and producer surplus minus the shadow costs of public funds mentioned above.

For the interpretation of the resulting pricing rules compare the following two simple approaches:

(i)   maximize $CS + (1-s)(R-C)$,   (47)

(ii)   maximize $CS + \gamma(R - C - \Pi^o)$,   (48)

where CS is consumer surplus, R is revenue and C is costs. γ is a Lagrangean parameter associated with a fixed budget constraint $R - C = \Pi^o$.

---

[66] See Feldstein (1974).

It is obvious that the resulting pricing formulas will look alike if only one replaces $(1-s)$ by γ. The only difference will be that s is exogenously given,[67] whereas γ is endogenous and hence depends on all variables and functions of the model.

2.5.4 Fully Exogenous Deficits and Profits

The arguments of the preceding subsection present a serious criticism of a full-information second-best model, in particular if it is a general-equilibrium planning model. Such a model assumes that an otherwise omniscient and omnipotent government faces some particular outside barrier which it cannot surpass or does not want to surpass.

In spite of this criticism, in most of this book I shall apply a fixed revenue-cost constraint,

$$\Pi = \Pi^{o}. \tag{49}$$

I consider this procedure satisfactory because an exogenously fixed budget constraint is by no means as implausible as sometimes suggested. One explanation relates Π^{o} to the past: the binding budget has been determined before the prices are set, that is, the budget of period t has been fixed in period $t-1$, hence in period t it is exogenously given. Another explanation relates Π^{o} to political forces which are strictly separable from the government's pricing decision. By way of an example, the railways may be allowed only a low deficit Π^{o} because in the negotiations on the federal budget it was seen as a priority to increase the expenditures for health and for education.

Finally, it should be mentioned that the exogenous budget constraint is traditional in models on pricing and price regulation, its roots in the history of economic thought may be traced back to Boiteux (1956), maybe even to Ramsey (1927).

---

[67] The value of s is determined in cost-benefit-analytical studies on government finance. Hence, in this approach (47) it is exogenous, but not determined by another agent than the government.

3
Normative Optimum Theory

3.1 The Actors and Their Instruments

When *Boiteux* published his seminal paper on the management of public
monopolies subject to budgetary constraints, he was not only a qualified economic theorist, but at the same time manager of the nationalized French
electricity industry.[1] He therefore did not visualize his approach as a purely
theoretical exercise in welfare economics. Rather, he speculated on the actual
applicability of his results and offered rules of thumb for an approximative numerical solution. The applicability of his original model was limited because
of the assumption of perfect competition or equivalent behavior in the non-
nationalized sector (Boiteux, 1971: 233–4). However, subsequent extensions
of his model and the version to be presented below allow for a monopolistic
private economy. Moreover, Boiteux's restriction to compensated demand is
not necessary and we can include income effects and consider pricing with
distributional objectives. For these reasons we have chosen an extended version of the Boiteux model as the best approach to deal with special pricing
principles, for both theoretical and empirical reasons.[2]

The main actor in the model is the *board* of a public enterprise which we
assume maximizes the welfare function

$$W(v^1, \ldots, v^H); \quad \partial W/\partial v^h > 0; \qquad h = 1, \ldots, H \qquad (1)$$

where $v^h(p, r^h)$ are the individual indirect utility functions.

The board has to consider the market economy on the one hand and the
government on the other hand.

Taking the market economy into account implies taking demand into
account, be it demand from consumers or producers. The board must be
aware of the existence of many private firms, mostly operating under some
sort of monopolistic competition. The following basic model imputes to the
board the explicit consideration of market-clearing conditions

---

[1] Boiteux' paper was originally published in French in 1956; an English translation
appeared in 1971.

[2] For other extensions of the Boiteux model see Drèze (1984), Drèze–Marchand (1976)
Hagen (1979), Marchand–Pestieau–Weymark (1982).

$$\sum_h x_i^h(p, r^h) - z_i - \sum_j y_i^j(p) = 0; \qquad i = o, \dots, n \qquad (2)$$

where positive x_i^h is private net demand,[3] positive y_i^j is net supply by a private enterprise and positive z_i is net supply by the public enterprise in question, produced according to a production function

$$g(z) = 0. \qquad (3)$$

In addition, we assume some superior authority outside the model, call it *government*. This authority has decided that a particular part of the economy's production has to be run by the public enterprise in question and has given the board of the enterprise the right to set prices of particular goods, which will be labelled $k \in K \subset I$. Moreover, the government has set the public enterprise's minimum profits or maximum deficits, and therefore the board has to act in accordance with the revenue-cost constraint

$$\sum_{i=o}^{n} p_i z_i = \Pi^o. \qquad (4)$$

Taking into account all these constraints, both from the market and from the government, leads to a realistic second-best model.[4] As mentioned above,[5] the institutional distribution of responsibility for price control is a complex phenomenon of decision sharing between government and public enterprise. In the following we adhere to the hypothesis that the government sets constraints and the board decides on the relevant instruments.[6] The instruments available to the board are as follows.

The *controlled prices* $\{p_k, k \in K \subset I\}$ are a subset of all prices. Prices of goods that are only supplied or demanded by the public enterprise will be controlled in any case. There may exist also non-regulated prices of publicly supplied or demanded goods where the public enterprise has to accept prices which are fixed by private enterprises or by government agencies outside our model. We exclude regulation of the wage rate p_o which serves as the numeraire.[7] The *uncontrolled prices* $\{p_i, i \notin K\}$, are exogenously given which

---

[3] Negative x_i^h is private net supply etc.

[4] As usual in Boiteux-type models, there is no explicit managerial-participation constraint. This type of constraint will however explicitly be introduced in the regulation models of part IV of the book.

[5] See subsection 1.2.3 above.

[6] This basic hypothesis will, for instance, be given up when we deal explicitly with the regulation of marginal-cost or Ramsey pricing. (See chapters 24 and 25 below.)

[7] except in chapters 21 and 26 below.

is a sensible assumption in a model which aims to show the appropriate adjustment of public-sector pricing to the given structures of the unregulated private economy.

The *controlled net production plans* $\{z_i, i \in I\}$ are, of course, a subset of all net production plans of the economy $\{z_i, y_i^j, i = o, \ldots, n; j = 1, \ldots, J\}$. Thus control of prices *and* control of production refer to parts of the economy only. These parts do not necessarily coincide.

For particular benchmark cases we will suppose that, in addition, the board is given the opportunity to fix *individual lump-sum incomes* $\{r^h, h = 1, \ldots, H\}$. Needless to say, the analysis is much more realistic if these far-reaching distributional activities are excluded.

3.2 Solving the Model[8]

In the following it will be convenient to follow a stepwise procedure, by first discussing welfare-maximizing prices and net production plans, and then extending the analysis to optimal lump-sum incomes.

(i) Optimal Prices and Quantities

Welfare-maximizing controlled prices and net production plans can be obtained by maximizing the following Lagrangean function:[9]

$$
\mathcal{F} = W(\cdot) - \sum_{i=o}^{n} \alpha_i \left[\sum_h x_i^h(p, r^h) - z_i - \sum_j y_i^j(p) \right] -
$$
$$
- \beta g(z) - \overline{\gamma} \left[\Pi^o - \sum_{i=o}^{n} p_i z_i \right]. \tag{5}
$$

---

[8] As usual in the public-economics literature, we leave open the questions whether: the second-order conditions for a maximum are fulfilled; there is a unique optimum; the optimum achieved is a local one only; the optimum derived can actually be realized by decentralized decisions of economic agents. Explicit answers to any of the above questions can be given only if very restrictive assumptions are fulfilled. (For some details see, for instance section 7.1.3 and 8.1.3 below.) As the restrictive assumptions cannot be justified by usual microeconomic theory, it is not sensible to treat the above questions in general theoretical analyses. In any empirical case, however, the restrictive assumptions are either fulfilled or not, whence the investigation of the above questions in empirical case studies is always appropriate.

[9] The politician must control at least three prices to avoid degeneration of the optimization approach because of insufficient degrees of freedom. Corner solutions are always excluded.

The necessary maximum conditions are as follows:

$$\frac{\partial \mathcal{F}}{\partial p_k} : \sum_h \frac{\partial W}{\partial v^h} \frac{\partial v^h}{\partial p_k} - \sum_i \alpha_i \left(\sum_h \frac{\partial x_i^h}{\partial p_k} - \sum_j \frac{\partial y_i^j}{\partial p_k} \right) + \overline{\gamma} z_k = 0; \quad k \in K, \quad (6)$$

$$\frac{\partial \mathcal{F}}{\partial z_i} : \alpha_i - \beta \frac{\partial g}{\partial z_i} + \overline{\gamma} p_i = 0; \quad i = o, \dots, n. \tag{7}$$

As further necessary optimum conditions we obtain the constraints $(2) - (4)$ by differentiating $\mathcal{F}$ with respect to the Lagrangean multipliers. Thus we get a system of as many equations as unknowns. Assuming regularity of this system of equations, the unknowns can be determined.

(ii) Optimal Lump-sum Incomes

In the next step we assume that the board also controls the distribution of lump-sum incomes. Hence it maximizes the Lagrangean function $\mathcal{F}$ not only with respect to prices and quantities, but also with respect to the lump-sum incomes.[10] The resulting additional marginal conditions are

$$\frac{\partial \mathcal{F}}{\partial r^h} : \frac{\partial W}{\partial v^h} \frac{\partial v^h}{\partial r^h} - \sum_i \alpha_i \frac{\partial x_i^h}{\partial r^h} = 0; \quad h = 1, \dots, H. \tag{8}$$

The unknown prices, quantities, lump-sum incomes and Lagrangean multipliers can be computed from (6), (7) and (8) plus the constraints of the optimization approach. Regularity is, once again, assumed.

3.3   The Conditions for Optimal Prices and Quantities

We first concentrate on prices and quantities alone, neglecting lump-sum incomes. In this case (6) and (7) plus constraints constitute the relevant system of equations. Substituting (7) into (6) we obtain

$$\sum_h \frac{\partial W}{\partial v^h} \frac{\partial v^h}{\partial p_k} - \sum_i \left(\beta \frac{\partial g}{\partial z_i} - \overline{\gamma} p_i \right) \left[\sum_h \frac{\partial x_i^h}{\partial p_k} - \sum_j \frac{\partial y_i^j}{\partial p_k} \right] + \overline{\gamma} z_k = 0. \tag{9}$$

---

[10] The number of controlled prices plus the number of consumers must exceed 2 so as to avoid degeneration of the optimization approach because of insufficient degrees of freedom.

We divide these equations by $\beta_o := \beta(\partial g/\partial z_o) > 0$[11] and furthermore define $\lambda^h := (\partial W/\partial v^h)/\beta_o$; $\gamma := \bar{\gamma}/\beta_o$; $c_i := (\partial g/\partial z_i)/(\partial g/\partial z_o)$.

$\lambda^h \geq 0$ is the 'normalized' marginal social welfare of individual utility. An equity-conscious politician will choose the welfare function W in such a way that the λ^h increase with decreasing individual utility.

γ is a 'normalized' measure of the welfare effects of the size of the public enterprise's deficit. If the revenue-cost constraint Π^o exceeds the unconstrained welfare-optimal profit, then $0 < \gamma < 1$.[12]

c_i is a shadow price which measures the marginal *labor* costs of publicly producing good i (for $z_i > 0$; otherwise it is a partial marginal rate of transformation). However, as most recent papers on the topic denote c_i as marginal costs, we will adhere to this convention.[13]

Using these new symbols, the conditions (9) can be rewritten as follows:

$$\sum_h \lambda^h \frac{\partial v^h}{\partial p_k} - \sum_i (c_i - \gamma p_i)\left[\sum_h \frac{\partial x_i^h}{\partial p_k} - \sum_j \frac{\partial y_i^j}{\partial p_k}\right] + \gamma z_k = 0. \qquad (10)$$

For a better economic interpretation we will use the price-cost differences $(p_i - c_i)$ instead of using $(\gamma p_i - c_i)$. For this purpose we proceed as follows. We add $(1-\gamma)\Sigma_i p_i[\Sigma_h(\partial x_i^h/\partial p_k) - \Sigma_j(\partial y_i^j/\partial p_k)]$ to both sides of the marginal conditions (10) and obtain:

$$\sum_h \lambda^h \frac{\partial v^h}{\partial p_k} - (1-\gamma)\sum_h\sum_i p_i \frac{\partial x_i^h}{\partial p_k} - \sum_i (c_i - p_i)\left[\sum_h \frac{\partial x_i^h}{\partial p_k} - \sum_j \frac{\partial y_i^j}{\partial p_k}\right] =$$

$$= -\gamma z_k - (1-\gamma)\sum_i\sum_j p_i \frac{\partial y_i^j}{\partial p_k}; \qquad k \in K. \qquad (11)$$

This equation consists of five terms which we shall consider in turn from left to right.

---

[11] Differentiate the Lagrangean function $\mathcal{F}$ with respect to initial endowments of labor z_o and y_o. Then $\alpha_o > 0$ and $\beta_o > 0$ follows from economic plausibility. See Drèze–Marchand (1976: 67).

[12] Remember that $\alpha_o > 0$ and $\beta_o > 0$. Now assume a fixed profit constraint Π^o which exceeds unconstrained welfare-optimizing profit. Differentiate $\mathcal{F}$ (in (5)) with respect to Π^o. $\partial\mathcal{F}/\partial\Pi^o = -\bar{\gamma} < 0$ follows from economic plausibility (and from the appropriate Kuhn-Tucker formulation of the problem). Therefore $\gamma > 0$. Moreover, (7) yields $\alpha_o/\beta_o = 1-\gamma$. Hence $1-\gamma > 0$ and $\gamma < 1$. If, on the other hand, Π^o falls below the unconstrained welfare-optimizing profit, $\gamma < 0$.

[13] The connection between c_i and the C_i, the marginal costs proper, has been treated in subsection 2.4.4 above.

3.3.1 *Distributional Objectives*

The first two terms reflect *distributional objectives*.

The first term, $\Sigma_h \lambda^h (\partial v^h / \partial p_k)$, is the social valuation of a change in price p_k. This term refers to the *price structure*, its absolute value being high for necessities and low for luxuries. This can be seen most easily after applying Roy's identity:

$$\sum_h \lambda^h \frac{\partial v^h}{\partial p_k} = -\sum_h \lambda^h x_k^h \cdot \frac{\partial v^h}{\partial r^h}; \qquad k \in K. \tag{12}$$

In the following it will be convenient to define a 'distributional characteristic' of any good $k \in K$ as a distributionally weighted sum of individual consumption shares:

$$F_k := \sum_h \lambda^h \frac{\partial v^h}{\partial r^h} \cdot \frac{x_k^h}{x_k}; \qquad k \in K. \tag{13}$$

The social valuation of changes in the individual lump-sum incomes, $\lambda^h (\partial v^h / \partial r^h)$, will be a decreasing function of individual incomes, thereby bringing about the distributional weighting mentioned above. For a similar argument see Feldstein (1972a,b,c) and Atkinson–Stiglitz (1980: 387, 469).

The second term refers to the *price level*. It does not include any particular distributional differentiation between necessities and luxuries. Its absolute value is larger, the smaller γ. Typically, a smaller γ will result from a lower Π^o. The lower Π^o, the lower the level of prices:[14] to take a simple example, the level of prices of a welfare-maximizing deficit enterprise will be lower than that of a perfect monopolist.

Formally, we apply the Slutsky equation to this second term[15]

$$(1-\gamma)\sum_h\sum_i p_i \frac{\partial x_i^h}{\partial p_k} = (1-\gamma)\left[\sum_h\sum_i p_i \frac{\partial \hat{x}_i^h}{\partial p_k} - \sum_h\sum_i p_i x_k^h \frac{\partial x_i^h}{\partial r^h}\right] =$$
$$= -(1-\gamma)\sum_h x_k^h, \tag{14}$$

where $\hat{x}_i^h$ denotes compensated demand. The reader should recall that for any individual h the compensated expenditures for all goods do not react to price changes

---

[14] 'Level of prices' may be interpreted as referring to some adequately defined price index. It does not necessarily imply $\partial p_k / \partial \Pi^o > 0$ for all $k \in K$.

[15] Low prices will typically imply high demand x_k, which reinforces the tendencies mentioned in the text.

$$\sum_i p_i(\partial \hat{x}_i^h / \partial p_k) = 0. \tag{15a}$$

Moreover, differentiating the individual budget constraint always yields

$$\sum_i p_i(\partial x_i^h / \partial r^h) = 1. \tag{15b}$$

Hence the first two terms can be rewritten as follows

$$-F_k x_k + (1 - \gamma)x_k, \tag{16}$$

the first term referring to the price structure and the second to the price level.

3.3.2 Allocation in the Public Sector

The third and the fourth terms of (11) reflect the problems of *allocation in the public sector*. They center on the question of whether and how far prices should deviate from marginal costs, as expressed by $(p_i - c_i)$. In recent decades theoretical interest has shifted from marginal-cost pricing to second-best prices which deviate from marginal costs. The Boiteux model itself is an important step in that direction, with its stress on the revenue-cost constraints of the public sector. In our version of Boiteux's model this constraint is represented by γz_k.

However, allocation in the public sector depends not only on the supply side but also on the price sensitivity of demand for publicly supplied goods. This can be clarified by defining $z_i^D(p)$[16] as 'demand for public supply' which implies

$$\frac{\partial z_i^D}{\partial p_k} := \sum_h \frac{\partial x_i^h}{\partial p_k} - \sum_j \frac{\partial y_i^j}{\partial p_k}. \tag{17}$$

Note that z_i^D is a normal, 'Marshallian' demand function and not a 'Hicksian' compensated one.

3.3.3 The Public Enterprise and the Private Sector

The fifth term in (11) reflects the *adjustment of public-firm pricing to monopolistic structures in the private unregulated economy*. The term vanishes if the

---

[16] The net supply z_i in the market clearing condition (2) does not depend directly on any other variable of the model because z_i is an instrument variable. After determining the optimal z_i from the optimization approach (5), we can define consumer net demand z_i^D as depending on prices.

private sector is perfectly competitive because profit-maximizing price-taking firms follow Hotelling's lemma which leads to

$$\sum_i p_i (\partial y_i^j / \partial p_k) = 0. \tag{18}$$

The term does not vanish if the private sector follows noncompetitive pricing. Such practices can best be described by price-cost margins which can be introduced into our analysis as follows. Consider $c_i^j := -dy_o^j / dy_i^j$, the marginal costs of producing good i in firm j at the optimum (for outputs $y_i^j > 0$; otherwise c_i^j is a partial marginal rate of transformation). c_i^j can be interpreted as 'producer prices'. In the case of efficient production

$$\sum_i c_i^j \frac{\partial y_i^j}{\partial p_k} = 0; \qquad j = 1, \dots, J. \tag{19}$$

Hence the following expansion is valid (Hagen, 1979):

$$(1 - \gamma) \sum_i \sum_j p_i \frac{\partial y_i^j}{\partial p_k} = (1 - \gamma) \sum_i \sum_j (p_i - c_i^j) \frac{\partial y_i^j}{\partial p_k}; \qquad k \in K \tag{20}$$

which clearly shows that private price-cost margins influence public prices. Incorporating these definitions and reformulations of the five terms in our basic marginal conditions, we can rewrite equation (11) as[17]

$$F_k x_k - (1 - \gamma) x_k + \sum_i (c_i - p_i) \frac{\partial z_i^D}{\partial p_k} =$$
$$= \gamma z_k - (1 - \gamma) \sum_i \sum_j (c_i^j - p_i) \frac{\partial y_i^j}{\partial p_k}; \qquad k \in K. \tag{21a}$$

For any good k which is neither supplied nor demanded by private firms, but by the public sector only ($z_k = x_k$), equation (21a) simplifies to

$$\sum_i (c_i - p_i) \frac{\partial z_i^D}{\partial p_k} = (1 - F_k) z_k - (1 - \gamma) \sum_i \sum_j (c_i^j - p_i) \frac{\partial y_i^j}{\partial p_k}; \qquad k \in K. \tag{21b}$$

---

[17] after multiplying by -1.

It seems natural to think of a public enterprise's policy within the general framework given by (21). This means that we

- look at the interaction between public and private supply;
- include distributional welfare judgments;
- use the usual, non-compensated demand for public supply.

It is rather surprising that the conventional literature did not follow this framework, which suggests itself naturally. It was not until 1956-57 that Lipsey–Lancaster stressed the interaction between the public and private sectors. And it was not until 1972 that Martin Feldstein stressed the distributional component of the problem. Moreover, the allocative elements of our framework have been narrowly analyzed by the exclusive concentration on compensated demand functions. The basic philosophy behind this emphasis on allocation is the underlying assumption that price control or price regulation are not appropriate instruments for redistribution. When dealing with compensated demand only, it is assumed that incomes are redistributed optimally by some sort of compensating lump-sum payments even though the empirical feasibility of such payments is at least questionable. The consumer-surplus approaches often employed do not make this basic redistributional procedure explicit, thereby hiding the implied value judgments.

Not only the importance of lump-sum transfers but also the conceptual weakness of this traditional procedure can be revealed by considering explicitly the redistribution required to obtain compensated demand functions in the Boiteux model.

3.4   Compensating for Income Effects

Consider now a board that controls the distribution of lump-sum incomes.[18] It computes the optimum on the basis of (6), (7), (8) and the relevant constraints. The marginal conditions (8)

$$\frac{\partial W}{\partial v^h}\frac{\partial v^h}{\partial r^h} - \sum_i \alpha_i \frac{\partial x_i^h}{\partial r^h} = 0; \qquad h = 1,\ldots,H \qquad (8)$$

can be transformed by substituting Roy's identity. We obtain

$$\frac{\partial W}{\partial v^h}\frac{\partial v^h}{\partial p_k} = -\sum_i \alpha_i x_k^h \frac{\partial x_i^h}{\partial r^h}; \qquad h = 1,\ldots,H; \quad k \in K. \qquad (8a)$$

---

[18] An implicit connection between the amount of lump-sum transfers and the public firm's deficit is guaranteed by the financial equilibrium of the economy, eq (2–14) on p. 44 of this book.

Incomes are redistributed in such a way that for each consumer the weighted sum of all income effects that result from changing price p_k is equated to the board's valuation of the individual's utility change because of the change in the price p_k. Hence, at this optimum, distributional valuations and all income effects cancel out. This implies the elimination of all distributional considerations from the pricing structure, the optimal income distribution being guaranteed by the optimal choice of lump-sum incomes, leaving only the task of allocation for the public pricing structure. At the same time all income effects are eliminated from the pricing structure, leading to a concentration on substitution effects, that is on compensated demand.

Formally we substitute (8a) into (6) and denote

$$\frac{\partial \hat{z}_i}{\partial p_k} := \left[\sum_h \left(\frac{\partial x_i^h}{\partial p_k} + x_k^h \frac{\partial x_i^h}{\partial r^h} \right) - \sum_j \frac{\partial y_i^j}{\partial p_k} \right]; \quad i = o, \ldots, n; \quad k \in K \quad (22)$$

where $\hat{z}_i(p)$ denotes the 'compensated aggregate demand' for public supply of good i.[19]

The resulting equations

$$-\sum_i \alpha_i \frac{\partial \hat{z}_i}{\partial p_k} + \overline{\gamma} z_k = 0; \qquad k \in K, \quad (23)$$

can be transformed analogously to the above 'non-compensated' case[20] to obtain

$$\sum_i (c_i - p_i) \frac{\partial \hat{z}_i}{\partial p_k} = \gamma z_k - (1 - \gamma) \sum_i \sum_j (c_i^j - p_i) \frac{\partial y_i^j}{\partial p_k}; \qquad k \in K. \quad (24)$$

These are the basic marginal conditions for the case of compensated demand.

---

[19] The reader should note that the integrability conditions are not necessarily fulfilled for demand $\hat{z}_i$. $\partial \hat{z}_i / \partial p_k$ equals $\partial \hat{z}_k / \partial p_i$ only if $\Sigma_j \partial y_i^j / \partial p_k = \Sigma_j \partial y_k^j / \partial p_i$ which is the case for perfect competition in the private economy only (Hotellings lemma). However, our model explicitly takes into account the possibility of private monopolistic pricing.

[20] The procedure is as follows: first substitute for α_i from equation (7) and divide by β_o. Then add $(1-\gamma) \Sigma_i p_i (\partial \hat{z}_i / \partial p_k)$ to both sides of the marginal conditions. For the further transformation of the right-hand side the reader may note that $\Sigma_i p_i (\partial \hat{z}_i / \partial p_k) = -\Sigma_i \Sigma_j p_i (\partial y_i^j / \partial p_k)$, because for compensated demand $\Sigma_i \Sigma_h p_i (\partial \hat{x}_i^h / \partial p_k) = 0$.

4
Positive Optimum Theory

4.1   Why Positive Theory?

The theory and application of welfare-optimal pricing have been criticized for
a number of reasons, in particular, for the normative character of the welfare
function, the excessive informational requirements and the lack of incentives
for efficiency.

Welfare Function
It is often argued that the Bergsonian welfare function should be abandoned
because it is a purely normative concept which requires far-reaching assumptions on individual utilities, namely cardinal utilities which can be compared
interpersonally.[1] Opponents of welfare economics argue that pricing theory
should be based on the actual objectives of the relevant economic agents. For
example, politicians may be interested in winning votes, bureaucrats in maximizing their budgets, output or revenue instead of welfare. Labor unions
may try to induce public enterprises to follow a policy which maximizes labor
inputs or wages (subject to relevant constraints).

Information Requirements
If we assume objectives which represent the interests of politicians and bureaucrats, the information requirements will be lower than those of the normative
approach since in most cases there is no need to go back to the social valuation of individual utilities. Moreover, we can also ignore lump-sum transfers
which, if they were to be made, would require data which could not be obtained. In contrast, if revenue or output is maximized, or if a Laspeyres price
index is minimized (always given some revenue-cost constraint), the required
data are readily available. This implies that ex post it is possible to ascertain
whether the objectives, e.g. of politicians and bureaucrats, have actually been
achieved.

Incentives
A typical board might find it both unattractive and infeasible to follow an
abstract guideline like 'maximum welfare'. In claiming managerial success
the board would prefer to be able to rely on high output or revenue figures

---

[1]   Recall, however, that we have shown in subsection 2.1.2 above that all normative
results of this book can also be interpreted as if they resulted from a pure Pareto approach
$max\, v^1$ subject to $v^h(\cdot)=v^{ho}$ for $h=2,...,H$.

of the preceding year, or the number of employees in public production. A board which only pleads that it worked for the public welfare might seem to be less dynamic and to be using 'welfare' as an excuse for its poor economic performance.

4.2   The Various Objectives

Positive theories investigate pricing policies which are actually applied in practice. We do not evaluate whether it is desirable that a public enterprise follows some particular positive-theory objective, but rather accept the objective and consider the consequences of optimizing such an objective. Often, however, these consequences can best be evaluated when compared with a normative-theory benchmark, in particular Ramsey pricing.

According to the above-mentioned pragmatic point of view, there are as many positive-theory objectives as the day-to-day practice of public enterprises brings about. However, the neoclassical paradigm of rational economic behavior reduces these objectives because there is only a finite number of agents involved and a finite number of economic variables and indicators which lend themselves as positive-theory objectives.

Consider first politically-minded agents. Local public enterprises may be used by policymakers to attract votes. This may be of particular interest if in some election public-sector pricing becomes one of the major questions of the political platforms (for instance if some incumbent or opponent promises not to increase local public transportation prices during his next term of office). Often, however, the political side of public-enterprise policy concentrates less on votes, and more on giving sinecures to party politicians – this typically is the basis of 'empire-building' bureaucratic procedures in public enterprises. Following Niskanen, budget maximization can be assumed as an appropriate description of such an enterprise's policy. And it is only a small step from budget maximization to output or revenue maximization, a grey zone between empire-building bureaucrats and market-share oriented technocrats in public enterprises.

Since profit maximization typically is forbidden for public enterprises, they are prone to the application of objectives which represent the 'political fashion of the day'. Energy-saving policies in the mid-seventies are as prominent an example as the minimization of the cost-of-living index by public-sector prices and the many proposals of zero pricing of local public transportation.

Positive-theory objectives may also be multiple objectives. Public enterprises' policies are influenced by various groups and the objective of the firm may therefore result from a compromise between such groups. As a case in point, in this book we deal with an objective function which combines the board's interest in output and a trade union's interest in wages and in jobs. (The latter is a multiple objective in itself – revealing the trade unions' willingness to ignore any trade-off between high wages and high employment.) Note that multiple objectives are nothing bad per se, as long as the weights of the various components of these objectives are well defined and known to the involved economic agents. In our theoretical model this is the case; those involved with public enterprises in practice, however, often complain about the fuzziness of multiple objectives.

The reader should not be puzzled about the diversity of positive-theory objectives – economic practice always is diverse, and according to the political and economic circumstances various positive-theory objectives will be applied. Even a single enterprise might apply various positive objectives in the course of time – an extreme example was London Transport which in the seventies and early eighties fundamentally changed its (positive) objectives several times. It moved from commercial pricing (1970–2) to a 'fare freeze' in order to contribute to the central government's target of fighting inflation (1972–5), to a policy of maximizing passenger miles (1975–81), then to a distributionally motivated 'fares fair' policy (from November 1981) which was ended by a doubling of fares in March 1982 as a consequence of a decision of the House of Lords.[2]

A detailed treatment and economic interpretation of positive-theory pricing structures will be given in chapters 17 – 22. In the present chapter we shall only present the theoretical derivation of the relevant marginal conditions based on an optimization approach which is formulated in so general a way that it comprises all of the various objectives mentioned in the preceding paragraphs. For this purpose we use $\Phi(p, z)$ as general notation for any objective function of positive pricing. Φ may be the number of votes, the size of the bureaucratic budget, output, revenue etc. A brief overview of the formal definitions of the various objectives $\Phi(p, z)$ is given in table 1 below. For details on these definitions the reader is referred to the chapters 17 – 22.

The environment in which the board is assumed to be working is treated in the same way as in the extended version of the Boiteux model we used in chapter 3. There is an economy with H utility-maximizing consumers, J private enterprises and a public sector. The board chooses prices $\{p_k, k \in K\}$ and production plans $\{z_i, i \in I\}$, given the production technology, market-clearing constraints and a revenue-cost constraint. Many political and bureaucratic objectives require explicit differentiation between inputs and outputs. We have to include such differentiation in our model. $z_i \leq 0; i = o, \ldots, d$ denote public inputs and $z_i \geq 0; i = d + 1, \ldots, n$ denote public outputs.

---

[2] For details see Bös (1989: 346–8).

Table 1: Positive Theory Objectives

objective	objective function to be maximized(Φ)[3]	explanation
votes (chapter 17)	$f(v^1, \ldots, v^H)$	The function f measures expected votes.
Laspeyres price index (ch. 18)[4]	$-\sum_{d+1}^{n} p_i x_i^o / \sum_{d+1}^{n} p_i^o x_i^o$	The superscript 'o' refers to the base period in which the 'basket' $\{x_i^o, i = d+1, \ldots, n\}$, was empirically determined.
'discretionary' budget (chapter 19)	$\sum_{d+1}^{n} p_i z_i + \mathcal{B}(z^+)$	Revenue from selling output and from a government grant $\mathcal{B}(z^+)$; $z^+ := (z_{d+1}, \ldots, z_n)$ is a vector of outputs.
output (chapter 20)	$\sum_{d+1}^{n} z_i$	The sum of several outputs, f.i. first-class and second-class passenger miles.
revenue (chapter 20)	$\sum_{d+1}^{n} p_i z_i$	The revenue from selling output; there is no government grant $\mathcal{B}(z^+)$.
energy (privately supplied, chapter 20)	$z_a - \sum_h x_a^h(\cdot) + \sum_{j \notin A} y_a^j(\cdot)$	a is the index of a single good 'energy'. A is the index set of energy-producing private firms.
combined bureaucrat - trade union interests (ch. 21)	$U^1(z_{d+1}, \ldots, z_n) + U^2(p_o, z_o)^5$	U^1 is the bureaucrat's utility, U^2 is trade-union's utility.

---

[3] We restrict ourselves to the regulation of output prices, $k = d+1, \ldots, n$. The only exceptions are energy pricing (chapter 20) and the explicit consideration of wage regulation if trade union interests are explicitly considered (chapter 21).

[4] We restrict ourselves to the analysis of a Laspeyres index which is the usual price index applied by statistical bureaus. Comparisons with a Paasche index or a true-cost-of-living index are straightforward. See Bös (1978a).

[5] In this case the numeraire must not be labor, but some other good.

Table 1: Continued

objective	$\partial\Phi/\partial z_i$		$\partial\Phi/\partial p_k$
votes (chapter 17)	0		$\sum_h \frac{\partial f}{\partial v^h} \cdot \frac{\partial v^h}{\partial p_k} < 0$
Laspeyres price index (ch. 18)	0		$-x_i^o / \sum_{d+1}^n p_i^o x_i^o < 0$
'discretionary' budget (chapter 19)	0 $p_i + \partial\mathcal{B}/\partial z_i > 0$	inputs outputs	$z_k > 0$
output (chapter 20)	0 1	inputs outputs	0
revenue (chapter 20)	0 $p_i > 0$	inputs outputs	$z_k > 0$
energy (privately supplied, chapter 20)	0 $\forall i \neq a$ 1 $i = a$		$-\left(\frac{\partial z_a^D}{\partial p_k} + \sum_{j \in A} \frac{\partial y_a^j}{\partial p_k}\right) > 0^6$
combined bureau-crat - trade union interests (ch. 21)	$U_z^2 < 0$ $i = o$ $U_i^1 > 0$ outputs		$U_p^2 > 0$ $i = o$ 0 outputs

---

[6] In chapter 20 we also explicitly deal with the case where energy is publicly supplied. – For both privately and publicly provided energy note that $\partial z_a^D/\partial p_k$ does not result from directly differentiating z_a, but from defining $\partial z_a^D/\partial p_k := \Sigma_h \partial x_a^h/\partial p_k - \Sigma_j \partial y_a^j/\partial p_k$. Now assume normally reacting demand for energy, $\partial z_a^D/\partial p_a < 0$, and complementarity of energy and other goods, $\partial z_a^D/\partial p_k < 0, k \neq a$. The above signs hold regardless of whether $z_a > 0$ (public energy supply case) or $z_a < 0$ (private supply case). Additionally we assume normally reacting supply of energy, $\partial y_a^j/\partial p_a < 0, j \in A$, and, once again, complementarity of energy and other goods, $\partial y_a^j/\partial p_k < 0, k \neq a, j \in A$.

4.3 The Marginal Conditions on Positive-Theory Prices

We impute to the board an optimization approach characterized by the following Lagrangean function

$$
\mathcal{F} = \Phi(p, z) - \sum_{i=o}^{n} \alpha_i \left[\sum_h x_i^h(p, r^h) - z_i - \sum_j y_i^j(p) \right] -
$$

$$
- \beta g(z) - \overline{\gamma} \left(\Pi^o - \sum_{i=o}^{n} p_i z_i \right).
\tag{1}
$$

Differentiating $\mathcal{F}$ with respect to prices and quantities[7] leads to the following system of necessary conditions for an optimum

$$
\frac{\partial \Phi}{\partial p_k} - \sum_{i=o}^{n} \alpha_i \frac{\partial z_i^D}{\partial p_k} + \overline{\gamma} z_k = 0; \qquad k \in K,
\tag{2}
$$

$$
\frac{\partial \Phi}{\partial z_i} + \alpha_i - \beta \frac{\partial g}{\partial z_i} + \overline{\gamma} p_i = 0; \qquad i = o, \ldots, n
\tag{3}
$$

where we have made use of the definition of $\partial z_i^D / \partial p_k$ as presented above in equation (3–17).

These marginal conditions can be transformed in the usual way. After dividing all conditions by $\beta_o := \beta(\partial g / \partial z_o)$, we transform eqs. (3) into

$$
\frac{\alpha_i}{\beta_o} = \left(c_i - \gamma p_i - \frac{1}{\beta_o} \frac{\partial \Phi}{\partial z_i} \right); \qquad i = o, \ldots, n
\tag{4}
$$

where $c_i := (\partial g / \partial z_i)/(\partial g / \partial z_o)$ and $\gamma := \overline{\gamma}/\beta_o$ as in chapter 3.

We will always define the chosen objective function $\Phi(p, z)$ in such a way that $\beta_o > 0$. γ will be positive if the objectives are defined as above and if the prescribed profit exceeds the unconstrained Φ-optimizing profit. $\gamma < 1$ can be deduced as usual as long as the objective function does not depend directly on labor inputs.

Substituting (4) into (2) we obtain the following conditions for optimal prices

$$
\sum_{i=o}^{n} \left(c_i - \gamma p_i - \frac{1}{\beta_o} \frac{\partial \Phi}{\partial z_i} \right) \frac{\partial z_i^D}{\partial p_k} = \gamma z_k + \frac{1}{\beta_o} \frac{\partial \Phi}{\partial p_k}; \qquad k \in K.
\tag{5}
$$

---

[7] We always implicitly assume that politicians use sufficiently many instruments as to avoid degeneration of the optimization approach because of a lack of degrees of freedom.

To obtain price-cost differences in the left-hand terms we simply subtract $(1 - \gamma)\Sigma_i p_i(\partial z_i^D/\partial p_k)$ on both sides of the marginal conditions. The result is as follows:

$$\sum_{i=o}^{n}\left(c_i - p_i - \frac{1}{\beta_o}\frac{\partial \Phi}{\partial z_i}\right)\frac{\partial z_i^D}{\partial p_k} =$$

$$= \gamma z_k - (1 - \gamma)\sum_{i=o}^{n}p_i\frac{\partial z_i^D}{\partial p_k} + \frac{1}{\beta_o}\frac{\partial \Phi}{\partial p_k}; \qquad k \in K. \tag{6}$$

Using eqs. (3–14) and (3–20), we obtain

$$\sum_i p_i\frac{\partial z_i^D}{\partial p_k} = \sum_i p_i\left[\sum_h \frac{\partial x_i^h}{\partial p_k} - \sum_j \frac{\partial y_i^j}{\partial p_k}\right] =$$

$$= -x_k - \sum_i\sum_j(p_i - c_i^j)\frac{\partial y_i^j}{\partial p_k}; \qquad k \in K. \tag{7}$$

Substituting the expression in (7) into equation (6) we obtain the general price conditions

$$\sum_{i=o}^{n}\left(c_i - p_i - \frac{1}{\beta_o}\frac{\partial \Phi}{\partial z_i}\right)\frac{\partial z_i^D}{\partial p_k} = \gamma z_k + (1 - \gamma)x_k +$$

$$+ (1 - \gamma)\sum_i\sum_j(p_i - c_i^j)\frac{\partial y_i^j}{\partial p_k} + \frac{1}{\beta_o}\frac{\partial \Phi}{\partial p_k}; \qquad k \in K. \tag{8}$$

The reader will note that in the above pricing rules the adjustment to monopolistic structures in the private unregulated economy follows the same lines as in the normative approach. Therefore we need not repeat explicitly all the results when dealing with positive approaches. It is more convenient to concentrate on those terms of the respective marginal conditions where positive approaches actually differ from normative ones. For that purpose we neglect all interdependencies between the public and the private sector. We therefore assume:

(i) only prices of publicly supplied goods are controlled;[8]

---

[8] This assumption could be given up to investigate public-sector pricing of goods which are only produced in the private sector. Such investigations, however, are beyond the scope of this book.

(ii) the private sector is perfectly competitive; goods with publicly controlled prices are neither supplied nor demanded by private firms ($z_k = x_k$).

Under these assumptions we obtain the following pricing structure

$$\sum_{i=o}^{n} \left(c_i - p_i - \frac{1}{\beta_o} \frac{\partial \Phi}{\partial z_i} \right) \frac{\partial z_i^D}{\partial p_k} = z_k + \frac{1}{\beta_o} \frac{\partial \Phi}{\partial p_k}; \qquad k \in K. \tag{9}$$

Part III, on positive public-enterprise economics, will concentrate on this system of marginal conditions.

It is interesting to note that γ does not appear in (9). Thus, the revenue-cost constraint does not influence the *structure* of prices, although it influences their *absolute values*. The conditions (9) even hold if there is no revenue-cost constraint at all! Let us briefly discuss what happens in positive-theory models in the absence of an explicit revenue-cost constraint. Of course we cannot expect marginal-cost pricing because we do not deal with welfare maximization. However, we could expect zero prices if output or a Laspeyres price index is minimized. It is interesting to note that this result typically will not occur. If at zero prices demand goes to infinity, the market-clearing conditions cannot be met. The financial equilibrium of the economy becomes an implicit revenue-cost constraint. The deficit of the public enterprise is restricted to

$$\Pi^o = \sum_{h} r^h - \sum_{j} \pi^j \tag{2--14}$$

where the sum of non-labor incomes $\Sigma_h r^h$ is exogenously given in our positive-theory models and the private entrepreneurs enjoy those intra-marginal profits $\Sigma_j \pi^j$ which accrue in a perfectly competitive economy.

5
Normative Piecemeal Theory

5.1   On the Difference Between Optimum and Piecemeal Policies

In chapter 3 we presented the conditions for optimal prices and lump-sum incomes. In practice, the prices set by a public enterprise which assumes lump-sum incomes are likely to be suboptimal. Switching to the optimal set of prices would typically require a total rearrangement of all relevant variables.

Such a one-shot policy may often be impossible or unwanted. Political reasoning might suggest the choice of some stepwise course, which is less exposed to criticism from the opposition and the media. Economically, the public enterprise's board might fear the disturbance of consumption habits by abrupt policy changes. The latter argument is closely connected to the informational requirements of pricing policies. A board which tries to achieve an optimum in a one-shot policy needs full information on market demand functions, its competitors' supply functions, and its own cost functions and those of its competitors. Even a well-informed board will have knowledge of these functions only in the neighborhood of its *present situation.*

The board facing the above problems will turn to a piecemeal policy. The optimum being unknown, and possibly far away, the board starts from given prices and lump-sum incomes, the level and structure of which will usually not be optimal, and searches for small price changes which increase welfare. If lump-sum incomes are available as instruments, we can also integrate the analysis of changes in lump sums into such a piecemeal framework. The welfare-increasing piecemeal policy in a Boiteux world must be market-clearing and technologically and financially feasible. Each small step has to consider the usual constraints, as treated in the previous chapters of this book.

A theory of piecemeal policy yields *sufficient* conditions for welfare improvements, as opposed to an optimum theory which yields *necessary* conditions which are fulfilled at the optimum. Let us give a simple example. The optimum Ramsey pricing policy tells us that it is a necessary condition for an optimum that price-cost margins are fixed according to an inverse-elasticity rule. A piecemeal Ramsey policy tell us that, given some public prices, near the optimum but still non-optimal, an increase of the price-cost margin of a price-inelastic good is a sufficient condition for a welfare improvement. However, this property need not always hold for all welfare-increasing price changes along a path from non-optimal prices to optimal prices. If the present situation is far from the welfare optimum, there are so many different ways to increase welfare that clear-cut rules, comparable to our optimum rules, usually will *not* be obtainable. Therefore the general results of a *theory* of piecemeal policy are disappointing. This does not mean that a theory of piecemeal policy is unimportant. After specifying all relevant functions, it may well serve as the basis for the board's decisions on how to proceed step by step.

As the general results are disappointing, it is not necessary to deal in full detail with all different possible cases of changing prices and lump-sum incomes. We shall restrict the analysis to one particular case, namely, to small changes of prices (and the corresponding small changes of quantities). The extension to changing lump-sum incomes is straightforward.

5.2   Welfare Improvements with Non-Tight Constraints

Welfare improvements are 'non-tight' if they are performed under inequality constraints. Consider a board which is guided by the welfare function

$$W(v^1, \ldots, v^H) \qquad (1)$$

where $v^h(p, r^h)$ are the indirect utilities which depend on variable prices and on constant lump-sum incomes.

At the starting point of our analysis, prices p_k and quantities z_i are set in a market-clearing and technologically and financially feasible way:

$$\sum_h x_i^h(p, r^h) - z_i - \sum_j y_i^j(p) = 0; \quad i = o, \ldots, n, \qquad (2)$$

$$g(z) = 0, \qquad (3)$$

$$\Pi^o = \sum_{i=o}^n p_i z_i. \qquad (4)$$

The board intends to increase welfare

$$\Delta W(v^1, \ldots, v^H) > 0 \qquad (5)$$

by small changes of prices $\Delta p_k, k \in K^1$ and of quantities $\Delta z_i, i \in I$, always remaining in the Boiteux world. Let us assume that along any path of price and quantity changes all markets must remain in equilibrium; the technology and budget constraints are weakened to inequalities.

---

[1] The uncontrolled prices are assumed to remain constant ($dp_i = 0 \ \forall i \notin K$).

The above problem is very complicated because we do not know the functional shape of the different 'reaction functions': neither do we know exactly how welfare reacts to price and quantity changes, nor do we know exactly how the constraints are altered. As shown in figure 7, $\Delta W = 0$ may be some arbitrary, non linear function in a $(\Delta p_1, \Delta p_2)$-space, going through the status quo point X.

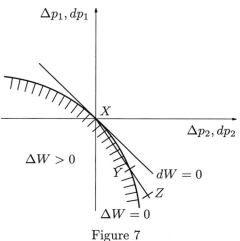

Figure 7

Usually, this problem is solved by linearizing all 'reaction functions', using the total differentials.[2] Then our problem consists of finding price changes dp_k and quantity changes dz_i which fulfill the following conditions:[3]

$$dW = \sum_h \sum_k \frac{\partial W}{\partial v^h} \frac{\partial v^h}{\partial p_k} dp_k > 0, \tag{6}$$

$$\sum_h \sum_k \frac{\partial x_i^h}{\partial p_k} dp_k - dz_i - \sum_j \sum_k \frac{\partial y_i^j}{\partial p_k} dp_k = 0; \qquad i = o, \ldots, n, \tag{7}$$

$$\sum_i \frac{\partial g}{\partial z_i} dz_i \leq 0, \tag{8}$$

$$-\sum_i p_i dz_i - \sum_k z_k dp_k \leq 0. \tag{9}$$

---

[2] Hammond (1984) takes into account also second-order terms.
[3] We assume enough prices and quantities are changed to avoid overdetermination.

Consider a feasible ray of price changes, represented by XYZ in the above figure 7.[4] As $\Delta W = 0$ is non-linear, a point like Z actually does not improve welfare although it is shown as welfare-improving under the approximation $dW > 0$. All points between X and Y, however, are welfare improving. Hence, if the step $(\Delta p_1, \Delta p_2)$ along any feasible ray is small enough, there will be a welfare improvement. Denoting proportional changes of both (all) prices along such a ray by 's' we obtain

$$\exists s > 0 : \forall s' < s \mid W(p) < W(p + s'dp); \quad s' > 0. \tag{10}$$

The above result implies that there is always some possible welfare improvement as long as the step taken is sufficiently small. This result is valid for all rays in the non-closed space $dW > 0$. It is not valid for $dW = 0$ which is tangential to $\Delta W = 0$. Therefore only $dW > 0$ is sensible, not $dW \geq 0$.

It is not only condition (6), $dW > 0$, which causes particular problems. Let us also examine conditions (7) – (9). These conditions are sensible because we assumed that the enterprise started from a market-clearing and technologically and financially feasible situation. Without this assumption, changing prices and quantities according to (7) – (9) would imply switching from an infeasible situation to another which may also be infeasible, and we have no economic rationale for such a change.

For *finite* changes of prices and quantities, conditions (7) – (9) normally do not guarantee that the new situation is still market-clearing and technologically and financially feasible. Only for infinitesimal changes dp_k and dz_i is such an outcome guaranteed.[5] For sufficiently small steps we may hope that the outcome is almost always welfare improving.

As welfare-improving finite price and quantity changes may lead away from allocative efficiency, one could even doubt that there is any connection between a piecemeal policy as described above and an optimum policy, given the formulation of a Boiteux-type model. Fortunately Farkas' 'theorem of the alternative' enables us to show that such a connection exists. For this purpose we condense the analysis to piecemeal-*pricing* policies, and assume that the piecemeal-quantity changes always secure market equilibria, given the price changes. The economic reasoning requires solving (7) explicitly for dz_i to obtain

$$dz_i = \sum_k \sum_h \frac{\partial x_i^h}{\partial p_k} dp_k - \sum_k \sum_j \frac{\partial y_i^j}{\partial p_k} dp_k = \sum_k \frac{\partial z_i^D}{\partial p_k} dp_k; \quad i = o, \ldots, n. \tag{11}$$

---

[4] The following analysis deals with W only, ignoring the constraints for welfare-improvement. They could easily be inserted into figure 7, but would not alter the economic reasoning in favor of $dW > 0$.

[5] The same holds trivially if all relevant functions in eqs. (7) – (9) are linear in p and z.

After substituting for the dz_i's in (8) and (9), we obtain the system

$$A_o^T(dp_k) = \left(\sum_h \frac{\partial W}{\partial v^h}\frac{\partial v^h}{\partial p_k}\right)^T (dp_k) > 0, \qquad (12)$$

$$A_1^T(dp_k) = \left(\sum_i \frac{\partial g}{\partial z_i}\frac{\partial z_i^D}{\partial p_k}\right)^T (dp_k) \leq 0, \qquad (13)$$

$$A_2^T(dp_k) = \left(-\sum_i p_i \frac{\partial z_i^D}{\partial p_k} - z_k\right)^T (dp_k) \leq 0 \qquad (14)$$

where (dp_k) is the vector[6] of price changes; A_o, A_1, A_2 are gradient vectors which are defined as can be seen in $(12) - (14)$.

It is convenient to denote the set of feasible welfare-improving price changes by $\Omega(dp_k)$:

$$\Omega(dp_k) = \left\{(dp_k) \mid A_o^T(dp_k) > 0; A_1^T(dp_k) \leq 0; A_2^T(dp_k) \leq 0\right\}. \qquad (15)$$

After this preparatory work we are ready to apply Farkas' theorem to our problem. This theorem belongs to the family of theorems which state that either a system of homogeneous linear equations has a solution or a related system of inequalities has a solution, but never both. For an exact mathematical presentation and comparison of the different 'theorems of the alternative' see Mangasarian (1969).

The special case of Farkas' theorem to be applied to our problem is as follows. For each given matrix $A = (A_1, A_2)^T$ and each vector A_o[7] either

(i) $A_o^T \varrho > 0$, $A^T \varrho \leq 0$ has a solution ϱ or
(ii) $A\chi = A_o$, $\chi \geq 0$[8] has a solution χ

but never both.

To apply the above theorem to our problem, we define $\varrho := (dp_k)$ and A_o, A_1, A_2 as before. Then it can be seen easily that the piecemeal policy conditions $(12) - (14)$ satisfy case (i) of Farkas' theorem.

---

[6] Principally we define vectors as column vectors; A^T means the transpose.

[7] $A_o \neq 0$ is a sort of trivial condition in our case; otherwise the whole problem of welfare improvement is not well-defined.

[8] $\chi \geq 0$ means that all components of vector χ must be non-negative, and so the case of all components equal to zero is not excluded.

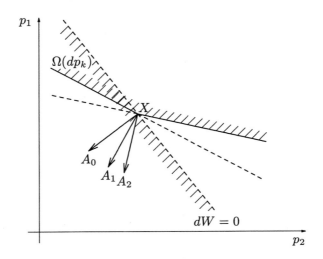

Figure 8a

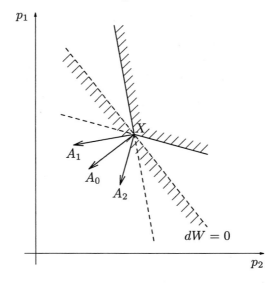

Figure 8b

What about case (ii) of Farkas' theorem? Defining $\chi \equiv (\beta, \overline{\gamma})^T$, this case implies

$$A_o - \beta A_1 - \overline{\gamma} A_2 = (0) \qquad (16a)$$

where (0) is an adequately defined vector consisting of zero elements. This system of equations can be written as

$$\left(\sum_h \frac{\partial W}{\partial v^h} \frac{\partial v^h}{\partial p_k} \right) - \beta \left(\sum_i \frac{\partial g}{\partial z_i} \frac{\partial z_i^D}{\partial p_k} \right) - \overline{\gamma} \left(-\sum_i p_i \frac{\partial z_i^D}{\partial p_k} - z_k \right) = (0)$$

or equivalently

$$\sum_h \frac{\partial W}{\partial v^h} \frac{\partial v^h}{\partial p_k} - \sum_i \left[\beta \frac{\partial g}{\partial z_i} - \overline{\gamma} p_i \right] \frac{\partial z_i^D}{\partial p_k} + \overline{\gamma} z_k = 0 \quad \text{for all} \quad k \in K. \quad (16b)$$

This result is identical with our necessary optimum conditions (3–9)! The application of Farkas' theorem to our problem, therefore, shows that either $(12) - (14)$ hold or (16), but never both. Hence, there is always a possibility for welfare-improving price changes unless the existing prices are welfare-optimal under the given constraints. This shows the connection between piecemeal and optimum theory.[9]

The economic content of the piecemeal-policy conditions $(12) - (14)$, and of their connection to the optimum conditions (16), can best be illustrated by means of a graphical exposition. Figure 8a shows the contours of the conditions $(12) - (14)$ for two price changes dp_1, dp_2. The hatching indicates the location of the halfspaces which are generated by the above conditions. All price changes that start from the status quo X and move into the set $\Omega(dp_k)$ are welfare-improving under the chosen constraints.

In the case of figure 8b the situation is rather different. The intersection of the three halfspaces generated by $(12) - (14)$ is empty.[10] No welfare-improving price changes are possible; point X is a welfare optimum. Graphically such a situation is always given if A_o lies between A_1 and A_2. Analytically, in that case A_o, A_1 and A_2 can be written as a non-negative linear combination

$$A_o = \beta A_1 + \overline{\gamma} A_2; \qquad \beta, \overline{\gamma} \geq 0 \qquad (17)$$

which is the well-known optimum condition.[11]

---

[9] Because of $\chi \geq 0$, the Lagrangean multipliers must be non-negative, $\beta, \overline{\gamma} \geq 0$.

[10] Remember that $dW = 0$ itself is *not* part of the halfspace generated by (12). Hence the intersection is actually empty. Otherwise the intersection would have consisted of point X.

[11] We do not explicitly deal with degenerate cases where either χ_1 or χ_2 equals zero.

5.3   Welfare Improvements with Tight Technology Constraint

Matters become more complicated if more of the relevant constraints have to hold as equalities. The best example is offered by the case of a tight technology constraint whence the welfare-improving price changes should satisfy the following conditions

$$A_o^T(dp_k) > 0,\tag{18}$$

$$A_1^T(dp_k) = 0,\tag{19}$$

$$A_2^T(dp_k) \leq 0,\tag{20}$$

where the vectors A_o, A_1, A_2 and (dp_k) have the same meaning as before. We denote the set of feasible welfare-improving price changes by $\widetilde{\Omega}(dp_k)$:

$$\widetilde{\Omega}(dp_k) = \{(dp_k) \mid A_o^T(dp_k) > 0; A_1^T(dp_k) = 0; A_2^T(dp_k) \leq 0\}.\tag{21}$$

In this case Farkas' theorem is inapplicable, but Motzkin's theorem of the alternative can be applied.[12] The special case of the theorem to be applied is as follows. For each of the given vectors A_o,[13] A_1 and A_2, either

(i) $A_o^T \varrho > 0, \quad A_1^T \varrho = 0, \quad A_2^T \varrho \leq 0 \quad$ has a solution ϱ or

(ii) $\chi_o A_o + \chi_1 A_1 - \chi_2 A_2 = 0; \quad \chi_o > 0, \chi_1 \gtreqless 0, \chi_2 \geq 0$ has a solution χ.

If the vector $\chi = (\chi_o, \chi_1, \chi_2)$ is normalized so as to yield $\chi = (1, -\beta, \overline{\gamma}),$[14] it can be seen easily that Motzkin's theorem is applicable to the above problem of tight welfare improvements. Once again, there is some possibility for welfare-improving price changes[15] according to (18) – (20) unless the prices are already optimal.

The graphical illustration of the piecemeal-policy conditions (18) – (20) is a bit more difficult than in the case of improvements under non-tight constraints because at least three prices must be changed and hence a three-dimensional presentation is required. However, there is a technique which

---

[12] See once again Mangasarian (1969) for mathematical details. Diewert (1978) and Weymark (1979) have applied Motzkin's theorem to tax reforms.

[13] Once again, $A_o \neq 0$ must be fulfilled. Not only for mathematical reasons, but also for economic reasons, as our problem is only well-defined for $A_o \neq 0$.

[14] Motzkin's theorem does *not* imply a particular sign of β; $\overline{\gamma} \geq 0$ is, once again, implied.

[15] At least three prices must be changed, otherwise the problem is overdetermined.

allows an easier graphical presentation. Consider changing three prices. We know that all price changes must take place along the plane $A_1(dp_k) = 0$. Typically this plane will intersect the two halfspaces which are generated by $A_o(dp_k) > 0$ and $A_2(dp_k) \leq 0$.

To draw figure 9 we rotate the plane $A_1(dp_k) = 0$ until it coincides with the page.[16] The figure shows the contours of conditions (18) and (20). $\vec{A}_o$ and $\vec{A}_2$ are projections of the gradient vectors into the plane $A_1(dp_k) = 0$. All price changes along this plane that start from the status quo X and move into the set $\widetilde{\Omega}(dp_k)$ are welfare-increasing under the chosen constraints.

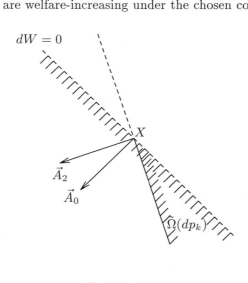

Figure 9

It is not easy to show graphically the typical optimum case.[17] Take again a three-price case where the conditions (18) – (20) are three-dimensional hyperplanes. Then in the typical optimum case all three planes intersect along one straight line, all three gradient vectors being vertical on this line. Looking vertically at the plane $A_1(dp_k) = 0$ yields figure 10a; looking vertically at the line of intersection of all three planes yields figure 10b. Since all planes intersect along the same line, two degrees of freedom are lost, in other words, A_o, A_1 and A_2 are linearly dependent:

---

[16] Because of this rotation we cannot explicitly denote axes of a system of coordinates in such a case.

[17] where χ_o, χ_1 and $\chi_2 \neq 0$.

$$A_o = -(\chi_1/\chi_o)A_1 + (\chi_2/\chi_o)A_2 \tag{22}$$

where $(\chi_1/\chi_o) = -\beta$ and $(\chi_2/\chi_o) = \overline{\gamma}$.

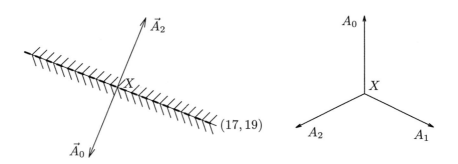

Figure 10a   Figure 10b

5.4   On Welfare–Improving Increases of Public Inefficiency[18]

Given an inefficient initial situation, one would a priori expect piecemeal recommendations for which welfare improvements are associated with reductions of inefficiency. This a priori expectation is wrong. It may well be that the first steps of piecemeal policy should go in the direction of further increases of inefficiency, and not toward decreasing inefficiency until some subsequent stage of policy.[19]

The above statement can be proved easily. Given tight market-clearing constraints,[20] but non-tight technology and budget constraints, i.e.

$$g(z) < 0, \tag{23}$$

$$\Pi^o - \sum_i p_i z_i < 0, \tag{24}$$

---

[18] See Peters (1985).

[19] Cfr. also Smith (1983).

[20] If market disequilibria are allowed, the normative-piecemeal theory does not lead to a meaningful analysis, in contrast to many cases of the positive-piecemeal theory. See subsection 6.2.2 below.

the first step of piecemeal policy should follow the steepest ascent of the objective function ('gradient-projection method'):[21]

$$(dp_k) = \sum_h \frac{\partial W}{\partial v^h} \frac{\partial v^h}{\partial p_k}. \tag{25}$$

The economic implications of this gradient-projection method are as follows. Substitute Roy's identity to obtain

$$(dp_k) = -\sum_h \frac{\partial W}{\partial v^h} \frac{\partial v^h}{\partial r^h} x_k^h. \tag{26}$$

The resulting price changes are higher, the higher the quantities consumed (x_k^h) and the higher the social valuation of consumption. The latter will typically imply larger price reductions of necessities.[22]

Any further economic interpretation of the above piecemeal policy has to explicitly consider the technology and the budget constraints. We rewrite these constraints using dummy variables $DV_1, DV_2 > 0$

$$\tilde{g}(z, DV_1) = g(z) + DV_1 = 0 \tag{27}$$

$$\tilde{\Pi}(z, p, DV_2) = \Pi^o - \sum_i p_i z_i + DV_2 = 0. \tag{28}$$

We postulate the validity of these constraints along any piecemeal-policy path and therefore the following linear approximations hold[23]

$$\sum_i \sum_k \frac{\partial \tilde{g}}{\partial z_i} \frac{\partial z_i^D}{\partial p_k} dp_k + \frac{\partial \tilde{g}}{\partial DV_1} dDV_1 = 0, \tag{29}$$

$$\sum_k \left[\sum_i \frac{\partial \tilde{\Pi}}{\partial z_i} \frac{\partial z_i^D}{\partial p_k} + \frac{\partial \tilde{\Pi}}{\partial p_k} \right] dp_k + \frac{\partial \tilde{\Pi}}{\partial DV_2} dDV_2 = 0. \tag{30}$$

To transform the above approximations, we first differentiate (27) and (28) with respect to z_i and DV_i, respectively:

---

[21] See Luenberger (1973: 247–54).

[22] The reader should compare eq. (26) on piecemeal-price changes, and the 'distributional characteristic' of the optimum policy, as defined in eq. (3–13).

[23] By substituting (11) we explicitly consider the market-clearing conditions.

$$\frac{\partial \tilde{g}}{\partial z_i} = \frac{\partial g}{\partial z_i} \; ; \; \frac{\partial \tilde{g}}{\partial DV_1} = 1, \tag{31}$$

$$\frac{\partial \tilde{\Pi}}{\partial z_i} = -p_i \; ; \; \frac{\partial \tilde{\Pi}}{\partial p_k} = -z_k \; ; \; \frac{\partial \tilde{\Pi}}{\partial DV_2} = 1. \tag{32}$$

Next we recall that price changes (dp_k) follow the gradient of the welfare function as shown in (26). Welfare-improving price changes, therefore, can be characterized by the following changes of the dummy variables:

$$dDV_1 = \sum_h \sum_i \sum_k \frac{\partial W}{\partial v^h} x_k^h \frac{\partial v^h}{\partial r^h} \frac{\partial g}{\partial z_i} \frac{\partial z_i^D}{\partial p_k}, \tag{33}$$

$$dDV_2 = \sum_h \sum_k \frac{\partial W}{\partial v^h} x_k^h \frac{\partial v^h}{\partial r^h} \left\{ -\sum_i p_i \frac{\partial z_i^D}{\partial p_k} - z_k \right\}. \tag{34}$$

Let us first interpret equation (33). The derivates on the right-hand side have different signs, namely

- $\partial W/\partial v^h \geq 0$ (value judgment in the welfare function)
- $\partial v^h/\partial r^h > 0$ (property of an indirect utility function)
- $\partial g/\partial z_i > 0$ (property of the production function)
- $\partial z_i^D/\partial p_k \gtrless 0$ (if z_i and z_k are outputs $i \neq k$: typically positive for substitutes, negative for complements).

Hence, the sign of dDV_1 cannot be determined: increasing inefficiency, $dDV_1 > 0$, cannot be excluded as a possible candidate for welfare-improving price changes.

The worst is yet to come: the paradoxical case of increasing inefficiency is likely to occur. Consider a single price change dp_k. Any tendencies toward $dDV_1 < 0$ come from the own price effect $\partial z_k^D/\partial p_k < 0$, or from the cross-price effects of complements. All cross effects with respect to substitutes tend toward $dDV_1 > 0$. The more disaggregated a model, the more likely the occurence of the above paradoxical result.

Figure 11a corroborates the probability of paradoxical results. For a one input - one output model of a public monopoly, we consider the technology frontier $g(z)$,[24] and an aggregate offer curve, connecting the consumption

---

[24] Without limitation of generality figure 11a uses a convex technology frontier.

bundles (z_o, z_1) the consumers would choose at different possible price ratios.[25] X_3 is the optimum. Any piecemeal policy which starts somewhere between X_1 and X_2 will first imply increasing inefficiency because the distance between the technology frontier and the offer curve increases if one moves from X_1 toward X_2. Only if the piecemeal policy starts somewhere between X_2 and X_3 will decreasing inefficiency be the appropriate choice.

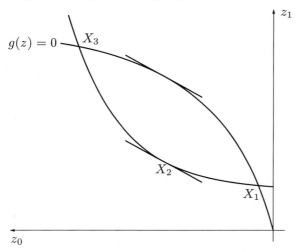

Figure 11a

Let us now turn to eq. (34). $dDV_2 > 0$ implies that the public enterprise's excess revenues $(\Sigma_i p_i z_i - \Pi^o)$ increase. Such a case seems to be a poor candidate for welfare improvements because typically we would expect this policy to be associated with higher public prices, which should reduce, and not increase, welfare. Once again, however, we cannot exclude paradoxical results. An example can be found easily. We know from (34) that $dDV_2 > 0$ if

$$z_k + \sum_i p_i \frac{\partial z_i^D}{\partial p_k} < 0 \qquad \text{for all } k. \tag{35}$$

Hence $dDV_2 > 0$ if the effects of complements are predominant and in addition if demand is highly responsive and if the output of publicly supplied goods is not too large. – However, one should not be too concerned about

---

[25] The positive intersect of the offer curve and the z_1-axis can be explained by assuming a positive Σr^h in the initial situation.

such a possibility. Empirical evidence indicates that the predominance of complements is rather unusual. Substitutes are found more often, and in the case where substitution effects are predominant the above paradoxical result will not hold.

5.5   Piecemeal-Policy Recommendations: General Rules for Some Special Cases

The theory elaborated above yields interesting insight into piecemeal improvements of welfare and its connection with optimum policy. However, the results on piecemeal price changes do not lend themselves to straightforward economic interpretation. They are valuable for practical application, but leave the neoclassical theoretician disappointed. There exist, however, some special cases where piecemeal pricing policies can be interpreted in an economically satisfactory way. The best-known case, to be treated in the present section, deals with price changes with optimal adjustments of quantities and lump-sum incomes.[26]

Consider the board of a public enterprise which intends to improve welfare by changing prices, quantities and lump-sum incomes. The condition for a welfare improvement can therefore be written as follows

$$dW = \sum_h \sum_k \frac{\partial W}{\partial v^h} \frac{\partial v^h}{\partial p_k} dp_k + \sum_h \frac{\partial W}{\partial v^h} \frac{\partial v^h}{\partial r^h} dr^h > 0. \tag{36}$$

The piecemeal policy may be constrained by the market-clearing and technology conditions. There is no budget limitation. We again linearize the relevant constraints by applying total differentiation:

$$\sum_h \sum_k \frac{\partial x_i^h}{\partial p_k} dp_k + \sum_h \frac{\partial x_i^h}{\partial r^h} dr^h - dz_i - \sum_j \sum_k \frac{\partial y_i^j}{\partial p_k} dp_k = 0; \quad i = o, \ldots, n, \tag{37}$$

$$\sum_i \frac{\partial g}{\partial z_i} dz_i = 0. \tag{38}$$

Solving (37) for dz_i and substituting into (38) yields

$$\sum_i \frac{\partial g}{\partial z_i} \left\{ \sum_k \frac{\partial z_i^D}{\partial p_k} dp_k + \sum_h \frac{\partial x_i^h}{\partial r^h} dr^h \right\} = 0. \tag{39}$$

---

[26] A second very special way to apply piecemeal-policy techniques uses an alleged similarity between the total differential of demand functions and the left-hand side of pricing formulas in compensated-demand cases. See section 8.3 below.

We could now apply Motzkin's theorem as above. However, this would not lead to further results on piecemeal-policy recommendations. Therefore, we restrict ourselves to a very special case of the above piecemeal-policy approach. For any given prices p we assume that the public enterprise chooses quantities z_i and incomes r^h in a welfare-maximizing way:

$$\max_{z_i, r^h} W \bigg|_p - \sum_i \alpha_i \left(\sum_h x_i^h - z_i - \sum_j y_i^j \right) - \beta g(\cdot). \tag{40}$$

The marginal conditions are

$$\alpha_i - \beta \frac{\partial g}{\partial z_i} = 0; \qquad i = o, \ldots, n, \tag{41}$$

$$\frac{\partial W}{\partial v^h} \frac{\partial v^h}{\partial r^h} - \sum_i \alpha_i \frac{\partial x_i^h}{\partial r^h} = 0; \qquad h = 1, \ldots, H. \tag{42}$$

These additional conditions enable us to transform $dW > 0$ as follows:

$$dW = \sum_h \sum_k \frac{\partial W}{\partial v^h} \frac{\partial v^h}{\partial p_k} dp_k + \sum_h \frac{\partial W}{\partial v^h} \frac{\partial v^h}{\partial r^h} dr^h$$

$$= -\sum_h \sum_k \frac{\partial W}{\partial v^h} \frac{\partial v^h}{\partial r^h} x_k^h dp_k + \sum_h \frac{\partial W}{\partial v^h} \frac{\partial v^h}{\partial r^h} dr^h$$

$$= \sum_h \frac{\partial W}{\partial v^h} \frac{\partial v^h}{\partial r^h} \left(dr^h - \sum_k x_k^h dp_k \right)$$

$$\overset{(42)}{=} \sum_h \sum_i \alpha_i \frac{\partial x_i^h}{\partial r^h} \left(dr^h - \sum_k x_k^h dp_k \right)$$

$$\overset{(41)}{=} \sum_h \sum_i \beta \frac{\partial g}{\partial z_i} \frac{\partial x_i^h}{\partial r^h} \left(dr^h - \sum_k x_k^h dp_k \right)$$

$$\overset{(39)}{=} -\sum_i \sum_k \beta \frac{\partial g}{\partial z_i} \left(\frac{\partial z_i^D}{\partial p_k} + \sum_h x_k^h \frac{\partial x_i^h}{\partial r^h} \right) dp_k$$

$$= -\sum_i \sum_k \beta \frac{\partial g}{\partial z_i} \frac{\partial \hat{z}_i}{\partial p_k} dp_k .$$

Therefore we can conclude

$$-\sum_{i=o}^{n}\sum_{k\in K}c_i\frac{\partial\hat{z}_i}{\partial p_k}dp_k > 0 \Rightarrow dW > 0. \qquad (43)$$

For an economic interpretation of the above condition we transform the left-hand side of (43) as follows. To obtain price-cost differences, we simultaneously add and subtract $\Sigma_i p_i(\partial\hat{z}_i/\partial p_k)$, for any good k, and use the property

$$\sum_i p_i\frac{\partial\hat{z}_i}{\partial p_k} = -\sum_i\sum_j p_i\frac{\partial y_i^j}{\partial p_k} \qquad (44)$$

(because $\Sigma_i p_i(\partial\hat{x}_i/\partial p_k) = 0$).

Now consider first a *perfectly-competitive private economy* for which $\Sigma_i p_i(\partial y_i^j/\partial p_k) = 0$ for any private firm. Price changes are welfare-improving in this case if

$$\sum_i\sum_k(p_i - c_i)\frac{\partial\hat{z}_i}{\partial p_k}dp_k > 0. \qquad (45)$$

We know from (45) that either welfare-improving price steps dp_k are possible, or that prices are optimal, in which case

$$\sum_{i=o}^{n}(p_i - c_i)\frac{\partial\hat{z}_i}{\partial p_k} = 0; \qquad k \in K. \qquad (46)$$

For a perfectly-competitive private economy the relevant optimum is the marginal-cost optimum. Details on the piecemeal policy on its way toward the marginal-cost optimum will be given in section 7.3 below.

Consider second a private economy which is not perfectly competitive but where the *private* enterprises realize profits, $\pi^j > 0$. Let the piecemeal policy dp_k be neutral with respect to private profits

$$d\pi^j = \sum_k\left\{y_k^j + \sum_i p_i\frac{\partial y_i^j}{\partial p_k}\right\}dp_k = 0; \qquad \text{for all } j \qquad (47)$$

and hence

$$\sum_i\sum_j p_i\frac{\partial y_i^j}{\partial p_k} = -\sum_j y_k^j = -y_k. \qquad (48)$$

Note that $\Sigma_k y_k dp_k$ is the impact incidence[27] on private profits of the piecemeal pricing policy. We obtain the following condition for welfare-improving price changes

$$\sum_k \left\{ \sum_i (p_i - c_i) \frac{\partial \hat{z}_i}{\partial p_k} - y_k \right\} dp_k > 0, \tag{49}$$

which shows a dependency on the price effects $\partial \hat{z}_i / \partial p_k$ and on the impact incidence on private profits of the piecemeal pricing policy.

The optimum which corresponds to the above piecemeal policy can be characterized by the marginal conditions

$$\sum_{i=o}^{n} (p_i - c_i) \frac{\partial \hat{z}_i}{\partial p_k} = y_k; \qquad k \in K. \tag{50}$$

It can be seen clearly that this optimum is *not* a marginal-cost optimum, but depends decisively on the impact incidence of public pricing on private-sector profits. The result, of course, rests on our assumption of constant private profits. Considering Walras' law this assumption is a type of substitute for a public-sector profit constraint and we therefore obtain a pricing rule which appears to resemble Ramsey pricing.

---

[27] In the sense of Musgrave (1959: 230).

Positive Piecemeal Theory

6.1 Improvements with Tight and Non-Tight Constraints

As we could expect, most positive piecemeal analyses lead to similar results as the normative analyses presented in chapter 5. Consider, for instance, an initial state where prices p_k and quantities z_i are fixed in a market-clearing, technologically and financially feasible way, the relevant constraints being fulfilled as equalities. Along any piecemeal-policy path all markets must remain in equilibrium; the technology and budget constraints are weakened to inequalities.

The value of an adequately chosen objective function $\Phi(p, z)$ will increase if price changes dp_k and quantity changes dz_i fulfill the following conditions:

$$d\Phi = \sum_k \frac{\partial \Phi}{\partial p_k} dp_k + \sum_i \frac{\partial \Phi}{\partial z_i} dz_i > 0, \tag{1}$$

$$\sum_h \sum_k \frac{\partial x_i^h}{\partial p_k} dp_k - dz_i - \sum_j \sum_k \frac{\partial y_i^j}{\partial p_k} dp_k = 0; \quad i = o, \ldots, n, \tag{2}$$

$$\sum_i \frac{\partial g}{\partial z_i} dz_i \leq 0, \tag{3}$$

$$-\sum_i p_i dz_i - \sum_k z_k dp_k \leq 0. \tag{4}$$

Solving the market-clearing conditions for dz_i, and substituting into (1), (3), and (4), we obtain

$$B_o^T(dp_k) = \left(\frac{\partial \Phi}{\partial p_k} + \sum_i \frac{\partial \Phi}{\partial z_i} \frac{\partial z_i^D}{\partial p_k} \right)^T (dp_k) > 0, \tag{5}$$

$$B_1^T(dp_k) = \left(\sum_i \frac{\partial g}{\partial z_i} \frac{\partial z_i^D}{\partial p_k} \right)^T (dp_k) \leq 0, \tag{6}$$

$$B_2^T(dp_k) = \left(-\sum_i p_i \frac{\partial z_i^D}{\partial p_k} - z_k\right)^T (dp_k) \leq 0. \qquad (7)$$

Clearly, Farkas' theorem can be applied to this system of conditions,[1] showing the connection between positive piecemeal and optimum theory. After replacing dW with $d\Phi$, figures 8a and 8b of the previous chapter apply directly. A similar line of reasoning applies in case of a tight-technology constraint, making use of Motzkin's theorem[2] and of figures 9 and 10 in the preceding chapter.

6.2 The Trade-Off Between Efficiency and Market Equilibrium

6.2.1 *Trends Toward Production Inefficiency with Markets in Equilibrium*

We saw in section 5.4 that increasing production inefficiency can be a necessary step to improve welfare. Let us now ask whether similar paradoxical results can occur in the positive piecemeal approach. The question is by no means trivial. It is often suggested in political discussions that positive pricing principles are preferable to normative approaches because the former postulate maximands which can be observed directly and therefore provide better incentives for efficiency in production. Such an argument sounds very plausible because many positive-theory objectives are directly linked to quantities produced. Welfare, on the other hand, is directly linked to quantities consumed and therefore we could expect market equilibria to be of greater importance in piecemeal normative than in piecemeal positive theory. The following analysis shows to what extent efficiency improvements are of greater importance in positive than in normative piecemeal theory. Consider an initial situation with tight market-clearing conditions

$$z_i = \sum_h x_i^h(p, r^h) - \sum_j y_i^j(p); \quad i = o, \ldots, n, \qquad (8)$$

but non-tight technology and budget constraints

$$\widetilde{g}(z, DV_1) = g(z) + DV_1 = 0 \qquad (9)$$

$$\widetilde{\Pi}(z, p, DV_2) = \Pi^o - \sum_i p_i z_i + DV_2 = 0 \qquad (10)$$

---

[1] See section 5.2 above.
[2] See section 5.3 above.

where $DV_1, DV_2 > 0$ are dummy variables, measuring the public firm's inefficiency and excess revenues. Assume these conditions hold not only in the initial situation, but also along any piecemeal-policy path. Direct application of the gradient-projection method to $\Phi(p, z)$ leads to a complicated result[3] which does not lend itself to further economic interpretation. Hence, we substitute the market equilibria $z_i = z_i^D(p, \cdot)$ into the objective function

$$\widetilde{\Phi}(p) := \Phi(p, z) \tag{11}$$

and let prices change along the steepest ascent of the objective function $\widetilde{\Phi}$

$$dp_k = \frac{\partial \widetilde{\Phi}}{\partial p_k} = \frac{\partial \Phi}{\partial p_k} + \sum_i \frac{\partial \Phi}{\partial z_i} \frac{\partial z_i^D}{\partial p_k} \tag{12}$$

where the derivatives $\partial\Phi/\partial z_i$ and $\partial\Phi/\partial p_k$ vary from objective function to objective function, as shown explicitly in table 1, chapter 4. As the non-tight technology and budget constraints are assumed to hold along any policy path, we obtain the following linear approximations:[4]

$$dDV_1 = -\sum_i \sum_k \frac{\partial g}{\partial z_i} \frac{\partial z_i^D}{\partial p_k} \frac{\partial \widetilde{\Phi}}{\partial p_k}, \tag{13}$$

$$dDV_2 = -\sum_i \sum_k \left\{ -p_i \frac{\partial z_i^D}{\partial p_k} - z_k \right\} \frac{\partial \widetilde{\Phi}}{\partial p_k} \tag{14}$$

where the market equilibria $z_i = z_i^D(p, \cdot)$ have been substituted.

Let us concentrate on decreasing or increasing inefficiency.[5] We know from (13) that changes in inefficiency depend on the relevant objective function, via $\partial\widetilde{\Phi}/\partial p_k \lessgtr 0$, on the price effects, $\partial z_i^D/\partial p_k \lessgtr 0$, and on the production effects, $\partial g/\partial z_i > 0$. Since these partial derivatives are multiplied by each other, it is impossible to obtain any general conclusions as to whether

---

[3] According to Luenberger (1973) the only binding constraints (8) determine the formula for the optimal price and quantity changes dp and dz as follows:
$$\begin{pmatrix} dp \\ dz \end{pmatrix} = \left\{ I - \nabla_M \left[\nabla_M^T \nabla_M \right]^{-1} \nabla_M^T \right\} \begin{pmatrix} \partial\Phi/\partial p \\ \partial\Phi/\partial z \end{pmatrix}$$
where I is a unit matrix, ∇_M is the gradient matrix of the market-clearing conditions with respect to prices and quantities, $\partial\Phi/\partial p$ and $\partial\Phi/\partial z$ are the gradient vectors of Φ.

[4] Analogously to section 5.4 above.

[5] The interpretation of (14) is similar to that of (13). However, it is even more complicated to obtain any results.

positive piecemeal theory requires decreasing or increasing inefficiency. We cannot exclude the paradoxical result that increasing inefficiency is best along some parts of the piecemeal-policy path, nor can we definitely conclude which positive-theory objectives provide the best incentives for efficiency.

Nevertheless, some typical characteristics of piecemeal policy can be shown with the help of two examples. Both examples describe some initial situation which is characterized by particular price responses. Results for such a situation can be found by applying eq. (13). The reader should always remember that the results which follow hold only for such an initial state. Along the path toward the optimum we expect all cases of decreasing inefficiency to vanish, at least at the very last step toward the optimum.[6] The two examples are as follows:

Case (I), 'predominant-substitute relations'
Assume the own-price effects of demand are not too high *and* predominant-substitutional relations are more likely than predominant-complementary relations.[7] Assume the price effects interact in such a way that the second term in (12) always takes the same sign as the components of $(\partial \Phi / \partial z)$, and dDV_1 takes the opposite sign to that of the components of $(\partial \widetilde{\Phi} / \partial p)$.[8]

Case (II), 'ignore the cross-elasticities'
$(\partial z_i^D / \partial p_k = 0; \partial z_k^D / \partial p_k < 0$ by excluding inverse reactions of demand.) This is just the opposite of case (I). The second term in (12) always takes the opposite sign as $\partial \Phi / \partial z_k$, and dDV_1 takes the same sign as the components of $(\partial \widetilde{\Phi} / \partial p)$.

Although the assumptions of case (I) seem to be realistic for many cases of public supply, case (II) has a historical tradition as an aid for interpreting public-sector pricing.[9]

Let us first interpret *case* (I). We obtain

$$\partial \widetilde{\Phi} / \partial p_k < 0 \qquad \text{for maximization of votes, and} \atop \text{for minimization of price indices;} \qquad (15)$$

$$\partial \widetilde{\Phi} / \partial p_k > 0 \qquad \text{for budget, output, revenue maximization,} \atop \text{and for energy saving;} \qquad (16)$$

$$\partial \widetilde{\Phi} / \partial p_k \lessgtr 0 \qquad \text{for the bureaucrat-trade union objective.} \qquad (17)$$

---

[6] As usual, we exclude the possibility of interior optima.

[7] Complementarities, for instance in the case of energy minimization, can easily disturb that pattern.

[8] Recall from table 1, chapter 4, that for any objective function all $\partial \Phi / \partial z_i$ are either positive or negative or zero, but never mixed. The same is valid for $\partial \Phi / \partial p_k$. The only exception is the combined bureaucrat-trade union objective.

[9] The 'inverse-elasticity rule' is the best-known application. See subsection 8.1.2.

Hence, we expect *increasing inefficiency* if votes are maximized or if price indices are minimized. These results are consistent with those derived from the welfare approach of chapter 5. The reason is that vote maximization refers explicitly to individual utilities, as does welfare. And it is well-known that every price index can be seen as a sort of welfare measure.[10] Therefore we should not be surprised that vote and price-index optimization imply similar tendencies toward efficiency as does welfare maximization.

On the other hand, we expect *decreasing inefficiency* if budget, output or revenue is to be maximized. This result shows the existence of higher efficiency incentives from those positive-theory objectives which concentrate on prices and quantities sold by the firm instead of on customers' utilities.

Energy saving is another objective which leads to decreasing inefficiency. This result could be expected if we think of inefficiency in terms of waste and energy inputs are assumed to be lower, the less waste occurs. Yet this result is also surprising since energy saving as such is an objective which discriminates between different inputs, and would be expected to cause inefficiencies.

The inefficiency incentives which result from the combined bureaucrat-trade union objective cannot be determined unambigously. There are two trade-offs:[11]

(i) a trade-off between the trade union's interest in wages and the bureaucrat's interest in output. Increasing inefficiency occurs if a trade union (over)accentuates wage policy in a public firm which is not too eagerly engaged in increasing its outputs;

(ii) a trade-off between the trade union's interest in employment and its interest in wages, the interest in employment pointing toward increasing efficiency and the interest in wages toward increasing inefficiency.

It should be noted that these trade-offs change considerably if market disequilibria are allowed, as the following subsection will show.

Let us now *consider case* (II) where all cross-price effects are neglected. In that case we obtain

$$\partial\widetilde{\Phi}/\partial p_k < 0 \qquad \text{for maximization of votes, minimization of} \\ \text{price indices, maximization of output;} \qquad (18)$$

$$\partial\widetilde{\Phi}/\partial p_k > 0 \qquad \text{for energy saving (public supply);} \qquad (19)$$

---

[10] The easiest way to grasp this connection is to compare a true cost-of-living index with the Hicksian compensating variation.

[11] Substituting from table 1, chapter 4, leads to $\partial\widetilde{\Phi}/\partial p_o=U_p^2+U_z^2(\partial z_o^D/\partial p_o)$ which will be positive if the union's interest in wages dominates ($U_p^2>0$), and negative if the union's interest in employment dominates ($U_z^2<0$), as $\partial z_o^D/\partial p_o$ is positive. $\partial\widetilde{\Phi}/\partial p_k=\Sigma_i U_i^1(\partial z_i^D/\partial p_k)<0$; $k,i=d+1,...,n$, on the other hand, depend on the firm's interest in output only ($U_i^1>0$). $\partial z_i^D/\partial p_k<0$ because of the complementary assumption of case (I).

$\partial \widetilde{\Phi} / \partial p_k \lessgtr 0$ for budget and revenue maximization,
energy saving (private supply),
combined bureaucrat – trade union interest.[12]   (20)

The results of case (II), therefore, are not simply opposite to those of case (I). The utility-related objectives, votes and price indices, indicate a tendency toward increasing efficiency. The same tendency prevails for output maximization, which thereby exhibits the most pronounced incentive for efficiency of all positive-theory objectives. Budget and revenue maximization may still exhibit incentives for efficiency if the own-price effect is not too low. The combined bureaucrat-trade union interest, again, leads to indeterminate results. – Once again, the usual reminder holds that the above tendencies need not prevail along the whole path of piecemeal policy.

6.2.2   Production Efficiency With Markets in Disequilibrium

Until now we have always assumed that markets are in equilibrium. The present subsection shows that the above-mentioned tendencies toward increasing inefficiency result from the necessity of observing the market equilibrium constraints. For this purpose we consider an initial situation with non-tight market, technology and budget constraints

$$\widetilde{m}_i(z_i, p, r, DV_{oi}) = \sum_h x_i^h(p, r^h) - z_i - \sum_j y_i^j(p) + DV_{oi} = 0, \quad (21)$$

$$\widetilde{g}(z, DV_1) = g(z) + DV_1 = 0, \quad (22)$$

$$\widetilde{\Pi}(z, p, DV_2) = \Pi^o - \sum_i p_i z_i + DV_2 = 0. \quad (23)$$

Employing the gradient-projection method, price *and* quantity changes are as follows:

$$dp_k = \frac{\partial \Phi}{\partial p_k}; \; dz_i = \frac{\partial \Phi}{\partial z_i}. \quad (24)$$

This piecemeal policy does not change the prevailing degree of inefficiency if votes are maximized or if a Laspeyres price index is minimized. Both objectives do not depend on quantities z_i and therefore (24) implies $dz_i = 0$.

---

[12] In this case $\partial \widetilde{\Phi} / \partial p_k < 0$ for $k \neq 0$; $\partial \widetilde{\Phi} / \partial p_k > 0$ for $k = 0$.

As the quantities remain unchanged, the degree of inefficiency represented by DV_1 in (22) also remains unchanged. There is no trade-off between inefficiency and market disequilibrium in the cases of vote and price index optimization.[13]

However, such a trade-off exists if positive-theory objectives depend on quantities z_i. For an analysis of these cases, we assume that the non-tight constraints (21) – (23) hold along any piecemeal-policy path. Therefore we obtain as linear approximations

$$dDV_{oi} = \frac{\partial \Phi}{\partial z_i} - \sum_k \frac{\partial z_i^D}{\partial p_k} \frac{\partial \Phi}{\partial p_k}; \qquad i = o, \dots, n, \tag{25}$$

$$dDV_1 = -\sum_i \frac{\partial g}{\partial z_i} \frac{\partial \Phi}{\partial z_i}, \tag{26}$$

$$dDV_2 = \sum_i p_i \frac{\partial \Phi}{\partial z_i} + \sum_k z_k \frac{\partial \Phi}{\partial p_k}. \tag{27}$$

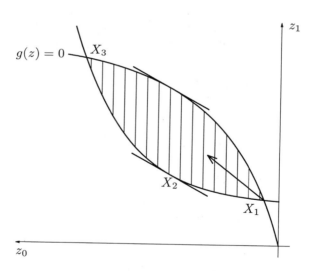

Figure 11b

Let us begin the economic interpretation with the most interesting result: if a positive-theory objective is monotonically increasing in z_i, there is a tendency toward decreasing inefficiency.[14] This result is based on eq. (26) where $dDV_1 < 0$ if all $(\partial g/\partial z_i) > 0$ and all $(\partial \Phi/\partial z_i) \geq 0$, strictly positive for at least one z_i. For a plausible explanation of this effect see figure 11b. There are two curves in figure 11b: the offer curve which represents the market equilibrium and the production-possibility frontier which represents efficiency. In previous analyses we followed the offer curve from X_1 to X_2, which yielded inefficiency. The present analysis allows us to approach more directly the production-possibility frontier by moving within the hatched lens between the two curves and ignoring the offer curve.

The only exception may result from the trade union's influence.[15] We encounter a trade-off between the trade union's interest in employment and the bureaucrat's in output. Too intensive accentuation of employment targets may drive the public firm into inefficiency unless it is quite conscious of its own output targets. The trade union's interest in wage increases does not influence this efficiency trade-off, but affects the equilibrium on the labor market.

Positive theory's higher incentives for efficiency may be questionable if they are attained at the cost of increasing market disequilibria $(dDV_{oi} > 0)$. As we could expect, this result occurs with certainty if output is maximized. Output-maximizing public firms, therefore, face the well-known bias of quantitatively producing as much as possible, but missing the market.

It is impossible to state in general which objectives will always lead to increasing or decreasing disequilibria in all markets. However tendencies toward a trade-off between efficiency and market equilibria are also prevalent in many other cases. Once again, cases (I) and (II) may serve as examples. The results are shown in table 2a.

Table 2a: Sign of dDV_{oi} [16]

Objective	Case (I)	Case (II)
Votes, Price index	+	−
Budget $(i = d + 1, \ldots, n)$	$\pm$	+
Output	+	+
Revenue $(i = d + 1, \ldots, n)$	$\pm$	+
Energy[17]	−	+

---

[14] There is only one exception which will be considered in the following paragraph.

[15] If $U_z^2 < 0$ outweighs the influence of the bureaucrat's $U_i^1 > 0, i = d+1,...,n$.

[16] + means $dDV_{oi} > 0$; − means $dDV_{oi} < 0$; $\pm$ means the sign is indeterminate.

[17] In case of privately supplied energy the above signs hold for $i \neq a$; if $i = a$ the private monopolistic supplier will always guarantee the equilibrium in the energy market.

Whereas most results of table 2a are self-evident, we should deal more extensively with the combined bureaucrat-trade union objective. In all markets but the labor market there is a tendency toward increasing disequilibria.

Table 2b: Sign of dDV_{oi}

Objective	Case (I)	Case (II)
Bureaucrat and trade union $i = 0$[18]	–	–
$\quad i = d+1, \ldots, n$	+	+

The reason is simple. The bureaucrat's part of this objective function is a monotonically increasing function of output. The union's part depends on the labor-market variables only. Hence for all markets but the labor market, this objective function has the same effect as output maximization. On the labor market, however, the union's interest involves a tendency toward decreasing market disequilibria.

It is fitting that we close this section by reminding the reader, once again, that caution is required when dealing with the above cases (I) and (II). A tendency toward increasing market disequilibria typically will not hold along the whole piecemeal-policy path. Somewhere along this path the above tendency has to switch, and piecemeal policy must imply decreasing market disequilibria, at least at the last step toward the optimum.

---

[18] If p_o is an instrument variable, this holds for $\partial z_o^D / \partial p_o > 0$ which is a little unrealistic.

PART TWO
NORMATIVE THEORY

PRICING POLICIES
FOR WELFARE MAXIMIZATION

A
Basic Rules

In chapter 3 we presented a fairly general normative theory of public-sector pricing. The result was presented in the marginal conditions (3–21) and (3–24). In chapter 3, however, we did not give an economic interpretation of these conditions. This is done in the present part of the book. We consider special cases of the above-mentioned marginal conditions. These cases result from imposing restrictive assumptions on the Boiteux-type model presented in chapter 3. Since these restrictions are unlikely to be fulfilled in economic practice, rules like marginal-cost pricing or Ramsey pricing should not necessarily be considered as direct instructions for practical policy. However, in any case they are most important as benchmark models. They teach us the basic lines we should follow when thinking about public-sector pricing, namely the dependence of prices on marginal costs, on price elasticities of demand, on distributional value judgments and on private monopolistic pricing. For didactical purposes these various dependencies are treated separately in the following four chapters of the book.

7
Marginal-Cost Pricing

7.1   Optimum Policy

7.1.1   Pricing in a First-Best Environment

We begin with the most restrictive case. Let us assume that

(i)   only prices of publicly produced goods are controlled; uncontrolled prices equal marginal costs c_i in the public sector;

(ii)   the private sector is perfectly competitive;

(iii)   the distribution of lump-sum incomes is optimally chosen, hence we deal with compensated demand;

(iv)   there is no revenue-cost constraint on the public sector.

Then the marginal conditions (3–24) reduce to

$$\sum_{i \in K}(p_i - c_i)\frac{\partial \hat{z}_i}{\partial p_k} = 0; \qquad k \in K. \tag{1}$$

This can be interpreted as a homogeneous system of equations in the unknown variables $(p_i - c_i)$. If we assume the matrix $\partial \hat{z}_i / \partial p_k$ to be regular,[1] we obtain the well-known marginal-cost pricing rule,

$$p_i = c_i(z); \qquad i \in K. \tag{2a}$$

This rule requires the enterprise to set all controlled prices equal to the marginal costs c_i which are defined as the marginal rates of transformation between output or input i and labor. Moreover, as all uncontrolled prices also equal the respective marginal costs c_i, production is always cost-minimizing, implying equality of c_i and C_i, the marginal costs proper.[2] Therefore

$$p_i = C_i(z); \qquad i \in K. \tag{2b}$$

This rule is normatively valid for any kind of public enterprise: for competitive public enterprises (nationalized steel industries, communal breweries etc.) as well as for natural monopolies (e.g. telephone, electricity, gas supply). With this in mind it is not surprising to find a wide range of proposals for the practical application of marginal-cost pricing:

(i)   nationalized enterprises in general (White Paper (1967) for the UK; the project failed – see NEDO (1976); the White Paper (1978) avoided any explicit pricing rule);

(ii)   electricity (papers by Boiteux and his team are collected in Nelson (1964); for Electricité de France see also Quoilin (1976); for the UK Turvey (1968, 1971));

(iii)   railways (frequently suggested since Hotelling's (1938) seminal paper);

(iv)   television (Samuelson (1964) opposing Minasian (1964) given the assumption of zero marginal costs for TV);

(v)   telephone, theater, airports etc.

7.1.2   Deficits Under Marginal-Cost Pricing

The marginal-cost pricing rule is a challenge for economists, both in theory and practice, because it provides a theoretical justification for public supply

---

[1]   The Slutsky matrix never has full rank. However, our approach deals with a part of the economy only ($k \in K$; $K \subset I$).

[2]   See subsection 2.4.4 above.

with permanent deficits. This consequence of marginal-cost pricing results if there exist strict local scale economies (as defined below). The concept of a 'welfare-optimal' deficit is contrary to the widespread belief that deficits always mean mismanagement of public enterprises. The theoretical justification of deficits provided by marginal-cost pricing does not justify mismanagement. Marginal-cost prices are only one part of the solution of an optimization model which also gives normative instructions for optimal quantities of outputs and inputs thereby prescribing cost minimization.[3]

Let us consider more closely the conditions required for such a welfare-optimal deficit. It can be shown that strict *local* increasing returns to scale are a necessary *and* sufficient condition for a marginal-cost pricing deficit. The proof is comparatively simple although we deal with a multiproduct enterprise. The reason for this simplicity lies in the particular definition of marginal costs in our Boiteux-type model which allows a straightforward definition of local increasing returns to scale which directly depends on marginal costs.[4]

For this purpose we solve the production function $g(z) = 0$ so as to obtain a labor-requirement function $z_o = z_o(z_1, \dots, z_n) = z_o(z.)$ whence $\partial z_o / \partial z_i = -(\partial g / \partial z_i)/(\partial g / \partial z_o) = -c_i$. We define strict local increasing returns to scale by an adequately chosen elasticity of production[5]

$$\varepsilon(z) = \lim_{s \to 1} \frac{s}{z_o(sz.)} \frac{\partial z_o(sz.)}{\partial s} < 1. \tag{3}$$

This is an elasticity of the labor input with respect to the scale parameter s. The production function exhibits increasing returns to scale if labor input increases by a smaller proportion than all netputs $z_1, \dots, z_n$.

Transforming the above definition yields

$$\varepsilon(z) = \lim_{s \to 1} \frac{s}{z_o(sz.)} \cdot \sum_{i=1}^{n} \frac{\partial z_o(sz.)}{\partial(sz_i)} \cdot z_i$$

$$= \frac{1}{z_o} \cdot \sum_{i=1}^{n} \frac{\partial z_o(z.)}{\partial z_i} z_i \tag{4}$$

$$= -\frac{1}{z_o} \cdot \sum_{i=1}^{n} c_i z_i.$$

---

[3] How to transpose these solutions into regulatory practice will be discussed extensively in chapter 24 below.

[4] The general proof is more complicated as shown by Baumol (1976, 1977) and Panzar–Willig (1977a).

[5] For a similar procedure see Intriligator (1971: 181–2).

Strict local increasing returns to scale are therefore given if[6]

$$z_o + \sum_{i=1}^{n} c_i z_i < 0. \tag{5}$$

From the marginal-cost pricing deficit

$$\sum_{i=o}^{n} p_i z_i = \sum_{i=o}^{n} c_i z_i = z_o + \sum_{i=1}^{n} c_i z_i < 0, \tag{6}$$

it can be seen that $\varepsilon(z) < 1$ is equivalent to the case of a marginal-cost pricing deficit.[7]

Strict *global* increasing returns, on the other hand, are only a sufficient, but not a necessary, condition for deficits under marginal-cost pricing in multiproduct enterprises. Deficits can also arise if returns to scale are decreasing in some parts and increasing in others.

7.1.3   Marginal-Cost Pricing and General Equilibria

In the eighties there has been a revival of interest in the theory of marginal-cost pricing under economies of scale.[8]

First, the *existence* of marginal-cost pricing equilibria was challenged:[9] how can such an optimum be achieved by decentralized decisions of economic agents? Will marginal-cost pricing firms go bankrupt because of losses? Will consumers go bankrupt if they are liable as shareholders of public enterprises? In the Boiteux approach this problem is solved by assuming (optimal) lump-sum taxes which finance possible deficits. Although this is a satisfactory way of dealing with an allocative optimum, it is not a satisfactory way of dealing with decentralization because there are no a priori arrangements that assure positive individual incomes, given any distributions of profits and endowments. To overcome this problem, one has to consider special distributions (Beato, 1982). Further research should concentrate on the existence of marginal-cost pricing equilibria if public deficits are financed by taxes on goods and factors which are inelastic in supply (the old Hotelling proposal) or by two-part tariffs, where the fixed parts, aggregated over all customers,

---

[6] Recall $z_o < 0$ when transforming $\varepsilon(z) < 1$.

[7] If the technology is represented by a cost function, the above result occurs for strictly decreasing ray average costs (see Baumol, 1976).

[8] The main points of this discussion will be mentioned briefly, although existence problems are not handled at all in the Boiteux framework. Mentioning those papers gives us an opportunity to stress some shortcomings of the Boiteux approach.

[9] Beato (1982), Cornet (1982), Dierker–Guesnerie–Neuefeind (1985).

must be such as to cover the difference between total costs and the revenue which would result from marginal-cost pricing.

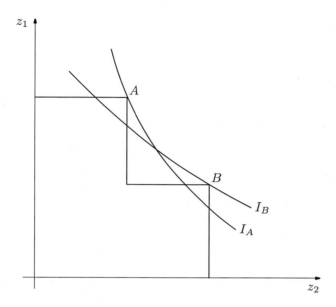

Figure 12

Second, the *optimality* of marginal-cost pricing was challenged.[10] If the production possibilities are non-convex, marginal-cost equilibria may fail to be Pareto optima. The literature tried to find conditions under which at least one equilibrium is Pareto efficient. However, there exist examples showing that even in very simple cases such conditions cannot be found. The best example can be given by using Brown–Heal's (1979) figure for a two-consumer, one-producer economy. Let the production possibility frontier of the non-convex economy be as shown in figure 12. The Scitovsky social indifference curve through A is denoted I_A. If endowments and the relative price change, the social indifference curve may shift, say from I_A to I_B. This implies a new equilibrium at B. Both A and B are equilibria because they fulfill the first-order conditions, but are not Pareto optimal. Whether such problems arise depends on the endowments of the consumers because they affect the social indifference curves and their possible intersection.

---

[10] Guesnerie (1975), Brown–Heal (1979, 1980a,b), Tillmann (1981), Dierker (1986).

For a further treatment of general equilibria when some firms follow marginal-cost pricing, the reader may be referred to Dierker–Guesnerie–Neuefeind (1985). In the present book, their approach is treated in subsection 8.1.3 on general equilibria with Ramsey pricing. However, their arguments hold also for marginal-cost pricing.

7.1.4   Long-Run Versus Short-Run Marginal-Cost Pricing; Joint Inputs; Social Costs

Depending on the particular specification of technology $g(z)$, there are different meanings that can be attributed to marginal costs:

(i) $g(z)$ can be defined in a short-run or in a long-run sense, depending on the variability of inputs over time. The resulting problems of short-run versus long-run marginal-cost pricing have been discussed intensively in the empirical literature.[11]

(ii) Similar problems arise if the technology $g(z)$ comprises specific inputs for any good to be produced *and* joint inputs which are necessary for the production of more than one good. The empirical literature explicitly stresses the importance of including the optimal capacity choice if marginal-cost pricing is to be applied.

(iii) It has often been postulated that marginal-cost pricing should equate prices to *social* marginal costs in the sense used in cost-benefit analysis. The application of marginal-cost pricing, then, gives rise to the usual practical problems: the empirical estimation of spillovers, intangibles, the choice of the rate of time preference or rate of opportunity costs. Of course, the technology $g(z)$ could be understood as including all the above effects. However, in the framework of our general model this procedure is by no means straightforward. There is no need to include *external effects*, as the interaction with the rest of the economy is explicitly modelled so as to ensure Pareto efficiency. *Intangibles* cannot be measured in any case. Hence, if necessary, we could include some warning of the presence of intangibles in verbal supplementary remarks, but it is not helpful to include intangibles in the model. The choice of the *discount factor*, on the other hand, remains of importance. However, our model is a static one. Elsewhere we have shown explicitly the importance of discount rates for pricing and for subsidizing of public enterprises.[12]

---

[11] Some of the problems of this discussion have been treated in subsection 2.4.5.

[12] Bös–Tillmann–Zimmermann (1984) present a dynamic duopoly model, the actors being a public utility and a public authority. All results depend heavily on the relation between the social time preference rate $\mathcal{PR}$, used to discount future revenues and welfare, and the social opportunity cost rate $\mathcal{O}$ which is applied if money is carried forward to the next period. If $\mathcal{O}=\mathcal{PR}$, prices and subsidies are constant over the whole horizon of time. Hence,

7.1.5 The Problem of Cross-Subsidization[13]

Before marginal-cost pricing can be applied in practice, we must always consider carefully what is to be understood as a 'good' in the sense of our analysis. In practice we can start from a comparatively narrow conception (e.g. different categories of seats in theaters) or from a comparatively broad conception (regional unitary tariffs for railways, electricity, gas and certain postal services). The term 'broad conception' means unitary pricing for a good, in spite of different costs for various parts of production, and in spite of differences in the demand for this good. Unitary pricing thereby leads to internal subsidization. If, for instance, a unitary tariff is collected for local traffic (determined by marginal costs of total local traffic), long-distance users will be subsidized by short-distance users and, as well, users of less frequented lines by users of heavily frequented lines, etc.

If such an internal subsidization is unwanted, we have to split our good into different goods with different prices depending on the marginal costs of the newly defined different goods. Usually, this will lead to cases of joint-cost production.

7.2 Consequences for Allocation, Distribution, and Stabilization

Owing to its derivation from the unconstrained maximization of welfare, marginal-cost pricing leads to what is called a *first-best allocation of resources*. This is the crux of the merit of marginal-cost pricing, and we should note in particular the following two consequences.

(i) Marginal-cost pricing leads to first-best utilization of capacity especially if we take into consideration the identity of short-run and long-run marginal costs in cases of optimal investment decisions of public enterprises.

(ii) If public *and* private enterprises follow marginal-cost pricing, the allocation between publicly and privately produced goods is first best.[14] Such a result influences the *size of the public sector*. In the case of increasing returns to scale it leads to an extension of the public sector beyond that associated with cost-covering prices, because in such a case marginal-cost prices have to be lower than cost-covering prices and demand for publicly supplied goods will be greater.

---

if the public utility and the public authority follow the usual tradition of discounting future benefits and costs by the opportunity cost rate $\mathcal{O}$, they should apply a policy of constant pricing and subsidizing over time.

[13] As cross-subsidization is of particular interest in the case of a given revenue-cost constraint, a more extended discussion of this problem may be found in subsection 8.1.4.

[14] If private enterprises set prices above marginal costs, the public enterprise can minimize welfare losses only by giving up marginal-cost pricing as well.

Income redistribution is not the main objective of marginal-cost pricing. This does not mean that marginal-cost pricing has no distributional consequences at all:

(i) In the case of increasing returns to scale, the comparatively low price level may be distributionally positive if the publicly supplied goods are mainly consumed by lower-income earners. However, because in our model the public deficits are financed by lump-sum taxes, a regressive impact of these taxes may offset the above mentioned positive effects.

(ii) Splitting up one good into different goods (as in the case of peak-load pricing[15]) may have distributional consequences, although in general we cannot say what these consequences will be. Comparing uniform marginal-cost pricing for a composite good with differentiated marginal-cost pricing for every single good we may point out the following distributional effects: typical peak-load pricing with higher peak prices will burden lower-income earners if the peak demand comes mainly from those groups (who cannot shift to off-peak demand as easily as higher-income earners). If the different goods are characterized by differences in quality,[16] marginal-cost pricing will favor lower-income earners if marginal costs of 'first class' goods exceed marginal costs of 'second class' goods at least in the neighborhood of the optimum. These possibilities show clearly that we cannot draw general conclusions.

As far as the *stabilization* aspects are concerned, it has often been asserted that marginal-cost pricing is a built-in stabilizer. The typical argument is as follows (Thiemeyer, 1964): assume a public one-product enterprise producing under increasing marginal costs at the point of intersection with average costs. Demand-compatible marginal-cost prices and average-cost prices then coincide (point A in fig. 13). If we start from this point, a fall in demand (recession) will lead to a fall in marginal-cost prices, but to a rise in average-cost prices as shown by the demand function $D''D''$ in fig. 13. If demand rises (boom), marginal-cost prices will rise more than average-cost prices as shown by demand function $D'D'$. The comparatively lower prices in recession and comparatively higher prices in boom periods can be regarded as anticyclical.

This built-in stabilizing effect is a special case and does not hold in general. If we consider the boom period only, we can see that:

(i) The above argument is not valid in the case of scale economies where both marginal and average costs decrease, marginal costs falling faster than average costs.

(ii) The argument applies to the short-run. In the long-run the public enterprise will start to invest in order to regain the point of minimum average costs.

---

15 For details see chapter 15.

16 For details see chapters 16 and 22.

(iii) We need to ask how the public enterprise spends the revenue it receives from selling its products at higher prises. If the revenue is spent on additional investment or labor, for instance on overtime, there is no decrease in total demand but only a lag effect.

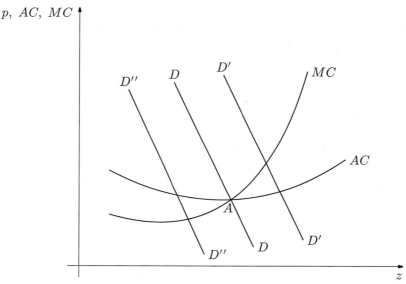

Figure 13

(iv) The stabilizing effects depend on the market structure. A monopolistic public enterprise, selling at higher prices to consumers, withdraws private purchasing power; selling at higher prices to producers, it reduces their profits or increases inflationary pressure: the effect on stabilization may be regarded as positive. Competitive public enterprises, on the other hand, selling at higher prices, allow other producers to increase their profits, and increase inflationary pressure: the effect on stabilization is negative.

7.3 Piecemeal Policy

In deriving marginal-cost pricing as a special result of the extended Boiteux model, we started from particular assumptions, (i) to (iv) in the first paragraph of this chapter. Let us now introduce the same assumptions into the piecemeal policy model and assume quantities and lump-sum incomes to be optimally adjusted to any price changes.

As shown in chapter 5, we then obtain eq. (5–45). Welfare will be increased by changing prices according to the sufficient condition

$$\sum_{i \in K} \sum_{k \in K} (p_i - c_i) \frac{\partial \hat{z}_i}{\partial p_k} dp_k > 0. \tag{5--45}$$

The above formula shows, once again, all the intricacy of piecemeal policy recommendations. After introducing so many restrictive assumptions we would have expected the result that welfare always increases if the price-cost margin of some good $k \in K$ is lowered in absolute value. Unfortunately, such a result cannot be corroborated by inequality (5--45). Consider the following example: there is some arbitrary initial situation where all prices in K are above the respective marginal costs. Some good, $k \in K$, is a substitute for all other goods in $K, \partial \hat{z}_i / \partial p_k > 0$. The own price response $\partial \hat{z}_k / \partial p_k < 0$ is small in absolute value. In that case welfare may increase if dp_k is positive, which implies increasing the deviation of p_k from c_k. Of course, such a result cannot hold along the complete path of price changes toward the optimum, but at least it cannot be excluded from the piecemeal policy analysis.

To obtain more appealing economic results, we need further (!) assumptions. Two well-known examples are shown in the following.[17]

Assume, *first*, that all prices change in proportion to the existing distortions $(dp_k = (p_k - c_k)ds)$. Welfare increases if

$$\sum_{i \in K} \sum_{k \in K} (p_i - c_i) \frac{\partial \hat{z}_i}{\partial p_k} (p_k - c_k) ds > 0 \tag{7}$$

which is only fulfilled if $ds < 0$:[18] an equal relative reduction of all marginal-cost differences increases welfare. If all prices move toward marginal costs in proportion to the existing distortions, welfare increases. Here, at last, is the long wished for result that welfare increases if marginal-cost pricing is approached.

Assume, *second*, some particular good $k \in K$ whose Lerner index $\mathcal{L}_k := (p_k - c_k)/p_k$ in the inital situation does not exceed the Lerner indices of its complements, but exceeds the Lerner indices of its substitutes. Let the other prices be constant.

---

[17] For further details of this approach see Dixit (1975), Green (1975), Hatta (1977), Hagen (1979), Kawamata (1974), Wiegard (1980).

[18] We assume that at least one price does not equal marginal costs. We postulate that the matrix $(\partial \hat{z}_i / \partial p_k)$ has full rank and is negative semidefinite. For the latter property consider $(\partial \hat{z}_i / \partial p_k) = (\partial \hat{x}_i / \partial p_k) - \Sigma_j (\partial y_i^j / \partial p_k)$, the first matrix being negative semidefinite as a part of the matrix of substitution effects, the second matrix being positive semidefinite as a sum of the matrices of the second derivatives of the individual firms' profit functions which is known to be convex in prices in case of perfect competition.

Then $dp_k < 0$ increases welfare. The proof is as follows. Split[19]

$$\sum_{i \in I} \mathcal{L}_i p_i \frac{\partial \hat{z}_i}{\partial p_k} dp_k > 0 \tag{8}$$

into complements and substitutes

$$\left\{ \sum_{i \in IC} \mathcal{L}_i p_i \frac{\partial \hat{z}_i}{\partial p_k} + \sum_{i \in IS} \mathcal{L}_i p_i \frac{\partial \hat{z}_i}{\partial p_k} \right\} dp_k > 0 \tag{9}$$

where

$$IC = \{i \mid \mathcal{L}_i \geq \mathcal{L}_k \; ; \; \partial \hat{z}_i / \partial p_k < 0\}$$
$$IS = \{i \mid \mathcal{L}_i < \mathcal{L}_k \; ; \; \partial \hat{z}_i / \partial p_k \geq 0\}$$
$$IC \cup IS = I.$$

Now recall that $\Sigma_i p_i (\partial \hat{z}_i / \partial p_k) = \Sigma_i p_i (\partial \hat{x}_i / \partial p_k) - \Sigma_i p_i (\partial y_i^j / \partial p_k)$. However, (i) for compensated demand we have $\Sigma_i p_i (\partial \hat{x}_i / \partial p_k) = 0$; (ii) for the perfectly competitive private sector Hotelling's lemma implies $\Sigma_i p_i (\partial y_i^j / \partial p_k) = 0$. Hence, $\Sigma_i p_i (\partial \hat{z}_i / \partial p_k) = 0$ and therefore

$$\mathcal{L}_k \left\{ \sum_{i \in IC} p_i \frac{\partial \hat{z}_i}{\partial p_k} + \sum_{i \in IS} p_i \frac{\partial \hat{z}_i}{\partial p_k} \right\} = 0. \tag{10}$$

Subtracting (10) from (9) yields

$$\left\{ \sum_{i \in IC} (\mathcal{L}_i - \mathcal{L}_k) p_i \frac{\partial \hat{z}_i}{\partial p_k} + \sum_{i \in IS} (\mathcal{L}_i - \mathcal{L}_k) p_i \frac{\partial \hat{z}_i}{\partial p_k} \right\} dp_k > 0. \tag{11}$$

Our assumptions imply that $dp_k < 0$ increases welfare. The intuitive appeal of this result can be seen if all $\mathcal{L}_i$ are positive: in this case welfare increases if some price p_k is lowered so as to approach the respective marginal costs c_k. Such a change brings $\mathcal{L}_k$ closer to the Lerner indices of the substitutes, but farther away from the Lerner indices of the complements.

---

[19] Recall $\mathcal{L}_i = 0$ for $i \notin K$ because of our assumption (ii) in subsection 7.1.1. That property enables us to proceed from (5–45) to (8).

8
Ramsey Pricing

8.1 Optimum Ramsey Policy

8.1.1 Pricing Subject to a Budget Constraint

Let us now consider the case where

(i)   only prices of publicly produced goods are controlled; uncontrolled prices equal marginal costs c_i in the public sector;[1]

(ii)   the private sector is perfectly competitive;

(iii)   the distribution of lump-sum incomes is optimally chosen, hence we deal with compensated demand;

(iv)   *the public enterprise is restricted by an exogenously fixed deficit or profit* Π^o.

Then the marginal conditions (3–24) reduce to

$$\sum_{i \in K} (p_i - c_i) \frac{\partial \hat{z}_i}{\partial p_k} = -\gamma z_k; \qquad k \in K \qquad (1)$$

where $\gamma \neq 0$. For the most relevant case where Π^o exceeds the unconstrained welfare-optimal profit, $0 < \gamma < 1$.[2]

Ramsey pricing is characterized by a particular trade-off between the level of prices and the structure of prices.

The *level of prices* is primarily influenced by the value of Π^o chosen. Ramsey pricing therefore can stand for low pricing as well as for high pricing policies, for deficit enterprises, cost-covering ones, or for profit-making enterprises. All or some prices can fall below marginal costs to bring about a deficit Π^o. The lower and the upper bounds of Π^o, as mentioned above, are widely separated. Hence, Ramsey prices range from zero tariffs to unconstrained profit maximizing prices. The economic consequences of pricing under revenue-cost constraints depend on the concrete choice of Π^o. The usual exclusive concentration on the structure of prices relegates to the background of the economic discussion that a low Π^o will imply a low pricing level and, if demands react normally, a comparatively large public sector. Low Π^o may

---

[1]   If only output prices are regulated, this assumption implies equality of c_i, and C_i for all netputs. See subsection 2.4.4 above.

[2]   See footnote 12 in chapter 3 above.

imply cheaper prices of publicly provided goods in order to help lower-income earners. This argument is mainly relevant if Π^o refers to a single public enterprise, the outputs of which are mainly demanded by lower-income earners.

What about the *structure of prices?* Recall that the enterprise has to observe a revenue-cost constraint and to meet all demand. Hence the board must consider the price elasticities of demand for the different goods. The less price elastic a good, the easier can its price be increased in order to achieve Π^o because the enterprise need not be too afraid of losing its customers. If, on the other hand, a good is comparatively price elastic, the customers will leave the market if the price is increased. The board will therefore refrain from large price increases of very price elastic goods.

Of course, cross-price elasticities may destroy this basic pattern. However, the above considerations suggest a similarity between the Ramsey price structure and the price structure of a profit-maximizing monopolist, which can be shown easily. Assume a monopolist who calculates his profit-maximizing prices $p_k, k \in K$, considering production possibilities $g(z) = 0$ and acting along compensated demand functions $\hat{z}_k(p)$. He will choose the following price structure:[3]

$$\sum_{i \in K}(p_i - c_i)\frac{\partial \hat{z}_i}{\partial p_k} = -\hat{z}_k; \qquad k \in K. \tag{2}$$

Therefore Ramsey pricing converges to monopoly pricing if $\gamma \to 1$ and if the monopolist takes account of compensated demand functions.

Hence a board which chooses Ramsey pricing behaves as if it were an unconstrained profit-maximizing monopolist who inflates all compensated price elasticities by a factor $1/\gamma$.[4]

---

[3] Following Drèze (1964: 31) we solve the production function $g(z)=0$ to obtain a labor-requirement function $z_o=z_o(z_1,...,z_n)$; $\partial z_o/\partial z_i=-(\partial g/\partial z_i)/(\partial g/\partial z_o)=-c_i$. A monopolist's optimization is as follows ($z_i=z_i(p)$!):

$$max_{p_k} \sum_{i=1}^{n}p_i z_i + p_o z_o(z_1,...,z_n).$$

Therefore

$$z_k+\sum_{i=1}^{n}p_i(\partial z_i/\partial p_k)+p_o\sum_{i=1}^{n}(\partial z_o/\partial z_i)(\partial z_i/\partial p_k)=0; \quad k \in K$$

which can be transformed into

$$\sum_{i=1}^{n}(p_i-c_i)(\partial z_i/\partial p_k)=-z_k; \quad k \in K.$$

Now remember that we always assume $p_i=c_i$ $\forall i \notin K$ and that the monopolist acts along compensated demand functions $\hat{z}_k(p)$.

[4] Divide (2) by γ and set $(\partial \hat{z}_i/\partial p_k)/\gamma=(\partial \hat{z}_i/\partial p_k)^{infl}\forall i,k$. The compensated price elas-

If Π^o exceeds the unconstrained welfare-optimal revenue-cost difference, the inflating factor is $1/\gamma > 1$. The board has to overestimate all price elasticities and thus react more carefully than a monopolist would, being more anxious not to lose customers, which implies a lower level of prices than for a profit-maximizing monopolist.[5]

This comparison between Ramsey and monopoly pricing is the most general and appealing way to interpret Ramsey pricing. Note in particular that it holds for the general case of a multiproduct enterprise and that all cross-price elasticities of demand have been included. However, the reader should be warned that the above-mentioned properties of Ramsey pricing should not be taken as the basis for *price regulation*.[6]

8.1.2   Alternative Transformations of the Ramsey-Pricing Condition

It is quite common to find the following transformations of the Ramsey condition, equation (1), in the public-economics literature:

$$a) \quad \sum_{i \in K} t_i S_{ik} = -\gamma \hat{z}_k; \qquad k \in K, \tag{1a}$$

where $t_i := p_i - c_i$ and $S_{ik} := \partial \hat{z}_i / \partial p_k$ is the substitution effect.[7] This transformation is well known from the theory of optimal indirect taxation.

$$b) \quad \sum_{i \in K} \mathcal{L}_i \eta_{ki} = -\gamma; \qquad k \in K. \tag{1b}$$

where $\mathcal{L}_i := (p_i - c_i)/p_i$ is the Lerner index and $\eta_{ki} := (\partial \hat{z}_k / \partial p_i)(p_i / \hat{z}_k)$ is the compensated price elasticity of demand.[8]

Applying Cramer's rule, this system of equations can explicitly be solved for the Lerner indices, yielding

---

ticities are then obtained by multiplying each partial derivative by the corresponding price/compensated quantity ratio. $\eta_{ik}^{infl} = (1/\gamma)\eta_{ik}$ follows.

[5] For the sake of completeness we must deal also with the case of Π^o below the unconstrained welfare-optimal revenue-cost difference. In this case the inflating factor $1/\gamma$ is negative. The board behaves like a monopolist who changes the signs of all price elasticities.

[6] See chapter 25 below.

[7] For these transformations remember that $z_k(p,(r^h(p,u^{h*}))) = \hat{z}_k(p,(u^{h*}))$, where u^{h*} is the individual utility at the firm's second-best optimum. (The star indicates that the consumer has maximized his utility taking account of the board's policy.) Hence at the optimum the right hand side of eqs. (1) equals $\hat{z}_k$.

[8] Recall that the substitution effects are symmetric, $\partial \hat{x}_i / \partial p_k = \partial \hat{x}_k / \partial p_i$. Because of assumption (ii) in the first paragraph of this chapter, moreover $\partial y_i^j / \partial p_k = \partial y_k^j / \partial p_i$ and therefore $\partial \hat{z}_i / \partial p_k = \partial \hat{z}_k / \partial p_i$.

$$c) \quad \mathcal{L}_k = \mathcal{R}_k; \qquad k \in K. \tag{1c}$$

Here $\mathcal{R}_k$ is a Ramsey-index which according to Cramer's rule is defined as

$$\mathcal{R}_k := \frac{det(\vec{\eta}_1, \ldots, \vec{\eta}_{k-1}, -\vec{\gamma}, \vec{\eta}_{k+1}, \ldots, \vec{\eta}_\mathcal{M})}{det\eta}, \tag{3}$$

where η is the $\mathcal{M}$ times $\mathcal{M}$-dimensional matrix of compensated price elasticities with column vectors $\vec{\eta}_1 \ldots \vec{\eta}_\mathcal{M}$.[9] $-\vec{\gamma}$ is a column vector consisting of $\mathcal{M}$ elements $-\gamma$. By *det* we denote the determinants of the relevant matrices.

The transformation (1c) lends itself to economic interpretations. 'Lerner *index equal to Ramsey index*' is an intuitive description of the economic contents of Ramsey pricing. Unfortunately, the right-hand side of (1c) becomes quite complicated as soon as more than two goods are considered. Hence, I prefer the general interpretation of Ramsey prices by comparison with monopoly prices, as stated in the previous subsection. 'Lerner index equal to Ramsey index', however, is a very enlightening formula if demand interdependencies can totally be neglected or if they refer to two goods only.

(i) In the case of *independent demand functions* $\hat{z}_k(p_k)$, the Ramsey index reduces to $\mathcal{R}_k = -\gamma/\eta_{kk}$ where η_{kk} is the own compensated price elasticity of demand. Hence we obtain the famous '*inverse-elasticity rule*'

$$\mathcal{L}_k = -\frac{\gamma}{\eta_{kk}}; \qquad k \in K \tag{4}$$

where η_{kk} is the own compensated price elasticity of demand. In this special case any Lerner index is proportional to its inverse price elasticity.

The Lerner index of a good is larger, the smaller the absolute value of its price elasticity. Since the own compensated price elasticities are always negative, all prices lie either above or below marginal costs. The case of positive Lerner indices may, for instance, be achieved by a break-even constraint for a public enterprise working under increasing returns to scale. The case of negative Lerner indices is plausible for public enterprises that have to follow 'low pricing procedures'.[10]

The economic consequences of the inverse-elasticity rule are different for positive and for negative Lerner indices. The case of positive Lerner indices leads to relatively higher prices of price-inelastic goods and to relatively lower

---

[9] $\mathcal{M}$ is the number of regulated prices.

[10] $\mathcal{L}_k = -\gamma/\eta_{kk}$ implies that, for prices above marginal costs, $\gamma > 0$, and for prices below marginal costs $\gamma < 0$. But, of course, this does not hold generally if all cross-price elasticities are taken into account, as in (1).

prices of price-elastic goods. The case of negative Lerner indices leads to the contrary. Now assume that goods mainly bought by lower-income consumers are comparatively price inelastic (whether this is the case must be ascertained empirically – Timmer, 1981). Then lower-income consumers are burdened in the case of positive Lerner indices and favored in the case of negative ones.

(ii) For a *two-product firm*, the Ramsey index becomes

$$\mathcal{R}_1 = -\gamma \frac{(\eta_{22} - \eta_{12})}{\eta_{11}\eta_{22} - \eta_{12}\eta_{21}} \tag{5}$$

and $\mathcal{R}_2$ is found analogously. This formula is not easy to interpret because of the interplay of direct and cross elasticities.[11] The Ramsey term can, however, be transformed so as to achieve a counterpart to the inverse-elasticity rule. For this purpose we transform

$$\left[\frac{\eta_{22} - \eta_{12}}{\eta_{11}\eta_{22} - \eta_{12}\eta_{21}} \right]^{-1} = \eta_{11} \left[\frac{1 - \dfrac{\eta_{12}\eta_{21}}{\eta_{11}\eta_{22}}}{1 - \dfrac{\eta_{21}}{\eta_{22}} \cdot \dfrac{p_2 z_2}{p_1 z_1}} \right] =: \mathcal{H}_{11} \tag{6}$$

and analogously for $\mathcal{H}_{22}$. The $\mathcal{H}_{kk}$ are called superelasticities.[12] 'Lerner index equal to Ramsey index' therefore implies

$$\mathcal{L}_k = -\frac{\gamma}{\mathcal{H}_{kk}}; \qquad k = 1, 2. \tag{7}$$

Hence, in a two-product firm $\mathcal{L}_k = \mathcal{R}_k$ can also be interpreted as implying an inverse-elasticity rule related to the superelasticities defined above. A more elaborate interpretation of $\mathcal{L}_k = -\gamma/\mathcal{H}_{kk}$ has to concentrate on the various price elasticities contained in $\mathcal{H}_{kk}$. This interpretation recognizes a tendency toward a larger Lerner index if

- the direct-price elasticity is low;
- the two goods are substitutes, $\eta_{ik} > 0$, because in that case the price increase of one good raises the revenue received on the other good.[13]

Finally, it should be noted that a particularly intuitive Ramsey formula for a two-product enterprise can be attained by dividing the respective Lerner indices, that is

$$\frac{\mathcal{L}_1}{\mathcal{L}_2} = \frac{\mathcal{H}_{22}}{\mathcal{H}_{11}} = \frac{\eta_{22} - \eta_{12}}{\eta_{11} - \eta_{21}}. \tag{8}$$

---

[11] See, for instance, Bös (1981: 56–7).
[12] See Rohlfs (1979), Brown–Sibley (1986: 42–3).
[13] Laffont–Tirole (1990: 10).

These formulas haven often been applied because the elimination of the Lagrangean parameter γ facilitates the economic interpretation.

8.1.3 Ramsey Pricing and General Equilibria

A recent paper by Dierker–Guesnerie–Neuefeind (1985) deals with the existence of a general equilibrium in an economy where some firms are price takers and others are price setters (with a possibly nonconvex technology). The price-setting firms apply special pricing rules like, for instance, Ramsey prices.[14] The possibility of non-existence of an equilibrium can best be illustrated by figure 14.

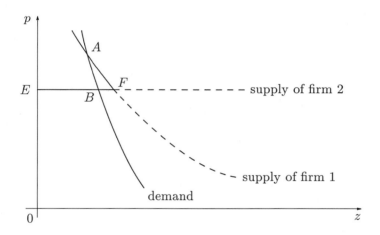

Figure 14
Source: Dierker–Guesnerie–Neuefeind (1985: 1374).

Consider an economy where the same good is produced by two firms. Firm 1 is a price setter who applies a nonconvex technology. Its average-cost curve is taken to be downward sloping and the application of cost-covering Ramsey prices, that is average-cost pricing, leads to a supply curve as illustrated in the figure. Firm 2 is a price taker operating under constant returns to scale, its supply curve is parallel to the horizontal axis. Now assume that

---

[14] The approach can also be extended to further pricing rules like Aumann–Shapley prices. (These prices are treated in chapter 23 below.)

aggregate demand intersects the individual supply functions in A and B, respectively. In that case there is no equilibrium with both firms in operation. This can be deduced directly from the fact that there is no point of intersection between the demand function and the total supply correspondence which is indicated by the dashed line in figure 14. Simply put: there is too much supply and not enough demand for an equilibrium with both firms in operation. Note that the points A and B are not equilibria. Point A is not an equilibrium because firm 1 would be underbid by firm 2. Point B is not an equilibrium either: firm 1 will not close down if it behaves according to the imposed Ramsey rule. Hence at price $0E$ there will be supply of firm 1 larger than B, according to point F.

Intuitively, the existence of an equilibrium can only be ensured if the gap between the graph of total supply and the price axis is bridged in order to obtain a point of intersection between supply and demand. Taking the same technologies as in figure 14 above, we require an extended total supply correspondence as indicated in figure 15. Here a point of interesection between demand and total supply exists.

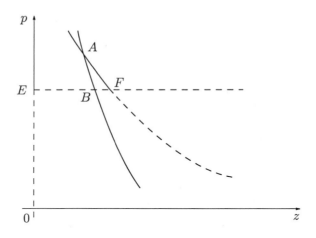

Figure 15
Source: Dierker–Guesnerie–Neuefeind (1985: 1377).

Mathematically, the supply graph has been connected with the price axis by a boundary condition on public pricing: if the good is not produced by the price setter, its price can be lowered. Economically, this boundary condition embodies a possibility of endogenously closing down the public firm. Point B becomes an equilibrium, since the price-setting firm can be closed down and need not produce at point F as the original Ramsey rule would require.[15]

The above has only been a brief heuristic treatment to show the main gist of the Dierker–Guesnerie–Neuefeind paper; we forwent any detailed presentation of the model[16] and the complex proof of the result.

After discussing the existence of equilibria with Ramsey firms, we should now turn to the *optimality* of Ramsey pricing. The famous Ramsey marginal conditions are only necessary for second-best optimality. Further special assumptions are needed to ensure sufficiency. This is a global problem, hence it cannot be solved by reference to the second-order conditions. According to Dierker (1991) the following three assumptions are needed (in addition to the usual assumptions of the Boiteux–Ramsey model[17]):

(i)   monotonicity: consumers buy more output if prices decline, 'but not so much more that no room is left for an increase in the consumption of the numeraire good', for instance leisure (Dierker, 1991: 121).

(ii)   convexity: if two output bundles are compatible with the firm's revenue-cost constraint, any linear combination of these two bundles must also be compatible.

(iii)   elasticity: compensated demand must be less elastic than supply.

These conditions become less stringent if the technology of the public enterprise is convex (up to some well-defined fixed costs).

---

[15] If not the same good, but close substitutes are supplied, the authors require that in the case of zero demand for the good of the price setter, an increase of the price does not lead to positive demand for that good. Basically this is an assumption that the relevant good is not Giffen.

[16] Of special interest are two assumptions: (i) the incomes must be distributed in such a way that each consumer stays above his subsistence level provided that the society can afford the particular pricing policy.   (ii) bankruptcy problems are excluded; these problems might result from the consumers transferring too many resources to the low-price planned sector, which are withdrawn from the other sectors of the economy whence consumers might not receive enough income to survive.

[17] Dierker (1991: 104) attaches great importance to the fact that he deals with Ramsey pricing within Pareto theory, that is he does not use a welfare function to capture distributional problems. This is fully compatible with the approach applied in this book as explicitly mentioned on pp. 39–40 above. More problematical seems Dierker's (1991: 104) explicit exclusion of any lump-sum redistribution. In the setting of this book, Ramsey pricing is no longer optimal if there is no such redistribution (unless the distribution of incomes r^h happens to be optimal by some unlikely coincidence). If there is no lump-sum redistribution, the public enterprise should charge Feldstein prices. However, Dierker's three additional assumptions would also be needed to prove second-best optimality of Ramsey pricing if there were lump-sum redistribution of incomes.

8.1.4 Cross-Subsidization

The cross-subsidization problem of multiproduct enterprises refers to the relation between the revenues and the costs that are attributed to the individual goods or to combinations of goods. The best presentation of the problem uses a game-theoretic approach (Faulhaber, 1975). If an enterprise produces n' goods, we denote by 'N' any 'coalition' of goods, either individual goods, or combinations of more than one good, or the 'coalition of the whole' n'. We denote an output vector z^{+N} with entries

$$z_i^{+N} = \begin{cases} z_i^+ & i \in N \\ 0 & \text{otherwise.} \end{cases} \tag{9}$$

Denote revenue of the enterprise by R and costs by C. Then for a *break-even* enterprise that is characterized by

$$R(z^{+n'}(p)) = C(z^{+n'}(p)) \tag{10}$$

we can identify 'subsidizers' for which

$$R(z^{+N}(p)) \geq C(z^{+N}(p)) \tag{11}$$

and subsidized coalitions where the contrary holds. This definition applies to any kind of cost function.[18] It follows that some good or some coalition of goods is a cross subsidizer if it can 'go it alone' and make a profit. The concrete computation of (11) is quite complicated for enterprises facing interrelated demand (z^{+N} always depends on all prices p!) and facing joint production.[19]

The break-even case, however, is only one particular case of Ramsey pricing. And there may well exist cross-subsidization in cases of public enterprises with deficits or profits. Therefore, we should extend Faulhaber's terminology. The straightforward extension is as follows. If the revenue-cost ratio of an enterprise is exogenously given, denoted by $\Pi^o(\Pi^o > 0)$:

$$\frac{R(z^{+n'}(p))}{C(z^{+n'}(p))} = \Pi^o, \tag{12}$$

---

[18] In contrast Faulhaber (1975) restricts his analysis to subadditive cost functions because he is mainly interested in price structures of break-even enterprises where no coalition is a subsidizer but all benefit from being part of the enterprise. This formulation of the cross-subsidization problem was the starting point of the discussion on substainability of natural monopolies.

[19] Recently developed cost-sharing algorithms that make computation of $C(z^{+N}(p))$ possible also follow game-theoretic approaches, especially the Shapley-value. See Littlechild (1970), Billera–Heath–Raanan (1978).

we can identify 'subsidizers' for which

$$\frac{R(z^{+N}(p))}{C(z^{+N}(p))} \geq \Pi^o \tag{13}$$

and subsidized coalitions for which the contrary holds. This definition again applies to any kind of cost function. And, needless to say, the computational problems are the same.

According to this extension, in deficit enterprises goods with a nearly cost-covering price subsidize goods with a price which covers only 50 percent of the costs attributed to the production although this problem cannot be handled by a 'go it alone'–test and there is no problem of a possible lack of sustainability. Moreover, it implies that in a profitable enterprise some goods may be subsidized although the prices are cost covering and they could 'go it alone'. In the long-run this problem will, of course, only exist if entry to this market is forbidden.

Let us conclude by pointing out that the problem of cross-subsidization is of no importance from the point of view of welfare economics. If optimal pricing includes any kind of cross-subsidization (of the Faulhaber type or of an extended type), then that cross-subsidization should be accepted.

8.2 Influence of Ramsey Prices on Allocation, Distribution, and Stabilization

It is impossible to derive general results on allocative, distributional, and stabilization effects of Ramsey prices because all the consequences will depend on the value of Π^o. Whether Ramsey prices will exceed or fall below marginal-cost prices will be determined by Π^o. Results can only be derived for given values of Π^o.

Considering $\Pi^o = 0$, in the case of increasing returns to scale, at least one Ramsey price will exceed marginal cost. If cross-price elasticities can be neglected, all Ramsey prices exceed marginal costs. With respect to an *optimal allocation* this will lead to a shrinking public sector as compared with marginal-cost prices, where a revenue-cost constraint does not exist.[20]

The *distributional consequences* of Ramsey pricing depend, first, on the *level of prices*. A public enterprise may, for instance, be constrained to work under deficit ($\Pi^o < 0$) to hold the price level of its products low in order to subsidize its lower-income customers. Second, the *price structure* has to be

---

[20] The same tendency will prevail if we compare Ramsey prices with optimal two-part tariffs. Whereas the fixed charge as a lump-sum tax does not influence the first-best marginal conditions, a Ramsey price higher than the marginal-cost prices will.

considered. Here we have to ask whether the prices are above or below their marginal costs, as shown above by the example of the 'inverse-elasticity rule'.

General results with respect to the *stabilization consequences* of Ramsey prices cannot be formulated. These consequences will depend on the relevant elasticities of demand in business cycles. It will not be possible to obtain concrete results unless we build a dynamic model to investigate the relevant cases. There will be quite different consequences for stabilization policy if we consider other types of revenue-cost constraints than cost-covering ones. In such cases we can assume $\Pi^o \neq 0$ to vary anticyclically and to cause stabilization effects by means of optimal price or quantity instructions to the public enterprise.

8.3　A Piecemeal-Policy Interpretation of the Ramsey Optimum

Some of the best-known interpretations of Ramsey pricing follow a piecemeal approach. Consider a situation where the controlled prices change by dp_k and the uncontrolled prices remain constant. Then the total differentials of the demand functions $\hat{z}_k = \hat{z}_k(p)$ are as follows

$$d\hat{z}_k(p) = \sum_{i \in K} \frac{\partial \hat{z}_k}{\partial p_i} dp_i; \qquad k \in K. \tag{14}$$

Let all price changes be proportional to the difference between price and marginal cost, that is,

$$dp_i = (p_i - c_i)ds; \qquad i \in K \tag{15}$$

where $ds < 0$ implies that prices move towards marginal costs[21] and $ds > 0$ implies the contrary. Substituting into (1) yields

$$-\gamma \hat{z}_k = \sum_{i \in K}(p_i - c_i)\frac{\partial \hat{z}_i}{\partial p_k} = \sum_{i \in K}(p_i - c_i)\frac{\partial \hat{z}_k}{\partial p_i} = \frac{1}{ds}\sum_{i \in K}\frac{\partial \hat{z}_k}{\partial p_i}dp_i = \frac{1}{ds}d\hat{z}_k(p) \tag{16}$$

and by rearranging we obtain

$$d\hat{z}_k = -\gamma \hat{z}_k ds; \qquad k \in K. \tag{17}$$

---

[21] Prices which exceed marginal costs are lowered; prices which are below marginal costs are increased.

This is one of Boiteux's (1956, 1971) main results for a second-best optimum: The price marginal-cost deviations are proportional to those infinitesimal variations in price that entail a proportional change in the demands for all publicly provided goods. This proportional change in demand may, however, imply that for some goods demand increases, although the own price decreases or vice versa.[22] Consider the following example: Π^o exceeds the unconstrained revenue-cost difference. Hence, $\gamma \in (0, 1)$. Assume $ds > 0$. Recall that, for a given Π^o, some prices may exceed marginal costs, some others may fall short of them. The proportional price changes then imply increasing as well as decreasing prices. But the quantities change in the same direction: demand decreases, even for those goods whose prices decrease. The reason for such a demand response is straightforward. If the relevant good k is relatively unresponsive to its own price, but quite responsive to the prices of other goods that are complements, its second-best price may fall below marginal costs even if other prices exceed marginal costs. In such a case the proportional price change implies increasing the prices of complements which may imply a fall in the demand for good k even though its own price decreases.

A very common alternative interpretation going back to Ramsey (1927) concerns the case of the transition from second-best to marginal-cost pricing:[23] at a second-best optimum the relative deviations of second-best quantities from those quantities that would have been demanded if the goods were sold at marginal-cost prices are equal for all goods. Usually the authors add some remarks on the empirical applicability of such a result: if the enterprise sells every good, not at the present price but at a price given by the marginal cost of the present production, it will not be in a state of second-best optimum if the relative shifts of demand for the various goods turn out to be different.

However, the Boiteux–Ramsey interpretation of second-best quantities is an approximation only, contrary to our interpretation of second-best prices. As we use the total differential (14), all following results are strictly valid only for infinitesimal deviations from marginal-cost pricing or for demand functions which are linear in prices. This raises the question whether the prominence given to this approach, for instance in papers on optimal commodity taxation (Diamond, 1975; Mirrlees, 1975), is warranted.

---

[22] Of course $\partial \hat{z}_k / \partial p_k$ is always negative. However, as we are considering simultaneous changes of all prices, the cross-price effects may overcompensate this direct effect.

[23] This is a special case of (13) where we start from marginal-cost pricing and integrate over ds from -1 (p^{MC}) to 0 (p^{Ramsey}). Then $[\hat{z}_i(p^{MC}) - \hat{z}_i(p^{Ramsey})]/\hat{z}_i(p^{Ramsey}) = \gamma \ \forall i$.

9
Pricing with Distributional Aims

9.1 Prices Versus Taxes

In many European countries public pricing is not only considered as an instrument of allocation policy, but also as an instrument of distribution policy. The most favorable conditions for this approach prevail if different classes of goods can be identified which typically are demanded by consumers with different incomes: first- and second-class railway or hospital accommodation provide good examples. We could think also of a nationalized enterprise producing small cars for low-income consumers and large cars for high-income consumers and deviating from allocatively optimal pricing by reducing the price of small cars at the expense of large cars.

Such a pricing policy favors low-income earners and it avoids the need for a direct means test and the associated costs of implementing such a system of distributional pricing. Moreover, the consumers are still given the freedom to choose the good they prefer. A rich person who likes to chat with the less affluent is not prohibited from using a second-class railway compartment.

However, we must examine the following two main objections against the use of public-sector pricing as means of income redistribution:

(i) First, *liberal economists* often oppose distributionally modified public pricing. They view progressive income taxation or income subsidies as the most effective instruments of income redistribution and wish to restrict public-sector pricing to the allocational objectives only. ('Why do you want to favor poor people simply because they travel by rail? If you regard them as poor give them money' as A.A. Walters formulated it in a personal discussion with the author some years ago.)

The traditional liberals argue that income taxation distorts the labor-leisure decision only, whereas distributional public prices distort relative prices throughout the economy. They contend that a rich person, reflecting upon the labor-leisure choice, does not only consider the marginal income tax rate on additional income, but also the additional expenditures for certain goods. By whatever means a dollar is taken away, the disincentive effect on labor effort will be the same. Hence, public pricing is an inferior instrument of redistribution. For the same degree of redistribution it leads to the same welfare losses from distorting labor-leisure choices as an income tax, but it leads to additional welfare losses because of distorted relative prices for goods (Ng, 1984).

However, this conclusion is not valid for the following reasons:

• If we assume a social welfare function with the usual distributional weighting of individual incomes, and that income taxation *and* public pricing are available policy instruments, the level of social welfare which can be achieved must be greater than or at least the same as that which can be attained when an income tax is the only policy instrument. This result takes account of the disincentive effects of both progressive taxation and distributional pricing. There is, however, a special case where optimal prices equal marginal costs. This implies that pricing is restricted to the allocative task and the redistribution task has to be achieved by the income tax only. The optimality of marginal-cost pricing, however, depends on very restrictive assumptions, namely, constant returns to scale and utility functions which are weakly separable between labor and all goods together. These assumptions are highly implausible and therefore public prices will usually have to consider distributional objectives and income taxation will not be the only, and hence superior, instrument of redistribution (Bös, 1984).

• It is worth noting that the argument of the liberal economists did not presuppose fiscal illusion. It seems likely that they would have found that this illusion varies with the way in which revenue is raised (taxes, prices etc.). Moreover, fiscal illusion can be particularly relevant when price differences are associated with quality differences. The absence of fiscal illusion in this case would require the purchaser to distinguish between that part of the higher price which is due to quality and that which is due to redistribution.

(ii) *Social democrats*, on the other hand, oppose distributional public prices because they do not depend on personal means unlike, for example, the payment of income taxes. The rich person in the second-class railway compartment offers a good example. Moreover, distributional price differentiation typically implies some quality differentiation which has often been critized for ideological reasons, which stress the merits of uniform public supply of schooling, health etc.

However, there are counter-arguments to these conclusions:

• distributional pricing can be tied to individual income by using an explicit means test;[1]

---

[1] For some of the problems which are created by means-tested pricing, see Bös (1985b): (i) The adjustment of consumers to means-tested public pricing leads to a 'gap in the income distribution'. There are many who decide to earn the threshold income, but nobody who earns an income which is just slightly above the threshold. (ii) It is impossible to obtain results referring to the size of the optimum threshold income. Both a low and a high threshold are plausible: the low one favors a selected group of the poor, the high one burdens a selected group of the rich.

- quality differentiation can be restricted to a few classes of different goods, or even totally be avoided if it seems appropriate for distributional reasons.

9.2 Feldstein Pricing

Let us consider the following special case of the generalized Boiteux model:

(i)   only prices of publicly produced goods are controlled;
(ii)   the private sector is perfectly competitive;
(iii)   *all lump-sum incomes are exogenously given, and we are dealing with non-compensated demand;*
(iv)   there is a revenue-cost constraint Π^o.

The reasons for combining the above assumptions are the following:

We must first ensure that public prices are the actual instruments of distribution policy. Therefore we have to exclude those lump-sum transfers which are the distributional instruments in the earlier sections on marginal-cost pricing and Ramsey pricing. Public pricing with distributional objectives must be located in a world of Marshallian demand functions, not in a world of compensated demand functions (assumption (iii) above).

Next we have to consider the financial difficulties the enterprise's board will encounter if it applies distributional pricing: revenue will tend to fall, perhaps below costs, because any internal subsidization of the poor is limited by the possibility that the rich may leave the market totally or switch to the consumption of lower-priced goods.[2] Large redistributional effects will thus lead to a marked increase in the demand for low-priced goods and a marked decrease in the demand for high-priced goods, implying a tendency toward a deficit. Hence, we must always include a profit constraint for the public enterprise (assumption (iv) above).

The financial difficulties would become even worse if private competitors were allowed to enter the public enterprise's markets. Needless to say, these competitors would concentrate on supplying those goods which are intended to play the role of internal subsidizers. This problem will become more important, the more profitably some of the publicly supplied goods can be priced.

Let us first exclude this particular problem by introducing the additional assumption that goods with publicly controlled prices are neither supplied nor demanded by private firms. Then, given assumptions (i) to (iv) the marginal conditions (3–21b) reduce to:

$$\sum_{i=o}^{n}(p_i - c_i)\frac{\partial z_i^D}{\partial p_k} = -(1 - F_k)z_k; \qquad k \in K. \tag{1}$$

---

[2] Compare Sah (1983) on the limits of redistribution through commodity taxes.

The reader should recall that z_i^D represents *non*-compensated demand and F_k the distributional characteristics (3–13)

$$F_k := \sum_h \lambda^h \frac{\partial v^h}{\partial r^h} \frac{x_k^h}{x_k}; \qquad k \in K. \tag{2}$$

The distributional characteristic of any good is higher, the larger is its share of consumption by lower-income consumers: quantities x_k^h of a necessity are given the higher weights λ^h; moreover $\partial v^h / \partial r^h$ will be higher for lower income. Hence F_k will usually be higher for a necessity than for a luxury, implying a tendency toward lower prices of necessities. Pricing according to (1) may be denoted 'Feldstein pricing' as Feldstein (1972a,b,c) was the first to emphasize distributional-equity considerations in public-sector pricing.

The most general interpretation of the distributional price structure (1) can once again be given by comparing this price structure with that of the perfect monopolist. The distributionally oriented board behaves as if it were a monopolist who inflates each price elasticity of demand ε_{ik} by $1/(1 - F_k)$.[3] This pricing behavior is more complicated than in the Ramsey case because typically there will exist as many different inflating factors as publicly priced goods. The operation of this procedure can be illustrated most easily if we neglect cross-price effects. Then the pricing rule is as follows:

$$(p_k - c_k) \frac{\partial z_k^D}{\partial p_k} = -(1 - F_k) z_k. \tag{3}$$

If we exclude inverse demand responses by assuming $\partial z_k^D / \partial p_k < 0$, then the price of good k will exceed the marginal costs c_k if $1 > F_k > 0$ and fall below c_k if $F_k > 1$.

For a price above marginal costs the inflating factors $1/(1 - F_k)$ will be positive and will increase with increasing F_k. The demand response must therefore be overestimated and the degree of overestimation increases with increasing social valuation of individual consumption as reflected in F_k. Above all, the demand response of necessities must be overestimated because monopolistic pricing always implies greater care in the pricing of goods with higher demand elasticities.

If, on the other hand, the price falls below marginal costs, the inflating factor $1/(1 - F_k)$ will be negative and will again increase with increasing F_k. This implies once again a tendency to reduce the price of necessities.

---

[3] Divide (1) by $(1-F_k)$ and define $(\partial z_i^D/\partial p_k)/(1-F_k)=(\partial z_i^D/\partial p_k)^{infl}$. Elasticities can then be obtained easily by multiplying each partial derivative with the corresponding price/quantity ratio p_k/z_i^D.

An interesting extension of the above distributional-pricing formula arises if the regulated goods are supplied or demanded also by private firms. Then public prices have to be determined according to a special case of (3–21a):

$$\sum_{i=o}^{n}(p_i - c_i)\frac{\partial z_i^D}{\partial p_k} = -(1 - F_k)x_k - \gamma(z_k - x_k); \qquad k \in K. \qquad (4)$$

As we could expect, this formula shows that prices are not only reduced for distributional reasons, but also because of competition by private firms. This trade-off can be seen directly by looking at eqs. (4).

Cheaper prices for necessities are brought about by higher F_k or, equivalently, by lower $(1 - F_k)x_k$. The price of good k is also reduced if $|z_k - x_k|$ increases, i.e. if the consumption from private supply is greater (for outputs $x_k > z_k$ and positive γ).

Competition by private firms becomes more important, the more profitably some publicly supplied goods can be priced. In the above formula this tendency is revealed by the influence of γ which typically will be higher, the higher the permitted public revenue-cost difference Π^o.

It is interesting to note that γ influences the pricing *structure*[4] only if private market entry is explicitly considered in the model. Eqs. (1) do not contain γ, but eqs. (4) do.

9.3   Comparing Distributional and Allocative Pricing

Assume a public enterprise which employs the Boiteux model to determine prices p_k and quantities z_i, the revenue-cost difference being restricted to Π^o. The enterprise's board is given the choice between Ramsey pricing (including the optimal determination of lump-sum incomes r^h) and 'Feldstein' pricing (accepting lump-sum incomes r^h as exogenously fixed).

- Ramsey pricing:
$$\sum_{i \in K}(p_i - c_i)\frac{\partial \hat{z}_i}{\partial p_k} = -\gamma z_k; \qquad k \in K \quad (8\text{–}1)$$

is usually thought of as 'the' pure allocative-pricing rule.

- 'Feldstein'pricing:[5]
$$\sum_{i \in K}(p_i - c_i)\frac{\partial z_i^D}{\partial p_k} = -(1 - F_k)z_k; \qquad k \in K \quad (5)$$

is usually thought of as 'the' distributional-pricing rule.

---

[4] γ does, of course, influence the optimal absolute values of the prices in any case.

[5] For this explicit comparison between Ramsey and Feldstein pricing we additionally assume that uncontrolled prices equal marginal costs c_i in the public sector.

Both pricing rules have been derived from the same basic model. There-fore, our first conclusion must be the following: if the social welfare function $W(v^1, \ldots, v^H)$ is the same in both cases, Ramsey prices are at least as effec-tive with respect to the achievement of distributional objectives as Feldstein prices. This weak distributional dominance of Ramsey pricing is due to the fact that both approaches optimize the same objective function under the same constraints, but with different instrument variables, the set of Feldstein instruments being a proper subset of the set of Ramsey instruments.

The above paradoxical result shows the importance of using compensated demand in the Ramsey case and non-compensated demand in the Feldstein case. However, it seems a little unfair to compare Ramsey and Feldstein pricing using the same welfare function. Let us therefore follow the usual tradition and compare

• Ramsey pricing as the policy of a distributionally neutral board of the firm, $\partial W/\partial v^h = 1$ for all h, and

• Feldstein pricing as the policy of a distributionally oriented board, $\partial W/\partial v^h > 0, \partial^2 W/\partial(v^h)^2 < 0$ for all h.

The revenue-cost difference Π^o is assumed to be identical in both cases.[6]

Needless to say, Feldstein pricing by definition leads to a distributionally optimal result with respect to the above objective function and the given constraints. But how good are these distributional results if they are compared with Ramsey prices? *Will Feldstein prices always favor necessities more than Ramsey prices?*

To examine this issue we restrict the analysis to two publicly priced goods:

• good 1 (for example, 'first class') is a luxury. A comparatively high percentage of the quantity x_1 is bought by higher-income consumers. It has a numerically high price elasticity of demand because of easy substitutability and because lower-income consumers of this good are very sensitive to price increases;

• good 2 (for example, 'second class') is a necessity. A comparatively high percentage of the quantity x_2 is bought by lower-income consumers. It has a numerically low price elasticity of demand.[7]

Moreover, we assume that income effects are not very important (ideally equal to zero), and cross-price elasticities are neglected.

Usually, the necessity will be favored if Feldstein pricing is applied. How-ever, there may exist perverse cases where the maximization of a distribution-ally oriented welfare function leads to higher prices for necessities than the

---

[6] The following text of this subsection is taken from Bös (1983).

[7] In practical applications of our theoretical model one should, however, always carefully check whether these assumptions are fulfilled.

maximization of the neutral welfare function under the same revenue-cost constraint. These perverse cases depend on the fact that favoring lower-income groups in this model does not differentiate between incomes but between goods.

Usually the shifts in the Lerner indices are used as proxies for the shifts in the prices. Let us for the moment accept this approximation. Let us consider only cases where both prices exceed marginal costs.[8] Then the necessity is favored if

$$\frac{\mathcal{L}_1^F}{\mathcal{L}_2^F} > \frac{\mathcal{L}_1^R}{\mathcal{L}_2^R} \tag{6}$$

where F refers to Feldstein and R to Ramsey. Substituting from the marginal conditions for Ramsey and for Feldstein pricing, therefore, the necessity is favored relatively if

$$\frac{\varepsilon_{22}}{\varepsilon_{11}} \cdot \frac{(1 - F_1)}{(1 - F_2)} > \frac{\eta_{22}}{\eta_{11}} \tag{7}$$

where the non-compensated elasticities ε_{ii} are considered at the Feldstein optimum, the compensated elasticies η_{ii} at the Ramsey optimum.

Looking at above inequality, we see that the necessity may be relatively expensive under Feldstein pricing for the following reasons:

(i) η_{22}/η_{11} may exceed $\varepsilon_{22}/\varepsilon_{11}$.

The distributional objectives aim at a lower price for the necessity. This typically implies a numerically lower elasticity ε_{22}. However, the allocative 'inverse-elasticity structure' which also is implied in the Feldstein rule, implies a tendency toward a price increase of the necessity. It can be seen immediately from (7) that such changes of the elasticities work against lower Feldstein prices of the necessity.

Usually this difficulty is overcome by the assumption that the elasticities are identical for the comparison (7), $\varepsilon_{ii} = \eta_{ii}$ for $i = 1, 2$. This assumption can be justified only if we restrict ourselves to cases where income effects do not matter and where a politician is unwilling to change prices abruptly for fear of political disturbances and therefore only compares Ramsey prices and Feldstein prices that are not far from one other. Needless to say there may exist many cases where this does not hold and where the above-mentioned change of elasticities may lead to unexpected results.

---

[8]   Other possible cases are dealt with in Bös (1981: 96–7, 100).

(ii)   Perverse Ranking of the 'Distributional Characteristics'.

Let us assume identical elasticities $\varepsilon_{ii} = \eta_{ii}$. Then inequality (7) reduces to $F_1 < F_2 < 1,$[9] which implies

$$\sum_h W_h \frac{x_1^h}{x_1} < \sum_h W_h \frac{x_2^h}{x_2} \tag{8}$$

where $W_h := \lambda^h (\partial v^h / \partial r^h)$ is the marginal social valuation of the individual lump-sum income r^h, and is assumed to be a decreasing function of income r^h.

There will exist many cases where this condition holds, because we have assumed that the weights W_h decrease with increasing income and that x_1 is demanded mainly by higher-income earners and x_2 mainly by lower-income earners. But we can easily think of combinations of x_i^h and W_h that do not fulfill these conditions. The reader should recall that we only assumed that 'a comparatively high percentage' of total demand comes from higher- or from lower-income earners, respectively. Therefore we have neither excluded purchases of necessities by higher-income earners nor purchases of luxuries by lower-income earners.

A simple numerical example for $F_1 > F_2$ is as follows: define a necessity as a good where more than 50 percent of the total quantity is consumed by lower-income earners, and conversely for a luxury. Take an economy with 5 income earners, $r = (10, 15, 20, 30, 35)$, which results in an average income of 22. Thus the first three income earners are lower-income earners. Assume that for the income distribution mentioned above the social marginal valuations of the individual incomes, W_h, are given by the vector $(1; 0.8; 0.6; 0.55; 0.5)$. Now choose consumption shares of the necessity as $(0.2; 0.1; 0.25; 0.225; 0.225)$ which implies that 55 percent of the consumption comes from lower-income earners. Choose consumption shares of the luxury as $(0.25; 0.1; 0.1; 0.275; 0.275)$ which implies that 55 percent of the consumption comes from higher-income earners. – The distributional characteristic for the luxury then is $F_1 = 0.68$, and for the necessity, $F_2 = 0.67$.

The comparison of Feldstein versus Ramsey pricing remains incomplete if it is restricted to the above considerations. Relaxing the earlier assumption on cross-price effects and the restriction of our comparison (7) to Lerner indices, we get the following additional reasons why Feldstein prices might make the necessity more expensive:

---

[9] The other mathematically possible solution of reducing (7) in case of $\varepsilon_{ii}=\eta_{ii}$ is excluded by the assumption that both prices exceed marginal costs.

(iii)   Influence of Cross-Price Elasticities

If the Lerner indices are assumed to depend on the cross-price elasticities of demand (allowing also for the income effects in case of the non-compensated elasticities ε_{ij}[10]), general conclusions on a comparison between Feldstein and Ramsey prices become next to impossible.

(iv)   Influence of Returns to Scale

Until now, our comparison has not focussed on the prices themselves, but on the ratios of price-cost margins, i.e. Lerner indices. However a lower Lerner index may imply a higher price if the marginal costs change correspondingly. This can be a further reason why Feldstein prices of a necessity may exceed Ramsey prices. If additional quantities of the necessity can only be produced at increasingly higher marginal costs, it will become more and more difficult to achieve distributional objectives by a low price of the necessity. This tendency will be reinforced if considerable economies of scale prevail in the production of the luxury.

---

[10] See Feldstein (1972a); corrected version of p. 33, footnote 7 in American Economic Review 62 (1972, 763).

10
Adjustment to Private Monopolistic Pricing

10.1 The Second-Best Issue: Adjustment to, Versus Interference in, Private Monopolistic Pricing

Let some prices in the private economy deviate from marginal costs because of the monopoly power of some entrepreneurs, because of the application of rule of thumb (e.g. mark-up) pricing, or because of commodity taxation.[1] Any of these cases will be called 'monopolistic pricing', the degree of monopoly being measured by the positive Lerner index

$$\mathcal{L}_i^j := (p_i - c_i^j)/p_i > 0; \qquad i = 1, \ldots, n; \quad j = 1, \ldots, J. \tag{1}$$

If these prices cannot be, or are not, brought down to marginal costs, then the second-best philosophy tells us that in general the prices of the remaining goods also must deviate from marginal costs in order to obtain maximal welfare. The rationale is that the attainable welfare in an economy is maximized if the price structure corresponds to the relative scarcity of goods. Such a correspondence will, in general, be approximated better if unavoidable distortions are compensated by other distortions than if the rest of the economy does not react to these distortions.[2]

Lipsey–Lancaster (1956-57) and Green (1962) were the first to articulate some challenging hypotheses on public-sector pricing in a monopolistic environment. This second-best approach to public-sector pricing was attacked subsequently because it seemed to take as unalterable the fact that prices in the private economy cannot be brought down to marginal costs and therefore required that public prices adjust to the private degrees of monopoly. In turn, this seemed to imply a public-pricing policy that did everything to enable private monopolists to make profits. If privately and publicly priced goods are substitutes, public prices must be increased to mitigate the competition against the monopoly. If they are complements, public prices must be reduced to make the joint purchase of both goods cheaper, which again helps

---

[1] In this case p_i are the consumer prices which differ from producer prices; the latter may well be identical to marginal costs. See, for instance Green (1962) and Wiegard (1979).

[2] In a second-best model *typically* all conditions for the optimum differ from the corresponding conditions for the Pareto optimum. The seminal paper by Lipsey–Lancaster (1956-57) is confusing in this respect. Page 11 incorrectly states that *all* Paretian conditions must be altered. Page 27 correctly states that this holds '*in general*'.

the private enterprise. Opponents argued that this meant the 'abdication of economic policy'.

These objections partly miss the point. They may be valid if a public enterprise actually adjusts its price structure to that of a perfect private monopolist. However, monopolistic pricing in the private sector, as defined above, refers to all enterprises whose prices exceed marginal costs. Usually there will exist many cases of politically acceptable positive Lerner indices. Then the chosen structure of public prices only implies the best possible way to restore price relations that indicate the relative scarcity of goods. Therefore, publicly priced substitutes have to be more expensive to restore at least partly the price relations that would have prevailed in the absence of private monopolistic pricing. On the other hand, publicly priced complements have to be cheaper: if public prices remained at marginal costs, the 'composite' price for both complements would be farther from the price relations that would have prevailed in the absence of private monopolistic pricing. In other words: if 'two goods are complements, ... second-best pricing involves offsetting exogenous distortions, not the sort of distortion matching one thinks of for substitutes.' (Schmalensee, 1981: 453).

Objections to adjusting public pricing to private monopolistic pricing can be criticized for yet another reason. It is true that this approach assumes private Lerner indices to be exogenously given and public ones to be endogenously adjusted. However, this does not imply that the public sector has no influence on the private economy. For example, assume the public Lerner indices are lower than those in a private substitute industry. This will decrease the demand for the privately supplied goods although the public sector does not follow marginal-cost pricing. One should always consider the adjustment of the private economy to public pricing which is also included in our approach. The importance of this feedback will, of course, depend on the relative size of the public and the private sectors of the economy.

The adjustment of public pricing to typical private pricing can be treated in general and in partial microeconomic models.

(i)   The interdependence between public and private pricing can first be treated in a *general microeconomic model*, in our case in the extended Boiteux-type model. Section 10.2 will be devoted to this approach.

(ii)   Recently, however, there has been particular interest in *partial analyses* which consider duopolistic or oligopolistic markets where one of the participants is a public enterprise. Such analyses show public and private pricing to depend on the different possible strategies of the economic agents involved. This problem of 'mixed markets' will be treated in chapter 34 below.

10.2   Public Prices in an Imperfect Market Economy

Dealing with a special case of the extended Boiteux model, we must once again clarify the particular assumptions which characterize the following analysis:

(i)   only prices of publicly produced goods are controlled;[3]
(ii)   *the unregulated private sector is not perfectly competitive;*
(iii)   the distribution of lump-sum incomes is optimally chosen, hence we shall deal with compensated demand;
(iv)   the revenue-cost difference is considered alternatively as constrained and as non-constrained.

Then the marginal-conditions (3–24) of the extended Boiteux-model hold:

$$\sum_i (p_i - c_i)\frac{\partial \hat{z}_i}{\partial p_k} = -\gamma z_k - (1-\gamma)\sum_i \sum_j (p_i - c_i^j)\frac{\partial y_i^j}{\partial p_k}; \quad k \in K. \qquad (2)$$

For the economic interpretation of this pricing structure we *first* assume a revenue-cost constraint which exceeds unconstrained profits ($\gamma > 0$). For any single price p_k equation (2) can be rewritten as

$$p_k = c_k - \frac{\gamma z_k}{\partial \hat{z}_k / \partial p_k} - \sum_{i \neq k}(p_i - c_i)\frac{\partial \hat{z}_i / \partial p_k}{\partial \hat{z}_k / \partial p_k} -$$
$$- (1-\gamma)\sum_i \sum_j (p_i - c_i^j)\frac{\partial y_i^j / \partial p_k}{\partial \hat{z}_k / \partial p_k}; \quad k \in K. \qquad (3)$$

Hence, the controlled price p_k will usually differ from marginal costs. The second term on the right hand side of (3) measures the effects of the revenue-cost constraint and implies the expected tendency for the price p_k to exceed the marginal costs of producing good k in the public sector (since $\gamma > 0$, $\partial \hat{z}_k / \partial p_k < 0$). The last two terms on the right hand side, the 'reallocation effects' (Hagen, 1979) imply a unique tendency for price p_k to exceed c_k if all prices exceed the respective marginal costs *and* if good k is a net substitute for all other goods ($\partial \hat{z}_i / \partial p_k > 0, \partial y_i^j / \partial p_k > 0 \; \forall i \neq k$). Complementarities between good k and (some) other goods point in the opposite direction; there is no general answer in this case.

Let us *secondly* consider public pricing without a binding budget constraint, but with given price distortions in the private economy. The general

---

[3] The analysis can be extended easily to price control of goods which are only produced privately. (Set $z_k = 0$ and $\partial \hat{z}_k / \partial p_k = 0$ in eqs. (2).)

interpretation of this case is straightforward and can be left to the reader. (Set $\gamma = 0$ in (3).) One special interpretation, however, must be treated more extensively. Assume the Lerner index for any good i to be identical for all private firms and for the public sector

$$\mathcal{L}_i = (p_i - c_i)/p_i = (p_i - c_i^j)/p_i; \quad i = 1, \dots, n; \ j = 1, \dots, J$$
$$\mathcal{L}_o = 0. \tag{4}$$

The theoretical literature on the topic usually tries to account for such parallel behavior by referring to identical commodity taxation. Then (2) can be written as follows

$$\mathcal{L}_k p_k \frac{\partial \hat{x}_k}{\partial p_k} = -\sum_{i \neq k} \mathcal{L}_i p_i \frac{\partial \hat{x}_i}{\partial p_k}; \quad k \in K. \tag{5}$$

Since the compensated expenditures for all goods do not respond to price changes $(\Sigma_i p_i (\partial \hat{x}_i / \partial p_k) = 0)$, we obtain

$$\mathcal{L}_k = \sum_{i \neq k} \mathcal{L}_i w_{ik}; \quad k \in K, \tag{6}$$

where

$$w_{ik} = p_i (\partial \hat{x}_i / \partial p_k) \bigg/ \sum_{b \neq k} p_b (\partial \hat{x}_b / \partial p_k); \quad \sum_{i \neq k} w_{ik} = 1. \tag{7}$$

The Lerner index $\mathcal{L}_k$ is a weighted average of all other $\mathcal{L}_i$. This implies that the optimal Lerner index lies somewhere between the minimum and the maximum Lerner index if good k is a net substitute for all other goods. With some modifications this result can be found in Green (1962), Bergson (1972), Hatta (1977), Kawamata (1977), Wiegard (1978, 1979), Hagen (1979).

It seems unlikely that this celebrated result merits the attention given to it, for two reasons:

(i) Exogenously fixing $\mathcal{L}_i = \mathcal{L}_i^j$ for all i and j implies the exogenous determination of variables that are endogenously determined in the model: the optimal values of $\mathcal{L}$ are the result of the optimization approach! Equality of $\mathcal{L}_i$ and $\mathcal{L}_i^j$ can only result by chance or from particular theoretical assumptions regarding the private sector which we have avoided deliberately in this section. Moreover, there is no economic justification for introducing this identity of Lerner indices as additional constraints in our optimization approach.

(ii)   The result is only valid if good k is a net substitute for all other goods, which is empirically not very plausible. There exist many net complementarities between regulated and non-regulated goods. Take, for instance, the example of demand for different goods that are relevant for producing transportation services. Publicly priced railway services are substitutes for private motor-car traffic, publicly priced toll roads or petrol are complements to private motor-car traffic. The demand for regulated airline tickets is complementary to the demand for hotel services, as often there is a joint demand for both.

B
Intermediate Goods

11
Optimal Pricing of
Publicly Supplied Intermediate Goods

Intermediate goods are not bought by consumers, but by firms as inputs of their production. Public utilities quite often sell both consumer goods and intermediate goods. Telephone calls, gas, electricity, and transportation services are demanded both by private and by business customers. In this chapter we define intermediate and final goods as different goods, even if in everyday language the goods would be considered identical. Hence, in our terminology, a business telephone call and a private telephone call are different goods and accordingly can be priced differently.[1]

11.1 Modifying the Basic Model

11.1.1 Reaction Functions of the Private Sector

In principle, public-sector pricing of intermediate goods is fully included in the basic model which we developed in chapter 3 above. Any one of the prices p_k could be the price of some good which is sold only to enterprises and not to consumers. The price of such an intermediate good, in the basic model, would not influence welfare in the usual direct way. After all, intermediate goods are not arguments of the individual direct utility functions. Intermediate-good pricing might, however, influence welfare in one of the following two ways. First because of cross-subsidization: higher rates for business may be used to lower rates for consumers (and these prices are arguments of the indirect utility functions). Second, there is a snowball-effect of intermediate-good pricing. Let a public firm increase the price of a good it sells to a private firm. Then the private firm will typically respond by increasing the

---

[1] This is the same practice which we shall also apply when dealing with peak-load pricing.

prices of its outputs. If these outputs are consumer goods, welfare will be affected. Unfortunately, this snowball-effect is excluded in our basic model by the assumption that all prices p_i, $i \neq k$ are exogenously given.[2] Hence, this assumption must be abandoned to deal adequately with public pricing of intermediate goods.[3] Two modifications of the basic model will therefore be introduced in this chapter.

(i)   First, we assume that the private monopolistic firms[4] increase the prices of their final consumption goods if they have to pay more for publicly provided intermediate goods. We do not explicitly present a model which explains how these price responses come about. There are many such models which we could investigate (and in chapter 34, on mixed markets, we will explicitly do so). For the moment, however, it seems preferable to assume that there exist reaction functions which link the prices of privately supplied final consumption goods to the prices of the inputs which the private firms buy from the public firm.[5] We assume that these reaction functions are known to the public enterprise when choosing its instruments.

(ii)   Second, the private monopolistic firms may shift part of the burden of price increases back to the public enterprise. This may occur if the public firm buys intermediate goods from private firms which themselves buy intermediate goods from the public firm. This feedback will be modelled by assuming the existence of reaction functions which link private intermediate-good prices to public intermediate-good prices.

11.1.2   A Synopsis of the Various Goods

It is appropriate to begin with a synopsis of the various goods of the model. We deal with a partition of all goods $i \subset I$ into five subsets:

(i)   Publicly provided intermediate goods. These goods are sold by the public utility and bought by private firms. They are indexed $k \in K \subset I$. Prices p_k and quantities $z_k > 0$ are instruments of the public enterprise. Our specification implies that $x_k^h = 0, y_k^j < 0$. We have $\Sigma_j y_k^j + z_k = 0$ as market-clearing conditions.

(ii)   Publicly provided consumption goods. These goods are sold by the public utility and bought by consumers. They are indexed $b \in B \subset I$. Prices

---

[2]   See pp. 74–5 above.

[3]   See Ebrill–Slutsky (1990: 419).

[4]   The term 'monopolistic' reflects a positive Lerner index, not necessarily a complete monopoly. See section 10.1 above.

[5]   Feldstein (1972c) assumes a fixed-coefficient technology. In his model the prices of private consumption goods depend on the wage and on the prices of publicly-provided inputs in a mark-up fashion.

p_b and quantities $z_b > 0$ are instruments of the public enterprise. We have $y_b^j = 0, x_b^h > 0$ and market-clearing conditions $\Sigma_h x_b^h = z_b$.

(iii) Privately provided intermediate goods. They are sold by the private firms and bought by the public firm.[6] These goods are indexed $a \in A \subset I$. We will assume that any single price p_a is functionally dependent on all regulated prices $p_k, k \in K$ and on the wage p_o. A shorthand notation for any such reaction function is $p_a(\cdot)$. We have market-clearing conditions $\Sigma_j y_a^j + z_a = 0$ where $y_a^j < 0, z_a > 0$. Of course $x_a^h = 0$ by definition.

(iv) Privately provided consumption goods. They are sold by the private firms and bought by consumers. We apply the index $m \in M \subset I$. Any single price p_m is functionally dependent on all regulated prices $p_k, k \in K$, and on the wage p_o. A shorthand notation for any such reaction function is $p_m(\cdot)$. The market-clearing conditions are $\Sigma_h x_m^h = \Sigma_j y_m^j$. Of course $z_m = 0$ by definition.

(v) Labor is supplied as usual with a market equilibrium $x_o = y_o + z_o$. Labor is the numeraire, hence the wage rate is $p_o = 1$.

When dealing with the optimization approach of the public enterprise, it is convenient to write sums over all i, although the above specifications imply that several quantities of goods are zero by definition, for instance $x_k^h = 0$.[7]

11.1.3   The Conditions for Optimal Prices and Quantities

The public enterprise maximizes the following Lagrangean function with respect to its netputs and the prices of both consumer and intermediate goods it sells to its customers:[8]

$$\mathcal{F} = W(\cdot) - \sum_i \alpha_i \left[\sum_h x_i^h(\cdot) - z_i - \sum_j y_i^j(\cdot) \right] - \\ - \beta g(z) - \overline{\gamma} \left[\Pi^o - \sum_i p_i z_i \right]. \tag{1}$$

The precise functional dependencies are determined by our assumptions on the different types of goods. Household consumption and consequently household utility depend directly on the prices of consumption goods and on the wage

---

[6] To avoid complications, we abstain from explicitly modelling privately provided intermediate goods which are bought by other private firms.

[7] Derivatives of those quantities with respect to prices etc. are also zero by definition.

[8] Lump-sum incomes $\{r^h, h=1,...,H\}$ will be treated as instruments in subsection 11.3.3 below.

rate, but the postulated reaction functions $p_m(\cdot)$, $m \in M$, also induce a dependence on the regulated prices p_k, $k \in K$. The production plans of the private firms depend on all prices, including the wage rate.

The necessary optimum conditions are as follows:

$$\sum_h \frac{\partial W}{\partial v^h} \frac{\partial v^h}{\partial p_b} - \sum_i \alpha_i \left(\sum_h \frac{\partial x_i^h}{\partial p_b} - \sum_j \frac{\partial y_i^j}{\partial p_b} \right) + \bar{\gamma} z_b = 0; \quad \forall b, \qquad (2)$$

$$\sum_h \sum_m \frac{\partial W}{\partial v^h} \frac{\partial v^h}{\partial p_m} \frac{\partial p_m}{\partial p_k} - \sum_i \alpha_i \left(\sum_h \sum_m \frac{\partial x_i^h}{\partial p_m} \frac{\partial p_m}{\partial p_k} - \sum_j \frac{dy_i^j}{dp_k} \right) + \bar{\gamma} z_k = 0; \quad \forall k, \qquad (3)$$

$$\alpha_i - \beta \frac{\partial g}{\partial z_i} + \bar{\gamma} p_i = 0; \quad \forall i. \qquad (4)$$

We have used the abbreviation

$$\frac{dy_i^j}{dp_k} := \frac{\partial y_i^j}{\partial p_k} + \sum_m \frac{\partial y_i^j}{\partial p_m} \frac{\partial p_m}{\partial p_k} + \sum_a \frac{\partial y_i^j}{\partial p_a} \frac{\partial p_a}{\partial p_k}. \qquad (5)$$

The above conditions clearly show a first result: prices of publicly provided consumption goods, $\{p_b, b \in B \subset I\}$, are chosen according to the very same principles as derived in the basic model of chapter 3 and as extensively interpreted in the preceding chapters:

$$\sum_i (p_i - c_i) \frac{\partial z_i^D}{\partial p_b} = -(1 - F_b) z_b - (1 - \gamma) \sum_i \sum_j (p_i - c_i^j) \frac{dy_i^j}{dp_b}; \quad \forall b, \qquad (6)$$

where F_b is Feldstein's distributional characteristic.[9] We did not include any lump-sum redistribution, hence income effects matter.

A different pricing structure, however, is obtained for the prices of publicly provided intermediate goods, $\{p_k, k \in K\}$. If we substitute equations

---

[9] Recall from (9–2), p. 145 above the definition of Feldstein's distributional characteristic $F_k := \sum_h (x_k^h / x_k) \lambda^h (\partial v^h / \partial r^h); \quad k \in K$.

(4) into (3) and transform in exactly the same way as in chapter 3 above,[10] we obtain the following result:[11]

$$\sum_{i}(p_i - c_i)\frac{\partial z_i^D}{\partial p_k} = -(1 - \text{INT}_k)z_k - (1 - \gamma)\sum_{i}\sum_{j}(p_i - c_i^j)\frac{dy_i^j}{dp_k}; \quad \forall k. \quad (7)$$

Here we have abbreviated

$$\text{INT}_k = \frac{1}{z_k}\cdot\left\{(1-\gamma)\left[z_k - \sum_{m}x_m\frac{\partial p_m}{\partial p_k}\right] + \sum_{m}x_m F_m\frac{\partial p_m}{\partial p_k}\right\}. \quad (8)$$

The reader should by now be familiar with this sort of pricing structure; it has been transformed in such a way as to reveal a formal similarity between the results of the basic model of chapter 3 and the intermediate-goods model of this chapter. Since we did not compensate for income effects, we do not have a Ramsey equivalent, but a Feldstein-pricing equivalent: equation (7) above exhibits the same formal structure as the result of our basic model (3–21b) which has extensively been interpreted in the chapters on distributional pricing and on the adjustment to monopolistic pricing in the private sector. Hence, we can apply the usual interpretation: the public enterprise behaves like a profit-maximizing monopolist who misestimates every single non-compensated response of demand by $1/(1 - \text{INT}_k)$.

Of particular interest, however, are special cases of the general formula (7) which also help us to understand the precise implications of the term INT_k. These special cases will be treated in the following sections. Before doing so, however, we should deal with the question whether intermediate-good pricing should be mainly considered as a distributional or as an allocative device.

11.2   Distributional or Allocative Pricing?

Since Feldstein's (1972c) paper the pricing of publicly provided intermediate goods has been associated with distributional aims. This is strange because

---

[10] pp. 76–81.

[11] In all definitions and derivations the term $\partial y_i^j / \partial p_k$ of chapter 3 is replaced by dy_i^j / dp_k. This holds in particular for $\partial z_i^D / \partial p_k := \Sigma_h\Sigma_m(\partial x_i^h / \partial p_m)(\partial p_m / \partial p_k) - \Sigma_j dy_i^j / dp_k$. It also holds for the condition for efficient production. For the latter recall that efficient production in any private firm requires that the technology $g^j(y_1^j,...,y_n^j) = 0$ holds if any price p_k changes. Taking the total differential of g^j with respect to prices p_k and denoting $c_i^j = -\partial y_o^j / dy_i^j$, we obtain $\Sigma_k\Sigma_i c_i^j(\partial y_i^j / \partial p_k)dp_k = 0$. Hence, efficient production in the private sector is given if $\Sigma_i c_i^j(dy_i^j / dp_k) = 0$.

intermediate goods are far removed from the consumers whose distributional position is at stake in public-sector pricing. Even in case of publicly-supplied consumer goods we had to deal with the argument that public-sector pricing is at best an indirect instrument of redistribution as opposed to income taxation or subsidization. The rich man in the second-class railway compartment was used as a typical example.[12] In case of intermediate goods the public prices are an even more indirect instrument of redistribution. The distributional consequences are diffuse. This can be seen directly by comparing the price formulas (6) and (7) above. In the pricing of consumer goods (6) the Feldstein characteristic of any single good matters for the price of that good; price elasticities are misestimated by $1/(1 - F_b)$. In the pricing of intermediate goods (7), the misestimation refers to $1/(1 - \text{INT}_k)$ and INT_k contains various terms, only one of which can be considered as distributionally relevant, namely $\Sigma_m x_m F_m (\partial p_m / \partial p_k)$. It is, however, precisely this term which proves the point of our criticism: only a weighted sum of Feldstein's distributional characteristics matters. This is just the diffusion of distributional effects mentioned some sentences above. Feldstein (1972c: 54) argues: 'The greater the proportion of the ... good used in the production of luxuries ..., the lower [the average distributional characteristic] will be and the greater the optimal excess of price over marginal costs.' If we think of publicly provided intermediate goods like gas, electricity, telecommunications, mail etc. it seems difficult to find such a case in economic practice. Is electricity mainly used for the production of luxuries in the daytime and for the production of necessities at night? Of course not. The case for distributional prices of intermediate goods seems pretty weak.

11.3   Allocative Pricing

In the following we begin with the interpretation of some special cases; these cases occur if some of the endogenously determined relationships of the model take on particular values, for instance if the private monopolistic prices p_m, $m \in M$, do not react to public intermediate prices p_k, $k \in K$. In the theoretical framework of a general equilibrium model it is highly unlikely that $\partial p_m / \partial p_k = 0$; such an assumption can only be taken for didactic reasons. If the model is to be applied in practice, however, there might well exist cases which can be approximated by $\partial p_m / \partial p_k = 0$.

11.3.1   No Response of Private Prices

Let us first consider the case where $\partial p_a / \partial p_k = 0$ and $\partial p_m / \partial p_k = 0$: the private prices do not respond to price changes of publicly provided interme-

---

[12] See p. 142 above.

162   *Normative Theory: Intermediate Goods*

diate goods. Non-response of private prices implies allocative pricing because the prices of the intermediate goods do not influence individual utilities and hence do not influence the welfare function which is the only part of our model reflecting distributional value judgements.[13]

A non-response of private prices could happen if the public enterprise sells intermediate goods which do not account for a high percentage of the private sector's inputs and if there is enough pressure from competition in the private sector as to prevent easy mark-up pricing. As a good example I might refer to the US National Institute of Standards and Technology, an institute which provides standard reference materials. They are sold as small quantities of materials with a certified standard which can be used by private producers, in particular to 'calibrate their instruments and measurement systems used to maintain quality control'.[14]

It can easily be seen that in the special case of non-responding prices p_a and p_m, the pricing formula for intermediate goods, equation (7), is reduced to

$$\sum_i (p_i - c_i) \sum_j \frac{\partial z_i^D}{\partial p_k} = -\gamma z_k - (1 - \gamma) \sum_i \sum_j (p_i - c_i^j) \frac{\partial y_i^j}{\partial p_k}; \qquad k \in K. \quad (9)$$

Since the intermediate goods' prices do not influence consumer demand, there is no consumer response $\partial x_i^h / \partial p_k$ and $\partial z_i^D / \partial p_k = -\Sigma_j \partial y_i^j / \partial p_k$. Hence public pricing depends only on the price elasticities of demand of the private firms. Otherwise the interpretation of equation (9) is straightforward: if the private economy were perfectly competitive, it would recommend Ramsey behavior to the public enterprise. In case of a monopolistic private economy, the prices of publicly provided intermediate goods, moreover, have to be adjusted to the private-sector price-cost margins.

---

[13] Note that in our model there are still prices of publicly provided consumption goods $\{p_b, b \in B\}$ which influence welfare. If a public enterprise sells only intermediate goods, the only way to model some direct influence on welfare is to assume a special wage policy, that is to split the labor market into the supply of and demand for labor in the public enterprise and in the rest of the economy.

[14] This is part of the official definition of standard reference materials by the Institute of Standards and Technology. Fuller (1991: 2) gives the following illustration: 'For example, a bottle of simulated rainwater contains exactly 2.69 milligrams of sulfate per liter, 0.205 milligrams of potassium, and a number of known quantities of other substances. The sample is intended to be used as a benchmark. Knowing its precise composition, a user can calibrate laboratory equipment for measuring acid rain.'

11.3.2 Distributional Neutrality of the Public Firm

We next turn to the case where $F_m = 1$ for all m. This occurs if the public firm is indifferent with respect to changes in the individual incomes, that is if $\lambda^h(\partial v^h/\partial r^h) = 1$ at the optimum. Allocative pricing results because there are no distributional objectives of the public enterprise. Pricing of publicly provided intermediate goods in that case follows the conditions

$$\sum_i (p_i - c_i)\frac{\partial z_i^D}{\partial p_k} = -\gamma\left(z_k - \sum_m x_m\frac{\partial p_m}{\partial p_k}\right) - (1-\gamma)\sum_i\sum_j (p_i - c_i^j)\frac{dy_i^j}{dp_k}; \quad \forall k.$$
(10)

The weighted average of distributional characteristics has vanished from the formula. The term $-\gamma z_k$ on the right hand side reflects the usual Ramsey structure and $\Sigma_m x_m(\partial p_m/\partial p_k)$ is an allocative correction term. It measures the changes in consumer expenditures which result from a change in price p_k. Let R be the aggregate expenditure function, then[15]

$$\frac{\partial R}{\partial p_k} = \frac{\sum_h \partial r^h(p, u^{ho})}{\partial p_k} = \sum_h\sum_m \hat{x}_m^h\frac{\partial p_m}{\partial p_k} = \sum_m x_m\frac{\partial p_m}{\partial p_k}; \quad k \in K. \quad (11)$$

Let us for the moment ignore the adjustment of public-sector pricing to private-sector monopolistic structures. We rewrite equation (10) as follows

$$\sum_i (p_i - c_i)\frac{\partial z_i^D}{\partial p_k} = -\gamma(1 - \Delta_k R)z_k; \quad k \in K \quad (12)$$

where we have defined $\Delta_k R := (\partial R/\partial p_k)/z_k$. The term $\Delta_k R$ is positive since we assume $\partial p_m/\partial p_k > 0, \forall k, m$. If the term $\Delta_k R$ converges to zero, we approach the case of the preceding subsection and obtain Ramsey prices which depend on the private sector's price elasticities. Otherwise, the public firm behaves as if it were a profit-maximizing monopolist who misestimates any non-compensated price elasticity by $1/\gamma(1 - \Delta_k R)$.

11.3.3 Compensation by Lump-sum Redistribution

Finally, we introduce the individual lump-sum incomes $\{r^h, h = 1, \ldots, H\}$ as further instruments. This implies allocative pricing because the redistribution is performed by choosing optimal r^h's, that is, by lump-sum taxation or

---

[15] For the far-right equality remember that $\hat{x}_i^h(p, u^{h*}) = x_i^h(p, r^h(p, u^{h*}))$, where u^{h*} is the individual utility at the firm's second-best optimum. (The star indicates that the consumer has maximized his utility taking account of the firm's policy.)

subsidization which compensates the consumer for all income effects which result from public-sector pricing.

We differentiate the Lagrangean function (1) with respect to the incomes $\{r^h, h = 1, \ldots, H\}$ and obtain the following necessary first-order conditions

$$\frac{\partial W}{\partial v^h} \frac{\partial v^h}{\partial r^h} - \sum_i \alpha_i \frac{\partial x_i^h}{\partial r^h} = 0; \quad h = 1, \ldots, H. \tag{13}$$

Combined with the marginal conditions for $\{p_k, k \in K\}$ and $\{z_i, i = o, \ldots, n\}$ we arrive at the following rule for publicly provided intermediate goods:

$$\sum_i (p_i - c_i) \frac{\partial \hat{z}_i}{\partial p_k} = -\gamma z_k - (1 - \gamma) \sum_i \sum_j (p_i - c_i^j) \frac{dy_i^j}{dp_k}; \quad k \in K. \tag{14}$$

It is interesting to note that precisely the same formula holds for the prices of publicly provided consumer goods, i.e. for $\{p_b, b \in B\}$. Pricing in the compensated demand case follows the basic-model rules of public sector pricing. Formula (14) above is identical to (3–24) which we derived when dealing with the basic model in chapter 3 above.

11.4   Distributional Pricing

The preceding section dealt with several cases of purely allocational pricing of intermediate goods. Let us now turn to the case of distributional pricing. Recall the definition of INT_k:

$$INT_k = \frac{1}{z_k} \cdot \left\{ (1 - \gamma) \left[z_k - \sum_m x_m \frac{\partial p_m}{\partial p_k} \right] + \sum_m x_m F_m \frac{\partial p_m}{\partial p_k} \right\}. \tag{8}$$

It is evident that distributional pricing results if

$$z_k = \sum_m x_m \frac{\partial p_m}{\partial p_k}. \tag{15}$$

If this condition holds, then INT_k is reduced to

$$INT_k = \frac{\sum_m x_m (\partial p_m / \partial p_k) \cdot F_m}{z_k} = \frac{\sum_m x_m (\partial p_m / \partial p_k) \cdot F_m}{\sum_m x_m (\partial p_m / \partial p_k)}. \tag{16}$$

Hence, INT_k becomes a weighted average of the distributional characteristics of the privately supplied consumption goods, with each term weighted by the changes in consumers' expenditures for good m which result from a change in price p_k.

As already mentioned, this implies a fairly indirect type of distributional policy. It is only a weighted average of distributional characteristics which matters and it can be doubted that some publicly provided intermediate goods are typically used in the production of luxuries and others in the production of necessities. However, such a distinction would be necessary to obtain values INT_k which distinctly differ from each other.

It is of particular interest to consider the conditions which must be met in order to achieve the case of distributional pricing: in other words, when will z_k actually be equal to $\Sigma_m x_m (\partial p_m / \partial p_k)$? The answer is: if the private industry shifts the whole burden of its increased costs to the consumers. This can be shown as follows.

Consider the cost functions of the private firms, $-c^j$.[16] Since we assume cost minimization in the private sector, we can apply Shephard's lemma to obtain

$$-\frac{\partial \Sigma_j c^j}{\partial p_k} = -\sum_j y_k^j = z_k. \tag{17}$$

The second equality is due to the market equilibrium. z_k, therefore, is the monetary equivalent of the increase in the firms' costs caused by an increase in price p_k.

Now assume that all consumer endowments r^h are exogenously given as is the public firm's profit Π^o. The financial equilibrium of the economy[17] therefore requires a constant sum of private profits $\Sigma_j \pi^j$. Hence an increase of costs by z_k must also imply an increase of the private firms' revenues by z_k. The increase in revenue, in turn, can result from higher sales to customers, y_m^j and from higher sales to the public firm, y_a^j.[18] Let us for the moment exclude the latter. Then the burden of the increased costs can only be shifted to the consumers. Since the increased revenues are increased by z_k, this shifting implies that the consumers' expenditures for the consumption goods m must also go up by an amount of z_k. However, their expenditures for these goods respond to a change of a price p_k als already shown in equation (11),

---

[16] Because of the netput concept positive costs are denoted by $-c_j = -\Sigma_i p_i y_i^j > 0$.

[17] See p. 44 above: $\Sigma_h r^h - \Pi^o - \Sigma_j \pi^j = 0$.

[18] Input changes y_o^j, y_k^j are integrated in Shephard's lemma.

$$\frac{\partial R}{\partial p_k} = \sum_m x_m \frac{\partial p_m}{\partial p_k}. \tag{11}$$

Hence, by simple equilibrium mechanics, we obtain $z_k = \Sigma_m x_m (\partial p_m / \partial p_k)$.

11.5   The Double Response of Private Firms

The private unregulated firms have two ways of responding to increasing prices $\{p_k, k \in K\}$: either by shifting the burden to the consumers by higher prices $\{p_m, m \in M\}$ or by shifting the burden back to the public enterprise through higher prices $\{p_a, a \in A\}$. Arguing along the same lines as in the preceding section we learn

$$z_k = \sum_m x_m \frac{\partial p_m}{\partial p_k} + \sum_a z_a \frac{\partial p_a}{\partial p_k}. \tag{18}$$

Therefore, the term INT_k in our pricing rules changes into

$$\mathrm{INT}_k = \frac{1}{z_k} \left\{ (1 - \gamma) \sum_a z_a \frac{\partial p_a}{\partial p_k} + \sum_m x_m F_m \frac{\partial p_m}{\partial p_k} \right\}. \tag{19}$$

This term clearly shows the feedback of the double response of the private sector to the price of publicly supplied intermediate goods.

C
Adjustment to Rationed Markets

The existence of rationed markets means that the market-clearing conditions of the Boiteux model are disturbed. The disturbances are caused by a lack of flexibility on the demand side or the production side of the economy, or both. Sticky prices may be one of the reasons for these failures.

The best way of modelling such failure is to take a typical second-best approach. The model does not explain the causes of failures of demand and production, but takes them as given. The resulting disturbances are introduced as exogenous influences in the model. By way of an example, we do not formulate explictly which demand or cost-side influences prevent some people from being employed. Rather we assume there is disequilibrium because of fixed prices for labor and (some) other goods in the private sector and therefore consumers are rationed in their employment decision.

There are many situations where rationed markets are relevant for public enterprises and public utilities. Two important cases are presented in the following two chapters.

12
Rationed Labor Market

12.1   Individual Employment Constraints

In the recent situation of public enterprises most Western European governments rank employment problems first. What is the role of public pricing in such a situation? Should the public enterprise reduce the prices of labor-intensive goods, thereby accepting the resulting welfare losses associated with departing from first-best pricing?

The high priority of employment problems suggests we must explicitly consider total employment as an instrument variable. Taking this approach we assume the public sector is large enough to warrant treating total employment L as a macro-variable instrument. To develop a realistic model of the recent economic situation we should abandon the usual equilibria in the labor and private commodity markets and instead deal with equilibria under rationing (Malinvaud, 1977).

Following Drèze (1984), we assume the individual supply of labor is constrained as follows[1]

$$x_o^h \geq \overline{x}_o^h(L); \qquad h = 1, \ldots, H; \qquad \sum \overline{x}_o^h = L, \qquad (1)$$

where $L < 0$ is total labor demand by private and public firms. $\overline{x}_o^h(L)$ is an exogenously given rationing function which is assumed to be differentiable. In the following we assume this constraint to be binding. The excess supply of labor is assumed to result from fixed prices of (some) privately supplied goods, and a fixed wage rate, respectively.

The consumer maximizes his direct utility $u^h(x^h)$ given the prices and his fixed labor and lump-sum income. The resulting individual demand functions are $x_i^h(p, r^h, \overline{x}_o^h(L)) =: x_i^h(p, r^h, L)$. The rationing of labor supply implies that the individual demand for any good depends on the total labor demand.

We assume excess supply of labor and therefore

$$\overline{w}^h < p_o = 1. \qquad (2)$$

The reservation wage $\overline{w}^h$ is defined as the marginal rate of substitution between labor and income

$$\overline{w}^h := \frac{\partial u^h / \partial x_o^h}{\partial u^h / \partial r^h}(\overline{x}_o^h). \qquad (3)$$

At the reservation wage the consumer voluntarily would supply $\overline{x}_o^h$. In the case of excess supply of labor $\overline{x}_o^h$ is lower in absolute value than the voluntary labor supply x_o^h; therefore the reservation wage must be lower than the market wage rate, which explains the assumption in (2).

The compensated employment effect of demand, $\partial \hat{x}_i^h / \partial L$, can be derived from the identity of Marshallian and Hicksian demand at the lump-sum income $r^h = R^h(p, \overline{x}_o^h, u^{h*}) : x_i^h(p, r^h, L) = \hat{x}_i^h(p, u^{h*}, L)$. Differentiation with respect to L yields

$$\frac{\partial x_i^h}{\partial L} + \frac{\partial x_i^h}{\partial r^h} \frac{\partial R^h}{\partial \overline{x}_o^h} \frac{\partial \overline{x}_o^h}{\partial L} = \frac{\partial \hat{x}_i^h}{\partial L}. \qquad (4a)$$

---

[1] If, for instance, an individual wants to work 40 hours per week, it is possibly constrained to work 20 hours only ($\overline{x}_o^h$) or less. For the direction of the inequality remember $x_o^h < 0$.

We differentiate the expenditure function $R(\cdot) = p_o \bar{x}_o^h + \Sigma_1^n p_i \hat{x}_i^h$ with respect to individual employment $\bar{x}_o^h$. Using the envelope theorem we obtain[2]

$$\frac{\partial R^h}{\partial \bar{x}_o^h} = p_o - \frac{\partial u^h / \partial \bar{x}_o^h}{\partial u^h / \partial r^h} = 1 - \bar{w}^h. \tag{5}$$

Substituting (5) into (4a) yields

$$\frac{\partial \hat{x}_i^h}{\partial L} = \frac{\partial x_i^h}{\partial L} + \frac{\partial x_i^h}{\partial r^h}(1 - \bar{w}^h)\frac{\partial \bar{x}_o^h}{\partial L}. \tag{4b}$$

The indirect utility function is $u^h(x_i^h(p, r^h, \bar{x}_o^h), \bar{x}_o^h) =: v^h(p, r^h, \bar{x}_o^h(L)) =: v^h(p, r^h, L)$. Its dependence on employment L is as follows. Recall that at the consumer optimum $v^h = u^{h*}$. Therefore

$$\frac{\partial v^h}{\partial r^h}\frac{\partial R^h}{\partial \bar{x}_o^h}\frac{\partial \bar{x}_o^h}{\partial L} + \frac{\partial v^h}{\partial L} = 0. \tag{6a}$$

Substituting (5) into (6a) we obtain

$$\frac{\partial v^h}{\partial L} = (\bar{w}^h - 1)\frac{\partial v^h}{\partial r^h}\frac{\partial \bar{x}_o^h}{\partial L}. \tag{6b}$$

The rationed labor supply, moreover, influences the net supply of private firms, and this relationship can be written as $y_i^j = y_i^j(p, L), i \geq 1$. The private firms' demand for labor, in turn, will typically be lower than their demand in the absence of rationing, and hence $y_o^j = y_o^j(p, L)$. Public net supply and demand are also influenced by the rationing of individual labor supply. However, the quantities z_i are taken as instruments and therefore the functional dependencies are not specified a priori, but well-defined at the optimum.

The board chooses optimal prices $p_k, k \in K$, optimal input and output quantities $z_i, i \in I$ (including public labor input z_o), optimal lump-sum transfers $r^h, h = 1, \ldots, H$ and optimal total employment L. The board considers the usual constraints, the rationed labor-market equilibrium being defined as follows:

$$L = z_o + \sum_j y_o^j(p, L). \tag{7}$$

---

[2] Consider the Lagrangean function: $\mathcal{F}=p_o\bar{x}_o^h+\Sigma_1^n p_i x_i^h-\lambda(u^h(\bar{x}_o^h,x_1^h,\ldots,x_n^h)-u^{h*})$, where $\lambda=\partial R/\partial u^{h*}$. Differentiating $\mathcal{F}$ with respect to $\bar{x}_o^h$ yields $\partial\mathcal{F}/\partial\bar{x}_o^h=p_o-\lambda(\partial u/\partial\bar{x}_o^h)=\partial R/\partial\bar{x}_o^h$ where the last equation is based on the envelope theorem.

Hence, the board maximizes the following Lagrangean function:

$$\mathcal{F} = W(v^1(p, r^1, L), \ldots, v^H(\cdot)) - \alpha_o \left[L - z_o - \sum_j y_o^j(p, L) \right] -$$

$$- \sum_{i=1}^{n} \alpha_i \left[\sum_h x_i^h(p, r^h, L) - z_i - \sum_j y_i^j(p, L) \right] - \tag{8}$$

$$- \beta g(z) - \bar{\gamma} \left[\Pi^o - \sum_{i=o}^{n} p_i z_i \right].$$

We obtain the following result:

$$\sum_{i=1}^{n} (\gamma p_i - c_i) \frac{\partial \hat{z}_i}{\partial L} = (1 - \gamma) \frac{\partial z_o}{\partial L} \tag{9a}$$

$$\sum_{i=1}^{n} (p_i - c_i) \frac{\partial \hat{z}_i}{\partial p_k} = -\gamma z_k - (1 - \gamma) \sum_{i=o}^{n} \sum_{j=1}^{J} (p_i - c_i^j) \frac{\partial y_i^j}{\partial p_k}; \quad k \in K. \tag{9b}$$

In (9a) the compensated response of demand z_i to total employment is defined as

$$\frac{\partial \hat{z}_i}{\partial L} := \sum_h \left[\frac{\partial x_i^h}{\partial L} + \frac{\partial x_i^h}{\partial r^h} (1 - \overline{w}^h) \frac{\partial \overline{x}_o^h}{\partial L} \right] - \sum_j \frac{\partial y_i^j}{\partial L}. \tag{10a}$$

The response of public-sector employment z_o to total employment is defined as

$$\frac{\partial z_o}{\partial L} = 1 - \sum_j \frac{\partial y_o^j}{\partial L}. \tag{10b}$$

Condition (9a) can be interpreted after some further transformations. We use the property of the compensated response $\partial \hat{z}_i / \partial L$

$$\sum_{i=1}^{n} p_i \frac{\partial \hat{z}_i}{\partial L} = - \sum_{h=1}^{H} \sum_{i=1}^{n} p_i \overline{w}^h \frac{\partial x_i^h}{\partial r^h} \frac{\partial \overline{x}_o^h}{\partial L} - \sum_{i=1}^{n} \sum_{j=1}^{J} p_i \frac{\partial y_i^j}{\partial L}$$

to obtain

$$\sum_{i=1}^{n}(p_i - c_i)\frac{\partial \hat{z}_i}{\partial L} = (1 - \gamma)\left[1 - \sum_{h=1}^{H}\sum_{i=1}^{n}p_i\overline{w}^h\frac{\partial x_i^h}{\partial r^h}\cdot\frac{\partial \overline{x}_o^h}{\partial L}\right] - \\ - (1 - \gamma)\sum_{i=o}^{n}\sum_{j=1}^{J}(p_i - c_i^j)\frac{\partial y_i^j}{\partial L}. \tag{9a'}$$

This formula reflects an adjustment of public-sector prices to the monop-olistic private pricing and also an adjustment to the labor-market disequilib-rium, as expressed by the first term of the right-hand side of (9a'). A general interpretation of this term cannot be given. A particular specification of the rationing scheme $\overline{x}_o^h(L)$ may therefore be helpful. The individual rationing is more serious the lower the individual reservation wage. Hence an increase in the overall employment should favor an employee more, the lower $\overline{w}^h$. A useful benchmark, therefore, is the following specification

$$\frac{\partial \overline{x}_o^h}{\partial L} = \frac{s}{\overline{w}^h}$$

where $s > 0$ is a proportionality factor. This factor is determined by the aggregation property

$$\sum_h\frac{\partial \overline{x}_o^h}{\partial L} = 1 \rightarrow s = \frac{1}{\sum_h(1/\overline{w}^h)}.$$

Hence the rationing depends on the relative reservation wages

$$\frac{\partial \overline{x}_o^h}{\partial L} = \frac{1}{\sum_{h'}(\overline{w}^h/\overline{w}^{h'})}.$$

Substituting this specification into (9a') we obtain

$$\sum_{i=1}^{n}(p_i - c_i)\frac{\partial \hat{z}_i}{\partial L} = (1 - \gamma)(1 - sH) - (1 - \gamma)\sum_{i=o}^{n}\sum_{j=1}^{J}(p_i - c_i^j)\frac{\partial y_i^j}{\partial L}. \tag{9a''}$$

H is the number of consumers. The factor $s \in (0, 1/H]$, and therefore $sH \in (0, 1]$. sH is higher, the higher overall employment. The adjustment of public-sector pricing to changes in the overall employment, therefore, depends on $(1 - \gamma)(1 - sH)$. For ease of exposition, we only consider prices which are greater than marginal costs.

We can see the following trade-off between employment and pricing policy. If we approach a high level of overall employment $(sH \to 1)$, the right-hand side of (9a″) becomes lower. This can only be achieved by also reducing the left-hand side. Such a reduction can be brought about by reducing the prices of complements to leisure $(\partial \hat{z}_i / \partial L > 0)$[3] and increasing the prices of complements to labor $(\partial \hat{z}_i / \partial L < 0)$. The result is an increase in the demand for leisure, and thus we can conclude that prices have been changed in order to reduce the overall employment. This interpretation suggests that typically we will obtain an interior solution for L which is somewhere below full employment. If, however, we approach a low level of overall employment $(sH \to 0)$, the right-hand side of (9a″) increases and the board will increase the prices of complements to leisure and reduce the prices of complements to labor. Prices are changed in order to increase the overall employment.

Let us now turn to the interpretation of the marginal conditions (9b). Surprisingly, they are identical with the conditions (10–2).[4] Hence, rationing individual labor supply does not influence the qualitative results on the structure of prices we have derived in chapter 10. Quantitatively, of course, prices will differ depending on the rationing scheme.

The result we have obtained depends decisively on the form of individual rationing. As labor is allocated according to a binding scheme $\overline{x}_o^h$, this labor allocation cannot be influenced by changes in the public prices. Hence there is no rationale for changing the structure of prices in order to influence the labor market. Such a rationale exists, however, if we are dealing with an economy where overall employment is constrained, but where the individuals are given the option of choosing the utility maximizing labor supply. This case is treated in the next subsection.

12.2   An Overall Employment Constraint

If we want to obtain a pricing structure which directly reflects the optimal response of public-sector pricing to a disequilibrium in the labor market, we should not treat overall employment as an instrument variable and we should not apply the individual rationing scheme of the Drèze model. We should rather assume that overall employment is exogenously given at a level $\overline{L}$. Hence, the public firm has to accept the constraint

---

[3] The definitions of complements to leisure and labor used in the text are unusual albeit the straightforward definitions to deal with equation (9a″).

[4] Recall $p_o = c_o$.

$$\overline{L} \leq \sum_h x_o^h(p, r^h). \tag{11}$$

The individuals are allowed to choose the utility maximizing labor supply x_o^h. We assume that in the absence of the constraint (11) the total labor supply Σx_o^h would be higher in absolute value than $\overline{L}$. Hence the labor-market constraint will be binding.

Prices, quantities and lump-sum incomes have to be chosen in such a way that the utility-maximizing labor supplies of the consumers add up to the exogenously given employment level $\overline{L}$. Consequently, the board of the firm maximizes the following Lagrangean function:

$$\mathcal{F} = W(v^1(p, r^1), \ldots, v^H(\cdot)) - \sum_{i=o}^{n} \alpha_i \left[\sum_h x_i^h(p, r^h) - z_i - \sum_j y_i^j(p) \right] -$$

$$- \alpha_{n+1} \left[\overline{L} - \sum_h x_o^h(p, r^h) \right] - \beta g(z) -$$

$$- \overline{\gamma} \left[\Pi^o - \sum_{i=o}^{n} p_i z_i \right]. \tag{12}$$

We obtain the following structure of public-sector pricing

$$\sum_{i=1}^{n} (p_i - c_i) \frac{\partial \hat{z}_i}{\partial p_k} = -\gamma z_k - \frac{\alpha_{n+1}}{\beta_o} \frac{\partial \hat{x}_o}{\partial p_k} -$$

$$- (1 - \gamma) \sum_{i=o}^{n} \sum_{j=1}^{J} (p_i - c_i^j) \frac{\partial y_i^j}{\partial p_k}; \qquad k \in K. \tag{13}$$

The ratio of Lagrangean multipliers, α_{n+1}/β_o is positive because $\alpha_{n+1} = -\partial W/\overline{L} > 0$ and $\beta_o := \beta(\partial g/\partial z_o) > 0$.[5] (13) is identical to (10–2) except for the term $(\alpha_{n+1}/\beta_o)(\partial \hat{x}_o/\partial p_k)$. The result in (13) reflects the adjustment of public-sector pricing to disequilibria in the private commodity markets (far right term) and the influence of the employment constraint:[6] there is a tendency to reduce the price of complements to leisure $(\partial \hat{x}_o/\partial p_k < 0)$ and to increase the price of complements to labor $(\partial \hat{x}_o/\partial p_k > 0)$.

---

[5] For the sign of α_{n+1} recall $\overline{L} < 0$. For $\beta_o > 0$ see section 3.3, footnote 11.

[6] The reader may explicitly solve (13) for a particular price p_k as we have done in (10–3). Then the following economic interpretation follows immediately.

If lump-sum incomes are not available instruments, the optimization of (12) with respect to public prices and quantities leads to a pricing structure which is identical with (3–21) except for the term $(\alpha_{n+1}/\beta_o)(\partial \hat{x}_o/\partial p_k)$, and the labor-market constraint influences the price structure in the same way as in the model presented in the text. However, for a direct comparison with the results of chapter 10 and of the preceding section 12.1 the inclusion of lump-sum incomes as instruments is necessary.

13
Capacity Limits of Public Transportation

Transportation-capacity limits are of critical importance during times of peak demand. Traffic demand for public buses or underground is rationed. Congestion causes queues at bus stops because of delayed arrival of buses. On the other hand, private peak traffic is also rationed. People anticipate traffic jams, and have to invest more time in travel. The following model integrates the rationing of public and private peak traffic.

We label public peak traffic by 'n'. Therefore $x_n^h > 0$ is consumer h's demand, $y_n^j < 0$ is private producer j's demand, $z_n > 0$ public supply. Public off-peak traffic is one of the many goods $i \in I$ which are part of the model, but in which we are not particularly interested.

In dealing with private traffic we have to distinguish between marketed and non-marketed services.

Marketed traffic services are produced by private enterprises and sold to consumers and to private and to public enterprises at a market price or at a regulated price (taxis etc.). These services are also included in our model as some of the many goods $i \in I$. To keep our model simple, we do not include these services explicitly into the capacity constraint.

Non-marketed private traffic is 'produced' by the traffic user at the moment of use. There is no market price or regulated price. In fact, demand for non-marketed private traffic is revealed in the demand for those goods and services the private consumer or producer needs for the 'production' of traffic. Hence, traffic demand is revealed indirectly as the demand for automobiles, petrol etc. Moreover, if a consumer or a private producer 'produces' such non-marketed traffic services, this production requires labor as an input. Private producers evaluate these labor inputs at the wage rate, $p_o = 1$. Consumers are assumed to ignore their own labor input.

We label private non-marketed peak traffic by $n + 1$ because it is a good which is revealed only indirectly by demand for, and supply of, other goods $i \in \{o, 1, \ldots, n\}$. There is no price for 'good $n+1$' and no 'market' equilibrium. However we specify two 'production functions', namely,

$$x_{n+1}^h = x_{n+1}^h(x_1^h, \ldots, x_{n-1}^h); \quad x_{n+1}^h > 0, \tag{1}$$

$$y_{n+1}^j = y_{n+1}^n(y_o^j, y_1^j, \ldots, y_{n-1}^j); \quad y_{n+1}^j < 0 \tag{2}$$

as the consumers'and the private producers' production functions.

Consumers' optimal consumption choices and producers' optimal input and output choices can be written as usual, referring to good $i = \{o, \dots, n\}$. Good $n + 1$ enters the consumption and production plans only indirectly, via consumption or input of automobiles, petrol etc.

Both public and private traffic require infrastructure. Public traffic, however, requires less infrastructure for the same quantity of passenger miles: for example, the present UK or US highways would provide sufficient infrastructure for motor traffic even during the summer holiday weekends if everybody used public buses instead of private cars. Hence we postulate the following demand function for infrastructure, i.e. for capacity

$$\mathcal{K} = \mathcal{K}(x_n - y_n; x_{n+1} - y_{n+1})^1$$
$$(\mathcal{K} > 0; \mathcal{K}_1, \mathcal{K}_2 > 0; \mathcal{K}_1 < \mathcal{K}_2). \tag{3}$$

This demand will not be met totally by the available capacity. Hence we assume an exogenously given capacity limit $\overline{K}$ which restricts the peak-transportation services

$$\overline{K} \geq \mathcal{K}(x_n - y_n; x_{n+1} - y_{n+1}). \tag{4}$$

As our analysis deals with peak traffic, we assume this constraint to be binding. – Let us now consider the Boiteux model for the case of constrained peak traffic. The board chooses optimal prices $p_k, k \in K$, quantities $z_i, i \in I$, and lump-sum transfers $r^h, h = 1, \dots, H$, maximizing the following Lagrangean function[2]

$$\mathcal{F} = W(v^1(p, r^1), \dots, v^H(\cdot)) - \sum_{i=o}^{n} \alpha_i \left[\sum_h x_i^h(p, r^h) - z_i - \sum_j y_i^j(p) \right] -$$

$$- \alpha_{n+1} \left[\overline{K} - \mathcal{K} \left(z_n; \sum_h x_{n+1}^h(p, r^h) - \sum_j y_i^j(p) \right) \right] - \tag{5}$$

$$- \beta g(z) - \overline{\gamma} \left[\Pi^o - \sum_{i=o}^{n} p_i z_i \right].$$

---

[1] As usual $x_i = \Sigma_h x_i^h$, $y_i = \Sigma_j y_i^j$.

[2] To avoid the tedious treatment of corner solutions, we assume every consumer to consume $x_n^h > 0$ and $x_{n+1}^h > 0$. This assumption can be justified by thinking of consumers as households where, e.g., the man uses the private car to go to business and the wife uses the public bus for shopping or vice versa.

We obtain the following structure of prices

$$\sum_{i=o}^{n}(p_i - c_i)\frac{\partial \hat{z}_i}{\partial p_k} + \frac{\alpha_{n+1}}{\beta_o}\left(K_1\frac{\partial \hat{z}_n}{\partial p_k} + K_2\frac{d(\hat{x},y)_{n+1}}{dp_k}\right) =$$

$$= -\gamma z_k - (1-\gamma)\sum_{i=o}^{n}\sum_{j=1}^{J}(p_i - c_i^j)\frac{\partial y_i^j}{\partial p_k}; \quad k \in K. \tag{6}$$

Prior to the detailed economic interpretation of this structure of prices we have to clarify the exact meaning of some of the symbols used.

First, α_{n+1}/β_o is a marginal rate of substitution between labor and capacity. This can be shown as follows. Remember that $\beta_o := \beta(\partial g/\partial z_o) = -\partial W/\partial \overline{z}_o > 0$, where $\overline{z}_o$ is the initial endowment of labor in the public sector. Differentiating the Lagrangean function $\mathcal{F}$ with respect to $\overline{K}$ yields $\alpha_{n+1} = -\partial W/\partial \overline{K} < 0$. Therefore the ratio of the parameters $\alpha_{n+1}/\beta_o = \partial \overline{z}_o/\partial \overline{K}$ (at constant W) is negative. This marginal rate of substitution between labor and capacity is large (in absolute value) if the social valuation of the capacity limit is large, which is more probable the lower the capacity limit $\overline{K}$. In such a case the welfare loss from forgoing one unit of capacity can only the compensated by a large increase in the available labor endowment in the public sector.

Second, we have defined a 'compensated' price effect of the non-marketed private peak traffic[3]

$$\frac{d(\hat{x},y)_{n+1}}{dp_k} := \sum_{h}\frac{dx_{n+1}^h}{dp_k} + \sum_{h}x_k^h\frac{dx_{n+1}^h}{dr^h} - \sum_{j}\frac{dy_{n+1}^j}{dp_k}. \tag{7}$$

In doing so we had to consider that the 'production functions' $x_{n+1}^h(\cdot)$ and $y_{n+1}^h(\cdot)$ depend on prices in the following way

$$\frac{dx_{n+1}^h}{dp_k} = \sum_{i=1}^{n-1}\frac{\partial x_{n+1}^h}{\partial x_i^h}\cdot\frac{\partial x_i^h}{\partial p_k} ; \quad \frac{dy_{n+1}^j}{dp_k} = \sum_{i=o}^{n-1}\frac{\partial y_{n+1}^j}{\partial y_i^j}\cdot\frac{\partial y_i^j}{\partial p_k}. \tag{8}$$

We assume the price effect $d(\hat{x},y)_{n+1}/dp_k$ to be positive for substitutes for private peak traffic, as for instance for public peak traffic. The effect is assumed to be negative for complements, for instance for petrol which can be

---

[3] We cannot use the symbol $d\hat{z}_{n+1}$, because ex definitione there is no public supply z_{n+1} in our model.

considered as one of the goods $k \in K$ if its price is controlled by the public sector.[4]

Let us now turn to the economic interpretation of public-sector pricing when peak traffic is constrained by a capacity limit. We transform (6) to obtain

$$
\begin{aligned}
p_k = c_k &- \frac{\gamma z_k}{\partial \hat{z}_k / \partial p_k} - \sum_{i \neq k}(p_i - c_i)\frac{\partial \hat{z}_i / \partial p_k}{\partial \hat{z}_k / \partial p_k} - \\
&- (1 - \gamma)\sum_{i=o}^{n}\sum_{j=1}^{J}(p_i - c_i^j)\frac{\partial y_i^j / \partial p_k}{\partial \hat{z}_k / \partial p_k} - \\
&- \frac{\alpha_{n+1}}{\beta_o(\partial \hat{z}_k / \partial p_k)}\left(\mathcal{K}_1 \frac{\partial \hat{z}_n}{\partial p_k} + \mathcal{K}_2 \frac{d(\hat{x}, y)_{n+1}}{dp_k}\right); \quad k \in K.
\end{aligned}
\tag{9}
$$

This pricing structure can be compared with equation (10–3). Public prices therefore depend on

- marginal costs;
- a 'Ramsey term', implying a dependence of prices on their own price elasticity of demand;
- the 'reallocation terms' which relate prices p_k to price-cost margins, both in the public and in the private sector; and
- a capacity term, measuring the influence of p_k on capacity utilization.

Both the Ramsey and the reallocation terms have the usual signs. The Ramsey term typically implies a tendency for p_k to exceed marginal costs. The reallocation terms would imply a tendency for p_k to exceed marginal costs if all other prices exceed the respective marginal costs *and* if public production is a net substitute for all other goods. If $k = n$, the latter assumption is very implausible. Transportation usually is complementary to many other goods. Hence, the reallocation terms might imply a tendency toward low public peak prices.

Let us now turn to the capacity term. It is this term which captures the particular characteristics of pricing under a capacity constraint. The more restrictive the capacity limit, the more relevant its influence on public-sector pricing.[5] However, this influence differs across goods. Hence, in the following

---

[4] We skip over all institutional details of controlling the petrol price like direct setting of the price or indirect control via taxation, and possible earmarking of tax revenues for the expansion of capacity.

[5] We also obtain the expected result that the capacity term is more important the larger the marginal rate of substitution between labor and capacity, in absolute value.

we distinguish among three different groups of goods which are publicly controlled: public peak traffic, substitutes for peak traffic, and complements to peak traffic.

The price of *public peak traffic* must be lower, the less public traffic influences capacity $(\mathcal{K}_1)$ and the more private traffic does $(\mathcal{K}_2)$. The influence of private utilization of capacity, moreover, depends on a ratio of price effects, reflecting the influence of changing p_n on both private and public peak traffic. The relevant price effects, however, are not independent of each other. An increase in p_n will typically *shift* traffic from the public to the private transportation modes; the more sensitively public traffic responds to p_n, the more sensitively will private traffic respond. This interdependence can be shown easily. We denote the total traffic volume by TV which consists of public and private traffic (all variables measured in the same units, for instance passenger miles):

$$TV = z_n + x_{n+1} - y_{n+1}. \tag{10}$$

Differentiation with respect to the public peak fare yields

$$\frac{\partial TV}{\partial p_n} = \frac{\partial z_n}{\partial p_n} + \frac{d(x,y)_{n+1}}{dp_n} \tag{11}$$

and we obtain

$$\frac{d(x,y)_{n+1}/dp_n}{\partial z_n/\partial p_n} = -1 + \frac{\partial TV/\partial p_n}{\partial z_n/\partial p_n}. \tag{12}$$

Since a reduction in public fares typically increases the traffic volume, we assume $\partial TV/\partial p_n < 0$.[6] Moreover, we assume income effects are small and therefore non-compensated price effects approximate compensated effects. Now substitute (12) into the capacity term for the public fare p_n, to determine the extent to which increases in the traffic volume, resulting from low public fares, restrict the use of low-fares policies.

Let us now consider publicly controlled *prices of peak-traffic substitutes* $(\partial \hat{z}_n/\partial p_k > 0,\ d(\hat{x},y)_{n+1}/dp_k > 0)$. They must be lower, the more public and private peak traffic influence capacity. The private utilization of capacity will have a greater effect because of $\mathcal{K}_2 > \mathcal{K}_1$. The resulting low prices for peak-traffic substitutes is a familiar result of the peak-load pricing literature.

---

[6] $(\partial TV/\partial p_n)/(\partial z_n/\partial p_n)<1$ is guaranteed by the assumption that public and private peak traffic are substitutes and that demand for public peak traffic does not react inversely to its own price. The influence of $\mathcal{K}_2$ on the fare of public peak traffic, therefore, cannot turn over to the contrary.

The peak-traffic substitutes are typically the off-peak transportation services, and their low prices are designed to shift demand from peak to off-peak times.

The opposite result is obtained for publicly controlled *prices of peak-traffic complements* $(\partial \hat{z}_n / \partial p_k < 0, \ d(\hat{x}, y)_{n+1}/dp_k < 0)$. They must be higher, the more public and private peak traffic influence capacity. Once again, $\mathcal{K}_2$ will be more influential. Furthermore, lower utilization of capacity by the public peak traffic leads to a lower price for petrol which, in turn, favors also the private peak traffic in spite of its heavy utilization of capacity.

D
Time-Dependent Pricing

14
Pricing Through Time and Adjustment Clauses

14.1 Optimum Pricing Policy and Inflation

Inflation erodes nominal prices. Hence nominal prices must be increased over time if some desired level of welfare or profit is to be maintained. If price adjustments were costless, the optimal policy would consist of continual nominal-price changes over time. In the presence of positive price-adjustment costs, however, a discontinual pattern of nominal-price adjustments is optimal.

The time pattern of price adjustments has attracted much attention in the practice of public (and private) enterprises.[1] Of particular interest is the question whether it is preferable to have few large price adjustments or many small price adjustments: should railway fares be increased every three months by, say, 1 percent or should the railway company wait and increase prices by 17.5 percent after four years?

Sheshinski and Weiss (1977) addressed the problem for a one-product monopoly which perfectly anticipates a constant rate of inflation.[2] Demand and hence profit or welfare depend on the real price of the good, that is on the nominal price divided by the general price level. The latter continuously increases with inflation. The authors assume price-adjustment costs which are the same no matter how small the price change. The optimal policy is (S, s):[3] there is a series of intervals during which the nominal price is held constant. If, due to inflationary erosion the real price falls to a lower threshold s, the nominal price is increased so that it corresponds to a real price S. Subsequently, the nominal price will once again be eroded and the policy will continue. The endogenous limits s and S depend, inter alia, on the rate of inflation and the price-adjustment costs. If inflation increases, the

---

[1] For a good survey of empirical studies on the topic see Weiss (1993).

[2] For stochastic inflation see Sheshinski–Weiss (1983).

[3] This policy is well-known from theories of optimal inventory adjustment.

interval $[S, s]$ also increases; however, only under additional assumptions will the frequency of price changes be increased. If adjustment costs increase, the frequency of price changes is reduced and consequently the firm chooses larger adjustments.

The price adjustment of multiproduct firms is extremely complicated. Sheshinski and Weiss (1992) show that for any individual price the optimal policy is once again (S, s). However, the timing of the various price adjustments is of particular interest: should price changes be bunched together, or should they be spread over time? Two effects must be taken into account to answer this question:

(i) The nominal price paths depend on the interaction in the profit function between prices. 'Positive interaction' means that an increase of real price p_i increases the marginal change in real profit which results from an increase of price $p_k, k \neq i$. If this is the case, there is a tendency to increase all prices simultaneously ('synchronization').

(ii) The nominal price paths also depend on the form of the price-adjustment costs. In the extreme case of 'menu costs', price adjustments cost the same, regardless of how many prices are changed. In this case there is a tendency toward synchronization of price changes. However, in the extreme case of 'decision costs', changing n prices is n times as costly as changing only one price. In this case there is a tendency towards a staggered policy where nominal prices are changed at different points in time.

14.2   Adjustment Clauses (Cost Pass-Through)

Adjustment clauses imply instantaneous adjustment of output prices over time: input-price increases can directly be passed on to consumers by output-price increases. The theoretical and practical discussion of adjustment clauses of public utilities was fueled (in the true sense of the word) by the first oil price shock in 1973. This led to particularly interesting proposals in the mid- and late-seventies. However, the interest in automatic adjustment clauses has not diminished, but has, for instance, been revived by the discussion on the British regulation of privatized utilities.

For a theoretical model of adjustment clauses let us assume symmetric but imperfect information in a regulatory setting: neither government nor the board of the public enterprise know whether some or all input prices will change at time t; there is uncertainty about future factor prices. The problems which arise from this uncertainty have been investigated explicitly for fuel-adjustment clauses which provide for automatic adjustment in output prices in response to changes in the factor prices of fuel and gas but not in response to other factor prices. Assume a technology where fuel and capital inputs can be substituted ex ante, but where their ratio is fixed ex post. The future price of fuel is uncertain at the time the fuel-capital ratio is chosen. The fuel-adjustment clause implies a sharing of the risk resulting from the uncertain factor price, reducing both the firm's expected profit and the regulator's expected welfare compared with the case of certainty (Baron–DeBondt, 1981). The fuel-adjustment clause can lead to an inefficient fuel-capital ratio. Moreover, the incentive to choose the least-cost fuel supply can be reduced. These problems are relevant primarily in cases of decreasing returns to scale because in this case the profit from increasing the output price exceeds the additional cost from the inefficient input combination. However, this effect appears only if the output price is adjusted immediately or after a short time. Hence, the above inefficiencies can be avoided by extending the 'collection lag' if the firm is not permitted to collect the adjusted price until after some time (Baron–DeBondt, 1979).

The *practical response* to these problems in the US has been to apply or to propose adjustment clauses for electricity utilities and the Bell telephone companies. They are either fuel-adjustment clauses, or general factor-price adjustment clauses, permitting the firm to adjust automatically to increases in all factor prices. The first type of adjustment clause weakens incentives for the efficient combination of inputs, whereas the latter avoids this bias. Both types of adjustment clauses, however, weaken incentives for the regulated firm to increase its productivity. Hence, some proposals permit automatic output price increases only in so far as the weighted input price increases exceed the rate of increase of productivity (Kendrick, 1975; Sudit, 1979). The price increase of any input is weighted by the respective share of that input in total costs. Productivity is measured either by man-hour per output (Kendrick) or by a Divisia index of total factor productivity change[4] (Sudit). To avoid controversies between firm and regulator over the accuracy and reliability of actual company-specific data, Sudit proposes that the adjustment clause be based on market reference input prices and industry-productivity trends.

In a multiproduct enterprise, moreover, the *many* adjustment paths of the different prices have to be compatible with the *overall* productivity incentives of the firm. Sudit therefore suggests (i) individual price changes which are determined by minimizing a quadratic loss function, postulating automatically adjusted price increases to be as close as possible to certain desirable levels of price changes, as defined by the regulator, *and* (ii) an overall adjustment formula which restricts the weighted sum of individual price changes to the weighted sums of input price changes minus factor productivity changes, the weights being the respective revenue and cost shares.

---

[4] This is the difference between the sum of the percentage changes in physical outputs weighted by their respective shares in total revenue and the sum of the percentage changes in physical inputs weightes by their respective share in total costs (Sudit, 1979: 60).

In recent UK privatizations various provisions for cost pass-through have been made. These provisions refer to increases in special cost factors which fluctuate considerably and are beyond the firm's control. The price regulation of British Gas provides two forms of cost pass-through: first, British Gas is enabled to pass on to tariff consumers the costs of approved energy efficiency schemes, second, British Gas is enabled to increase its average revenue not only by the retail price index minus X, but also by the costs of purchasing gas from suppliers where these costs are measured by a gas-purchasing index minus an efficiency gain.[5] The regional electricity companies, which directly supply electricity to customers, may pass on the cost of electricity purchases, of transmission and distribution charges they themselves have to pay to the electricity generation and transmission companies.[6]

The advantages and disadvantages of the practical application of adjustment clauses have been discussed intensively. Proponents argue that damage to firms from regulatory lags is reduced and competitiveness between regulated and non-regulated industries is restored. Opponents, on the other hand, stress the implied abandonment of regulatory control, the resulting inefficiencies and the reduction of built-in-stabilizing effects of regulatory lags. They argue that problems like profit squeeze of regulated firms could equally well be diminished by granting them interim relief.

---

[5] For details on the regulation of British Gas see Helm (1988), Letwin (1988: 130–41) and Price (1993). Since the average price per therm and the average cost of gas refer to the same year, some special correction for forecast errors is necessary. See, for instance, Helm (1988: 116) or Vickers–Yarrow (1988: 263–4).

[6] For further details on the regulation of electricity in the UK see Vickers–Yarrow (1991), Weyman-Jones (1992) and McGowan (1993).

15
Peak-Load Pricing

15.1   Presenting the Problem

Consider goods for which *demand* fluctuates cyclically over time, both daily and seasonally. Electricity or gas demand peaks in the morning, at noon and in the evening, and is highest in winter. Local bus and underground services are used most intensively between 7 and 9 a.m. and 4 to 7 p.m. Air and rail traffic have a holiday demand peak; telecommunication has a business demand peak.In all these cases it is impossible to use off-peak production to serve peak demand because the goods are not storable, at least not at reasonable costs.

The *supply* side of such goods also has special features. The production typically is characterized by high fixed costs and low variable costs; there are many cases of increasing returns to scale. In other words, the characteristics of 'natural monopolies' are often present: enterprises producing those goods could keep others out of the market by their pricing policy and still make profits. For these reasons the goods are produced either by nationalized or by regulated public utilities.

In practice such public utilities are often required to meet all demand, however high it may be. (There are some theoretical arguments to justify this requirement.) A public utility which charges only one price for its output will therefore face a trade-off between fairly high capacity costs and a fairly high price. To cope with this trade-off, profit-maximizing as well as welfare-maximizing monopolies have used systems of price differentiation.[1]

The *simplest rule of thumb* in our peak-load case is based upon the distinction between operating and capacity costs: only consumers who are responsible for the capacity costs should pay for them. Hence peak demand pays operating plus capacity costs whereas off-peak demand pays the low operating costs only. This price structure is designed to encourage a more uniform utilization of capacity by reducing peak demand and increasing off-peak demand. Welfare gains result from the fact that consumers are not driven from the market completely, but rather are enticed to shift their demand from peak to off-peak times.

---

[1] A particularly well-known empirical study is Glaister (1976) which deals with the Channel tunnel. The proposed peak-load pricing would have reduced the investment required in terminal facilities, rolling stock, track signalling etc. to almost one third of the official unitary-price design.

The welfare optimality of this rule of thumb has been verified by Steiner (1957) and Williamson (1966), but under very restrictive assumptions. They assume at least two periods of fixed length, each characterized by a given demand function $x_k(p_k)$. For a given price, demand within any period is assumed to be constant ('time-independent demand'). The chosen cost function is of the simplest possible type, namely that resulting from a fixed-proportions technology, leading to constant operating costs and constant capacity costs.

There is, however, an interesting counterexample to this simple model. Assume that peak and off-peak demand do not differ very much and that capacity costs are very high. At a single price there may be an undesired peak/off-peak structure of demand. The public utility introduces peak-load pricing and follows the above mentioned rule of thumb. The off-peak price falls drastically because the capacity costs are assumed to be very high. The peak price increases drastically. This may induce a *shifting peak* where the former off-peak demand becomes the new peak demand and vice versa. An empirical example was the German 'moonlight-tariff' for phoning after 10 p.m. It was abolished in 1981 because it led to an extraordinary demand peak between 10 and 11 p.m. Under the restrictive assumptions on cost functions mentioned above, welfare-optimal pricing requires price discrimination which equates peak and off-peak demand. This implies that off-peak demand has to pay for its operating costs plus some share of capacity costs. The peak price is reduced by that share of capacity cost carried by off-peak demand.

The plausibility of the above mentioned rules should not prevent us from recognizing that their validity rests on their very restrictive assumptions. They do not remain valid if we work with the usual neoclassical cost functions (Panzar, 1976), or allow for time-dependent demand.

We therefore require a more general model of the peak-load problem. A priori we might consider applying the usual Boiteux model of public pricing. This would involve classifying demand in different periods as different goods so that demand is time-independent within each period. We obtain peak-load marginal-cost pricing rules, peak-load Ramsey-pricing rules etc. The peak-load problem turns out to be a special case of joint production and by always considering the optimal input choice we can find a price which leads to an optimal mix between paying for operating and for capacity costs.

Practical problems can arise if too many periods are distinguished, but the approach seems to provide a straightforward theoretical solution of the peak-load problem (Bös, 1981: 31–3). It is, however, a bit superficial to treat the peak-load problem in this way. Were the approach appropriate, it would be difficult to understand the immense interest in the peak-load problem (as surveyed in Crew–Kleindorfer (1979), Mitchell–Manning–Acton (1977) and Turvey–Anderson (1977), to mention a few outstanding books).

What, then, is the reason for developing a special theory of peak-load pricing? It is the following peak-load trilemma:

• First, the government does not want too many prices because this leads to high information and administrative costs and to uncertainty for consumers.[2] Hence the length of the periods chosen is such that demand does not depend on prices alone, but fluctuates within the periods as well, either stochastically,[3] or deterministically depending on an index of time ('time-dependent demand').

• Second, the government wants to avoid high peak prices, mainly because of distributional considerations. High peak prices for local transport may disadvantage the lower-income working population most and not the more affluent car owner.

• Third, the government wants to meet all demand because reliability is an important quality characteristic of public supply.

The direct application of the Boiteux model does not come to terms with time-dependent demand although it deals adequately with points two and three. Hence we must extend our usual approach to the case of time-dependent demand. Moreover, recent peak-load theory avoids condition three of the trilemma and accepts excess demand and rationing, arguing that it may be welfare optimal to accept excess demand to avoid excessive spending on the capacity of public utilities or applying peak prices which are too high.

15.2   A Model with Excess Demand and Rationing

We treat the peak-load problem in the following model. There is a public utility producing one good, say electricity. The market demand for this good varies among the periods of the day. These periods are labelled $k \in K$. The number of periods and their respective length, $L(k)$, are exogenously fixed. The board uses the instruments $p_k, k \in K$ and $z_i, i = o, \ldots, n$ to maximize welfare under relevant constraints.

We want to show the trade-off between rationing by price and rationing by quantity. This trade-off could not be shown clearly if the board were allowed to apply lump-sum transfers,[4] as such transfers would introduce a further means of rationing: 'rationing by redistribution', shifting purchasing power from peak to off-peak demand. Let us therefore exclude lump-sum transfers.

To deal with the peak-load problem we define all demand and supply quantities x_k and z_k per unit of time in a period (say, demand in one second).

---

[2] With microprocessing, the technical possibilities of adequate metering would allow for many more periods than was the case previously.

[3] Electricity demand, for instance, depends heavily on weather.

[4] Either r^h or $r_k^h, h = 1, \ldots H, k \in K$.

This method of definition enables us to come to terms with fluctuations of demand within a given period $k \in K$. Quantities of all other goods $i \notin K$ are defined as usual.

The *quantity demanded per unit of time*, x_k, depends on the period price and on time in an additively separable way (Dansby, 1975):[5] [6]

$$x_k(p_k, t_k) = x_k(p_k) + \tau(t_k); \qquad k \in K. \tag{1}$$

The demand depends on the price p_k which is the same for all units of time of period k. It does not depend on prices in other periods: no cross price elasticities enter our formulas.[7] On the other hand, demand is allowed to fluctuate within the period, depending on t_k, the index of units of time (moments) of period $k, t_k \in k$. The price effect of demand is invariant with respect to time and the time effect is invariant with respect to the period price.

The time-dependent demand $\tau(t_k)$ is defined over the interval $[0, \tau_k^{max}]$. Both $\tau = 0$ and $\tau = \tau_k^{max}$ may occur at one, or more than one, moment of time in the interval k. In other words, there may be one, or more than one, cyclical movement of demand $\tau(t_k)$ during period t_k. We assume that the board observes all these fluctuations. Hence it can compute the density function $f_k(\tau)$ of time-dependent demand. This density function measures the relative frequency of a particular demand τ, taken together from all cyclical fluctuations in period t_k. The corresponding distribution function may be denoted $F_k(\tau)$.

The *quantity supplied per unit of time*, z_k, is assumed to be time-independent. It is constant within a period, but may differ between periods. As we deal with outputs only, $z_k \geq 0$. With respect to the other quantities $z_i, i \notin K$, all our conventions hold. They are defined with respect to the usual time horizon of production, i.e. over all periods $k \in K$. Hence the production function equals

$$g(z) = g(z_k L(k), z_i|_{i \notin K}) = 0 \tag{2}$$

and we can define marginal costs

---

[5] The derivations of our model can be applied analogously to the case of stochastic demand $x_k = x_k(p_k, u)$, where u is a random variable. Our specification corresponds to the additive stochastic demand function $x_k = x_k(p_k) + u$. For further discussion of these problems see Brown–Johnson (1969), Visscher (1973), and Carlton (1977).

[6] It is possible to give up the additive structure of time-dependent demand and to prove most results for more general demand functions (Watzke, 1982).

[7] They can be introduced easily into our derivations. However, the interpretation of the resulting price structure (18) becomes far more complicated. Hence we follow the usual tradition of the stochastic pricing literature and suppress them.

$$c_k = \frac{\partial g / \partial (z_k L(k))}{\partial g / \partial z_o} > 0; \quad c_i |_{i \notin K} = \frac{\partial g / \partial z_i}{\partial g / \partial z_o} > 0. \tag{3}$$

The market for the good of the public utility may be *in equilibrium or in disequilibrium*.[8] Both excess demand and excess supply are possible, resulting in rationing of demand or supply. The extent of demand rationing, however, will be constrained for political reasons. The welfare-optimal choice of output may well imply that during some periods demand is always rationed. Consumers, however, would not be willing to accept a telecommunications system which is rationed all day long and unrationed between 0 and 5 a.m. only. As a matter of fact, such a low level of electricity, gas or telephone supplies in single periods is undesirable and usually leads to adverse reactions from customers. The quality structure of public utilities' supply is obviously influenced by political considerations. The government will be afraid of losing votes, of protests against electricity blackouts etc. Hence it requests that the enterprise's board explicitly considers *reliability constraints*. The straightforward choice of a reliability constraint in our model is:[9]

$$z_k - x_k(p_k) \geq 0; \quad k \in K. \tag{4}$$

This constraint obliges the board to cover at least the time-independent basic demand $x_k(p_k)$ in any period. Demand rationing is restricted to the time-dependent demand $\tau(t_k)$.

For expositional clarity we split supply z_k into the 'minimum' supply z_k^m which just covers the time-independent basic demand, and the 'additional' supply z_k^a which is consumed by time-dependent demand:

$$z_k^m = x_k(p_k); \quad z_k^m + z_k^a = z_k; \quad k \in K. \tag{5}$$

Rationing of demand refers to supply z_k^a only. Therefore, at any point in time the public enterprise will sell the following quantity

$$S(k, t_k) := z_k^m + \min[\tau(t_k), z_k^a]; \quad k \in K. \tag{6}$$

---

[8] For all goods $i \notin K$ the market equilibria are assumed to hold as usual.

[9] As these constraints will reduce the extent of rationing, they can be thought of as a surrogate for explicitly regarding administrative rationing costs (Crew–Kleindorfer, 1979: 91). – In stochastic models of peak-load pricing such constraints have been dealt with since Meyer (1975) by saying that the probability of excess demand at any moment k must not exceed a level ε_k.

Accordingly, its revenue-cost constraint is as follows:

$$\sum_{k \in K} p_k \int_{t_k \in k} S(k,t)dt + \sum_{i \notin K} p_i z_i = \Pi^o \qquad (7)$$

or equivalently

$$\sum_{k} p_k L(k) \left\{ z_k^m + \int_0^{z_k^a} \tau f(\tau)d\tau + z_k^a (1 - F(z_k^a)) \right\} + \sum_{i \notin K} p_i z_i = \Pi^o. \qquad (8)$$

Let us now turn to demand rationing and its social valuation. Demand is rationed if there is excess demand, $E > 0$, where

$$E(k, t_k) := \max \left\{ \tau(t_k) - z_k^a, 0 \right\}; \qquad k \in K. \qquad (9)$$

The usual peak-load literature deals with different *theoretical* alternatives to rationing: consumers are either excluded randomly or with respect to their willingness to pay, usually measured by the individual consumer's surplus or by the compensating variation. In the latter case rationing may exclude people in order of the lowest or highest willingness to pay until capacity is exhausted.

These are theoretical solutions to the rationing problem. They can be handled nicely in the peak-load calculus. Practical rationing, for instance of telephone calls etc., follows other criteria. Hence we will not adopt one of these concepts, but use a more general concept to capture the welfare losses of rationing. We start from a *social welfare function per unit of time* $W(p, t_k)$ depending on both controlled and uncontrolled prices. According to the usual definition, welfare is defined on the assumption that all consumers who are willing to pay the price p_k are being served. Hence, welfare accrues unreduced in moments without excess demand. With respect to moments of rationing, however, the board has to consider an adequately reduced welfare $\Gamma(E(k, t_k)) \cdot W(p, t_k)$ where $\Gamma(E)$ can take values between 0 and 1. This is a fairly general formulation of welfare losses from rationing: the function $\Gamma(E)$ may represent individual consumers' actually accruing welfare losses but also the board's valuation of such losses. By normalization $\Gamma(E) = 1$ if there is no excess demand. However, the board may decide to set $\Gamma(E) = 1$ even if $E > 0$, thus totally ignoring welfare losses from rationing. On the other hand, the board may decide to value welfare losses from rationing at more than the individual consumer losses; in the limiting case assuming $\Gamma(E) = 0$ as soon as $E > 0$. Usually, the board will follow some middle course, in particular it may take into account the actual losses.[10]

---

[10] Some particular cases of rationing cannot be expressed directly by $\Gamma(E)$ if the board

Aggregating over all moments of time and over all periods we obtain the board's total welfare measure

$$\widetilde{W}(p,z) = \sum_{k \in K} \int_{t_k \in k} \Gamma(E(k,t)) \cdot W(p,t)dt$$

$$= \sum_{k \in K} L(k) \left\{ \Gamma(0) \int_0^{z_k^a} W(p,\tau)f(\tau)d\tau \right. \tag{10}$$

$$\left. + \int_{z_k^a}^{\tau_k^{max}} \Gamma(\tau - z_k^a)W(p,\tau)f(\tau)d\tau \right\}.$$

We follow the usual peak-load literature and assume the social welfare function to be a consumer surplus, that is

$$\frac{\partial W}{\partial p_k} = -x_k(p_k, t_k). \tag{11}$$

15.3 The Optimization Problem

We now substitute the special welfare function $\widetilde{W}$ into the Boiteux model, and consider the reliability constraints (4), the rationed-market equilibrium of public supply (5) and the revenue-cost constraint (7). The board of the firm maximizes the following Lagrangean function with respect to prices $p_k, k \in K$ and quantities $z_i, i \notin K; z_k, z_k^m, z_k^a, k \in K$:

$$\mathcal{F} = \widetilde{W}(p,z) - \sum_{k \in K} \alpha_k(x_k(p_k) - z_k^m) -$$

$$- \sum_{i \notin K} \alpha_i \left[\sum_h x_i^h(p) - z_i - \sum_j y_i^j(p) \right] -$$

$$- \beta g(z) - \overline{\gamma} \left[\Pi^o - \sum_{k \in K} p_k \int_{t_k \in k} S(k,t)dt - \sum_{i \notin K} p_i z_i \right] - \tag{12}$$

$$- \sum_{k \in K} \delta_k(z_k - z_k^m - z_k^a).$$

---

takes the actual individual losses as a measure of the relevant social welfare losses. Random rationing, for instance, can only be expressed by a function $\Gamma(E,x)=(1-E/x)$. The extension of our derivations to such a case is straightforward, albeit a little tedious.

The following first-order conditions hold:

$$\frac{\partial \mathcal{F}}{\partial p_k} : - \int\limits_{t_k \in k} \Gamma(E) x_k(\cdot) dt - \alpha_k \frac{\partial x_k}{\partial p_k} - \sum_{i \notin K} \alpha_i \frac{\partial z_i^D}{\partial p_k} +$$

$$+ \overline{\gamma} L(k) \left[z_k^m + \int\limits_0^{z_k^a} \tau f(\tau) d\tau + z_k^a (1 - F(z_k^a)) \right] = 0; \quad k \in K, \quad (13)$$

$$\frac{\partial \mathcal{F}}{\partial z_i} : \alpha_i - \beta \frac{\partial g}{\partial z_i} + \overline{\gamma} p_i = 0; \quad i \notin K, \tag{14}$$

$$\frac{\partial \mathcal{F}}{\partial z_k} : -\beta \frac{\partial g}{\partial (z_k L(k))} L(k) - \delta_k = 0; \quad k \in K, \tag{15}$$

$$\frac{\partial \mathcal{F}}{\partial z_k^m} : \alpha_k + \overline{\gamma} p_k L(k) + \delta_k = 0; \quad k \in K, \tag{16}$$

$$\frac{\partial \mathcal{F}}{\partial z_k^a} : -L(k) \int\limits_{z_k^a}^{\tau_k^{\max}} \Gamma'(\tau - z_k^a) W(p, \tau) f(\tau) d\tau +$$

$$+ \overline{\gamma} L(k) p_k \left[1 - F(z_k^a) \right] + \delta_k = 0; \quad k \in K. \tag{17[11]}$$

What is the economic interpretation of these marginal conditions? First, they show that in our model it is *welfare optimal to have excess demand*. This can be proved by contradiction. Assume an optimum without any excess demand, where $z_k^a = \tau_k^{\max}$. Then the integral in (17) vanishes, and so does $\overline{\gamma} L(k) p_k [1 - F(z_k^a)]$, because by definition $F(\tau_k^{\max}) = 1$. Therefore eqs. (17) could only be fulfilled if $\delta_k = 0$. But, because of (15), $\delta_k = 0$ implies $c_k = 0$ which contradicts our assumption $c_k > 0$. Therefore $z_k^a = \tau_k^{\max}$ is ruled out and there must exist excess demand at the welfare optimum. Only if demand is time-independent, supply always equals demand, because $z_k^a = 0$ and $z_k^m = z_k = x_k(p_k)$ from eq. (5).[12]

Second, the marginal conditions have implications for pricing. Applying the usual type of transformations we obtain the following pricing rule:

---

[11] After cancelling $\Gamma(0) W(p, z_k^a) f(z_k^a) - \Gamma(z_k^a - z_k^a) W(p, z_k^a) f(z_k^a)$ in the derivation of the welfare function, and $z_k^a f(z_k^a) - z_k^a F'(z_k^a)$ in the derivation of the profit constraint.

[12] In this case the aggregation constraints on z_k must be omitted in the optimization approach (12).

$$(c_k - p_k)\frac{\partial x_k}{\partial p_k}L(k) + \sum_{i \notin K}(c_i - p_i)\frac{\partial z_i^D}{\partial p_k} =$$

$$= \int_{t_k} \left[\gamma S(k,t) - \frac{\Gamma(E)}{\beta_o}x_k \right] dt - \tag{18}$$

$$- (1-\gamma)\left[p_k\frac{\partial x_k}{\partial p_k}L(k) + \sum_{i \notin K}p_i\frac{\partial z_i^D}{\partial p_k} \right]; \quad k \in K.$$

The particular properties of peak-load pricing can be seen more easily if we follow the usual peak-load literature and suppress the relations to other public outputs or inputs. Our interpretation therefore focuses on the price structure

$$(c_k - p_k)\frac{\partial x_k}{\partial p_k}L(k) = \int_{t_k}\left[\gamma S(k,t) - \frac{\Gamma(E)}{\beta_o}x_k \right] dt -$$

$$- (1-\gamma)p_k\frac{\partial x_k}{\partial p_k}L(k); \quad k \in K. \tag{19}$$

The main economic meaning of this formula will be indicated for the limiting case $\gamma = 1$. (It is left to the reader to consider further limiting cases.) If in such a case the board is so sensitive to rationing as to set $\Gamma(E) = 0$ if $E > 0$,[13] the pricing rule reduces to

$$(c_k - p_k)\frac{\partial x_k}{\partial p_k} = \frac{L(\Psi_k)}{L(k)}z_k + \frac{\beta_o - 1}{\beta_o}\frac{L(\Psi_k^c)}{L(k)}\bar{x}_k^c; \quad k \in K, \tag{20}$$

where $L(\Psi_k)$ is the time span of excess demand, and $L(\Psi_k^c)$ is its complement, $L(\Psi_k) + L(\Psi_k^c) = L(k)$. $\bar{x}_k^c$ is the average demand per unit of time in period Ψ_k^c. The right-hand side of (20) is a weighted average of $S(k, t_k)$. A profit-maximizing monopolist who faces the reliability constraints follows similar conditions, but uses the arithmetic mean of $S(k, t_k)$. For $\beta_o \to \infty$ therefore welfare maximization and profit maximization lead to the same result. Hence,

---

[13] Differentiability, in that case, can be achieved by replacing the discontinuous function $\Gamma(E)$ by a sequence Γ_S of differentiable functions converging to $\Gamma(E)$. Under the assumption that the sequence of quantities is convergent, the limit system of quantities can be characterized by (20).

for large β_o the board concentrates on rationing by high prices, reducing the extent of rationing by quantity.

If, on the other hand, the board is totally insensitive to rationing [that is, $\Gamma(E) = 1$ if $E > 0$], the pricing formula becomes:

$$
\begin{aligned}
(c_k - p_k)\frac{\partial x_k}{\partial p_k} &= \frac{L(\Psi_k)}{L(k)}(z_k - \bar{x}_k/\beta_o) + \frac{\beta_o - 1}{\beta_o}\frac{L(\Psi_k^c)}{L(k)}\bar{x}_k^c = \\
&= \frac{\beta_o - 1}{\beta_o}\bar{x}_k^{act} - \overline{E}(k); \quad k \in K,
\end{aligned}
\tag{21}
$$

where $\bar{x}_k$ is the average demand per unit of time in period Ψ_k; $\bar{x}_k^{act}$ is the actual demand per unit of time, $\bar{x}_k^{act} = \int_{t_k} x_k(t)dt/L(k)$; $\overline{E}(k)$ is the average excess demand per unit of time, $\overline{E}(k) = \int_{t_k} E(k,t)dt/L(k)$. For small β_o (that is, $\beta_o < 1$), prices fall below marginal costs. We obtain low prices: the board concentrates on rationing by quantity, reducing the extent of rationing by prices. Prices above marginal costs are obtained if $\beta_o > 1$ and if the excess demand is not too large.

One central question remains: will peak prices exceed off-peak prices in our model? There is no general answer to this question, but we can show when such a result may occur.

Consider two periods only, k(peak) and k(off-peak), and assume the following relations to hold:

$$
z_{k(\text{peak})} \geq x_{k(\text{peak})}^m > z_{k(\text{off-peak})} \geq x_{k(\text{off-peak})}^m.
\tag{22}
$$

Now consider the right-hand side of the pricing rule (19). z_k increases if we switch from off-peak to peak. This implies a *tendency* for the difference quotient

$$
\Delta(\text{right-hand side of (19)})/\Delta x_k^m,
\tag{23}
$$

to be positive. There always exist values of γ which are large enough and of $\Gamma(E)$ which are small enough to ensure that this tendency becomes effective for the whole difference quotient (23). In this case

$$
\Delta(\text{left-hand side of (19)})/\Delta x_k^m > 0
\tag{24}
$$

must also hold.

This implies a higher difference between price and marginal cost in the peak period *if* the price effect $\partial x_k/\partial p_k$ is unchanged or does not change too sharply in spite of the change from off-peak to peak. And if, additionally, marginal peak costs exceed marginal off-peak costs, higher peak prices are obtained.

The following conditions are sufficient for higher peak than off-peak prices:

- the government fixes a sufficiently high budget requirement;
- the enterprise's board is sufficiently sensitive to excess demand and rationing;
- β_o is not too low;
- the price effect of peak demand does not differ too much from that of off-peak demand;
- marginal peak costs do not fall below marginal off-peak costs.

This result indicates the crucial importance of the particular assumptions of those older theories on peak-load pricing according to which higher peak prices were always superior.

E
Pricing When Quality Matters

16
Different Approaches Toward Optimal Quality

16.1   How to Model Quality

16.1.1   Quality I: Distinguishing Different Goods

According to the Arrow–Debreu tradition a good must be described exhaustively with respect to time, location and quality. This definition of a good is more precise than the colloquial definition. Goods of different quality constitute different goods which can be sold at different prices.

Quality differentiation very often can be described adequately in the above manner. First, those nationalized firms which are competitive with private enterprises offer the usual differentiated supply, be it different types of automobiles, sorts of steel, etc. Second, public utilities often subdivide the market by distinguishing between different goods. Examples include electric current for business and for households (with different reliability of supply), special or normal delivery of letters, and all applications of peak-load pricing. Some public utilities, moreover, apply a particular sort of monopolistic price differentiation by distinguishing between different classes of goods, like first and second class railway or hospital accommodation.

Assuming goods of different quality to be different goods, labelled $k \in K$ or $i \in K$, we can apply all pricing rules which we have treated in the previous chapters. However, some special problems arise with respect to this application.

A preliminary question relates to the *degree of differentiation*: to what extent should the public enterprise subdivide its market by distinguishing between different goods? This question has to be answered before applying models of optimal allocation because optimal allocation can be defined for any degree of differentiation. From a theoretical point of view it is always possible to increase welfare by further differentiation. However such a procedure leads to additional costs. At the optimal degree of differentiation the welfare gains equal the marginal costs of further differentiation. In practice the rule of thumb is to stop if further differentiation does not change the result significantly. Very often, however, only two goods are distinguished, e.g. day and night electricity, or peak and off-peak traffic.

The optimal extent of monopolistic quality discrimination is treated in several industrial-organization papers;[1] particularly well-known is Mussa–Rosen (1978). They show that a monopolist enlarges the quality spectrum: the socially optimal quality is purchased by consumers with high valuation of quality, whereas a suboptimal quality is sold to the consumers who value quality less.[2]

Further questions relate to the *specific properties of supply and demand* in case of quality differentiation:

• The relevant goods are typically substitutes for each other; then in applying various models of the previous chapters we have to take the substitute case. This implies, inter alia, a high probability of welfare-optimal increases in *inefficiency* (section 5.4).

• In many cases of quality differentiation, the cross-price elasticities will be comparatively high; in those cases we must not apply approaches which neglect cross elasticities.

• The differentiated-quality case often lends itself to price differentiation with distributional objectives.

• We typically deal with joint production, and all the difficult problems of imputation of fixed costs arise.

• Adding up quantities of different goods makes economic sense if these goods 'satisfy the same wants' at different levels of quality. It is this property alone of public supply which allows multiproduct enterprises to follow a strategy of maximizing total output.[3]

• Goods which are only distinguished by quality are typically close substitutes. Hence in special cases demand for good i can be met by supply of good j, for instance if second-class railway passengers are allowed to use first-class seats at a second-class price after all second-class seats have been occupied.[4]

---

[1] In this chapter we deal with the quality choice of a monopolistic multi-product firm. Hence, we only mention in passing that recently many papers treated two-stage duopoly games where in the first stage each firm chooses the value of the quality of its product and in the second stage engages in price or quantity competition. For an overview of these studies see Tirole (1988: 296–8).

[2] See also O'Keefe (1981). For a textbook presentation see Tirole (1988: 96–7, 149–52).

[3] See chapter 20 below.

[4] The usual market-clearing conditions, in that case, would have to be replaced with one condition only, implying $\Sigma_k \Sigma_h x_k^h - \Sigma_k z_k - \Sigma_k \Sigma_j y_k^j = 0$ with Lagrangean parameter α whence $c_k - \gamma p_k = \alpha/\beta_o$ has to be constant for all goods k included in the above market-clearing constraint.

16.1.2   *Quality II: Using Continuous Quality Indicators*

Separate Indicators Versus Quantity-Augmenting Quality

Consider a transport enterprise deciding whether the deficit should be reduced by increasing fares or by decreasing the frequency of bus or train service. It is not very sensible to assume different goods in such a case, x_1 being 'bus with 4 minutes waiting time', x_2 being 'bus with 4.5 minutes waiting time' etc., under the explicit constraint that one and only one of the above goods can actually be supplied. In such cases, the straightforward approach is to proceed by explicitly defining continuous quality indicators. In this context quality is typically measured by a one-dimensional variable, and there are several ways to introduce such one-dimensional quality indicators into the analysis:

(i)   The approach applied in this book assumes that quality indicators enter the individual utility and demand functions, and the public enterprises' production functions. If q is a vector of one-dimensional quality indicators $q := (q_o, \ldots, q_n)$, then consumer utility depends on both quantities and qualities, $u^h = u^h(x^h, q)$. Going back to the example of bus demand, and for the moment ignoring cross effects, bus demand depends on price and on a quality indicator measuring waiting time which is treated as continuously variable by the transport enterprise. Similarly, we define technology as depending on quantities and qualities, $g(z, q) = 0$.

Assuming that the relevant functions are differentiable with respect to the quality indicators, such a procedure allows an explicit modelling of the optimal quality choice, and of the quality-price trade-off, in a way which is easily tractable by calculus.

(ii)   An alternative approach is based on Lancaster's assumption that consumers derive utility not from a quantity consumed, but from various 'characteristics' of the good. Drèze and Hagen (1978) therefore assume that consumer utility depends on characteristics which are defined as $\mathcal{X}_i^h = q_i x_i^h$, where x_i^h are the consumed quantities and q_i is a one-dimensional quality indicator. Quality thus is a quantity-augmenting factor and consumer utility does not directly depend on quantities, but on characteristics, $u^h = u^h(\mathcal{X}^h)$. The quality indicator can also be defined as a random variable: a consumer who buys x_i^h units of good i of quality q_i receives a random level of service $\mathcal{X}_i^h = q_i x_i^h$, depending on the distribution of q_i. This definition of quality is particularly appropriate for the modelling of reliability of supply. See Nelson (1991), Falkinger (1991, 1992).

Use of one-dimensional quality indicators is a superior approach if the explicit quality-price trade-off is a central concern of a public enterprise. Such a theory is best suited to answer questions of the following type (always taking account of the permissible deficit):

- should the bus fare be increased or should the number of buses serving the route be decreased?
- should the electricity price per kw-h be increased or should the reliability of supply be decreased?
- should the fees of some school be increased or should the student-teacher ratio be increased?

The restriction to *one-dimensional* quality indicators could be seen as a major deficiency of the analysis. However, as we shall argue in what follows, there is reason to believe that this restriction is not too serious in the case of publicly supplied goods.

Quality Standardization for Publicly Supplied Private Goods[5]

Nationalized automobile enterprises or communal breweries provide good examples of cases where quality is determined by actual or potential competition between public and private enterprises. Mostly, however, public supply of private goods occurs in politically determined or natural monopolies, without free market entry.

Thus, political and technological constraints determine the quality pattern of many publicly supplied private goods: for instance, equity considerations against too intensive quality differentiation, regulation-induced biases (for instance safety prescriptions, obligation to cover a particular basic supply), bureaucratic constraints, technological constraints (reducing quality differentiation to exploit increasing returns to scale) and too restrictive or insufficiently restrictive financial constraints.

The quality pattern that results from these constraints will generally imply the production of only one or a few standard levels of quality, which may, but need not, match private tastes. Problems of this kind are well-known in the case of natural monopolies (railway, telephone, motorways, airlines), urban transport, public utilities (electricity, water, refuse collection), health care and hospitals.

Ex Ante and Ex Post Quality

Consider a board of a public enterprise which has to decide how to build a new motorway or a new hospital. It can choose the quality of a motorway in terms of the number of lanes, the width of the lanes, the material to be used; or, in the case of a hospital, the installation of modern medical instruments. These choices at the planning stage determine the overall quality of the output. Once

---

[5] The subsections on quality standardization and on ex ante versus ex post qualities are taken from Bös–Genser–Holzmann (1982).

the public investment is made, the general quality level is fixed, although the manager or the politician may introduce minor quality variations around this given level.

Let us concentrate on the determination of the overall quality level, since variations around this level are of minor importance in the case of public supply. For instance, quality differentiation within a given hospital (e.g., first- versus second-class) is marginal in comparison with the quality difference between technologically well-equipped university hospitals and a provincial hospital. Local public transport offers another good example in which the ex ante decision for a particular technology establishes a particular quality level, whereas further changes in comfort, travelling time, etc., are possible only within a limited range.

In these examples the technology fixes the quality level which, once se- lected, has the characteristic of a public good in that the same level of quality is available to all consumers and does not decrease if the number of consumers increases. (We disregard congestion effects.) Given the fixed quality level of the good, each consumer can make a quantity choice, for instance the num- ber of trips using local transport, the number of telephone calls and, within certain limits, even the length of hospital treatment. The above situation can be described most easily by using a one-dimensional quality indicator for each of the goods of our model (Spence, 1975; Sheshinski, 1976). Concentrating on one dimension of quality implies no loss of generality if we regard the cho- sen indicator as the parameter of a technologically feasible quality path in an n-dimensional quality space. For practical purposes, it is often sufficient to interpret the chosen indicator as the facet of quality that is dominant with respect to individual evaluations, for instance the travelling time of public transport (Glaister and Collings, 1978; Glaister, 1982), or the reliability of supply of electricity (Telson, 1975; Falkinger, 1991, 1992).

Quality Indicators for 'Public Good' Properties

As mentioned above, quality indicators can also be taken as indicators for typical 'public good' properties of public supply, e.g. the level of education or of health care. Schools or hospital services can then be treated as publicly supplied private goods, where the individually varying demand depends on the quality level, prices and individual income. In my view the above treatment is empirically much more realistic than the assumption of schools or hospital services being public goods, consumed to the same extent by everybody.[6]

---

[6] See the discussion of Usher's (1977) model in section 1.3 above.

16.2 The Conditions for Optimal Quality

16.2.1 On Consumers' Quality Choice

In this chapter we assume that every good is not only associated with a particular price, but also with a particular one-dimensional quality indicator q_i. Let $q := (q_o, \ldots, q_n)$ be a vector of these indicators. For the individual consumer the qualities are given and he adjusts his demand accordingly. Hence we have indirect utility functions exhibiting the dependence of the individual optimum utility on prices, on lump-sum income *and on the qualities of public supply:*

$$v^h(p, q, r^h) := \max_{x^h} u^h(x^h, q) \quad s.t. \quad \sum_{i=o}^{n} p_i x_i^h = r^h; \qquad h = 1, \ldots, H. \quad (1)$$

This optimization leads to Marshallian demand functions $x_i^h(p, q, r^h)$.

Modelling quality is complicated because there is no counterpart to the usual duality between prices and quantities. The same price typically refers to quantity and quality, and there is no differentiation between a quantity and a quality price, which would facilitate the analysis. For the above reasons it is necessary to deduce some fundamental properties of consumers' and producers' quality choice before transforming the relevant marginal conditions.

First we must extend *Roy's identity* so as to include qualities.[7] Consider an optimum state of the world, characterized by prices p^*, qualities q^* and optimal incomes $r^{h*}, h = 1, \ldots, H$. Consumer h can attain optimum utility u^{h*}. Now consider the dual problem. The expenditure function $R^h(p, q, u^{h*})$ denotes the minimal expenditures which enable the consumer to attain the constant utility level u^{h*}:

$$R^h(p, q, u^{h*}) = \min_{x^h} \left\{ \sum_i p_i x_i^h \mid u^h(x^h, q) = u^{h*} \right\}. \quad (2)$$

Hence the following identity holds[8]

$$u^{h*} = v^h(p, q, R^h(p, q, u^{h*})). \quad (3)$$

The interpretation of this equation is that for any arbitrary set of prices and qualities, the consumer can achieve optimum utility u^{h*} if he is given the

---

[7] For the case without quality see e.g. Varian (1978: 93).

[8] By starting from this specification of v^h we make sure that we obtain Marshallian demand functions in what follows.

minimal income which he needs to obtain u^{h*}. Let us now differentiate this identity with respect to some quality q_k :

$$0 = \frac{\partial v^h(p^*, q^*, r^{h*})}{\partial q_k} + \frac{\partial v^h(p^*, q^*, r^{h*})}{\partial r^h} \cdot \frac{\partial R^h(p, q, u^{h*})}{\partial q_k}. \tag{4}$$

Rearranging (4) we obtain a formula similar to Roy's identity, that is

$$\frac{\partial v^h(\cdot)/\partial q_k}{\partial v^h(\cdot)/\partial r^h} = -\frac{\partial R^h(\cdot)}{\partial q_k}. \tag{5}$$

This result, although interesting in itself, raises further issues: what interpretation can be given to $\partial R^h/\partial q_k$ and can this partial derivative be rearranged to obtain a relationship similar to $\partial R^h/\partial p_k = \hat{x}_k^h$? There are several ways of approaching this problem.

(i)   At the optimum, prices will depend on qualities. Under the strong assumption that the inverse demand functions

$$p_i = f_i^h(q, x^h, r^h) \tag{6}$$

exist, we can consider the expenditure functions at the optimum

$$R^h(f^h(q, x^h, r^h), q, u^{h*}). \tag{7}$$

Now let the consumer optimally adjust to qualities, that is let him behave as if he could choose the cost-minimizing quality levels q_k. Minimizing R^h with respect to q_k implies

$$\sum_i \frac{\partial R^h}{\partial p_i} \cdot \frac{\partial f_i^h}{\partial q_k} + \frac{\partial R^h}{\partial q_k} = 0. \tag{8}$$

Using Shephard's lemma we obtain

$$\frac{\partial R^h}{\partial q_k} = -\sum_i \nu_{ik}^h x_i^h \tag{9}$$

where the $\nu_{ik}^h = \partial f_i^h/\partial q_k$ measure the price-quality effects. If some particular quality influences its own price only, the above result reduces to

$$\frac{\partial R^h}{\partial q_k} = -\nu_{kk}^h x_k^h \tag{10}$$

which is nicely analogous to the differentiation of an expenditure function with respect to a single price: once again, the influence is the greater, the higher consumer's consumption of the respective good. The parameter ν_{kk}^h gives the necessary transformation from the quality to the quantity and expenditure spaces. For consumption goods $x_i > 0$, the price-quality effect ν_{kk}^h is usually expected to be positive (Sheshinski, 1976).[9] Hence $\partial R^h / \partial q_k$ will typically be negative: utility is maintained at lower expenditures, the consumer being compensated by the higher quality level.

(ii) A further interpretation of $\partial R^h / \partial q_k$ assumes an individual quality-quantity trade-off as follows

$$\widetilde{f}^h(q, x^h) \leq 0. \tag{11}$$

According to this constraint, the consumer's options are not only restricted by an income ceiling but also by particular limitations in the choice of qualities. The best example refers to quality levels q which are measured in units of time, as is usual in transportation economics where lower waiting and travelling times are taken as the best proxies for higher quality. In these cases the constraint (11) simply reads as

$$\sum_k q_k x_k^h \leq Q - Q(\neg k) \tag{12}$$

where $k \in K$ are the goods supplied by the transportation enterprise, Q is an upper limit of time for any flow of consumption, say 24 hours, and $Q(\neg k)$ is time devoted to consumption of non-transportation goods and leisure. The usual analysis treats both Q and $Q(\neg k)$ as exogenous variables (Glaister, 1982).

Given such a quality-transformation constraint, the consumer is restricted in minimizing his expenditures so as to achieve utility u^{h*}. Consider, therefore, the expenditure function at the optimum and let the consumer optimally adjust to qualities, that is let him behave as if he could choose the optimal quality levels q_k

$$\min_{q_k} R^h(p, q, u^{h*}) \quad \text{subject to} \quad \widetilde{f}^h(q, x^h) \leq 0. \tag{13}$$

Restricting ourselves to interior solutions we obtain the following necessary conditions for the expenditure function to be optimal with respect to qualities

$$\frac{\partial R^h}{\partial q_k} = \nu^h \left(\frac{\partial \widetilde{f}^h}{\partial q_k} + \sum_i \frac{\partial \widetilde{f}^h}{\partial x_i^h} \cdot \frac{\partial x_i^h}{\partial q_k} \right); \qquad k \in K \tag{14}$$

---

[9] The second derivative of the inverse demand function $\partial f_i^h / \partial q_i \partial x_i^h$ is more complicated. If this derivative is negative, quality and quantity can be regarded as substitutes; if it is positive, they can be regarded as complements (Sheshinski, 1976).

where $\nu^h \leq 0$ is the Lagrangean multiplier of the above optimization approach. The optimum conditions become more appealing if we concentrate on a public-transportation enterprise which is constrained by (12). Then the expenditure function follows the condition

$$\frac{\partial R^h}{\partial q_k} = \nu^h \left(x_k^h + \sum_{i \in K} q_i \frac{\partial x_i^h}{\partial q_k} \right); \qquad k \in K. \tag{15}$$

16.2.2   On the Producer's Quality Choice

The production side of our model must also be extended by explicitly including the quality indicators q. Hence the public enterprise has a production function

$$g(z, q) = 0. \tag{16}$$

In equilibrium, production will be influenced by qualities in a twofold way:

• it costs more to produce a given quantity of some good the higher its quality. This *direct influence* is expressed by c_{qk}, the marginal labor costs of an increase in quality q_k

$$c_{qk} := \frac{\partial g / \partial q_k}{\partial g / \partial z_o}; \tag{17}$$

• changing quality leads to changing demand which, in turn, influences the costs of production. This *indirect influence* is expressed by

$$\sum_i c_i \frac{\partial z_i^D}{\partial q_k} \quad \text{in the case of non-compensated demand} \tag{18}$$

or, alternatively, by

$$\sum_i c_i \frac{\partial \hat{z}_i}{\partial q_k} \quad \text{in the case of compensated demand} \tag{19}$$

where $\partial z_i / \partial q_k$ is defined in a similar way to that in which $\partial z_i / \partial p_k$ was defined in chapter 3. The exact definitions follow in the next subsection.

It is a little more complicated to deal with quality influences on private-enterprise production. We assume that private enterprises adjust to those qualities q_k which are determined by the public enterprise. Consider the production function of the j-th private enterprise, $g^j(y^j, q) = 0$. Since efficiency is maintained for all price and quality changes, we obtain the following condition

$$\sum_k \left(\sum_i \frac{\partial g^j}{\partial y_i^j} \cdot \frac{\partial y_i^j}{\partial p_k} \right) dp_k + \sum_k \left(\frac{\partial g^j}{\partial q_k} + \sum_i \frac{\partial g^j}{\partial y_i^j} \cdot \frac{\partial y_i^j}{\partial q_k} \right) dq_k = 0 \qquad (20)$$

which, after division by $\partial g^j / \partial y_o^j$, is fulfilled if

$$\sum_i c_i^j \frac{\partial y_i^j}{\partial p_k} = 0; \qquad k \in K \qquad (21)$$

and

$$c_{qk}^j + \sum_i c_i^j \frac{\partial y_i^j}{\partial q_k} = 0; \qquad k \in K. \qquad (22)$$

$c_{qk}^j := (\partial g^j / \partial q_k)/(\partial g^j / \partial y_o^j)$ are marginal costs of increasing quality at constant quantities y_i^j (direct influence). $\Sigma_i c_i^j (\partial y_i^j / \partial q_k)$ measures the indirect influence on costs,[10] via changing y_i^j.

16.3   Optimal Qualities, Prices and Quantities

16.3.1   The Optimization Approach

In order to show the basic consequences of an optimal quality choice, let us go back to chapter 3 and extend the analysis by the explicit inclusion of quality. As in chapter 3, we assume that the board controls prices $\{p_k, \ k \in K \subset I\}$, netputs $\{z_i, \ i \in I\}$ and, occasionally, lump-sum incomes $\{r^h, h = 1, \ldots, H\}$. In this chapter the board also controls a subset of all *qualities* $\{q_k, k \in K \subset I\}$. It is plausible to assume that the board controls the qualities of those, and only those, goods whose prices it controls.[11] Private enterprises which supply or demand goods $k \in K$ have to take the publicly fixed quality as given (in the same way as they have to accept the publicly fixed price). We assume that the board has information on the net supply functions $y_i^j (p, q)$ and that these functions always exist even if the private firms are monopolies.

Since it is more convenient for the reader, let us present the entire optimization approach instead of continually referring to chapter 3. The board of

---

[10] Recall $c_i^j := (\partial g^j / \partial y_i^j)/(\partial g^j / \partial y_o^j)$.

[11] Our model can be extended easily to quality regulation of goods which are supplied only privately, e.g. DIN-norms referring to $q_i, i \notin K$. Such problems, however, are beyond the scope of this book.

the firm maximizes the following Lagrangean function:[12]

$$\mathcal{F} = W(\cdot) - \sum_{i=o}^{n} \alpha_i \left[\sum_h x_i^h(\cdot) - z_i - \sum_j y_i^j(\cdot) \right] -$$

$$- \beta g(\cdot) - \overline{\gamma} \left[\Pi^o - \sum_{i=o}^{n} p_i z_i \right]. \tag{23}$$

The necessary maximum conditions are as follows:

$$\sum_h \frac{\partial W}{\partial v^h} \frac{\partial v^h}{\partial p_k} - \sum_i \alpha_i \left(\sum_h \frac{\partial x_i^h}{\partial p_k} - \sum_j \frac{\partial y_i^j}{\partial p_k} \right) + \overline{\gamma} z_k = 0; \quad k \in K, \tag{24}$$

$$\alpha_i - \beta \frac{\partial g}{\partial z_i} + \overline{\gamma} p_i = 0; \quad i = o, \dots, n, \tag{25}$$

$$\frac{\partial W}{\partial v^h} \frac{\partial v^h}{\partial r^h} - \sum_i \alpha_i \frac{\partial x_i^h}{\partial r^h} = 0; \quad h = 1, \dots, H, \tag{26}$$

$$\sum_h \frac{\partial W}{\partial v^h} \cdot \frac{\partial v^h}{\partial q_k} - \sum_i \alpha_i \left(\sum_h \frac{\partial x_i^h}{\partial q_k} - \sum_j \frac{\partial y_i^j}{\partial q_k} \right) - \beta \frac{\partial g}{\partial q_k} = 0; \quad k \in K. \tag{27}$$

16.3.2   *Optimal Qualities in the Non-compensated Case*

Since this is the more realistic case, let us first exclude any redistribution of lump-sum incomes. We substitute (25) into (27), transform as usual, and obtain

$$\sum_h \lambda^h \frac{\partial v^h}{\partial q_k} - (1 - \gamma) \sum_h \sum_i p_i \frac{\partial x_i^h}{\partial q_k} - \sum_i (c_i - p_i) \left[\sum_h \frac{\partial x_i^h}{\partial q_k} - \sum_j \frac{\partial y_i^j}{\partial q_k} \right] =$$

$$= c_{qk} - (1 - \gamma) \sum_i \sum_j p_i \frac{\partial y_i^j}{\partial q_k}; \quad k \in K. \tag{28}$$

---

[12] Needless to say, the conditions of avoiding degeneration must be changed accordingly. (Cfr. Footnotes 9 and 10 in chapter 3.)

These are the basic equations on qualities in the same way as eqs. (3–11) are the basic equations on prices. 'Basic' means that the economic interpretation of eqs. (28) centers on quality whereas the interpretation of eqs. (3–11) centers on prices (nothwithstanding the fact that qualities, prices, and quantities are always determined together by the same system of equations). The degree of complexity of eqs. (28) is similar to eqs. (3–11). They consist of five terms which we shall consider now, reading from left to right.

Social Valuation of Quality Changes

The first term describes the social valuation of changing quality. It is convenient to denote

$$Q_k := -\sum_h \lambda^h \frac{\partial v^h}{\partial q_k}; \qquad k \in K. \tag{29}$$

Q_k can be transformed by using the extended version of Roy's identity we described in the last subsection. Applying the general formula (5) we obtain

$$Q_k = \sum_h \lambda^h \frac{\partial v^h}{\partial r^h} \frac{\partial R^h}{\partial q_k}; \qquad k \in K. \tag{30}$$

The social valuation of changing lump-sum incomes, $\lambda^h(\partial v^h/\partial r^h)$, will usually decrease with increasing lump-sum income, reflecting the distributional considerations of the enterprise's board. However $\partial R^h/\partial q_k$ is very likely to increase with increasing lump-sum income, reflecting the higher sensitivity to quality of higher-income earners. Hence, in general we cannot say whether Q_k is higher or lower for a typical necessity than for a luxury.

This is not a surprising result. If higher-income earners are more sensitive to quality, the explicit inclusion of quality in our optimization must imply a stronger weighting of higher-income earners' tastes. A board which does not want to indirectly favor higher-income earners in this way must choose a W which gives a higher value to $\partial W/\partial v^h$ for lower-income earners. Hence, the achievement of a particular degree of redistribution[13] calls for different social welfare functions depending on the inclusion or exclusion of quality problems.[14]

---

[13] The degree of redistribution is meant to be defined with respect to some concentration measure (Lorenz, Gini etc.) applied to the individual utilities v^h.

[14] As we could well expect, substituting for $\partial R^h/\partial q_k$ does not help to solve the above problems but only shows them up once again. Therefore it may be left to the reader as an exercise to insert either (9), or (10), or (14), or (15) into (30) and to consider the consequences.

For reasons of completeness let us next mention the second term of (28). It is very easy to handle. Differentiating the individual consumer's budget constraint $\Sigma_i p_i x_i^h - r^h = 0$ with respect to quality q_k, we can see that

$$\sum_i p_i \frac{\partial x_i^h}{\partial q_k} = 0; \qquad k \in K. \tag{31}$$

Therefore this second term vanishes.

Quality Allocation in the Public Sector

The third and the fourth terms of (28) reflect the problems of quality allocation in the public sector, and the influence of quality allocation on the Lerner indices (price-cost margins). The third term can be rewritten by defining

$$\frac{\partial z_i^D}{\partial q_k} := \sum_h \frac{\partial x_i^h}{\partial q_k} - \sum_j \frac{\partial y_i^j}{\partial q_k}; \qquad k \in K, \tag{32}$$

similarly to (3–17). The fourth term, c_{qk}, is already given in its definitive form.

The interpretation of the third and fourth terms of (28) is complicated because the qualities q_k do not appear explicitly, but in the optimum influence all relevant variables, even the prices p. Moreover, $(c_i - p_i)$ also are of central importance in the marginal conditions (3–11), and thus we should always interpret the marginal conditions (3–11) and (28) together, for instance by substituting for $(c_i - p_i)$ from (3–11) into (28). In the general formulation the result of such a procedure is a tedious formula which cannot be interpreted straightforwardly, but in special cases the procedure may lead to nice results as shown later in the book with examples of particular price-quality choices.

The Public Enterprise and the Private Sector

The fifth term in (28) reflects the adjustment of the public enterprise to the private economy. The problems of interpretation are similar to those just mentioned. Generally the economic interpretation is easier if eq. (22) is added to obtain a corrected fifth term as follows

$$(1 - \gamma) \sum_j c_{qk}^j + (1 - \gamma) \sum_i \sum_j (c_i^j - p_i) \frac{\partial y_i^j}{\partial q_k}. \tag{33}$$

The Basic Equation Rewritten

Introducing the new definitions and reformulations above we can rewrite (28), the basic equations on qualities, in the following way

$$\sum_i (c_i - p_i) \frac{\partial z_i^D}{\partial q_k} =$$

$$= -[c_{qk} + Q_k] - (1 - \gamma) \sum_j c_{qk}^j - (1 - \gamma) \sum_i \sum_j (c_i^j - p_i) \frac{\partial y_i^j}{\partial q_k} \tag{34}$$

which corresponds to (3–21) above.

16.3.3 Compensating for Income Effects

Let us now give the board the right to control the distribution of lump-sum incomes $\{r^h, h = 1, \dots, H\}$. The basic equations on qualities (28) can be transformed by the use of the optimum conditions for lump-sum incomes[15] which after substituting the quality extended version of Roy's identity equal

$$\frac{\partial W}{\partial v^h} \cdot \frac{\partial v^h}{\partial q_k} = -\sum_i \alpha_i \frac{\partial R^h}{\partial q_k} \frac{\partial x_i^h}{\partial r^h}; \qquad h = 1, \dots, H; \qquad k \in K. \tag{35}$$

The incomes are redistributed in such a way that for each consumer the weighted sum of all quality induced income effects is equated to the board's valuation of the quality induced utility change. Hence, the board's valuation and the quality induced income effects cancel. Formally, we substitute (35) into (28) and define

$$\frac{\partial \hat{z}_i}{\partial q_k} := \left[\sum_h \left(\frac{\partial x_i^h}{\partial q_k} + \frac{\partial R^h}{\partial q_k} \cdot \frac{\partial x_i^h}{\partial r^h} \right) - \sum_j \frac{\partial y_i^j}{\partial q_k} \right]; \qquad k \in K \tag{36}$$

where $\hat{z}_i$ is compensated demand, compensation referring to prices and qualities. The basic conditions on quality can then be written as follows:[16]

$$\sum_i (c_i - p_i) \frac{\partial \hat{z}_i}{\partial q_k} = -\left[c_{qk} + (1 - \gamma) \sum_h \frac{\partial R^h}{\partial q_k} \right] -$$

$$- (1 - \gamma) \sum_j c_{qk}^j - (1 - \gamma) \sum_i \sum_j (c_i^j - p_i) \frac{\partial y_i^j}{\partial q_k}; \qquad k \in K. \tag{37}$$

---

[15] Equations (26) above.

[16] Differentiating the budget constraint $\Sigma_i p_i x_i^h = r^h$ we obtain $\Sigma_i p_i(\partial x_i^h / \partial r^h) = 1$. This property is used to transform $(1-\gamma)\Sigma_h(\partial R^h / \partial q_k)\Sigma_i p_i(\partial x_i^h / \partial r^h) = (1-\gamma)\Sigma_h(\partial R^h / \partial q_k)$.

These are the basic equations on qualities in the same way as eqs. (3–24) are the basic equations on prices, if in both cases income effects are excluded. (Although, of course, qualities, quantities, prices and lump-sum incomes are determined simultaneously by the same system of equations.)

Comparing (34) and (37) shows that the optimal lump-sum redistribution leads to a shift from non-compensated to 'quality compensated' demand. It also excludes the social valuations of individual incomes, which can easily be seen by substituting $Q_k = \Sigma_h \lambda^h (\partial v^h / \partial r^h)(\partial R^h / \partial q_k)$ for $(1-\gamma)\Sigma_h(\partial R^h / \partial q_k)$. Hence, optimal qualities and optimal prices no longer reflect those distributional features which tend to favor necessities and to burden luxuries.

16.4   Basic Rules for Optimal Quality

Recall the treatment of basic rules for optimal prices in chapters 7 to 10. This section presents the analogue for optimal qualities. Starting point of the analysis are the equations (34) for the non-compensated case and (37) for the compensated base. Unfortunately, quality q_k itself never appears explicitly in the marginal conditions, it only has an implicit influence on other variables, as shown by the respective partial derivatives such as $\partial z_i / \partial q_k$. Hence, any statement on quality q_k can only be of an indirect type. Prices p_k, on the contrary, always appear directly in the marginal conditions, which allows statements of a direct type. This does not mean that the consideration of quality indicators is without interest. First, the introduction of quality indicators shows the restricted validity of the marginal-cost or Ramsey rules etc. Second, the theory is very useful if the relevant quality responses are specified, that is for any econometric investigation.

Because of the above difficulties of interpretation, the following analysis is restricted to the question of how the best-known basic rules of public sector pricing change if quality indicators are considered. For this purpose remember the four assumptions we used to deduce basic rules from the general model of chapter 3. The narrowest formulation was presented at the beginning of chapter 7 on marginal-cost pricing:

(i)   only prices of publicly produced goods are controlled; uncontrolled prices equal marginal costs c_i in the public sector;[17]

(ii)   the private sector is perfectly competitive;

(iii)   the distribution of lump-sum incomes is optimally chosen, hence we deal with compensated demand;

(iv)   there is no revenue-cost constraint on the public sector.

---

[17]   If only output prices are regulated, this assumption implies equality of c_i and C_i for all net outputs. See subsection 2.4.4 above.

16.4.1 The Case that Corresponds to Marginal-Cost Pricing

To deal with optimal quality, we maintain all four assumptions (i) to (iv). The board of the firm has to consider the marginal conditions (7–1)

$$\sum_{i \in K}(p_i - c_i)\frac{\partial \hat{z}_i}{\partial p_k} = 0; \qquad k \in K \qquad (7\text{--}1)$$

and the following special case of the marginal conditions (37)[18]

$$\sum_{i \in K}(p_i - c_i)\frac{\partial \hat{z}_i}{\partial q_k} = c_{qk} + \sum_{h}\frac{\partial R^h}{\partial q_k}; \qquad k \in K. \qquad (38)$$

Let us assume both matrices $(\partial \hat{z}_i/\partial p_k)$ and $(\partial \hat{z}_i/\partial q_k)$ have full rank. The optimal prices and qualities can then be obtained by solving the total system of marginal conditions which consists of the two subsystems that have been presented above. In that case, (7–1) directly implies marginal-cost prices, whence a solution of the whole system of marginal conditions can only be achieved if

$$c_{qk} = -\sum_{h}\frac{\partial R^h}{\partial q_k}; \qquad k \in K. \qquad (39)$$

Thus we obtain a marginal condition for first-best qualities. In the marginal-cost price optimum the qualities have to be expanded until the marginal quality costs equal the sum of marginal utility gains as measured by the changes of the expenditure functions. This condition reflects the public-good properties of the qualities. c_{qk} is the marginal rate of transformation between quality and labor, see eq. (17). As the wage rate is normalized to unity, it is also a marginal rate of transformation between quality and income earned in the public sector $(p_o z_o)$. Each individual $\partial R^h/\partial q_k$ is a marginal rate of substitution between quality and the individual lump-sum income, see eq. (5). The first-best qualities, therefore, require the equality of a marginal rate of transformation and the sum of individual marginal rates of substitution, both rates defined between quality and income. This condition resembles the Samuelson condition on public goods. The relevant incomes, however, are defined differently in the transformation rate and in the substitution rates.

---

[18] Recall $c_{qk}^j + \Sigma_i c_i^j(\partial y_i^j/\partial q_k) = 0$ from (22). For perfect competition in the private sector, moreover, $\Sigma_i p_i(\partial y_i^j/\partial q_k) = 0$. Moreover, because of assumption (iv) we obtain $\gamma = 0$.

16.4.2   The Case that Corresponds to Ramsey Prices

Recall once more our usual four assumptions, and abandon assumption (iv). We consider an optimal quality choice in the presence of a fixed revenue-cost constraint Π^o. The resulting pricing rule is the corresponding case to Ramsey pricing. We have to consider the marginal conditions (8–1)

$$\sum_{i \in K} (p_i - c_i) \frac{\partial \hat{z}_i}{\partial p_k} = -\gamma z_k; \qquad k \in K \tag{8–1}$$

and the following special case of the marginal conditions (37)

$$\sum_{i \in K} (p_i - c_i) \frac{\partial \hat{z}_i}{\partial q_k} = c_{qk} + (1 - \gamma) \sum_h \frac{\partial R^h}{\partial q_k}; \qquad k \in K. \tag{40}$$

We assume, once again, both matrices $(\partial \hat{z}_i / \partial p_k)$ and $(\partial \hat{z}_i / \partial q_k)$ have full rank. The Ramsey prices and qualities can then be obtained by solving the total system of marginal conditions which consists of the two subsystems that have been presented above.

How to interpret the resulting qualities and prices? Remember the interpretation of Ramsey pricing in chapter 8: if an enterprise's board applies Ramsey prices, it behaves like a monopolist who miscalculates all price elasticities of demand by the same factor $1/\gamma$. We could therefore expect a similar result to hold if a profit-maximizing monopolist and a welfare-maximizing public enterprise under a budget constraint do not only set optimal prices, but also optimal qualities.

Consider a monopolist who calculates his profit maximizing prices p_k, and qualities q_k, $k \in K$, considering production possibilities $g(z, q) = 0$ and acting along compensated demand functions $\hat{z}_k(p, q)$. His profit optimum is characterized by the following two systems of marginal conditions[19]

$$\sum_{i \in K} (p_i - c_i) \frac{\partial \hat{z}_i}{\partial p_k} = -z_k; \qquad k \in K, \tag{41}$$

$$\sum_{i \in K} (p_i - c_i) \frac{\partial \hat{z}_i}{\partial q_k} = c_{qk}; \qquad k \in K. \tag{42}$$

---

[19] Write the production function as $z_o = z_o(z_1(p,q),...,z_n(p,q),q)$ and consider $\partial z_o / \partial z_i = -(\partial g / \partial z_i)/(\partial g / \partial z_o) = -c_i$ and $\partial z_o / \partial q_k = -(\partial g / \partial q_k)/(\partial g / \partial z_o) = -c_{qk}$. The monopolistic optimum then follows from an optimization approach $max_{p_k, q_k} \Sigma_{i=1}^n p_i z_i(\cdot) + p_o z_o(\cdot)$. Remember that $p_i = c_i$ for all $i \notin K$ and that the monopolist applies compensated demand functions.

Hence we can still conclude that the welfare-maximizing board behaves as if it were an unconstrained profit-maximizing monopolist who inflates all compensated price elasticities by $1/\gamma$. In the usual case of $1/\gamma > 1$[20] the board will react more carefully in the price space than a monopolist would, overaccentuating consumers' price responses. With respect to quality, the profit maximizer neglects consumer welfare gains, the welfare maximizer takes them into account. As these gains are measured by the negative $\Sigma_h \partial R^h / \partial q_k$, we may conclude that the welfare maximizer behaves like a monopolist who underestimates the marginal quality costs c_{qk} which implies a tendency toward higher qualities.

16.4.3   Pricing with Distributional Aims

We now abandon assumption (iii). Hence, we deal with the optimal quality choice in the presence of a revenue-cost constraint Π^o and in the presence of uncompensated demand. As the distribution of lump-sum incomes is exogenously given, the distributional value judgments of the board of the firm cannot lead to a redistribution of incomes, but are explicitly reflected by the public price and quality structure. We exclude private demand and supply of publicly controlled goods k. This additional assumption could easily be given up, as shown for optimal pricing in chapter 9. Consider the marginal conditions (9–1)

$$\sum_{i \in K}(p_i - c_i)\frac{\partial z_i^D}{\partial p_k} = -(1 - F_k)z_k; \qquad k \in K \tag{9-1}$$

and the following special case of conditions (34)

$$\sum_{i \in K}(p_i - c_i)\frac{\partial z_i^D}{\partial q_k} = Q_k + c_{qk}; \qquad k \in K. \tag{43}$$

As in the case of Ramsey pricing, we can compare these two systems of equations with the corresponding equations which result from profit maximization. The welfare-maximizing board behaves as if it were a profit maximizer who inflates all price elasticities by factors $1/(1 - F_k)$. With respect to quality the profit maximizer neglects the welfare gains of the consumers, Q_k, which are explicitly considered by the welfare maximizer. As in the Ramsey case this implies an underestimation of the marginal quality costs ($Q_k < 0$) which in turn implies a tendency toward higher qualities.

---

[20] Π^o exceeds the unconstrained welfare-optimal revenue-cost difference.

16.4.4   *Adjustment to Private Monopolistic Pricing*

Consider the pricing rule which includes the possibility that uncontrolled prices deviate from their respective marginal costs in the public and in the private sector. We deal with compensated demand, obtaining the systems of equations (37) and (10–2):

$$\sum_i (p_i - c_i) \frac{\partial \hat{z}_i}{\partial p_k} = -\gamma z_k$$

$$- (1 - \gamma) \sum_i \sum_j (p_i - c_i^j) \frac{\partial y_i^j}{\partial p_k}; \quad k \in K, \qquad (10\text{–}2)$$

$$\sum_i (p_i - c_i) \frac{\partial \hat{z}_i}{\partial q_k} = c_{qk} + (1 - \gamma) \sum_h \frac{\partial R^h}{\partial q_k} + (1 - \gamma) \sum_j c_{qk}^j$$

$$- (1 - \gamma) \sum_i \sum_j (p_i - c_i^j) \frac{\partial y_i^j}{\partial q_k}; \quad k \in K. \qquad (3\text{–}53)$$

The optimal prices and qualities can be found by simultaneously solving these two systems of equations.

PART THREE
POSITIVE THEORY

PRICING POLICIES FOR
POLITICAL AND BUREAUCRATIC AIMS

17
Winning Votes[1]

17.1 How to Define Expected Votes[2]

Pricing of public utilities tends to be one of the major determinants of the political climate in local communities. Local politicians try to postpone any price increases for local public transportation, gas and electricity until after the next election. The popularity of any local politician seems to be at stake if local public utilities work inefficiently or if price increases are in the offing.

Consider a politician who chooses public prices so as to maximize votes. In a democratic context the political choice is only well-defined if there are at least two alternatives. Consider therefore *two price systems*, p and p^o, both market clearing and technologically feasible and subject to the same profit constraint Π^o. Because of the identical constraints, vote maximization has to consider the trade-off frontier where some prices p_i are lower than p_i^o, and some others are higher. The trivial cases of $p \ll p^o$ or $p \gg p^o$ are excluded.

Assume $\{p_k, k \in K\}$ to be the instruments of a politician who wants to maximize votes and $\{p_k^o, k \in K\}$ to be a given reference price system. Various institutional stories can be told to rationalize this reference price system. We have, for example, at least the following two possibilities: according to one we treat public pricing in a two-party competition model, according to the other we treat it in the context of a monopoly approach of public choice. In the first, p^o would be the price system offered to the voter by the other political party.[3] In the second, p^o would be a sort of 'reversion policy' that will apply if the price system p is not supported by a majority, similar to

---

[1] Parts of this chapter are taken from Bös–Zimmermann (1987).

[2] On the surface the approach of the present chapter bears some resemblance to the theory of probabilistic voting, see in particular the recent book by Coughlin (1992). This theory imputes to any individual a probabilistic choice where the probabilities are proportional to utility. Each individual has a probabilistic voting density function which characterizes his choice probabilities and this density function is also his utility function. Hence the individual decides on the basis of a density function and the politician has to take account of this individual probabilistic behavior. Probabilistic voting is very different from our approach where the individual applies a neoclassical utility function which, generally, has nothing to do with a density function. It is only at the next stage of the analysis that a density function is introduced into our approach: the politician who is imperfectly informed about the influence of personality factors (sympathy) on the voters' decisions, applies a density function of individual utility as far as sympathy is concerned.

[3] This implies Nash-type behavior of the political duopolists. Note that we do not

Romer–Rosenthal's (1979) agenda-setter model. Finally p^o can simply mean the present system of prices. In that case we describe a referendum on public pricing or a demoscopic opinion poll.

Regardless of which of the above versions we adopt, any politician will always be interested in finding that platform p which the greatest possible number of voters prefers to p^o.[4]

Voters, however, do not make their decision based on economic criteria alone. Therefore, we assume an individual h to vote for a price system p if

$$\omega^h + s^h \geq 0. \tag{1}$$

ω^h measures the 'economic' component of the voter's decision, the utility gain or loss from price system p

$$\omega^h(p, r^h) := v^h(p, r^h) - v^h(p^o, r^h). \tag{2}$$

s^h, on the other hand, measures the 'sympathy' or 'antipathy' component of his decision. Some individual might not be willing to vote for platform p which increases his utility because he 'does not like' the politician who proposes price system p. On the other hand, somebody may be willing to vote for platform p which diminishes his utility because the proposal comes from 'his party'.[5]

Now turn to the *vote-maximizing politician*. The indicator function μ 'counts' yes-votes by awarding a 1 each time the yes-condition is fulfilled and a 0 when it is not:

$$\mu(\omega^h + s^h) = \begin{cases} 1 & \text{if } \omega^h + s^h \geq 0 \\ 0 & \text{if } \omega^h + s^h < 0 \end{cases}. \tag{3}$$

Every voter, of course, knows the exact values of his ω^h and s^h. The politician, however, is imperfectly informed of the individual voters' characteristics. Let us assume he knows the exact economic consequences of his

---

deal with a voting equilibrium where both parties react to each other. Only under very restrictive assumptions will such equilibria exist.

[4] If p^o happens to be the vote-maximizing price system, the politician will apply $p=p^o$. This case of indifference is excluded in the text.

[5] In Ungern-Sternberg (1983) the voters consider both their loyalty to a particular party and the economic consequences of a one-dimensional platform. Each voter is fully informed of his loyalty, the politicians know the density function of loyalty. The policy outcome of a two-party competition is shown to depend on the shape of the loyalty function, dealing with the polar cases of a uniform, a symmetric U-shaped and a symmetric inverted U-shaped distribution. Our model is further elaborated than Ungern-Sternberg's; it is multi-dimensional instead of one-dimensional; we concentrate on the variance of sympathy instead of on the shape.

pricing policy, as expressed by the utility differences w^h. He does not know exactly whether some particular person likes or dislikes him. He only knows that there is some distribution of sympathy and antipathy among the voters. For the politician, therefore, s is a random variable, $\tilde{s}$. Let him assume, without limitation of generality, that $\tilde{s}$ is normally distributed with density function $f(s^h)$, expected value zero and variance σ^2

$$f(s^h) = \frac{1}{\sigma\sqrt{2\pi}} \exp\left[-\frac{1}{2}\left(\frac{s^h}{\sigma}\right)^2\right]. \tag{4}$$

For any single individual the imperfectly informed politician assumes sympathy s^h to be distributed with $f(s^h)$.

Not being informed about the exact values of s^h, but only knowing that $\tilde{s}$ is a normally distributed random variable, the politician can only rely upon the expected value of any single vote. Replacing $w^h + s^h =: \Omega^h$, we obtain

$$\Phi_h(w^h) = \int_{-\infty}^{+\infty} \mu(w^h + s^h) f(s^h) ds^h = \int_{-\infty}^{+\infty} \mu(\Omega^h) f(\Omega^h - w^h) d\Omega^h \tag{5}$$

as shown in figure 16.

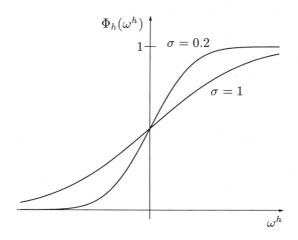

Figure 16

Figure 16 shows how an individual with utility difference ω^h can be expected to vote. For $\sigma^2 \to 0$ the voters would be expected to be pure homines oeconomici, deciding according to their utility difference only

$$\Phi_h(\omega^h) = \mu(\omega^h) = \begin{cases} 1 & \text{if } \omega^h \geq 0 \\ 0 & \text{if } \omega^h < 0 \end{cases}. \tag{6}$$

The higher σ^2, on the other hand, the more sympathy and antipathy will count, as shown in figure 16 for $\sigma = 0.2$ and $\sigma = 1$.

The objective function of the vote-maximizing politician results from aggregating the expected value of votes

$$\Phi(p) = \sum_{h=1}^{H} \Lambda(r^h)\Phi_h(\omega^h(p, r^h)), \tag{7}$$

where $\Lambda(r^h)$ measures the relative frequency of the expected value Φ_h in the population,[6] the population being subdivided into $h = 1, \ldots, H$ groups of identical people, $\Sigma_h \Lambda(r^h) = 1$.

Differentiating this objective function leads to

$$\frac{\partial\Phi}{\partial p_k} = \sum_{h=1}^{H} \Lambda(r^h) \int_{-\infty}^{+\infty} \mu(\Omega^h)\frac{\partial}{\partial p_k} f(\Omega^h - \omega^h)d\Omega^h. \tag{8}$$

Excluding all ranges where $\mu(\Omega^h) = 0$ we obtain

$$\frac{\partial\Phi}{\partial p_k} = \sum_{h=1}^{H} \Lambda(r^h) \int_{0}^{\infty} \frac{\partial}{\partial p_k} f(\Omega^h - \omega^h)d\Omega^h$$

$$= -\sum_{h=1}^{H} \Lambda(r^h) \int_{0}^{\infty} f'(\Omega^h - \omega^h)\frac{\partial\omega^h}{\partial p_k}d\Omega^h. \tag{9}$$

---

[6] Any bracket $\Lambda(r^h)$ consists of many people, which allows us to concentrate on the expected value alone, ignoring the variance.

Hence

$$\frac{\partial \Phi}{\partial p_k} = -\sum_{h=1}^{H} \Lambda(r^h) \frac{\partial v^h}{\partial p_k} \left[f(\Omega^h - \omega^h) \right]_0^\infty$$

$$= \sum_{h=1}^{H} \Lambda(r^h) \frac{\partial v^h}{\partial p_k} f(\omega^h).$$

(10)

For voters who follow economic reasoning only, $\sigma^2 = 0$, the differentiation (10) will degenerate. All $\omega^h \neq 0$ do not contribute to the sum. Therefore $\partial \Phi / \partial p_k \neq 0$ can only occur if there happen to be individuals whose income r^* leads to $\omega^h(r^*) = 0$. Then the whole weight of $f(\omega^h)$ is attached to those individuals and $\partial \Phi / \partial p_k = \infty$. Hence $\partial \Phi / \partial p_k$ varies erratically between 0 and ∞, depending not only on the incomes but also on the price vector p. For $\sigma^2 = 0$ it is therefore impossible to employ the usual optimization approach. Only if we assume a continuum of consumers, does everything work nicely (Bös–Zimmermann, 1987). Assuming this continuum to be an approximation of $H \to \infty$, we can treat the case of $\sigma^2 = 0$ as well as the case of $\sigma^2 > 0$ in the following pricing rules.

The influence of changing price p_k on the objective function according to (10) depends on the individual utility responses $\partial v^h / \partial p_k$ weighted by the number of individuals with the respective utility and on the politician's attention paid to the individual utility difference $f(\omega^h)$ as illustrated in figure 17.

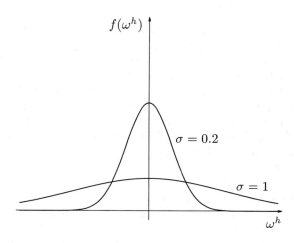

Figure 17

Note that originally we introduced $f(s^h)$ as the density function of the individual 'sympathy' variable s^h. In the course of the above differentiation we obtained $f(\omega^h)$ which can best be interpreted as the 'politician's attention': for any pair of p and p^o the politician must pay most attention to utility differences in a close neighborhood of $\omega^h = 0$. This includes voters with both small negative and small positive ω^h. The first group may represent the votes of tomorrow; the votes of the second can be lost easily. Both groups may be floating voters at the next election. Less attention is paid to sufferers whose ω^h is large and negative, but also to beneficiaries with large positive ω^h. The sympathy of the first can be won only at disproportionate effort; the votes of the second seem almost certain.

17.2   On Prices Which Maximize Expected Votes

Which price structure will a politician employ who follows the political strategy of maximizing $\Phi(p)$? As a special case of our general rule (4–9) we obtain

$$\sum_{i=o}^{n}(p_i - c_i)\frac{\partial z_i^D}{\partial p_k} = -(1 - POL_k)z_k; \qquad k \in K, \tag{11}$$

where (after inserting Roy's identity) POL_k equals

$$POL_k = \frac{1}{\beta_o}\sum_{h=1}^{H}\Lambda(r^h)f(\omega^h(p,r^h))\frac{\partial v^h}{\partial r^h}\cdot\frac{x_k^h}{x_k}; \qquad k \in K. \tag{12}$$

There is a striking formal similarity between distributionally oriented pricing (9–1) and political pricing (11). This raises the question whether democratic maximization of political sympathy and votes is a good vehicle for achieving distributionally desirable results.

Remember first that F_k in (9–1) weighted the individual consumption shares by $\lambda^h(\partial v^h/\partial r^h)$, which is always assumed to be a decreasing function of individual incomes. Weighting by such a decreasing function can be found also in POL_k. In POL_k, however, only the individual marginal utilities $(\partial v^h/\partial r^h)$ are of relevance, which excludes many of the typical features of distribution policy as represented by λ^h, for instance Rawlsian policy.

Can we argue that $\Lambda(\cdot)f$ replace the social valuation λ^h? $\Lambda(r^h)$ is an approximation to a density function of the income distribution. From empirical estimates we know that such a function increases for lower and decreases for higher incomes. Hence weighting with $\Lambda(r^h)$ will typically not imply particular emphasis on the *poor*. However, as there are usually more lower-income than higher-income earners, the $\Lambda(r^h)$-values favor policies beneficial to lower-income earners.

Finally, we have to emphasize the role of f. It stresses the importance of fishing for political sympathy and of being afraid of losing 'uncertain' voters. In other words, it stresses the interests of floating voters. If we assume a continuum of consumers we can let $\sigma^2 \to 0$ and look at the results. Then POL_k depends only on those individuals whose utility difference is just equal to zero. The vote-maximizing politician will therefore reduce the price of those goods that are mainly demanded by the floating voters. No particular distributional components remain in POL_k. The result has nothing to do with distribution policy. Unfortunately, in our general model we lack specific information as to which income earners are the floating voters and which publicly supplied goods are bought primarily by floating voters.

Summarizing, there are some plausible arguments which suggest that distributionally 'desirable' results may follow from political pricing. However, no general conclusions can be drawn.

18
Minimizing Price Indices

In countries with large public-enterprise sectors, the government may be in a position to significantly influence price indices through the pricing policies of its enterprises: indeed, attempts are sometimes made to reduce at least the reported rate of inflation in this manner (Bös, 1978a). The policies of the Heath government in Great Britain or of the Austrian governments of the end-forties and fifties provide appropriate examples. The incentives for aiming public pricing at the target of index minimization are greater, the higher the inflation rate and the greater the impact of indexed expenditures (for instance transfers whose annual increase is tied to a price index) on the budget.

The simplest attempt to reduce a price index drastically is by setting public prices of zero. However, such a policy is usually excluded in our general approach, since we explicitly consider a revenue-cost constraint. In our case the enterprise's board will consider one of the statistical price indices, as computed and published by some statistical office. Such indices compare quantities of money that can purchase a constant basket of commodities at changed prices. Thus substitution by consumers is ignored in the analysis (which leads to an overestimation of effective price changes when Laspeyres indices are used and an underestimation when Paasche indices are used). The most common index follows Laspeyres and takes as fixed some base period's basket of consumer goods. The index compares those expenditures which at changing prices are necessary to enable a representative consumer to buy an unaltered basket of consumer goods, $x_i^o > 0, i = d + 1, \ldots, n$. We denote variables of the base period by the superscript 'o' and define the board's objective function as follows

$$\Phi(p) = -\sum_{i=d+1}^{n} p_i x_i^o \Big/ \sum_{i=d+1}^{n} p_i^o x_i^o. \tag{1}$$

It is quite natural to assume a Laspeyres price index as the objective function of a positive theory of public-sector pricing. First, the statistical offices typically estimate time series only of Laspeyres price indices. Second, minimization of a true cost of living index would require a redistribution of non-labor incomes which we intentionally have excluded from positive-theory models.[1]

Minimizing a Laspeyres index in our positive-theory framework leads to a special case of the general pricing rule (4–9).[2] Prices have to be set according to

$$\sum_{i=o}^{n}(p_i - c_i)\frac{\partial z_i^D}{\partial p_k} = -(1 - L_k)z_k; \qquad k \in K, \qquad (2)$$

where

$$L_k = \frac{x_k^o}{x_k} \cdot \frac{1}{\Sigma p_i^o x_i^o} \cdot \frac{1}{\beta_o}; \qquad k \in K. \qquad (3)$$

According to the common practice of statistical offices x_i^o is always of the order of magnitude of individual demand, whereas $z_k (= x_k)$ is total supply. This problem can be taken into account by transforming (3) into

$$L_k = \frac{x_k^o}{\bar{z}_k} \cdot \frac{1}{H\Sigma p_i^o x_i^o} \cdot \frac{1}{\beta_o}; \qquad k \in K, \qquad (4)$$

where $\bar{z}_k = z_k/H$, with H as the number of consumers.

The periodical index revisions for developed countries have shown a shifting of consumption from necessities toward non-necessities. Hence, L_k is high for such goods where lower-income groups account for large shares of total consumption.

Therefore, the economic interpretation of eqs. (2) is analogous to the interpretation of eqs. (9–1). Qualitatively, minimizing a Laspeyres price index has the same distributional effects as maximizing a welfare function of a board with distributional aims! This result is due to the fact that, in minimizing a Laspeyres index account is taken of the weights of the base period in which necessities bought by lower-income groups get higher weights than those which would correspond to present consumption. This is a 'desirable' distributional consequence of the 'politician's error', i.e. of acting on the basis of past consumption patterns. It ought, perhaps, to induce second thoughts regarding

---

[1] If such a redistribution of non-labor incomes is taken into account, minimizing a true cost of living index leads to welfare-optimal, i.e. Ramsey pricing. For details see Bös (1978a).

[2] In chapters 18, 20 and 21 we use linear objective functions. Thus, there may arise particular problems in the case of constant returns to scale and with respect to corner solutions, but these will be ignored.

the frequent 'a priori' rejection of an index-minimization strategy for public pricing.

Furthermore, we have to bear in mind that, with a constant basket of commodities, the distributionally 'desirable' effects increase quantitatively with the passage of time, because deviations of actual consumption from the corresponding proportions of the basket of the base period increase with time. Therefore, after some years, minimizing a Laspeyres index may not only imply qualitatively equal, but also quantitatively similar, results as maximizing a distributionally weighted welfare function.

Before concluding this chapter let us deal with the following interesting question: what happens if in our model there is no revenue-cost constraint and the public firm still is instructed to minimize a Laspeyres index? One could expect zero prices as the natural outcome of such a procedure. However, this is not correct. If at zero price demand goes to infinity, the market-clearing conditions cannot be met. Hence, the market equilibria prevent zero prices and low positive prices will result from minimizing the price index. How low will they be? Once again[3] we have to refer the reader to the financial equilibrium of the economy. So there is an implicit revenue-cost constraint which restricts the profit of the public firm to the difference between the sum of lump-sum incomes and the private intramarginal profits.

---

[3] See p. 90 above.

19
Maximizing Budgets

An investigation of the political determination of price setting must not be restricted to vote maximization. It may be even more realistic to assume that a majority-seeking politician does not set the prices himself, but delegates this task to the bureaucracy of a ministry or of a public utility. The government becomes the 'sponsor', the price-setting board becomes the 'bureaucracy'. The government as owner or regulator in this full-information approach is able to perfectly control the bureaucracy.[1] Hence it could well hinder the bureaucracy to maximize output. However, it has decided not to do so but to fully accept the bureaucratic objective. Government's reluctance to accept this objective is only articulated by the amount of money the government (sponsor) is willing to award to the firm.

Bureaucrats attempt to build their own empires. If a bureaucrat wants to maximize his influence, his prestige, his income, he can do so most successfully by maximizing the number of his subordinates, the amount of money he can decide upon, in short: by maximizing his budget (Niskanen, 1971). However, the sponsor who has to grant the bureaucrat's budget will not appropriate any amount the bureaucrat applies for. The budget $\mathcal{B}$ the sponsor is willing to grant will depend on the output the bureau is offering

$$\mathcal{B} = \mathcal{B}(z_{d+1}, \ldots, z_n); \quad \mathcal{B}_k = \partial \mathcal{B}/\partial z_k > 0, \quad \partial^2 \mathcal{B}/\partial z_k^2 < 0, \tag{1}$$

where $z_k \geq 0, k = d+1, \ldots, n$, are the outputs of the bureau. For the one-service bureau with which he deals almost exclusively, Niskanen specifies $\mathcal{B}$ as a quadratic function of output, thus assuming a linearly decreasing marginal valuation of the bureau's service. This political valuation may be rooted in arguments about political sustainability. Needless to say, there exist many other possible explanations but we do not consider them here, because in this chapter we are interested mainly in the bureaucrat's behavior.

Consider a bureaucrat whose budget comes from two sources: the revenue from selling services to customers and from a grant $\mathcal{B}$. This is Niskanen's 'mixed bureau' (1971: 87–105) where the bureaucrat faces 'two separate demands' for any particular good: a market demand $x_k(p)$ and a 'sponsor demand' $\mathcal{B}_k$. However, there is a great difference between these 'demand'

---

[1] This is in contrast to Niskanen's (1971) approach. The assumption of full information will be given up in chapter 33 below.

functions: the sponsor does not consume any quantity of good z_k, but only pays for it. Hence, we shall characterize $\mathcal{B}_k$ as a political valuation function rather than as a demand function.

The mixed bureau can be interpreted as a public enterprise which sells goods or services at prices which do not cover costs and expects some ministry to cover its deficit. The most interesting economic feature of such a bureau is the particular demand-cost balance. In extreme situations the mixed bureau may be constrained by demand only: customers and sponsor are willing to grant a budget that altogether exceeds the costs. (Assume that a unique optimum exists in such a case because of the satiation properties of customers' and sponsor's demand.) Usually, however, the mixed bureau will be constrained by the deficit limit (or profit prescription) Π^o:

$$\sum_{i=o}^{n} p_i z_i + \mathcal{B}(z_{d+1}, \dots, z_n) = \Pi^o. \tag{2}$$

This revenue-cost constraint implies an interesting twofold political influence on the bureau. On the one hand, the sponsor is willing to appropriate grants $\mathcal{B}$, depending on the quantities produced. On the other hand, the bureau is expected to break even, or to avoid excessive deficits or to achieve a profit (depending on the sign of Π^o).

Given the revenue-cost constraint, the market-equilibrium conditions and its technology, the mixed bureau will maximize its budget, consisting of revenue plus grant

$$\Phi(p, z) = \sum_{i=d+1}^{n} p_i z_i + \mathcal{B}(z_{d+1}, \dots, z_n). \tag{3}$$

Note that in applying (4–9) we have not only to consider $\partial\Phi/\partial z_i$ and $\partial\Phi/\partial p_k$, but also to replace c_i with $c_i - \gamma\mathcal{B}_i$ for all outputs because of the unusual revenue-cost constraint (2). The resulting price structure for all output prices $k \in \{d+1, \dots, n\}^2$ can be written as

$$\frac{\beta_o}{1+\beta_o} \sum_{i=o}^{d} (p_i - c_i) \frac{\partial z_i^D}{\partial p_k} +$$
$$+ \sum_{i=d+1}^{n} \left[p_i - \left(\frac{\beta_o}{1+\beta_o} \right) c_i + \left(\frac{1+\beta_o\gamma}{1+\beta_o} \right) \mathcal{B}_i \right] \frac{\partial z_i^D}{\partial p_k} = -z_k. \tag{4}$$

---

[2] As already mentioned in chapter 4, footnote 3, we do not explicitly consider the regulation of input prices $k \in \{1,\dots,d\}$. The instruments of the bureaucrat therefore are all quantities $z_i, i \in I$, but only the output prices $p_k, k \in \{d+1,\dots,n\}$.

For the economic interpretation we compare this pricing structure with that of a profit-maximizing monopolist who maximizes $\Sigma_{i=o}^{n} p_i z_i$.[3] Monopoly pricing implies

$$\sum_{i=o}^{n}(p_i - c_i)\frac{\partial z_i^D}{\partial p_k} = -z_k; \qquad k \in \{d+1,\ldots,n\}. \tag{5}$$

Obviously, there are two main differences between the pricing structures (4) and (5):

(i) Budget maximization leads to output prices which are related not to marginal costs c_i, but to modified marginal costs

$$C_i := \delta_1 c_i - \delta_2 \mathcal{B}_i; \quad i \in \{d+1,\ldots,n\}; \quad 0 < \delta_1, \delta_2 < 1. \tag{6}$$

The exact meaning of δ_1 and δ_2 can be seen in (4). The 'social-cost function' in (6) demonstrates that the bureaucrat adopts a cost-benefit attitude, taking the political marginal valuation of output as a sort of external social benefit which reduces the marginal production costs. This may even imply negative social costs C_i.

How production economics and political economics are integrated depends on the coefficients δ_1 and δ_2. *Production-cost considerations* are determined by production-side problems only as we could well expect. (δ_1 depends on β_o only.) The more sensitively the achievable budget reacts to additional endowments of labor, the larger the influence of production costs on public pricing. (δ_1 is increasing in β_o.) the *political considerations*, on the other hand, depend on the demand-cost balance of the bureau. The percentage δ_2 is lowest if the budget constraint is non-binding ($\gamma = 0$) which is the demand-constrained case. The more customers and sponsor are willing to pay, the less necessary it is for the bureaucrat to concentrate on the political valuation of its outputs. How much the political valuation is taken into account in the limiting, demand-constrained, case depends on production-side arguments only. If, on the other hand, the required budget becomes larger (heuristically speaking, if γ increases), then the political valuation of outputs has to be considered increasingly. This structure of public pricing reveals the sponsor's political dilemma: he loses influence on public pricing the more money he is willing to pay for it.

(ii) Budget maximization distorts the input-output relations because the objective function relates to outputs only. Profit maximization does not lead to such a distortion because it weights inputs and outputs equally. This implies that the budget maximizer does not care so much about costs as the profit

---

[3] For a detailed treatment see subsection 8.1.1 above.

maximizer does and implies wasteful use of inputs which is only restrained by the revenue-cost constraint. Formally, in equation (4) the deviations of input prices from the respective shadow prices c_i are multiplied by $\beta_o/(1+\beta_o) < 1$. This is not the case in equation (5). This can be illustrated by rewriting equation (4) for a single output price p_k

$$
\begin{aligned}
p_k = C_k &- \frac{z_k}{\partial z_k^D/\partial p_k} - \frac{\beta_o}{1+\beta_o} \sum_{i=o}^{d}(p_i - c_i)\frac{\partial z_i^D/\partial p_k}{\partial z_k^D/\partial p_k} - \\
&- \sum_{\substack{i=d+1\\i\neq k}}^{n} (p_i - C_i)\frac{\partial z_i^D/\partial p_k}{\partial z_k^D/\partial p_k}; \qquad k \in \{d+1,\ldots,n\}.
\end{aligned}
\tag{7}
$$

The two reallocation effects, terms three and four on the right-hand side of the equation, clearly show that the input-related feedback of changes in p_k is weighted less than the output-related one.

20
Maximizing Output or Revenue, Saving Energy

Proving success with reference to output or revenue data is of particular interest for public enterprises. The latter are often prevented from seeking maximum profits and therefore the firm's success cannot be appraised with respect to profit data. An interesting example of the practical application of *output maximization* by a public enterprise is the maximization of passenger miles pursued by London Transport some years ago (Glaister–Collings, 1978; Bös, 1978b).

Although economists would argue that adding quantities of different goods does not make any sense, in practice such targets can often be found. For example consider patients of hospitals who receive first class (z_1) and second class (z_2) treatment, respectively, or rail passengers travelling first class (z_1) or second class (z_2). It can be seen that, under certain circumstances, the maximization of a sum of different quantities makes sense.

The board's objective function is as follows

$$\Phi(z) = \sum_{i=d+1}^{n} z_i. \tag{1}$$

As usual, we label the public enterprise's outputs by $i = d + 1, \ldots, n$. Maximizing the sum of outputs leads to a special case of the general pricing rule (4–9). For any output price p_k, $k \in \{d+1, \ldots, n\}$ we obtain a pricing structure

$$\sum_{i=o}^{d}(p_i - c_i)\frac{\partial z_i^D}{\partial p_k} + \sum_{i=d+1}^{n}\left(p_i - \left(c_i - \frac{1}{\beta_o}\right)\right)\frac{\partial z_i^D}{\partial p_k} = -z_k. \tag{2}$$

The board behaves as if it were a monopolist but underestimates the marginal costs ($c_i - 1/\beta_o$ instead of c_i). As each marginal-cost term is reduced by the same absolute amount, high-cost goods will be favored relatively less than low-cost goods, leading to the expected result of increasing the sales of the latter. The maximum output will therefore consist of too much low-cost output as compared with the welfare-optimal mix.

Let us now turn to *revenue maximization*. Revenue is a somewhat superficial indicator of economic success. Public enterprises are often inclined to use such an objective mainly because, due to the rapid growth in the past decades, these figures were growing at an impressive rate. Attempting to show business success with respect to revenue data is also of interest in private enterprises. Baumol (1959: 47–8) has pointed out that in business, any 'program which explicitly proposes any cut in sales volume, whatever the profit considerations, is likely to meet a cold reception'. Let us now investigate the economic consequences of revenue maximization as another possible objective of our board

$$\Phi(p, z) = \sum_{i=d+1}^{n} p_i z_i. \tag{3}$$

For any output price p_k, $k \in \{d+1, \dots, n\}$ we obtain the following pricing structure

$$\frac{\beta_o}{1 + \beta_o} \sum_{i=o}^{d} (p_i - c_i) \frac{\partial z_i^D}{\partial p_k} + \sum_{i=d+1}^{n} \left(p_i - \frac{\beta_o}{1 + \beta_o} c_i \right) \frac{\partial z_i^D}{\partial p_k} = -z_k, \tag{4}$$

which, as might be expected, equals the budget-maximizing result, except for the sponsor demand $\mathcal{B}_k$. Comparing the result of revenue maximization to monopoly pricing, we recognize two main differences:

(i)   the board behaves as if it were a monopolist, but relates output prices to underestimated marginal costs $C_i := [\beta_o/(1 + \beta_o)]c_i < c_i$. As every marginal-cost term is reduced by the same relative amount, there is no inherent tendency to mass produce low-cost goods, in contrast to the case of output maximization;

(ii)   the input-output relations are distorted because the objective of revenue maximization relates to outputs only in contrast to profit maximization which treats inputs and outputs symmetrically. (In equation (4) the deviations of input prices from the respective shadow costs c_i are multiplied by $\beta_o/(1 + \beta_o) < 1$).

Another simple objective of recent interest is *energy saving*.[1] Let good a be energy, supplied by private firms, $j \in A$. The board is interested in minimizing energy inputs and consumption. Hence it maximizes

$$\Phi = z_a - \sum_h x_a^h(\cdot) + \sum_{j \notin A} y_a^j(\cdot); \qquad a \in \{1, \dots, d\}. \tag{5}$$

---

[1]   For an overview on recent literature on energy conservation see the introduction of Lewis–Sappington (1992).

The energy-saving pricing structure is as follows

$$\sum_{i=o}^{n}(p_i - c_i)\frac{\partial z_i^D}{\partial p_k} - \frac{1}{\beta_o}\sum_{j\in A}\frac{\partial y_a^j}{\partial p_k} = -z_k; \quad k \in K = \{d+1,\dots,n\}. \quad (6)$$

The economic significance of this pricing structure can be seen best if we neglect cross-price elasticities among outputs, and therefore

$$\left[p_k - \left(c_k + \frac{1}{\beta_o}\frac{\Sigma_{j\in A}\partial y_a^j/\partial p_k}{\partial z_k^D/\partial p_k}\right)\right]\frac{\partial z_k^D}{\partial p_k} = -z_k; \quad k \in K. \quad (7)$$

Let us assume normal reaction of demand, $\partial z_k^D/\partial p_k < 0$, and complementarity of energy and other goods, $\partial y_a^j/\partial p_k < 0, j \in A$.[2] The more energy-intensive the production of some good, the higher in absolute value is the sum $\Sigma_{j\in A}\,\partial y_a^j/\partial p_k$.

Therefore, a board that follows pricing rule (7) behaves as if it were adhering to monopolistic pricing but overestimates the marginal costs. The more energy-intensive the production, the more the respective marginal costs must be overestimated, which leads to higher prices of energy-intensive goods.

The same results can be obtained if the only supplier of energy is the public sector. The objective of saving energy, then, is as follows:

$$\Phi = -\sum_h x_a^h(\cdot) + \sum_j y_a^j(\cdot); \quad a \in \{1,\dots,d\}. \quad (8)$$

The resulting price structure

$$\sum_{i\in G}(p_i - c_i)\frac{\partial z_i^D}{\partial p_k} - \frac{1}{\beta_o}\frac{\partial z_k^D}{p_k} = -z_k; \quad k \in G = \{a, d+1,\dots,n\} \quad (9)$$

can be interpreted analogously to the above case of private energy supply. (The complementarity of energy and other outputs implies $\partial z_a^D/\partial p_k < 0$, $a \neq k$; normally reacting demand implies $\partial z_k^D/\partial p_k < 0$, $k \in G$.)[3]

Moreover, the equations (9) imply a particular energy-pricing rule, If, for explanatory clarity, cross-price effects are once again suppressed, the following holds

---

[2] Recall footnote 6 of table 1, chapter 4.
[3] Recall, once again, footnote 6 of table 1, chapter 4.

$$\left[p_a - \left(c_a + \frac{1}{\beta_o} \right) \right] \frac{\partial z_a^D}{\partial p_a} = -z_a. \tag{10}$$

We obtain the expected tendency toward increasing energy prices because of 'overestimated' marginal costs. As could be expected, the input-minimizing pricing rule is just the reverse of the output-maximizing rule, as can easily be seen by comparing eqs. (2) and (10).

21
The Influence of Unions

The influence of employee pressure groups on nationalized enterprises or public utilities differs widely from country to country. A first extreme are labor-managed firms, like in the former Yugoslavia, the pressure groups being the workers' councils. They typically try to maximize value added per employee and the disincentive effects of such a policy are well-known from both practice and theory. Labor unions, taking a broader view, will oppose the job restrictions that often result from such a firm's policy. The other extreme are nationalized firms which behave in the same way as private firms without any special influence of labor unions.

Typically, however, nationalized enterprises or public utilities will follow a middle course. Their objectives will be some compromise between those of the board of the firm and the union. Such a result need not only follow from close contacts between representatives of public enterprises and unionists although such contacts will often be found. Additionally, representatives of a public firm may be less resistant to pressure from labor unions, since they may also be receiving pressure from the 'owner' – the government – to support employment goals similar to those advocated by the unions. In any case, unions will take a special interest in public firms, since they are usually large firms whose policy has a great influence on the whole economy.

We formulate the compromise between the bureaucratically-minded board of the firm and the representatives of some labor union in the following simple way. The board may be thought of as aiming to maximize output, while the union's utility may be assumed to depend on the number of working hours and on the real wage rate (Gravelle, 1984; Rees, 1984b). Hence, we impute to the public sector the following objective:

$$\Phi(p, z) = \sum_{i=d+1}^{n} z_i + \delta U(p_o, z_o) \tag{1}$$

where the first part describes the bureaucratic interest in output, the second part describes the union's interest in wage rate and working hours. The partial derivatives of the union's utility function are $U_p > 0$ and $U_z < 0$ (additional plausible assumptions are that $U_{pp} < 0$ and $U_{zz} > 0$).[1] $\delta > 0$ is a

---

[1] U_p is short-hand for $\partial U / \partial p_o$; similar interpretations hold for U_z, U_{pp}, U_{zz}.

parameter measuring the strength of the union's influence, which depends on its bargaining power (Rees, 1984b).

As usual, we treat inputs and outputs $\{z_i, i \in I\}$ and prices $\{p_k, k \in K\}$ as instruments. Additionally, the board has to fix the wage rate p_o. Choosing p_o as instrument gives rise to two special assumptions we need in modelling:

(i)   We relax the assumption of chapter 4 that 'goods with publicly controlled prices are neither supplied nor demanded by private firms $(z_k = x_k)$.' In this chapter we only assume $z_k = x_k$, $\forall k \neq o$. Otherwise the above assumption would exclude labor inputs of private firms.

(ii)   Instead of labor, good n is chosen as the numeraire good, $p_n = 1$. When applying (4–9) to our case, therefore, marginal costs are defined as $c_i := (\partial g/\partial z_i)/(\partial g/\partial z_n)$. Moreover, we define $\gamma = \overline{\gamma}/\beta_n$ with $\beta_n := \beta(\partial g/\partial z_n) > 0$.

We obtain the following price structure

$$\sum_{i=o}^{n} \left(p_i - \left(c_i - \frac{1}{\beta_n} \frac{\partial \Phi}{\partial z_i} \right) \right) \frac{\partial z_i^D}{\partial p_k} = -z_k; \quad k = d+1, \ldots, n, \qquad (2a)$$

$$\sum_{i=o}^{n} \left(p_i - \left(c_i - \frac{1}{\beta_n} \frac{\partial \Phi}{\partial z_i} \right) \right) \frac{\partial z_i^D}{\partial p_o} = -\gamma z_o - (1 - \gamma)x_o - \frac{\delta U_p}{\beta_n}, \qquad (2b)$$

where

$$\frac{\partial \Phi}{\partial z_i} = \begin{cases} \delta U_z & \text{for } i = o \\ 0 & \text{for } i = 1, \ldots, d \\ 1 & \text{for } i = d+1, \ldots, n \end{cases}.$$

The economic interpretation of this pricing structure is a little complicated. How regulated output prices deviate from marginal costs can be seen best if (2a) is transformed as follows

$$p_k - c_k = -\frac{z_k}{\partial z_k^D/\partial p_k} - \sum_{\substack{i=o \\ i \neq k}}^{n}(p_i - c_i)\frac{\partial z_i^D/\partial p_k}{\partial z_k^D/\partial p_k} - \sum_{i=d+1}^{n} \frac{1}{\beta_n} \cdot \frac{\partial z_i^D/\partial p_k}{\partial z_k^D/\partial p_k} -$$

$$- \frac{\delta U_z}{\beta_n} \cdot \frac{\partial z_o^D/\partial p_k}{\partial z_k^D/\partial p_k}; \quad k = d+1, \ldots, n. \qquad (3a)$$

The first two terms on the right-hand side can be interpreted similarly to the corresponding terms in eq. (10–3) above. There is, first, a *monopolistic tendency* for p_k to exceed c_k if demand reacts normally $(\partial z_k^D/\partial p_k < 0)$. There is, second, a *reallocation effect* toward p_k beyond c_k if all prices exceed the respective marginal costs and if good k is a 'substitute' for all other goods in the sense that $\partial z_i^D/\partial p_k > 0 \; \forall i \neq k$.

The third term reflects the *bureaucratic interest in output maximization*, again implying a tendency for p_k to be above c_k if good k is a 'substitute' for all other goods in the sense mentioned above.

The fourth term reflects the *union's interests*. It implies a tendency for lower p_k if decreasing p_k increases public labor input $(\partial z_o^D/\partial p_k > 0)$. This, in turn, implies a tendency toward lower prices of relatively labor-intensive goods. The economic intuition for these effects is as follows: let good k be labor intensive and let its price decrease. If demand reacts normally, z_k^D increases. Hence the use of inputs in the public sector will be shifted to a higher percentage of labor inputs. This tendency will be intensified if we consider the demand for other goods which will also be influenced by changing p_k.

The typical influence of a union's policy, summarized in the fourth term, will be stronger the greater the union's bargaining power (δ) and the more interested the union is in securing jobs (U_z). The influence will be counterbalanced by production-side effects (β_n).

It may be noted that one cannot deduce unambiguously whether an increase in the union's influence leads to wage increases or decreases. The reader may solve (2b) for $p_o - c_o$, to obtain a counterpart to equation (3a). In this new equation, call it (3b), the influence of the union on the wage level p_o is reflected by $(\delta/\beta_n)[U_z + U_p/(\partial z_o^D/\partial p_o)]$. If the public firm's labor demand reacts normally on wages, $\partial z_o^D/\partial p_o > 0$, the sign of this term is indeterminate given our assumptions $\delta > 0, U_z < 0, U_p > 0$ and given $\beta_n > 0$. As could be expected, what matters it is the relative weight of wages versus employment in the union's utility function.

22
Quality in Positive-Theory Models

The preceding chapters have described optimal positive-theory pricing when quality levels are held constant. Let us now consider how optimal quality levels are determined in the positive approach. How does optimal quality depend on the objective chosen? Will a vote maximizer choose a higher quality level than an output maximizer?

To answer such questions we choose a procedure which is analogous to that of chapter 16 where we dealt with quality in the context of welfare maximization. We assume that individual utility $v^h(p, q)$ depends on a vector of prices and on a vector of one-dimensional qualities. Since we deal with positive theory, we do not include any lump-sum redistribution and therefore drop the endowments r^h in the analysis.

The quality problem arises in all positive-theory approaches treated in the preceding chapters 17–21. For a comprehensive analysis of all the various objectives treated in these chapters, we impute to the board of the enterprise an objective function $\Phi(p, q, z)$. Details of the various meanings of this objective function have been given in chapter 4, table 1.

The instruments of the board are prices $\{p_k, \ k \in K\}$, netputs $\{z_i, \ i \in I\}$ and qualities $\{q_k, \ k \in K\}$. Private enterprises adjust to the publicly chosen quality levels as shown by their net supply functions $y_i^j(p, q)$. The board maximizes the following Lagrangean function

$$\mathcal{F} = \Phi(p, q, z) - \sum_{i=o}^{n} \alpha_i \left[\sum_h x_i^h(p, q) - z_i - \sum_j y_i^j(p, q) \right] -$$
$$- \beta g(q, z) - \overline{\gamma} \left[\Pi^o - \sum_{i=o}^{n} p_i z_i \right]. \tag{1}$$

To shorten the presentation we present only those marginal conditions which result from differentiating the above Lagrangean function with respect to q_k,[1]

$$\frac{\partial \Phi}{\partial q_k} - \sum_{i=o}^{n} \alpha_i \frac{\partial z_i^D}{\partial q_k} - \beta \frac{\partial g}{\partial q_k} = 0; \qquad k \in K. \tag{2}$$

---

[1] For $\partial \mathcal{F} / \partial p_k$ see (16–24) and for $\partial \mathcal{F} / \partial z_i$ see (16–25).

As usual, we substitute for α_i from the $\partial \mathcal{F}/\partial z_i$ conditions and divide by $\beta_o := \beta(\partial g/\partial z_o)$. We get the following result

$$\sum_{i=o}^{n} \left(c_i - \gamma p_i - \frac{1}{\beta_o} \frac{\partial \Phi}{\partial z_i} \right) \frac{\partial z_i^D}{\partial q_k} = -c_{qk} + \frac{1}{\beta_o} \frac{\partial \Phi}{\partial q_k}; \qquad k \in K \qquad (3)$$

where $c_{qk} := (\partial g/\partial q_k)/(\partial g/\partial z_o)$. Next we subtract $(1-\gamma)\Sigma_i p_i(\partial z_i^D/\partial q_k)$ on both sides of the marginal conditions and obtain

$$\sum_{i=o}^{n} \left(c_i - p_i - \frac{1}{\beta_o} \frac{\partial \Phi}{\partial z_i} \right) \frac{\partial z_i^D}{\partial q_k} =$$

$$= -c_{qk} - (1-\gamma)\sum_{i=o}^{n} p_i \frac{\partial z_i^D}{\partial q_k} + \frac{1}{\beta_o} \frac{\partial \Phi}{\partial q_k}; \qquad k \in K. \qquad (4)$$

However, applying eqs. (16–22) and (16–31), we learn that

$$\sum_i p_i \frac{\partial z_i^D}{\partial q_k} = \sum_j c_{qk}^j - \sum_i \sum_j (p_i - c_i^j) \frac{\partial y_i^j}{\partial q_k}; \qquad k \in K. \qquad (5)$$

Substituting (5) into (4), we obtain the general quality conditions

$$\sum_{i=o}^{n} \left(c_i - p_i - \frac{1}{\beta_o} \frac{\partial \Phi}{\partial z_i} \right) \frac{\partial z_i^D}{\partial q_k} = -c_{qk} - (1-\gamma)\sum_j c_{qk}^j +$$

$$+ (1-\gamma)\sum_i \sum_j (p_i - c_i^j) \frac{\partial y_i^j}{\partial q_k} + \frac{1}{\beta_o} \frac{\partial \Phi}{\partial q_k}; \qquad k \in K. \qquad (6)$$

Similar to the case of positive public-sector pricing (chapter 4), the reader will note that the adjustment of public qualities to monopolistic structures in the private economy follows the same lines as in the normative approach. Hence, let us skip this interpretation and neglect all interdependencies between the public and the private sector. We therefore assume:

(i) only prices of publicly supplied goods are controlled;[2]
(ii) the private sector is perfectly competitive; goods with publicly controlled prices are neither supplied nor demanded by private firms.

---

[2] This assumption could be given up to investigate the public quality regulation of goods which are only produced in the private sector.

Under these assumptions we obtain the following structure of qualities[3]

$$\sum_{i=o}^{n} \left(p_i - c_i + \frac{1}{\beta_o} \frac{\partial \Phi}{\partial z_i} \right) \frac{\partial z_i^D}{\partial q_k} = c_{qk} - \frac{1}{\beta_o} \frac{\partial \Phi}{\partial q_k}; \qquad k \in K. \tag{7}$$

Let us compare the public firm's quality choice with the corresponding marginal condition of a profit-maximizing monopolist

$$\sum_{i=o}^{n} (p_i - c_i) \frac{\partial z_i^D}{\partial q_k} = c_{qk}; \qquad k \in K. \tag{8}$$

There is a formal identity of both quality rules if we impute to the public firm the following modified marginal costs

$$\tilde{c}_i = c_i - \frac{1}{\beta_o} \frac{\partial \Phi}{\partial z_i} \qquad \text{quantity marginal costs} \tag{9}$$

$$\tilde{c}_{qk} = c_{qk} - \frac{1}{\beta_o} \frac{\partial \Phi}{\partial q_k} \qquad \text{quality marginal costs.} \tag{10}$$

Hence we are once again left with the result that the public firm behaves as if it were a profit-maximizing monopolist who misestimates costs. The direction of miscalculation depends on $\partial \Phi / \partial z_i$ and $\partial \Phi / \partial q_k$ respectively[4] and varies from one objective function to the other. The miscalculation of marginal costs will, most probably, influence prices and qualities in the following way:

$$\frac{\partial \Phi}{\partial z_i} < 0 \Rightarrow \tilde{c}_i > c_i \text{ (higher quantity marginal costs)} \Rightarrow \text{higher price} \tag{11}$$

$$\frac{\partial \Phi}{\partial q_k} < 0 \Rightarrow \tilde{c}_{qk} > c_{qk} \text{ (higher quality marginal costs)} \Rightarrow \text{lower quality} \tag{12}$$

where 'higher' and 'lower' refers to the price and quality choice of a profit-maximizing monopolist.

The signs of $\partial \Phi / \partial z_i$ have explicitly been presented in table 1 in chapter 4. With respect to $\partial \Phi / \partial q_k$, we do not need another table, because for most

---

[3] Recall $c_{qk}^j + \Sigma_i c_i^j (\partial y_i^j / \partial q_k) = 0$ from (16–22). For perfect competition in the private sector, moreover, $\Sigma_i p_i (\partial y_i^j / \partial q_k) = 0$.

[4] $\partial \Phi / \partial p_k$ influences the quality choice because both prices and qualities result from the system of equations (4–9) and (22–7).

positive-theory objectives this derivative is equal to zero. There are only two exceptions: the vote-maximizer faces a positive $\partial\Phi/\partial q_k$ – his expected vote increases if some quality is increased. On the other hand, an energy-saving utility[5] faces a negative $\partial\Phi/\partial q_k$ – higher quality increases demand whence more energy is needed. Hence, we can conclude as follows: there is a tendency toward higher quality in political models of vote-maximizers, there is a tendency toward lower quality in case of energy saving.[6] The other positive theory objectives are neutral.

Therefore, the answer to one of the introductory questions is as expected: a vote maximizer will tend to choose a higher quality level than an output maximizer.

---

[5] Regardless of whether energy is publicly or privately supplied.

[6] In the energy-saving case, the signs of $\partial\Phi/\partial q_k$ rest on the assumptions of normal reaction of demand with respect to its own price, and of complementarity between energy and all other goods $k\neq a$.

23

A Set of Axioms for Prices to Achieve
a Fair Allocation of Costs

This chapter is devoted to a theory of pricing that differs conceptually from all the other approaches outlined in this book. Cost-axiomatic pricing does not assume that some objective function is optimized subject to production feasibility, a revenue-cost constraint, and the conditions for market equilibria. Rather it proceeds by formulating some basic axioms to which prices should correspond and seeks those pricing rules that are uniquely determined by these axioms. The theoretical deduction is rather advanced, but the basic ideas of the approach as presented below, are easily understandable. Moreover, cost-axiomatic pricing is not a purely theoretical exercise of the l'art pour l'art sort, but has actually been applied in practice.

Some economists at Cornell University were asked to compute fair internal telephone billing rates for their university (Billera–Heath–Raanan, 1978). Problems arose because costs for long distance calls followed different schedules, consisting of different basic fees and variable charges the university had to pay to the telephone company (direct distance dialing – DDD, foreign exchange lines – FX, wide area telecommunications service – WATS). Thus two people calling Chicago at the same time may have caused different costs for the university, if one used the FX-line, the other DDD, because the computer routed the first call to the cheaper FX-line and the second, which came in some seconds later, to DDD, as FX and all WATS-lines were occupied. Is it fair to charge different internal billing rates in such a case?

The authors solved the problem by applying the Shapley-value of nonatomic games (Aumann–Shapley, 1974). Billera–Heath (1979), Mirman–Tauman (1982) and Samet–Tauman (1982) then redefined the game-theoretic axioms as axioms on the relation between prices and cost functions. They succeeded in finding a set of axioms that is understandable on its own even by readers who are not familiar with sophisticated game theory. Thus they created a new, generally applicable, theory of pricing which has been further developed in Mirman–Samet–Tauman (1983), Bös–Tillmann (1983) and Samet–Tauman–Zang (1981).

The most striking feature of cost-axiomatic pricing is that it starts from axioms on the relation between prices and cost functions and hence needs no information on consumer tastes. However, it is not a priori guaranteed that the application of such price schedules will always lead to equilibria between demand and supply of the relevant goods. And if market clearing under cost-axiomatic prices is to obtain, the estimation of private tastes enters again.

Consider a producer who has to produce particular quantities of consumption goods $\zeta = (\zeta_1, \ldots, \zeta_n); \zeta_i > 0$. Total costs of producing ζ are given by $C(\zeta)$, a continuously differentiable long-run cost function (all inputs are treated as variable, $C(0) = 0$). Input prices are fixed. Increasing returns to scale are included. The quantities ζ are to be sold at prices $p = (p_1(C, \zeta), \ldots, p_n(C, \zeta))$ that fulfill the following four axioms (Samet–Tauman, 1982):

Axiom 1 (Rescaling): The price should be independent of the unit's measurement. Let G and C be two cost functions and

$$G(z_1, \ldots, z_n) = C(s_1 z_1, \ldots, s_n z_n); \qquad s_i > 0; \qquad \forall i. \tag{1}$$

Then for each ζ and each $i = 1, \ldots, n$

$$p_i(G, \zeta) = s_i p_i(C, (s_1 \zeta_1, \ldots, s_n \zeta_n)). \tag{2}$$

The rationale for this axiom is trivial: the price of ζ_i if measured in tons, has to be 1000 times the price of ζ_i if measured in kilos.

Axiom 2 (Consistency): The same price shall be charged for goods which have the same influence on costs in the following sense: if G is a one-variable cost function and if for every z

$$C(z_1, \ldots, z_n) = G(\Sigma_i z_i), \tag{3}$$

then for every i and every ζ

$$p_i(C, \zeta) = p(G, \Sigma_i \zeta_i). \tag{4}$$

Typical examples are red and blue cars which should be sold at the same price. Objections to this axiom stress different situations of demand: if, at the same prices, red cars can and blue cars cannot be sold, it makes sense to sell blue cars at a lower price.

Axiom 3 (Additivity): If the cost function can be broken into subcosts, the prices can be found by adding the prices determined by the subcosts. If C, G^1 and G^2 are cost functions and for each z

$$C(z_1, \ldots, z_n) = G^1(z_1, \ldots, z_n) + G^2(z_1, \ldots, z_n), \tag{5}$$

then for each ζ

$$p(C, \zeta) = p(G^1, \zeta) + p(G^2, \zeta). \tag{6}$$

Axiom 3 refers only to cases where the cost function is separable. Then there are no interdependencies between subcosts and the additivity of pricing makes sense.

Axiom 4 (Positivity): The price of a commodity, the production of which requires investment, is not negative.

Let ζ be given. If C is non-decreasing at any $z \leq \zeta$, then $p(C, \zeta) \geq 0$.   (7)

The reasoning is straightforward.

Samet–Tauman (1982) prove that prices which correspond to these four axioms are of the form

$$p_i(C, \zeta) = \int_0^1 C_i(s\zeta)d\mu(s); \qquad i = 1, \ldots, n; \qquad \zeta \neq 0. \tag{8}$$

This rather complicated mathematical formulation can be grasped most easily if one interprets the prices p as 'some average' of the marginal costs C_i where the measure $\mu(s)$ denotes how 'the average' is to be computed.[1] We can clarify this further if we show how, by changing μ, we can generate, as polar cases of the same pricing formula, the 'pure' marginal-cost prices as well as the 'Aumann-Shapley' break-even prices:

(i) Marginal-Cost Pricing

Axiom 4 is strengthened in order to obtain Axiom 4*.

Axiom 4* (Positivity)

Let ζ be given. If C is non-decreasing in a neighborhood of ζ, then $p(C, \zeta) \geq 0$.   (9)

This requires that prices be non-negative at ζ even if C is nondecreasing in a neighborhood of ζ only.

If axioms 1 to 3 and 4* are fulfilled,[2] the price mechanism reduces to

$$p_i(C, \zeta) = C_i(\zeta) \tag{10}$$

which is the marginal-cost pricing rule as a special case of the above general pricing rule.

---

[1] More precisely, μ is a non-negative measure on $([0,1], B)$, B being the Borel σ-algebra. We define $\bar{\mu} := \mu([0,1])$ and assume $0 < \bar{\mu} < \infty$, i.e. μ is positive and finite.

[2] Some additional normalization is necessary as shown in Samet–Tauman (1982: 905).

(ii) Aumann–Shapley Pricing
We add a break-even axiom.

Axiom 5 (Break even)

$$\sum_i p_i(C, \zeta)\zeta_i = C(\zeta); \qquad \text{for each } \zeta > 0. \tag{11}$$

If axioms 1 to 5 (including 4, but not 4*) are fulfilled, the pricing rule is

$$p_i(C, \zeta) = \int_0^1 C_i(s\zeta)ds. \tag{12}$$

The reader should be aware that (12) does not mean the usual kind of average-cost pricing. Since we are dealing with more than one good, the average is found by proportionate variations s of all quantities ζ along a ray going from 0 to ζ.

Thus cost-axiomatic prices include marginal-cost prices and cost-covering prices as special cases. We recall that welfare-maximizing prices also include marginal-cost and cost-covering prices as special cases. What, then, is the *difference between pricing according to these two approaches?*

First, *marginal costs* enter the pricing rules in different ways. All kinds of welfare-maximizing pricing, following the general rules (3–21) or (3–24) depend on the marginal costs c_i at the optimum – and only at the optimum. Cost axiomatic pricing, following eqs. (8) also depends on alternative production possibilities, on the values of the respective marginal costs for any quantity along a ray between 0 and ζ. This difference is interesting with respect to the whole philosophy of pricing rules. Perhaps one should think of pricing rules as depending also on further alternative production possibilities, e.g. the production of higher quantities ($C_i(s\zeta)$ for $s > 1$).

Only in the case of pure marginal-cost pricing does this particular difference between the welfare approach and the cost-axiomatic approach disappear.

Second, the *demand side* is treated differently. The welfare approach typically assumes an equilibrium between quantities demanded and supplied (the only exception in this book being the peak-load model). No such constraint enters the cost-axiomatic approach. However, will prices that are determined only by cost axioms always be 'demand compatible'? Or will demand at given prices exceed or fall short of supply? Mirman and Tauman (1982) have already shown that Aumann–Shapley prices are demand compatible and Bös–Tillmann (1983) have shown that *all* cost-axiomatic prices are demand compatible if the financing of deficits of public utilities is explicitly included in an equilibrium approach.

The proof has, of course, extended the applicability of cost-axiomatic pricing to a considerable extent. Only with this general proof of the demand compatibility of cost-axiomatic pricing can these price schedules be treated as an equivalent and perhaps superior alternative to welfare-maximizing price schedules.

Generally, it will be difficult to decide which approach is superior. Compare, for example, Ramsey and Aumann–Shapley prices. Both are cost-covering. However, one cannot expect these prices to coincide. If there are different price elasticities of demand for two goods that have the same influence on costs (in the sense of axiom 2 above), Ramsey prices of these two goods will differ, Aumann–Shapley prices will be equal. In such a case, someone who adheres to the welfare approach will stress the welfare losses caused by Aumann–Shapley prices. Someone who adheres to the above axioms on costs will stress the weaknesses of social welfare functions. There is no generally accepted result concerning the superiority of one of these two approaches.

PART FOUR

PRICE REGULATION

A

Can Welfare-Optimal Prices be Achieved by Simple Rules?

Let us consider a two-person setting. A regulator wants to maximize welfare, the management of the regulated firm wants to maximize profits, revenue, or output, instead of welfare. (If the regulated firm is privately owned, we expect its managers will maximize profits. If the firm is a public enterprise, output or revenue maximization are quite plausible managerial strategies.)

In the following two chapters we will deal with the question whether welfare-optimal prices can be achieved if the regulator imposes some simple rules on the regulated firm. Regulation by simple rules has often been applied in practice, for instance by explicitly instructing public utilities to sell at long-run marginal costs[1] or to meet all demand. Many recent theoretical proposals also attempt to solve the problems of regulation by the application of simple rules - prominent examples are the regulatory models of Loeb–Magat (1979), and Vogelsang–Finsinger (1979).

Note that the following two chapters attempt to make the results of normative pricing theory directly applicable for practical price regulation. If the simple rules of the following two chapters were sufficient to bring about the welfare optimum, we would have found the philosopher's stone. Unfortunately, we shall see that the simple rules fail to achieve optimal prices.

24

Regulating Marginal-Cost Prices

Marginal-cost pricing was treated as one of the basic pricing principles in chapter 7 above. Under specific (and restrictive) assumptions, the welfare-optimal prices were developed as the solution of the following system of equations:

---

[1] The UK White Paper (1967) is a good example.

$$\sum_{i \in K}(p_i - c_i)\frac{\partial \hat{z}_i}{\partial p_k} = 0; \qquad k \in K. \tag{1}$$

The present chapter deals with some particular aspects of regulating a firm so as to induce the marginal-cost prices.

24.1   Competitive Public Enterprises

If prices are determined by the market, and a public enterprise produces under decreasing returns to scale, profit maximization will directly lead to marginal-cost pricing; if additionally all other enterprises produce under non-increasing returns to scale the welfare optimum can be easily decentralized.

This is not valid if the public enterprise produces under increasing returns to scale. Economic theory offers different solutions for the case in which an enterprise produces under a deficit.

Assume that all potential firms have the same technology $g(z)$ and that input prices are given. Now define $\mathcal{A}$ as the locus where ray-average costs[2] are minimal along each ray in the $z_1 - z_2-$space. Below $\mathcal{A}$ we therefore face strictly decreasing ray-average costs which corresponds to economies of scale. Moreover, below $\mathcal{A}$ we postulate the presence of transray-convex costs which encourage the production of more than one good.[3] These cost attributes are sufficient for a natural monopoly below $\mathcal{A}$.

Now consider the region of all output vectors that can generate total revenue equal to or exceeding the total costs of the industry. The location of this region depends on the interrelation between demand and costs. If this region is outside and far to the right of $\mathcal{A}$ in figure 18 $(T(z^I))$, production by more than one enterprise will be optimal (cost minimizing). If in such a case the enterprises that are actually in the market make profits, these profits will be restrained by potential entrants. If they have deficits, the marginal producers will leave the market. In the long run, the producers will produce along $\mathcal{A}$ and break even. This mechanism solves the deficit problem and determines the optimal number of firms.

---

[2] This concept deals with cost changes along a ray, that is, for proportionate variations of the outputs of a firm. Allowing all outputs to change to the s-fold ($s>1$) leads to total costs $C(sz^+)$. Then ray-average costs are denoted by $RAC:=C(sz^+)/s$ where z^+ 'is the unit bundle for a particular mixture of outputs – the arbitrary bundle assigned the value 1' (Baumol–Panzar–Willig, 1982: 48).

[3] See Baumol–Panzar–Willig (1982).

In the case of region $T(z^{II})$ such a solution cannot be found and the elimination of marginal producers will continue until one firm prevails as a monopoly. In contestable markets the monopolist sets Ramsey prices which are sustainable.[4] If the government prefers to set marginal-cost prices, it has to regulate the enterprise and to finance the firm's deficit.

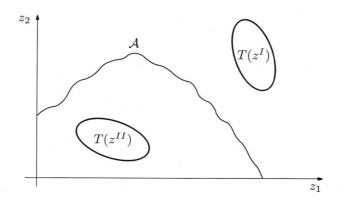

Figure 18

24.2   Regulating Natural Monopolies

24.2.1   *Counting Equations*

Many simple rules which are imposed on a natural monopoly are insufficient for welfare maximization because they leave too many degrees of freedom to the manager of the firm which he can use to maximize profit or output, say. Hence, these rules can be eliminated from the list of successful regulatory approaches. In the following we will start by evaluating several rules with respect to these degrees of freedom, i.e., we will 'count equations'.

The assumption under which this counting-equations approach has been invented, is that of a fully-informed regulator. Hence, the approach fails if the regulator lacks information on costs or demand. In such a case the welfare optimum, that is, marginal-cost pricing, cannot be achieved by simply imposing so many simple rules on the manager that no degrees of freedom are

---

[4] See section 25.1 below.

left. If the regulator cannot observe whether the rules were actually obeyed, the better informed manager can get off unpunished if he fails to abide by the regulatory rules.

Nevertheless it is interesting to see how these simple rules look. We shall begin with the most general case and subsequently introduce one simple rule after the other.

To investigate the regulation of marginal-cost pricing in an empirically relevant environment, we exclude lump-sum redistribution from the following analysis.[5] Available instruments are the $n + 1$ quantities $(z_o, \ldots, z_n)$ and the $\mathcal{M}$ regulated prices $(p_1, \ldots, p_\mathcal{M})$ which we always assume to refer to net outputs.[6]

(i) First case of regulation: delegating the maximization of social welfare to the regulated firm, giving the firm the right to optimize welfare in the Boiteux framework, by means of prices $p_k, k \in K$, and quantities $z_i, i \in I$, taking into account those particular assumptions which lead to marginal-cost pricing.[7]

The firm's incentives to maximize welfare are low because the firm is left with $\mathcal{M} + n + 1$ degrees of freedom, $\mathcal{M}$ prices and $n + 1$ quantities, which can be used to maximize profits, output or revenue. Profit maximization might be detected easily by government control since we deal with monopolies and hence profit-maximizing prices will be far from welfare-maximizing ones. But if a regulated public enterprise chooses output or revenue maximization, this is much more complicated to detect by someone who is not fully informed of the relevant demand and cost functions, because these objectives lead to low-pricing strategies of the firm, which might be difficult to distinguish from welfare-optimal low pricing. To deal with the lack of incentives of the firm, the government will tend to be more precise in its regulatory activities, as shown in the next case.

(ii) Second case of regulation: the government sets $\mathcal{M}$ welfare-optimal output prices, the regulated firm chooses $n + 1$ netput quantities.

The firm's incentives for welfare maximization are not particularly high. Assuming all z_i are used as instruments of the enterprise, the firm is given

---

[5] The optimality of marginal-cost pricing must therefore be justified by one of the usual arguments of applied studies: either by assuming negligible income effects or assuming a representative consumer.

[6] We exclude the difficult problem that, for instance, in cases of increasing returns to scale, there might exist no unique solution of the model or no solution at all and treat the problems of regulation only for cases where a unique welfare optimum exists.

[7] Theoretically, lump-sum incomes $r^h, h=1,\ldots,H$, are assumed to be optimally fixed by the government. From a more practical point of view income effects are neglected.

exactly $n + 1$ degrees of freedom. The firm could use these degrees of freedom to maximize revenue or outputs, which would typically imply some distortions.

The same problems as in the price-setting case arise if the government sets a certain amount of welfare-optimal netput quantities, say m, whereas the firm chooses $\mathcal{M}$ prices and the remaining $n + 1 - m$ quantities. Hence, this kind of regulation does not help either.

Therefore, apart from setting prices or quantities, the government has to instruct the board to follow particular regulatory rules. These rules should be as simple as possible, but they must be sufficient to guarantee the welfare optimum.

(iii) Third case of regulation: the government sets $\mathcal{M}$ prices[8] and particular regulatory rules which must be obeyed by the regulated firm.

The best-known of these rules is called the *MC-rule*: the government instructs the firm to extend production until marginal costs are equal to the fixed prices

$$c_k(z) = p_k = \overline{p}_k; \qquad k \in K, \tag{2}$$

the bar indicating that prices p_k are exogenously given to the firm.

The firm's degrees of freedom are clearly reduced by the MC-rule. However, there remain many degrees of freedom because $c_k(z)$ depends on all outputs and inputs. If all z_i are used as instruments, the firm is given as many degrees of freedom as the number of all goods minus the number of regulated prices. Hence, the MC-rule is not sufficient to guarantee the achievement of the marginal-cost-pricing welfare optimum by independent decisions of the government and of the firm. Let us therefore proceed to some more restrictive forms of regulatory activity.

The *efficiency rule*, to be added to the MC-rule, is as follows. The government instructs the firm to achieve the welfare-optimal profit or deficit Π^{*}[9] and to produce efficiently.

The firm, then, has to follow the production function $g(z) = 0$, or equivalently the labor-requirement function $z_o = z_o(z_1, \ldots, z_n) = z_o(z.)$ with the well-known property $\partial z_o / \partial z_i = -(\partial g / \partial z_i)/(\partial g / \partial z_o) = -c_i$. As the profit or deficit is exogenously fixed, the firm faces the following constraint

$$\Pi^{*} = z_o + \sum_{i=1}^{n} p_i z_i \; ; \; d\Pi^{*} = 0. \tag{3}$$

---

[8] The case of the government setting m quantities could be treated analogously.

[9] The government optimizes welfare without any revenue-cost constraint. The resulting marginal-cost prices imply a particular welfare-optimal profit or deficit Π^{*}. For the regulated enterprise, facing the efficiency rule, this profit or deficit Π^{*} is exogenously given.

But then

$$d\Pi^* = \sum_{i=1}^{n} \frac{\partial z_o}{\partial z_i} dz_i + \sum_{i=1}^{n} p_i dz_i = \sum_{i=1}^{n} (p_i - c_i) dz_i = 0. \qquad (4)$$

This condition can only be met if the MC-rule is fulfilled and if $p_i = c_i$ for all $dz_i, i \notin K$, which guarantees the achievement of the welfare optimum. The remarkable feature of such a regulatory rule is the necessity of informing the enterprise about the deficit or profit it has to achieve.

The combination of the MC-rule and the efficiency rule seems to be quite common in regulatory practice, in particular for public enterprises. The reason is simple: the government always has to plan its budget in advance. Therefore it is always sensible to instruct the public enterprise to achieve that deficit which is provided for in the budget.

Although the above way of regulating marginal-cost prices leads to the welfare optimum and implies reasonable incentives for the firm, one is inclined to search for regulatory procedures with even better incentives for the firm. The straightforward candidate for this is the *profit rule*, to be added to the MC-rule: the government obliges the enterprise to choose all $z_i, i \notin K$, in a profit-maximizing way,

$$\text{choose } \Pi^{**} = \max_{z_i(i \notin K)} \left\{ \sum_i p_i z_i \mid g(z) = 0 \right\}. \qquad (5)$$

Since the prices $p_i, i \notin K$, are given by the market, a quasi-equilibrium situation arises,[10] and the firm will choose netputs so as to equate marginal costs $c_i, i \notin K$, to prices. Unfortunately, however, the firm might have an incentive not to follow this approach. In case of non-increasing returns to scale, everything goes the right way, the above rules implying a profit maximum. In the case of increasing returns to scale, however, the above marginal conditions imply a profit *minimum*, as can be seen from the second-order conditions.[11]

For this purpose, we solve the production function for z_o and differentiate $\Pi = z_o(z_1, \ldots, z_n) + \sum_1^n p_i z_i$ with respect to $z_i, i \notin K$. The first-order conditions

$$\left(\frac{\partial z_o}{\partial z_i} + p_i \right) = (p_i - c_i) = 0; \qquad i \notin K, \qquad (6)$$

---

[10] This presumes that the regulated firm is not a monopoly, but perfectly competitive, with respect to all goods $i \notin K$.

[11] If the management of the firm is obliged to minimize costs by using $z_i, i \notin K$, the approach leads to a cost maximum in the case of increasing returns to scale.

added to the MC-rule, lead to second-order conditions

$$d\Pi^2 = dz.^T \nabla^2_{z.} dz. \tag{7}$$

where $\nabla^2_{z.} = (\partial^2 z_o)/(\partial z_i \partial z_k)$ is the Hessian matrix of the labor-requirement function $z_o = z_o(z_1, \ldots, z_n)$. In the case of increasing returns to scale, $z_o(\cdot)$ is a convex function, $\nabla^2_{z.}$ is positive semidefinite and hence $d\Pi^2 \geq 0$. Therefore the optimum achieved is a profit minimum. In the case of non-increasing returns to scale the contrary is true.

However, we do not believe that on the basis of the above result regulated firms should be instructed to *minimize* profits[12] because the practice of such a regulation will typically induce the firm to produce inefficiently, neglecting our theory which explicitly excludes inefficiencies. Therefore regulation by combining the MC-rule and the profit rule should only be applied for non-increasing returns to scale industries, in which case the firm actually achieves the welfare optimum by finding its profit maximum.

Finally, we should discuss the common regulation of combining the MC-rule and the *'meet-all-demand' rule*: the firm is instructed to sell as much of each net output as customers demand and to buy as much of each net input as they offer. The latter instruction could also be termed a *'buy-all-supply'* rule. Hence, quantity rationing of customers' demand or supply is forbidden by the meet-all-demand rule. Price rationing, on the other hand, is forbidden by the MC-rule.

Recall that the MC-rule leaves us with $n + 1 - \mathcal{M}$ degrees of freedom. Additionally introducing the $\mathcal{M}$ equations of the meet-all-demand rule,[13]

$$z_k = x_k - y_k; \qquad k \in K, \tag{8}$$

we obtain a system of equations which is either underdetermined or overdetermined depending on whether $\mathcal{M} \gtrless n + 1 - \mathcal{M}$. In the case of underdetermination, there may still be distortions if a firm uses some or all of the remaining degrees of freedom to maximize, say, output or revenue. In the case of overdetermination, the enterprise cannot follow all regulatory rules. Only if $\mathcal{M} = n + 1 - \mathcal{M}$, there are no degrees of freedom left.

(iv) Fourth case of regulation: the government does not set prices or quantities, but regulatory rules only. The regulated firm chooses prices $p_k, k \in K$, and quantities $z_i, i \in I$.

---

[12] Other authors are sometimes willing to accept profit minimization as a regulatory rule, see Wiegard (1978).

[13] As usual, x_k is total consumer demand for good k, whereas y_k is total quantity of good k produced by other (private) firms than the regulated enterprise.

The combination of three regulatory rules, namely

- choose prices at marginal costs,
- achieve a given profit or deficit Π^* by efficient production, *and*
- meet all demand at the resulting prices,

is sufficient to eliminate degrees of freedom which could be used by the firm to deviate from the welfare optimum. In the case of non-increasing returns to scale, the MC-rule, profit-rule, and meet-all-demand rule, taken together, can be used as an alternative system of regulation to achieve the marginal-cost pricing optimum.

As already mentioned, the counting-equations approach breaks down if the regulator is not fully informed. By way of an example, the application of the MC-rule is futile unless the regulator knows the firm's marginal-cost function, which implies that he knows whether the firm has operated X-efficiently. The manager of the firm has no incentive to provide the regulator with these informations and hence the regulator will be unable to assess whether his simple rule has actually been obeyed.

Regulation by simple rules, therefore, can only be successful if the problems of the regulator's lack of information are overcome. In the following we shall present two approaches which recently have been developed to achieve marginal-cost prices of the regulated firm in spite of the regulator's lack of information.

24.2.2   Loeb–Magat Regulation

Loeb and Magat (1979) were the first to suggest that the regulator should make the manager the residual claimant to welfare. For a one-good public utility they suggest a subsidy of the following type

$$\mathcal{S}(p) = CS(p) - LS \tag{9}$$

where CS is consumer surplus and LS is a lump-sum charge which does not depend on the price. The manager of the regulated firm will maximize the profit defined as revenue minus cost plus government subsidy,

$$\max_{p} pz(p) + \mathcal{S}(p) - C(z(p)). \tag{10}$$

The particular choice of the subsidy guarantees that the manager maximizes

$$CS(p) + pz(p) - C(z(p)) - LS \tag{11}$$

which leads to marginal-cost prices according to the first-order condition

$$\left(p - \frac{\partial C}{\partial z} \right) \frac{\partial z}{\partial p} = 0. \tag{12}$$

The advantages of the Loeb–Magat regulatory scheme are straightforward. The welfare optimum is achieved by cleverly reckoning on the manager's incentives; and the lump-sum payment makes is possible to extract the ex-ante rents of the manager.[14] On the other hand, as already mentioned in chapter 1 of this book,[15] there are some noteworthy drawbacks to the procedure: in particular, Loeb–Magat regulation fails to be optimal if there is asymmetric information and if the manager is risk-averse. These, however, are the most interesting cases of regulation and, therefore, in this book the chapters on the new economics of regulation will concentrate on regulation under asymmetric information (chapters 28–32) and on regulation of risk-averse agents (chapter 33). Since it is very important to make clear that the Loeb–Magat mechanism does not yield optimal results in these cases, let us briefly elaborate the problems which arise:

(i)   Asymmetric Information

If the regulator is perfectly informed, he can achieve the first best without paying any information rent to the manager. If he is not perfectly informed, however, the regulator faces a trade-off: how much inefficiency should he accept and how large an information rent should he pay? The Loeb–Magat mechanism guarantees that the manager chooses the first best. However, in case of asymmetric information such a policy would not be optimal, because it would imply that excessive information rents be paid to the manager. The lump-sum payment which the manager would have to pay to the regulator, would have to be low to guarantee the participation of even the worst type of manager and therefore would involve high information rents in all other situations.[16] It is preferable not to choose Loeb–Magat's mechanism in case of asymmetric information, but to accept a certain degree of inefficiency and avoid excessive information rents. (This is different in case of symmetric information where the manager is willing to participate if his *expected* information rent is zero.)

---

[14] Regardless of uncertainty, the subsidy must be financed, for instance, by taxation which will be distortionary; hence the net subsidy should be low. See Sharkey (1979).

[15] See subsection 1.5.3.

[16] It may be noted that the Clark–Groves mechanism for the revelation of preferences faces a similar problem: it guarantees perfect revelation of preferences but violates the balanced-budget requirement. (See Fudenberg–Tirole, 1991: 271–3, where the similarity between Clark–Groves and Loeb–Magat becomes clear.) Note, however, that Clark-Groves deal with a mechanism without individual rationality (participation constraints): the citizens must participate in the Clark–Groves mechanism.

(ii)   Risk-Aversion of the Manager

For expositional clarity, our presentation of the Loeb–Magat approach excluded any uncertainty. In practice, however, such uncertainty always exists and it must be questioned how the Loeb–Magat mechanism works in such a case. All the uncertainty, and hence all the risk is contained in consumer and producer surplus. The lump-sum payment to the government, on the other hand, is risk-free. Hence, the Loeb–Magat mechanism shifts all the risk to the manager and leaves no risk for the government. Risk-neutrality of both regulator and manager is sufficient to guarantee that the Loeb–Magat mechanism induces the first best. If, however, the manager is risk-averse, the government's lump-sum charge must be reduced and then Loeb–Magat ceases to be the optimal mechanism and other ways of regulation are preferable.

24.2.3   The Subsidy-Adjustment Process

There have been several follow-ups to the Loeb–Magat approach.[17] A nice dynamic formulation is the subsidy-adjustment process of Finsinger–Vogelsang (1981). The management wishes to maximize the discounted flow of profits, including government subsidies. We assume demand and cost functions to be constant over time. The firm chooses its prices at the beginning of any period and meets all demand which arises at these prices. Let us restrict the presentation to the usual case of initial prices $p(0)$ above marginal costs. These prices are thought of as representing the state of the world without regulation.

The government does not restrict the firm's free choice of prices, but gives subsidies which increase with decreasing prices. It begins with a first period subsidy of

$$\mathcal{S}(1) = z^+(0) \cdot [p(0) - p(1)] \tag{13}$$

and afterwards always pays

$$\mathcal{S}(t) = \mathcal{S}(t-1) + z^+(t-1) \cdot [p(t-1) - p(t)]; \quad t = 2, \ldots, \tag{14}$$

where t is the index of time, $\mathcal{S}$ is the subsidy and z^+ is the vector of publicly supplied outputs. After successively substituting for the earlier periods, in any period T the subsidy can be written as

$$\mathcal{S}(T) = \sum_{t=1}^{T} z^+(t-1) \cdot [p(t-1) - p(t)]; \quad T = 1, \ldots. \tag{15}$$

To calculate this subsidy, the regulator only needs information about quantities of the previous period and about the prices (set by the firm) of the

---

[17] See also Chamley–Marchand–Pestieau (1989).

previous and of the present period. He does not need any information about demand or cost functions.

The management is motivated to maximize welfare. The subsidy (15) consists of accumulated rectangles under the demand functions, and therefore approximates consumer surplus, measured between the starting prices $p(0)$ and the present prices $p(T)$. The after-subsidy profits of the firm are therefore an approximation to the sum of consumer and producer surplus in period T. The maximum of this sum is obtained at marginal-cost prices. Hence, it always pays for the firm to lower its prices until they equal marginal costs. The firm will prefer to lower the prices in small steps in order to skim off the consumer surplus as far as possible. However, as future subsidies and profits are discounted, these small steps are prevented from becoming infinitesimally small.

Besides the usual points of criticism against any regulatory scheme of the Loeb–Magat type,[18] it should be noted that the firm's incentives are achieved by paying total consumer surplus to the firm, which may imply unwanted distributional consequences. (Finsinger–Vogelsang do not include a lump-sum charge to be paid by the firm.) The amount of subsidy paid to the firm will depend on the firm's initial prices $p(0)$ and therefore we expect the firm to try to start from prices chosen as high as possible.[19]

24.2.4 Yardstick Regulation

A 'yardstick regulator' constitutes an indirect competition between firms. He links the regulatory rules for some firm to performance indicators of other firms in similar position.[20] By way of an example, in the US Medicare system hospitals are reimbursed for a specific treatment on the basis of the average costs of this treatment in similar hospitals. In the UK, yardstick regulation has been proposed in the Littlechild Report (1986) on the regulation of water authorities.[21] It was also discussed when British Gas was privatized and when the several UK electricity distribution companies were set up in the process of privatization. There are many other possible cases where yardstick regulation of public utilities could be thought of, in particular all cases of local

---

[18] See the preceding subsection.

[19] If the management is not interested in maximizing the firm's profit, but in maximizing its own income, similar incentives can be obtained by paying the managers an additional income which approximates the changes of consumer and producer surplus (Finsinger–Vogelsang, 1981: 399–401).

[20] There is a close connection between yardstick regulation and managerial incentive incomes based on relative performance have been treated in several papers on tournaments (starting with Lazear and Rosen, 1981), or on team competition (Holmström, 1982).

[21] See Vickers–Yarrow (1988: 415–9).

or regional public utilities like fire departments, garbage collection and local transportation services.

Yardstick regulation is meaningful if its application helps to solve the problem of the regulator's lack of information about certain unobservable characteristics. By way of an example, if some general shock hits the costs of all firms, then information about the costs of some firm can be useful for the regulation of any other firm. The situation is clearly different if an idiosyncratic shock hits one firm only. Special information about how the costs of this firm responded to the shock are irrelevant for the regulation of any other firm. Yardstick regulation is only meaningful in the presence of general shocks,[22] otherwise each firm must be regulated separately.[23]

The best-known paper on yardstick regulation is Shleifer (1985). In his model, the regulator applies a revelation mechanism similar to Groves' and Ledyard's mechanisms on the revelation of preferences for public goods. The basic idea is to regulate everybody on the basis of data provided by the other agents. Since every agent knows that the announcement of his own costs is only used to regulate others, he has no incentive to cheat and will truthfully inform the regulator about its costs. By assuming identical firms, Shleifer ensures that it is meaningful to regulate firms on the basis of information about other firms' costs.

Let us briefly present Shleifer's basic model.[24] Consider an economy with many identical public utilities located in separate geographical areas. Each utility is a one-good monopoly in its area and faces the same downward-sloping demand function in a separate market,

$$z = z(p); \frac{dz}{dp} < 0; \tag{16}$$

where z is output and p price. Each firm faces initial constant marginal costs c_o. It can reduce these marginal costs to a value of $c < c_o$ if it spends $R(c)$, where higher investment yields lower costs,

$$R(c_o) = 0; R'(c) < 0; R''(c) > 0. \tag{17}$$

The manager of each firm wants to maximize profit,

$$\pi = (p - c)z(p) + \mathcal{T} - R(c), \tag{18}$$

---

[22] This is made particularly clear in Laffont–Tirole (1993: 84–5).

[23] The approaches presented in chapters 28–31 below are characteristic for this kind of regulation.

[24] Shleifer (1985: 323–4).

where T is a lump-sum transfer. No manager will be willing to sign a contract with the regulator if this imposes deficits. Hence, the participation constraint of every manager is $\pi \geq 0$.

The regulator is interested only in optimal allocation. He does not care about distributional problems. Hence, in his objective function the lump-sum transfer T and the taxes which finance this transfer cancel out. The regulator's objective function for any single firm, therefore, is as follows:

$$W = cs(p) + (p - c)z(p) - R(c), \tag{19}$$

where consumer surplus cs depends on this firm's price p. For n identical firms, the regulator has n identical objective functions which look like (19).

If the regulator were fully informed, he would proceed according to the following benchmark approach:

$$\underset{c,p,T}{\text{maximize}}\, W \text{ subject to } \pi \geq 0. \tag{20}$$

The full-information benchmark optimum is characterized by the marginal conditions

$$R(c^*) = T^*; \; p^* = c^*; \; -R'(c^*) = z(p^*). \tag{21}$$

This command optimum, however, cannot be implemented directly because the regulator does not know what the R&D technology is. The manager has no incentive to inform the regulator about the true R&D technology because such truth-telling would result in zero profits regardless of costs and in such a case the manager prefers not to reduce costs. (Shleifer assumes that the manager maximizes profits, but as long as profits are not at stake, he exerts as little effort as possible. Hence he chooses $c = c_o$ instead c^* if he knows that his profits will be zero anyhow.)

The first-best optimum can, however, be achieved by yardstick regulation, choosing the following sequence of the regulator's and agents' strategies:

Stage 1: the regulator announces regulatory rules for prices and transfers; in particular, for each firm $i = 1, \ldots, n$ he announces that he will set prices according to the mean of the marginal costs of all other firms,

$$p_i = \bar{c}_i := \frac{1}{n-1} \sum_{j \neq i} c_j. \tag{22}$$

Moreover, he announces a transfer rule

$$T_i = \bar{R}_i := \frac{1}{n-1} \sum_{j \neq i} R(c_j). \tag{23}$$

The regulator must fully commit himself to these rules which may well imply deficits or even bankruptcy of inefficient firms.

Stage 2: each firm invests $R_i(c_i)$; the regulator observes both cost levels c_i and cost-reduction expenditures $R(c_i)$. This observation is made possible because no firm has an incentive to hide information on c_i and $R(c_i)$.[25]

Stage 3: on the basis of these observations, the regulator calculates both p_i and $\mathcal{T}_i$ according to (22) and (23).

Stage 4: each firm produces, sells at price p_i and receives the transfer $\mathcal{T}_i$.

It can be shown that there exists a unique[26] Nash equilibrium where each firm operates at the first-best level of marginal costs and cost-saving R&D investments.[27]

It is fascinating to see how this approach overcomes the regulator's difficulties in obtaining information. He announces the regulatory rules without having any information on costs. Then the firms give him correct information on costs, because giving this information does not affect their profits. On the basis of his correct information the regulator sets the prices. Each firm has incentives to minimize costs because any cost reduction is in the firm's own best interests; the advantages accruing to the firm are not taken away by regulation. A firm which operates more efficiently than the other firms has a clear advantage because of its better performance, hence each firm has an incentive to operate efficiently.

Unfortunately, the fascinating clarity and straightforwardness of Shleifer's approach is flawed if the actual application is considered. The main counterarguments are as follows:

(i)   The model loses much of its elegance if firms do not have uniform characteristics. Shleifer[28] proposes a 'reduced-form regulation' which uses predicted costs on the basis of a regression analysis linking marginal costs and exogenous characteristics of all firms. The reduced-form regulation is exact if the regression explains 100 percent of the variance of costs among the firms. Typically, however, this will not be the case. Moreover, regulation leads to undesired consequences if one or more of the exogenous characteristics can

---

[25]   Note that this is a one-shot game. It is not too unreasonable, however, to assume that rapid technical progress would quickly erode any knowledge of the R&D-technology which the regulator had won when deciding on regulation some 3 or 4 years ago.

[26]   Shleifer (1985) in his highly stylized setting of identical one-product firms succeeded in proving the uniqueness of the Nash equilibrium for marginal-cost prices. As soon as an explicit break-even constraint is added to the model, however, this proof breaks down. Shleifer (1985: 324) with laconic brevity remarks in a footnote: 'Uniqueness of equilibrium under average cost pricing remains to be established.'

[27]   The following paragraphs are taken from Bös (1991a: 82–3).

[28]   Shleifer (1985: 324–5).

be strategically influenced by the firms.

(ii)   Collusion among the firms leads to a break-down of the model. In the case of privatization, the contacts between the various new firms will be very close, therefore collusion could occur easily. There may also be a problem of parallel inefficient behavior, without explicit collusion, following those rules of thumb which had been applied in the public firm prior to privatization.

(iii)   The regulator must commit himself to not helping the firms if inefficient production leads to difficulties or even leads to bankruptcy.[29]   It is difficult to understand how a regulator of a privatized firm can commit himself in such a way. It would not be credible if the government threatened to let some privatized water authorities go bankrupt.

*

We have seen in this chapter that regulation by simple rules fails to achieve marginal-cost prices. Unfortunately, the same holds for Ramsey prices as will be shown in the following chapter.

---

[29]   Shleifer (1985: 323).

25
Regulating Ramsey Prices

Ramsey prices are one of the best-known paradigms of regulatory pricing. In chapter 8 above, we showed that Ramsey prices result from a general welfare-type of pricing model under some specific assumptions. These assumptions are even more restrictive than the assumptions which yield marginal-cost prices, because of the additional assumption of an exogenously given profit Π^o. Accordingly, Ramsey prices result if the following system of equations is solved with respect to prices $p_k, k \in K$, and the parameter γ:

$$\sum_{i \in K}(p_i - c_i)\frac{\partial \hat{z}_i}{\partial p_k} = -\gamma z_k; \qquad k \in K,$$

$$\sum_{i=o}^{n} p_i z_i = \Pi^o. \tag{1}$$

The present chapter deals with some particular aspects of regulating a firm so as to induce Ramsey prices.

25.1 Regulation by Changing the Environment

Baumol and others[1] have stressed the contestability of natural monopolies. Assume a monopoly which works under particular cost advantages: strictly decreasing ray-average costs and transray-convex costs. These modern concepts[2] correspond to economies of scale and of scope, respectively. What kind of pricing will protect the monopoly from losing its monopolistic position through new entrants into the market? If we define sustainability as 'a stationary equilibrium set of product quantities and prices which does not attract rivals into the industry', it can be proved that Ramsey prices are sufficient for sustainability if the natural monopoly's profit does not exceed the sunk entry costs of potential rivals.[3]

If the sustainability approach were correct, the government would not have to bother about price regulation of natural monopolies. Privatization

---

[1] Baumol–Bailey–Willig (1977), Panzar–Willig (1977b), Baumol–Panzar–Willig (1982).

[2] For details of these concepts see Baumol–Panzar–Willig (1982). Ray-average costs, moreover, are explicitly defined in footnote 2 in chapter 24 above.

[3] For further details see Baumol–Bailey–Willig (1977: 350).

coupled with market entry would prevent any consumer exploitation.[4] However, recent literature has shown that this view is overly optimistic. First, entry-deterring prices are always possible as long as there are sunk costs associated with market entry. If entry costs are high, the incumbent prices will also be high. The over-accentuation of the contestability of monopolies, as presented in many papers in the late seventies and early eighties, has only resulted from the assumption of zero sunk costs of market entry. Second, the theory of contestability in the late seventies and early eighties assumed that incumbents and potential entrants have the same access to the most recent technical development and therefore can operate under identical cost functions. By the same token, full information of both incumbent and entrant was assumed. This is clearly unrealistic. An incumbent, in contrast to an unexperienced newcomer, often has an informational advantage based on past production experience. – Recent theories which explicitly consider sunk entry costs, strategic entry deterrence, and asymmetric information are typically game-theoretic. They highlight the strategic interactions, giving many more weapons to both incumbent and entrant than the theory of contestable markets, which dealt with market entry as if the incumbent's production possibility frontier were the only relevant problem.

25.2 Regulation in a Given Environment

25.2.1 Counting Equations

Many simple regulatory rules have been suggested in a full-information framework where the regulator wants to achieve Ramsey prices but faces a manager who wants to maximize profits or output. The manager will use any degree of freedom which is left to him given the regulatory rules. The regulator on the other hand will combine so many rules as to leave no degrees of freedom for the manager. Such a simple-rules approach to Ramsey prices can be treated in the same way as the regulation of marginal-cost prices in the preceding chapter.

First case of regulation: the government totally shifts the Ramsey optimization problem to the regulated firm. The government's information requirements are low, but equally low are the firm's incentives to maximize welfare. Hence, this case of regulation is not likely to be successful.

Second case of regulation: the government sets prices or netput quantities. The firm is still left with many degrees of freedom which can be used, for example, to maximize profits.

Third case of regulation: the government sets $\mathcal{M}$ prices *and* particular regulatory rules. The MC-rule has to be replaced with the *Ramsey-rule* which

---

[4] The rest of this paragraph is taken from Bös (1991a: 69–70).

consists of $\mathcal{M}$ rules on the pricing structure and one rule on the price level, that is the revenue-cost constraint which determines whether prices on average have to be low or high. The *Ramsey rule*, therefore is described by the system of equations (1), where the prices $p_i, i \in K$ are given for the firm.[5]

If the firm faces fixed prices *and* the Ramsey rule, it is left with as many degrees of freedom as the number of all goods minus the number of regulated prices. Hence, once again, further regulatory rules should be added to the above Ramsey rule to obtain the optimum. The *efficiency rule* – produce efficiently at given Π^*[6] – absorbs the degrees of freedom which remain after fixing prices and imposing the Ramsey rule because the firm will equate marginal costs $c_i, i \notin K$ to those prices p_i which are given exogenously by the market. Hence, by decentralized decisions of the government and of the firm, precisely that welfare optimum is attained which we discussed above.[7]

If a *meet-all-demand* rule is added to the Ramsey rule, the system of equations will usually be over- or underdetermined, as in our earlier case of the regulation of marginal-cost pricing.[8]

Fourth case of regulation: the government does not set prices or quantities, but regulatory rules only. Here, the government has to combine the Ramsey rule, the efficiency rule and the meet-all-demand rule so as to obtain the desired welfare optimum.

Unfortunately, lack of information on the part of the regulator will prevent any such combination of rules from success. The efficiency rule, for instance, cannot be successfully applied by the regulator because he will lack the necessary information on the firm's technology and the manager has no incentive to inform him. Let us therefore consider some further simple rules which have been suggested to overcome the problems which result from the regulator's lack of information.

25.2.2 *The Drèze–Marchand Approach*

Let us assume the government makes use of the similarity between the Ramsey-price structure and the perfect monopoly pricing structure, and advises the firm to inflate all demand elasticities by a common factor $1/\gamma > 1$ and then to behave like a profit-maximizing monopolist (Drèze–Marchand, 1976).

There are three main objections to this proposal: first, the information requirements do not differ from those in the cases of setting prices or setting

---

[5] The case of the government fixing m quantities could be treated analogously.

[6] See eqs. (24–2) and (24–3).

[7] See section 8.1.

[8] A *profit rule* is meaningless in the Ramsey case as maximizing profit under a given profit constraint makes no sense.

quantities, as the Ramsey optimization problem must be solved by the government to find the exact value of γ. Second, any profit maximizer will apply Marshallian demand functions and not compensated ones. Hence, the firm always has an incentive to deviate from the above rule to optimize normal instead of compensated profit. Correct incentives could only be achieved by inflating factors which vary by commodity, depending on the varying income effects. Third, the proposal seems to include a strategy for the firm to cheat itself by computing profits on the basis of elasticities which the enterprise knows to be wrong. Thus there will always be a tendency for the firm's management to switch to the correct elasticities or to give false information to the government agency.

25.2.3   The Vogelsang–Finsinger Approach

Finally, we must mention the *regulatory adjustment process* discussed by Vogelsang and Finsinger (1979). This process, applicable to enterprises under increasing returns to scale, reduces the government's information requirements and is based on the profit-maximizing behavior of the firm, thus yielding positive incentive effects. The government regularizes the set of prices the enterprise is allowed to choose. These prices are at most cost covering if applied to the quantities sold in the period before. Let p_i and $z_i > 0$ be the present prices and outputs, whereas quantities z_i^o refer to the period before. Then the set of regulatory adjusting prices, RAP, is defined as follows:

$$\text{RAP} := \left\{ p \ \middle| \ \sum_i p_i z_i^o - C(z^o) \le 0 \right\}. \tag{2}$$

The demand functions $z_i(p)$ and the cost function $C(z)$ are assumed to be constant over time. Prices are set by the firm at the beginning of any period. The firm meets all demand at these prices. The regulated firm then maximizes the profits of the present period

$$\max_{p \in RAP} \left[\sum_i p_i z_i(p) - C(z(p)) \right] \tag{3}$$

which may be positive. The profit-maximizing quantities of the present serve as the basis for finding the prices of the next period. It can be shown that this iterative process converges to break-even Ramsey-prices.

The basic rationale of Vogelsang–Finsinger's adjustment process is as follows. It is evident that maximization of profit subject to a constraint on consumer welfare is dual to the Ramsey problem and therefore achieves the Ramsey optimum. The RAP-constraint (2) is not a direct constraint on consumer welfare. However, it is immediately evident that it protects consumers from high prices. More technically, RAP is a hyperplane which is tangent to the indifference surface of the welfare function. The convexity of welfare allows Vogelsang and Finsinger in their iterative process to substitute the tangent hyperplane RAP for the indifference surface of the welfare function. Each change of RAP in the iterative process is equivalent to an increase in the welfare level which the firm has to attain (and the assumption of increasing returns to scale prevents overshooting). Thus, step by step welfare increases until the Ramsey optimum is attained.[9]

Unfortunately, as shown in Sappington (1980), the Vogelsang–Finsinger approach implies undesirable incentives for the firm to increase costs in the long-run, for instance by undersupplying cost-reducing innovations.[10] Waste today in the Vogelsang–Finsinger approach increases the permitted level of prices tomorrow[11] and hence the long-run profits.

Moreover, if the iterative process were to be applied in practice, then the length of time between price reviews should be short (for instance, one month only). Otherwise, the demand and cost functions will cease to remain constant and the optimum will not be attained. This problem has found particular attention in some recent studies which exploit the similarities between the dynamic effects of price-cap regulation and the Vogelsang–Finsinger mechanism.[12] These studies will explicitly be treated when we deal with the dynamic problems of price-cap regulation (section 27.3 below).

*

The simple-rules approach applied to Ramsey regulation has failed in the same way as when applied to marginal-cost-price regulation. Hence, let us give up the dream of a simple rule which achieves welfare-optimal pricing. Therefore, we shall turn to a treatment of those regulatory constraints which are the most common in regulatory practice, namely rate-of-return and price-cap constraints. This practice accepts that there will be no welfare-optimal outcome. Accordingly, in the following two chapters we shall always deal with a profit-maximizing manager under regulatory constraint. The welfare-maximizing prices under the same constraint are also presented because they constitute useful benchmarks.

---

[9] Whereas Vogelsang–Finsinger (1979) apply a dual approach to attain a Ramsey optimum, their subsidy-adjustment process uses a direct approach to achieve marginal-cost prices. For an explicit treatment of this process see subsection 24.2.2 above.

[10] See also Gravelle (1981, 1982b, 1985).

[11] Vickers–Yarrow (1988: 106).

[12] See Brennan (1989), Neu (1993).

B
Practical Regulatory Constraints

26
Rate-of-Return Regulation

26.1   An Intuitive Introduction

Since a fixed profit constraint Π^o is exogenous for the firm, it involves frequently recurring regulatory review processes, especially in inflationary times. Asking a government to change constraints is always a tedious procedure, leading to regulatory lags and a waste of time and other resources by the firm's management. Thus, it seems to be a more economical and flexible procedure if the government regulates the firm by constraining the rate of return on investment in real terms.[1] This procedure can be found often in regulatory practice, e.g. in the United States and in different proposals of the British White Papers on Nationalised Industries (1967, 1978). Moreover, this kind of regulation has been the subject of intensive analysis from the early paper by Averch and Johnson (1962) to the book by Bailey (1973) and the recent monograph by Train (1991).

Rate-of-return regulation is relevant for public as well as for regulated private enterprises. Public enterprises may consider the rate-of-return limitation as a constraint on welfare maximization in the framework of our Boiteux-type model. Regulated private enterprises will typically treat it as a constraint on profit maximization. The results of both approaches can be compared.

The concept of a rate of return *on investment* requires a separation between capital inputs on the one side and the rest of the inputs on the other side. Typically, a dichotomization is chosen, restricting the analysis to only two inputs, capital and labor. We shall follow this tradition and assume that labor $z_o < 0$ and capital $z_1 < 0$ are used to produce outputs $z_i > 0$, $i = 2, \ldots, n$. In what follows I shall present the usual definition of a rate-of-return constraint. The reader will recognize that this constraint in its usual formulation refers to

---

[1] Other profit constraints which are partly endogenous include fixing a 'fair' mark-up on cost or fixing a 'fair' profit per unit of output. See Bailey–Malone (1970) for the resulting allocational inefficiencies.

a partial analysis, not to a general-equilibrium model: in contrast to a general equilibrium, where there could not be two prices for capital, this is assumed in the rate-of-return model. We shall return to that point after presenting the usual definition of a rate-of-return constraint.

A 'fair' rate of return on investment is earned if gross revenue minus operating expenses are sufficient to compensate the firm for its investment in plant and capital. For this purpose let us define:[2]

$$\text{Rate of Return} = \frac{\text{Gross Revenue - Labor Costs - Depreciation - Taxes}}{\text{Capital Acquisition Costs - Cumulated Depreciation}}. \quad (1)$$

To simplify the analysis we shall assume that depreciation is zero (both the value of the annual depreciation in the numerator and the cumulative value of depreciation in the denominator). We also exclude taxation. Then the rate base is reduced to the capital acquisition costs, $-p_A z_1$, where p_A are the acquisition costs per unit of capital. These unit costs p_A differ from p_1, the opportunity costs of resources tied up in plant and equipment. In the case of borrowed capital p_1 are interest costs, in the case of own capital p_1 is the return the firm could earn by lending out its capital.[3] All factor prices, p_o, p_1 and p_A, are exogenously given. We define capital in such a way that the acquisition price is equal to unity, $p_A = 1$.

Using the above assumptions we obtain the following formula for the rate of return ρ:

$$\rho = \frac{\sum_{i=2}^{n} p_i z_i + p_o z_o}{-z_1}. \quad (2)$$

Consider now the profit of the regulated firm, defined by using the opportunity costs of capital, not the acquisition costs, $\Pi = \Sigma_{i=o}^{n} p_i z_i$. Then the above definition of a rate of return can be rewritten as follows

$$\Pi = (\rho - p_1)(-z_1). \quad (3)$$

This shows that the rate of return on investment can always directly be transformed into the profit of the firm. Accordingly, any rate-of-return con-

---

[2] This is the definiton given by Averch–Johnson (1962: 1054); extended by the inclusion of taxes, see Berg–Tschirhart (1988: 298–9).

[3] See Train (1991: 34). An alternative interpretation considers z_1 as the physical capital with a price of one dollar per unit, whence p_1 'is the percentage – reflecting the cost of financial capital, which is then used for the acquisition of physical capital' (Berg–Tschirhart, 1988: 299). In Boiteux-type models, however, we do not have this distinction between physical and financial capital.

straint is a profit constraint.[4] However, whether a minimum or a maximum profit is prescribed by regulation depends on the objective of the regulated firm. Let us restrict the analysis to rate-of-return constraints which imply a profit above the unconstrained welfare-maximizing level and below the unconstrained profit-maximizing level. Therefore, a profit maximizer must be regulated so as to avoid excessive profits

$$\Pi \le (\rho - p_1)(-z_1). \tag{4}$$

On the other hand, a welfare maximizer must be regulated so as to keep his profits from becoming too low, as would result from welfare-optimally low prices. Hence in that case the constraint must be defined the other way round:

$$\Pi \ge (\rho - p_1)(-z_1). \tag{5}$$

Note that a profit constraint which exceeds the profit level of the unconstrained welfare maximum does not necessarily imply positive profits. Hence, we cannot conclude a priori whether $(\rho - p_1)$ is positive or negative.

Any such profit constraint evidently differs from a 'neutral' constraint Π^o because of its asymmetric treatment of the inputs. Compared to the neutral constraint, rate-of-return regulation will typically distort the capital-labor input ratio. The output prices of the multiproduct public sector or regulated private enterprise will be distorted as well.

Since this book considers pricing and price regulation in a static general-equilibrium framework, we have to face the problem that the usual rate-of-return model assumes two prices of capital, p_1 and p_A. If there were a perfect capital market, these two prices would coincide; in contrast, rate-of-return theorists usually assume that they differ. However, in order to retain the flavor of the rate-of-return literature in the presentation of this chapter, I prefer to give up parts of the general-equilibrium framework than to equalize p_1 and p_A. Hence, in this chapter I refrain from assuming equilibrium at the market for capital, and let p_1 and p_A differ.

There is yet another problem which arises from choosing capital as the numeraire, $p_A = 1$. Since labor no longer has the price of unity, we cannot choose the usual definition of marginal costs. For this purpose we solve the technology $g(z) = 0$ to obtain a capital-requirement function

$$z_1 = z_1(z_o, z_2, \ldots, z_n). \tag{6}$$

This allows to write marginal costs c_i as follows

---

[4] Cfr. Bailey–Malone (1970).

$$\frac{\partial z_1}{\partial z_i} = -\frac{\partial g/\partial z_i}{\partial g/\partial z_1} = -c_i. \tag{7}$$

Here c_i are shadow prices which measure the marginal *capital* costs of producing good i (for z_o it is a partial marginal rate of transformation). These 'marginal costs' are evaluated at capital acquisition costs, $p_A = 1$. The connection between c_i and C_i, the marginal costs proper, can be treated analogously to the case of the marginal *labor* costs, which are denoted by c_i in the rest of the book. For convenience, we shall always speak of c_i as the *marginal costs*.

26.2   Rate of Return and Welfare Maximization

Let us consider a Boiteux-type model: let profit, however, be constrained by prescribing a minimum rate of return. Some further restrictive assumptions are made because it is the main aim of this chapter to compare a welfare maximizer and a profit maximizer who face the same rate-of-return constraint. The welfare maximizer's instruments are its labor input z_o and its output quantities $z_i^+, i = 2, \ldots, n$. Capital input z_1 is indirectly chosen via the capital requirement function $z_1(z_o, z^+)$. It is well possible that the firm is a price setter for some of its outputs and a price taker for some others; hence its price instruments are $p_k, k \in K \subseteq \tilde{I}$ where $\tilde{I} := I \backslash \{0, 1\}$. We exclude redistribution of the non-labor incomes $r^h, h = 1, \ldots, H$. (Would you give any profit maximizer the right to redistribute by lump-sum transfers?) The board of the enterprise cares about the equilibria of the output markets, but not of the labor and capital markets[5] (as seems a sensible assumption for a regulated profit maximizer). Finally, we assume perfect competition in the rest of the economy. The board of the enterprise maximizes the following Lagrangean function:

$$\mathcal{F} = W(v^1(p, r^1), \ldots, v^H(\cdot)) - \sum_{i=2}^{n} \alpha_i [x_i(\cdot) - z_i - y_i(\cdot)]$$

$$- \gamma \left[-(\rho - p_1)z_1 - \sum_{i=o}^{n} p_i z_i \right]. \tag{8}$$

---

[5] Equilibrium in the labor market can be introduced without changing anything in our analysis. Postulating equilibrium at the capital market would lead to some minor complications of the analysis since z_1 could not be chosen as direct instrument and hence there would be no $\partial \mathcal{F}/\partial z_1$ equation which could be used to replace α_1 in the $\partial \mathcal{F}/\partial p_k$ equations. Due to this complication, one more term would appear in the pricing formulas, which made the interpretation more tedious without leading to new economic insight.

We have assumed that the minimum rate of return has been fixed so as to achieve a profit which exceeds the unconstrained welfare-maximizing profit. Therefore, the welfare-maximizing firm will reduce its output prices as much as possible and the rate-of-return constraint will always be binding. Accordingly, the Lagrangean parameter $\gamma \geq 0$ (Kuhn-Tucker). Moreover, since at the optimum $\partial \mathcal{F}/\partial \rho = \gamma z_1 < 0$, we know that the parameter is strictly positive.

We obtain the following pricing structure[6]

$$\sum_{i=2}^{n}(p_i - \rho c_i)\frac{\partial z_i^D}{\partial p_k} = -(1 - F_k)z_k; \qquad k \in K, \tag{9}$$

where we have assumed $x_k = z_k$. The distributional characteristics are defined slightly differently from the usual case, however, there is no difference in the qualitative properties of the F_k's,

$$F_k := \sum_h \frac{(\partial W/\partial v^h)}{\gamma}\frac{\partial v^h}{\partial r^h} \cdot \frac{x_k^h}{x_k}. \tag{10}$$

The pricing structure (9) resembles the Feldstein result, replacing c_i with ρc_i. Hence, the firm will behave like a profit-maximizing monopolist who inflates price elasticities by the factors $1/(1-F_k)$. Moreover, the input allocation is distorted. The most eye-catching interpretation of this input distortion can be given if we assume a perfect capital market and therefore $p_1 = 1$. In that case $\Pi = (\rho - 1)(-z_i)$ and profits or deficits of the enterprise are associated with a rate of return above or below unity. If the firm is obliged to earn a positive profit, we have $\rho > 1$, then the marginal capital requirements c_i are overestimated and the firm will *undercapitalize* compared with the efficient capital-labor ratio. This implies that prices for labor-intensive goods are too low and vice versa. A cost-covering welfare maximizer, however will use the inputs efficiently, because $\rho = 1$ and therefore there is no distortion in the marginal capital requirements. Finally, if the firm is allowed to run a deficit, we have $\rho < 1$, the marginal capital requirements c_i are underestimated and the firm will *overcapitalize*.

The exogenous profit constraint Π^o, on the other hand, always leads to an efficient capital-labor ratio because it treats inputs symmetrically. This is an important theoretical advantage of Ramsey–Feldstein regulation as compared to rate-of-return regulation. This theoretical advantage, however, has to be balanced against the practical disadvantages mentioned in the introduction to

---

[6] Labor inputs are determined according to $p_o = \rho c_o$.

this chapter. These disadvantages may be more important for practical applications, as we do not know the exact empirical relevance of the theoretically inefficient input choices.

26.3   Rate of Return and Profit Maximization

US rate-of-return regulation is directed at profit maximizers rather than welfare maximizers. Hence, we should compare this approach to the case of a welfare maximizer. For this purpose we consider a profit-maximizing regulated firm, setting prices $p_k, k \in K \subseteq \tilde{I}$, labor inputs z_o and output quantities $z_i^+, i \in \tilde{I}$. We exclude lump-sum transfers. This exclusion can be justified ideologically: we do not want to give the profit-maximizing enterprise the right to control the income distribution in order to maximize its profits. Hence, the enterprise is restricted to one-part tariffs and is not allowed to set different income deductions and transfers for individuals as the fixed part of a two-part tariff.

The firm considers the market equilibria for all outputs. In our partial approach, however, there is no need for the firm to consider the equilibrium of the labor and capital markets. The technology is introduced into the model by applying the capital requirement function $z_1(z_o, z_2 \ldots, z_n)$.

The maximum profit the firm is allowed to make depends on the rate of return, as fixed by the *government*. To deal with the most relevant case, we assume this rate of return to exceed the opportunity costs of resources p_1, since otherwise the enterprise would have to run a deficit (and a private enterprise would leave the market). On the other hand, the rate of return must be chosen in such a way that the profit permitted falls below the unconstrained monopoly profit. Under these conditions the profit constraint will always be binding and the Lagrangean parameter will satisfy $\gamma \leq 0$ (Kuhn–Tucker).

Hence, the firm maximizes the following Lagrangean function:

$$\mathcal{F} = \sum_{i=o}^{n} p_i z_i - \sum_{i=2}^{n} \alpha_i [x_i(p) - z_i - y_i(p)]$$
$$- \gamma \left[-(\rho - p_1)z_1 - \sum_{i=o}^{n} p_i z_i \right]. \tag{11}$$

This yields the first-order conditions[7]

$$\sum_{i=2}^{n} \left(p_i - \frac{1 + \gamma\rho}{1 + \gamma} c_i \right) \frac{\partial z_i^D}{\partial p_k} = -z_k; \qquad k \in K. \tag{12}$$

---

[7] Labor inputs are determined according to $p_o = c_o \cdot (1+\gamma\rho)/(1+\gamma)$.

Inputs are not treated symmetrically, rather the marginal capital require-ments c_i are distorted by $(1 + \gamma\rho)/(1 + \gamma)$. This term depends on the rate of return ρ and on the Lagrangean parameter γ which lies in the interval $(-1, 0]$, the limiting cases occurring for zero profits $(\gamma = -1; \ \rho = p_1)$ and for monopoly profits $(\gamma = 0)$.[8,9] For the following it is convenient to deal only with cases where the distortionary term is positive.

The marginal capital requirements are underestimated if the rate of re-turn ρ exceeds unity, that is $\rho > 1$. In this case the rate-of-return regu-lated profit maximizer behaves as if he were an unconstrained monopolist who underestimates the marginal capital requirements. This property of our pricing formula corresponds to the well-known Averch–Johnson effect of over-capitalization resulting from this kind of regulation.[10] The resulting price structure reduces the prices of capital-intensive goods. The rate-of-return regulation, therefore, does not only imply a suboptimal structure of inputs but also a suboptimal structure of outputs because of a distortion of output prices resulting from regulation. This effect vanishes if the constraint is non-binding as then the enterprise will follow the usual perfect-monopoly price structure which does not imply any miscalculation of the marginal capital requirements. (If $\gamma = 0$, the distorting term $(1 + \gamma\rho)/(1 + \gamma)$ is equal to unity.) This reveals a puzzling feature of the rate-of-return regulation: if the regulated firm is restricted in its ability to maximize profits, it will misallo-cate inputs and outputs. If it is not so restricted, it will allocate inputs and outputs X-efficiently, albeit monopolistically.

If we assume a perfect capital market with opportunity costs of resources $p_1 = 1$, then in our model the Averch–Johnson effect vanishes if the rate of return is equal to the opportunity costs of capital. (If $\rho = 1$, then once again $(1+\gamma\rho)/(1+\gamma)$ is equal to unity.)[11] While the original Averch–Johnson model failed to reach this intuitive result, it has meanwhile been established in some other papers, in particular in Bawa–Sibley (1980).

---

[8] The sign and range of this Lagrangean multiplier are a much discussed aspect of the Averch–Johnson literature. For details see Bailey (1973: 25–8; 73–4; 80).

[9] $\gamma=0$ for monopoly profits is straightforward. $\gamma=-1$ for zero profits can be derived as follows. Set $\rho=p_1$. Then, applying the envelope theorem, consider $\partial\mathcal{F}/\partial z_1=0=p_1(1+\gamma)$ which yields $\gamma=-1$ because $p_1\neq0$. – It should be mentioned that the restriction of the range of γ does not necessarily imply $\partial\gamma/\partial(\rho-p_1)>0$ although the above mentioned interpretation may suggest that.

[10] There is no clear-cut empirical evidence that the Averch–Johnson effect actually mat-ters. See Joskow–Noll (1980) for further references.

[11] If ρ were smaller than unity, the firm would overestimate the cost of capital and undercapitalize. However, this would imply a deficit of the private firm and hence we do not deal with that special case.

26.4   Dynamic Problems of Rate-of-Return Regulation

The rate of return will be reviewed in regular intervals to cope with technology changes. The time period between two regulatory reviews is called 'regulatory lag' and causes intricate dynamic problems of rate-of-return regulation.[12]

Consider a regulator who sets prices on the basis of some fair rate of return and a regulated firm which reduces costs in order to increase its profits. Between the reviews the firm enjoys the profits from its cost reductions. At the review, however, the prices are set so as to shift the gains of the efficiency increases from the producer to the consumer (Baumol–Klevorick, 1970: 184–8). Hence the regulatory-lag problem resembles the problem of patent lifetimes (Bailey, 1974).[13] If the time span between two reviews is too short, there are not many incentives for the firm to undertake innovative activities, since the firm is not given the opportunity to enjoy the gains from innovation long enough. On the other hand, if the regulatory lag is too long, there are high incentives for innovation but the consumers are exploited because the cost reductions from innovations are not passed on to consumers by lower prices quickly enough.

Particular problems arise if the regulated firm is imperfectly informed. It may for instance only know some exogenous probability of regulatory review (Klevorick, 1973) and, accordingly be more careful in its policy of overcapitalization. More sophisticatedly, the probability of regulatory review may be endogenized. Bawa and Sibley (1980) assume that the probability of review depends on the amount of current profits in excess (or deficit) of the fair profits allowed by rate-of-return regulation. The probability increases with any increase in current profits. The resulting stochastic model converges to that price where there is no excess of current over fair profit. Moreover, cost minimization is achieved.

Finally, if the principal is imperfectly informed, the regulatory lag may cause the firm to behave strategically. The firm knows that at the next regulatory review the rate of return will be set so as to guarantee a fair profit to the firm. The basis for the calculation of this fair profit is the production possibilities at the very moment of the review. Insofar as cost-reducing innovations are reversible, the firm has an incentive to be a high-cost firm at the moment of the regulatory reviews, but a low-cost firm in between. A sawtooth profile of the firm's cost-reducing innovations will result.

The preceding paragraph implicitly assumed a long-term regulatory contract. Such a long-term contract may be infeasible because it may be impossible to adequately describe the future technological development today. In

---

[12] For a short overview see Vickers–Yarrow (1988: 85–8).

[13] See also Lesourne (1976) and Bailey (1976).

that case regulation necessarily consists of repeated short-term games. Laffont and Tirole (1987, 1988) consider a two-period version of such a game. The regulator is now in a position to update his beliefs on the productivity of the regulated firm at the end of the first period and to offer a new regulatory scheme for the second period. The regulator learns from the behavior of the firm in period 1, for instance he infers from low-cost production that the firm has high productivity. The regulated firm, however, fears that true revelation of its productivity would induce the regulator to extract all rents from the firm in the second period. Hence the firm has an incentive not to produce at the boundary of its production possibilities in period 1 (*ratchet effect*). Accordingly, in such a regulatory setting, pooling equilibria in the first period are a likely outcome at the perfect equilibria of the game. In such an equilibrium more productive firms behave like less productive ones to prevent the regulator from learning their true productivity. If the regulator attempts to avoid such phenomena by offering a large transfer to a highly productive firm in period 1, he may face another problem: it may now be worthwhile for a less productive firm to mimic the behavior of the more productive firm, cash-in the large transfer and terminate the relationship at the beginning of the second period (*take-the-money-and-run strategy*).

27
Price-Cap Regulation

27.1   Price Caps and the Case of RPI − X[1]

The rate-of-return regulation which has been applied in many countries for
many years has been critized:[2]

(i)   for its lack of incentives for cost reduction and technological innovation,
because increasing capital inputs imply an increase in the allowed profit;

(ii)   for its capital-distorting effects: since the allowed rate of return is
defined as a percentage of the capital inputs, profit can be increased by producing too capital-intensively. This is known as the Averch–Johnson effect;

(iii)   because of its high information requirements for the regulatory authority: since the profit allowed is defined as a percentage of the capital inputs, the
regulator has to determine which depreciation policy is appropriate, and how
joint capital costs are allocated between regulated and unregulated services,
and between the various regulated services.[3]

The US Federal Communications Commission, FCC (1987, 1988), proposed replacing rate-of-return regulation with 'price-cap' regulation in the
market for local and long-distance telephone service. Meanwhile, many US
states have adopted price-cap regulation of intrastate telephone services provided by AT&T, and the FCC has recently begun to apply price caps on
AT&T's prices for interstate services.[4] Price caps are typically applied only
to prices for monopolistically supplied goods. A separate price cap can be
defined for every single good in monopolistic supply. If the index m denotes
monopolistically supplied goods, a profit-maximizing firm faces constraints
$p_m \leq \overline{p}_m$, where the price ceilings $\overline{p}_m$ are set by the regulator and the firm
can choose any price p_m up to the limit $\overline{p}_m$. However, the flexibility of the
regulated firm can be greatly enhanced if a joint price ceiling is defined for
a basket of services supplied by the firm. The best-known example of such
a joint ceiling is the $RPI − X$ regulation: an average price of some bundle of

---

[1]   The following two paragraphs are taken from Bös (1991a: 65–6).

[2]   For a recent survey comparing rate-of-return and price-cap regulation see Liston
(1993).

[3]   See, e.g., Littlechild (1988: 55), and Braeutigam and Panzar (1989).

[4]   Mathios and Rogers (1989) present an empirical investigation comparing AT&T's
prices for intrastate, direct dial, long-distance telephone services in states that apply price-
cap regulation with those services in states which continue to use rate-of-return regulation.

the firm's products must not exceed the retail price index minus an exogenously fixed constant X. This form of price regulation has been proposed by Littlechild (1983) and is the basis for the regulation of, among others, British Telecom, British Gas, and the UK public electricity suppliers (i.e. the twelve area companies responsible for the local distribution of electricity).

In the following two sections we shall deal with both a welfare maximizer and a profit maximizer who face an $RPI - X$ constraint. We shall restrict the analysis to the practically relevant cases, that is we shall deal with constraints that imply a profit which exceeds the unconstrained welfare-maximizing level but falls below the unconstrained profit-maximizing level. In this range, a profit maximizer must be prevented from exploiting the consumers by a constraint

$$P \leq RPI - X, \tag{1}$$

where P is a price index of the monopolistically supplied outputs of the firm, in our models an average of the regulated prices $\{p_k, k \in K\}$. This is one of the most usual price-cap regulations for privatized firms. On the other hand, a welfare maximizer must be prevented from reducing his prices too sharply. Hence his $RPI - X$ constraint must be defined the other way round,

$$P \geq RPI - X. \tag{2}$$

Let us first repeat the definition of the retail price index, RPI.[5] This is a Laspeyres index of the usual type, which compares those expenditures which at changing prices are necessary to enable a representative consumer to buy an unaltered basket of consumer goods, $x_i^o > 0$, $i = d + 1, \ldots, n$. As usual, we apply the superscript 'o' to define variables of the base period in which the fixed commodity basket of the index was empirically determined.

$$RPI = \frac{\sum_{i=d+1}^n p_i x_i^o}{\sum_{i=d+1}^n p_i^o x_i^o} = \frac{\sum_{i=d+1}^n p_i x_i^o}{D^o}, \tag{3}$$

where we have introduced the abbreviation $D^o := \sum_{i=d+1}^n p_i^o x_i^o$, which will be convenient in the following derivations.

Let us next define the price index P and the 'X' percent to be deducted from the retail price index. We will always assume that the index P is a subindex of the retail price index.[6] Hence the index P is also a Laspeyres price index,

---

[5] See chapters 4 and 18 above.

[6] Other procedures are a bit strange, for instance taking as weights revenues of the relevant classes of business. For that practice see Bös (1991a: 126, 131-2).

$$P = \frac{\sum_{k \in K} p_k x_k^o}{\sum_{k \in K} p_k^o x_k^o} = \frac{\sum_{k \in K} p_k x_k^o}{P^o}, \qquad (4)$$

where we have introduced the abbreviation $P^o := \Sigma_{k \in K} p_k^o x_k^o$.

Another problem is the setting of X. Fewest distortions arise if X is taken as exogenously given for the regulated firm. We will call that 'political regulation'. However, from the very conception of the $RPI - X$ regulation, another interpretation has also been prevalent, according to which X should be chosen as an estimate of the firm's increase in productivity,[7]

$$X_t = \frac{\sum_{i=o}^{n} p_i^{t-1}(z_i^t - z_i^{t-1})}{\sum_{i=o}^{n} p_i^{t-1} z_i^{t-1}} = \frac{\sum_{i=o}^{n} p_i^{t-1} z_i^t}{I^{t-1}} - 1 \qquad (5)$$

where $t, t - 1$ are indices of time. X_t is a sum of weighted output increases minus a sum of weighted input increases. If X is endogenous for the firm as in (5) we speak of a 'productivity-related regulation'.

27.2   RPI – X and Welfare Maximization

In this section we employ the Boiteux framework. The fixed revenue-cost constraint, however, is replaced by an $RPI - X$ constraint. To be regulated are the output prices $p_k, k \in K$, all other prices are exogenously given for the regulated welfare-maximizing firm. We assume perfect competition in the unregulated private sector.

Since the index P is a subindex of the retail price index, we can rewrite the $RPI - X$ constraint as follows:

$$\sum_k p_k x_k^o \geq \mathcal{J}(X) \qquad (6)$$

where

$$\mathcal{J}(X) := \frac{D^o P^o}{D^o - P^o} \left[\frac{\sum_{\substack{i=d+1 \\ i \neq k}}^{n} p_i x_i^o}{D^o} - X \right]. \qquad (7)$$

Note that the prices $p_i, i \neq k$ are exogenously given. Hence in the case of political regulation $\mathcal{J}(X) = \mathcal{J}^o$ is a constant. In the case of productivity-related regulation it depends on the firm's production plans $\{z_i, i = o, \ldots, n\}$. $\mathcal{J}(X)$ is always positive. First, $D^o - P^o > 0$ because the sum D^o contains

---

[7] For this definition see Vogelsang (1989: 34).

more outputs than P^o. Moreover, the term in square brackets is positive because the 'rest-index' referring to goods $i \neq k$ is much larger than X.[8]

27.2.1 Political Regulation

Let the percentage X be exogenously given for the enterprise. Then it maximizes the following Lagrangean function with respect to prices $p_k, k \in K$, netputs $z_i, i = o, \dots, n$, and, possibly, lump-sum incomes $r^h, h = 1, \dots, H$:

$$
\mathcal{F} = W(v^1(p, r^1), \dots, v^H(\cdot)) - \sum_{i=o}^{n} \alpha_i \left[\sum_h x_i^h(p, r^h) - z_i - \sum_j y_i^j(p) \right] -
$$
$$
- \beta g(z) - \overline{\gamma} \left[\mathcal{J}^o - \sum_{k \in K} p_k x_k^o \right].
$$
(8)

Since we have assumed that the $RPI - X$ constraint implies a profit which exceeds the unconstrained welfare-maximizing profit, the firm will always wish to reduce prices as much as possible. The constraint, therefore, is always binding and the Lagrangean parameter $\overline{\gamma} \geq 0$ according to the Kuhn-Tucker theorem.

We obtain the following structures of pricing:[9]

(i)   for the non-compensated case (equivalent to equation (3–21b))[10]

$$
\sum_{i=o}^{n} (p_i - c_i) \frac{\partial z_i^D}{\partial p_k} = - \left(1 - F_k + \gamma \frac{x_k^o}{x_k} \right) z_k; \quad k \in K.
$$
(9)

(ii) for the compensated case (equivalent to equation (3–24))

$$
\sum_{i=o}^{n} (p_i - c_i) \frac{\partial \hat{z}_i}{\partial p_k} = -\gamma \frac{x_k^o}{x_k} z_k; \quad k \in K.
$$
(10)

---

[8] RPI is a figure like 1.07. The term X is a figure like 0.04. The numerator of RPI is reduced by the sum $\Sigma_k p_k x_k^o$. However, this sum is only some small part of the total revenue of the economy, depending on the size of the regulated firm in question.

[9] The derivation follows the usual lines of chapter 3. However, since $\alpha_i = \beta(\partial g/\partial z_i)$, we have to proceed as follows. Since
$\Sigma_h \lambda^h (\partial v^h/\partial p_k) = -F_k \Sigma_h x_k^h = F_k \Sigma_i \Sigma_h p_i (\partial x_i^h/\partial p_k)$,
we obtain
$\Sigma_i (p_i F_k - c_i) \Sigma_h (\partial x_i^h/\partial p_k) - \Sigma_i c_i (\partial y_i^j/\partial p_k) = -\gamma x_k^o$.
Now add on both sides $(1-F_k)\Sigma_i p_i \Sigma_h (\partial x_i^h/\partial p_k)$ and recall that perfect competition implies
$\Sigma_i p_i (\partial y_i^j/\partial p_k) = 0$.

[10] We have assumed $z_k = x_k$.

Let us begin with the interpretation of the non-compensated case. Income effects matter and are expressed by the distributional characteristics F_k which are positive and higher for necessities than for luxuries.[11] However, there is a countervailing effect which reduces the distributional consequences of the distributional characteristics. The term $\gamma(x_k^o/x_k)$ is non-negative and is higher for necessities than for luxuries. This results from the empirical facts of growing economies where the percentage of necessities consumed shrinks over time whereas the percentage of luxuries increases. Hence the ratio of consumption of some base period and the present period x_k^o/x_k is higher for necessities. Since $\gamma > 0$,[12] this *RPI*-effect counteracts the consequences of the distributional characteristics.

At first sight it seems strange that an $RPI - X$ constraint reduces the distributionally positive consequences of welfare-maximizing pricing. Didn't we learn in chapter 18 that the minimization of a retail price index given a fixed-profit constraint yields distributionally positive results, i.e., leads to the same pricing structure as the profit-constrained welfare maximization if income effects matter? In both cases it is the overly high weights of necessities in the *RPI* basket of the base period which drives the result. However, if necessities are given too high a weight in the objective function, the welfare maximizer cares particularly about necessities and reduces their prices. If, on the other hand, necessities are given too high a weight in the constraint, then these weights hinder the welfare maximizer from reducing the prices of necessities as much as he would like.

The distributionally negative consequences of the $RPI - X$ constraint can also be seen in the compensated case. This case is to be compared with Ramsey pricing. In contrast to the Ramsey rule, however, on the right-hand side of equation (10) the *RPI*-effect x_k^o/x_k matters. The consequences can most clearly be seen if we consider a special case of the pricing formula, assuming two goods and no cross-price elasticities. Then the compensated pricing rule for the $RPI - X$-constrained welfare maximizer is as follows:

$$\frac{\mathcal{L}_1}{\mathcal{L}_2} = \frac{(x_1^o/x_1)\eta_{22}}{(x_2^o/x_2)\eta_{11}}, \tag{11}$$

where $\mathcal{L}_i$ are the Lerner-indices and η_{ii} the compensated price elasticities of demand. Let good 1 be a luxury and good 2 a necessity. Therefore $x_2^o/x_2 > x_1^o/x_1$. Both the *RPI*-effect and the consequences of the inverse elasticities lead to a higher Lerner index of the necessity.

---

[11] Compare chapter 9 above.

[12] Since $\partial \mathcal{F}/\partial \mathcal{J}^o = -\overline{\gamma} < 0$ and $\beta(\partial g/\partial z_o) > 0$.

27.2.2 *Productivity-Related Regulation*

Next we investigate a variant of $RPI - X$ regulation where X is chosen as an increase of the firm's increase in productivity, as specified in equation (5) above. The optimization approach remains the same as in the case of political regulation, only $\mathcal{J}^o$ is replaced by $\mathcal{J}(X)$. The marginal conditions $\mathcal{F}_{p_k} = 0$ are the same as before, because the productivity index is independent of the present-period prices. However, the marginal conditions $\mathcal{F}_{z_i} = 0$ become

$$\alpha_i = \beta(\partial g/\partial z_i) - \overline{\gamma}\frac{D^o P^o}{D^o - P^o} \cdot \frac{p_i^{t-1}}{I^{t-1}}; \quad i = o, \dots, n. \tag{12}$$

This implies that the right-hand side of the pricing formulas[13] remains the same as in the case of political regulation and the distributionally negative $RPI - X$ effect still prevails. On the left-hand side of the pricing formulas, however, the $(p_i - c_i)$-terms are replaced with

$$\left(p_i - c_i + \gamma\frac{D^o P^o}{D^o - P^o} \cdot \frac{p_i^{t-1}}{I^{t-1}} \right); \quad i = o, \dots, n. \tag{13}$$

Two effects are combined in this change:

(i) Output prices $p_i, i \in K$, are determined on the basis of underestimated costs

$$\tilde{c}_i = c_i - \gamma\frac{D^o P^o}{D^o - P^o} \cdot \frac{p_i^{t-1}}{I^{t-1}} \le c_i; \quad i \in K. \tag{14}$$

The higher the output price of the preceding period, p_i^{t-1}, the greater the underestimation of costs and the more pronounced the tendency to lower the output price of the present period p_i.

(ii) For the inputs $i \notin K$ let us define modified prices

$$\tilde{p}_i = p_i + \gamma\frac{D^o P^o}{D^o - P^o} \cdot \frac{p_i^{t-1}}{I^{t-1}} \ge p_i; \quad i \notin K. \tag{15}$$

The welfare maximizer calculates inputs at excessively high prices which means that too little input is used. The associated increase in productivity lowers the output prices which fits with the output-increasing tendencies mentioned in point (i) above.

We forgo any explicit treatment of the complicated dynamic system of regulation which is revealed by (14) and (15).

---

[13] Equations (9) and (10) above.

The above interpretation concentrated on the left-hand side of the regulatory pricing formulas. The right-hand side is unchanged as in equations (9) and (10) and is distributionally unfavorable. In conclusion, we face a trade-off. If a productivity-related $RPI - X$ constraint is added to a welfare-maximization approach, this increases productivity at the expense of burdening lower-income consumers.

27.3   RPI – X and Profit Maximization

Let us now compare the welfare maximizer with a profit maximizer who operates in exactly the same environment: he is obliged to consider market equilibria in all markets,[14] applies the technology $g(z) = 0$ and faces an $RPI - X$ constraint. Once again we assume perfect competition in the private sector.

The $RPI - X$ constraint can be written as

$$\sum_k p_k x_k^o \leq \mathcal{J}(X), \tag{16}$$

where $\mathcal{J}(X)$ is defined as in the preceding section.[15] Depending on $\mathcal{J}$ being constant or not, we once again distinguish between political regulation and productivity-related regulation.

27.3.1   Political Regulation

The profit-maximizing firm sets prices $p_k, k \in K$, input and output quantities $z_i, i = o, \ldots, n$. For ideological reasons the firm is not given the right to redistribute lump-sum incomes in order to maximize profits. The percentage X is exogenously given for the firm and hence it maximizes the following Lagrangean function:

$$\mathcal{F} = \sum_{i=o}^{n} p_i z_i - \sum_{i=o}^{n} \alpha_i \left[\sum_h x_i^h(p, r^h) - z_i - \sum_j y_i^j(p) \right] - $$
$$- \beta g(z) - \overline{\gamma} \left[\mathcal{J}^o - \sum_k p_k x_k^o \right]. \tag{17}$$

The $RPI - X$ constraint is always binding, since the constraint was chosen in such a way that the permitted profit falls below the unconstrained monopoly

---

[14] In Bös (1991a: 127–33) the firm takes care of the equilibria of the output markets only. Qualitatively the same result is achieved as in the present section.

[15] See equation (7) above.

profit. This implies that the Lagrangean multiplier $\bar{\gamma} \leq 0$ according to the Kuhn-Tucker theorem. The following structure of regulatory pricing results:[16]

$$\sum_{i=o}^{n}(p_i - c_i)\frac{\partial z_i^D}{\partial p_k} = -\left(1 + \gamma\frac{x_k^o}{x_k}\right) z_k; \quad \forall k, \tag{18}$$

where we have assumed $z_k = x_k$. Since $\gamma \leq 0$ and x_k^o/x_k is higher for necessities, the effect is distributionally positive. The $RPI - X$ effect has the same qualitative properties as the distributional characteristics of the Feldstein-type. Whereas $RPI - X$ hindered a welfare maximizer in his distributional policy, $RPI - X$ favors lower-income consumers if imposed on a profit maximizer. There are two explanations for this surprising result:

(i)   The overly high weights of necessities in the RPI basket of the base period drive the result. Since necessities are given too much weight in the constraint, these weights hinder the profit maximizer from increasing the prices of necessities as far as he would like. The high weights of necessities always constrain the firm – the welfare maximizer cannot reduce prices as much as he would like and the profit maximizer cannot increase them as far as he would like. This explains why the same constraint can have distributionally positive or negative effects, depending on the objective function.

(ii)   The maximization of profit given an $RPI - X$ constraint with constant X is precisely the dual approach of the minimization of RPI given a fixed profit constraint. Therefore the results are the same as in chapter 18 above where we explicitly dealt with the minimization of price indices.

27.3.2   Productivity-Related Regulation

Finally, we consider the productivity-related variant of the percentage X as defined in equation (5) above. The optimization approach remains the same, however $\mathcal{J}$ changes from $\mathcal{J}^o$ to $\mathcal{J}(X)$. Consequently, on the left-hand side of the pricing formula the $(p_i - c_i)$-terms are replaced with

$$\left(p_i - c_i + \gamma\frac{D^o P^o}{D^o - P^o} \cdot \frac{p_i^{t-1}}{I^{t-1}}\right); \quad i = o, \ldots, n. \tag{19}$$

This result is just opposite to the case of welfare maximization because $\gamma \leq 0$. Hence output prices are determined on the basis of overestimated costs which

---

[16]   Once again, the derivation follows the lines of chapter 3. Note that $\partial \mathcal{F}/\partial z_i$ yields $\alpha_i = -p_i + \beta(\partial g/\partial z_i)$ and therefore after substituting into $\partial \mathcal{F}/\partial p_k$ and dividing by $\beta(\partial g/\partial z_o)$ we have to add $\Sigma_{i=o}^{n}(p_i - p_i/\beta_o)(\partial z_i^D/\partial p_k)$ to both sides of the equation.   Then recall $\Sigma_i\Sigma_h p_i(\partial x_i^h/\partial p_k) = -x_k$ and $\Sigma_i\Sigma_j p_i(\partial y_i^j/\partial p_k) = 0$ from the assumption of perfect competition.

is output reducing. On the other hand, the inputs are calculated at too low prices which means that too much input is used.[17] The associated reduction in productivity pushes output prices upwards. This is exactly the result we expected from the explicit introduction of factor productivity in the price-cap regulation of a profit maximizer. If productivity increases are deducted from *RPI* when calculating the maximum increases of output prices, the firm is punished for productivity increases. Consequently the firm will keep the productivity increases lower and maximize its profits by increasing output prices. The implications of this result are straightforward. X must remain an exogenously given constant to maintain the firm's incentives for efficient input policy.

The right-hand side of the regulatory pricing formula remains unchanged as in (18) and therefore we can summarize: if a productivity-related $RPI - X$ constraint is added to a profit-maximization approach, lower-income consumers are favored at the expense of reduced productivity.

27.4   Dynamic Problems of RPI − X Regulation

From the qualitative point of view, the dynamic problems of $RPI - X$ regulation are the same as those of a rate-of-return regulation. For a profit maximizer, typically there is an incentive to produce more efficiently because the firm can retain the gains from cost reductions until the next review. It may, however, be worthwhile to stop innovating activities in good time before the next review in order to induce a less restrictive review which would enable the firm to achieve higher profits after the review. The welfare maximizer, however, who is not permitted to reduce prices below some limits, cannot reap the welfare gains from cost reductions by low prices. His only incentive for cost reduction is the possibility of inducing a regulatory review which increases X and hence allows lower prices after the next review.

If cost-reducing innovations are induced by a 'price cap minus X' constraint, there is a discontinuity problem as shown by Cabral–Riordan (1989) for the case of a profit-maximizing firm. In their model, R&D effort is increasing in X, but only up to a critical level X^*. If the constraint is tightened beyond X^*, that is $X > X^*$, there will be no R&D effort at all. Cost reductions which increase in X can be explained by the 'Arrow effect': the lower the price, the higher the quantity supplied and the higher the savings from a reduction in unit costs.[18] However, this effect breaks down at the critical level X^* because for higher X's the price is not high enough to cover the expenses for R&D effort.

---

[17]   The rest of this paragraph is taken from Bös (1991a: 133).
[18]   Arrow (1962).

Most of the recent literature on incentives for cost reduction under price-cap regulation deals with asymmetric information – typically it is assumed that the management of the firm has some private information on parameters which influence the technology.[19],[20] The more uncertain the costs of the firm, the higher the price ceilings must be set in order to keep the regulated firm profitable. At high levels of uncertainty, cost-plus regulation will be preferred to price-cap regulation, in particular if the regulator's objective is to maximize consumer surplus. If the objective is to maximize total welfare, which includes the firm's profits, cost-plus may be less preferred than price caps because the higher price limits are less damaging to the objective (Schmalensee, 1989). Since asymmetric information is intrinsic to price regulation, it may be a good idea to let the firm choose between various forms of regulation so as to exploit its private knowledge about its capabilities and cost-reducing activities. In Lewis and Sappington (1989) the firm chooses between a modified rate-of-return regulation and a modified price-cap regulation. Firms with a potential for large productivity improvements self-select for price caps.

When dealing with price-cap regulation under asymmetric information, particular attention has been directed to the similarities between the dynamic effects of price-caps and the Vogelsang–Finsinger (1979) mechanism treated in chapter 25 above. Recall for outputs $z_i > 0$ Vogelsang–Finsinger's set of regulatory adjusting prices

$$RAP := \left\{ p \;\middle|\; \sum_i p_i z_i^o - C(z^o) \leq 0 \right\}. \tag{25--2}$$

The relevant inequality can easily be transformed into a price-cap constraint

$$\sum_i [p_i - (1 - X)p_i^o] z_i^o \leq 0 \tag{20}$$

where $X = \Pi(p_o)/\Sigma p_i^o z_i^o$.[21] If this price-cap constraint is applied over time, prices converge to Ramsey pricing if the assumptions of Vogelsang and Finsinger hold. If these assumptions are violated, then of course this convergence property fails to hold. Neu (1993) investigates this problem for the case of exogenous growth factors of demand for the various goods in question.[22] As

---

[19] The rest of this paragraph is taken from Bös (1991a: 66–7).

[20] The optimal regulatory lag under price-cap regulation has been investigated in Armstrong–Rees–Vickers (1991).

[21] See Bradley and Price (1988), Neu (1993).

[22] That means Vogelsang–Finsinger's assumption of stationary demand over time is violated.

Neu shows, convergence to Ramsey pricing will only occur if the regulatory mechanism directly depends on forecasts for the quantities of the present period instead of on quantities of the past, and if these forecasts turn out to be correct.[23]

The above connection between price-cap regulation and regulatory adjustment processes did not refer to the $RPI - X$ constraint. However, for outputs $z_i > 0$ this constraint can be rewritten as

$$\sum_i [p_i - (RPI - X)p_i^o] z_i^o \leq 0 \qquad (21)$$

for arbitrary X. If this constraint is applied, pricing over time does not converge to Ramsey pricing. However, as Vogelsang (1989) shows, such a convergence can be obtained by an improved regulatory adjustment process. Vogelsang suggests differentiation between two types of adjustment. A long-term adjustment by means of profit-based examination occurs only at multi-year intervals. This long-term adjustment determines the average caps. Between any two long-term regulatory reviews, however, short-term adjustments take place which are constrained by the $RPI - X$ constraint (21). Regulation which combines this long-term and short-term adjustments converges to Ramsey prices (given the strong assumptions of the Vogelsang–Finsinger mechanism, in particular stationary demand and cost functions).

---

[23] See also Brennan (1989: 138–41).

C
The New Economics of Price Regulation

28
The Principal-Agent Framework

28.1 Information Setting and Revelation Principle

The regulator in the preceding two chapters was assumed to be fully informed. In practice, however, this will not be the case. The information will be asymmetric, with a fully informed management of the regulated firm and with an imperfectly or incompletely informed regulator.[1] His lack of information results from lack of observation. Certain actions of the management cannot be observed directly by the regulator or, alternatively, cannot be verified by a court which has to decide on the case. This is the case of hidden action and the management will exploit the informational deficit of the regulator to maximize its own objectives. Alternatively or cumulatively, certain information about the state of the world may be observable (verifiable) only by the management, not by the regulator. This is the case of hidden information.

If the case in question is the regulation of a public utility, hidden action and hidden information typically occur simultaneously. The regulator cannot observe the management's effort (hidden action) and also cannot observe some relevant variables which determine the economic outcome (hidden information).

Let us give some examples of hidden information as it shall be treated in the following chapters. This hidden information will always be captured by a one-dimensional parameter θ.[2]

---

[1] If the regulated firm is a public enterprise, it is natural to assume the two-person setting of regulator and management. If the regulated firm is privately owned, the private owners might enter as third person to be considered, see for instance table 1 on privatization (p. 25 above). We will assume, however, that the private owners have no influence in the regulatory game (which, for instance, is a good description of the UK situation). The regulated firm's profit constraint guarantees the private owners' participation, hence for a private regulated firm $\Pi^o \geq 0$ is required.

[2] For a recent extension to the case of multidimensional parameters see Armstrong (1993).

- In a first case, θ refers to the productivity of a regulated firm. It characterizes the type of the firm, from more productive to less productive firms as expressed by a technology $g(\theta, e, z) = 0$ with e as managerial effort and z as vector of inputs and outputs.

- In a second case, θ refers to certain demand characteristics. It measures in which way the willingness of consumers to pay for the firm's products deviates from the usual price- and income-dependent willingness to pay. We have individual demand functions $x_i^h(\theta, p, r^h)$, where p is a price vector and r^h is non-labor income.

- In a third case, θ measures the softness of a budget constraint. The regulator instructs the management to act as a lobbyist, persuading the government or the parliament to appropriate a higher budget for the regulated firm. The success of the management depends on the lobbying effort e and on the toughness of the government or parliament. We capture the degree of toughness by θ and define the firm's budget as $\Pi(\theta, e)$.

In all of the above-mentioned examples, it is plausible that the management of the regulated firm is better informed about θ than the regulatory agency.

In the following chapters we shall deal with the interplay of a regulator as the principal and the management of the regulated firm as the agent. Crucial for any such approach is the sequencing of information and of actions. Table 3 illustrates the sequencing which will be chosen in the following chapters.

Table 3

Sequencing of information and actions of manager and regulator

Manager	Time	Regulator
θ known	0	$F(\theta)$ known
contract acceptance	1	contract offer
information revelation	2	θ known
$e(\theta)$ chosen	3	
production, sale	4	payment of agent's compensation

Consider some parameter θ. Ex ante, the regulator has only prior beliefs on this parameter, as expressed by the distribution function $F(\theta)$. The manager, on the other hand, knows the precise value of θ. This informational asymmetry, which is a standard assumption in the literature, can be motivated by the particular professional experience of the manager, referring to technology, customers, competitors, but also referring to the manager's own personal abilities.

In the traditional principal-agent framework, the interplay between regulator and management is modelled as follows. The management attempts to exploit its informational advantage in order to maximize its income and to minimize its effort. When stipulating the management's income, the regulator has to take into account the management's interests. It would be futile to instruct the management to work at some effort level e^* which maximizes the regulator's objective: since effort is unobservable and some cost- or demand characteristics are also unobservable, the management would lie to the regulator. A typical lie would be to tell the regulator that unexpectedly the hired workers were less efficient than they actually were and hence the management's effort had to be higher than it actually was. Even if a regulator observes the output of the firm, he cannot detect such a lie if cleverly conceived (see below) and hence will pay income based on the assumption of an incorrectly low workers' efficiency and an incorrectly high management effort. Clearly such a lie would be in the interest of the management, but not in the interest of the regulator.

In this situation, there are many possible contracts the regulator can offer. This could therefore be the starting point of a complicated search for the optimal contract. Fortunately, the so-called revelation principle[3] shows that there is one special class of contracts whose result is always at least as good for the regulator as any other contract he could conceive. Therefore, the analysis of the following chapters can be restricted to this special type of contracts, namely those which constitute a 'direct mechanism'. In this type of contract, the principal asks the agent for his private information and bases the incentive income on this announcement. This class of contracts can be described in more detail as follows:[4]

(i)   After learning the precise value of θ, the manager is required to announce which value has occurred. We denote this announced value by $\hat{\theta}$.

---

[3] This principle was developed by Gibbard (1973), Green–Laffont (1977), Myerson (1979) and Dasgupta–Hammond–Maskin (1979). For good textbook treatments see, for instance, Mas-Colell–Whinston–Green (1993, chapter 14) and Fudenberg–Tirole (1991, chapter 7).

[4] See Myerson (1982). The description in the text closely follows Mas-Colell–Whinston–Green (1993).

(ii)   The contract specifies the incentive income $t(\hat{\theta})$, depending on the announced characteristic $\hat{\theta}$. The contract is calculated on the basis of an effort level $e(\hat{\theta})$ which the manager should take.

(iii)   The management reports truthfully, that is it announces $\hat{\theta} = \theta$, where θ is the actual value of the characteristic. Moreover, the management actually chooses effort $e(\theta)$ in state θ.

The incentive income must be chosen by the regulator in such a way that the truthful revelation of θ is guaranteed. The regulator knows that he cannot apply the ideal income schedule he would choose if he were fully informed. This income schedule would be

$$\text{incentive pay} = \begin{cases} t & \text{if } e = e^* \\ 0 & \text{otherwise.} \end{cases} \tag{1}$$

However, it is futile to stipulate a transfer t which the management gets only if it works with effort e^*. Since the effort is non-observable, the management will always insist on having worked with effort e^* and the regulator cannot prove the contrary. Moreover, even if effort is observable, it cannot be verified in court.   Hence income must be conditioned on observable variables, for instance on profit, output or total costs. Let us assume for the moment that the regulator observes total costs and therefore stipulates a managerial income according to

$$\text{incentive pay} = \begin{cases} t & \text{if } C = C(\hat{\theta}) \\ 0 & \text{otherwise,} \end{cases} \tag{2}$$

where $\hat{\theta}$ is that value of the characteristic θ which has been announced by the management. The incentive income (2) has to be chosen in such a way that the management always has an incentive to inform the regulator truthfully. Such a contract is called incentive-compatible.

Note that truthful revelation of θ implies that after signing the contract the regulator comes to know the correct value of θ. However, he cannot use this knowledge to exploit the manager.[5] He can only obtain the knowledge on the basis of an incentive-compatible contract which has to be signed at a moment when he is still uninformed. If the regulator does not enter into such a contract, he risks failing to obtain correct information about the relevant cost- or demand parameter. When the contract is to be fulfilled, the regulator is stuck with the dilemma that he knows the actual value of θ but has to comply with a contract which is based on his not knowing θ at the moment of contracting. (This setting excludes renegotiations.)

---

[5]   The following four sentences are in part taken from Bös–Peters (1991a: 31).

28.2   The Objectives of Management and Regulator

Imagine the regulator faces a single manager with utility

$$U = U(t, e), \tag{3}$$

where t is the reward paid to the manager and e is his effort. $U_1 > 0$ is the marginal utility of income and $U_2 < 0$ the marginal disutility of effort. $U(t, e)$ is a direct utility function. It depends, first, on the manager's consumption which is represented by his income t, and secondly, on his labour supply which is represented by his effort e.[6]

Since the regulator cannot run the enterprise himself, he has to consider the manager's participation constraint

$$U \geq U^o. \tag{4}$$

If the regulated firm would act exactly as a private firm in its business behavior, then we could simply assume that the manager would not stay at his job unless the contract offers a utility higher than the utility of the best alternative job. In such a case the reservation utility is exogenous as determined by the market. At least in Europe, however, for a manager in a regulated firm the reservation utility U^o may well be lower than the reservation utility for somebody who is employed in an equivalent position in the private economy. This holds in particular for public enterprises, where a special civil-servant ethos might prevent a manager from leaving although he could earn more in some private alternative job. Some public-enterprise managers may enjoy the power and the public attention which comes with running a public enterprise. Particular public-sector fringe benefits which are not explicitly modelled may also be relevant for the manager's reservation utility.

We assume $U(0, 0) < U^o$. This implies that work pays. The participation constraint holds only for positive effort and consequently for positive managerial reward (Bös–Peters, 1991a: 31).

Let us next turn to a brief treatment of the regulator's objective. In a normative theory of price regulation, the regulator is assumed to maximize welfare. In a positive theory, we impute to the regulator the maximization of votes, output, the budget etc. In this and in the following chapters (29–32) we shall derive the basic principles of price regulation for a welfare-maximizing regulator. The extension to the positive theory of price regulation is straightforward and will be sketched in chapter 33.

---

[6] See Bös–Peters (1991a: 31).

The treatment of managerial utility in a welfare context is tricky. Best known are the following traditional procedures:

(i) In partial welfare analyses the regulator maximizes the sum of consumer and producer surplus. Here the influence of every single consumer, including the manager, is infinitesimally small and does not require explicit modelling. This is the easiest way to treat, or better to circumvent, the problem.[7]

(ii) Another procedure is chosen in Laffont–Tirole (1990: 5). They explicitly consider the sum of consumers' and manager's welfare, where the managers' utility is specified according to $U = t - \psi(e), \psi', \psi'' \geq 0$. However, while the manager's utility is assumed to increase total welfare, his income is deducted as welfare-reducing as are the opportunity costs of financing this income. If $\gamma > 0$ are the exogenously given shadow costs of public funds, the regulator's objective is as follows:

$$W(z^+) + U - (1+\gamma)t, \tag{5}$$

where $W(z^+)$ is the social value associated with the public outputs z^+. Substituting the definition of the manager's utility, we obtain

$$W - \gamma U - (1+\gamma)\psi. \tag{6}$$

Total welfare is decreasing in the manager's utility: this results from adding U but deducting more than 100 percent of his compensation t. The regulator is therefore interested in reducing the manager's utility as far as possible, that is he would wish to set $U = 0$. Unlike any other consumer, the manager is not treated as a human being whose utility is of interest for a social planner. He is only treated as a mechanism, needed for production (participation constraint) and for the acquisition of information (incentive-compatibility constraint). Managers are only granted positive utility if this is unavoidable for the above two reasons.

In this book, however, we plead for social symmetry between consumers and managers. Accordingly, we shall apply the following specification of a welfare function which depends on the utility of every single person, including the manager:

$$W(v^1, \ldots, v^h, \ldots, v^H; \underline{U}); \quad \partial W/\partial v^h > 0, \partial W/\partial \underline{U} =: W_U > 0. \tag{7}$$

Here $v^h(p, r^h)$ are the individual indirect utility functions of the consumers $h = 1, \ldots, H$ and $\underline{U} \geq U^\circ$ is the basic utility of the manager of the regulated

---

[7] See, for instance Bös–Peters (1991a).

firm. According to this specification welfare is increasing in the manager's basic utility, but not in his information rent $U - \underline{U}$. This is tantamount to saying that the regulator wishes to minimize the information rent: the full-information optimum can be approached more closely the cheaper the information can be extracted from the manager. Hence $U - \underline{U}$ should be as low as possible. The manager's personal well-being, on the other hand, is captured by $\underline{U}$ and enters the welfare function in the same way as the utility of every single consumer.

The relation between the manager's basic utility and his informational rent may further be clarified by an analogy from another area of economics.[8] The owner of a monopoly has conflicting interests as to his roles as consumer and monopolist. As consumer he favors efficient production whereas as monopolist he benefits from a high price and monopoly profits. From society's point of view efficient production is conducive to maximizing welfare and the monopolist could be compensated for the loss of monopoly profit to the extent that all benefit. Analogously by awarding him a higher basic utility the manager of our model can be compensated for his loss of information rent to such an extent that all benefit.

28.3 Incentive Compatibility

In all of the following chapters the incentive-compatibility constraints will be derived in the same way. According to the specifications this always looks quite complicated. However, the basic procedure is simple to grasp. This section presents this procedure, detailed elaborations will be given whenever the incentive-compatibility constraints are derived for particular applications.

Consider an agent who has private information on some characteristic $\theta \in [\underline{\theta}, \overline{\theta}]$ where $\overline{\theta}$ is that realization which is best for the firm. If the agent truthfully announces θ, his utility depends on θ, say $V(\theta)$. However if he announces some arbitrary $\hat{\theta}$, his utility is $U(\theta, \hat{\theta})$, since some variables like the manager's income depend only on $\hat{\theta}$, others like his effort depend on θ and $\hat{\theta}$ because the effort-saving effect of the manager's lying in the announcement of θ depends on both θ and $\hat{\theta}$. A typical specification would therefore be $U(\theta, \hat{\theta}) = U(e(\theta, \hat{\theta}), t(\hat{\theta}))$.

Any income schedule which induces truthtelling behavior of the manager requires that lying must never lead to higher utility than telling the truth,

$$\mathcal{D}(\theta, \hat{\theta}) := V(\theta) - U(\theta, \hat{\theta}) \geq 0. \tag{8}$$

Formally, the regulator chooses the managerial income in such a way that the distance function $\mathcal{D}$ is minimized with respect to $\hat{\theta}$. The best lie must be the truth: this requires that at the optimum we have $\theta = \hat{\theta}$.

---

[8] I owe this analogy to Kåre Hagen.

This is illustrated in figure 19 for two distance functions which depend on the announced $\hat{\theta}$. The agent always chooses that $\hat{\theta}$ which minimizes $\mathcal{D}$. In the first case he announces $\hat{\theta}_1^*$, which is a lie. Since the agent's best response is a lie, the distance function $\mathcal{D}_1$ is based on a compensation scheme which is not incentive compatible. In the second case, however, the agent announces $\hat{\theta}_2^*$: his best response is the truth. This directly implies that the distance function $\mathcal{D}_2$ is based on an incentive-compatible compensation of the agent. The principal will proceed according to $\mathcal{D}_2$, thus eliciting truthful revelation from the agent.

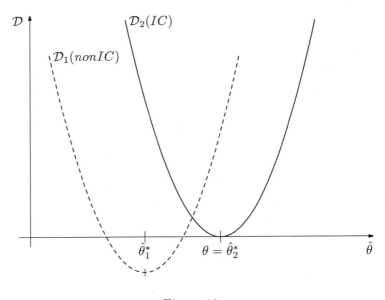

Figure 19

Let us now turn to a more precise presentation of the agent's incentive-compatibility problem. Minimizing the distance function with respect to $\hat{\theta}$ yields the first-order condition

$$\frac{\partial U}{\partial \hat{\theta}} = 0. \tag{9}$$

Consider now changes in utility with respect to θ if the announced characteristic is true. We obtain

$$\dot{U}(\theta) := \frac{dU}{d\theta} = \frac{\partial U}{\partial \theta} + \frac{\partial U}{\partial \hat{\theta}}\bigg|_{\hat{\theta}=\theta}. \tag{10}$$

Substituting equation (9) into (10) yields

$$\dot{U}(\theta) = \frac{\partial U}{\partial \theta}. \tag{11}$$

Equation (11) is the incentive-compatibility condition of the manager. We shall need particular information requirements to apply the above derivation of the incentive-compatibility constraint. This will be treated in detail in the following chapters. Here we only want to present the basic structure of the argument which will be repeated in the various approaches to follow.

Let us finally consider the second-order condition

$$\frac{\partial^2 U}{\partial \hat{\theta}^2} \leq 0. \tag{12}$$

This condition typically cannot be shown to hold generally, because the second derivative of managerial utility contains second derivatives like $\partial^2 t / \partial \theta^2$ whose sign is indeterminate. However, the following procedure often helps in the interpretation.[9] Take the total differential of the first-order conditions (9)

$$\frac{\partial^2 U}{\partial \hat{\theta}^2} d\hat{\theta} + \frac{\partial^2 U}{\partial \hat{\theta} \partial \theta} d\theta = 0. \tag{13}$$

Since the truthtelling property must be retained, the terms $d\hat{\theta}$ and $d\theta$ cancel out and we directly recognize that the second-order condition holds if and only if

$$\frac{\partial^2 U}{\partial \hat{\theta} \partial \theta} \geq 0. \tag{14}$$

It is often possible to find plausible economic assumptions for this inequality to hold, in contrast to the original second-order condition. Some interesting examples will be given in the next section.

28.4 The Single-Crossing Property

In special cases the second-order condition of the manager's optimization holds iff the so-called single-crossing property is fulfilled. In the following I shall

---

[9] Guesnerie–Laffont (1984: 336–41).

present such a special case. For this purpose we consider the following regulatory environment. It is common knowledge that the costs of producing outputs z^+ are given by the function

$$C = C(\theta, e, z^+). \tag{15}$$

Costs can be reduced by the manager's effort, but also through some outside event θ. The regulator is able to observe the total costs and the quantities z^+, but neither e nor θ. When the manager is asked to announce a particular value of θ, he realizes that the same value of C can be achieved by announcing the true value of θ and working $e(\theta)$ or by announcing a false value, $\hat{\theta}$, and adjusting the effort in such a way that the same costs are achieved. We denote this effort level by $e(\theta, \hat{\theta})$. Formally, an identical value of C can be achieved either by a false or by a true announcement:

$$C = \begin{cases} C(\theta, e(\theta, \hat{\theta}), z(\hat{\theta})) & \text{if } \hat{\theta} \neq \theta \\ C(\hat{\theta}, e(\hat{\theta}), z(\hat{\theta})) & \text{if } \hat{\theta} = \theta. \end{cases} \tag{16}$$

A false announcement therefore is detected by the regulator unless the manager combines an announcement $\hat{\theta}$ and effort $e(\theta, \hat{\theta})$ in such a way that equations (16) are fulfilled for the announced $\hat{\theta}$ and C is the same in both equations.

In this setting let us now consider the second-order condition of the manager's optimization problem. We require $U_{\hat{\theta}\theta} \geq 0$ as mentioned in the preceding section. The manager's utility is given by $U(e(\theta, \hat{\theta}), t(\hat{\theta}))$, where $e(\hat{\theta}, \theta)$ is defined implicitly by

$$C(\text{observed}) = C(\theta, e(\theta, \hat{\theta}), z(\hat{\theta})) = C(\hat{\theta}, e(\hat{\theta}), z(\hat{\theta})). \tag{17}$$

For the following derivations let us assume that $\partial e(\theta, \hat{\theta})/\partial \hat{\theta}$ depends only on $\hat{\theta}$, but not on θ. A simple example where $\partial e(\theta, \hat{\theta})/\partial \hat{\theta}$ does not depend on θ is as follows. Assume marginal costs which are observable and defined as $MC = MC^o - \theta - e$. A consistent lie requires identity of

$$MC = \begin{cases} MC^o - \theta - e(\hat{\theta}, \theta) & \text{if } \hat{\theta} \neq \theta \\ MC^o - \hat{\theta} - e(\hat{\theta}) & \text{if } \hat{\theta} = \theta \end{cases} \tag{18}$$

and accordingly

$$e(\theta, \hat{\theta}) = e(\hat{\theta}) + (\hat{\theta} - \theta). \tag{19}$$

Here $\partial e(\theta, \hat{\theta})/\partial \hat{\theta} = \partial e(\hat{\theta})/\partial \hat{\theta} + 1$, which depends only on $\hat{\theta}$ and not on θ.[10]

---

[10] In the following chapters we will typically apply general specifications which do not exclude the dependency of $\partial e/\partial \hat{\theta}$ on θ.

For the presentation of the single-crossing property let us start from an implicit specification of the relevant functions, that is

$$\frac{\partial U}{\partial e}(\theta, \hat{\theta}); \ \frac{\partial e}{\partial \hat{\theta}}(\hat{\theta}); \ \frac{\partial U}{\partial t}(\theta, \hat{\theta}); \ \frac{\partial t}{\partial \hat{\theta}}(\hat{\theta}). \tag{20}$$

Then the second-order condition requires

$$\frac{\partial^2 U}{\partial \hat{\theta} \partial \theta} = \frac{\partial^2 U}{\partial e \partial \theta}\frac{\partial e}{\partial \hat{\theta}} + \frac{\partial^2 U}{\partial t \partial \theta}\frac{\partial t}{\partial \hat{\theta}} \geq 0. \tag{21}$$

The first-order condition, equation (9) can be rewritten as

$$\frac{\partial U}{\partial \hat{\theta}} = \frac{\partial U}{\partial e}\frac{\partial e}{\partial \hat{\theta}} + \frac{\partial U}{\partial t}\frac{\partial t}{\partial \hat{\theta}}\bigg|_{\hat{\theta}=\theta} = 0. \tag{22}$$

This equation can be used to eliminate $\partial t/\partial \hat{\theta}$ in the inequality (21) yielding[11]

$$\left[\left[\frac{\partial^2 U}{\partial e \partial \theta}\frac{\partial U}{\partial t} - \frac{\partial^2 U}{\partial t \partial \theta}\frac{\partial U}{\partial e}\right] \Big/ \frac{\partial U}{\partial t}\right]\frac{\partial e}{\partial \hat{\theta}} \geq 0. \tag{23}$$

Now assume that $\partial e/\partial \hat{\theta} < 0$, that is, the manager only increases the announcement of θ if this reduces his effort. Then the condition (23) is equivalent to postulating

$$\frac{\partial}{\partial \theta}\left(\frac{\partial U/\partial e}{\partial U/\partial t}\right) \leq 0. \tag{24}$$

The manager's marginal rate of substitution between effort and income must be decreasing in the characteristic θ. This is known as single-crossing property because it means that the slope of the manager's indifference curves in the (e, t)-space decreases in θ, as illustrated in figure 20 on the overleaf page.

Another interesting implication of the second-order condition can be presented if in our special example we start from an explicit specification of the relevant functions, that is

$$\frac{\partial U}{\partial e}\left[e(\theta, \hat{\theta}), t(\hat{\theta})\right]; \ \frac{\partial e}{\partial \hat{\theta}}(\hat{\theta}); \ \frac{\partial U}{\partial t}\left[e(\theta, \hat{\theta}), t(\hat{\theta})\right]; \ \frac{\partial t}{\partial \hat{\theta}}(\hat{\theta}). \tag{25}$$

Then the second-order condition requires

$$\frac{\partial^2 U}{\partial \hat{\theta} \partial \theta} = \frac{\partial^2 U}{\partial e^2}\frac{\partial e}{\partial \theta}\frac{\partial e}{\partial \hat{\theta}} + \frac{\partial^2 U}{\partial t \partial e}\frac{\partial e}{\partial \theta}\frac{\partial t}{\partial \hat{\theta}} \geq 0. \tag{26}$$

---

[11] See, for instance, Fudenberg–Tirole (1991: 258–60).

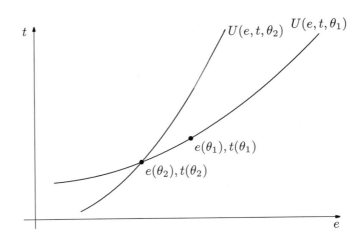

Figure 20 $(\theta_2 < \theta_1)$
Source: Fudenberg–Tirole (1991: 260).

Once again, the first-order condition (22) can be used to eliminate $\partial t/\partial\hat\theta$ in the above inequality and we obtain

$$\frac{\partial e}{\partial\hat\theta}\frac{\partial e}{\partial\theta}\left(\frac{\partial^2 U}{\partial t\partial e}-\frac{\partial U/\partial t}{\partial U/\partial e}\frac{\partial^2 U}{\partial e^2}\right)\le 0. \tag{27}$$

The term in brackets is negative if consumption is a normal good.[12] Hence, the second-order condition is fullfilled if consumption is normal, if $\partial e/\partial\hat\theta < 0$ and, moreover, $\partial e/\partial\theta < 0$, for instance if θ is a factor influencing agricultural production costs and higher θ indicates better weather.[13] However, whereas $\partial e/\partial\hat\theta < 0$ is a straightforward assumption resulting from the revelation principle, $\partial e/\partial\theta < 0$ is by no means straightforward.[14] Hence there may well be

---

[12] An explicit derivation of this condition is rarely found in microeconomic textbooks. An exception is Otani–El-Hodiri (1987: 39–43). For the connection between normality of consumption and the single-crossing condition see also Ebert (1992: 50).

[13] It may be noted in passing that in the following chapters the most difficult part of proving the second-order condition will be the determination of the sign of $\partial e/\partial\theta$.

[14] In Bös–Peters (1991a: 47), for instance, in our simulation analysis we show that effort follows a U-shaped curve if θ increases.

cases where the single-crossing property holds although consumption is not a normal good.

28.5 Bunching

28.5.1 A Simple Example

To establish incentive compatibility, the manager must be induced to announce the correct value of θ. This requires the validity of the first-order and of the second-order conditions of the manager's individual utility maximization. If the second-order conditions fail to hold, it ceases to be optimal for the regulator to adjust his instruments to every single value of θ. Rather it is better 'to throw away information' and to choose identical realizations of instruments for different θ's. This is called 'bunching'.[15]

    In a general-equilibrium framework of the Boiteux type it is impossible to find general analytical criteria for the validity of the second-order conditions. Therefore, in what follows, we present a simple example.[16] We assume that the manager's disutility from effort depends inversely on some variable θ, which can take two values $\underline{\theta}$ and $\overline{\theta}$. By way of an example, θ may be the ability of the manager. For simplification, the manager's disutility from effort is specified as e/θ and accordingly the manager's utility function equals

$$U = t - e/\theta. \tag{28}$$

The principal is imperfectly informed about θ and has to pay an incentive reward to induce the manager to announce the correct value of θ. In this example incentive compatibility requires[17]

$$\overline{t} - \overline{e}/\overline{\theta} \geq \underline{t} - \underline{e}/\overline{\theta}, \tag{29a}$$

$$\underline{t} - \underline{e}/\underline{\theta} \geq \overline{t} - \overline{e}/\underline{\theta}. \tag{29b}$$

Adding these two inequalities yields

$$(\underline{e} - \overline{e})(\underline{\theta} - \overline{\theta})/\overline{\theta}\underline{\theta} \geq 0. \tag{30}$$

Since $\underline{\theta} - \overline{\theta} < 0$ and $\theta\overline{\theta} > 0$, this inequality holds if

---

[15] Guesnerie and Laffont (1984) were the first to address this question for the case of regulation under asymmetric information. Their approach afterwards was applied to the special problems of 'unknown demand' in a paper by Lewis and Sappington (1988).

[16] This example follows the lines of Caillaud–Guesnerie–Rey–Tirole (1988: 16).

[17] Where $\overline{t}:=t(\overline{\theta})$ and $\overline{e}:=e(\overline{\theta})$ and analogous for $\underline{\theta}$.

$$\overline{e} \geq \underline{e}. \tag{31}$$

Hence, bunching is excluded if the manager chooses high effort when his disutility from effort is low and vice versa. Although this is very plausible, it cannot be ruled out that the manager chooses high effort when his disutility of effort is high. The reason for this behavior would be a high incentive income which outweighs the high disutility from effort.[18] In the latter case bunching is optimal for the principal.

28.5.2   Output Maximization

Managers of public enterprises often are not interested in profit maximization, but in other objectives of positive theory such as budget or output maximization. Let us therefore briefly discuss the potential bunching problem facing the regulator of an output-maximizing manager. Once again we consider a one-good case and specify output as

$$x(\theta, p) = \theta x(p). \tag{32}$$

We assume that x is both the demanded and the supplied quantity. The incentive-compatibility constraints for $\overline{\theta}$ and $\underline{\theta}$ are

$$\overline{\theta} x(\overline{p}) \geq \overline{\theta} x(\underline{p}), \tag{33a}$$

$$\underline{\theta} x(\underline{p}) \geq \underline{\theta} x(\overline{p}). \tag{33b}$$

Adding them together, we obtain

$$(x(\overline{p}) - x(\underline{p}))(\overline{\theta} - \underline{\theta}) \geq 0 \tag{34}$$

which holds if $x(\overline{p}) \geq x(\underline{p})$.

This condition is always fulfilled in case of decreasing marginal costs; as figure 21 illustrates, typically it will also hold in the case of increasing marginal costs. Hence bunching is unlikely to occur if a manager is interested in output (in contrast to the case of profit maximization which will be treated in the following subsection).

---

[18] For this possibility see Bös–Peters (1991a) where in a simulation analysis both $e_\theta < 0$ and $t_\theta < 0$ result for some interval of θ.

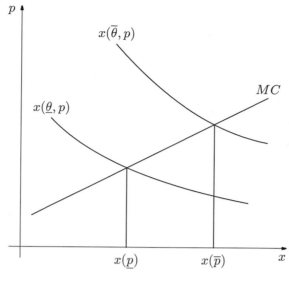

Figure 21

28.5.3   The Lewis–Sappington Case

In Lewis–Sappington (1988) a welfare-maximizing regulator is imperfectly informed about the demand for a single good $x(\theta, p)$. He only knows the distribution of θ. Moreover, he is unable to observe the quantity x.[19] The manager
of the regulated firm wants to maximize profits which consist of revenue minus
costs plus a transfer T. The regulator's instruments are the price p and the
transfer T. To present the gist of Lewis–Sappington's arguments, we assume
that profit can be specified as

$$\pi(p, \theta) = \theta \mathcal{N}(p) + T(\theta) \qquad (35)$$

where $\mathcal{N}(p)$ is the net revenue, i.e. revenue minus costs. There are only two
economic situations, $\underline{\theta}$ and $\bar{\theta}$. In that case incentive-compatibility requires[20]

$$\bar{\theta} \mathcal{N}(\bar{p}) + \overline{T} \geq \bar{\theta} \mathcal{N}(\underline{p}) + \underline{T}, \qquad (36a)$$

$$\underline{\theta} \mathcal{N}(\underline{p}) + \underline{T} \geq \underline{\theta} \mathcal{N}(\bar{p}) + \overline{T}. \qquad (36b)$$

---

[19] This is a somewhat artificial assumption.
[20] where $\bar{p} := p(\bar{\theta})$ etc.

Adding these conditions yields

$$\left(\mathcal{N}(\overline{p}) - \mathcal{N}(\underline{p})\right)\left(\overline{\theta} - \underline{\theta}\right) \geq 0. \tag{37}$$

Accordingly, there is no problem with incentive compatibility if we have $\mathcal{N}(\overline{p}) \geq \mathcal{N}(\underline{p})$. This directly leads to the basic message of Lewis and Sappington:

- in case of increasing marginal costs, no bunching occurs;[21]
- in case of decreasing marginal costs, we would have $\mathcal{N}(\overline{p}) < \mathcal{N}(\underline{p})$ if we had not imposed any incentive-compatibility constraint (this is the deficit problem of marginal-cost pricing). Hence the same price and the same transfer payment are implemented for both $\underline{\theta}$ and $\overline{\theta}$.[22]

28.6   Where Does Asymmetric Information Matter in Price Regulation?

Recall that in part I of this book we presented a basic full-information model of pricing. It described the problem as follows:[23]

- maximization of either welfare or political or bureaucratic aims

subject to

- market-clearing conditions,
- the enterprise's technology, and
- a revenue-cost constraint.

Asymmetric information of a regulator can refer to each of the four points above. In the following four chapters, therefore, these four types of asymmetric information are treated. We begin with the best-known paradigm – managers will often have private information on their firm's technology. Hence, chapter 29 deals with regulation under asymmetric information on costs. However, the demand side may just as well be the source of an asymmetric-information problem: in chapter 30, therefore, we treat managerial marketing efforts whose precise extents are private information of the managers. The revenue-cost constraint also is prone to problems of asymmetric information. Consider a regulator who is discontent with the deficit limit which has been fixed by the government for a particular fiscal year. Hence he employs a lob-

---

[21] For an exception see Lewis–Sappington (1988: 994–5, figure 2 which erroneously is denoted figure 3).

[22] Condition (37) requires $\mathcal{N}(\overline{p}) = \mathcal{N}(\underline{p})$ and therefore $\overline{p} = \underline{p}$. Then, however, conditions (36a) and (36b) can only hold if $\overline{T} = \underline{T}$.

[23] See the introduction of chapter 2 above.

byist whom he pays to engage in renegotiations with the government.[24] It is likely that the amount of effort which the lobbyist devotes to achieving a higher deficit will be unknown to the regulator. This is one of the central features of soft budget constraints which we investigate in chapter 31. Finally, imperfect information may also directly influence the regulator's objective function. This happens if he cannot directly distinguish the types of consumers. In such a case non-linear pricing will be the adequate procedure to deal with the regulator's lack of knowledge. We will devote chapter 32 to this problem. For convenience, all approaches of chapters 28–32 assume that the regulator is a welfare maximizer, that is, they deal with a normative approach to regulation. The extension to a positive theory of regulation is straightforward as shown in chapter 33.

---

[24] Note that there are two renegotiation problems which must be distinguished. First, the possible renegotiation of the budget as investigated in chapter 31 below. This renegotiation refers to the relation between the regulator and his sponsor (be it the parliament, the government, or some minister). Second, possible renegotiation of the contract between the regulator and the lobbyist, which is excluded in the analysis of chapter 31. When in section 28.1 above we explicitly excluded renegotiation, we referred only to the second problem.

29
Asymmetric Information on Costs

29.1 The Model

29.1.1 The Information Setting

In this chapter we deal with the best-known paradigm of regulation under asymmetric information.[1] The manager is better informed on the technology than the regulator. We assume that the technology depends on some productivity parameter which characterizes the type of the enterprise. The manager always knows the actual value of θ; the regulator only knows the density function $f(\theta)$. We normalize θ by defining $\theta \in [\underline{\theta}, \overline{\theta}]$, where $\underline{\theta}$ is the worst type. Asymmetric information does not only prevail with respect to the type of firm, but also with respect to the manager's effort e: it cannot be observed by the regulator.

On the other hand, we shall apply a sort of Laffont–Tirole approach by assuming that the regulator is able to observe inputs, outputs, and prices.[2] The ex-post observability of outputs and prices is a very plausible assumption. It requires a little more sophistication to establish the ex-post observability of inputs. We could for instance refer to inside information: a representative sent to the board of a public enterprise by the regulator may have gained direct knowledge of the input quantities. If the regulated firm is privately owned, the observation of outputs and inputs results from some outside monitoring.

Finally, as usual in models of this type, we assume that the shape of all relevant functions is common knowledge. Hence, the regulator knows the exact functional shape of the technology, of the manager's utility function, of the demand functions etc. The regulator, therefore, is extremely well informed; only effort e and parameter θ are hidden from his knowledge.

29.1.2 The Technology

We start from a neoclassical technology

$$g(\theta, e, z) = 0. \tag{1}$$

---

[1] The paper which introduced this paradigm is Baron–Myerson (1982); well-known further papers are Freixas–Laffont (1985), Laffont–Tirole (1986) and Laffont–Tirole (1990). Laffont (1994) gives a good overview of the problem.

[2] If lump-sum incomes are chosen as control variables, the regulator is also able to observe these incomes.

This implicit production function denotes the relation among productivity θ, managerial effort e, and the netputs $(z_o, \ldots, z_n) =: z$. Since, from its very conception, effort is a non-negative variable, it is a sort of alien element in a netput model where every single good can alternatively be an output or an input, depending on its sign. Effort, however, can only be an input. We could explicitly introduce a non-negativity constraint on e in this and in the following chapters. However, the qualitative results remain unchanged if we refrain from this tedious introduction of a further constraint and assume that at the regulator's optimum we always have $e > 0$.

We solve the production function to obtain a labor-requirement function[3]

$$z_o = z_o(\theta, e, z_1, \ldots, z_n). \tag{2}$$

This function determines the minimal labor input which is necessary in a firm of type θ to combine managerial effort and non-labor inputs in the production of output goods. Labor is taken as the numeraire, $p_o = 1$.[4] Moreover, we define an effort-requirement function

$$E(\theta; z_o; z_1, \ldots, z_n); \quad E_\theta < 0, \ E_{zi} > 0, \tag{3}$$

where $E_{zi} := \partial E / \partial z_i$. This function determines the minimal effort which is necessary in a firm of type θ to combine inputs and outputs. Accordingly we have[5]

$$z_o \equiv z_o(\theta; E(\theta, z); z_1, \ldots, z_n). \tag{4}$$

Thus we have given four descriptions of the technology which will be used in our model:

(i) the neoclassical technology (1) which will be applied as usual, that is as a description of the firm's production possibilities.

(ii) the labor-requirement function (2) which will not explicitly be applied in the model; instead $z_o(\theta)$ will be treated as an instrument variable. Note that the labor-requirement function depends on the actually used ('supplied') effort e.

---

[3] Cfr. Drèze (1964: 31). See also pp. 131 (ch. 8) and 253 (ch. 24) above.

[4] This enables us to define marginal costs $c_i := -(\partial z_o / \partial z_i) = (\partial g / \partial z_i)/(\partial g / \partial z_o)$.

[5] This is a simple identity, cfr. Laffont–Tirole (1990: 5). As an example let us assume a labor-requirement function $-z_o = z_1 - \theta e$ with z_1 as single output which is produced by a combination of labor and effort. Then the effort-requirement function is $E = (z_1 + z_o)/\theta$ and equation (4) is given by $-z_o \equiv z_1 - \theta[(z_1 + z_o)/\theta] = -z_o$. This procedure cannot be applied if the technology is described by the implicit function $g(\theta, e, z)$; therefore, we apply the labor-requirement function, equation (2).

(iii) the effort-requirement function (3) which will be applied to define the incentive-compatibility constraint. It depends on the effort E which is required ('demanded').

(iv) Needless to say, definition (4) is only the implicit determination of E and not used in the optimization approach. However, it can be useful for some comparative-static analysis at the optimum.[6]

For understandable reasons, the reader might wonder why we choose such a complicated description of technology. The reason is the following: in this chapter we want to show how incentive compatibility influences public-sector pricing. Therefore, in the pricing formulas which we intend to derive, there should be some term which explicitly shows how the manager's incentive-compatibility constraint influences the prices. Hence marginal conditions resulting from maximization with respect to netputs (or prices) must explicitly be influenced by the incentive-compatibility problem. This can only be achieved if the incentive-compatibility condition explicitly depends on the firm's netputs (or prices). As we shall see in the following, it is just the effort-requirement function (3) which establishes this direct link between incentive compatibility and firm's netputs.[7]

29.1.3 Incentive Income

The principal wants to induce the management to announce the correct value of the productivity characteristic θ. This is achieved by choosing a management reward scheme

---

[6] See subsection 29.3.2 below.

[7] It might be interesting for the specialized reader to learn that in one of the previous attempts to write this chapter, I followed the same procedure as in Bös–Peters (1991a). I inverted manager utility $U(e,t)$ into an effort-requirement function $E(t,V)$. The incentive-compatibility condition was $\dot{V}=U_1(E(t,V),t)\cdot e_\theta(t,V)$. Then, as state variable I chose managerial utility V and as control variables the managerial compensation t, the regulated prices, the firm's netputs and, possibly, consumers' lump-sum incomes. For a formal presentation see Appendix 1 of this chapter. In such a modelling there is no explicit link between incentive compatibility and netputs or prices. The pricing formulas, therefore, are identical with those of chapter 3 of this book, only that they are shifted by the consideration of incentive compatibility. And, unfortunately, in such a model it is impossible to say in which way they are shifted. Hence, it is preferable to employ the effort-requirement function (3) to see explicitly how pricing rules are shifted to ensure incentive compatibility. For the economic interpretation, however, one should always keep in mind that there is another consistent way of presenting the problem according to which the structure of public-sector pricing is not changed by the asymmetric information, but only the absolute values of prices and quantities (and lump-sum incomes if they are used as instruments).

$$\text{incentive pay} = \begin{cases} t(\hat{\theta}) & \text{if } p_k = p_k(\hat{\theta}), r^h = r^h(\hat{\theta}) \text{ and} \\ & z_i = z_i(\hat{\theta}) \text{ for } k \in K, \text{ and } \forall h, i \\ 0 & \text{otherwise.} \end{cases} \qquad (5)$$

Given this offer, the manager decides to announce a particular value $\hat{\theta}$. The management would not have any degree of freedom if the principal knew the actual value of $\hat{\theta}$ and could monitor the management's behavior according to this knowledge. But since this is not the case, the management could announce a false θ if that value implies higher utility. However, when telling lies, the management must be cautious. The principal is able to observe prices, lump-sum incomes, inputs and outputs. Hence, the effects of effort, and the actual and announced values of θ must always be consistent with those prices, incomes and quantities which the principal will be able to observe. This characterization of the incentive-pay schedule presupposes that prices, inputs and outputs and possibly lump-sum incomes are set by the manager. If the regulator chooses these variables as control variables, he does so to anticipate the manager's setting of these variables.[8] The actual instrument of the regulator, however, is the managerial incentive income.

29.1.4 The Manager's Optimization

We impute to the manager a utility function of the following type[9]

$$U = t - \psi(e). \qquad (6)$$

Utility from income is linear implying that the management is risk-neutral over income lotteries. We can make this assumption because our main interest is in the influence of asymmetric information on pricing rules. We are not studying the implicit insurance which an income schedule provides for a risk-averse manager. The disutility from effort is measured by the money metric $\psi(e)$. The manager dislikes high effort, $\psi'(e) > 0$, with an ever-increasing intensity, $\psi''(e) > 0$.[10]

---

[8] In a similar way effort is chosen as control variable to anticipate the manager's behavior.

[9] This type of utility function is very usual in the literature, see for instance Laffont–Tirole (1990).

[10] Additionally $\psi''' \geq 0$. This technical assumption prevents the optimality of stochastic incentive schemes. See Laffont–Tirole (1990: 5).

The optimization of the manager's utility must be taken into account by the regulator; that means he has to consider the manager's incentive-compatibility and participation constraints.

(i) Incentive Compatibility

The manager's preferred announcement $\hat{\theta}$ results from the minimization of the distance function

$$\mathcal{D} := \left[t(\theta) - \psi(E(\theta, z(\theta))) \right] - \left[t(\hat{\theta}) - \psi(E(\theta, z(\hat{\theta}))) \right]. \tag{7}$$

Inputs and outputs are observable by the regulator and are used as control variables. Hence we write $z(\theta)$. The observability, however, restricts the manager when announcing some $\hat{\theta}$. Because of the technology, the labor requirement z_o in any case depends on the actual θ. Now consider a manager who announces a false $\hat{\theta}$, that is he pretends to work in a worse type of firm than is actually the case. This allows him to reduce his effort. However, to be trustworthy, the manager has to choose his effort in such a way that in spite of his working in a better firm and in spite of his reduced effort, the firm uses just that labor input z_o which is observed and which corresponds to the falsely announced $\hat{\theta}$. More formally, the manager chooses effort $e(\theta, \hat{\theta})$ in such a way that $z_o(\hat{\theta})$ results. Therefore, a consistent lie of the manager implies a labor requirement function

$$z_o(\hat{\theta}) = z_o(\theta, e(\theta, \hat{\theta}), z_1(\hat{\theta}), \ldots, z_n(\hat{\theta})), \tag{8}$$

where $e(\theta, \hat{\theta})$ has been chosen in such a way that it exactly compensates for the influence of the actual θ as given by the first argument of the labor-requirement function.

For our special case we now apply the same procedure we described in a general way in chapter 28 above. Minimizing the distance function $\mathcal{D}$ with respect to the announced $\hat{\theta}$ yields a first-order condition

$$\frac{dt}{d\hat{\theta}} - \psi' \sum_{i=o}^{n} E_{zi} \frac{dz_i}{d\hat{\theta}} = 0. \tag{9}$$

Moreover, we consider changes in utility which result from changes in the actual θ:

$$\dot{U}(\theta) := \frac{dU}{d\theta} = \frac{dt}{d\theta} - \psi' E_\theta - \psi' \sum_{i=o}^{n} E_{zi} \frac{dz_i}{d\theta}. \tag{10}$$

At the optimum we have $\theta = \hat{\theta}$, and observability implies

$$\frac{dz_i}{d\theta} = \frac{dz_i}{d\hat{\theta}}. \tag{11}$$

Since inputs and outputs are observable, the manager must always lie in such a way that (11) holds. Moreover, we have

$$\frac{dt}{d\theta} = \frac{dt}{d\hat{\theta}}, \tag{12}$$

as a property of the income schedule which is set by the regulator and therefore trivially is observable. Hence we can substitute equation (9) into equation (10) to obtain

$$\dot{U}(\theta) = -\psi' E_\theta > 0 \tag{13}$$

which is the manager's incentive-compatibility constraint.

The second-order condition $U_{\hat{\theta}\theta}^2 \geq 0$ takes the form[11] (at $\theta = \hat{\theta}$)

$$-\psi'' E_\theta \sum_{i=o}^{n} E_{zi} \frac{dz_i}{d\theta} - \psi' \sum_{i=o}^{n} E_{zi\theta} \frac{dz_i}{d\theta} \geq 0, \tag{14}$$

where $E_{zi\theta} := \partial E_{zi}/\partial\theta = \partial(\partial E/\partial z_i)/\partial\theta$. In our model we have assumed $\psi' > 0, \psi'' > 0$; moreover, $E_{zi} > 0$ and $E_\theta < 0$. Then $E_{zi\theta} < 0$ and $dz_i/d\theta \geq 0$ are sufficient for the second-order condition to hold.[12]

(ii)   Participation

In our model we distinguish between[13]

• the manager's reservation utility U^o which is exogenously given; if the manager's utility were to fall below this level, he would leave the firm. This must be avoided since the regulator needs the manager for production.

• the manager's basic utility $\underline{U} \geq U^o$ which refers to some minimally acceptable combination of income and effort. This basic utility will be chosen optimally by the regulator.

• the total managerial utility U which weakly exceeds the basic utility by an information rent $U - \underline{U}$. Total managerial utility will be treated as a state variable of our model.

---

[11] For this formulation of the second-order condition see section 28.3 above. For the differentiation note that in the first-order condition (9) $dt/d\hat{\theta}$ and $dz_i/d\hat{\theta}$ do not depend on θ, but only on $\hat{\theta}$. This also holds for $dz_o/d\hat{\theta}$ – if θ changes, this is corrected by changing $e(\theta,\hat{\theta})$. However, $\psi'(e)$ and $E_{zi}(\theta)$ depend on the actual θ, via $E(\theta,z(\hat{\theta}))$, and are differentiated with respect to the actual θ.

[12] Cfr. in a similar context Laffont–Tirole (1990: 32).

[13] Cfr. Section 28.2 above.

Since the information rent $U - \underline{U}$ is weakly positive, the regulator's choice of managerial utility is constrained as follows

$$U \geq \underline{U} \geq U^o. \tag{15}$$

Hence, for the worst type of firm the regulator will set the information rent $U - \underline{U}$ equal to zero and therefore

$$U(\underline{\theta}) = \underline{U}. \tag{16}$$

For all better types of firms the constraint must not be binding to ensure incentive compatibility,

$$U(\theta) > \underline{U} \qquad \text{for all } \theta > \underline{\theta}. \tag{17}$$

Note that the manager's basic utility $\underline{U}$ is bounded from above, since the manager's total income is included in the regulator's budget constraint. Hence even if the regulator esteems the manager's basic utility $\underline{U}$ highly, he has to face the budgetary consequences of increasing $\underline{U}$ too much.

29.1.5   Market Equilibria

We postulate that markets are in equilibrium for every single θ. Formally, this implies that we consider infinitely many market equilibria, one for each θ. In any case this procedure is preferable to Laffont–Tirole (1990: 27–8) who assume 'that there is a continuum of regulated firms producing goods 1 through n'. Of course their procedure makes it possible to define market equilibria in expected values, but how meaningful is regulation if there is a continuum of firms? Regulation is rooted in monopolistic market positions. If there are infinitely many producers, their competition should make regulation superfluous.

We apply the usual notation. There are h consumers, $h = 1, \ldots, H$ and j unregulated private firms, $j = 1, \ldots, J$, whose demand and supply meet with that of the regulated firm at the markets. Household demand or supply is denoted by x_i^h, household lump-sum incomes by r^h, inputs or outputs of any unregulated firm by y_i^j. The market equilibria are as follows:

(i)   input and output markets, $i = o, \ldots, n - 1$.

$$\sum_h x_i^h (p(\theta), r^h(\theta)) - z_i(\theta) - \sum_j y_i^j (p(\theta)) = 0, \quad \forall \theta, \tag{18}$$

where the vector $p(\theta)$ consists of both regulated prices $p_k(\theta), k \in K$, and exogenously given non-regulated prices $p_i, i \neq k$.

(ii)   output market, $i = n$. To make the problem more tractable, we assume that the manager consumes only good n, and therefore

$$x_n^{man}(\theta) = t(\theta)/p_n. \tag{19}$$

The regulator does not optimize with respect to the manager's consumption x_n^{man}, but with respect to his income $t(\theta)$. The price of good n is given for the regulator and for the manager. We postulate market equilibrium

$$\sum_h x_n^h(p(\theta), r^h(\theta)) + x_n^{man}(\theta) - z_n(\theta) - \sum_j (y_n^j(p(\theta))) = 0, \quad \forall \theta. \tag{20}$$

In the regulator's optimization problem we shall substitute

$$x_n^{man}(\theta) = t(\theta)/p_n = [U(\theta) + \psi(e(\theta))]/p_n. \tag{21}$$

29.1.6   Financial Equilibrium

As usual in models of the Boiteux tradition, the market equilibria imply a financial equilibrium of the economy. We multiply every single market-clearing condition by its respective price. The resulting 'monetary-market-equilibrium' equations are then summed up. After appropriate substitution we obtain

$$\sum_h r^h(\theta) - (\Pi(\theta) - t(\theta)) - \sum_j \pi^j(\theta) = 0; \quad \forall \theta \tag{22}$$

where $\Pi(\theta) - t(\theta)$ is the net profit of the regulated enterprise of type θ and $\Sigma \pi^j$ are the private profits in the economy.

29.1.7   The Regulator's Budget Constraint

The regulator's revenue-cost constraint is postulated to hold for any individual type of firm

$$\sum_{k \in K} p_k(\theta) z_k(\theta) + \sum_{i \notin K} p_i z_i(\theta) - t(\theta) = \Pi^o; \quad \forall \theta. \tag{23}$$

In the optimization problem we shall once again substitute for $t(\theta)$. Hence the budget constraint will be written as follows

$$\sum_{k \in K} p_k(\theta) z_k(\theta) + \sum_{i \notin K} p_i z_i(\theta) - U(\theta) - \psi(e(\theta)) = \Pi^o; \quad \forall \theta. \tag{24}$$

The constraint has been imposed on the regulator by some superior government authority. It is this authority which has decided that the budget constraint must always be binding and that there is one and only one value of Π^o for all realizations of θ. This profit or deficit Π^o exceeds those profits or deficits $\Pi^*(\theta)$ which would result if the regulator solved exactly the same optimization approach without any budget constraint. The latter assumption is appropriate for the following reason. If $\Pi^o < \Pi^*(\theta)$ for any θ, then both welfare and profit could be increased by ignoring the budget constraint for these values of θ. If the government authority insists on such a Π^o for these θs, it must be guided by non-welfare, non-profit objectives. Maybe it is vote-maximizing to choose the correspondingly low prices. We exclude such government behavior by the assumption of $\Pi^o > \Pi^*(\theta)$ for all θ.

29.2   The Optimization Problem

29.2.1   *Objective, Constraints, Control and State Variables*

The regulator maximizes the expected value of the welfare function

$$\int_{\underline{\theta}}^{\overline{\theta}} W(v^1(p(\theta), r^1(\theta)), \dots, v^H(p(\theta), r^H(\theta)); \underline{U}) f(\theta) d\theta \tag{25}$$

subject to the following constraints[14]

- market equilibria for every single θ,
- the technology constraint $g(\cdot) = 0$ for every single θ,
- the budget constraint for every single θ,
- the manager's incentive-compatibility constraint,
- the manager's participation constraint.[15]

This is an optimal control problem with

- state variable U and
- control variables e,
$$p_k; k \in K, k \neq o, n,$$
$$r^h; h = 1, \dots, H,$$
$$z_i; i = o, \dots, n.$$

Initial and terminal condition of the state variable $U(\theta)$ are as follows:

- initial condition $U(\underline{\theta}) = \underline{U}$, where the basic managerial utility $\underline{U}$ is optimally chosen by the regulator, and exceeds the reservation utility U^o,
- terminal condition $U(\overline{\theta})$ free.

---

[14] We do not explicitly introduce non-negativity constraints on prices $p_k, k \in K$, and on effort e, but assume interior solutions in what follows.

[15] The participation constraint is not explicitly added to the Hamiltonian, but considered by postulating the respective transversality condition for $\theta = \underline{\theta}$. For this procedure see Seierstad–Sydsæter (1987: 185–6).

We assume that the constraint qualifications[16] hold along the optimal path of control and state variables.

29.2.2   The Hamiltonian

In the following generalized[17] Hamiltonian the Lagrangean multipliers for the market equilibria and for the regulator's budget depend on θ, since there is an individual constraint for every single θ and the associated Lagrangean multipliers are denoted by explicit reference to that particular θ. The vector p refers to all prices, both regulated and non-regulated.

$$
\begin{aligned}
H = {} & W(v^1(p, r^1), \ldots, v^H(p, r^H); \underline{U}) f(\theta) \\
& - \sum_{i=o}^{n-1} \alpha_i(\theta) \left[\sum_h x_i^h(p, r^h) - z_i - \sum_j y_i^j(p) \right] \\
& - \alpha_n(\theta) \left[\sum_h x_n^h(p, r^h) + \frac{U}{p_n} + \frac{\psi(e)}{p_n} - z_n - \sum_{j=1}^J y_n^j(p) \right] \\
& - \beta(\theta) g(\theta, e, z_o, z_1, \ldots, z_n) \\
& - \overline{\gamma}(\theta) \left[\Pi^o - \sum_{i=o}^n p_i z_i + U + \psi(e) \right] \\
& + \mu(\theta) \left[-\psi'(e) E_\theta(\theta, z_o, z_1, \ldots, z_n) \right].
\end{aligned}
\tag{26}
$$

29.2.3   The Marginal Conditions

The necessary conditions for the regulator's optimum are the following (where the dependencies on θ typically are suppressed).

$$
\frac{\partial H}{\partial e} : - \left(\frac{\alpha_n}{p_n} + \overline{\gamma} \right) \psi' - \beta \frac{\partial g}{\partial e} - \mu \psi'' E_\theta = 0,
\tag{27}
$$

---

[16] These are conditions on the rank of the matrix of partial derivatives of the 'mixed constraints' on state and control variables, that is, the market equilibria, the technology and the budget constraint(s). See, for instance Seierstad–Sydsæter (1987: 276, 278, 280, 334).

[17] Strictly defined, the Hamiltonian would be $Wf(\theta) - \mu\psi' E_\theta$. The constraints which do not refer to the differential equation on the state variable are added to achieve a generalized Hamiltonian (alternatively, the generalized Hamiltonian is called the Lagrangean). For this terminology see Seierstad–Sydsæter (1987: 270–1).

$$\frac{\partial H}{\partial p_k} : \sum_h \frac{\partial W}{\partial v^h} \frac{\partial v^h}{\partial p_k} f - \sum_{i=o}^{n} \alpha_i \left(\sum_h \frac{\partial x_i^h}{\partial p_k} - \sum_j \frac{\partial y_i^j}{\partial p_k} \right) + \overline{\gamma} z_k = 0, \quad (28)$$

$$\frac{\partial H}{\partial r^h} : \frac{\partial W}{\partial v^h} \frac{\partial v^h}{\partial r^h} f - \sum_{i=o}^{n} \alpha_i \frac{\partial x_i^h}{\partial r^h} = 0, \quad (29)$$

$$\frac{\partial H}{\partial z_i} : \alpha_i - \beta \frac{\partial g}{\partial z_i} + \overline{\gamma} p_i - \mu \psi' \frac{\partial E_\theta}{\partial z_i} = 0, \quad (30)$$

$$-\frac{\partial H}{\partial U} = \dot{\mu}(\theta) \Longleftrightarrow \dot{\mu}(\theta) = \frac{\alpha_n(\theta)}{p_n} + \overline{\gamma}(\theta). \quad (31)$$

The transversality conditions are[18]

$$\mu(\underline{\theta}) \leq -W_U := -\int_{\underline{\theta}}^{\overline{\theta}} \frac{\partial W}{\partial \underline{U}} f(\theta) d\theta, \quad (32)$$

$$\mu(\overline{\theta}) = 0. \quad (33)$$

29.2.4   *The Signs of Lagrangean Multipliers*

(i) $\alpha_o > 0$.
See above, chapter 3, note 11.

(ii) $\alpha_n > 0$.
Based on the same procedure which we applied to achieve $\alpha_o > 0$.

(iii) $\overline{\gamma} > 0$.
See above, chapter 3, note 12.

(iv) $\mu(\theta) < 0$ for $\underline{\theta} \leq \theta < \overline{\theta}$.
Since $\alpha_n, \overline{\gamma} > 0$, equation (31) implies that μ is increasing in θ. However, for the best type of firm, the transversality condition (33) is $\mu(\overline{\theta}) = 0$. Hence $\mu(\theta) < 0$ for all $\theta < \overline{\theta}$. This is compatible with the transversality condition (32) which establishes $\mu(\underline{\theta}) \leq -W_U < 0$.

29.3   Pricing Rules

29.3.1   *The Connection Between Lerner-, Ramsey- and Incentive Terms*

As 'incentive corrections' we denote those derivatives of the incentive-compatibility constraint which constitute the central distinction between full-information models and asymmetric-information models. In our model, pricing is explicitly influenced by the incentive-correction term[19]

---

[18] See Seierstad–Sydsæter (1987: 185–6).
[19] Recall from chapter 3 that $\beta_o := \beta(\partial g / \partial z_o)$.

$$\mathcal{I}_i := -\frac{\mu}{\beta_o}\frac{\partial \dot{U}}{\partial z_i} = \frac{\mu}{\beta_o}\psi'\frac{\partial E_\theta}{\partial z_i}. \tag{34}$$

As we shall see in what follows, it is this incentive-correction term $\mathcal{I}_i$ (and only this term) which distinguishes the asymmetric-information case from the full-information case of chapter 3.

After some straightforward transformations,[20] our asymmetric-information model yields the following pricing rules for all prices $p_k, k \in K; \ k \neq o, n$:

(i) Let us first assume that the consumers have exogenous initial endowments $r^h, h = 1, \ldots, H$. Prices and quantities are optimally chosen. Then we obtain an incentive-corrected pricing rule of the Feldstein type with adjustment to monopolistic structures in the private economy. (F_k is Feldstein's distributional characteristic: it is higher the more good k is consumed by lower-income earners.[21]) This rule is equivalent to equation (3–21b), where we have assumed $x_k = z_k$,

$$\sum_{i=o}^{n}(p_i - c_i - \mathcal{I}_i)\frac{\partial z_i^D}{\partial p_k} = -(1 - F_k)z_k - (1 - \gamma)\sum_{i=o}^{n}\sum_{j=1}^{J}(p_i - c_i^j)\frac{\partial y_i^j}{\partial p_k}. \tag{35}$$

(ii) If, furthermore, an optimal lump-sum redistribution is chosen, then we obtain an incentive-corrected pricing rule of the Ramsey type with adjustment to monopolistic structures in the private economy. This rule is equivalent to equation (3–24),

$$\sum_{i=o}^{n}(p_i - c_i - \mathcal{I}_i)\frac{\partial \hat{z}_i}{\partial p_k} = -\gamma z_k - (1 - \gamma)\sum_{i=o}^{n}\sum_{j=1}^{J}(p_i - c_i^j)\frac{\partial y_i^j}{\partial p_k}. \tag{36}$$

---

[20] The derivation corresponds to the usual way which we applied in chapter 3 above. Hence in this chapter we do not present all the tedious details of the transformation. However, some instructions may be helpful to the reader. (i) If initial endowments r^h are exogenous, we solve the $\partial H/\partial z_i$ conditions with respect to the α_i's and substitute into the $\partial H/\partial p_k$ conditions. As usual in the Boiteux framework, we have $c_i := (\partial g/\partial z_i)/(\partial g/\partial z_o)$ as the 'marginal costs' of the public utility. Non-compensated demand for the products of the public utility is denoted by defining $\partial z_i^D/\partial p_k := \Sigma_h x_i^h/\partial p_k - \Sigma_j \partial y_i^j/\partial p_k$. y_i^j and c_i^j are netputs and marginal costs of the j-th private firm. F_k is Feldstein's distributional characteristic for good k. It is defined as $F_k := \Sigma_h(\partial W/\partial v^h)(\partial v^h/\partial r^h)(x_k^h/x_k)(1/\beta_o)f(\theta)$ with $\beta_o := \beta(\partial g/\partial z_o)$. (ii) If initial endowments r^h are endogenous, the $\partial H/\partial r^h$ conditions are also taken into consideration. Compensated demand for the products of the public utility is denoted by defining $\partial \hat{z}_i/\partial p_k := [\Sigma_h(\partial x_i^h/\partial p_k + x_k^h(\partial x_i^h/\partial r^h)) - \Sigma_j \partial y_i^j/\partial p_k]$.

[21] For details of these distributional characteristics see section 9.2 above.

As can be seen directly, the asymmetrically-informed regulator chooses the same pricing structure as the fully-informed firm of chapter 3, but replaces marginal costs c_i with $c_i + \mathcal{I}_i$. This means that the regulator relates prices to both costs of production and costs of 'buying' the information about the value of θ. It is interesting to note that this interpretation reduces the problem of asymmetric information on costs to a problem of higher costs facing the principal. Thus, pricing under imperfect information follows the same basic principles as pricing under full information. The regulator applies the usual rules of public-sector pricing: marginal-cost prices, Ramsey prices, Feldstein prices, adjustment to monopolistic private firms etc., always taking account of the increased costs of gathering information from the manager. (The level of any single price, of course, is influenced by the higher compensation which is given to the manager in the asymmetric-information case.)

This interpretation bridges the gap between the model presented in the present chapter and that employed in Bös–Peters (1991a). There, an effort-requirement function $E(t, V)$ was used and the pricing rules were exactly equal to those of chapter 3. In the present chapter we use an effort-requirement function $E(\theta, z)$ and also find pricing rules which follow the basic principles of chapter 3. The particular choice of the $E(\theta, z)$, however, explicitly shows how these basic pricing rules are adapted to cope with the regulator's imperfect information on technology.

Let us finally compare the result of our model with Tirole–Laffont (1990: 2–3, 8–9). This comparison can most easily be performed using the example of Ramsey pricing. In case of asymmetric information our model yields

$$\sum_{i \in K}(\mathcal{L}_i - \mathcal{I}_i/p_i)\eta_{ki} = -\gamma; \quad k \in K, \tag{37}$$

where $\mathcal{L}_i$ is the Lerner index, $\mathcal{L}_i := (p_i - c_i)/p_i$. By applying Cramer's rule, this system of equations can be solved to attain

$$\mathcal{L}_k - \mathcal{I}_k/p_k = \mathcal{R}_k; \qquad k \in K. \tag{38}$$

Here $\mathcal{R}_k$ is a Ramsey index, for instance $\mathcal{R}_k := -\gamma/\eta_{kk}$ for independent demands or $\mathcal{R}_k := -\gamma/\mathcal{H}_{kk}$ for a two-product firm with $\mathcal{H}_{kk}$ as the superelasticity we have defined in chapter 8 above.[22] The message of the formula (38) is clear: the requirement of incentive compatibility drives a wedge between

---

[22] As already shown in subsection 8.1.2 above, the precise definition of the Ramsey index is

$$\mathcal{R}_k := [det(\vec{\eta}_1, ..., \vec{\eta}_{k-1}, -\vec{\gamma}, \vec{\eta}_{k+1}, ..., \vec{\eta}_{\mathcal{M}})]/det\eta,$$

where η is the $\mathcal{M}$ times $\mathcal{M}$-dimensional matrix of compensated price elasticities with column vectors $\vec{\eta}_1...\vec{\eta}_{\mathcal{M}}$. ($\mathcal{M}$ is the number of regulated prices.) $-\vec{\gamma}$ is a column vector consisting the Lerner index and the Ramsey index which would have been equated in the full-information model. This is exactly Laffont–Tirole's result. We shall see later on, that no such separability between Lerner index, Ramsey index and incentive-correction term is possible if the regulator's lack of information refers to demand or budget instead of costs.

29.3.2   How Incentive Corrections Influence Prices[23]

A positive incentive-correction term favors a high price. This case occurs if $\partial E_\theta / \partial z_i < 0$.[24] Equivalently this occurs if an increase in z_i increases the marginal rate of transformation between effort and firm productivity θ in the labor-requirement function: an increase in output makes it easier for the manager to exploit an improvement in θ by reducing effort e. This can be proved as follows.[25] Consider the labor-requirement function,

$$z_o \equiv z_o(\theta, E(\theta, z), z_1, \ldots, z_n). \tag{39}$$

Differentiation with respect to θ yields[26]

$$0 = \frac{\partial z_o}{\partial \theta} + \frac{\partial z_o}{\partial e} E_\theta \tag{40}$$

or, equivalently

$$E_\theta = -\frac{\partial z_o / \partial \theta}{\partial z_o / \partial e} =: MRT\,(e, \theta). \tag{41}$$

This marginal rate of transformation between effort and productivity θ is negative which fits in with the assumption $E_\theta < 0$. It consists of two effects. $\partial z_o / \partial \theta > 0$ because the labor requirement is lower the better the type of the firm.[27] In the same way $\partial z_o / \partial e > 0$ because the labor requirement is lower the higher the manager's effort.

Given the equivalence of E_θ and the marginal rate of transformation, a high price is favored if

---

of $\mathcal{M}$ elements $-\gamma$. By *det* we denote the determinants of the relevant matrices. – Unfortunately, the Ramsey index becomes very complicated if the firm produces more than two goods where demands are interdependent.

[23] The special case of a vanishing incentive correction at the top, $\bar\theta$, will be treated in section 29.5 below.

[24] Since $\psi' > 0$, $\beta_o > 0$, and $\mu < 0$ for all θ except $\bar\theta$.

[25] Cfr. Laffont–Tirole (1990: 15–6).

[26] This is a comparative-static analysis at the optimum: how does an infinitesimal change of θ influence the labor-requirement function ceteris paribus, i.e. holding constant all variables z at their optimal level.

[27] Recall that $z_o < 0$.

$$\frac{\partial MRT\,(e,\theta)}{\partial z_i} < 0. \tag{42}$$

Hence, if MRT is large in absolute value, improvements in θ can be exploited by more intense effort reductions. This characterizes the high-cost case.

29.3.3 *Incentive-Pricing Dichotomy*

Similar to Laffont–Tirole (1990: 15–7) we have $\mathcal{I}_i = 0$ if $\partial E_\theta/\partial z_i = 0$. This can be called an 'incentive-pricing dichotomy' since the incentive correction $\mathcal{I}_i$ vanishes in the price equation – on superficial inspection pricing seems to be independent of the asymmetric information. However, this is incorrect. The condition for optimal effort still depends on $\mu\psi'' E_\theta$ and since the principal solves an interdependent system of equations, the incentive problem is still relevant for the prices which are chosen.

It is still of some interest to find the special form of technology which yields $\partial E_\theta/\partial z_i = 0$.[28] This is the case if the trade-off between effort e and productivity θ in the technology does not depend on the input and output quantities, that is

$$g(f(\theta,e), z_o, \dots, z_n) = 0. \tag{43}$$

Total differentiation with respect to θ and e then yields

$$E_\theta = -\frac{f_\theta}{f_e}. \tag{44}$$

We see directly that in this case E_θ is independent of $z_i, i = o, \dots, n$.

29.4 Optimal Effort

To understand the condition on optimal effort, equation (27), we need some benchmark models. Let us first begin with cost minimization under full information:[29]

$$\underset{e, z_{\overline{k}}, U}{\text{minimize}} -z_o(e, z_1, \dots, z_n) - \sum_i p_i z_i^- + U + \psi(e)$$

subject to

$$U \geq U^o.$$

$$\tag{45}$$

---

[28] See Laffont–Tirole (1990: 16).
[29] Cfr subsection 2.4.4 above.

Here U^o is the reservation utility of the manager which is exogenous in the benchmark model. Let ϕ be the Lagrangean parameter which is associated with the participation constraint. Then the necessary optimum conditions are

$$\frac{\partial z_o}{\partial e} = \psi', \tag{46}$$

$$\frac{\partial z_o}{\partial z_k^-} = -p_k, \tag{47}$$

$$\phi = 1. \tag{48}$$

Consider in particular the first condition above. According to this condition, to achieve a cost minimum, labor is replaced with effort until the marginal disutility of effort is equated to the marginal rate of transformation between labor and effort (measured along the labor-requirement function). Effort is lower the higher its marginal disutility. Note that $\partial z_o / \partial e > 0$ follows from the usual properties of the technology $g(\cdot) = 0$.

Consider next a principal-agent model where the regulator is fully informed about θ and is able to observe and hence to directly enforce the second-best welfare-maximizing effort. In this model there is no incentive-compatibility constraint, and the participation constraint $t - \psi(e) = \underline{U}$ is always binding. θ is known, hence all functions are evaluated at the value of the correct θ (no control theory needed). The regulator's objective function is W at the correct value of θ (no expectation). Market equilibria, technology and budget constraint are formulated in the same way as in the asymmetric-information model of this chapter. They are always evaluated at θ. A brief formal presentation of this model is given in appendix 2 of this chapter.

In this full-information benchmark model the necessary condition for effort is

$$\frac{\partial z_o}{\partial e} = \left(\frac{\alpha_n}{p_n} + \overline{\gamma} \right) \frac{\psi'}{\beta_o}, \tag{49}$$

where $\partial z_o / \partial e = -(\partial g / \partial e)/(\partial g / \partial z_o)$. Obviously the optimum effort in this model is not cost-minimizing. Effort in the full-information benchmark model is lower the higher its normalized marginal disutility ('normalization' referring to the parameters by which ψ' is multiplied in (49)).

Let us finally turn to the condition on optimal effort under asymmetric information. We rewrite equation (27) to obtain

$$\frac{\partial z_o}{\partial e} = \left(\frac{\alpha_n}{p_n} + \overline{\gamma} \right) \frac{\psi'}{\beta_o} + \frac{\mu}{\beta_o} \psi'' E_\theta. \tag{50}$$

Once again, effort is not cost minimizing. There is even a tendency that it will be lower than in the full-information principal-agent model, caused by the additional costs of incentive compatibility, as expressed by the derivative of the incentive-compatibility constraint $((\mu/\beta_o)\psi'' E_\theta > 0)$.[30]

29.5   Incentives at the Top

The transversality condition requires $\mu(\overline{\theta}) = 0$. Hence, in the most efficient firm the incentive corrections vanish in both the price and the effort formula. This type of result is pretty well-known in asymmetric-information models. It is the same type of result which postulates that the most able consumer should have to pay a marginal income-tax rate of zero or an undistorted non-linear price, equal to marginal costs, for some commodity supplied by public utilities.

Let us first ponder why this result is achieved.[31] It depends on the informational asymmetry. Recall that the manager's utility must be increasing in θ to guarantee incentive compatibility. Therefore, any decision of the regulator at some level $\widetilde{\theta}$ influences the decisions at all levels of $\theta > \widetilde{\theta}$. Such an 'external effect' on other decisions occurs as long as there are further θ's in excess of $\widetilde{\theta}$. This is not the case at the top. Consequently, for the most-productive firm, the incentive corrections vanish.

It is interesting to see that the least-productive firm is faced with incentive corrections, although the regulator knows that in this type of firm the manager has no incentive to lie: lies pay only if a $\hat{\theta}$ can be announced which falls below the actual value. Knowing this, the regulator could enforce the equivalent to a full-information contract for $\theta = \underline{\theta}$. However, this is not the regulator's optimal policy. He rather accepts incentive corrections in the least-productive firm. Enforcing efficiency at the bottom would be too costly because of the 'external effects' on all other realizations of θ.

It should be clear that the vanishing incentive corrections do not imply that in the best-type firm the same manager income and prices are optimal in case of full and in case of asymmetric information. At the top some marginal conditions are identical in these two approaches. But the incentive compatibility, of course, implies feedbacks on the regulator's policy for the most-productive firm, driving a wedge between asymmetric and full-information incomes, prices etc.[32]

---

[30] Recall $\psi''>0$, $E_\theta<0$, and $\mu<0$ for all θ except $\overline{\theta}$. Moreover, $\beta_o>0$. Note that we can only speak of a 'tendency' because it cannot be said whether $[(\alpha_n/p_n)+\overline{\gamma}][\psi'/\beta_o]$ is larger in the full-information setting or under asymmetric information.

[31] See Bös–Peters (1991a: 38–9).

[32] More formally: if a full-information model is set up as formally described in appendix 2

Appendix 1:
A Benchmark Model with Effort Requirement E(t,V)

We specify managerial utility as

$$U(e, t); \qquad U_1 < 0, \quad U_2 > 0.$$

The value $\hat{\theta}$, which is announced by the manager, results from minimizing the following distance function with respect to $\hat{\theta}$:

$$\mathcal{D} := V(e(\theta), t(\theta)) - U(e(\theta, \hat{\theta}), t(\hat{\theta}))$$

This leads to a first-order condition

$$-U_1 e_{\hat{\theta}} - U_2 t' = 0.$$

We combine this marginal condition with

$$\dot{U}(\theta) = U_1(e_\theta + e_{\hat{\theta}}) + U_2 t'$$

to obtain the incentive-compatibility condition

$$\dot{U}(\theta) = U_1 e_\theta > 0.$$

Now invert the managerial utility $U(e, t)$ to obtain the following effort-requirement function

$$e = E(t, V); \quad E_t = -U_2/U_1 > 0; \quad E_V = \frac{1}{U_1} < 0.$$

The constraints are chosen analogous to the optimization approach treated in the text. We formulate an optimal control problem with

- state variable V and
- control variables $p_k, \ k \in K, \ k \neq o, n,$

---

of this chapter, some marginal conditions of this model and of the asymmetric-information model in the case of $\theta = \bar{\theta}$ are identical, namely equations (27) to (30) above, since the incentive corrections in equations (27) and (30) vanish. However, there are some remaining marginal conditions which are different in the two compared models. In the asymmetric-information model we have the incentive-compatibility setting

$\dot{\mu} = (\alpha_n/p_n)(\bar{\theta}) + \bar{\gamma}(\bar{\theta}),$ (31)

$\mu(\underline{\theta}) = -W_U,$ (32)

$\mu(\bar{\theta}) = 0.$ (33)

In the full-information model these three conditions are replaced by the condition:

$W_U - \phi = \alpha_n/p_n + \bar{\gamma}$

where ϕ is the Lagrangean multiplier of the managerial participation constraint.

$$r^h, \ h = 1, \ldots, H,$$

$$t,$$

$$z_i, \ i = o, \ldots, n.$$

The Hamiltonian is as follows

$$
\begin{aligned}
H = {}& W(v^1(p(\theta), r^1(\theta)), \ldots, v^H(p(\theta), r^H(\theta)); \underline{V}) f(\theta) \\
& - \sum_{i=o}^{n-1} \alpha_i(\theta) \left[\sum_h x_i^h(p(\theta), r^h(\theta)) - z_i(\theta) - \sum_j y_i^j(p(\theta)) \right] \\
& - \alpha_n(\theta) \left[\sum_h x_n^h(p(\theta), r^h(\theta)) + \frac{t(\theta)}{p_n} - z_n(\theta) - \sum_{j=1}^J y_n^j(p(\theta)) \right] \\
& - \beta g(\theta, E(t(\theta), V(\theta)), z(\theta)) \\
& - \overline{\gamma}(\theta) \left[\Pi^o - \sum_{i=o}^n p_i(\theta) z_i(\theta) + t(\theta) \right] \\
& + \mu(\theta) \left[-U_1(E(t(\theta), V(\theta)), t(\theta)) \cdot e_\theta(t(\theta), V(\theta)) \right].
\end{aligned}
$$

It can directly be seen that the conditions $H_p = 0$, $H_r = 0$, $H_z = 0$ are formally identical with the respective conditions of chapter 3.[33] Hence the pricing formulas are identical to those of chapter 3.[34] However, prices, quantities and lump-sum incomes will not be same as in the optimization problem of chapter 3, because the regulator has to solve an interdependent system of equations which does not only consist of the conditions $H_p = 0, H_r = 0, H_z = 0$, but also of $H_t = 0, H_v = -\mu$ and the transversality conditions.

Appendix 2:
A Benchmark Model with Fully-Informed Regulator

This benchmark model is used in sections 29.4 and 29.5. The regulator knows the value of θ and therefore evaluates all functions at θ. The manager is not given an information rent, hence, $U = \underline{U} \geq U^o$, where U is total managerial utility, $\underline{U}$ is basic utility and U^o is the reservation utility. The regulator maximizes

$$W = W(v^1, \ldots, v^H, U),$$

---

[33] Eqs (3–6), (3–7), (3–8).

[34] Eqs (3–21) if only $H_p=0$ and $H_z=0$ are considered, eqs (3–24) if $H_r=0$ is also taken into account.

where $U = \underline{U}$ has been substituted. The optimization is subject to the following constraints:

- market equilibria,
- technology,
- budget constraint,
- the manager's participation constraint.

The instrument variables are

$e,$
$p_k, k \in K, k \neq o, n,$
$r^h, h = 1, \ldots, H,$
$z_i, i = o, \ldots, n,$
$U.$

The Lagrangean function, therefore, is as follows:

$$
\mathcal{F} = W(v^1, \ldots, v^H, U)
$$

$$
- \sum_{i=o}^{n-1} \alpha_i \left[\sum_h x_i^h(p, r^h) - z_i - \sum_j y_i^j(p) \right]
$$

$$
- \alpha_n \left[\sum_h x_n^h(p, r^h) + \frac{U}{p_n} + \frac{\psi(e)}{p_n} - z_n - \sum_j y_n^j(p) \right]
$$

$$
- \beta g(e, z)
$$

$$
- \overline{\gamma} \left[\Pi^o - \sum_{i=o}^{n} p_i z_i + U + \psi(e) \right]
$$

$$
- \phi [U - U^o].
$$

30
Asymmetric Information on Demand

30.1   The Model

30.1.1   The Information Setting

In this chapter we deal with asymmetric information on the demand for the outputs of the regulated firm. We assume that there is a *firm-specific* parameter θ which influences demand for any single output of the enterprise. θ measures how hostile or favorable the economic environment which the firm faces when selling any of its goods. It ranges from a gloomy $\underline{\theta}$ to a booming $\overline{\theta}$. Alternatively, we could have assumed *good-specific* parameters θ_b, varying across the firm's outputs $z_b > 0$ where $b = d + 1, \ldots, n$. Then, however, the model would have become too complicated.

As in the preceding chapter, the regulator is able to observe inputs, outputs and prices. However, the manager's effort and the actual value of θ are private information of the firm's management. The regulator only knows the density function $f(\theta)$. The shape of all relevant functions is common knowledge.

30.1.2   Demand Functions

The manager of the regulated firm responds to the situation θ with marketing efforts that influence consumer demand for the firm's outputs. This demand is denoted by $x_b^h > 0$, $b = d + 1, \ldots n$. The efforts are $e_b \geq 0$.[1] We assume that marketing always refers to a particular good and proportionally increases every consumer's demand for that good:

$$x_b^h = \mathcal{X}_b^h \left(\theta, p, r^h \right) \cdot \varphi_b(\theta, e_b); \quad b = d + 1, \ldots, n; \; h = 1, \ldots, H. \qquad (1)$$

Note that θ influences both the basic demand $\mathcal{X}_b^h$ and the marketing term φ_b. Naturally we have $\varphi_b(\theta, 0) = 1$ and otherwise $\varphi_b(\theta, e_b) > 1$. We assume

---

[1] The model could easily be extended by efforts $e_i > 0$, $i \neq o, b$ which stimulate the demand for privately supplied complements to the outputs of the public firm. This would imply that the regulator is not only responsible for the public utility but has a wider influence in the economy as is characteristic for Boiteux-type models of public-sector pricing. This would be the same basic philosophy of regulatory planning which imposes on the regulator the additional task of achieving market equilibria for all goods in the economy.

$$\frac{\partial x_b^h}{\partial \theta} > 0, \quad \frac{\partial x_b^h}{\partial p_b} < 0, \quad \frac{\partial x_b^h}{\partial e_b} > 0, \quad \frac{\partial x_b^h}{\partial r^h} > 0; \qquad b = d+1, \dots, n; \ \forall h. \qquad (2)$$

Our model excludes cross-marketing effects while including cross-price effects. This is not implausible. While a price increase directly affects the consumers' budgets, no such direct effect occurs in case of marketing efforts. Hence any cross-marketing effects would have to work their way through complicated psychological mechanisms whose modelling is beyond the scope of this book.

On the basis of effort-dependent demand an effort-requirement function can be defined as follows. The effort which is required to induce total demand $x_b = \Sigma_h x_b^h$ at prices p, lump-sum incomes r and a particular value of θ, can be written as

$$E_b = E_b(\theta, p, r, x_b); \qquad b = d+1, \dots, n, \qquad (3)$$

where r is the vector of lump-sum incomes r^h. The derivatives of the effort-requirement functions follow from (2), namely

$$\frac{\partial E_b}{\partial \theta} < 0, \quad \frac{\partial E_b}{\partial x_b} > 0; \qquad b = d+1, \dots, n. \qquad (4a)$$

Consider next the influence of an increasing price p_b on effort. Partially differentiating $E_b(\theta, p, r, x_b)$ with respect to p_b implies changing price while holding constant the firm-specific parameter θ, incomes r and demand x_b. This requires more effort and therefore

$$\frac{\partial E_b}{\partial p_b} > 0; \qquad b = d+1, \dots, n. \qquad (4b)$$

Cross-price derivatives depend on whether the relevant goods are complements or substitutes. Consider an increase in price p_k. Assume that this lowers the demand for good k. Hence, there is a downward pressure on the demand for the complement good b. This implies that more effort is needed to sell quantity x_b whence we can conclude

$$\frac{\partial E_b}{\partial p_k} > 0; \qquad \text{for complements, } b \neq k, \qquad (4c)$$

$$\frac{\partial E_b}{\partial p_k} < 0; \qquad \text{for substitutes, } b \neq k, \qquad (4d)$$

where $b = d + 1, \ldots, n$ and $k \in K$.[2] Finally, consider a change in consumer h's income r^h. Since higher income makes it easier to sell the same quantity at the same price in the same economic environment, we have

$$\frac{\partial E_b}{\partial r^h} < 0; \qquad b = d + 1, \ldots, n, \qquad h = 1, \ldots, H. \tag{4e}$$

The effort-requirement functions are implicitly defined by

$$x_b \equiv x_b(\theta, E_b(\theta, p, r, x_b), p, r); \qquad b = d + 1, \ldots, n. \tag{5}$$

In what follows we shall use the demand functions $x_b^h(\theta, e_b(\theta), p, r^h)$ for the description of the market-equilibria and the effort-requirement functions for the treatment of incentive compatibility.

Let us impute to the consumers quasi-linear preferences.[3] This implies that the consumers' indirect utility functions are as follows:

$$v^h := cs^h(\theta, e, p) + r^h; \qquad h = 1, \ldots, H, \tag{6}$$

where cs^h is an individual consumer surplus and $e := (e_{d+1}, \ldots, e_n)$. According to this specification we have

$$\frac{\partial v^h}{\partial p_k} = \frac{\partial cs^h}{\partial p_k} = -x_k^h; \quad \frac{\partial v^h}{\partial r^h} = 1; \quad \frac{\partial v^h}{\partial e_b} > 0, \tag{7}$$

where $b = d + 1, \ldots, n$ and $k \in K$. The derivative $\partial cs^h / \partial p_k = -x_k^h$ is a well-known property of consumer surplus. The derivative $\partial v^h / \partial r^h = 1$ is straightforward. The sign of $\partial v^h / \partial e_b > 0$ results from the chosen specification of consumer demand. Consider the integral over $\mathcal{X}_b^h(\theta, p, r^h)$ for constant θ and r^h. This is an area under a demand function (and is well-defined by our assumption of quasi-linear utilities). Now consider an increase in e_b. Since $\partial x_b^h / \partial e_b > 0$, this implies an outward shift of the demand function for good b and therefore an increase in consumer surplus.

30.1.3 Incentive Income

The manager is paid an income which induces him to announce the correct value of the parameter θ. This reward scheme must be chosen as follows:

---

[2] Only prices p_k, $k \in K$, change in our model.
[3] See Varian (1992: 164–6).

$$\text{incentive pay} = \begin{cases} t(\hat{\theta}) & \text{if } p_k = p_k(\hat{\theta}), r^h = r^h(\hat{\theta}) \text{ and} \\ & x_b = \Sigma_h x_b^h(\hat{\theta}) \text{ for } k \in K, \text{ and } \forall h, b, \\ \\ 0 & \text{otherwise.} \end{cases} \quad (8)$$

The manager who if offered this incentive reward decides to announce a particular value $\hat{\theta}$. In doing so he must avoid being caught lying. The principal is able to observe prices, lump-sum incomes and the quantities demanded. Hence, the effects of effort and the actual and announced values of θ must always lead to precisely those prices, incomes and quantities which the principal will be able to observe. Conditioning the reward on the vectors p, r and x is sufficient, because it also implies the correct setting of the vectors $y(p)$ and $z(p)$.[4]

Since every single quantity x_b depends only on e_b, and there are no cross effects, the manager will correctly disaggregate his effort among the various goods. This is achieved by the incentive reward which indirectly depends on the vector of efforts; notwithstanding the fact that the manager's disutility from effort is the same across all efforts, that is $\psi(\Sigma e_b)$.[5]

In this chapter we deal with one principal and one general manager who is responsible for all the various marketing efforts. As a possible alternative, let us briefly consider a decentralized internal organization of the firm, where the principal faces many product managers, each of whom is responsible for marketing a single output.

In that case we would no longer have a single θ for all outputs b, but rather assume separate parameters θ_b. Otherwise there would be moral hazard on the side of the principal. In order to elicit the true value of θ, he would not need to offer a separate contract to every single product manager. He rather would only have to offer one contract to one of the managers to learn θ and on the basis of this knowledge the principal could fully monitor all other managers.[6]

---

[4] Recall that in models of the Boiteux type the quantities z_i are chosen as instruments. In the transformation of the marginal conditions, however, the functional dependency $z(p)$ is introduced by substituting $\partial z/\partial p$ for $\partial x/\partial p - \partial y/\partial p$.

[5] As in the preceding chapter we assume $\psi' > 0, \psi'' > 0, \psi''' \geq 0$.

[6] Obviously, the principal can be prevented from such a policy by institutional arrangements which enforce simultaneous contracting between the principal and every single product manager. Such an arrangement could, for instance, result from bargaining between the principal and a trade union which represents the product managers' interests. If such an arrangement holds, bribing a single product manager would be the principal's only way to get the information on θ more cheaply than by contracting with all managers.

In the presence of parameters θ_b, the reward schedule for any single product manager b would be as follows:

$$\text{incentive pay of product manager} = \begin{cases} t_b(\hat{\theta}) & \text{if } x_b = \Sigma_h x_b^h(\hat{\theta}_b) \\ 0 & \text{otherwise.} \end{cases} \quad (9)$$

The optimal prices and lump-sum incomes would have to be chosen by the principal. Hence they do not enter the managerial-reward functions.

The economic story behind this multiple-agent model is convincing. However, in the present chapter I shall adhere to the story of the general manager with an incentive reward according to (8). The reason is simple: the multiple-agent approach is more cumbersome to model and does not lead to further economic insight.[7]

The awkwardness is the disadvantage of decentralization. For every product manager we would have to postulate an incentive-compatibility constraint and a participation constraint. Every single incentive-compatibility constraint would depend on a single θ_b, given the exogenous cumulative distribution $F(\theta_b, \theta_{-b})$ where θ_{-b} is the vector of all θ's excluding θ_b. The policy maker would have to formulate expected welfare for the cumulative distribution $F(\theta_{d+1}, \ldots, \theta_n)$. All prices, lump-sum incomes and netputs of the regulated firm would depend on the entire θ vector. This implies that the market-clearing conditions and the budget constraint would have to hold for each possible combination of realizations of the various θ_b.

30.1.4   The General Manager's Optimization

(i)   Incentive Compatibility
For a general manager with utility $U = t - \psi$, the preferred announcement $\hat{\theta}$ results from the minimization of the distance function

$$\mathcal{D} := [t(\theta) - \psi(E(\theta))] - \left[t(\hat{\theta}) - \psi(E(\theta, \hat{\theta}))\right]. \quad (10)$$

Here $E(\theta, \hat{\theta})$ is a shorthand for $\Sigma E_b(\theta, p(\hat{\theta}), r(\hat{\theta}), x_b(\hat{\theta}))$. As in the preceding chapter, effort $E_b(\theta, \hat{\theta})$ has been chosen in such a way that a falsely announced $\hat{\theta}$ and an actual θ combine in order to give $x_b(\hat{\theta})$ which is observable by the regulator and precisely corresponds to the announced $\hat{\theta}$ (consistent lie).

---

[7] After adequately redefining some incentive-correction terms the economic message would be the same.

Differentiating $\mathcal{D}$ with respect to the announced $\hat{\theta}$ leads to the following necessary first-order condition[8]

$$\frac{dt}{d\hat{\theta}} - \psi' Z(\hat{\theta}, \theta) = 0, \tag{11}$$

where

$$Z(\hat{\theta}, \theta) := \sum_b \left[\frac{\partial E_b}{\partial x_b} \frac{dx_b}{d\hat{\theta}} + \sum_k \frac{\partial E_b}{\partial p_k} \frac{\partial p_k}{\partial \hat{\theta}} + \sum_h \frac{\partial E_b}{\partial r^h} \frac{dr^h}{d\hat{\theta}} \right]. \tag{12}$$

We proceed as usual and consider changes in the manager's utility which result from changes in the actual θ,

$$\dot{U}(\theta) := \frac{dU}{d\theta} = \frac{dt}{d\theta} - \psi' E_\theta - \psi' Z(\theta, \theta), \tag{13}$$

where we have abbreviated $E_\theta := \Sigma \partial E_b / \partial \theta$.

At $\theta = \hat{\theta}$, all differential quotients in Z are observable for the regulator, and so is $dt/d\theta$. Hence the manager will choose his efforts in such a way that all of these differential quotients are equal in (11) and (13). Therefore, these equations can be combined to obtain the manager's incentive-compatibility condition

$$\dot{U}(\theta) = -\psi' E_\theta > 0. \tag{14}$$

The manager always has an incentive to understate θ: 'the economic situation is so bad, therefore I had to work so hard …' Hence, it is plausible that the manager's utility must be increasing in θ to induce him to report the correct θ.

The second-order condition $U_{\hat{\theta}\theta}^2 \geq 0$ is[9] (at $\theta = \hat{\theta}$):

$$-\psi' \frac{dZ}{d\theta} - Z\psi'' E_\theta \geq 0. \tag{15}$$

Sufficient for the second-order condition to hold, therefore, are $Z \geq 0$ and $dZ/d\theta \leq 0$. However, recall the definition of Z in equation (12) above. While some of the terms in Z have a plausible sign, it is absolutely impossible to determine the sign of

---

[8] Because of $E_b(\theta, \hat{\theta})$, the terms $\psi'(E)$ and $\partial E_b / \partial \xi$, $\xi = x_b^h, p_k, r^h$ depend on both the announced value $\hat{\theta}$ and the actual value θ. Hence, we denote $Z(\hat{\theta}, \theta)$.

[9] For this formulation of the second-order condition see section 28.3 above. For the differentiation note that in the first-order condition (11) $dt/d\hat{\theta}$ and $d\xi/d\hat{\theta}, \xi = x_b, p_k, r^h$, are independent of θ; they depend only on $\hat{\theta}$. On the other hand, $\psi'(e)$ and $\partial E_b / \partial \xi, \xi = x_b, p_k, r^h$, depend on the actual θ because we have $E_b(\theta, \hat{\theta})$.

$$\sum_b \sum_k \frac{\partial E_b}{\partial p_k} \frac{dp_k}{d\theta}. \tag{16}$$

Effort responds to price changes in a positive or negative way, depending on complementary or substitutional relationships between goods. Moreover, it is unclear whether better economic environment reduces or increases prices in our model. Correspondingly, not only is $dp_k/d\theta$ indeterminate, but also $dx_b/d\theta$.

If there is not even a set of plausible assumptions which supports $Z \geq 0$, it is utterly hopeless to find plausible assumptions which imply $dZ/d\theta \leq 0$. Whereas in the case of asymmetric information on costs it was easy to establish the validity of the second-order condition,[10] this is not the case if the asymmetric information refers to demand characteristics. In the rest of this chapter we shall assume that the second-order condition holds. However, the reader should always be aware of the possibility of bunching as treated in section 28.4 above.[11]

(ii)   Participation

The enterprise cannot be run by the regulator, but only by the manager whose participation is guaranteed if

$$U(\underline{\theta}) = \underline{U}, \tag{17a}$$
$$U(\theta) > \underline{U} \qquad \text{for all } \theta > \underline{\theta}. \tag{17b}$$

Incentive-compatibility requires total manager utility in excess of the basic utility $\underline{U}$ for all demand characteristics except the worst case $\underline{\theta}$.

30.1.5   Technology, Markets, Regulatory Budget Constraint[12]

After extensively presenting the particular features of asymmetric information on demand, we now close the model according to the Boiteux tradition. Let us begin by characterizing the price space of the model. The vector $p(\theta)$ refers to all prices, both the regulated prices $p_k(\theta), k \in K$, and the exogenously given non-regulated prices $p_i, i \notin K$. Labor is the numeraire, hence $p_o = 1$. The price of the n-th good p_n is given and not regulated.

---

[10] See subsection 29.1.4 (i) above.

[11] Lewis–Sappington (1988) address this problem in their paper as briefly sketched in subsection 28.5.3 above.

[12] We assume that the constraint qualifications hold along the optimal path of control and state variables. Refer to subsection 29.2.1 above.

We postulate that market-clearing conditions, technology and regulatory budget constraint hold for every single θ. Such a general assumption is necessary because every netput z_i, $i = o, \ldots, n$ depends on θ. Hence we define

(i)   the technology

$$g(z(\theta)) = 0, \tag{18}$$

(ii)   the regulatory budget constraint

$$\sum_{k \in K} p_k(\theta) z_k(\theta) + \sum_{i \notin K} p_i z_i(\theta) - U(\theta) - \psi(\Sigma e_b(\theta)) = \Pi^o. \tag{19}$$

(iii)   the market-clearing conditions

$$\sum_h x_i^h(\cdot) - z_i(\theta) - \sum_j y_i^j(\cdot) = 0; \qquad i = o, \ldots, n - 1, \tag{20a}$$

$$\sum_h x_n^h(\cdot) + [U(\theta) + \psi(\Sigma e_b(\theta))]/p_n - z_n(\theta) - \sum_j y_n^j(\cdot) = 0. \tag{20b}$$

In these formulas we have abbreviated the following specifications:

- $x_i^h(\cdot) = x_i^h(p(\theta), r^h(\theta))$ for $i = o, \ldots, d$,
- $x_b^h(\cdot) = \mathcal{X}_b^h(\theta, p(\theta), r^h(\theta)) \cdot \varphi_b(\theta, e_b(\theta))$ for $b = d + 1, \ldots, n$,
- $y_n^j(\cdot) = y_n^j(p(\theta))$.

To simplify the market-clearing conditions, we have assumed that only the demand of private consumers is influenced by special efforts of the firm's manager. Demand and supply of unregulated private firms depend on the prices p only. The manager, as in the preceding chapter, only consumes good n. As usual, the market equilibria constitute a financial equilibrium.[13]

30.2   The Optimization Problem

30.2.1   Objective, Constraints, Control and State Variables

The regulator maximizes expected welfare

$$\int_{\underline{\theta}}^{\bar{\theta}} W(v^1(\theta, e(\theta), p(\theta), r^1(\theta)), \ldots, v^H(\cdot); \underline{U}) f(\theta) d\theta \tag{21}$$

subject to the following constraints:[14]

---

[13] The formula is identical with that given in subsection 29.1.6 above.

[14] Moreover, the non-negativity of the efforts e_b is to be considered. In contrast to chapter 29 this problem is explicitly treated (although not by means of explicit constraints) because otherwise $e_b < 0$ for some b seems to be a probable outcome of the optimization. Once again, however, we do not explicitly introduce non-negativity constraints on prices p_k, but assume interior solutions.

- market equilibria for every single θ,
- the technology constraint $g(\cdot) = 0$ for every single θ,
- the budget constraint for every single θ,
- the manager's incentive-compatibility constraint,
- the manager's participation constraint.[15]

This is an optimal control problem with

- state variable U and
- control variables e_b; $b = d+1, \ldots, n$,

$$p_k; \ k \in K, \ k \neq o, n,$$
$$r^h; \ h = 1, \ldots, H,$$
$$z_i; \ i = o, \ldots, n.$$

30.2.2 The Generalized Hamiltonian[16]

$$H = W(v^1(\theta, e, p, r^1), \ldots, v^H(\cdot); \underline{U})f(\theta)$$
$$- \sum_{i=o}^{d} \alpha_i(\theta) \left[\sum_h x_i^h(p, r^h) - z_i - \sum_j y_i^j(p) \right]$$
$$- \sum_{b=d+1}^{n-1} \alpha_b(\theta) \left[\sum_h x_b^h(\theta, e_b, p, r^h) - z_b - \sum_j y_b^j(p) \right]$$
$$- \alpha_n(\theta) \left[\sum_h x_n^h(\theta, e_n, p, r^h) + \frac{U}{p_n} + \frac{\psi(\Sigma e_b)}{p_n} - z_n - \sum_j y_n^j(p) \right]$$
$$- \beta(\theta)g(z)$$
$$- \overline{\gamma}(\theta) \left[\Pi^o - \sum_{i=o}^{n} p_i z_i + U + \psi(\Sigma e_b) \right]$$
$$+ \mu(\theta) \left[-\psi'(\Sigma e_b) \sum_b \frac{\partial E_b}{\partial \theta}(\theta, p, r, x_b(\theta, e_b, p, r)) \right]. \tag{22}$$

---

[15] The participation constraint is not explicitly added to the generalized Hamiltonian, but considered by postulating the respective transversality condition for $\theta = \underline{\theta}$. For this procedure see Seierstad–Sydsæter (1987: 185–6). – The term 'generalized Hamiltonian' is explained in Seierstad–Sydsæter (1987: 270–1); see also footnote 17 in chapter 29 above.

[16] The vector p refers to all prices, both regulated and non-regulated.

30.2.3   The Marginal Conditions

The necessary conditions for the regulator's optimum are the following (where the dependencies on θ typically are suppressed).

$$\frac{\partial H}{\partial e_b} : \sum_h \left(\frac{\partial W}{\partial v^h} \frac{\partial v^h}{\partial e_b} f - \alpha_b \frac{\partial x_b^h}{\partial e_b} \right) - \left(\frac{\alpha_n}{p_n} + \overline{\gamma} \right) \psi' - \mu \frac{d(\psi' E_\theta)}{de_b} \leq 0, \quad (23a)$$

$$\frac{\partial H}{\partial e_b} \cdot e_b = 0, \quad e_b \geq 0, \quad (23b)$$

$$\frac{\partial H}{\partial p_k} : \sum_h \frac{\partial W}{\partial v^h} \frac{\partial v^h}{\partial p_k} f - \sum_{i=o}^{n} \alpha_i \left(\sum_h \frac{\partial x_i^h}{\partial p_k} - \sum_j \frac{\partial y_i^j}{\partial p_k} \right) + \overline{\gamma} z_k$$

$$- \mu \frac{d(\psi' E_\theta)}{dp_k} = 0, \quad (24)$$

$$\frac{\partial H}{\partial r^h} : \frac{\partial W}{\partial v^h} \frac{\partial v^h}{\partial r^h} f - \sum_{i=o}^{n} \alpha_i \frac{\partial x_i^h}{\partial r^h} - \mu \frac{d(\psi' E_\theta)}{dr^h} = 0, \quad (25)$$

$$\frac{\partial H}{\partial z_i} : \alpha_i - \beta \frac{\partial g}{\partial z_i} + \overline{\gamma} p_i = 0, \quad (26)$$

$$-\frac{\partial H}{\partial U} = \dot{\mu}(\theta) \quad \Longleftrightarrow \quad \dot{\mu}(\theta) = \frac{\alpha_n(\theta)}{p_n} + \overline{\gamma}(\theta). \quad (27)$$

The transversality conditions are[17]

$$\mu(\underline{\theta}) \leq -W_U := \int_{\underline{\theta}}^{\overline{\theta}} \frac{\partial W}{\partial \underline{U}} f(\theta) d\theta, \quad (28)$$

$$\mu(\overline{\theta}) = 0. \quad (29)$$

For the moment we assume that the second-order conditions of the manager's incentive problem are fulfilled and will start to interpret the marginal conditions for that case.

30.2.4   The Signs of Lagrangean Multipliers

As in the preceding chapter we have

$$\alpha_o, \alpha_n > 0, \quad \overline{\gamma} > 0, \quad \mu < 0. \quad (30)$$

---

[17] See Seierstad–Sydsæter (1987: 185–6).

30.3   Pricing and Effort Rules

30.3.1   *Optimal Prices When Incentive Corrections Matter*

After some transformations[18] we obtain the following pricing rules for all prices $p_k, k \in K; k \neq o, n$:

(i)   A regulator who accepts as exogenous the initial endowments r^h, but chooses optimal prices and quantities, adheres to a pricing rule which resembles Feldstein's, including the adjustment to monopolistic structures in the private economy. (F_k are Feldstein's distributional characteristics.[19]) The prices are determined according to the following, which is equivalent to equation (3–21b):[20]

$$\sum_{i=o}^{n}(p_i - c_i)\frac{\partial z_i^D}{\partial p_k} = -(1 - F_k - \mathcal{I}_k)z_k - (1 - \gamma)\sum_{i=o}^{n}\sum_{j=1}^{J}(p_i - c_i^j)\frac{\partial y_i^j}{\partial p_k}; \quad (31)$$

(ii)   If, furthermore, optimal lump-sum redistribution is chosen, pricing is similar to Ramsey pricing with adjustment to monopolistic structures in the private economy. The prices are determined according to the following, which is equivalent to equation (3–24):

$$\sum_{i=o}^{n}(p_i - c_i)\frac{\partial \hat{z}_i}{\partial p_k} = -(\gamma - \widehat{\mathcal{I}}_k)z_k - (1 - \gamma)\sum_{i=o}^{n}\sum_{j=1}^{J}(p_i - c_i^j)\frac{\partial y_i^j}{\partial p_k}. \quad (32)$$

We see directly that the pricing structure in the case of asymmetric information on demand is a straightforward extension of the usual price structure, be it marginal-cost, Ramsey or Feldstein pricing. The only significant difference are the incentive-correction terms

$$\mathcal{I}_k := \frac{\mu}{\beta_o} \cdot \frac{d(\psi' E_\theta)}{dp_k} \cdot \frac{1}{z_k}, \quad (33a)$$

$$\widehat{\mathcal{I}}_k := \frac{\mu}{\beta_o} \cdot \left[\frac{d(\psi' E_\theta)}{dp_k} + \sum_h x_k^h \frac{d(\psi' E_\theta)}{dr^h}\right] \cdot \frac{1}{z_k}. \quad (33b)$$

---

[18]   The transformation corresponds to the usual way which we applied in chapter 3 above. Some helpful instructions and definitions are also given in footnote 20 in chapter 29.

[19]   For details of these distributional characteristics see section 9.2 above.

[20]   We have assumed $x_k = z_k$.

Remember that asymmetric information on costs affected the cost side of the pricing rules – marginal costs c_i typically were increased by an efficiency correction $\mathcal{I}_i$. In the case of asymmetric information on demand, the demand side of the pricing rules is affected – in a Ramsey-type model, the regulator behaves as if he were a profit-maximizing monopolist who misestimates the compensated price elasticities of demand by $1/(\gamma - \widehat{\mathcal{I}}_k)$ instead of by $1/\gamma$;[21] in a Feldstein-type of model, as if he were a profit maximizer who misestimates the non-compensated elasticities by $1/(1 - F_k - \mathcal{I}_k)$ instead of by $1/(1 - F_k)$.[22]

Note that the incentive-correction term and the Ramsey index are not additively separable as in the case of asymmetric information on costs. Let us consider the example of Ramsey pricing. Even for the case of independent demand, such a separation is impossible, since we have

$$\mathcal{L}_k = -\frac{\gamma - \widehat{\mathcal{I}}_k}{\eta_{kk}}. \tag{34}$$

Price elasticities of demand and incentive-correction terms are even 'less separable' if demand is interdependent. Consider the two-product firm, where usually a superelasticity formula can be found which resembles the inverse-elasticity rule. This is impossible in the case of asymmetric information on demand. Proceeding as usual, for good 1 we obtain:

$$\mathcal{L}_1 = -\cfrac{1}{\cfrac{1 - \cfrac{\eta_{12}\eta_{21}}{\eta_{11}\eta_{22}}}{(\gamma - \widehat{\mathcal{I}}_1) - (\gamma - \widehat{\mathcal{I}}_2)\cfrac{\eta_{21}}{\eta_{22}}\cfrac{p_2 z_2}{p_1 z_1}}} \tag{35}$$

where the denominator on the right-hand side resembles the usual superelasticity but inseparably depends on both price elasticities and incentive-correction terms.

It seems straightforward that asymmetric information on costs directly influences the cost side of the model, and asymmetric information on demand directly influences the demand side. However, the reader should recall that any form of asymmetric information increases costs because the manager receives an information rent. Hence, one would not have been too surprised if any case of asymmetric information could have been interpreted as a simple increase in marginal costs. In this respect our result offers a new insight into the consequences of regulator's incomplete information.

---

[21] Cfr. pp. 131–2 above.
[22] Cfr. p. 145 above.

Unfortunately, the signs of both incentive-correction terms $\mathcal{I}_k$ and $\widehat{\mathcal{I}}_k$ are indeterminate, because[23]

$$\frac{d(\psi' E_\theta)}{dp_k} = \psi' \cdot \sum_b \left(\frac{\partial^2 E_b}{\partial\theta\partial p_k} + \frac{\partial^2 E_b}{\partial\theta\partial x_b} \frac{\partial x_b}{\partial p_k} \right) \gtrless 0, \qquad (36a)$$

$$\frac{d(\psi' E_\theta)}{dr^h} = \psi' \cdot \sum_b \left(\frac{\partial^2 E_b}{\partial\theta\partial r^h} + \frac{\partial^2 E_b}{\partial\theta\partial x_b} \frac{\partial x_b}{\partial r^h} \right) \gtrless 0. \qquad (36b)$$

There is no reason why all $\partial^2 E_b/\partial\theta\partial p_k$ should be positive or negative; and the same holds for both $\partial^2 E_b/\partial\theta\partial r^h$ and $\partial^2 E_b/\partial\theta\partial x_b$.

Let us briefly discuss a particular response $\partial^2 E_b/\partial\theta\partial x_b$ (for simplification the subscripts are dropped in figure 22). In figure 22a this derivative is negative – the dispersion of effort is increasing in x. In figure 22b the contrary holds. Both cases seem plausible and, above all, there is no reason why all effort levels E_b should respond in the same way. Hence, our conclusion that the sign of the incentive-correction terms are indeterminate.

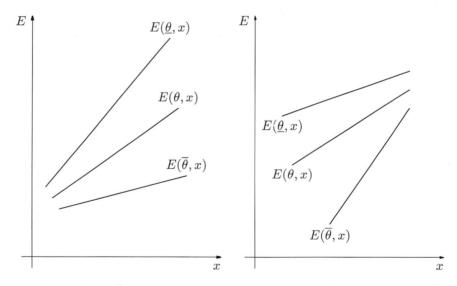

Figure 22a: $\partial^2 E/\partial x\partial\theta < 0$ Figure 22b: $\partial^2 E/\partial x\partial\theta > 0$

---

[23] Note the precise specification $\psi' E_\theta = \psi'(e)\Sigma(\partial E_b/\partial\theta)(\theta,p,r,x_b(\theta,e_b(\theta),p,r))$.

If the incentive-correction terms $\mathcal{I}_k$, $\widehat{\mathcal{I}}_k$ are zero, we have an incentive-pricing dichotomy in the sense of Laffont–Tirole (1990).[24] Note, however, that the conditions for optimal effort still depend on derivatives of the incentive-compatibility constraint and since the regulator solves an interdependent system of equations, the incentive problem remains relevant for the prices chosen. Formally, the incentive-correction terms are zero if for every consumer the demand functions equal

$$x_b^h = \mathcal{X}_b^h \left(p, r^h \right) \cdot \varphi_b(\theta, e_b); \quad h = 1, \ldots H, b = d+1, \ldots, n. \quad (37)$$

In that case the individual trade-offs between effort e_b and the firm-specific parameter θ in the demand functions do not depend on prices and lump-sum incomes.[25] It is only the outcome of the marketing effort which is uncertain.

30.3.2 The Optimal Choice of Effort

Let us finally consider the incentive correction referring to the optimal choice of effort. We start from a benchmark model where the regulator is fully informed about θ and observes all efforts e_b. (No incentive compatibility problems, binding participation constraint; otherwise everything is identical to the model we treat in this chapter.)[26] For interior solutions we obtain the following necessary condition for effort:

$$\sum_h \left(\frac{\partial W}{\partial v^h} \frac{\partial v^h}{\partial e_b} f - \alpha_b \frac{\partial x_b^h}{\partial e_b} \right) = \left(\frac{\alpha_n}{p_n} + \overline{\gamma} \right) \psi' = W_U \psi'; \quad b = d+1, \ldots, n. \quad (38)$$

Here $W_U \psi'$ is the social marginal disutility of effort e_b. This disutility is equated to the net social marginal valuation of e_b. It is net in the sense of measuring the social benefit of increasing e_b while allowing for the marginal shadow costs of adjusting the market equilibrium for good b. (α_b can be interpreted as a shadow price which measures the social valuation of a change in initial endowments of good b.)

In the asymmetric-information model, the corresponding equation is

$$\sum_h \left(\frac{\partial W}{\partial v^h} \frac{\partial v^h}{\partial e_b} f - \alpha_b \frac{\partial x_b^h}{\partial e_b} \right) = \left(\frac{\alpha_n}{p_n} + \overline{\gamma} \right) \psi' + \mu \frac{d(\psi' E_\theta)}{de_b}; \quad \forall b \quad (39)$$

---

[24] Compare subsection 29.3.3 above.

[25] Consider constant demand, $\mathcal{X}_b^h(p, r^h) \cdot \varphi_b(\theta, e_b) =$ const. Total differentiation with respect to θ and e then yields $dE_b/d\theta = -\varphi_\theta/\varphi_e$ which clearly is independent of prices and lump-sum incomes. For details see, for instance, Phlips (1983: 66–71).

[26] Compare section 29.4 above.

with the incentive correction

$$\mu \frac{d(\psi' E_\theta)}{de_b} = \psi'' E_\theta + \psi' \sum_b \frac{\partial E_b}{\partial \theta \partial x_b} \frac{\partial x_b}{\partial e_b}. \tag{40}$$

Unfortunately, once again the sign of the incentive correction is indeterminate. Hence we can conclude that the asymmetric information on demand distorts the decision of optimal effort. We cannot, however, say in which direction the decision is distorted.

31
Soft Budget Constraints

The concept of the soft budget constraint was developed by Kornai (1980, 1986). He used this term to describe an Eastern European system of redistribution between public enterprises, from the profitable to the non-profitable. This system consisted of rules of subsidization and taxation which were negotiable between government and enterprises. Kornai's concept meanwhile has often been used to characterize particular inefficiencies of the former socialist countries. In several papers the transition from socialist to market economies has been seen as a process of hardening the soft budget constraint. Privatization of public enterprises in the process of transition was said to harden the budget constraint because the owner's commitment to close a non-viable firm is credible if the firm is privately owned in contrast to the case of public ownership (Schmidt, 1991; Schmidt–Schnitzer, 1992). The installation of a social security system was said to harden the budget constraint because the government can more credibly commit itself to not bailing out private or public firms if in case of closure of the firm the laid-off workers are taken care of by a social security net (Hardy, 1992).

As already stated by Kornai himself, the softness of budget constraints is also a problem in Western market economies where renegotiations of public firms' budget constraints or of the price paid for a public investment are nothing out of the ordinary. (Each reader – of whatever Western country – will certainly recall some examples of rail or mail deficits higher than originally budgeted or the most recent scandal on the excessive costs of building a new public hospital.) The soft budget constraint of Western-type public utilities is treated in the present chapter.

Since models of the Boiteux type are rather complicated, we shall forgo the explicit modelling of a multistage game with renegotiation of the budget constraint. Instead we shall analyze a reduced-form approach of a soft budget constraint.

In this reduced-form framework, the soft budget constraint becomes a problem of asymmetric information on the budget, which has a formal structure similar to that of problems of asymmetric information on costs and on demand. It is not the very process of renegotiation which is modelled, but the lack of information facing the regulator who does not precisely know a priori how large a deficit the public utility will achieve.

Soft budget constraints have a bad reputation. As we shall show in this chapter, this bad reputation is not always deserved: budget renegotiations may well be the weapon of a welfare-oriented regulator against short-sighted political forces.

31.1   The Model

31.1.1   *Presenting the Problem*

Assume that in the budget for a particular fiscal year a deficit of Π^o dollars has been designated for some public utility. This deficit has, for instance, been set by the parliament or the government on the basis of political pressures. Maybe general elections are coming up and too high a deficit would be detrimental to the majority party. We assume that the budgeted deficit is smaller than that deficit which would result if welfare were to be maximized without a budget constraint. Note that this is the typical assumption which underlies Ramsey pricing. Because of increasing returns to scale marginal-cost prices would result in a deficit which is considered too high for political reasons.

The welfare-oriented regulator is dissatisfied with the deficit limit. A typical example would be the regulator of some railway company who would like not to close some branch lines which, however, he would have to if the budget constraint were strict. Now let us assume that this is not the case. Supplementary budgets can be passed by the parliament or the government, increasing the allowed deficits of public utilities. The regulator, therefore, employs a lobbyist whom he pays to engage in deficit-seeking activities. This assumption is similar in spirit to Goldfeld and Quandt (1988, 1990) who assume that the firm employs 'specialized bailout labor to 'whine' in the appropriate bureaucratic corridors.' The lobbyist is the agent of the regulator. His success can be expressed in dollars of additional money which as supplementary budget are appropriated to the firm. To get these additional appropriations the lobbyist has to convince either the parliament or the government or both, depending on who is competent to appropriate additional funds. The success of the lobbyist's activities depends on his effort and on a parameter θ. This parameter refers, for instance

- to political changes in the parliament (some by-election might bring more welfare-oriented members into the parliament),
- to the susceptibility of members of parliament to the lobbyist,
- to changes in the composition of government (maybe a minister will be replaced by some new person who is less experienced in dealing with professional lobbyists or who evaluates the services of a public utility more highly),
- to the toughness of the government (Schaffer, 1989).

We assume that the lobbyist is better informed about the uncertainties of renegotiations than the regulator. This superior knowledge is due to his previous experiences in similar renegotiations and to his special instinct developed over many years of budgetary discussions. In our model, therefore, we assume that the lobbyist knows the precise value of θ. The regulator lacks this precise knowledge and knows only the density function $f(\theta)$. Moreover, the regulator cannot observe the lobbyist's effort or, at least, cannot verify this effort before a court. The lobbyist, therefore, has an incentive to hide the information on θ and to earn a higher compensation by pretending that his effort was higher than it actually was. – As usual in models of this type, we assume that the shape of all relevant functions is common knowledge. The regulator's perfect knowledge of the technology and of the demand for the firm's products enables him to effectuate efficient production and efficient satisfaction of demand. This implies that the soft budget constraint in our model is neither driven by inefficiency of production nor by not responding to the market. Hence the analysis concentrates on the lobbying problem.

31.1.2 The Actual Deficit

The actual deficit facing the regulated firm is

$$\Pi = \Pi(\theta, e) < 0; \quad \Pi_\theta < 0, \Pi_e < 0. \tag{1}$$

The lobbyist's effort increases the deficit in absolute terms as does an increase in θ. Naturally, we have $\Pi(\underline{\theta}, 0) = \Pi^o$, the budgeted deficit.

The minimal effort, which is required to achieve an actual deficit of Π if the effectiveness of effort is θ, can be written as

$$E = E(\theta, \Pi); \quad E_\theta < 0, E_\Pi < 0. \tag{2}$$

This effort-requirement function is implicitly defined by

$$\Pi \equiv \Pi(\theta, E(\theta, \Pi)). \tag{3}$$

In the following we shall use this effort-requirement function to define the incentive-compatibility constraint.

31.1.3 Incentive Income

The lobbyist is paid an income which induces him to announce the correct value of the effectiveness of his activities θ. He is offered a reward scheme which depends on the regulated prices, on the regulated firm's netputs and, if they are taken as regulatory instruments, also on the consumers' lump-sum incomes:

$$\text{incentive pay} = \begin{cases} t(\hat{\theta}) & \text{if } p_k = p_k(\hat{\theta}), r^h = r^h(\hat{\theta}) \text{ and} \\ & \quad z_i = z_i(\hat{\theta}) \text{ for } k \in K, \text{ and } \forall h, i \\ \\ 0 & \text{otherwise.} \end{cases} \tag{4}$$

The total actual deficit Π will be determined by $\Sigma_i p_i z_i$ and the lobbyist's reward. In announcing θ, the lobbyist must be aware of the regulator's ability to observe prices, quantities and lump-sum incomes.

31.1.4   The Lobbyist's Optimization

(i)   Incentive Compatibility

A lobbyist with utility[1] $U = t - \psi(e)$ will announce the correct value of the effectiveness parameter θ if his incentive reward has been chosen so as to minimize the following distance function

$$\mathcal{D} := \left[t(\theta) - \psi(E(\theta, \Pi(\theta))) \right] - \left[t(\hat{\theta}) - \psi(E(\theta, \Pi(\hat{\theta}))) \right]. \tag{5}$$

After differentiating $\mathcal{D}$ with respect to the announced $\hat{\theta}$, the lobbyist considers the first-order condition

$$\frac{dt}{d\hat{\theta}} - \psi' E_\Pi \Pi_{\hat{\theta}} = 0. \tag{6}$$

Now consider changes in the lobbyist's utility which result from changes in the actual θ:

$$\dot{U}(\theta) := \frac{dU}{d\theta} = \frac{dt}{d\theta} - \psi' E_\theta - \psi' E_\Pi \Pi_\theta. \tag{7}$$

The regulator is able to observe prices and quantities and, trivially, the realizations of his own instrument t. Hence the lobbyist must in any case have chosen the announcement of θ so as to ensure the identity of all differential quotients in (6) and (7) at the optimum $\theta = \hat{\theta}$. Accordingly, we can combine (6) and (7) to obtain the lobbyist's incentive-compatibility constraint

$$\dot{U} = -\psi' E_\theta > 0. \tag{8}$$

It is intuitive that the lobbyist's utility must be increasing in θ. The lobbyist is always inclined to exaggerate how difficult it is to persuade parliament and government to appropriate a supplementary budget for the firm. If the regulator falls for this lie, the lobbyist can overstate his effort and get a higher reward. Therefore, the lobbyist is inclined to announce too low a θ. Hence he must be given an incentive to announce a higher value of θ which is just the content of the incentive-compatibility constraint.

---

[1]   As usual we assume $\psi' > 0$, $\psi'' > 0$, $\psi''' \geq 0$.

Let us next turn to the second-order condition $U_{\hat\theta\hat\theta}^2 \geq 0$.[2] At the optimum $(\theta = \hat\theta)$ this condition equals[3]

$$-\psi'' E_\theta E_\Pi \Pi_\theta - \psi' E_{\Pi\theta}\Pi_\theta \geq 0. \tag{9}$$

It is difficult to find plausible assumptions which are sufficient for this condition to hold. This problem can be seen most clearly if the single-crossing property is examined in our case. We obtain

$$\frac{d}{d\theta}\left(\frac{\partial U/\partial e}{\partial U/\partial t}\right) = -\psi''(E_\theta + E_\Pi \Pi_\theta) \leq 0. \tag{10}$$

There is the following trade-off: the profit effect $-\psi'' E_\Pi \Pi_\theta$ is negative, that is it points in the right direction; however, the direct effect of θ, that is $-\psi'' E_\theta$, is positive and therefore points in the wrong direction.

In the following we shall assume that the second-order condition holds; as in chapter 30, however, one should always be aware of the probability of bunching.

(ii) Participation

Since the regulator needs the lobbyist, he must ensure his participation. If the political circumstances are least favorable to budget renegotiations, the lobbyist's utility can be reduced to the basic utility $\underline{U}$, that is

$$U(\underline{\theta}) = \underline{U}. \tag{11}$$

The incentive-compatibility condition, however, makes it necessary to award an information rent to lobbyists who face a more favorable environment. Therefore we have

$$U(\theta) > \underline{U} \qquad \text{for all } \theta > \underline{\theta}. \tag{12}$$

31.1.5 Regulatory Budget Constraint, Technology and Markets[4]

For every single θ, the regulator has to consider the (soft) budget constraint. The actual deficit results from the firm's loss due to sales and the lobbyist's compensation,

---

[2] See section 28.3 above.

[3] In the first-order condition (6) $dt/d\hat\theta$ and $\Pi_{\hat\theta}$ do not depend on θ, but only on $\hat\theta$. However, $\psi'(e)$ and E_Π depend on the actual θ, via $E(\theta,\hat\theta)$, and are differentiated with respect to the actual θ.

[4] We assume that the constraint qualifications hold along the optimal path of control and state variables. Compare subsection 29.2.1 above.

$$\sum_{k \in K} p_k(\theta) z_k(\theta) + \sum_{i \notin K} p_i z_i(\theta) - t(\theta) = \Pi(\theta, e(\theta)). \tag{13}$$

As usual, in the treatment of the budget constraint, we shall replace $t(\theta)$ with $U(\theta) + \psi(e(\theta))$.

After presenting the particulars of the soft budget constraint, the model is now closed according to the Boiteux tradition. The firm produces efficiently according to the technology

$$g(z(\theta)) = 0. \tag{14}$$

For each and every θ the regulator furthermore considers the market equilibria:

(i)   input and output markets, $i = o, \ldots, n - 1$,

$$\sum_{h} x_i^h(p(\theta), r^h(\theta)) - z_i(\theta) - \sum_{j} y_i^j(p(\theta)) = 0, \tag{15a}$$

where $p(\theta)$ is the vector of the regulated prices $p_k(\theta), k \in K$, and the non-regulated ones, p_i, $i \notin K$. As usual, labor is the numeraire, hence $p_o = 1$.

(ii)   output market, $i = n$. Similar to the preceding chapters we assume that the lobbyist consumes only good n. The price of this good is given for both regulator and lobbyist. Accordingly, we postulate a market equilibrium

$$\sum_{h} x_n^h(p(\theta), r^h(\theta)) + (U(\theta) + \psi(e(\theta)))/p_n - z_n(\theta) - \sum_{j} y_n^j(p(\theta)) = 0. \tag{15b}$$

As usual, the market equilibria also imply a financial equilibrium of the economy. In our case we obtain

$$\sum_{h} r^h(\theta) - (\Pi(\theta) - t(\theta)) - \sum_{j} \pi^j(\theta) = 0, \quad \forall \theta, \tag{16}$$

which includes the actual deficit of the regulated firm $\Pi(\theta)$ and the lobbyist's incentive pay $t(\theta)$.

31.2   The Optimization Problem

31.2.1   *Objective, Constraints, Control and State Variables*

The regulator maximizes the expected value of the welfare function

$$\int_{\underline{\theta}}^{\overline{\theta}} W(v^1(p(\theta), r^1(\theta)), \ldots, v^H(p(\theta), r^H(\theta)); \underline{U}) f(\theta) d\theta \tag{17}$$

subject to the following constraints[5]

- market equilibria for every single θ,
- the technology constraint $g(\cdot) = 0$ for every single θ,
- the budget constraint for every single θ,
- the lobbyist's incentive-compatibility constraint,
- the lobbyist's participation constraint.[6]

This is an optimal control problem with

- state variable U and
- control variables e,

$$p_k; k \in K, k \neq o, n,$$
$$r^h; h = 1, \ldots, H,$$
$$z_i; i = o, \ldots, n.$$

Initial and terminal condition of the state variable $U(\theta)$ are specified as usual, namely:

- initial condition $U(\underline{\theta}) = \underline{U}$, where the lobbyist's basic utility $\underline{U}$ is optimally chosen by the regulator, and exceeds the reservation utility U^o,
- terminal condition $U(\overline{\theta})$ free.

31.2.2   The Generalized Hamiltonian[7]

$$H = W(v^1(p, r^1), \ldots, v^H(p, r^H); \underline{U}) f(\theta)$$
$$- \sum_{i=o}^{n-1} \alpha_i(\theta) \left[\sum_h x_i^h(p, r^h) - z_i - \sum_j y_i^j(p) \right]$$
$$- \alpha_n(\theta) \left[\sum_h x_n^h(p, r^h) + \frac{U}{p_n} + \frac{\psi(e)}{p_n} - z_n - \sum_j y_n^j(p) \right]$$
$$- \beta(\theta) g(z)$$
$$- \overline{\gamma}(\theta) \left[\Pi(\theta, e) - \sum_i p_i z_i + U + \psi(e) \right]$$

---

[5] We also require non-negativity of e although not by means of explicit constraints but by postulating the respective Kuhn–Tucker conditions. Non-negative prices are always assumed to result from the optimization.

[6] The participation constraint is not explicitly added to the generalized Hamiltonian, but considered by postulating the respective transversality condition for $\theta = \underline{\theta}$. For this procedure see Seierstad–Sydsæter (1987: 185–6). – The term 'generalized Hamiltonian' is explained in Seierstad–Sydsæter (1987: 270–1); see also footnote 17 in chapter 29 above.

[7] The vector p refers to all prices, both regulated and non-regulated.

$$+ \mu(\theta) \left[-\psi'(e) E_\theta \left(\theta, \sum_i p_i z_i - U - \psi(e) \right) \right]. \tag{18}$$

31.2.3   The Marginal Conditions

The necessary conditions for the regulator's optimum are the following (where the dependencies on θ typically are suppressed).

$$\frac{\partial H}{\partial e} : -\frac{\alpha_n}{p_n} \psi' - \overline{\gamma} \Pi_e - \overline{\gamma} \psi' - \mu \left[\psi'' E_\theta - (\psi')^2 E_{\theta \Pi} \right] \leq 0, \tag{19a}$$

$$\frac{\partial H}{\partial e} \cdot e = 0, \; e \geq 0, \tag{19b}$$

$$\frac{\partial H}{\partial p_k} : \sum_h \frac{\partial W}{\partial v^h} \frac{\partial v^h}{\partial p_k} f - \sum_{i=o}^n \alpha_i \left(\sum_h \frac{\partial x_i^h}{\partial p_k} - \sum_j \frac{\partial y_i^j}{\partial p_k} \right)$$
$$+ (\overline{\gamma} - \mu \psi' E_{\theta \Pi}) z_k = 0, \tag{20}$$

$$\frac{\partial H}{\partial r^h} : \frac{\partial W}{\partial v^h} \frac{\partial v^h}{\partial r^h} f - \sum_{i=o}^n \alpha_i \frac{\partial x_i^h}{\partial r^h} = 0, \tag{21}$$

$$\frac{\partial H}{\partial z_i} : \alpha_i - \beta \frac{\partial g}{\partial z_i} + (\overline{\gamma} - \mu \psi' E_{\theta \Pi}) p_i = 0, \tag{22}$$

$$-\frac{\partial H}{\partial U} = \dot{\mu}(\theta) \Longleftrightarrow \dot{\mu}(\theta) = \frac{\alpha_n(\theta)}{p_n} + \overline{\gamma}(\theta) - \mu(\theta) \psi' E_{\theta \Pi}. \tag{23}$$

The transversality conditions are[8]

$$\mu(\underline{\theta}) \leq -W_U, \tag{24}$$

where

$$W_U := \int_{\underline{\theta}}^{\overline{\theta}} \frac{\partial W}{\partial \underline{U}} f(\theta) d\theta > 0. \tag{25}$$

$$\mu(\overline{\theta}) = 0. \tag{26}$$

---

[8] See Seierstad–Sydsæter (1987: 185–6).

31.2.4 The Signs of the Lagrangean Multipliers

Unfortunately, the sign of μ is indeterminate, except for $\underline{\theta}$ and $\bar{\theta}$ where it follows from the transversality conditions. The signs of the other multipliers can easily be determined. $\alpha_o, \alpha_n > 0$ can be proved as usual. $\bar{\gamma} > 0$ follows from the respective Kuhn–Tucker condition assuming that

$$0 > \Pi^o \geq \Pi(\theta, e) > \Pi^W. \tag{27}$$

(This implies that the realized deficit exceeds that deficit Π^W which would have resulted from maximizing welfare in the absence of a budget constraint.)

31.2.5 The Sign of $(\gamma - \mathcal{I})$

As the experienced reader might have recognized when reading the marginal conditions, there is a particular term which exactly plays the role of $\bar{\gamma}$ in the usual conditions,[9] that is $(\bar{\gamma} - \mu\psi' E_{\theta\Pi})$. It will be convenient to define an incentive-correction term

$$\mathcal{I} := \frac{\mu}{\beta_o} \psi' E_{\theta\Pi}. \tag{28}$$

We restrict the analysis to the case where Π exceeds the unconstrained welfare-optimal profit. Then, like $\gamma = \bar{\gamma}/\beta_o$ in the usual setting,[10] the term $(\gamma - \mathcal{I})$ is positive and lies between zero and unity, as can be shown in two steps.

(i) Starting from the budget constraint (13) let us assume that the firm has to pay an exogenously fixed, infinitesimally small amount of $\bar{\Pi}$ to some outside institution which destroys the money. Hence, the new budget constraint equals

$$\Pi(\theta, e) = \sum_i p_i z_i - t - \bar{\Pi}. \tag{29}$$

Then we obtain

$$\left.\frac{\partial H^*}{\partial \bar{\Pi}}\right|_{\bar{\Pi}=0} = -(\bar{\gamma} - \mu\psi' E_{\theta\Pi}) = -(\gamma - \mathcal{I})\beta_o. \tag{30}$$

Recall the assumption that the regulator wants to increase the deficit from the politically fixed Π^o in the direction of the higher deficit which would be welfare optimal in the absence of a budget constraint. Now assume additionally that

---

[9] Compare the $\partial H/\partial p_k$ and $\partial H/\partial z_i$ conditions of this chapter with the $\partial \mathcal{F}/\partial p_k$ and $\partial \mathcal{F}/\partial z_i$ conditions of chapter 3 to recognize that $\bar{\gamma}$ is replaced with $(\bar{\gamma} - \mu\psi' E_{\theta\Pi})$.

[10] See footnote 12 in chapter 3 above.

the efforts of the lobbyist have led to a deficit $\Pi(\theta, e)$ which lies between Π^o and Π^W. Then the payment of $\overline{\Pi}$ is welfare reducing and we have $\partial H^*/\partial \overline{\Pi} < 0$ in (30). This result implies $(\gamma - \mathcal{I}) > 0$, since $\beta_o > 0$.

(ii) Consider

$$\frac{\partial H}{\partial z_o} : \quad \frac{\alpha_o}{\beta_o} - 1 + (\gamma - \mathcal{I}) = 0. \tag{31}$$

Hence $(\gamma - \mathcal{I}) < 1$.

31.3 Optimal Pricing and Effort

31.3.1 Pricing Rules

After some transformations[11] we obtain the following pricing rules for all prices $p_k, k \in K, k \neq o, n$.

(i) Let us first assume exogenous lump-sum incomes. From optimally choosing prices and quantities, we obtain an incentive-corrected equivalent to Feldstein pricing adjusted to private monopolistic pricing. (F_k are the distributional characteristics.[12]) Let us first assume $x_k \neq z_k$. The resulting rule is equivalent to equation (3–21a):

$$\sum_{i=o}^{n}(p_i - c_i)\frac{\partial z_i^D}{\partial p_k} = -(\gamma - \mathcal{I})z_k - (1 - (\gamma - \mathcal{I}))x_k + F_k x_k$$

$$- (1 - (\gamma - \mathcal{I}))\sum_{i=o}^{n}\sum_{j=1}^{J}(p_i - c_i^j)\frac{\partial y_i^j}{\partial p_k}. \tag{32a}$$

If goods k are neither supplied nor demanded by private firms ($z_k = x_k$), this equation reduces to

$$\sum_{i=o}^{n}(p_i - c_i)\frac{\partial z_i^D}{\partial p_k} = -(1 - F_k)z_k - (1 - (\gamma - \mathcal{I}))\sum_{i=o}^{n}\sum_{j=1}^{J}(p_i - c_i^j)\frac{\partial y_i^j}{\partial p_k} \tag{32b}$$

which is equivalent to equation (3–21b).

(ii) If, furthermore, an optimal lump-sum redistribution is chosen, we obtain an incentive-corrected equivalent to Ramsey pricing adjusted to private

---

[11] The transformation corresponds to the usual way which we applied in chapter 3 above. Some helpful instructions and definitions are also given in footnote 20 in chapter 29.

[12] For details of these distributional characteristics see section 9.2 above.

monopolistic pricing. Prices are determined according to the following, which is equivalent to equation (3–24):

$$\sum_{i=o}^{n}(p_i - c_i)\frac{\partial \hat{z}_i}{\partial p_k} = -(\gamma - \mathcal{I})z_k - (1 - (\gamma - \mathcal{I}))\sum_{i=o}^{n}\sum_{j=1}^{J}(p_i - c_i^j)\frac{\partial y_i^j}{\partial p_k}. \quad (33)$$

In the presence of a soft budget constraint the asymmetrically informed regulator chooses the same pricing structure as the fully-informed firm of chapter 3, but replaces the shadow price of the strict budget, γ, by the incentive-corrected term $(\gamma - \mathcal{I})$. As we have already shown, if Π exceeds the unconstrained welfare-optimal profit the term $(\gamma - \mathcal{I})$ lies between zero and unity, just as the shadow price γ.

The incentive-correction term influences all prices in the same way, contrary to the other cases of asymmetric information which we treated in the preceding chapters. The reason is straightforward: the lack of information of the regulator refers to the total deficit and not to single quantities or prices, as in the case of asymmetric information on costs or demand.

An 'incentive dichotomy' à la Tirole–Laffont (1990) occurs if $E_{\theta\Pi} = 0$. Then $(\gamma - \mathcal{I})$ is reduced to γ and the usual pricing formulas of chapter 3 prevail, although prices are of course shifted because the regulator still has to cope with his lack of information. Incentive dichotomy, for instance, arises if the public utility's deficit is specified as in the following simple example

$$\Pi = \Pi^o - e - \theta. \quad (34)$$

Note once again that the incentive-correction term and the Ramsey index are not additively separable as in the case of asymmetric information on costs. If we take the example of Ramsey pricing, for the cases of independent demand and two-product firms we obtain respectively

$$\mathcal{L}_k = -\frac{\gamma - \mathcal{I}}{\eta_{kk}}; \quad \mathcal{L}_k = -\frac{\gamma - \mathcal{I}}{\mathcal{H}_{kk}} \quad (35)$$

where $\mathcal{H}_{kk}$ are the 'superelasticities'.[13]

31.3.2   The Lobbyist's Effort in the Presence of a Soft Budget Constraint

To see the countervailing effects which determine the choice of *effort*, let us consider the special conditions which may totally discourage a lobbyist in his deficit-seeking activities. Note that it may well be worthwhile for a regulator

---

[13] If more than two goods are considered, the right-hand sides become more complicated.

not to fire a lobbyist whose effort is zero. The lobbyist is rewarded for two services which he renders to the regulator: effort and information. The value of the lobbyist's information may be high enough to justify his income even if his effort is zero.

Zero effort results if the relevant marginal condition (19a) holds as a strict inequality, that is

$$-\frac{\alpha_n}{p_n} - (\gamma - \mathcal{I})\beta_o - \mu(\psi''/\psi')E_\theta - \beta_o(\gamma/\psi')\Pi_e < 0. \qquad (36)$$

The corner solution $e = 0$ is attained if the negative terms in (36) outweigh the positive ones. Accordingly we should expect zero effort to be associated with the following effects:

(i) high social valuation of the lobbyist's consumption good n, that is a high value of α_n/p_n; if the lobbyist's consumption is very costly in terms of welfare, it is plausible that he be given a low reward which discourages his effort.

(ii) high prices, that is a high value of $(\gamma - \mathcal{I})$; this is plausible since we expect lower deficits in case of zero effort;

(iii) a fairly strict budget constraint, that is a low value of Π_e; it is directly clear that the lobbyist is more encouraged in his deficit seeking the softer the budget constraint;

(iv) a high degree of absolute risk aversion, that is a high Arrow–Pratt measure ψ''/ψ' if the political environment is particularly hostile to renegotiations (θ near its lower threshold and therefore $\mu < 0$). This effect is reversed if $\mu > 0$; the risk aversion of the regulator, however, is of no importance at all if the political environment is most favorable to renegotiation ($\mu = 0$ at $\theta = \bar{\theta}$).

32
Non-Linear Pricing

32.1 The Model

32.1.1 Presenting the Problem[1]

Pricing schedules can follow very different patterns. A uniform price per unit of quantity is only one alternative and, although very common, it is an extreme case. Natural monopolies whose products cannot be resold will typically tend to some sort of price differentiation. Uncertainty and administrative costs may prevent firms from fixing different prices for individual customers. However, some standardized forms of price differentiation can be found everywhere in public-utility pricing, the best-known being two-part and block tariffs.

In the case of *two-part tariffs* the customer pays a basic fee for the right to buy any desired amount of the relevant goods at given unit prices. Such tariffs have often been proposed as a means of break-even pricing for decreasing cost industries: the variable charge should equal marginal cost, and the deficit should be financed by the fixed charge, ideally a perfectly discriminating lump-sum tax (Coase, 1946). Such a pricing procedure is welfare optimal unless we explicitly regard the number of customers as endogenous.[2] The analysis can be extended by explicitly taking into account the consumption externality which tends to arise in telecommunications: the more customers are attracted to the network, the more valuable is participation in the network.[3] Moreover, distributional objectives of the regulator can be included in the analysis, leading to two-part social tariffs.[4]

Block-tariffs define a sequence of prices for successive intervals of quantity demanded. Increasing the number of blocks increases the number of pricing instruments and will therefore never decrease the maximum welfare attainable (Leland–Meyer, 1976).

A price structure which is interesting both theoretically and practically is one which gives the individual customer the right to choose between two different two-part tariffs, usually a low fixed charge and higher unit prices or

---

[1] For a good recent overview see Mitchell–Vogelsang (1991: 73–117). The most recent advanced monograph on the topic is Wilson (1993).

[2] See Oi (1971), Ng–Weisser (1974), Spremann (1978), Schmalensee (1981), Brander–Spencer (1985).

[3] See, for instance, Einhorn (1990).

[4] See Feldstein (1972b), Auerbach–Pellechio (1978).

vice versa (*optional tariff*). In the more interesting case the consumer has
to declare *ex ante* which tariff he chooses. This choice of tariff implies a
self-selection of consumers.[5]

All these problems of institutional practice lead to the theoretical question of how to relate the quantities bought to the customer's expenditure in an
optimal manner. Consider any customer's expenditures for the consumption
of price-regulated goods. These expenditures depend on quantities purchased
and on prices, following a functional relationship that must be uniquely defined over all quantities and prices respectively. The functional relationship
is not necessarily fixed a priori. We call this a *price schedule*.[6] Now consider
the regulator of a public utility who wants to choose the functional form of
this price schedule in a welfare-maximizing way. The welfare-optimal price
schedule will not necessarily be linear in quantities. Hence, we speak of '*non-
linear pricing*' (Spence, 1977; Roberts, 1979). Formally, this problem is the
same as that of finding a welfare-maximizing direct-tax function.

32.1.2   The Consumers' Optimization Problem

There is a continuum of consumers whose tastes are denoted by $\theta \in [\underline{\theta}, \overline{\theta}]$. It is
common knowledge that they have identical, twice differentiable and strictly
concave utility functions

$$u = u(\theta, x); \quad u_\theta > 0, u_{x_i} > 0, \ i = o, \ldots, n, \qquad (1)$$

where $x := (x_o, \ldots, x_n)$ are the consumption plans. The regulator cannot
observe the individual θ's but knows the density of preferences $f(\theta)$.

Price regulation refers to a subset of the goods, indexed by $k \in K \subset I$.
Resale of these goods is impossible, hence price discrimination across customers makes sense. The price-regulated goods are traded at a price schedule
$\mathcal{PS}(\theta)$. A customer who buys a bundle of these goods, pays the sum $\mathcal{PS}(\theta)$
which is not necessarily linear in the quantities.[7] It is convenient to define
$\mathcal{PS}(\theta)$ as a set of two-part tariffs, where different tariffs are chosen for consumers with different tastes. Choosing this set of two-part tariffs is equivalent
to choosing a general non-linear price schedule.[8] Hence, without loss of generality, we can restrict the analysis to price schedules of the following type:

[5] This type of tariff has been investigated by Faulhaber–Panzar (1977), Willig (1978),
Ordover and Panzar (1980) and Sharkey and Sibley (1991).

[6] Some authors call that an outlay schedule, for instance Brown–Sibley (1986) and
Mitchell–Vogelsang (1991).

[7] Similarly the model could be applied to the case of a supplier who receives the sum
$\mathcal{PS}$ for selling inputs to the public enterprise.

[8] See Roberts (1979: 69).

$$\mathcal{PS}(\theta) := B(\theta) + \sum_{k \in K} p_k(\theta) x_k. \qquad (2)$$

A consumer with taste parameter θ pays a basic fee $B(\theta)$ and marginal prices $p_k(\theta)$. The basic fee replaces the lump-sum incomes which otherwise are used in models of the Boiteux type.

The consumer buys both goods with regulated and with non-regulated prices. The latter are linear in quantities. Hence, a consumer of type θ maximizes utility given a budget constraint

$$\mathcal{PS}(\theta) + \sum_{i \notin K} p_i x_i = 0. \qquad (3)$$

As a result of the utility maximization the consumer chooses particular quantities $x_i(\theta, B(\theta), p(\theta))$, where the price vector $p(\theta)$ consists of the marginal prices $p_k(\theta)$, $k \in K$, and of the exogenously given non-regulated prices p_i, $i \neq k$.

Since the regulator does not know θ, he has to set incentive-compatible prices. Moreover, the participation of the consumers must be taken into account when the optimal price schedules are determined.

(i)   Incentive Compatibility

To simplify the derivation of these constraints, we abbreviate $x(\theta, B(\theta), p(\theta))$ as $x(\theta)$. We assume that the regulator is able to observe the quantities x. Hence, if a consumer wants to lie about his type, he has to lie in a consistent way. When announcing his taste parameter, the consumer minimizes a distance function

$$\mathcal{D} := u(\theta, x(\theta)) - u(\theta, x(\theta, \hat{\theta})). \qquad (4)$$

Therefore, he announces $\hat{\theta}$ according to the necessary first-order condition

$$\sum_i \frac{\partial u}{\partial x_i} \frac{dx_i}{d\hat{\theta}} = 0, \qquad (5)$$

where $dx_i/d\hat{\theta}$ includes all partial derivatives which result from differentiating $x_i(\cdot)$ with respect to $\hat{\theta}$. As usual,[9] we consider changes in utility with respect to θ if the announced taste parameter is the actual one, i.e. $\theta = \hat{\theta}$. We obtain

$$\dot{u}(\theta) := \frac{du}{d\theta} = \sum_i \frac{\partial u}{\partial x_i} \frac{dx_i}{d\theta} + \frac{\partial u}{\partial \theta}. \qquad (6)$$

---

[9] See section 28.3 above.

Substituting (5) into (6) yields the incentive-compatibility constraint,

$$\dot{u}(\theta) = \frac{\partial u}{\partial \theta} > 0. \tag{7}$$

Let us next consider the second-order conditions. In our case these conditions require

$$\frac{\partial}{\partial \hat{\theta}} \left[-\sum_i \frac{\partial u}{\partial x_i}(\theta, x(\theta, \hat{\theta})) \frac{dx_i}{d\hat{\theta}}(\hat{\theta}) \right] \geq 0. \tag{8}$$

Differentiation yields

$$\sum_{i \in I} \sum_{a \in I} \frac{\partial^2 u}{\partial x_i \partial x_a} \frac{dx_a}{d\hat{\theta}} \frac{dx_i}{d\hat{\theta}} + \sum_{i \in I} \frac{\partial u}{\partial x_i} \frac{d^2 x_i}{d\hat{\theta}^2} \leq 0. \tag{9}$$

Sufficient for this inequality to hold are the following plausible assumptions:[10]

• consumption must be concave in dependence on θ, that is, $dx_i/d\hat{\theta} > 0$, $d^2 x_i/d\hat{\theta}^2 < 0$.[11]

• the utility function must be strictly quasi-concave in the consumption goods x.[12]

(ii)   Participation

The participation constraint, in this model, means that the customers actually buy at the regulated prices. We will require that prices are chosen such that all customers participate. Hence we stipulate

$$u(\theta, x(\theta)) \geq \overline{u}(\theta), \qquad \forall \theta. \tag{10}$$

The utility level $\overline{u}(\theta)$ is exogenously given for the regulator's problem. It is the maximum utility achievable by consumer of type θ if he does not buy any quantities x_k. That is

$$\overline{u}(\theta) = \max_{\{x_i\}} u(\theta, x_o, \ldots, x_i, \ldots, x_n \mid i \notin K) \text{ s.t.} \sum_{i \notin K} p_i x_i = 0. \tag{11}$$

---

[10] If one of these assumptions fails to hold, bunching might occur. See, for instance, Maskin and Riley (1984).

[11] For a critical discussion see, for instance, Mirman and Sibley (1980: 661–2). In case of linear prices $\partial x_i/\partial \theta > 0$ follows from the assumption that consumption x_i is normal.

[12] This assumption ensures that the first term in (9) is weakly negative. See, for instance, Barten and Böhm (1982: 404–5).

The utility $\bar{u}(\theta)$ corresponds to the 'outside option' of the consumer. It is exogenous for the regulator because it does not depend on any of his control or state variables: if somebody does not buy any of the price-regulated goods, his demand for the other goods depends neither on the basic fee, which he does not pay, nor on the regulated prices, which he also does not pay. $\bar{u}(\theta)$, moreover, neither depends on the public utility's deficit, nor on the netputs of the utility. For any θ, the regulator is able to calculate $\bar{u}(\theta)$ and take it as an exogenous basis of a participation constraint.

In this general setting, unfortunately, the customers' participation constraint cannot be simplified by using the incentive-compatibility condition. Both sides of the constraint depend on quantities which result from particular optimization approaches and therefore incentive compatibility does not automatically ensure that the participation constraint holds for every θ if it holds for $\underline{\theta}$. This is in contrast to the manager's participation constraint of the preceding chapters. An example is illustrated in figure 23, where the constraint is binding at only one intermediate value $\tilde{\theta}$.

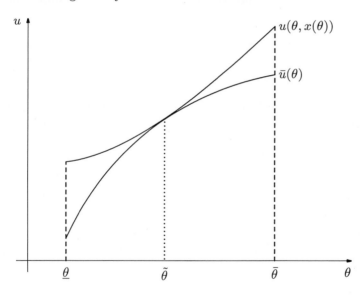

Figure 23

32.1.3 Technology, Markets, Regulatory Budget Constraint

The regulator's non-linear pricing policy is embedded into a model of the Boiteux type. Accordingly, the usual type of constraints have to be considered.

(i)   First, the regulated firm is characterized by the technology

$$g(z) = 0. \tag{12}$$

(ii)   Second, the regulator considers the market clearing conditions. For this purpose we assume that the public utility has a complete monopoly on the sale of the goods $k \in K$. This assumption helps to avoid the resale problem which could arise if some private non-regulated competitor were to enter the market. This competitor would buy the relevant goods at a cheap price from customers whom the regulator intends to subsidize by lower prices and sell them to those customers whom the regulator wants to burden (for instance because of their high income).

The treatment of the private sector causes many more problems. Consider a public utility which is the sole supplier of goods $k \in K$. Now let private firms respond to the non-linear price schedule of the public utility, either by buying goods from the utility or by supplying complements or substitutes to the goods k. The explicit treatment of this response would require the modelling of a differential game. The paths of both netputs z_i and y_i in dependence on θ would have to be modelled, taking into account welfare and profit as the objectives of the players. In the present chapter we will not choose such a complicated approach. We rather assume that the private sector is perfectly competitive and private firms neither sell nor buy goods k. Accordingly, the private firms' supply and demand functions depend only on the non-regulated prices $\{p_i, i \neq k\}$ which are exogenously given for every single private firm. We will denote the vector of these exogenous prices by p, in contrast to $p(\theta)$, which includes all prices. For notational convenience y_i will always be explicitly included in all market-clearing conditions with the understanding that $y_k \equiv 0$ for $k \in K$. Hence we have

$$\int_{\underline{\theta}}^{\overline{\theta}} x_i(\theta, B(\theta), p(\theta)) f(\theta) d\theta = z_i + y_i(p); \quad i = o, \dots, n. \tag{13}$$

As usual, the market equilibria imply a financial equilibrium of the economy.

(iii)   Let us finally turn to the regulator's budget constraint

$$\int_{\underline{\theta}}^{\overline{\theta}} \left[B(\theta) + \sum_{k \in K} p_k(\theta) x_k(\theta, B(\theta), p(\theta)) \right] f(\theta) d\theta + \sum_{i \notin K} p_i z_i(\theta) = \Pi^o. \tag{14}$$

In order to apply the maximum principle, the constraints will have to be rewritten. The rather technical details will be presented in the next subsection.

32.2 The Optimization Problem[13]

32.2.1 Objective, Constraints,[14] Control and State Variables

(i) State Variable I: Consumers' Utility

The individual consumers' optimization leads to indirect utility functions

$$u(\theta, x(\theta, B(\theta), p(\theta)) \equiv V(\theta, B(\theta), p(\theta)), \tag{15}$$

where $p(\theta)$ is the vector of both regulated and unregulated prices. For the following it is convenient to invert the utility functions to obtain

$$B = B(\theta, p(\theta), V(\theta)); \quad \frac{\partial B}{\partial p_k} = -x_k; \quad \frac{\partial B}{\partial V} = \frac{1}{\partial V / \partial B}. \tag{16}$$

In accordance with this inversion the regulator's welfare objective is written as

$$W = \int_{\underline{\theta}}^{\overline{\theta}} W(V(\theta)) f(\theta) d\theta. \tag{17}$$

The reason for this procedure is straightforward. The consumers' incentive-compatibility constraint is a differential equation in individual utility. This makes utility a candidate for a state variable. However, $u(\theta, x(\theta))$ is functionally specified and hence cannot directly be chosen as state variable. By inverting utility, the functional specification is shifted to another variable, namely B,[15] and therefore $V(\theta)$ is free to be chosen as a state variable.

The state variable V cannot be free at both $\underline{\theta}$ and $\overline{\theta}$. This can be shown as follows. If optimal values of B and p have been found, the incentive-compatibility constraint is $\dot{V}^* = u_\theta(\theta, x^*(\theta))$ where $x^*(\theta) = x(\theta, B^*(\theta), p^*(\theta))$. Hence $V^*(\underline{\theta})$ and $V^*(\overline{\theta})$ are linked to each other and cannot both be free. In the following we fix $V^*(\underline{\theta}) = u(\underline{\theta}, x^*(\underline{\theta})) =: \underline{U}$. Hence

$$V(\underline{\theta}) = \underline{U} \tag{18}$$

serves as an initial condition for the state variable V.

---

[13] For the formulation of this control-theoretic problem I gratefully acknowledge the advice of Norbert Christopeit, Bonn.

[14] We assume that the constraint qualifications hold along the optimal path of control and state variables. Compare subsection 29.2.1 above.

[15] Although functionally specified, $B(\theta, p(\theta), V(\theta))$ can, however, be chosen as control variable of our problem.

(ii)   State Variable II: Consumption

Let us next consider the individual consumption $x_i(\theta, B(\theta, p(\theta), V(\theta)), p(\theta))$. In order to apply the maximum principle, we write the market-clearing conditions (13) as differential equations

$$\frac{d\xi_i}{d\theta} = x_i(\cdot)f(\theta) \tag{19}$$

with starting and terminal conditions

$$\xi_i(\underline{\theta}) = 0; \ \xi_i(\overline{\theta}) = z_i(\overline{\theta}) + y_i(p, \overline{\theta}), \tag{20}$$

where $y_k \equiv 0$ holds for $k \in K$. As part of the terminal conditions, the regulator also has to consider the public utility's technology

$$g(z(\overline{\theta})) = 0, \tag{21}$$

or, after substitution from (20),

$$g(\xi(\overline{\theta}) - y(p, \overline{\theta})) = 0, \tag{22}$$

where ξ and y are appropriately defined vectors. Note that this terminal condition depends only on the terminal values of state variables, namely $\{\xi_i(\overline{\theta}), i = o, \ldots, n\}$, not on any values of control variables. The netputs $\{y_i(p, \overline{\theta}), i \notin K\}$ do not react to any of the regulator's instruments.

(iii)   State Variable III: Budget

Finally, we also write the regulatory budget constraint as a differential equation

$$\frac{d\Pi}{d\theta} = \left[B(\theta) + \sum_{k \in K} p_k(\theta)x_k(\cdot) \right] f(\theta) \tag{23}$$

with starting and terminal conditions

$$\Pi(\underline{\theta}) = 0; \ \ \Pi(\overline{\theta}) = \Pi^o - \sum_{i \notin K} p_i z_i(\overline{\theta}). \tag{24}$$

Once again, we substitute for $z_i(\overline{\theta})$ to obtain

$$\Pi(\overline{\theta}) = \Pi^o - \sum_{i \notin K} p_i(\xi_i(\overline{\theta}) - y_i(p, \overline{\theta})). \tag{25}$$

This terminal condition does not depend on any control variable. Π^o and $\{y_i(p, \overline{\theta}), i \notin K\}$ are exogenous for the regulatory problem.

(iv) Control Variables: Basic Fee and Marginal Prices

The control variables of our approach are the basic fee B and the marginal prices $\{p_k, k \in K\}$. Note that the quantities $\{z_i, i = o, \ldots, n\}$ are not chosen as controls, they are eliminated by substitution.

Summarizing, the regulator solves an optimal-control problem with

- state variables V,

  Π,

  $\xi_i; \ i = o, \ldots, n.$

- control variables B,

  $p_k; \ k \in K.$

32.2.2 The Hamiltonian, the Initial and Terminal Conditions

The Hamiltonian is based on the welfare function and on the differential equations governing the behavior of the state variables V, Π and ξ_i. We obtain:[16]

$$
\begin{aligned}
H = &\, W(V)f(\theta) \\
&+ \sum_i \alpha_i(\theta) \left[x_i\,(\theta, B, p) \right] f(\theta) \\
&+ \overline{\gamma}(\theta) \left[B + \sum_{k \in K} p_k x_k\,(\theta, B, p) \right] f(\theta) \\
&+ \mu(\theta) u_\theta \left[\theta, x\,(\theta, B, p) \right].
\end{aligned}
\tag{26}
$$

The corresponding Lagrangean combines the Hamiltonian and the 'pure state constraint' which refers to the participation of the consumers. Denote this constraint by $\mathcal{Q}(\theta, V(\theta)) := V(\theta) - \overline{u}(\theta) \geq 0$ with $\mathcal{Q}(\theta, V) = V - \overline{u}(\theta)$. Then the constraint $\mathcal{Q}(V)$ is included in the optimization approach by the following Lagrangean:[17]

$$
\begin{aligned}
\mathcal{F} &= H - \phi(\theta) \left[\mathcal{Q}_\theta + \mathcal{Q}_V u_\theta(\theta, x(\theta, B, p)) \right] \\
&= H - \phi(\theta) \left[u_\theta(\theta, x(\theta, B, p)) - \overline{u}_\theta \right].
\end{aligned}
\tag{27}
$$

---

[16] Since in the Hamiltonian and in the Lagrangean we always suppress that state and control variables depend on θ, it may be worthwhile to note that in $x(\theta, B, p)$ the vector p refers to all prices, both regulated and non-regulated. Recall that in $y(p, \overline{\theta})$ the vector p denotes non-regulated prices only.

[17] For this procedure see Hestenes (1966: 352–74). It is incorrect to include the pure state constraint by postulating $\mathcal{F} = H - \phi(\theta)[V - \overline{u}(\theta)]f(\theta)$. Unfortunately, this procedure can often be found, for instance in Seierstad–Sydsæter (1987: 358).

The transformation results from the derivatives $\mathcal{Q}_\theta = -\overline{u}_\theta$ and $\mathcal{Q}_V = 1$. Furthermore, the regulator has to consider the following initial and terminal conditions:

$$V(\underline{\theta}) = \underline{U} \tag{28}$$

$$\xi_i(\underline{\theta}) = 0; \quad g(\xi(\overline{\theta}) - y(p, \overline{\theta})) = 0. \tag{29}$$

$$\Pi(\underline{\theta}) = 0; \quad \Pi(\overline{\theta}) = \Pi^o - \sum_{i \notin K} p_i(\xi_i(\overline{\theta}) - y_i(p, \overline{\theta})). \tag{30}$$

32.2.3   The Optimum Conditions[18]

Suppressing the dependencies on θ, we obtain

$$\frac{\partial \mathcal{F}}{\partial B} : \sum_i \alpha_i \frac{\partial x_i}{\partial B} + \overline{\gamma}\left(1 + \sum_{i \in K} p_i \frac{\partial x_i}{\partial B}\right) + \frac{\mu - \phi}{f} \frac{du_\theta}{dB} = 0, \tag{31}$$

$$\frac{\partial \mathcal{F}}{\partial p_k} : \sum_i \alpha_i \frac{\partial x_i}{\partial p_k} + \overline{\gamma}\left(x_k + \sum_{i \in K} p_i \frac{\partial x_i}{\partial p_k}\right) + \frac{\mu - \phi}{f} \frac{du_\theta}{dp_k} = 0, \tag{32}$$

$$-\frac{\partial \mathcal{F}}{\partial V} = \dot{\mu} = -\frac{\partial W}{\partial V}(V^*(\theta)), \tag{33}$$

$$-\frac{\partial \mathcal{F}}{\partial \Pi} = \dot{\overline{\gamma}} = 0 \Rightarrow \overline{\gamma}(\theta) = \overline{\gamma} \quad \forall \theta, \tag{34}$$

$$-\frac{\partial \mathcal{F}}{\partial \xi_i} = \dot{\alpha}_i = 0 \Rightarrow \alpha_i(\theta) = \alpha_i \quad \forall \theta. \tag{35}$$

The differential quotients du_θ/dB and du_θ/dp_k comprise the dependencies of u_θ on B and on p_k, respectively, via all demand functions $x_i(\theta, B, p)$.

For the transversality conditions recall first that the state variable V is free at $\overline{\theta}$. Hence the costate variable μ is zero at $\overline{\theta}$,

$$\mu(\overline{\theta}) = 0. \tag{36}$$

The transversality conditions with respect to $\xi_i(\overline{\theta})$ are obtained as[19]

---

[18] See Seierstad–Sydsæter (1987: 390–3).

[19] Note that we assume $u(\overline{\theta}) > \overline{u}(\overline{\theta})$ and hence there is no positive parameter 'β_j' in Seierstad–Sydsæter's notation of theorem 6–13, according to their formula (6–12).

$$\alpha_i + \beta \frac{\partial g}{\partial z_i} - \delta p_i = 0; \qquad i \notin K, \tag{37a}$$

$$\alpha_i + \beta \frac{\partial g}{\partial z_i} = 0; \qquad i \in K, \tag{37b}$$

where the parameters $\beta \geq 0$ and $\delta \geq 0$ have been associated with the terminal conditions which have been defined in (29) and (30) above.[20] Finally, let us turn to the transversality condition with respect to $\Pi(\overline{\theta})$ which is

$$\overline{\gamma} = \delta. \tag{38}$$

Substituting this equality into (37a) yields terminal conditions which are similar to those marginal conditions which in chapter 3 were derived by differentiating the respective Lagrangean function with respect to netputs z_i.[21]

32.2.4   *The Adjoint Variables and the Lagrangean Multiplier ϕ*

(i) $\overline{\gamma} \geq 0$ results from the transversality condition (38), because $\delta \geq 0$.
(ii) $\mu > 0$ for $\theta < \overline{\theta}$, since $\mu(\overline{\theta}) = 0$ and $\dot{\mu} = -\partial W / \partial V < 0$.
(iii) The multiplier $\phi(\theta)$ is piecewise continuous, right continuous on $[\underline{\theta}, \overline{\theta}]$,[22] increasing, constant on every interval on which $Q(\theta, V^*(\theta)) > 0$, that is $V^*(\theta) > \overline{u}(\theta)$,[23] and continuous at every point of continuity of $(B^*(\theta), p^*(\theta))$; moreover $\phi(\overline{\theta}) \leq 0$. Therefore, $\phi \leq 0$ for $\theta < \overline{\theta}$.
(iv) Denote $\nu := \mu - \phi$. The above results imply $\nu(\theta) > 0$ for all $\theta < \overline{\theta}$, because $\nu(\underline{\theta}) > 0$, $\dot{\nu} < 0$ and $\nu(\overline{\theta}) \geq 0$.

32.3   Pricing Rules

In the following the dependency of variables on θ will be depressed to the extent that there is no danger of misunderstandings arising. The reader may remember that in our model we have both endogenous regulated prices $p_k(\theta), k \in K$, and exogenous non-regulated prices $p_i, i \neq k$. One may keep in mind that the perfectionistic notation would be $(p_k(\theta) - c_k(\theta))(dx_i/dp_k)(\theta)$ etc.

---

[20] This is based on the assumption that the constraints (29) and (30) originally are defined as inequalities $g(z(\overline{\theta})) \leq 0$ and $\Pi(\overline{\theta}) - \Pi_o + \Sigma_{i \notin K} p_i z_i(\overline{\theta}) \geq 0$ which are binding at the optimum.
[21] See equation (3–7) above.
[22] Assuming that controls $B(\theta), p(\theta)$ are piecewise continuous and right continuous.
[23] The star denotes values on the optimal path.

32.3.1 *Pricing in the Presence of Incentive Corrections*

Since the private sector does not respond to the public utility's policy, reactions of consumer demand are always equal to reactions of the demand for supply of the public utility, for instance $dx_i/dp_k = dz_i^D/dp_k$. This leads to fairly simple pricing rules which can easily be interpreted.

Let us first exclude the marginal condition for the basic fee. Prices are determined according to the following equation:[24]

$$\sum_i (p_i - c_i) \frac{\partial x_i}{\partial p_k} = -z_k - \mathcal{I}_k; \qquad k \in K. \tag{39}$$

Of special interest in this pricing rule are the incentive-correction terms

$$\mathcal{I}_k := \frac{\mu - \phi}{f \beta_o} \frac{du_\theta}{dp_k}; \qquad k \in K. \tag{40}$$

These terms account for the truthful revelation of θ, as expressed by the derivative of the incentive-compatibility constraint. They may be zero for the consumer with the highest taste parameter because $\nu(\bar\theta) := \mu(\bar\theta) - \phi(\bar\theta) \geq 0$. If $\nu(\bar\theta)$ actually is zero, then all incentive-related distortions are excluded from the marginal prices at the top. Interestingly, it is not a 'marginal price equals marginal cost' result which we achieve at the top. There is more resemblance to the pricing structure of a profit-maximizing perfect monopoly. This is not too surprising: in the present model welfare depends only on the state variable $V(\theta)$, not on any of the control variables. Therefore, no welfare weights of the Feldstein type can be found in the pricing rules.[25] It should be noted that the above result holds for the non-compensated case, i.e. if the regulator does not use basic fees $B(\theta)$ as controls. We shall see that the inclusion of optimal basic fees drastically changes the result for the top consumer.

For the other types of consumers, unfortunately, a more detailed interpretation of the incentive corrections is impossible. β_o and du_θ/dp_k may depend on θ in many different ways.

Let us next explicitly include the marginal condition for the basic fee.[26]

---

[24] The transformations are simple. Basically, we solve the transversality conditions for $\xi_i(\bar\theta)$ with respect to the α_i's and substitute into the $\partial \mathcal{F}/\partial p_k$ conditions. Then we divide the resulting equations by $\beta_o := \beta \cdot (\partial g/\partial z_o)$ and denote $c_i := (\partial g/\partial z_i)/(\partial g/\partial z_o)$ as 'marginal costs'. (Recall $p_o = 1$.) Then we add $(1-\gamma)\Sigma_i p_i (\partial x_i/\partial p_k)$ to both sides. On the right-hand side we substitute $\Sigma_i p_i (\partial x_i/\partial p_k) = -x_k = -z_k$ since $y_k \equiv 0$ for $k \in K$.

[25] The reader should be aware of the fact that this does not imply the absence of a distributional orientation of prices if required by the welfare function.

[26] Multiply the condition $\partial \mathcal{F}/\partial B = 0$ by x_k and subtract it from the respective $\partial \mathcal{F}/\partial p_k = 0$ condition. Then substitute for the α_i's from the transversality conditions. Finally, di-

For the consumer this basic fee is negative income, and therefore we can define the following compensated derivatives,

$$\frac{\partial \hat{x}_i}{\partial p_k} := \frac{\partial x_i}{\partial p_k} - x_k \frac{\partial x_i}{\partial B}; \quad \frac{d\hat{u}_\theta}{dp_k} := \frac{du_\theta}{dp_k} - x_k \frac{du_\theta}{dB}. \tag{41}$$

The resulting price structure is as follows:

$$\sum_i (p_i - c_i) \frac{\partial \hat{x}_i}{\partial p_k} = -\widehat{\mathcal{I}}_k, \quad \text{where } \widehat{\mathcal{I}}_k := \frac{\mu - \phi}{f\beta_o} \frac{d\hat{u}_\theta}{dp_k}; \quad k \in K. \tag{42}$$

Consider first the consumer with the highest taste parameter. He may face marginal prices which are marginal-cost prices.[27] This is the counterpart to one of the celebrated results of the theory of optimal income taxation.[28] Of course the result does not imply that the extreme type of consumer faces a basic fee of zero (which, once again, is analogous to the theory of optimal income taxation).

Let us next deal with some particularities of marginal prices for intermediate tastes. There are several ways to interpret the pricing formula (42) in these cases. First, if we restrict the analysis to a two-good enterprise, we obtain

$$\frac{p_1 - c_1}{p_2 - c_2} = \frac{\hat{u}_{1\theta}\hat{x}_{22} - \hat{u}_{2\theta}\hat{x}_{21}}{\hat{u}_{2\theta}\hat{x}_{11} - \hat{u}_{1\theta}\hat{x}_{12}} \tag{43}$$

where $\hat{u}_{i\theta} := d\hat{u}_\theta/dp_i$ and $\hat{x}_{ik} := \partial \hat{x}_i/\partial p_k$, $i = o, \dots, n$, $k \in K$. This formula is similar both to the Ramsey 'inverse-elasticity' approach and to the 'Pareto condition' which can be found in the optimal taxation literature.[29]

Second, consider the transition from marginal-cost prices to the present case of marginal prices which differ from marginal cost and denote this difference by

$$dp_i := p_i - c_i; \quad i \in K. \tag{44}$$

If the marginal prices are near to the marginal-cost prices, we can approximate the left-hand side of the pricing formula as follows

---

vide by β_o and add $(1-\gamma)\Sigma p_i(\partial \hat{x}_i/\partial p_k)$ to both sides. On the right-hand side substitute $\Sigma p_i(\partial \hat{x}_i/\partial p_k)=0$.

[27] We assume that non-regulated prices equal marginal costs c_i in the public sector.

[28] Typically, this result is associated with the papers by Sadka (1976a) and Seade (1977). For non-linear pricing see Roberts (1979: 72).

[29] See, for instance Mirrlees (1976: 337–8). See also Mirman and Sibley (1980: 664–5) for the special case of optimal non-linear pricing. This Pareto condition would be as follows: $(u_i-c_i)/(u_k-c_k)=\hat{u}_{i\theta}/\hat{u}_{k\theta}$ with $u_i:=\partial u/\partial x_i$. If u were consumer surplus, $u_i=p_i$. It has always been clear that the economic meaning of this 'Pareto condition' is difficult to grasp.

$$\sum_{i\in K}(p_i-c_i)\frac{\partial\hat{x}_i}{\partial p_k}=\sum_{i\in K}(p_i-c_i)\frac{\partial\hat{x}_k}{\partial p_i}=\sum_{i\in K}\frac{\partial\hat{x}_k}{\partial p_i}dp_i=d\hat{x}_k(p); \qquad k\in K. \quad (45)$$

where the first equality comes from the symmetry of substitution effects, the second from equation (44) and the third from applying the total differential of the demand functions for $\hat{x}_k=\hat{x}_k(p)$.[30] The pricing formula can therefore be written as

$$d\hat{x}_k=-\widehat{I}_k; \qquad k\in K. \quad (46)$$

The compensated quantity changes which result from moving from marginal-cost prices to the marginal prices of our present model are equated to the incentive corrections.

Although this is a nice result, the usual caveat against this type of interpretation is valid. Since we use the total differential, all results are approximations unless we deal with infinitesimal deviations from marginal-cost pricing or with demand functions which are linear in prices.[31]

32.3.2   The Basic Fee

Let us define the consumer's expenditure function as depending on the marginal prices,[32]

$$R(p,u):=\min_{x}\left[\sum_{i}p_ix_i|u(\theta,x)\geq u\right]. \quad (47)$$

Since there is no non-labor income of the consumers, their personal budget constraints imply

$$B(\theta)=-R(p(\theta),u(\theta)). \quad (48)$$

Differentiation yields

$$\frac{dB}{d\theta}=-\sum_{k}\frac{\partial R}{\partial p_k}\frac{\partial p_k}{\partial\theta}-\frac{\partial R}{\partial u}\frac{\partial u}{\partial\theta}. \quad (49)$$

Applying the special properties of the expenditure function[33] we obtain

$$\frac{dB}{d\theta}=\frac{\partial B}{\partial\theta}\bigg|_{u}-\sum_{k}x_k\frac{\partial p_k}{\partial\theta}. \quad (50)$$

---

[30] Cfr. section 8.3 above for a similar transformation of the Ramsey pricing formula. Once again, non-regulated prices are assumed to be equal to marginal costs c_i in the public sector.

[31] Cfr. p. 141 above.

[32] Cfr. Roberts (1979: 69).

[33] $\partial R/\partial p_k=x_k$; $\partial R/\partial u=-1/(\partial u/\partial B)$.

Changes in the taste parameter θ influence the basic fee in a way similar to the Slutsky equation: there is a 'substitution effect' and an 'income effect', the latter referring to the 'marginal expenditures' for the goods of the regulated enterprise, i.e. $\Sigma_k p_k x_k$.

(i) 'Substitution effect'. Recall that an increase in θ increases the individual utility because of the incentive-compatibility requirement. To keep the utility constant, the basic fee must be increased. Hence $(\partial B / \partial \theta)|_u > 0$. Higher θ's can be exploited by increasing the basic fee B.

(ii) 'Income effect'. A higher taste parameter θ can be exploited by increasing prices p_k, as illustrated in figure 24.

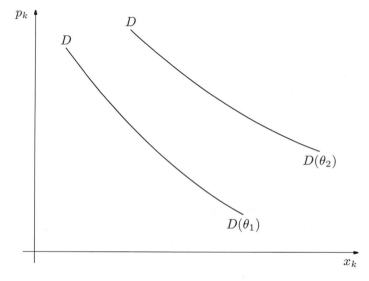

Figure 24

Shift in Demand for $\theta_2 > \theta_1$

In this figure we have assumed $\partial p_k / \partial \theta > 0$ and $\partial x_k / \partial \theta > 0$, both of which need not necessarily hold. However, if the marginal expenditures are increasing in θ, which is very plausible, then the higher marginal prices can be used to reduce the basic fee. This explains the negative sign of the 'income effect' and clarifies the trade-off of the two effects which constitute $dB/d\theta$.

33

Positive Theory of Price Regulation

33.1   Criteria of Positive Theory

In full-information models on pricing, it was easy to distinguish between normative and positive theories: in normative theories the government maximized welfare, in positive theories it optimized some other objectives like votes or output. In the asymmetric-information models on price regulation, this distinction is more complicated to draw. There are three main criteria which should be used to distinguish positive from normative theories:

  (i)   the objective of the regulator,
  (ii) the objective of the manager,
  (iii) the relationship between regulator and manager.

These three criteria will be treated in the following subsections.

33.1.1   The Objective of the Regulator

In this subsection we will briefly discuss how prices will be regulated if the regulator applies positive-theory objectives instead of maximizing welfare objectives. Examples include maximization of votes, of budgets or of output. These objectives have been explained extensively in other parts of this book.[1]

Let $\Phi(p(\theta), z(\theta))$ denote any positive-theory objective function with prices $p(\theta)$ and netputs $z(\theta)$ as the regulator's instruments.[2] Now consider any of the models of chapters 29–32, replacing welfare with the objective function Φ. Otherwise, the models remain unchanged, in particular the information setting. Hence the random parameter θ could refer to technology, demand, budget or type of consumer.

It is not necessary to repeat any details of the control-theoretic optimization. We always obtain extensions of the positive-theory pricing rules which we explicitly derived in chapter 4 above. Recall that these conditions are as follows:

---

[1]   See chapters 4 and 17–21 above.

[2]   Since we deal with positive theory, we will not include lump-sum incomes in the list of the regulator's instruments. Pricing formulas therefore refer only to non-compensated consumer demand.

$$\sum_{i=o}^{n}\left(c_i - p_i - \frac{1}{\beta_o}\frac{\partial\Phi}{\partial z_i}\right)\frac{\partial z_i^D}{\partial p_k} = \gamma z_k + (1-\gamma)x_k +$$

$$+ (1-\gamma)\sum_i\sum_j(p_i - c_i^j)\frac{\partial y_i^j}{\partial p_k} + \frac{1}{\beta_o}\frac{\partial\Phi}{\partial p_k}; \quad k \in K, \tag{4-8}$$

$$\sum_{i=o}^{n}\left(c_i - p_i - \frac{1}{\beta_o}\frac{\partial\Phi}{\partial z_i}\right)\frac{\partial z_i^D}{\partial p_k} = z_k + \frac{1}{\beta_o}\frac{\partial\Phi}{\partial p_k}; \quad k \in K. \tag{4-9}$$

The second formula is derived from the first by assuming that regulation is restricted to the firm in question, that the unregulated private sector is perfectly competitive and that goods with regulated prices are neither supplied nor demanded by non-regulated private firms ($z_k = x_k$).

Asymmetric information requires the explicit consideration of incentive-correction terms in the pricing formulas. These terms are defined in precisely the same way as in the preceding chapters.[3] They enter at precisely the same parts of the pricing formulas as shown in the preceding chapters and accordingly, the economic interpretation of their influence on price regulation is the same in normative- and in positive-theory models. By way of an example, if the regulator lacks information about the technology of the firm, an incentive correction term $\mathcal{I}_i$ has to be added to the marginal costs, so the left-hand side of (4–8) and (4–9) has to be replaced by $\Sigma(p_i - c_i - \mathcal{I}_i - (1/\beta_o)(\partial\Phi/\partial z_i))(\partial z_i^D/\partial p_k)$. The economic message, once again, would be that the problem of asymmetric information about costs constitutes a problem of higher costs facing the regulator; but otherwise the special properties of positive-theory pricing remain unchanged.

33.1.2 The Objective of the Manager

The theory of price regulation usually imputes to the manager a utility function $U(t,e)$ where t is his compensation and e his effort. If one is willing to accept utility functions as a part of a positive theory, then $U(t,e)$ is a good candidate. It is a direct utility function of the most usual microeconomic type. The manager consumes two goods: first, a composite commodity on which he spends all his income t; second, leisure, represented by his effort e.

This type of managerial objective has, however, sometimes been criticized by public-enterprise theorists, for instance by Rees (1984a,b, 1986, 1988). This

---

[3] That is, (29–34), (30–33), (31–28) and (32–40, 42).

criticism considers $U(t, e)$ as the typical objective of a manager of a private firm, be it regulated or not. Using income as an incentive to increase effort is said to be characteristic for private, but not for public enterprises, where the managers' satisfaction about properly doing their job should be enough of an incentive. This satisfaction typically is measured by output, by revenue, or by the budget of the enterprise. Accordingly, the public-firm manager is described by the optimization of $U(e, z^+)$ or $U(e, \kappa)$ where z^+ is a vector of outputs and κ the investment (capital inputs).

Moreover, instead of concentrating on a single representative manager's utility, the 'public-enterprise objective function' sometimes is described as the result of a compromise between the bureaucratically-minded board of the firm and the representatives of some trade union. The reader of this book is acquainted with this approach because in the full-information pricing models we already presented it as one of the positive-theory objectives[4] (chapter 21). The 'public-enterprise objective function' in this specification depends on output, employee wages and employment. Neither managerial income nor managerial effort enter into this objective.

The author of this book believes that a utility function like $U(e, z^+)$ or $U(e, \kappa)$ could in some circumstances adequately describe the objective of a European public-enterprise manager with civil-servant status whose income is paid regardless of his activities and increases automatically every second year, say. If this manager, however, is able to seek promotion to a higher-ranking, better-paid job, the total neglect of his compensation turns out to be a mistake of such a theory.[5] The neglect of both effort and compensation in the combined bureaucrat-trade union objective function, makes this function unrealistic as a managerial utility function, whereas it may be well acceptable as a public-enterprise utility function in a full-information model or, to a lower extent, as a regulator's objective function.

It is, of course, possible to set up principal-agent models where the regulator maximizes welfare or votes, whereas the regulated firm maximizes $U(e, z^+)$, or $U(e, \kappa)$ or the combined bureaucrat-trade union objective. Since there is no incentive income in these models, 'inducements to reveal information (would have to) take the form of resource allocations rather than straightforward money transfers'. (Rees, 1986: 257.) By way of an example, if the managerial objective is $U(e, \kappa)$, the regulator will have to endow the public enterprise with excessive capital to elicit truthful revelation of the manager's private information.

---

[4] $\Phi(p, z) = \Sigma_{i=d+1}^{n} z_i + \delta U(p_o, z_o)$.

[5] Hence, $U(t, e, z^+)$ or $U(t, e, \kappa)$ are better candidates for utility functions of public managers who are interested in the firm and not only in their own well-being. See Bös (1991a: 108–14).

33.1.3 The Relationship Between Regulator and Manager (Non-optimal Incentive Incomes)

If positive theory is to be a realistic description of economic reality, then there is another part of our control-theoretic models which does not really reflect the business practice in regulated firms. This point of criticism refers to the endogenous choice of the compensation $t(\theta)$ in control-theoretic models. In business practice, however, linear compensation schedules prevail.[6] Nonlinear schedules, if chosen, are specified as simply as possible, regardless of the specification which a control-theoretic optimization approach would require. Hence, a positive theory of price regulation should explicitly consider the consequences of non-optimal incentive incomes, particularly of linear schemes. This is an important subject of investigation even if, from a normative point of view a positive-theory objective could be improved by choosing an optimal endogenous compensation scheme as done in subsection 33.1.1 above.

33.2 Dealing with Non-Optimal Incentive Pay

The preceding section dealt with three criteria which distinguish positive theory from normative theory. The replacement of the regulator's objectives could be treated by showing what the relevant marginal conditions look like and how they can be interpreted in analogy to the chapters 29–32. The replacement of the manager's objectives was treated by surveying Rees' models. However, we did not exhaustively deal with the consequences of non-optimal incentive pay. Hence, it seems worthwhile to present a simple model[7] which shows the main effects of various schemes of managerial pay which have been used in public and private regulated firms.

33.2.1 The Public Utility

Let us consider a one-product monopoly which faces a demand function expressed as

$$z = z(p); \qquad \frac{dz}{dp} < 0, \tag{1}$$

where z is the output and p the price. We assume market-clearing behavior, therefore z measures both the demanded and the supplied quantity. Producing output z induces the following costs

---

[6] See, for instance, Gaynor (1992).

[7] See Tirole (1988: 39–40) with further references. More recently see Chamley–Marchand–Pestieau (1989) and Bös (1991a: 93–123).

$$C = C(\theta, e, z(p)),$$

$$\frac{\partial C}{\partial e} < 0; \quad \frac{\partial^2 C}{\partial e^2} > 0; \quad \frac{\partial C}{\partial e}(\theta, 0, z) = -\infty; \quad \frac{\partial C}{\partial e}(\theta, 1, z) = 0; \tag{2}$$

$$\frac{\partial C}{\partial \theta} < 0; \quad \frac{\partial C}{\partial z} > 0.$$

The cost function is monotonically decreasing and strictly concave in effort e, which we normalize to the $[0, 1]$–interval. The first unit of effort applied leads to an immense reduction in costs; the last unit of effort does not help any more in reducing costs. Second, there is a random factor $\theta > 0$ whose increase reduces costs. Later on we shall assume that at the moment of contracting θ is unknown to both regulator and manager.

The regulated monopoly is run by a manager whose utility depends on income and effort. Since the linear specification of the previous chapters would exclude many interesting characteristics of our problem, we impute to the manager the general utility function

$$V(t, e); \qquad \partial V/\partial t > 0, \ \partial V/\partial e < 0. \tag{3}$$

The manager's marginal rate of substitution between income and effort is defined as follows:

$$MRS := -\frac{\partial V/\partial e}{\partial V/\partial t}$$

$$\frac{\partial MRS(t, e)}{\partial e} > 0; \quad MRS(t, 0) = 0; \quad MRS(t, 1) = \infty. \tag{4}$$

We have assumed that the marginal rate of substitution is increasing in effort: the higher the manager's effort, the more income he must be given to allow him to remain at the same utility level. For the first unit of effort, an infinitesimally small increase in income is sufficient to keep his utility constant (for simplification we assume $MRS(t, 0) = 0$); to induce him to work at 100 percent effort an immensely large increase in income is necessary to keep his utility constant (for simplification we assume $MRS(t, 1) = \infty$).

The regulator needs the manager to run the firm. Hence the manager's expected utility must not fall below his reservation utility V^o which is exogenously given by some outside option which is not explicitly modelled in the following partial analysis. The manager, alternatively, will be treated as risk-neutral or risk averse. He signs the contract if $\mathcal{E}V(\cdot) \geq V^o$, which implies that he decides according to his expected utility; the variance of utility is not relevant for his participation constraint. The manager's attitudes toward risk, however, are expressed by the properties (concavity) of his utility function.

The public utility is subject to regulation. The distortions which are caused by the non-optimal incentive pay can most clearly be demonstrated if we impute to the regulator the objective of maximizing expected welfare (where the expectation refers to θ). The type of distortions, however, is exactly the same if any positive-theory objective is chosen instead of welfare. In our partial analysis we describe welfare as the sum of consumer and producer surplus

$$W = CS(p) + \mathcal{N} - t, \tag{5}$$

where CS is consumer surplus, $\partial CS/\partial p = -z$, and $\mathcal{N}$ is net revenue, that is, revenue minus costs.

The interplay between regulator and public utility can best be understood if we first present a full-information benchmark model, which afterwards will serve as the basis of comparison for the evaluation of the imperfect-information principal-agent model.

33.2.2 A Full-Information Benchmark Model

The precise meaning of efficiency in our setting becomes clear if we consider a regulator who is fully informed about all relevant variables and functional relationships. The regulator's instruments in this case are the price p, the effort level e and the managerial income t. Since the principal is fully informed, he chooses the managerial income as a lump-sum compensation. The agent's income is functionally independent of his effort.

In a full-information model, there is no problem of incentive compatibility. The participation of the manager, however, must explicitly be ensured. The relevant participation constraint is always binding. As long as the agent's utility were to exceed his reservation-utility level V^o, the regulator could always increase welfare by reducing the agent's income or by instructing him to work harder, until his utility is brought down to the reservation level. We associate a shadow price ϕ with the participation constraint and characterize the regulator's optimization problem by the following Lagrangean function:

$$\mathcal{F} = W - \phi(V(t,e) - V^o). \tag{6}$$

The regulator's optimization yields two rules on efficiency:

(i) The allocative-efficiency rule. This rule is obtained by differentiating the Lagrangean with respect to price. It instructs the regulator to choose marginal-cost pricing

$$\left(p - \frac{\partial \mathcal{C}}{\partial z}\right)\frac{dz}{dp} = 0. \tag{7}$$

(ii) The X-efficiency rule.[8] This rule results from differentiating the Lagrangean function with respect to managerial effort and income. Our assumptions on the cost function and on the marginal rate of substitution ensure an interior and unique effort level of the manager.

$$-\frac{\partial \mathcal{C}}{\partial e} - \phi \frac{\partial V}{\partial e} = 0, \tag{8}$$

$$-1 - \phi \frac{\partial V}{\partial t} = 0. \tag{9}$$

Taken together, these conditions yield the X-efficiency rule:

$$\frac{\partial V/\partial e}{\partial V/\partial t} = \frac{\partial \mathcal{C}}{\partial e}. \tag{10}$$

This rule requires the equalization of the manager's marginal rate of substitution (left-hand side) and of the firm's marginal rate of transformation (right-hand side).[9]

33.2.3 The Information Setting in the Imperfect-Information Model

The information setting with respect to θ is as follows. When the regulator and the manager negotiate about the managerial compensation, their knowledge is restricted to the density function $f(\theta)$. Neither can observe the actual value of θ. Hence at this moment both can only plan in terms of expected utility or welfare. Therefore, when the manager decides to work for the regulator, he is willing to sign the contract if his expected utility exceeds the reservation level. Only after starting to work can the manager observe the actual value of θ. He then sets his effort level according to θ and thereby maximizes his personal utility. Finally, production takes place, the regulator observes output and total costs and compensates the manager according to the previously negotiated contract. Table 4 gives a summary of the sequencing of information and actions of manager and regulator.

The above informational setting raises the question as to why the manager agrees to sign a contract at a point in time when he is badly informed and therefore unable to extract an information rent from the regulator. It seems more rational for the manager to wait until he observes θ and only then to

---

[8] Following Gravelle (1982a) we define X-efficiency according to a cost function instead of the production-possibility frontier.

[9] After dividing by the derivative of total costs with respect to managerial income, $\partial(\mathcal{C}+t)/\partial t = 1$.

sign the contract. The chosen informational setting, however, becomes quite plausible if we assume that the precise value of θ is only learned on the job, in the firm. If the manager does not sign the contract, he never learns the actual value of θ. Note that in such a situation there is no need for a direct mechanism since at the moment of contracting the manager has nothing to reveal to the regulator.[10]

Table 4

Sequencing of information and actions of manager and regulator

Manager	Time	Regulator
$f(\theta)$ known; contract acceptance	1	$f(\theta)$ known; contract offer; regulator sets price and parameters of linear incentive pay
θ observed;	2	
$e(\theta)$ chosen	3	
production, sale	4	output and total costs observed; payment of managerial income

In what follows, we shall investigate two different income schedules,

$$\text{(i)} \quad t = \bar{t}, \tag{11a}$$
$$\text{(ii)} \quad t = B - \delta(\mathcal{C}/z); \quad \delta > 0, \tag{11b}$$

The first schedule stipulates an a priori fixed income $\bar{t}$. By way of an example, the manager starts with a basic income which increases automatically over time regardless of his effort. The second schedule stipulates a two-part income: the lower the firm's average costs, the higher the managerial income. Conditioning incomes on average costs is possible because the regulator is able to observe total costs $\mathcal{C}$ and output z. If a performance-related income is stipulated, the average costs are deducted from a basic income B; hence the managerial participation constraint guarantees that $B \geq 0$.

---

[10] For an explanation of direct mechanisms see section 28.1 above.

In business practice profit-related compensations can often be found; this would imply[11]

$$\text{(iii)} \quad t = B_\mathcal{N} + \delta_\mathcal{N}\mathcal{N}; \quad B_\mathcal{N} \geq 0; \quad 0 < \delta_\mathcal{N} \leq 1. \tag{11c}$$

However, since in our model the regulator sets the price which directly determines output $z(p)$, there is no qualitative difference between a performance-related and a profit-related incentive pay and therefore we can forgo the explicit treatment of the latter.

The regulator is not given the right to choose that managerial-pay schedule he would prefer. Somewhen in the past there has been a particular law or some compromise with the manager's union which cannot be altered by the regulator. If, for instance, the regulator has been instructed to apply schedule (11b), his only degrees of freedom are the choices of the parameters B and δ.

As usual, we assume that the shape of all relevant functions is common knowledge. The regulator knows the exact functional shape of the cost function, the demand function, the manager's utility, in short, he knows all functions which have been presented in subsection 33.2.1 above. This enables him to choose as instruments not only the parameters of the incentive-pay schedule, but also the optimal price.[12]

33.2.4   The Manager's Optimization

We begin with the analysis of the second stage of our game, that is, with the managerial optimization. The manager takes as given the observed value of θ and the parameters of the income schedule, and maximizes his utility with respect to effort:

$$\max_{0 \leq e \leq 1} V(t, e). \tag{12}$$

---

[11] If the price is high enough to achieve a profit of the regulated firm, then it is possible that the optimal regulatory policy would require a very low B ($B \rightarrow -\infty$) and a very high δ ($\delta \rightarrow +\infty$) to induce very high effort. This would be an unrealistic result; hence the constraint $B_\mathcal{N} \geq 0$. This constraint is a typical second-best constraint of a positive theory: a pay scheme with negative B does not occur in business practice, B always is a positive basic income. There are only rare occasions where an 'entrance fee' $B < 0$ must be paid by a manager. Mondragon in Spain is one of these exceptions. See Hinds (1990: 45–6).

[12] Alternatively, we could assume that the regulator calculates that price which maximizes expected welfare and forces the manager to actually set the price by stipulating the following income schedule:

$$\text{incentive pay} = \begin{cases} t & \text{if } p = p^* \\ 0 & \text{otherwise,} \end{cases}$$

where t is specified according to one of the alternatives (11).

For the two alternative schedules defined in (11) the manager obtains the following marginal conditions:

(a) fixed managerial income $(t = \bar{t})$:

$$\frac{\partial V}{\partial e} \leq 0; \qquad \text{if } e = 0,$$

$$\frac{\partial V}{\partial e} = 0; \qquad \text{if } 0 < e < 1, \qquad (13a)$$

$$\frac{\partial V}{\partial e} \geq 0; \qquad \text{if } e = 1.$$

If we follow the typical assumption $\partial V/\partial e < 0$, the manager will exert minimal effort.

(b) performance-related pay $(t = B - \delta(\mathcal{C}/z))$:

$$\frac{\partial V/\partial e}{\partial V/\partial t} = \frac{\delta}{z} \frac{\partial \mathcal{C}}{\partial e}. \qquad (13b)$$

Once again, our assumptions on the cost function and on the marginal rate of substitution ensure an interior and unique effort level of the manager. Since only $0 < e < 1$ holds, it is sufficient to present the condition (13b) as an equality.

Comparing the manager's effort choice with the full-information benchmark effort,[13] we recognize that the manager's choice of effort is X-inefficient unless $\delta = z$. In such a case the manager cashes in on every reduction of costs which result from his effort, since his income is $t = B - \mathcal{C}$. Hence, he is a sort of 'residual claimant' and this leads to X-efficiency. Later on we shall explicitly treat the welfare-optimal choice of the parameters B and δ by the regulator who anticipates the manager's choice of effort. Then we shall investigate whether $\delta = z$ is optimal for the regulator or whether it is welfare superior to accept X-inefficient behavior.

33.2.5 The Regulator's Policy: The Principles

Let us finally turn to the regulator's optimization approach. The regulator maximizes expected welfare. In doing so, he is constrained in a twofold way. First, he has to consider the manager's participation constraint. Second, he has to anticipate the manager's choice of effort. Since we always have an exogenously given functional form of the incentive income, the regulator

---

[13] See equation (10) above, $(\partial V/\partial e)/(\partial V/\partial t)=\partial \mathcal{C}/\partial e$.

can use equations (13) to calculate the manager's reaction function e^* which results from the manager's utility maximization. In the following we use the abbreviation $e^*(\cdot)$ to denote alternatively:

- $e^*(\cdot) = 0,$ \hfill (14a)
- $e^*(\cdot) = e^*(\theta, B, \delta).$ \hfill (14b)

The first reaction function refers to the case of a fixed managerial income, the second to the performance-related pay.

Given these reaction functions, it is not necessary to apply control theory, rather it is sufficient to substitute the relevant reaction function whenever effort e enters any function that has to be taken into account by the regulator. In particular, $e^*(\cdot)$ is substituted in $\mathcal{W}$ and in V.

Consequently, the regulator's optimization approach is as follows:

$$\underset{p,\mathcal{G}}{\text{maximize}} \ \ \mathcal{E}\mathcal{W}(\cdot) \ \text{subject to} \ \mathcal{E}V(\cdot) \geq V^o, \qquad (15)$$

where $(\cdot)$ signals the substitution of $e^*(\cdot)$ and $\mathcal{E}$ is the expectation operator with respect to θ. The regulator's instruments are the price p and the parameters $\mathcal{G}$ of the income schedule. If the managerial income is independent of effort, $\mathcal{G} = \bar{t}$; for the performance-related pay we have $\mathcal{G} = (B, \delta)$. To simplify the presentation we do not explicitly consider the positivity constraint on the range of δ, which we have presented in equation (11b). We always assume that this condition is fulfilled.

To solve the optimization problem we formulate the Lagrangean function

$$\mathcal{F} = \mathcal{E}\mathcal{W}(\cdot) - \phi[\mathcal{E}V(\cdot) - V^o]. \qquad (16)$$

The resulting Kuhn–Tucker conditions are as follows:

$$\frac{\partial \mathcal{F}}{\partial p} = 0; \quad \frac{\partial \mathcal{F}}{\partial \mathcal{G}} = 0, \qquad (17)$$

$$\mathcal{E}V - V^o \geq 0; \quad \phi(\mathcal{E}V - V^o) = 0; \quad \phi \leq 0. \qquad (18)$$

The first set of Kuhn–Tucker conditions refers to the regulator's choice of price and managerial pay. The second set refers to managerial participation. The conflict of interest between the regulator and the manager implies that, starting from the optimum, an exogenous increase of the reservation utility V^o reduces the regulator's objective. Hence $\phi < 0$,[14] which implies that the

---

[14] For this sort of interpretation of Lagrangean parameters see Panik (1976: 225).

participation constraint is always binding. If the managerial income is independent of his effort, there is no uncertainty about managerial utility and the income $\bar{t}$ can immediately be found by solving the participation constraint $V(\bar{t}, 0) = V^o$ to obtain $\bar{t}$. If, however, managerial income is performance-related, it is the manager's *expected* utility which is depressed to his reservation utility. Unfortunately, this implies that *ex post* the manager may have to fulfill a contract which gives him less than his reservation utility.[15] This is the result of formulating the participation constraint in expected utility. If the manager had known the precise value of θ at the moment of contracting, the principal would have had to guarantee participation for any possible value of θ, not only with respect to some expected value. In that case the manager would have had a stronger position when signing the contract.[16]

33.2.6   The Regulator's Policy I: Fixed Managerial Income

If the managerial income is independent of effort, the manager chooses minimal effort $e = 0$, and the regulator adjusts to this decision. The regulator's choice of price and managerial income can be described by the following marginal conditions[17]

$$\left(p - \mathcal{E}\frac{\partial \mathcal{C}}{\partial z}\right)\frac{\partial z}{\partial p} = 0, \tag{19}$$

$$-1 - \phi\frac{\partial V}{\partial t} = 0. \tag{20}$$

We have *ex ante* marginal-cost pricing, because the price is equated to the *expected* marginal costs; *ex post* the price may significantly deviate from the *realized* marginal costs. Moreover, the expected marginal costs are too high, because the effort level is zero and hence is suboptimally low. The X-inefficiency directly influences the allocative inefficiency and all this shows the undesirable consequences of a managerial income which does not give any incentive for higher effort.

---

[15] A special problem of the manager's participation refers to the danger of ruin. To avoid this problem, we assume that any incentive schedule is fixed in such a way that the manager's income is never negative. This allows us to avoid the clumsiness of adding an explicit no-ruin constraint to the optimization problem.

[16] In models where the agent knows θ when contracting, his utility must be an increasing function of θ; the participation constraint is binding only for the lowest possible value of θ.

[17] For this and the following marginal conditions note which variables or functions are non-stochastic: (i) $p, z(p), \partial z/\partial p$; (ii) $\bar{t}, \partial V/\partial t$ in case of fixed income; (iii) the parameters of the performance-related income schedule; (iv) the Lagrangean parameter ϕ.

33.2.7   The Regulator's Policy II: Performance-Related Managerial Income

Let us first present the regulator's decision on the *price*. The respective marginal condition equals

$$\left(p - \mathcal{E}\frac{\partial\mathcal{C}}{\partial z}\right)\frac{dz}{dp} + \frac{\delta}{z}\mathcal{E}\left[\left(1 + \phi\frac{\partial V}{\partial t}\right)\left(\frac{\partial\mathcal{C}}{\partial z} - \frac{\mathcal{C}}{z}\right)\right]\frac{dz}{dp} = 0. \tag{21}$$

If the firm faces a constant-cost technology, then the price is chosen equal to the expected marginal costs (ex post, however, the price may well deviate from the realized marginal costs). Otherwise, unfortunately, there is no clear-cut result with respect to the price-cost difference. This shows how crucial it is for the results if various analyses on managerial incentive incomes begin by assuming constant costs. Note that only constant costs lead to the above result. Equality of expected marginal and average costs at the optimum is not sufficient for the result if these expected-cost terms differ at non-optimal quantities.[18]

Let us next deal with the *optimal compensation* which is paid to the manager. At an optimum the following marginal conditions hold:

$$\mathcal{E}\frac{\partial W}{\partial B} - \phi\mathcal{E}\left[\frac{\partial V}{\partial t}\left(1 - \frac{\delta}{z}\frac{\partial\mathcal{C}}{\partial e}\frac{\partial e}{\partial B}\right)\right] - \phi\mathcal{E}\left(\frac{\partial V}{\partial e}\frac{\partial e}{\partial B}\right) = 0, \tag{22a}$$

$$\mathcal{E}\frac{\partial W}{\partial\delta} - \phi\mathcal{E}\left[\frac{\partial V}{\partial t}\left(-\frac{\mathcal{C}}{z} - \frac{\delta}{z}\frac{\partial\mathcal{C}}{\partial e}\frac{\partial e}{\partial\delta}\right)\right] - \phi\mathcal{E}\left(\frac{\partial V}{\partial e}\frac{\partial e}{\partial\delta}\right) = 0. \tag{22b}$$

Substituting the condition for the manager optimum

$$\frac{\partial V}{\partial e} = \frac{\partial V}{\partial t}\frac{\delta}{z}\frac{\partial\mathcal{C}}{\partial e}, \tag{13b}$$

the above marginal conditions can be simplified considerably:

$$\mathcal{E}\frac{\partial W}{\partial B} - \phi\mathcal{E}\frac{\partial V}{\partial t} = 0, \tag{23a}$$

$$\mathcal{E}\frac{\partial W}{\partial\delta} + \phi\mathcal{E}\left(\frac{\partial V}{\partial t}\frac{\mathcal{C}}{z}\right) = 0. \tag{23b}$$

---

[18] Recall that $\phi\mathcal{E}(\partial V/\partial t)(\partial\mathcal{C}/\partial z - \mathcal{C}/z)(\partial z/\partial p) = \phi\{\mathcal{E}(\partial V/\partial t)[\mathcal{E}(\partial\mathcal{C}/\partial z) - \mathcal{E}(\mathcal{C}/z)](\partial z/\partial p)\} + \phi\{[cov(\partial V/\partial t;\partial\mathcal{C}/\partial z) - cov(\partial V/\partial t;\mathcal{C}/z)](\partial z/\partial p)\}$. If expected marginal and average costs are only equal at the optimum, the difference of the covariances does not vanish.

Let us further determine the derivatives of welfare. We use the fact that δ and z are non-stochastic and obtain[19]

$$\mathcal{E}\frac{\partial \mathcal{W}}{\partial B} = \left(\frac{\delta - z}{z}\right)\mathcal{E}\frac{\partial \mathcal{C}}{\partial B} - 1, \tag{24a}$$

$$\mathcal{E}\frac{\partial \mathcal{W}}{\partial \delta} = \left(\frac{\delta - z}{z}\right)\mathcal{E}\frac{\partial \mathcal{C}}{\partial \delta} + \mathcal{E}\frac{\mathcal{C}}{z}. \tag{24b}$$

We substitute these equations into (23) and combine (23a) with (23b) to obtain

$$\left(\frac{\delta - z}{z}\right)\left[\mathcal{E}\frac{\partial \mathcal{C}}{\partial \delta} + \frac{\mathcal{E}\left(\frac{\partial V}{\partial t}\frac{\mathcal{C}}{z}\right)}{\mathcal{E}\frac{\partial V}{\partial t}}\mathcal{E}\frac{\partial \mathcal{C}}{\partial B}\right] = -\mathcal{E}\frac{\mathcal{C}}{z} + \frac{\mathcal{E}\left(\frac{\partial V}{\partial t}\frac{\mathcal{C}}{z}\right)}{\mathcal{E}\frac{\partial V}{\partial t}}. \tag{25}$$

If the manager is risk neutral, the right-hand side of (25) is equal to zero[20] and the regulator chooses $\delta = z$.[21] In this case the manager enjoys the full rewards of his performance, since his income is $t = B - C$. On the other hand, the manager bears the full risk. From our analysis of the manager's optimization we know that for $\delta = z$, X-efficiency is achieved.

It is important to note that $\delta = z$ is not necessarily optimal if the manager is risk-averse or risk-loving. If the manager is risk-averse, we expect $\delta < z$ to be optimal, since this implies that the risk-averse manager bears less risk than the risk-neutral manager.[22] In such a case, the risk is shared between regulator and manager. Since in this case at the managerial optimum we have $MRS < -\partial \mathcal{C}/\partial e$, the effort level is suboptimally low.[23]

---

[19] Abbreviating $\partial \mathcal{C}/\partial B := (\partial \mathcal{C}/\partial e)(\partial e/\partial B)$ and analogously for $\partial \mathcal{C}/\partial \delta$.

[20] Compare Chamley–Marchand–Pestieau (1989). By way of an example, consider the linear utility function which we applied in the chapters 28–31, $V = t - \psi(e)$. It can directly be seen that this specification implies $\partial V/\partial t = 1$. Hence the right-hand side of equation (25) becomes zero.

[21] Assuming that the term in square brackets is not zero.

[22] If the objective of the regulator is Φ and the incentive pay of the manager is $B + \delta\Phi$, then it can be proved that $\delta \leq 1$ is always optimal for a risk-averse manager. See for instance Chamley–Marchand–Pestieau (1989: 236–7) who use a proof that follows the Rothschild–Stiglitz (1970) and Stiglitz (1974) line. Our case however is different and the Chamley–Marchand–Pestieau proof holds only under restrictive additional assumptions.

[23] The manager chooses effort according to equation (13b), that is $MRS = -(\delta/z)(\partial \mathcal{C}/\partial e)$. If $\delta < z$, we have $(\delta/z) < 1$ and hence $MRS < -\partial \mathcal{C}/\partial e$.

D
Regulation Through Competition

34
Mixed Markets

In this chapter we deal with oligopolistic markets in which at least one public firm and at least one private firm compete with each other. Such a 'mixed' public-private market can be the result of privatization, of nationalization, or of market entry. In the first case, some but not all public firms of an oligopolistic market have been privatized in order to increase productive efficiency. In the second case some but not all private firms have been nationalized in order to improve welfare. In the third case either a private firm enters the market of a public incumbent or vice versa.

We speak of 'regulation through competition' because all cases mentioned in the preceding paragraph are the result of government policy. It is the government which decides on privatization or nationalization. It is also the government which decides on market entry, for instance by allowing private firms to enter markets which hitherto had legally been declared public monopolies or oligopolies.[1]

34.1 A Duopoly Model for Public Prices

There are different optimal adjustments of welfare to private monopolistic pricing in a duopoly model, depending on the different types of behavior of the duopolists. The economic intuition behind these different concepts can be shown best if we restrict ourselves to the following simplified analysis. Consider two players of a game:

- a public enterprise whose board maximizes welfare by choosing prices $\{p_k, k \in K\}$, netputs $\{z_i, i \neq m\}$, and lump-sum incomes $\{r^h, h = 1, \ldots, H\}$

---

[1] The German TV market provides a good example. It had been a public oligopoly. Then market entry was allowed. Several private TV companies were established and began to compete with the publicly owned TV companies, resulting in a mixed market.

in a market-clearing and technologically feasible way; as usual $g(z) = 0$ describes the technology of the public firm.

- a private firm, setting prices $p_m, m \in M \subset I$, where $K \cap M = \emptyset$. The firm is interested in maximizing profits, defined as its revenue-cost difference $\pi_m = \Sigma_i p_i y_i^m$.

The following optimization approaches will be presented analytically in a comparatively general manner. The analytical presentation deals with substitutes as well as complements, decreasing as well as increasing cost functions, and various assumptions about the behavior of demand. However, typical neoclassical 'well behaved' functions are assumed to exist. – Figure 25 on p. 387 illustrates a typical configuration for substitute goods, increasing marginal costs of both enterprises, and well-behaved demand functions.

We define the duopoly problem over the budget space. Thus, any action of the public firm depends on its own price p_k and on the price $p_m^E(p_k)$ which the private firm is expected to set when responding to the public firm's price. Similarly, any action of the private firm depends on its own price p_m and on the price $p_k^E(p_m)$ the public firm is expected to set when responding to private firm's price. 'E' stands for 'expected response' because any firm when setting its own price uses some particular assumption of how the other firm will respond.

Hence, the public enterprise maximizes the following Lagrangean function with respect to its netputs, prices and lump-sum incomes:

$$\mathcal{F} = W(v^1(p_k, p_m^E(p_k), r^1), \ldots, v^H(\cdot)) - \sum_{i \neq m} \alpha_i \left[\sum_h x_i^h(p_k, p_m^E(p_k), r^h) \right.$$

$$\left. -z_i - \sum_j y_i^j(p_k, p_m^E(p_k)) \right] - \beta g(z) - \overline{\gamma} \left[\Pi^o - \sum_i p_i z_i \right] \tag{1}$$

where all variables which are held constant are suppressed in the notation of the functional dependencies.[2] $z_m = 0$ implies the assumption that good m is not used as an input of the public firm. It is only the price reactions which constitute the particular duopoly problem. The resulting price structure is relatively complicated, as it contains all possible reactions of the firm.[3]

---

[2] $v^h(p_k, p_m^E(p_k), r^h) := v^h(\overline{p}_o, \overline{p}_1, \ldots, p_k, \ldots, p_m^E(p_k), \ldots, \overline{p}_n, r^h)$ and analogously for the demand functions $x_i^h(\cdot)$ and $y_i^j(\cdot)$.

[3] The transformation corresponds to the usual way which we applied in chapter 3. Hence, in this chapter we do not present details of the transformation. The equations (2) result from a particular combination of the marginal conditions $\partial \mathcal{F}/\partial p_k = 0, \partial \mathcal{F}/\partial z_i = 0, i \neq m$,

$$\sum_{i \neq m}(p_i - c_i)\left(\frac{\partial \hat{z}_i}{\partial p_k} + \sum_m \frac{\partial \hat{z}_i}{\partial p_m}\cdot\frac{\partial p_m^E}{\partial p_k}\right) = -\gamma\left(z_k + \sum_m z_m \frac{\partial p_m^E}{\partial p_k}\right)$$

$$- (1-\gamma)\left\{\sum_{i \neq m}\sum_j (p_i - c_i^j)\left(\frac{\partial y_i^j}{\partial p_k} + \sum_m \frac{\partial y_i^j}{\partial p_m}\cdot\frac{\partial p_m^E}{\partial p_k}\right)\right. \qquad (2)$$

$$\left. + \sum_m (p_m - c_m^m)\left(\frac{\partial \hat{x}_m}{\partial p_k} + \frac{\partial \hat{x}_m}{\partial p_k}\cdot\frac{\partial p_m^E}{\partial p_k}\right)\right\}; \qquad k \in K.$$

The price structure becomes much simpler if a particular form of strategic behavior of the private firm is assumed by specifying $p_m^E(p_k)$. Before doing so, however, we must treat the private firm's optimization in a general form. We substitute $x_m = y_m^m$, $m \in M$ because of the monopolistic market structure ($z_m = 0$). Then the private firm's profit is as follows:[4]

$$\sum_m p_m x_m(p_k^E(p_m), p_m) + \sum_{i \notin M} p_i y_i^m \quad s.t. \quad g^m(x_m(\cdot), y_{i \notin M}^m) = 0, \qquad (3)$$

where $g^m(\cdot) = 0$ is the private firm's technology. Maximizing this profit with respect to prices p_m and netputs y_i^m leads to the following price structure[5]

$$\sum_{i \in M}(p_i - c_i^m)\left(\frac{\partial x_i}{\partial p_m} + \sum_k \frac{\partial x_i}{\partial p_k}\frac{\partial p_k^E}{\partial p_m}\right) = -x_m; \qquad m \in M \qquad (4)$$

which is the extension of the monopolistic-pricing rule we expected after including the reaction of the public firm.

We have now defined the general framework for duopoly pricing. We are interested in the type of behavior the duopolists will choose within this

---

and $\partial \mathcal{F}/\partial r^h = 0$. Recall the definitions of marginal costs, $c_i := (\partial g/\partial z_i)/(\partial g/\partial z_o)$ and of compensated demand for the products of the public enterprise, $\partial \hat{z}_i/\partial p_k := [\Sigma_h(\partial x_i^h/\partial p_k + x_k^h(\partial x_i^h/\partial r^h)) - \Sigma_j \partial y_i^j/\partial p_k]$.

[4] $x_m(\cdot) = x_m(\overline{p}_o, \overline{p}_1, \ldots, p_k^E(p_m), \ldots, p_m, \ldots, \overline{p}_n, \overline{r}^1, \ldots, \overline{r}^H)$.

[5] Differentiation of the respective Lagrangean $\mathcal{F}$ with respect to y_i^m yields $p_i - \lambda(\partial g^m/\partial y_i^m) = 0 \quad i \notin M$.

We use one of these marginal conditions, namely
$$\lambda(\partial g^m/\partial y_o^m) = p_o = 1$$
to replace λ in the conditions resulting from $\partial \mathcal{F}/\partial p_m$, and define as usual
$$c_k^m = (\partial g^m/\partial y_k^m)/(\partial g^m/\partial y_o^m) = (\partial g^m/\partial x_k)/(\partial g^m/\partial y_o^m).$$

framework. The first approach we shall examine assumes *Nash-type behavior* of both firms: each firm treats the price of the other firm as fixed at each stage of the pricing process. The public firm assumes that prices p_m do not respond to changes of p_k, and the private firm assumes that prices p_k do not respond to changes of p_m:

$$\frac{\partial p_m^E}{\partial p_k} = 0; \quad \frac{\partial p_k^E}{\partial p_m} = 0; \qquad k \in K, m \in M. \tag{5}$$

Under these assumptions the general pricing rules (2) and (4) reduce to

$$\sum_{i \neq m}(p_i - c_i)\frac{\partial \hat{z}_i}{\partial p_k} = -\gamma z_k - (1 - \gamma)\left\{\sum_{i \neq m}\sum_j(p_i - c_i^j)\frac{\partial y_i^j}{\partial p_k} + \right.$$
$$\left. + \sum_m(p_m - c_m^m)\frac{\partial \hat{x}_m}{\partial p_k}\right\}; \qquad k \in K. \tag{6}$$

$$\sum_{i \in M}(p_i - c_i^m)\frac{\partial x_i}{\partial p_m} = -x_m; \qquad m \in M. \tag{7}$$

Equation (6) resembles the usual welfare-optimal adjustment of public to private pricing as shown in equation (10–2). Its interpretation could, therefore, follow the lines of chapter 10 above. Equation (7) is the well-known monopoly-pricing rule, where prices will usually exceed marginal costs, depending on the uncompensated demand elasticities.

For a graphical representation consider figure 25 where (6) and (7) refer to the equations above. (6) connects the welfare-maximizing prices p_k if p_m is given. $W^{o'}$ and $W^{o''}$ are iso-welfare lines. Point W is the welfare maximum. Of course an upper limit for p_k exists where the public enterprise loses all customers ($z_k = 0$). (7) connects the profit-maximizing prices p_m if p_k is given. $\pi_m^{o'}$ and $\pi_m^{o''}$ are iso-profit lines. Since the figure is drawn for substitute goods, the absolute profit maximum is located on the line $z_k = 0$ where the public enterprise has left the market (point π_m).

Given Nash-type behavior of both firms, the resulting prices can be obtained analytically by solving (6) and (7) for p_k and p_m; graphically we obtain point A in figure 25.

The following alternative approach is due to Stackelberg. *Stackelberg-type behavior* is asymmetric. One duopolist takes the active position, while the other duopolist adjusts to the actions of the active player.

Suppose, first, the *public enterprise is the active player*. Taking the active position means it expects the private firm to respond to the public prices. The passive position, as taken by the private firm, means it does not expect the public firm to respond to the private firm's price changes:

$$\frac{\partial p_m^E}{\partial p_k} \neq 0 \quad \text{(active position)};$$

$$\frac{\partial p_k^E}{\partial p_m} = 0 \quad \text{(passive position)}; \qquad k \in K, m \in M. \tag{8}$$

Analytically we obtain prices according to the marginal conditions (2) and (7). Graphically the result is point B in figure 25 which is the welfare maximum given the private firm's adherence to eq. (7).[6]

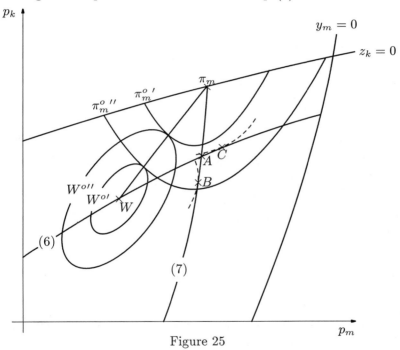

Figure 25

If the *private enterprise is the active player*, the contrary holds. The active private firm expects public prices to respond to private prices. The

---

[6] In figure 25, playing actively leads to higher welfare (profit) than playing passively. However, there exist situations where the contrary may result. For example, if quantities are used as strategic variables and the public enterprise has constant marginal costs, welfare is higher when the public enterprise plays passively. See Beato–Mas-Colell (1984).

passive public firm, however, does not expect private prices to respond to public ones:

$$\frac{\partial p_k^E}{\partial p_m} \neq 0 \quad \text{(active position)};$$

$$\frac{\partial p_m^E}{\partial p_k} = 0 \quad \text{(passive position)}; \qquad k \in K, m \in M. \tag{9}$$

Analytically, eqs. (4) and (6) result from this sort of Stackelberg-type behavior. Graphically point C in figure 25 is obtained, which is the profit maximum, given the public firm's adherence to eq. (6).

A somewhat different approach to the duopoly game assumes that the players behave so as to reach the *welfare-profit frontier*, where increasing welfare is only possible at the expense of decreasing profit and vice versa. (In figure 25 the welfare-profit frontier is represented by the contract curve $W\pi_m$.)

This situation can be seen as the equilibrium of an infinitely repeated game which is played by the private and the public enterprises. Such an equilibrium can be sustained e.g. by 'trigger strategies', i.e. history-dependent strategies that entail the punishment of behavior that induces a deviation from the contract curve. The punishment consists of setting Nash-prices (corresponding to point A in figure 25) in all future periods.[7] In practice, the selection of a given point on the welfare-profit frontier depends on the bargaining power of both firms. In a mixed duopoly there are good reasons to believe that most of the power lies in the hand of the public enterprise. Let us therefore assume that the public firm is able to restrain the profit of the private enterprise to a level π_m^o,

$$\pi_m = \sum_i p_i y_i^m \leq \pi_m^o; \qquad 0 < \underline{\pi}_m^o \leq \pi_m^o < \overline{\pi}_m^o, \tag{10}$$

where $\underline{\pi}_m^o$ is the threshold value of profit necessary for the private enterprise to stay in the market, and $\overline{\pi}_m^o$ is the pure monopoly profit.

Let us now turn to the prices which result if the public firm enforces a profit limitation of the private firm. The private firm is expected to maximize profits, given the constraint imposed by the public firm. The constraint can be regarded as binding for the optimization approach of the public enterprise. Hence we obtain

---

[7] This is an application of the Folk theorem. For a good explanation of this theorem in the context of repeated games with trigger strategies see Friedman (1986: 85–94).

$$\sum_{i \in M} \frac{\partial \pi_m}{\partial p_i} dp_i + \sum_{b \in K} \frac{\partial \pi_m}{\partial p_b} dp_b = 0. \tag{11}$$

If only one public price and one monopoly price change, we obtain a special case of (11):

$$\left. \frac{dp_m}{dp_k} \right|_{\pi_m^o} = \frac{\partial p_m^E}{\partial p_k} = -\frac{\partial \pi_m / \partial p_k}{\partial \pi_m / \partial p_m} (\pi_m^o). \tag{12}$$

The public enterprise, on the other hand, is not expected to respond to the private firm's price, as it takes the active position. Hence, in the case of (12), we have

$$\frac{\partial p_m^E}{\partial p_k} = -\frac{\partial \pi_m / \partial p_k}{\partial \pi_m / \partial p_m} (\pi_m^o) \qquad \text{(active position)};$$

$$\frac{\partial p_k^E}{\partial p_m} = 0 \qquad \text{(passive position)}; \qquad k \in K, m \in M. \tag{13}$$

Analytically we are once again back to solving conditions (2) and (7), but with the special specification of the private firm's price response due to its profit limitation.

The above approach precludes the usual objections to the idea that public enterprises adjust to private pricing because it accentuates the active position of the public enterprise and its ability and willingness to prevent exploitation of consumers by the private firm.

34.2 A Survey of Recent Papers on Mixed Markets[8]

34.2.1 Nash Versus Stackelberg Behavior

Typically, models on mixed markets deal with a duopoly consisting of one private and one public enterprise. The private firm maximizes profit, the public firm maximizes welfare. Both participants in the market are perfectly informed. Then the welfare properties of the various duopoly solutions are compared. If the public firm takes the Stackelberg leader position, welfare typically is improved over the Nash equilibrium (Vickers and Yarrow, 1988:

---

[8] With some changes in the text this section is taken from Bös (1991a: 72–8, 199–201), as is the first paragraph of this chapter. Newly written text are the presentations of the models of Corneo and Jeanne (1994), De Fraja and Delbono (1989), of Fershtman (1990) and Nett (1994a,b). – For another survey on the topic see Nett (1993) who also quotes further references.

51–2).[9] In special cases, however, the Stackelberg follower position can be welfare-superior to the leader position (Beato and MasColell, 1984). This is an interesting result, because it contradicts the usual second-best paradigm. The Stackelberg-follower position of a welfare-maximizing public firm implies marginal-cost pricing, although there is a market distortion caused by the private duopolist's profit maximization.

De Fraja and Delbono (1989) present an interesting special case where there are many private profit-maximizing firms and one welfare-maximizing public firm. All firms apply the same technology to produce a homogeneous good, imposing a positive fixed cost, increasing marginal costs and no capacity constraint. Figure 26 displays their results: social welfare as a function of the number of private firms n.[10]

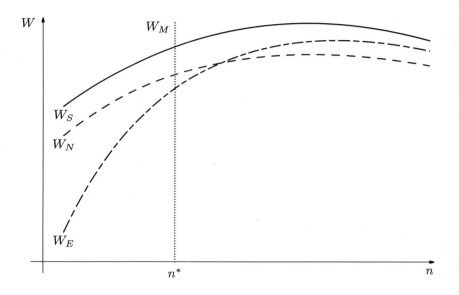

Figure 26
Source: De Fraja and Delbono (1989: 309)

The various curves refer to the following oligopoly settings:

- W_N – the public firm is a Nash player and maximizes welfare,
- W_S – the public firm is a Stackelberg leader and maximizes welfare,
- W_E – the public firm is a Nash player and maximizes profit,
- W_M – the whole industry is nationalized; produced quantities and number of private firms are chosen welfare-optimally.

The curves in figure 26 are inverted U's for the following reason: if the economy becomes more competitive (n increases), this reduces the distance between price and marginal costs of the various firms and thus enhances welfare. However, if n exceeds some threshold, a further increase in the number of firms has a negative effect on welfare due to the presence of fixed costs. De Fraja and Delbono's most striking result is $W_E > W_N$ if n is high enough. This result can be interpreted as follows. Assume that the public firm cannot obtain the welfare-desirable Stackelberg leader position. If in this case the market is competitive enough, then higher welfare is attained if the public firm maximizes profit instead of welfare. The public firm produces less than it would have under its welfare objective, but induces a welfare-enhancing expansion in the output of the private firms.

34.2.2 Mixed Markets and Differences in Costs

Consider an economy with n firms producing a homogeneous good. m of the n firms are publicly owned and choose welfare-maximizing break-even quantities. The other firms are privately owned and maximize profit. The analysis is restricted to Cournot–Nash equilibria. If the cost functions were identical, the welfare maximum would be attained in an economy with public firms only.[11]

In a recent paper, however, Cremer, Marchand, and Thisse (1989)[12] introduce an asymmetry in the cost functions: in public firms the employees are paid a premium over the market wages prevailing in the private firms.[13] Starting point of their analysis is an economy comprised exclusively of pri-

---

[11] As, for instance, in Merrill and Schneider (1966: 409–10).

[12] See also De Fraja (1991).

[13] Some critics feel uneasy about the authors' treatment of the wage premium. This premium does not enter the consumer surplus which the firm wants to maximize. However, it is taken into account in the break-even constraints of the individual public firms. This specification implies that the wage premium is treated as a pure transfer. The public firm has an objective function which consists of the sum of consumer and producer surplus where, at the optimum, the producer surplus including the wage premium is equal to zero. Hence, in writing down the objective function, the producer surplus including the wage premium can be omitted and only consumer surplus is maximized. Obviously, the optimal quantities depend on the wage premium.

vate firms. The authors investigate how many firms should be transferred into public ownership to achieve a welfare maximum. It is welfare-improving to nationalize one firm: the behavior of the public firm leads to higher aggregate output which is sold at a lower market price. Now consider the nationalization of further enterprises. At the non-cooperative solution of the game the nationalized firms behave as if they were cooperating; i.e., they behave like one institution. Hence it is welfare-superior to have only one public break-even firm rather than two or more, because each public firm has to finance the same amount of sunk costs. Therefore it is welfare-optimal to nationalize only one firm.

In Cremer, Marchand, and Thisse, higher public-sector pay is exogenously introduced by assuming a premium over the market wages prevailing in private firms. However, the theory of mixed markets can also be used for an endogenous explanation of higher public-sector pay. De Fraja (1993b) deals with a two-stage game: in the first stage a public and a private enterprise simultaneously and independently bargain with a trade union to determine wages. The public firm maximizes welfare, the private firm maximizes profits. The bargaining solution is of the Nash type. In the second stage the two firms are engaged in non-cooperative Cournot competition on the output market. The outcome of the second stage is perfectly anticipated in the first stage. As a result of the two-stage game, the public firm chooses higher wages.[14]

The public-wage premium is due to asymmetric firm responses to wage increases of the other duopolist. Higher wages always imply a higher market price and, hence, a lower overall quantity sold. However, an increase in private wages leads to a significantly higher level of output by the welfare-maximizing public firm and, in turn, to a significant reduction of the residual demand left for the private firm. An increase in public wages, on the other hand, implies much less increase in output by the profit-maximizing private firm and, consequently, has less influence on the residual demand left for the public firm. Therefore, the public firm loses relatively less by wage increases. This is then exploited by the trade union in wage negotiations.

Multistage games can also be used to endogenously explain the choice of technology by private and public firms. Nett (1994b) considers a profit-maximizing private firm and an output-maximizing public enterprise. Both are given the option to invest in R&D which requires a certain amount of fixed costs but allows output to be produced at lower variable costs. If a mixed duopoly comes into being, the private firm has an incentive to invest more in R&D, that is, to operate at lower variable but higher fixed costs than the public firm.

---

[14] This is the outcome of De Fraja's simulation analyses except for extreme values of the relevant parameters where the private wage may be higher.

34.2.3 Market Entry

As already mentioned, market entry is one of the ways mixed markets may come into being. In Western economies it is typically a private firm which enters into the market of a public enterprise. A particularly well-known model of this problem is Ware's (1986) two-stage game. There is one public incumbent and one potential entrant. In stage one of the game the incumbent chooses his capacity, i.e. the maximum quantity he can produce in the second stage of the game. This is the strategic advantage of the incumbent: in stage two his capacity costs are sunk costs, whereas an entrant must commit new capacity prior to entry.

At the beginning of stage two the potential entrant faces the decision of whether or not to enter the market. If he enters, incumbent and entrant play Cournot–Nash, where the Cournot–Nash solution depends on the capacity chosen by the incumbent, because it is this capacity which determines the incumbent's reaction function. Hence, depending on the capacity of the incumbent, the potential entrant may enter or stay out of the market. By choosing a high capacity in stage one, the incumbent can reduce the entrant's profits. There may even exist investment policies which totally deter entry.

Consider a 'natural monopoly' situation. According to Ware, a monopoly is natural if supply by one firm leads to maximal welfare. This is not the usual definition of a natural monopoly because it explicitly takes account of both cost- and demand-side properties of the market. In the one-input, one-output case, subadditive costs are a sufficient but not a necessary condition to have a natural monopoly in Ware's sense. Hence his definition is less stringent than the one which is usually found, for instance in Sharkey (1982). In a 'natural monopoly' situation, according to Ware, a public incumbent always deters private entry by offering the welfare-maximizing output.

Now assume a U-shaped average cost function and consider an increase in demand. At some point it becomes welfare-optimal to have the relevant good supplied by two firms and we have a 'natural duopoly'. However, given Ware's specifications, at that point an entrant would accrue a deficit, hence no private firm would enter, although supply by two firms would be welfare-optimal. The market is stuck in an 'unnatural monopoly'. The welfare orientation of the public firm makes market entry unprofitable for the private firm, because too high a capacity is chosen and too high a quantity is supplied by the incumbent. The point of an 'unnatural monopoly' seems interesting. However, if it is welfare-optimal to have two firms, why doesn't the government simply establish a second public firm in the case of an 'unnatural monopoly'? Why does it wait for a private entrant?

Moreover, privatization of the incumbent firm could be seen as a way to induce an efficient two-firm market structure and to escape from the 'unnatural monopoly'. However, Ware (1986: 651–2) argues that the welfare-oriented public firm will have chosen such a high capacity in stage one of the game that privatization at the end of stage one comes too late. Given the capacity inherited from the public firm, the privatized firm still produces too much and therefore entry is unprofitable. An interesting feature of Ware's model is the accentuation of how much privatized firms can be affected by their public past. Unfortunately, however, Ware's proposition on privatization is based on a solution which is not subgame-perfect. The public firm starts with a capacity which is built up under the assumption of the firm's remaining public. Then, unexpectedly, privatization occurs at the beginning of stage two and the privatized firm makes the best of the given capacity. Ware's proposition may break down if the public firm correctly anticipates its being privatized at the beginning of stage two and sets capacity so as to guarantee maximum welfare (i.e. entry) in stage two.

Ware's public incumbent does not face a budget constraint. Hence capacity installment which induces sunk costs in stage two (the market game), does not reduce the flexibility of the public firm. If, however, a budget constraint is explicitly considered, the public incumbent's capacity choice restricts the firm in pursuing its objectives, as shown in Nett (1994a). The public firm, in his model, aims at maximizing output. Hence in the first stage of the game it has to install a high capacity which allows high output in the second stage. However, given the zero-deficit budget constraint, higher investment costs imply less flexibility of the firm. This is exploited by the private firm which wants to enter into the market. Hence, contrary to Ware's case, it is a disadvantage of the public firm that it has to precommit its capacity in stage one of the game.

34.2.4 *Regulated Firms in Oligopolistic Markets*

In this subsection we deal with oligopolistic markets where one participant is a regulated public utility. The other firms in the market are private and unregulated.

Let us first deal with a duopoly where a private firm competes with a firm in mixed public-private ownership. For this purpose consider a public utility where the government holds Θ percent of the shares. The government, therefore, places its own representatives on the firm's board of directors. We assume that these representatives have been instructed to promote the government's welfare interests. Hence, at the board of the firm, some compromise must be found to balance profit and welfare interests. Since the government still keeps its hold on the firm, we consider this firm as 'regulated'; one could speak of 'internal regulation' because the welfare interests are pushed through from within the firm. We index this 'partly nationalized firm' as firm 1 and its (potential) private competitor as firm 2. Fershtman (1990) deals with quantity competition à la Cournot–Nash between firms 1 and 2 and also treats the problem of market entry if firm 1 is the incumbent. This firm compromises between profit and welfare by choosing the following reaction function

$$z_1 = \Theta z_1^W(z_2) + (1 - \Theta)z_1^\Pi(z_2), \tag{14}$$

where $z_i, i = 1, 2$, are the quantities of a homogeneous good and $z_1^W(\cdot)$ and $z_1^\Pi(\cdot)$ are the reaction functions which would result if firm 1 were a pure welfare maximizer or a pure profit maximizer, respectively.[15] The author reaches the following main results:

(i) Fershtman shows that at the Cournot–Nash equilibrium the partly nationalized firm 1 earns the higher profit and the private firm 2's profit is below the regular Cournot profit which would have accrued if firm 1 had also maximized profit. This is in contrast to the usual economic convention that nationalization reduces profit, whence the partly nationalized firm should earn less than a private profit maximizer.

(ii) Potential market entry will be influenced by the ownership of the incumbent, since the profitability of market entry depends on firm 1's reaction function. A potential entrant prefers to enter a market with a profit-maximizing incumbent than with a partly nationalized one because his profit will be higher in the first case, as mentioned in point (i) above. It is possible that a partly nationalized firm does not have to deviate from its behavior as a monopolist in order to deter entry,[16] whereas a profit-maximizing incumbent would have to.

Let us next turn to a duopoly where a private profit maximizer competes with a profit-maximizing utility which is regulated with respect to its prices, for instance by price-cap regulation. This is a very common situation if the government privatizes a utility and wants to protect the consumers by promoting market entry *and* regulating the prices. A good example is British Telecom which faces competition from Mercury *and* is subject to $RPI - X$ regulation. There is a trade-off in the government's instruments: the lower prices of the privatized firm make market entry less profitable, so the regulated firm must be allowed high enough profits to attract market entrants. There is not much special literature on entry into regulated markets;[17] Bös–Nett (1990) is one of the few contributions. In this paper the authors deal with a privatized firm facing potential market entry. The firm has inherited

---

[15] For a similar way to model compromises between profit and welfare see Bös (1988) and Bös (1991a: 135–48, 252–60).

[16] Fershtman (1990: 324) calls this a natural monopoly.

[17] The problem is briefly addressed in Cave and Trotter (1990: 74–82).

excess capacity from its public past. Hence, in contrast to all other market entry models, the incumbent will not build up capacity, but rather will reduce it. Consequently, we have a game with asymmetric costs. The incumbent has zero capacity installation costs since we assume that capacity reduction is costless. The entrant, on the other hand, must install new capacity and, therefore, incurs positive capacity installation costs.

In the subgame-perfect equilibria of a four-stage game, the incumbent and the entrant decide first on capacities and subsequently on prices. In both cases the incumbent moves first. The authors are particularly interested in the influence on entry of price regulation of the incumbent. As a first step in such an analysis they consider the pure market entry game in the absence of a price constraint. The results of this game are different for high, medium, and low capacity costs of the entrant. In the case in which the entrant faces high capacity costs the incumbent is able to deter market entry. In cases in which the entrant faces medium and low capacity costs, market entry always occurs because a high-capacity incumbent faces an entrant who is able to set a capacity which induces the incumbent to set a higher price than the entrant. Consequently, the entrant enjoys a positive profit and the incumbent faces a lower profit the higher his capacity.

There is no other recent paper in which these results have been derived. Kreps and Scheinkman (1983) implicitly proposed that there is almost no difference between the results of the classical Cournot-duopoly model and their two-stage game, where in the first stage two identical firms simultaneously build up their capacities, whereas in the second stage both firms simultaneously set prices. By contrast, in Bös–Nett (1990) the incumbent has a first-mover advantage. Therefore, one would expect that the outcome of our model should be equivalent to the outcome of the classical Stackelberg-duopoly model. However, this is not always the case. For medium and low capacity costs of the entrant, the results of the Bös–Nett model differ from those of a Stackelberg duopoly with the incumbent as the leading firm. This is an important result for the theoretical literature on entry in duopolistic markets.

In a second main part of their paper, Bös–Nett (1990) impose a price constraint on the incumbent. As a consequence the incumbent chooses higher capacity and output the lower the binding price. Market entry can be prevented by the regulator even in the case of low and medium capacity costs if the incumbent has to choose a regulated price which is lower than the entrant's capacity costs per unit. Two special results of the game with price regulation deserve attention.

(i) If the price constraint is binding and market entry occurs, the entrant sells at a higher price than the incumbent. This is an empirically realistic result which cannot be derived from Cournot- or Bertrand-duopoly models on market entry.

(ii) A binding price constraint does not necessarily lead to an increase in capacity and output. In the case of low and medium capacity costs the authors observed particular intervals of prices where a tighter price constraint only induces a lower price of the incumbent, while leaving the supply unchanged. This 'capacity trap' does not occur in any other model on price regulation.

Another interesting contribution to the topic is due to Estrin and de Meza (1988). They deal with an incumbent who is regulated so as to choose average-cost pricing and an entrant who wants to maximize profits. In the first stage the incumbent monopoly produces a single good under increasing returns to scale. At the beginning of the second stage the other firm enters if entry is profitable. If entry occurs, in the second stage the duopoly game is one of either Bertrand or Cournot competition. The entrant produces a single good which may be a close or a distant substitute[18] for the incumbent's good. The entrant's costs may be higher or lower than those of the incumbent. Both players are fully informed about each other's demand and cost functions and about the strategies to be chosen.

Let us first deal with the authors' results in the case of *Cournot competition*. When both firms sell an identical good and there are economies of scale throughout, entry will not occur if the incumbent is at least as efficient as any potential entrant. Moreover, the authors show that entry typically leaves the consumer worse off. The only exception is a case where the incumbent is expelled from the market and the entrant 'has a truly enormous cost advantage' (Estrin and de Meza, 1988: 72). Simulation analyses for linear demand functions and quadratic cost functions are performed by the authors to evaluate more complicated settings. The quantitative results show that entry is more likely to occur if the firms compete with distant substitutes and if the entrant has considerable cost advantages.

Since *Bertrand competition* is more aggressive, in many cases the incumbent does not survive. The gist of the simulations seems to be as follows: while there are some cases of profitable entry which are socially undesirable, on the whole profitability and increases in social welfare go hand in hand. The reason is that cost advantages for the entrant have to be huge to allow entry, while product differentiation is a new positive feature of successful entry. The latter tends to raise welfare, measured by consumer surplus, as well as to dissipate scale economies.

---

[18] The authors define a substitute to be distant if, for a demand function $p_i = \alpha - \beta z_i + \gamma z_e$, the absolute value of β is significantly different from γ. In the demand function the index i denotes the incumbent, the index e refers to the entrant.

There are many more possible cases of regulated oligopolistic markets, depending on the various types of regulation. Telecommunications or electricity distribution firms may be obliged to connect other licensed firms to their public network or grid. Privatized railway companies may be obliged to allow the common use of tracks and signalling facilities. Many further case studies will be necessary to understand strategic behavior in such regulated oligopolistic markets.

34.2.5   International Mixed Markets

There are many situations in which public firms operating in a mixed market face the possibility of international competition. The country where the firm is located may import the good or service offered by the public firm, and the public firm itself may be willing to export a part of its production. An interesting special case is that of a common market where public and private firms of different countries compete with each other in the absence of trade barriers. The deregulation of an industry where national markets were previously segmented may lead to market structures of this type. Conversely, an international mixed market may be the outcome of the disintegration of a centralized economy, in which local public bodies take hold of local utilities.

Mixed markets may work in a different way when they are plunged into an international setting. When a proportion of consumers and producers is constituted by foreigners, social welfare may cease to be the objective of the public firm since this is a *national* entity. Rather, the welfare of nationals only may be maximized. This raises the question of how public firms compete with foreign private and public firms, and to what extent regulation through competition is still feasible.

Corneo–Jeanne (1994) offer an interesting analysis of this type of situation. They study a mixed oligopoly in a common market for a homogeneous good. There are n countries and each of them may have any number of firms, one of which is possibly a public enterprise. Private firms maximize their profits whereas public firms maximize national surplus. All firms have access to the same technology and face identical constant marginal costs. Cournot–Nash competition occurs.

When an industry exhibits constant returns to scale, it is well known that in the Cournot–Nash equilibrium of a mixed market only the public firm produces in such a way that the price equals the marginal cost. As shown by Corneo–Jeanne (1994), this simple result vanishes in a common market, where it turns out that public firms limit their production so as to keep the price above the marginal cost. Instead, the behavior of public firms can be expressed uniquely in terms of an *export* target. More precisely, the optimal rule for public firms is the following: choose a production plan such that the country's exports amount to what is produced by an individual private firm.

To get the intuition, consider what happens when the public firm produces one extra unit of the good. First, national producers sell more at the given price, which increases national producer surplus. Second, the price level decreases, with an ambiguous impact on national surplus: it is negative for the producers but positive for the consumers. For units sold to domestic consumers, these two effects cancel out. Thus the net price effect is to decrease national producer surplus on exported units. If the country's external trade is balanced, the total effect reduces to the quantity effect, which induces the public firm to raise its production. When the country is exporting, the price effect only applies to profits on exported units. Hence, the optimal quantity of exports is equal to the production of a private, profit-maximizing, firm. Provided that at least one country has no public firm, the price level is strictly higher than the marginal cost and the social welfare in the common market is lower than in the first best.

Further interesting results in Corneo–Jeanne (1994) concern the welfare effects of privatization, nationalization, and creation of a public firm. These effects are shown to depend crucially on the pattern of international trade in the common market. Their most striking finding is that the interests of exporting countries run counter to the collective interest: an exporting country is always hurt by policies in other countries that increase social welfare for the common market as a whole. In fact, a policy that leads to an increase of social welfare involves a price decrease and some adjustment in national productions. The net price effect is to decrease the national surplus of each exporting country (its firms lose more in terms of profits than its consumers gain in terms of surplus). Furthermore, national production, be it private or public, is adjusted downwards, which also tends to decrease the national surplus of exporting countries.

These results suggest that the regulatory role of public firms in imperfectly competitive markets is preserved when the economy is open; however, optimal behavior is characterized by very different rules, and the normative implications of privatization or market entry can be more subtle than in a closed economy. Extending the analysis of mixed international markets to the case where cost functions differ across countries and to the case of international cross-ownership of firms may provide further valuable insights on this important topic.

Appendix 1   The Size of the Public Enterprise Sector in Europe

Table A1

Employment, gross value added and gross fixed-capital formation of public enterprises[1] in European economies, excluding the agricultural sector (1991)

Country	Employees thousands	Employees %	Value added %	GFCF %
France	1783	13.4	15.1	24.2
Germany (FRG)[2]	1687	8.3	10.0	14.9
Italy	1485	13.5	20.0	23.5
Great Britain	747	4.3	4.0	5.0
Spain	407	6.0	8.0	12.8
Portugal	216	10.6	21.5	30.0
Belgium	200	9.8	7.5	8.4
Netherlands	157	5.1	8.0	9.2
Greece	179	14.7	17.0	30.0
Denmark	115	8.2	8.7	17.6
Ireland	67	8.7	11.5	16.9
Luxembourg	5	3.2	5.2	4.6
Size of the public enterprise sector in the European economy, excluding the agricultural sector[3]	7048	8.9	10.9	15.6

Source: A. Bizaguet, *L'evolution de l'impact economique des entreprises a participation publique dans l'Europe des douze depuis 1988*, presented at the 1994-CEEP congress in Seville.

---

[1] According to a recent accounting convention of EUROSTAT, the public enterprise sector includes not only firms in full or partial ($\geq$ 50%) public ownership, but also firms where the government exerts a 'determining influence on the firm's general policy'.

[2] Provisional estimations, excluding the former German Democratic Republic (GDR).

[3] Excluding the former German Democratic Republic (GDR).

Table A1 (continued)

Average of three criteria (employment, gross value added, gross fixed-capital formation), 1982–1991

Country	1991 %	1988 %	1985 %	1982 %
France	17.6	18.3	24.0	22.8
Germany (FRG)[2]	11.1	11.6	12.4	14.0
Italy	19.0	19.6	20.3	20.0
Great Britain	4.5	7.4	12.7	16.2
Spain	9.0	10.0	12.0	12.0
Portugal	20.7	24.0	22.7	23.9
Belgium	8.6	10.3	11.1	12.1
Netherlands	7.5	9.6	9.0	9.0
Greece	20.6	20.8	23.2	22.3
Denmark	11.5	11.9	11.4	12.0
Ireland	12.4	14.4	15.3	15.1
Luxembourg	4.4	4.9	4.5	5.0
Size of the public enterprise sector in the European economy, excluding the agricultural sector[3]	11.8	13.3	15.3	16.4

Source: A. Bizaguet, *loc.cit.*

---

[2] Provisional estimations, excluding the former German Democratic Republic (GDR).
[3] Excluding the former German Democratic Republic (GDR).

Appendices

Table A2

Sectoral employment of public enterprises in the European economy, excluding the agricultural sector[1] (thousands of employees and percent of sector; 1991)

	Energy		Industry		Transport and Telecom.	
	Employ-ment	% of sector	Employ-ment	% of sector	Employ-ment	% of sector
France	202	88.0	465	11.1	783	58.8
Germany (FRG)[2]	290	63.0	120	1.1	930	60.0
Italy	172	89.0	312	10.0	705	82.5
Great Britain	103	23.5	8	0.2	262	34.0
Spain	61	45.0	79	3.0	228	50.0
Portugal	26	36.9	40	3.0	92	41.0
Belgium	10	27.3	5	0.5	160	64.3
Netherlands	2	3.5	–	–	154	42.2
Greece	35	90.0	6	1.3	76	37.8
Denmark	18	90.0	3	0.6	89	53.6
Ireland	14	68.0	3	1.1	46	52.0
Luxembourg	–	–	–	–	3	32.8
Public Enterprise Sector of the 12[3]	933	55.0	1041	3.4	3728	58.0

Source: A. Bizaguet, *L'evolution de l'impact economique des entreprises a participation publique dans l'Europe des douze depuis 1988*, presented at the 1994-CEEP congress in Seville.

---

[1] For the definition of the public enterprise sector see footnote 1 of Table A1.
[2] Provisional estimations, excluding the former German Democratic Republic.
[3] Excluding the former German Democratic Republic.

Table A2 (continued)

Sectoral employment of public enterprises in the European economy, excluding the agricultural sector[1] (thousands of employees and percent of sector; 1991)

	Financial Sector		Other Services and Trade		Total of National Public Sectors
	Employ-ment	% of sector	Employ-ment	% of sector	Employ-ment
France	193	32.0	140	2.4	1783
Germany (FRG)[2]	279	30.0	68	2.0	1687
Italy	249	50.0	48	2.0	1485
Great Britain	13	1.0	161	3.0	747
Spain	20	6.0	19	1.2	407
Portugal	49	65.3	8	0.8	216
Belgium	24	7.4	1	0.3	200
Netherlands	1	0.1	–	–	157
Greece	40	60.0	22	4.0	179
Denmark	–	–	6	1.0	115
Ireland	4	5.0	–	–	67
Luxembourg	2	9.3	–	–	5
Public Enterprise Sector of the 12[3]	874	20.0	473	1–2	7048

Source: A. Bizaguet, *loc.cit.*

[1] For the definition of the public enterprise sector see footnote 1 of Table A1.
[2] Provisional estimations, excluding the former German Democratic Republic.
[3] Excluding the former German Democratic Republic.

Appendix 2   The Size of the Government and Regulated Enterprise Sector in the United States[1]

Table A3

Government and Regulated Enterprises' Share of US GDP

	Government enterprises %	Transportation %	Communication %	Public utilities (electricity, gas, sanitary services) %	Finance and insurance[2] %	GDP (billion $ [3])
1982	1.34	3.46	2.81	3.01	4.76	3149.6
1983	1.35	3.48	2.89	3.22	5.29	3405.0
1984	1.37	3.49	2.77	3.24	5.07	3777.2
1985	1.44	3.37	2.79	3.20	5.50	4038.7
1986	1.46	3.32	2.81	3.09	6.06	4268.6
1987	1.47	3.36	2.81	3.07	6.39	4539.9
1988	1.49	3.34	2.76	2.97	6.09	4900.4
1989	1.50	3.22	2.66	2.94	6.04	5250.8
1990	1.51	3.19	2.65	2.84	6.14	5546.1
1991	1.60	3.16	2.71	2.98	6.61	5722.9

Source: Survey of current business, November 1993

---

[1] The following tables are based on the U.S. Department of Commerce's monthly survey of current business. Whereas the definition of a *government enterprise* is straightforward, the delimitation of the *regulated sector* is much more complicated. There are no comprehensive data sources which give separate information for US regulated and non-regulated industries. Hence we have selected figures for US sectors where the most intensive regulation takes place. However, it should be kept in mind that recent deregulation activities make any delimitation based on these data a little superficial.

[2] Excluding real estate.

[3] In current prices.

Table A4

Full-Time Equivalent Employees in US Government and Regulated Enterprises

	Govern-ment enter-prises	Transpor-tation	Communi-cation	Public utilities (electricity, gas, sanitary services)	Finance and insurance[1]	Total full-time equivalent employees
	%	%	%	%	%	(millions)
1982	1.79	3.11	1.57	0.99	4.99	84.8
1983	1.79	3.06	1.52	0.99	5.08	85.2
1984	1.77	3.08	1.36	0.96	4.96	91.2
1985	1.76	3.08	1.30	0.95	5.00	93.7
1986	1.76	3.08	1.25	0.94	5.16	95.4
1987	1.75	3.11	1.21	0.92	5.23	98.1
1988	1.68	3.15	1.16	0.90	5.12	101.6
1989	1.67	3.16	1.13	0.88	5.03	103.6
1990	1.67	3.18	1.15	0.89	5.02	105.0
1991	1.67	3.19	1.15	0.91	5.04	103.5
1992	1.66	3.19	1.12	0.91	4.98	103.6

Source: Survey of current business, July 1984, July 1988, July 1992, August 1993

---

[1] Excluding real estate.

Table A5

Expenditures for New Plant and Equipment by US Regulated[1] Enterprises

	Transportation	Public utilities (electricity, gas, sanitary services)	All Industries[2]
	%	%	(billion $ [3])
1982	4.23	14.84	282.71
1983	4.16	15.57	269.22
1984	4.66	13.39	354.44
1985	4.65	12.61	387.13
1986	4.96	12.22	379.47
1987	4.84	11.52	389.67
1988	3.65	13.25	455.49
1989	3.71	13.06	507.40
1990	4.03	12.62	532.61
1991	4.29	12.60	528.39
1992	4.14	13.21	546.60
1993	3.83	12.83	584.64
1994	3.39	13.21	616.50[4]

Source: Federal Reserve Bulletin, December 1984, 1986, 1988, 1990, 1992, March 1994

---

[1] The above source does not contain figures of government enterprises. Figures on 'transportation' and on 'finance and insurance' are not explicitly reported in the above source, but are contained in 'all industries'. Unfortunately, there is no recent printed report on new plant and equipment in the 'Survey of Current Business' although this survey is quoted as the primary source of the data published in the 'Federal Reserve Bulletin'!

[2] The row labelled 'All industries' in the primary source 'Survey of Current Business' is erroneously labelled 'Total nonfarm business' in the current source.

[3] In current dollars.

[4] Figures are amounts anticipated by business.

List of Symbols

a	index of commodities
b	index of commodities
c	marginal costs (with respect to quantity as defined in section 3.3: $c_i := (\partial g/\partial z_i)/(\partial g/\partial z_o)$; with respect to quality as defined in section 16.2: $c_{qk} := (\partial g/\partial q_k)/(\partial g/\partial z_o)$)
cs	individual consumer surplus
$d + 1$	number of inputs of public or regulated firm $(i = o, \ldots, d$ in chapters 4, 6, 18–22, 27, 30)
e	effort
f	function, in particular density function
g	production function (public firm $g(\cdot)$; private firms $g^j(\cdot)$)
h	index of consumers $(h = 1, \ldots, H)$
i	index of commodities $(i = o, \ldots, n)$
j	index of private producers $(j = 1, \ldots, J)$
k	index of regulated prices and qualities $(k \in K)$
ℓ	labor input $(\ell := -z_o)$
m	– index of private monopoly prices
	– index of minimal supply (chapter 15)
$n + 1$	number of commodities $(i = o, \ldots, n)$
p	price
q	quality
r	lump-sum (non-labor) income
s	– factor of proportional variation of different variables
	– political sympathy variable (chapter 17)
t	– index of time
	– price-marginal cost difference $(t_i := p_i - c_i$, chapter 8)
	– compensation of the agent (chapters 28–32)

u	direct individual utility function
v	indirect individual utility function
w	weights which add up to unity, for instance the weights in 10.2
$\overline{w}$	reservation wage (chapter 12)
x	consumer net demand (if positive), consumer net supply (if negative)
y	net output of private producers (if positive), net input of private producers (if negative)
z	net output of the public or regulated enterprise (if positive), net input of the public enterprise (if negative)
z^+	output of the public or regulated enterprise ($z^+ > 0$)
z^-	input of the public or regulated enterprise ($z^- < 0$)
A	– set of privately provided intermediate goods (chapter 11)
	– set of energy-producing private firms (chapter 20)
B	– set of publicly provided consumption goods (chapter 11)
	– basic fee (chapter 32)
C	cost function
CS	aggregate consumer surplus
D	$D^o := \Sigma^n_{i=d+1} p^o_i x^o_i$ (chapter 27)
DV	dummy variable (chapters 5, 6)
E	– excess demand (chapter 15)
	– effort-requirement function (chapters 28–31)
F	Feldstein's distributional characteristic (defined in subsection 3.3.1: $F_k := \Sigma_h \lambda^h (\partial v^h/\partial r^h)(x^h_k/x_k)$)
$F_k(\tau)$	distribution function of time-dependent demand (chapter 15)
G	– production possibility frontier (chapter 2)
	– cost function (chapter 23)
H	number of consumers ($h = 1,\ldots,H$)
I	– set of all commodities, $I = \{o,\ldots,n\}$
	– indifference curve

	$- I^{t-1} := \Sigma_i p_i^{t-1} x_i^{t-1}$ (chapter 27)
J	number of private producers $(j = 1, \ldots, J)$
K	set of regulated prices (resp. qualities), $K \subset I$
L	$-$ monopoly welfare loss (chapter 2)
	$-$ total employment (chapter 12)
	$-$ length of period (chapter 15)
	$-$ weights (chapter 18: minimization of a Laspeyres price index)
LS	lump-sum charge (Loeb–Magat mechanism, chapter 24)
M	$-$ set of privately provided consumption goods (chapter 11)
	$-$ set of prices, fixed by the private firm (chapter 34)
MRS	marginal rate of substitution
MRT	marginal rate of transformation
N	number of coalitions (subsection 8.1.4)
P	$-$ price index (chapter 27)
	$- P^o := \Sigma_{k \in K} p_k^o x_k^o$ (chapter 27)
POL	political weights (chapter 17)
Q	quality characteristic (defined in subsection 16.3.2: $Q_k := \Sigma_h \lambda^h (\partial v^h / \partial r^h)(\partial R^h / \partial q_k))$
R	$-$ expenditure function
	$-$ cost-saving expenditures (chapter 24)
RAC	ray-average costs (chapter 24)
RAP	set of regulatory adjusting prices (chapters 25, 27)
RPI	retail price index
S	$-$ substitution effect
	$-$ quantity sold at any point of time (chapter 15)
T	$-$ index which indicates transposed vectors or matrices
	$-$ index of time
TV	traffic volume (chapter 13)
U	$-$ individual utility function
	$-$ union's utility function (chapters 21, 33)

V	individual utility function
W	welfare function (defined in section 2.1)
X	in $RPI - X$: percentage to be deducted (chapter 27)
Y	individual income (subsection 2.4.2)
Z	term in incentive-compatibility conditions (chapter 30)

$\mathcal{A}$	locus where ray-average costs are minimal (chapter 24)
$\mathcal{B}$	budget (chapter 19)
$\mathcal{C}$	cost function (chapter 33)
$\mathcal{D}$	distance function (chapters 28–32)
$\mathcal{E}$	expectation operator (chapter 33)
$\mathcal{F}$	Lagrangean function
$\mathcal{G}$	parameters of incentive pay (chapter 33)
$\mathcal{H}$	superelasticity (chapters 8, 29–31)
$\mathcal{I}$	incentive-correction term (chapters 28–32)
$\mathcal{J}$	term in the $RPI - X$ constraint (chapter 27)
$\mathcal{K}$	capacity (chapter 13)
$\mathcal{L}$	Lerner index, $\mathcal{L}_i := (p_i - c_i)/p_i$
$\mathcal{M}$	number of regulated prices ($k = 1, \ldots, \mathcal{M}$) (chapters 8, 24)
$\mathcal{N}$	net revenue (chapters 28, 33)
$\mathcal{O}$	social opportunity cost rate
$\mathcal{PR}$	social time preference rate
$\mathcal{PS}$	price schedule (chapter 32)
$\mathcal{Q}$	pure state constraint (chapter 32)
$\mathcal{R}$	Ramsey index
$\mathcal{S}$	subsidy
$\mathcal{T}$	transfer (chapters 24, 28)
$\mathcal{W}$	welfare function (chapter 33)
$\mathcal{X}$	characteristic of consumed quantities (chapters 16, 30)

α	Lagrangean parameters (market-clearing conditions)
β	– Lagrangean parameter (public or regulated enterprise's technology)
	– $\beta_o := \beta(\partial g/\partial z_o)$
γ	Lagrangean parameter (budget constraint)
Γ	rationing function (chapter 15)
δ	– weights (chapters 19, 21)
	– Lagrangean multiplier (chapters 15, 32)
	– parameter of managerial income schedule (chapter 33)
Δ	– difference
	– finite changes of variables
ε	non-compensated price elasticity of demand
ζ	netput of public enterprise or public utility (chapter 23)
η	compensated price elasticity of demand
θ	private-information parameter in principal-agent models (chapters 28–33)
Θ	degree of privatization (in case of partial privatization)
κ	capital input
λ	social valuation of individual utility (defined in section 3.3: $\lambda^h := (\partial W/\partial v^h)/\beta(\partial g/\partial z_o)$)
Λ	– distribution of incomes r^h (chapter 17)
	– social valuation of individual utility (defined in subsection 2.1.2: $\Lambda^h := \partial W/\partial v^h$)
μ	– voter's decision function (chapter 17)
	– Lagrangean parameter (chapters 29–32)
	– measure (chapter 23)
ν	– shadow price of quality (section 16.2)
	– $\nu := \mu - \phi$ (chapter 32)
ξ	consumer demand (chapter 32)
π	private (unregulated) firm's profit

Π	revenue-cost constraint
ρ	rate of return
ϱ	vectors of price changes (dp_k) (chapter 5)
σ	variance of the political sympathy variable s^h (chapter 17)
Σ	sum of variables
τ	time-dependent demand (chapter 15)
φ	marketing influence on demand (chapter 30)
ϕ	Lagrangean parameter (chapters 29, 32, 33)
Φ	objective function, positive theory
χ	vectors in Farkas' and Motzkin's theorem (chapter 5)
ψ	effort disutility function (chapters 28–31)
Ψ	set of all moments of excess demand (chapter 15)
ω	individual voter's utility difference (chapter 17)
Ω	transformed variable $\Omega^h := \omega^h + s^h$ (chapter 17)

References

Aharoni, Y. (1986): *The Evolution and Management of State-Owned Enterprises*. Cambridge, Mass.: Ballinger.

Armstrong, M. (1993), 'Regulating a Multiproduct Firm with Unknown Costs', Economic Theory Discussion Papers, University of Cambridge, UK.

Armstrong, M., Rees, R., and Vickers, J. (1991), 'Optimal Regulatory Lag under Price Cap Regulation', mimeo: Nuffield College, Oxford.

Arrow, K.J. (1962), 'Economic Welfare and the Allocation of Resources for Invention', in National Bureau of Economic Research, *The Rate and Direction of Inventive Activity*. Princeton: Princeton University Press.

Atkinson, A.B., and Stiglitz, J.E. (1980), *Lectures on Public Economics*. Maidenhead: McGraw-Hill.

Attali, J. (1978), 'Towards Socialist Planning', in S. Holland (ed.), *Beyond Capitalist Planning*. Oxford: Basil Blackwell, 34–46.

Auerbach, A.J., and Pellechio, A.J. (1978), 'The Two-Part Tariff and Voluntary Market Participation', *Quarterly Journal of Economics* 92: 571–87.

Aumann, R.J., and Shapley, L.S. (1974), *Values of Non-Atomic Games*. Princeton, N.J.: Princeton University Press.

Averch, H., and Johnson, L.L. (1962), 'Behavior of the Firm Under Regulatory Constraint', *American Economic Review* 52: 1052–69.

Báger, G. (1993), 'Privatization in Hungary', in V.V. Ramanadham (ed.), *Constraints and Impacts of Privatization*. London and New York: Routledge, 93–101.

Bailey, E.E. (1973), *Economic Theory of Regulatory Constraint*. Lexington, MA: Heath.

Bailey, E.E. (1974), 'Innovation and Regulation', *Journal of Public Economics* 3: 285–95.

Bailey, E.E. (1976), 'Innovation and Regulation: A Reply', *Journal of Public Economics* 5: 393–4.

Bailey, E.E., and Malone, J.C. (1970), 'Resource Allocation and the Regulated Firm', *Bell Journal of Economics and Management Science* 1: 129–42.

Baron, D.P., and De Bondt, R.R. (1979), 'Fuel Adjustment Mechanisms and Economic Efficiency', *Journal of Industrial Economics* 27: 243–61.

Baron, D.P., and De Bondt, R.R. (1981), 'On the Design of Regulatory Price Adjustment Mechanisms', *Journal of Economic Theory* 24: 70–94.

Baron, D.P., and Myerson, R.B. (1982), 'Regulating a Monopolist with Unknown Costs', *Econometrica* 50: 911–30.

Barten, A.P., and **Böhm, V.** (1982), *Consumer Theory*, in K.J. Arrow and M.D. Intriligator, *Handbook of Mathematical Economics, Vol. II*. Amsterdam: North-Holland, 381–429.

Baumol, W.J. (1959), *Business Behavior, Value and Growth*. New York: Macmillan.

Baumol, W.J. (1976), 'Scale Economies, Average Cost, and the Profitability of Marginal Cost Pricing', in R.E. Grieson (ed.), *Public and Urban Economics, Essays in Honor of William S. Vickrey*. Lexington, Mass.: Heath, 43–57.

Baumol, W.J. (1977), 'On the Proper Cost Tests for Natural Monopoly in a Multiproduct Industry', *American Economic Review* 67: 809–22.

Baumol, W.J., **Bailey, E.E.**, and **Willig, R.D.** (1977), 'Weak Invisible Hand Theorems on the Sustainability of Multiproduct Natural Monopoly', *American Economic Review* 67: 350–65.

Baumol, W.J., and **Bradford, D.F.** (1970), 'Optimal Departures from Marginal Cost Pricing', *American Economic Review* 60: 265–83.

Baumol, W.J., and **Klevorick, A.K.** (1970), 'Input Choices and Rate-of-Return Regulation: An Overview of the Discussion', *Bell Journal of Economics and Management Science* 1: 162–90.

Baumol, W.J., **Panzar, J.C.**, and **Willig, R.D.** (1982), *Contestable Markets and The Theory of Industry Structure*, rev. edn. 1988. New York: Harcourt Brace Jovanovich.

Bawa, V.S., and **Sibley, D.S.** (1980), 'Dynamic Behavior of a Firm Subject to Stochastic Regulatory Review', *International Economic Review* 21: 627–42.

Beato, P. (1982), 'The Existence of Marginal Cost Pricing Equilibria with Increasing Returns', *Quarterly Journal of Economics* 97: 669–88.

Beato, P., and **Mas-Colell, A.** (1984), 'The Marginal Cost Pricing Rule as a Regulation Mechanism in Mixed Markets', in M. Marchand, P. Pestieau, and H. Tulkens (eds.), *The Performance of Public Enterprises: Concepts and Measurement*. Amsterdam: North-Holland, 81–100.

Beesley, M.E. (1992), *Privatization, Regulation and Deregulation*. London: Routledge.

Berg, S.V., and **Tschirhart, J.** (1988), *Natural Monopoly Regulation: Principles and Practice*. Cambridge, UK: Cambridge University Press.

Bergson, A. (1972), 'Optimal Pricing for a Public Enterprise', *Quarterly Journal of Economics* 86: 519–44.

Bergson, A. (1973), 'On Monopoly Welfare Losses', *American Economic Review* 63: 853–70.

Billera, L.J., and **Heath, D.C.** (1979), 'Allocation of Shared Costs: A Set of Axioms Yielding a Unique Procedure', mimeo, Cornell, Ithaca, NY.

Billera, L.J., Heath, D.C., and **Raanan, J.** (1978), 'Internal Telephone Billing Rates – A Novel Application of Non-Atomic Game Theory', *Operations Research* 26: 956–65.

Blanchard, O., Dornbusch, R., Krugman, P., Layard, R., and **Summers, L.** (1991), *Reform in Eastern Europe*. Cambridge, Mass.: MIT Press.

Boardman, A.E., and **Vining, A.R.** (1989), 'Ownership and Performance in Competitive Environments: A Comparison of the Performance of Private, Mixed and State-Owned Enterprises', *Journal of Law and Economics* 32: 1–33.

Boiteux, M. (1956, 1971), 'Sur la gestion des monopoles publics astreints à l'equilibre budgétaire', *Econometrica* 24: 22–40. (English edition: 'On the Management of Public Monopolies Subject to Budgetary Constraints', *Journal of Economic Theory* 3: 219–40.)

Bolton, P., and **Roland, G.** (1992), 'Privatization in Central and Eastern Europe', *Economic Policy* 7 (issue 15): 275–309.

Borcherding, T.E. (1980), 'Toward a Positive Theory of Public Sector Supply Arrangements', mimeo, Simon Frazer University, Burnaby, B.C., Canada.

Borcherding, T.E., Pommerehne, W.W., and **Schneider, F.** (1982), 'Comparing the Efficiency of Private and Public Production: The Evidence from Five Countries', in D. Bös, R.A. Musgrave, and J. Wiseman (eds.), *Public Production*. Vienna: Springer. (Zeitschrift für Nationalökonomie/Journal of Economics, Supplement 2), 127–56.

Borensztein, E., and **Kumar, M.S.** (1991), 'Proposals for Privatization in Eastern Europe', *IMF Staff Papers* 38: 300–26.

Bös, D. (1978a), 'Cost of Living Indices and Public Pricing', *Economica* 45: 59–69.

Bös, D. (1978b), 'Distributional Effects of Maximisation of Passenger Miles', *Journal of Transport Economics and Policy* 12: 322–9.

Bös, D. (1981), *Economic Theory of Public Enterprise*. Berlin–Heidelberg: Springer.

Bös, D. (1983), 'Public Pricing With Distributional Objectives', in J. Finsinger (ed.), *Public Sector Economics*. London: Macmillan, 171–88.

Bös, D. (1984), 'Income Taxation, Public Sector Pricing and Redistribution', *Scandinavian Journal of Economics* 86: 166–83.

Bös, D. (1985a), 'Public Sector Pricing', in A. Auerbach and M. Feldstein (eds.), *Handbook of Public Economics, Vol. I*, 129–211. 'Corrigendum', *Vol. II*, 1093–4. Amsterdam: North-Holland.

Bös, D. (1985b), 'Means Tested Public Pricing', Discussion Paper A–22, University of Bonn.

Bös, D. (1988), 'Recent Theories on Public Enterprise Economics', *European Economic Review* 32: 409–14.

Bös, D. (1989), *Public Enterprise Economics (Advanced Textbooks in Economics, Vol. 23)*. 2nd edition. Amsterdam: North-Holland.

Bös, D. (1991a), *Privatization: A Theoretical Treatment*. Oxford: Oxford University Press.

Bös, D. (1991b), 'Privatization and the Transition from Planned to Market Economies: Some Thoughts About Germany 1991', *Annals of Public and Cooperative Economics* 62: 183–94.

Bös, D. (1992), 'Privatization in East Germany: A Survey of Current Issues', IMF Working Paper, Washington D.C. Reprinted in V. Tanzi (ed.) (1993), *Transition to Market: Studies in Fiscal Reform*. Washington, D.C.: International Monetary Fund, 202–23.

Bös, D. (1993), 'Privatisation in Europe: A Comparison of Approaches', *Oxford Review of Economic Policy* 9(1): 95–111. Reprinted in E.E. Bailey and J. Rothenberg Pack (eds.) (1994), *The Political Economy of Privatization and Deregulation*. Cheltenham: Elgar.

Bös, D., Genser, B., and Holzmann, R. (1982), 'On the Quality of Publicly Supplied Goods', *Economica* 49: 289–96.

Bös, D., and Kayser, G. (1992), 'The Last Days of the Treuhandanstalt', mimeo, University of Bonn.

Bös, D., and Nett, L. (1990), 'Privatization, Price Regulation, and Market Entry: An Asymmetric Multistage Duopoly Model', *Journal of Economics/Zeitschrift für Nationalökonomie* 51: 221–57.

Bös, D., and Peters, W. (1991a), 'A Principal-Agent Approach on Manager Effort and Control in Privatized and Public Firms', in A. Ott and K. Hartley (eds.), *Privatization and Economic Efficiency*. Aldershot UK: E. Elgar, 26–52.

Bös, D., and Peters, W. (1991b), 'Privatization of Public Enterprises/A Principal-Agent Approach Comparing Efficiency in Private and Public Sectors', *Empirica* 18: 5–16.

Bös, D., and Tillmann, G. (1983), 'Cost-Axiomatic Regulatory Pricing', *Journal of Public Economics* 22: 243–56.

Bös, D., Tillmann, G., and Zimmermann, H.-G. (1984), 'Bureaucratic Public Enterprises', in D. Bös, A. Bergson, and J. R. Meyer (eds.), *Entrepreneurship*. Vienna: Springer (*Zeitschrift für Nationalökonomie/Journal of Economics*, Supplement 4), 127–76.

Bös, D., and Zimmermann, H.-G. (1987), 'Maximizing Votes under Imperfect Information', *European Journal of Political Economy* 3: 523–53.

Bös, J. (1956), 'Volksaktie als Versprechen, Hoffnung und Wirklichkeit', *Berichte und Informationen*, no. 520: 1–3.

Bouin, O. (1992), 'The Voucher Privatization's Auctioning Process in Czechoslovakia: Basic Mechanisms and Preliminary Results', mimeo, Centre Français de Recherche en Sciences Sociales, Prague.

Bouin, O. (1993), 'Privatization in Czechoslovakia', in V.V. Ramanadham (ed.), *Constraints and Impacts of Privatization.* London and New York: Routledge, 115–38.

Boyd, C.W. (1986), 'The Comparative Efficiency of State-Owned Enterprise', in A.R. Negandhi, H. Thomas, and K.L.K. Rao (eds.), *Multinational Corporations and State-Owned Enterprises: A New Challenge in International Business (Research in International Business and International Relations,* Greenwich, Conn.: JAI Press, 179–94.

Bradley, I., and **Price, C.** (1988), 'The Economic Regulation of Private Industries by Price Constraints', *The Journal of Industrial Economics* 37: 99–106.

Braeutigam, R.R., and **Panzar, J.C.** (1989), 'Diversification Incentives Under "Price-based" and "Cost-based" Regulation', *Rand Journal of Economics* 20: 373–91.

Brander, J.A., and **Spencer, B.J.** (1985), 'Ramsey Optimal Two Part Tariffs: The Case of Many Heterogeneous Groups', *Public Finance/Finances Publiques* 40: 335–46.

Brennan, T.J. (1989), 'Regulating by Capping Prices', *Journal of Regulatory Economics* 1: 133-47.

Brown, D.J., and **Heal, G.** (1979), 'Equity, Efficiency and Increasing Returns', *Review of Economic Studies* 46: 571–85.

Brown, D.J., and **Heal, G.** (1980a), 'Two-Part Tariffs, Marginal Cost Pricing and Increasing Returns in a General Equilibrium Model', *Journal of Public Economics* 13: 25–49.

Brown, D.J., and **Heal, G.** (1980b), 'Marginal Cost Pricing Revisited', mimeo, Econometric Society World Congress, Aix-en-Provence.

Brown, G. Jr., and **Johnson, M.B.** (1969), 'Public Utility Pricing and Output Under Risk', *American Economic Review* 59: 119–28.

Brown, S.J., and **Sibley, D.S.** (1986), *The Theory of Public Utility Pricing,* Cambridge, UK: Cambridge University Press.

Buccola, S.T., and **Sukume, C.** (1993), 'Social Welfare of Alternative Controlled-Price Policies', *Review of Economics and Statistics* 75: 86–96.

Cabral, L.M.B., and **Riordan, M.H.** (1989), 'Incentives for Cost Reduction under Price Cap Regulation', *Journal of Regulatory Economics* 1: 93–102.

Caillaud, B., Guesnerie, R., Rey, P., and **Tirole, J.** (1988), 'Government Intervention in Production and Incentives Theory: A Review of Recent Contributions', *Rand Journal of Economics* 19: 1–26.

Carlin, W., and **Mayer, C.P.** (1992), 'The Treuhandanstalt: Privatization by State and Market', mimeo, NBER, Cambridge, Mass.

Carlton, D.W. (1977), 'Peak Load Pricing With Stochastic Demand', *American Economic Review* 67: 1006–10.

Cave, M., and **Trotter, S.** (1990), 'The Regulation of Competition and Entry in Markets for U.K. Telecommunications Services', in D. Elixmann and K.-H. Neumann (eds.), *Communications Policy in Europe*. Berlin–Heidelberg: Springer, 57–84.

Caves, D.W., and **Christensen, L.R.** (1980), 'The Relative Efficiency of Public and Private Firms in a Competitive Environment: The Case of Canadian Railroads, *Journal of Political Economy* 88: 958–76.

Chamley, C., Marchand, M., and **Pestieau, P.** (1989), 'Linear Incentive Schemes to Control Public Firms', *European Journal of Political Economy* 5: 229–43.

Charzat, M.M. (1981), *Rapport no. 456, Assemblée Nationale 1981–1982, au nom de la Commission Spéciale Chargée d'Examiner le Projet de Loi de Nationalisation (no. 384), Vol. I: Présentation Génerale*. Paris: Imprimerie de l'Assemblee Nationale.

Chipman, J.S., and **Moore, J.C.** (1976), 'The Scope of Consumer's Surplus Arguments', in A. Tang, F. Westfield, and J. Worley (eds.), *Evolution, Welfare and Time in Economics*. Lexington, Mass.: Heath, 69–124.

Cieslik, J. (1993), 'Privatization in Poland', in V.V. Ramanadham (ed.), *Constraints and Impacts of Privatization*. London and New York: Routledge, 93–114.

Coase, R.H. (1946),'The Marginal Cost Controversy', *Economica* 13: 169–82.

Corneo, G., and **Jeanne, O.** (1994), 'Mixed Oligopoly in a Common Market', DELTA, wp # 9217. French translation: 'Oligopole Mixte Dans un Marché Commun', *Annales d'Economie et de Statistique* 33: 73–90.

Cornet, B. (1982), 'Existence of Equilibria in Economies with Increasing Returns', Working Paper, University of California at Berkeley.

Coughlin, P. (1992), *Probabilistic Voting Theory*, Cambridge, UK: Cambridge University Press.

Cowling, K., and **Mueller, D.C.** (1978), 'The Social Costs of Monopoly Power', *Economic Journal* 88: 727–48.

Cowling, K., and **Mueller, D.C.** (1981), 'The Social Costs of Monopoly Power Revisited', *The Economic Journal* 91: 721–5.

Cremer, H., Marchand, M., and **Thisse, J.F.** (1989), 'The Public Firm as an Instrument for Regulating an Oligopolistic Market', *Oxford Economic Papers* 41: 283–301.

Crew, M.A., and **Kleindorfer, P.R.** (1979), *Public Utility Economics*. London: Macmillan.

Dansby, R.E. (1975), 'Welfare Optimal Peak-Load Pricing and Capacity Decisions With Intraperiod Time Varying Demand', Economic Discussion Paper 39, Bell Laboratories.

Dasgupta, P., Hammond, P.J., and Maskin, E. (1979), 'The Implementation of Social Choice Rules: Some Results on Incentive Compatibility', *Review of Economic Studies* 46: 185–216.

Davies, D.G. (1981), 'Property Rights and Economic Behavior in Private and Government Enterprises: The Case of Australia's Banking System', in R.O. Zerbe (ed.), *Research in Law and Economics*, Vol. 3, Greenwich, Conn.: JAI Press, 111–42.

De Borger, B. (1993), 'The Economic Environment and Public Enterprise Behaviour: Belgian Railroads, 1950–86', *Economica* 60: 443–63.

De Fraja, G. (1991), 'Inefficiency and Privatisation in Imperfectly Competitive Industries', *Journal of Industrial Economics* 39: 311–21.

De Fraja, G. (1993a), 'Productive Efficiency in Public and Private Firms', *Journal of Public Economics* 50: 15–30.

De Fraja, G. (1993b), 'Unions and Wages in Public and Private Firms: A Game-Theoretic Analysis', *Oxford Economic Papers* 45: 457–69.

De Fraja, G., and Delbono, F. (1989), 'Alternative Strategies of a Public Enterprise in Oligopoly', *Oxford Economic Papers* 41: 302–11.

Delors, J. (1978), 'The Decline of French Planning', in S. Holland (ed.), *Beyond Capitalist Planning*. Oxford: Basil Blackwell.

Dervis, K., and Condon, T. (1992), 'Hungary: An Emerging "Gradualist" Success Story?', mimeo, NBER, Cambridge, Mass.

Diamond, P.A. (1975), 'A Many-Person Ramsey Tax Rule', *Journal of Public Economics* 4: 335–42.

Dierker, E. (1986), 'When Does Marginal Cost Pricing Lead to Pareto Efficiency', *Journal of Economics/Zeitschrift für Nationalökonomie* Supplement 5: 41–66.

Dierker, E. (1991), 'The Optimality of Boiteux–Ramsey Pricing', *Econometrica* 59: 99–121.

Dierker, E., Guesnerie, R., and Neuefeind, W. (1985), 'General Equilibrium When Some Firms Follow Special Pricing Rules', *Econometrica* 53: 1369–93.

Diewert, W.E. (1978), 'Optimal Tax Perturbations', *Journal of Public Economics* 10: 139–77.

Dixit, A. (1975), 'Welfare Effects of Tax and Price Changes', *Journal of Public Economics* 4: 103–23.

Drèze, J.H. (1964), 'Some Postwar Contributions of French Economists to Theory and Public Policy with Special Emphasis on Problems of Resource Allocation', *American Economic Review* 54 (no. 4, part 2, suppl.), 1–64.

Drèze, J.H. (1984), 'Second-Best Analysis with Markets in Disequilibrium: Public Sector Pricing in a Keynesian Regime', in M. Marchand, P. Pestieau, and H. Tulkens (eds.), *The Performance of Public Enterprises: Concepts and Measurement*. Amsterdam: North-Holland, 45–79.

Drèze, J.H., and **Hagen, K.P.** (1978), 'Choice of Product Quality: Equilibrium and Efficiency', *Econometrica* 46: 493–513.

Drèze, J.H., and **Marchand, M.** (1976), 'Pricing, Spending, and Gambling Rules for Non-Profit Organizations', in R.E. Grieson (ed.), *Public and Urban Economics. Essays in Honor of William S. Vickrey*. Lexington, Mass.: D.C. Heath, 59–89.

Ebert, U. (1992), 'A Reexamination of the Optimal Nonlinear Income Tax', *Journal of Public Economics* 49: 47–73.

Ebrill, L.P., and **Slutsky, S.M.** (1990), 'Production Efficiency and Optimal Pricing in Intermediate-Good Regulated Industries', *International Journal of Industrial Organization* 8: 417–42.

Einhorn, M.A. (1990), 'Regulatory Biases in Network Pricing with Access and Usage Externalities', mimeo.

Estrin, S. (1991), 'Privatization in Central and Eastern Europe', *Annals of Public and Cooperative Economics* 62: 159–82.

Estrin, S., and **de Meza, D.** (1988), 'Should the Post Office's Statutory Monopoly be Lifted?', mimeo, London School of Economics.

Falkinger, J. (1991), 'The Impact of Quality and Reliability on Demand', Research Memorandum 9107, University of Graz.

Falkinger, J. (1992), 'The Role of Quality and Reliability for the Demand of New Products', Research Memorandum 9203, University of Graz.

Färe, R., and **Grosskopf, S.** (1987), 'On Price Efficiency', Discussion Paper A–119, University of Bonn.

Färe, R., **Grosskopf, S.**, and **Nelson, J.** (1990), 'On Price Efficiency', *International Economic Review* 31: 709–20.

Färe, R., **Grosskopf, S.**, **Yaisawarng, S.**, **Li, S.K.**, and **Wang, Z.** (1990), 'Productivity Growth in Illinois Electric Utilities', *Resources and Energy* 12: 383–98.

Faulhaber, G.R. (1975), 'Cross-Subsidization: Pricing in Public Enterprises', *American Economic Review* 65: 966–77.

Faulhaber, G.R., and **Levinson, S.B.** (1981), 'Subsidy-Free Prices and Anonymous Equity', *American Economic Review* 71: 1083–91.

Faulhaber, G.R., and **Panzar, J.C.** (1977), 'Optimal Two-Part Tariffs with Self-Selection', Economic Discussion Paper 74, Bell Laboratories.

Federal Communications Commission (1987), 'Policy and Rules Concerning Rates for Dominant Carriers', CC Docket no. 87–263.

Federal Communications Commission (1988), 'Further Notice of Proposed Rulemaking', CC Docket no. 87–313.

Feldstein, M.S. (1972a) 'Distributional Equity and the Optimal Structure of Public Prices', *American Economic Review* 62: 32–6. (Corrected version of p. 33, footnote 7: *American Economic Review* 62: 763.)

Feldstein, M.S. (1972b) 'Equity and Efficiency in Public Sector Pricing: The Optimal Two-Part Tariff', *Quarterly Journal of Economics* 86: 175–87.

Feldstein, M.S. (1972c) 'The Pricing of Public Intermediate Goods', *Journal of Public Economics* 1: 45–72.

Feldstein, M.S. (1973) 'On the Optimal Progressivity of the Income Tax', *Journal of Public Economics* 2: 357–76.

Feldstein, M.S. (1974) 'Financing in the Evaluation of Public Expenditure', in W.L. Smith, and J.M. Culbertson (eds.), *Public Finance and Stabilization Policy*, Essays in Honour of Richard A. Musgrave. Amsterdam: North-Holland, 13–36.

Fershtman, C. (1990), 'The Interdependence between Ownership Status and Market Structure: The Case of Privatization', *Economica* 57: 319–28.

Finsinger, J., and **Vogelsang, I.** (1981), 'Alternative Institutional Frameworks for Price Incentive Mechanisms', *Kyklos* 34: 388–404.

Foster, C.D. (1976), 'The Public Corporation: Allocative and X-Efficiency', in J.A.G. Griffith (ed.), *From Policy to Administration*, Essays in Honour of W.A. Robson. London, 139–73.

Foster, C.D. (1992), *Privatization, Public Ownership and the Regulation of Natural Monopoly*. Oxford and Cambridge, Mass.: Blackwell.

Frantz, R.S. (1988), *X-Efficiency. Theory, Evidence and Applications*. Boston–Dordrecht: Kluwer.

Freixas, X., and **Laffont, J.-J.** (1985), 'Average Cost Pricing versus Marginal Cost Pricing under Moral Hazard', *Journal of Public Economics* 26: 135–46.

Friedman, J.W. (1986), *Game Theory with Applications to Economics*. Oxford: Oxford University Press.

Frydman, R., and **Rapaczynski, A.** (1991), 'Markets and Institutions in Large-Scale Privatizations: An Approach to Economic and Social Transformation in Eastern Europe', in V. Corbo, F. Coricelli, and J. Bossak (eds), Part VII in *Reforming Central and Eastern European Economies: Initial Results and Challenges*. Washington D.C.: World Bank.

Fudenberg, D., and **Tirole, J.** (1991), *Game Theory*. Cambridge, Mass.: MIT Press.

Fuller, S. (1991), *The Optimal Pricing of Standard Reference Materials*, mimeo, U.S. Department of Commerce, National Institute of Standards and Technology, Gaithersburg, MD.

Garner, M.R. (1983), 'Outline of Course Gv 220 – Public Enterprise', mimeo, London School of Economics and Political Sciences.

Gathon, H.-J., and **Pestieau, P.** (1991), 'Autonomy and Performance in Public Enterprises: The Case of European Railways', Working Paper 04, CIRIEC, University of Liége.

Gathon, H.-J., and **Pestieau, P.** (1992), 'Decomposing Efficiency into its Managerial and its Regulatory Components: The Case of European Railways', Working Paper 07, CIRIEC, University of Liége.

Gaynor, M. (1992), 'More on Moral Hazard in Organizations', *Public Choice* 74: 257–62.

Georgescu-Roegen, N. (1968–69), 'Revisiting Marshall's Constancy of Marginal Utility of Money', *Southern Economic Journal* 35: 176–81.

Gibbard, A. (1973), 'Manipulation of Voting Schemes: A General Result', *Econometrica* 41: 587–601.

Glaister, S. (1974), 'Generalised Consumer Surplus and Public Transport Pricing', *Economic Journal* 84: 849–67.

Glaister, S. (1976), 'Peak Load-Pricing and the Channel Tunnel: A Case Study', *Journal of Transport Economics and Policy* 10: 89–112.

Glaister, S. (1982), 'Urban Public Transport Subsidies: An Economic Assessment of Value for Money', Technical Report and Summary Report (Department of Transport, London).

Glaister, S., and **Collings, J.J.** (1978), 'Maximisation of Passenger Miles in Theory and Practice', *Journal of Transport Economics and Policy* 12: 304–21.

Goldfeld, S.M., and **Quandt, R.E.** (1988), 'Budget Constraints, Bailouts, and the Firm Under Central Planning', *Journal of Comparative Economics* 12: 502–20.

Goldfeld, S.M., and **Quandt, R.E.** (1990), 'Output Targets, the Soft Budget Constraint and the Firm Under Central Planning', *Journal of Economic Behavior and Organization* 14: 205–22.

Gravelle, H.S.E. (1981), 'Public Enterprise Management Incentive Mechanisms: Some Difficulties', Discussion Paper 75, Queen Mary College, London.

Gravelle, H.S.E. (1982a), 'Incentives, Efficiency and Control in Public Firms', in D. Bös, R.A. Musgrave, and J. Wiseman (eds.), *Public Production*. Vienna: Springer. (*Zeitschrift für Nationalökonomie/Journal of Economics*, Supplement 2), 79–104.

Gravelle, H.S.E. (1982b), 'Reward Structures in a Planned Economy: Comment', Discussion Paper 83, Queen Mary College, London.

Gravelle, H.S.E. (1984), 'Bargaining and Efficiency in Public and Private Sector Firms', in M. Marchand, P. Pestieau, and H. Tulkens (eds.), *The Performance of Public Enterprises*. Amsterdam: North-Holland, 193–220.

Gravelle, H.S.E. (1985), 'Reward Structures in a Planned Economy: Some Difficulties', *Quarterly Journal of Economics* 100: 271–8.

Green, H.A.J. (1962), 'The Social Optimum in the Presence of Monopoly and Taxation', *Review of Economic Studies* 29: 66–78.

Green, H.A.J. (1975), 'Two Models of Optimal Pricing and Taxation', *Oxford Economic Papers* 27: 352–82.

Green, J., and **Laffont, J.-J.** (1977), 'Characterization of Satisfactory Mechanisms for the Revelation of Preferences for Public Goods', *Econometrica* 45: 427–38.

Griliches, Z., and **Mairesse, J.** (1993), *Productivity Issues in Services at the Micro Level*. Boston–Dordrecht: Kluwer.

Guesnerie, R. (1975), 'Pareto Optimality in Non-Convex Economies', *Econometrica* 43: 1–29.

Guesnerie, R. (1980), 'Second-Best Pricing Rules in the Boiteux Tradition: Derivation, Review and Discussion', *Journal of Public Economics* 13: 51–80.

Guesnerie, R. (1988), 'Regulation as an Adverse Selection Problem. An Introduction to the Literature', *European Economic Review* 32: 473–81.

Guesnerie, R., and **Laffont, J.-J.** (1984), 'A Complete Solution to a Class of Principal-Agent Problems with an Application to the Control of a Self-Managed Firm', *Journal of Public Economics* 25: 329–69.

Gulledge, T., and **Lovell, K.** (1992), *International Applications of Productivity and Efficiency Analysis*. Boston–Dordrecht: Kluwer.

Hagen, K.P. (1979), 'Optimal Pricing in Public Firms in an Imperfect Market Economy', *Scandinavian Journal of Economics* 81: 475–93.

Hammond, P.J. (1977), 'Dual Interpersonal Comparisons of Utility and the Welfare Economics of Income Distribution', *Journal of Public Economics* 7: 51–71.

Hammond, P.J. (1984), 'Approximate Measures of Social Welfare and the Size of Tax Reform', in D. Bös, M. Rose, and C. Seidl (eds.), *Beiträge zur neueren Steuertheorie*. Berlin–Heidelberg: Springer, 95–115.

Hanson, A.H. (1965), *Public Enterprise and Economic Development*, 2nd edition. London: Routledge & Kegan Paul.

Harberger, A.C. (1954), 'Monopoly and Resource Allocation', *American Economic Review*, Papers and Proceedings 44: 77–87.

Hardy, D.C. (1992) 'Soft Budget Constraints, Firm Commitments, and the Social Safety Net', *IMF Staff Papers*, 39: 310–29.

Hare, P., and **Révész, T.** (1992), 'Hungary's Transition to the Market: The Case Against a 'Big-Bang' ', *Economic Policy* 7 (issue 14): 227–56.

Hart, O., and **Moore, J.** (1990), 'Property Rights and the Nature of the Firm', *Journal of Political Economy* 98: 1119–58.

Hatta, T. (1977), 'A Theory of Piecemeal Policy Recommendations', *Review of Economic Studies* 44: 1–21.

Heald, D. (1980), 'The Economic and Financial Control of U.K. Nationalised Industries', *Economic Journal* 90: 243–65.

Helm, D.R. (1988), 'Regulating the Electricity Supply Industry', in S. Estrin, and C.M.E. Whitehead (eds.), *Privatisation and the Nationalised Industries.* London: ST/ICERD, London School of Economics, 51–66.

Hestenes, M.R. (1966), *Calculus of Variations and Optimal Control Theory.* New York: J. Wiley & Sons.

Hinds, M. (1990), 'Issues in the Introduction of Market Forces in Eastern European Socialist Economies', Internal Discussion Paper, The World Bank, Washington.

Holland, S. (1975), *The Socialist Challenge.* London: Quartet Books.

Holland, S. (1978), 'Planning Disagreements', in S. Holland (ed.), *Beyond Capitalist Planning.* Oxford: Basil Blackwell, 137–61.

Holmström, B.R. (1982), 'Moral Hazard in Teams', *Bell Journal of Economics* 13: 324–40.

Holmström, B.R., and **Tirole, J.** (1989), 'The Theory of the Firm', in R. Schmalensee and R.D. Willig, *Handbook of Industrial Organization, Vol. I,* Amsterdam: North-Holland, 61–133.

Hotelling, H. (1938), 'The General Welfare in Relation to Problems of Taxation and of Railway and Utility Rates', *Econometrica* 6: 242–69.

Howell, D. (1981), *Freedom and Capital: Prospects for the Property-Owning Democracy.* Oxford: Basil Blackwell.

Intriligator, M.D. (1971), 'Mathematical Optimization and Economic Theory', Prentice-Hall, Englewood Cliffs, NJ.

Jenny, F., and **Weber, A.-P.** (1983), 'Aggregate Welfare Loss Due to Monopoly Power in the French Economy', *Journal of Industrial Economics* 32: 113–30.

Joskow, P., and **Noll, R.** (1980), 'Theory and Practice in Public Regulation: A Current Overview', Conference Paper 64, National Bureau of Economic Research, Cambridge, Mass.

Kahn, A.E. (1988), *The Economics of Regulation. Principles and Institutions.* New Edition with a Foreword by P.L. Joskow and a new Introduction by the Author. Cambridge, Mass.: MIT Press.

Kamerschen, D.R. (1966), 'An Estimation of the "Welfare Losses" From Monopoly in the American Economy', *Western Economic Journal* 4: 221–36.

Kamien, M.I., and **Schwartz, N.L.** (1981), *Dynamic Optimization: The Calculus of Variations and Optimal Control in Economics and Management.* Amsterdam: North-Holland.

Kawamata, K. (1974), 'Price Distortion and Potential Welfare', *Econometrica* 42: 435–60.

Kawamata, K. (1977), 'Price Distortion and the Second Best Optimum', *Review of Economic Studies* 44: 23–9.

Kay, J.A. (1983), 'A General Equilibrium Approach to the Measurement of Monopoly Welfare Loss', *International Journal of Industrial Organization* 1: 317–31.

Kendrick, J.W. (1975), 'Efficiency Incentives and Cost Factors in Public Utility Automatic Revenue Adjustment Clauses', *Bell Journal of Economics* 6: 299–313.

Klevorick, A.K. (1973), 'The Behavior of a Firm Subject to Stochastic Regulatory Review', *Bell Journal of Economics* 4: 57–88.

Koren, S. (1964), 'Sozialisierungsideologie und Verstaatlichungsrealität in Österreich', in W. Weber (ed.), *Die Verstaatlichung in Österreich.* Berlin: Duncker & Humblot, 9–339.

Kornai, J. (1980), *Economics of Shortage*, Amsterdam: North-Holland.

Kornai, J. (1986), 'The Soft Budget Constraint', *Kyklos* 39: 3–30.

Kreps, D.M., and **Scheinkman, J.A.** (1983), 'Quantity Precommitment and Bertrand Competition Yield Cournot Outcomes', *Bell Journal of Economics* 14: 326–37.

Labour Party (1973), *Labour's State Holding Company.* Opposition Green Paper. London: Labour Party.

Laffont, J.-J. (1994): 'The New Economics of Regulation Ten Years After', Presidential Address of the Econometric Society, *Econometrica* 62: 507–37.

Laffont, J.-J., and **Tirole, J.** (1986), 'Using Cost Observation to Regulate Firms', *Journal of Political Economy* 94: 614–41. Reprinted in Laffont, J.-J., and Tirole, J. (1993), chapters 1 and 2.

Laffont, J.-J., and **Tirole, J.** (1987), 'Comparative Statics of the Optimal Dynamic Incentive Contract', *European Economic Review* 31: 901–26. Reprinted in Laffont, J.-J., and Tirole, J. (1993), chapter 9.

Laffont, J.-J., and **Tirole, J.** (1988), 'The Dynamics of Incentive Contracts', *Econometrica* 56: 1153–75. Reprinted in Laffont, J.-J., and Tirole, J. (1993), chapter 9.

Laffont, J.-J., and **Tirole, J.** (1990), 'The Regulation of Multiproduct Firms. Part I: Theory', *Journal of Public Economics* 43: 1–36; 'Part II: Applications to Competitive Environments and Policy Analysis', *Journal of Public Economics* 43: 37–66. Reprinted in Laffont, J.-J., and Tirole, J. (1993), chapters 2 and 3.

Laffont, J.-J., and **Tirole, J.** (1991), 'Privatization and Incentives', *Journal of Law, Economics, and Organization* 7: 84–105. Reprinted in Laffont, J.-J., and Tirole, J. (1993), chapter 17.

Laffont, J.-J., and **Tirole, J.** (1993), *A Theory of Incentives in Procurement and Regulation.* Cambridge, Mass.: MIT Press.

426   *References*

Langohr, H.M., and **Viallet, C.J.** (1986), 'Compensation and Wealth Transfers in the French Nationalizations 1981–1982', *Journal of Financial Economics* 17: 273–312.

Lazear, E., and **Rosen, S.** (1981), 'Rank Order Tournaments as Optimum Labor Contracts', *Journal of Political Economy* 89: 841–64.

Leibenstein, H. (1966), 'Allocative Efficiency vs. "X-Efficiency"', *American Economic Review* 56: 392–415.

Leibenstein, H. (1969), 'Organizational or Frictional Equilibria, X-Efficiency, and the Rate of Innovation', *Quarterly Journal of Economics*, 83: 600–23.

Leibenstein, H. (1976), *Beyond Economic Man.* Cambridge, Mass.: Harvard University Press.

Leland, H.E., and **Meyer, R.A.** (1976), 'Monopoly Pricing Structures With Imperfect Discrimination', *Bell Journal of Economics* 7: 449–62.

Lesourne, J. (1976), 'Innovation and Regulation: A Comment', *Journal of Public Economics* 5: 389–92.

Letwin, O. (1988), *Privatising the World.* London: Cassell.

Lewis, T.R., and **Sappington, D.E.M.** (1988), 'Regulating a Monopolist with Unknown Demand', *American Economic Review* 78: 986–98.

Lewis, T.R., and **Sappington, D.E.M.** (1989), 'Regulatory Options and Price-Cap Regulation', *Rand Journal of Economics* 20: 405–16.

Lewis, T.R., and **Sappington, D.E.M.** (1992), 'Incentives for Conservation and Quality-Improvement by Public Utilities', *American Economic Review* 82: 1321–40.

Lipsey, R.G., and **Lancaster, K.** (1956–57), 'The General Theory of Second Best', *Review of Economic Studies* 24: 11–32.

Lipton, D., and **Sachs, J.** (1990a), 'Creating a Market Economy in Eastern Europe: The Case of Poland', *Brookings Papers on Economic Activity*, The Brookings Institution, Washington D.C., no. 1: 75–133.

Lipton, D., and **Sachs, J.** (1990b), 'Creating a Market Economy in Eastern Europe: The Case of Poland', *Brookings Papers on Economic Activity*, The Brookings Institution, Washington D.C., no. 2: 293–341.

Liston, C. (1993), 'Price-Cap versus Rate-of-Return Regulation', *Journal of Regulatory Economics* 5: 25–48.

Littlechild, S.C. (1970), 'A Game Theoretic Approach to Public Utility Pricing', *Western Economic Journal* 8: 162–6.

Littlechild, S.C. (1979), 'Controlling the Nationalised Industries: Quis Custodiet Ipsos Custodes?' Series B Discussion Paper no. 56, University of Birmingham.

Littlechild, S.C. (1981), 'Misleading Calculations of the Social Costs of Monopoly Power', *Economic Journal* 91: 348–63.

Littlechild, S.C. (1983), *Regulation of British Telecommunications' Profitability.* London: HMSO.

Littlechild, S.C. (1986), *Economic Regulation of Privatised Water Authorities.* London: HMSO.

Littlechild, S.C. (1988), 'Economic Regulation of Privatised Water Authorities and Some Further Reflections', *Oxford Review of Economic Policy* 4(2): 40–68.

Loeb, M., and **Magat, W.A.** (1979), 'A Decentralized Method for Utility Regulation', *Journal of Law and Economics* 22: 399–404.

Loesch, A. von (1983), *Privatisierung öffentlicher Unternehmen: Ein Überblick über die Argumente.* Baden-Baden: Nomos.

Luenberger, D.C. (1973), *Introduction to Linear and Nonlinear Programming.* Reading, Mass.: Addison-Wesley.

Malinvaud, E. (1977), *The Theory of Unemployment Reconsidered.* Oxford: Basil Blackwell.

Mangasarian, O.L. (1969), *Nonlinear Programming.* New York: McGraw-Hill.

Marchand, M., **Pestieau, P.**, and **Tulkens, H.** (1984), 'The Performance of Public Enterprises: Normative, Positive and Empirical Issues', in M. Marchand, P. Pestieau, and H. Tulkens (eds.), *The Performance of Public Enterprises: Concepts and Measurement.* Amsterdam: North-Holland, 3–42.

Marchand, M., **Pestieau, P.**, and **Weymark, J.A.** (1982), 'Discount Rates for Public Enterprises in the Presence of Alternative Financial Constraints', in D. Bös, R.A. Musgrave, and J. Wiseman (eds.), *Public Production.* Vienna: Springer. (*Zeitschrift für Nationalökonomie/Journal of Economics*, Supplement 2), 27–50.

Marchand, M., **Pestieau, P.**, and **Weymark, J.A.** (1984), 'Discount Rates for Public Enterprises in the Presence of Alternative Financial Constraints: A Correction', *Zeitschrift für Nationalökonomie/Journal of Economics* 44: 289–91.

Mas-Colell, A., **Whinston, M.D.**, and **Green, J.R.** (1993), *Microeconomic Theory*, to be published by Oxford University Press.

Maskin, E., and **Riley, J.** (1984), 'Monopoly with Incomplete Information', *Rand Journal of Economics* 15: 171–96.

Masson, R.T., and **Shaanan, J.** (1984), 'Social Costs of Oligopoly and the Value of Competition', *Economic Journal* 94: 528–30.

Mathios, A.D., and **Rogers, R.P.** (1989), 'The Impact of Alternative Forms of State Regulation of AT&T on Direct-Dial, Long-Distance Telephone Rates', *Rand Journal of Economics* 20: 437–53.

Mayer, C.P., and **Meadowcroft, S.A.** (1985), 'Selling Public Assets: Techniques and Financial Implications', *Fiscal Studies* 6(4), 42–56. (Reprinted in J.A. Kay, C.P. Mayer, and D.J. Thompson (eds.), *Privatisation and Regulation: The UK Experience.* Oxford: Clarendon Press, 1986.)

McGowan, F. (1993), 'Electricity – The Experience of OFFER', in T. Gilland and P. Vass (eds.), *Regulatory Review 1993.* London: Centre for the Study of Regulated Industries, 73–87.

Merrill, W.C., and **Schneider, N.** (1966), 'Government Firms in Oligopoly Industries: A Short-Run Analysis', *Quarterly Journal of Economics* 80: 400–12.

Meyer, R.A. (1975), 'Monopoly Pricing and Capacity Choice Under Uncertainty', *American Economic Review* 65: 326–37.

Milanovic, B. (1989), *Liberalization and Entrepreneurship*. New York: M.E. Sharpe.

Millward, R., and **Parker, D.M.** (1983), 'Public and Private Enterprise: Comparative Behaviour and Relative Efficiency', in R. Millward, D.M. Parker, L. Rosenthal, M.T. Sumner, and N. Topham (eds.), *Public Sector Economics*. London: Longman, 199–274.

Minasian, J.R. (1964), 'Television Pricing and the Theory of Public Goods', *Journal of Law and Economics* 7: 71–80.

Mirman, L.J., Samet, D., and **Tauman, Y.** (1983), 'An Axiomatic Approach to the Allocation of a Fixed Cost Through Prices', *Bell Journal of Economics* 14: 139– 51.

Mirman, L.J., and **Sibley, D.S.** (1980), 'Optimal Nonlinear Prices for Multiproduct Monopolies', *Bell Journal of Economics* 11: 659–70.

Mirman, L.J., and **Tauman, Y.** (1982), 'Demand Compatible Equitable Cost Sharing Prices', *Mathematics of Operations Research* 7: 40–56.

Mirrlees, J.A. (1975), 'Optimal Commodity Taxation in a Two-Class Economy', *Journal of Public Economics* 4: 27–33.

Mirrlees, J.A. (1976), 'Optimal Tax Theory: A Synthesis', *Journal of Public Economics* 6: 327–58.

Mitchell, B.M., Manning Jr., W.G., and **Acton, J.P.** (1977), 'Electricity Pricing and Load Management, Foreign Experience and California Opportunities', Rand Corporation, Study R-2106, Santa Monica, CA.

Mitchell, B.M., and **Vogelsang, I.** (1991), *Telecommunications Pricing. Theory and Practice*. Cambridge, UK: Cambridge University Press.

Moore, J. (1992), 'The Firm as a Collection of Assets', *European Economic Review* 36: 493–507.

Mueller, D.C. (1989), *Public Choice II. A revised edition of Public Choice*. Cambridge, UK: Cambridge University Press.

Musgrave, R.A. (1959), *The Theory of Public Finance*. New York: McGraw-Hill.

Mussa, M., and **Rosen, S.** (1978), 'Monopoly and Product Quality', *Journal of Economic Theory* 18: 301–17.

Myerson, R.B. (1979), 'Incentive Compatibility and the Bargaining Problem', *Econometrica* 47: 61–74.

Myerson, R.B. (1982), 'Optimal Coordination Mechanisms in Generalized Principal-Agent Problems', *Journal of Mathematical Economics* 10: 67–81.

NEDO (National Economic Development Office) (1976), 'A Study of U.K. Nationalised Industries' (Report, appendix volume and several background papers), Her Majesty's Stationery Office, London.

Nelson, J.R. (ed.) (1964), *Marginal Cost Pricing in Practice*. Englewood Cliffs, NJ: Prentice-Hall.

Nelson, J. (1991), 'Quality as a Substitute for Quantity: Do More Reliable Products Ever Sell for Less?', *Economics Letters* 36: 239–43.

Nett, L. (1993), 'Mixed Oligopoly with Homogeneous Goods', *Annals of Public and Cooperative Economics* 64: 367–93.

Nett, L. (1994a), 'The Role of Sunk Cost in Entry Deterrence in a Mixed Oligopolistic Market', *Annales d'Économie et de Statistique* 33: 113–31.

Nett, L. (1994b), 'Why Private Firms are More Innovative than Public Firms', *European Journal of Political Economy*, forthcoming.

Neu, W. (1993), 'Allocative Inefficiency Properties of Price-Cap Regulation', *Journal of Regulatory Economics* 5: 159–82.

Ng, Y.-K. (1982), 'A Dollar is a Dollar: Efficiency, Equality, and Third-Best Policy', mimeo, Monash University, Clayton, Vic.

Ng, Y.-K. (1984), 'Quasi-Pareto Social Improvements', *American Economic Review* 74: 1033–50.

Ng, Y.-K., and **Weisser, M.** (1974), 'Optimal Pricing With a Budget Constraint – The Case of the Two-Part Tariff', *Review of Economic Studies* 41: 337–45.

Niskanen, W.A., Jr. (1971), *Bureaucracy and Representative Government*. Chicago: Aldine.

Niskanen, W.A., Jr. (1975), 'Bureaucrats and Politicians', *Journal of Law and Economics* 18: 617–43.

Nutzinger, H.G., and **Backhaus, J.** (eds.) (1988), *Codetermination: A Discussion of Different Approaches*. Berlin–Heidelberg: Springer.

Oi, W.Y. (1971), 'A Disneyland Dilemma: Two-Part Tariffs for a Mickey Mouse Monopoly', *Quarterly Journal of Economics* 85: 77–96.

O'Keefe, M. (1981), 'Quality and Price Discrimination', Ph.D. thesis, Harvard University.

Olson, D.O., and **Bumpass, D.L.** (1984), 'An Intertemporal Analysis of the Welfare Costs of Monopoly Power', *Review of Industrial Organization* 1: 308–23.

Ordover, J.A., and **Panzar, J.C.** (1980), 'On the Nonexistence of Pareto Superior Outlay Schedules', *Bell Journal of Economics* 11: 351–4.

Otani, Y., and **El-Hodiri, M.** (1987), *Microeconomic Theory*. Berlin–Heidelberg: Springer.

Oum, T.H., and **Yu, C.** (1993), 'Economic Efficiency of Railways and Implications for Public Policy: A Comparative Study of the OECD Countries' Railways', forthcoming in *Journal of Transport Economics and Policy*.

Panik, M.J. (1976), *Classical Optimization: Foundations and Extensions*. Amsterdam: North-Holland.

Panzar, J.C. (1976), 'A Neoclassical Approach to Peak Load Pricing', *Bell Journal of Economics* 7: 521–30.

Panzar, J.C., and **Willig, R.D.** (1977a), 'Economies of Scale in Multi-Output Production', *Quarterly Journal of Economics* 91: 481–93.

Panzar, J.C., and **Willig, R.D.** (1977b), 'Free Entry and the Sustainability of Natural Monopoly', *Bell Journal of Economics* 8: 1–22.

Parris, H., **Pestieau, P.**, and **Saynor, P.** (1987), *Public Enterprise in Western Europe*. London: Croom Helm.

Peltzman, S. (1990), 'How Efficient is the Voting Market?', *Journal of Law and Economics* 33: 27–63.

Perelman, S., and **Pestieau, P.** (1988), 'Technical Performance in Public Enterprises: A Comparative Study of Railways and Postal Services', *European Economic Review* 32: 432–41.

Perelman, S., and **Pestieau, P.** (1994), 'A Comparative Performance Study of Postal Services: A Productive Efficiency Approach', *Annales d'Économie et de Statistique* 33: 187–202.

Perry, M.K. (1989), 'Vertical Integration: Determinants and Effects', in R. Schmalensee and R.D. Willig (eds.), *Handbook of Industrial Organization, Vol. I.* Amsterdam: North-Holland, 183–255.

Peters, W. (1985), 'Can Inefficient Public Production Promote Welfare?', *Zeitschrift für Nationalökonomie/Journal of Economics* 45: 395–407.

Peters, W. (1988), 'Cost Inefficiency and Second Best Pricing', *European Journal of Political Economy* 4: 29–45.

Phlips, L. (1983), *Applied Consumption Analysis (Advanced Textbooks in Economics, Vol. 5).* 2nd edition. Amsterdam: North-Holland.

Pigou, A.C. (1937), *Socialism Versus Capitalism.* London: Macmillan.

Pint, E.M. (1990), 'Nationalization and Privatization: A Rational-Choice Perspective on Efficiency', *Journal of Public Policy* 10: 267–98.

Pint, E.M. (1991), 'Nationalization vs. Regulation of Monopolies: The Effects of Ownership on Efficiency', *Journal of Public Economics* 44: 131–64.

Pint, E.M. (1992), 'The Effects of Privatization on Firm Objectives: U.K. Evidence', mimeo, Nuffield College, Oxford.

Posner, R.A. (1975), 'The Social Costs of Monopoly and Regulation', *Journal of Political Economy* 83: 807–27.

Price, C. (1993), 'Gas – A Review of 1992', in T. Gilland and P. Vass (eds.), *Regulatory Review 1993.* London: Centre for the Study of Regulated Industries, 33–44.

Quoilin, J. (1976), 'Marginal Cost Selling in Électricité de France', *Annals of Public and Co-operative Economy* 47: 115–41.

Ramanadham, V.V. (ed.) (1988), *Privatisation in the UK.* London and New York: Routledge.

Ramsey, F. (1927), 'A Contribution to the Theory of Taxation', *Economic Journal* 37: 47–61.

Rees, R. (1976, 1984), *Public Enterprise Economics*, 1st and 2nd edition. London: Weidenfeld and Nicolson.

Rees, R. (1984a), 'The Public Enterprise Game', *Economic Journal* 94, Supplement, 109–23.

Rees, R. (1984b), 'A Positive Theory of the Public Enterprise', in M. Marchand, P. Pestieau, and H. Tulkens (eds.), *The Performance of Public Enterprises: Concepts and Management.* Amsterdam: North-Holland, 179–91.

Rees, R. (1986), 'Incentive Compatible Discount Rates for Public Investment', *Journal of Public Economics* 30: 249–57.

Rees, R. (1988), 'Inefficiency, Public Enterprise and Privatisation', *European Economic Review* 32: 422–31.

Reid, G. L., and **Allen, K.** (1970), *Nationalized Industries*. Harmondsworth: Penguin.

Roberts, K.W.S. (1979), 'Welfare Considerations of Nonlinear Pricing', *Economic Journal* 89: 66–83.

Roberts, K.W.S. (1980a), 'Interpersonal Comparability and Social Choice Theory', *Review of Economic Studies* 47: 421–39.

Roberts, K.W.S. (1980b), 'Possibility Theorems with Interpersonally Comparable Welfare Levels', *Review of Economic Studies* 47: 409–20.

Rohlfs, J.H. (1979), 'Economically-Efficient Bell System Pricing', Bell Laboratories Economics Discussion Paper No. 138.

Romer, T., and **Rosenthal, H.** (1979), 'Bureaucrats Versus Voters: On the Political Economy of Resource Allocation by Direct Democracy', *Quarterly Journal of Economics* 93: 563–87.

Rothschild, M., and **Stiglitz, J.E.** (1970), 'Increasing Risk: I, A Definition', *Journal of Economic Theory* 2: 225–43.

Sachs, J. (1991), 'Accelerating Privatization in Eastern Europe', mimeo, World Bank Annual Conference on Development Economics, Washington, D.C.

Sadka, E. (1976a), 'On Income Distribution, Incentive Effects and Optimal Income Taxation', *Review of Economic Studies* 43: 261–8.

Sadka, E. (1976b), 'Social Welfare and Income Distribution', *Econometrica* 44: 1239–51.

Sah, R.K. (1983), 'How Much Redistribution is Possible Through Commodity Taxes?', *Journal of Public Economics* 20: 89–101.

Samet, D., and **Tauman, Y.** (1982), 'The Determination of Marginal Cost Prices Under a Set of Axioms', *Econometrica* 50: 895–909.

Samet, D., Tauman, Y., and **Zang, I.** (1981), 'An Application of the Aumann–Shapley Prices for Cost Allocation in Transportation Problems', Working Paper 803, The University of British Columbia, Vancouver.

Samuelson, P.A. (1964), 'Public Goods and Subscription TV: Correction of the Record', *Journal of Law and Economics* 7: 81–3.

Sappington, D.E.M. (1980), 'Strategic Firm Behavior under a Dynamic Regulatory Adjustment Process', *Bell Journal of Economics* 11: 360–72.

Schaffer, M.E. (1989), 'The Credible-Commitment Problem in the Center-Enterprise Relationship', *Journal of Comparative Economics* 13: 359–82.

Scherer, F.M., and **Ross, D.** (1990), *Industrial Market Structure and Economic Performance*. 3rd edition. Boston: Houghton Mifflin Company.

Schmalensee, R. (1979), *The Control of Natural Monopolies*. Lexington, Mass.: Heath.

Schmalensee, R. (1981), 'Monopolistic Two-Part Pricing Arrangements', *Bell Journal of Economics* 12: 445–66.

Schmalensee, R. (1989), 'Good Regulatory Regimes', *Rand Journal of Economics* 20: 417–36.

Schmidt, K.M. (1991), 'The Costs and Benefits of Privatization', Discussion Paper A–330, University of Bonn.

Schmidt, K.M., and **Schnitzer, M.** (1992), 'Privatization and Management Incentives in the Transition Period in Eastern Europe', Working Paper No. 92-17, Massachusetts Institute of Technology, Cambridge, Mass.

Schwartzman, D. (1960), 'The Burden of Monopoly', *Journal of Political Economy* 68: 627–30.

Seade, J.K. (1977), 'On the Shape of Optimal Tax Schedules', *Journal of Public Economics* 7: 203–35.

Seidl, C. (1983), 'Gerechtigkeit und Besteuerung unter besonderer Berücksichtigung der Optimalsteuertheorie', in D. Pohmer (ed.), *Zur optimalen Besteuerung*, Schriften des Vereins für Socialpolitik N.F. 128. Berlin: Duncker & Humblot, 163–259.

Seierstad, A., and **Sydsæter, K.** (1987), *Optimal Control Theory with Economic Applications.* Amsterdam: North-Holland.

Sen, A.K. (1970), *Collective Choice and Social Welfare.* San Francisco, CA: Holden-Day; Edinburgh: Oliver & Boyd.

Shapiro, C., and **Willig, R.D.** (1990), 'Economic Rationales for the Scope of Privatization', in E.N. Suleiman, and J. Waterbury (eds.), *The Political Economy of Public Sector Reform and Privatization.* Boulder, Colorado: Westview Press, 55–87.

Sharkey, W.W. (1979), 'A Decentralized Method for Utility Regulation: A Comment', *Journal of Law and Economics* 22: 405–7.

Sharkey, W.W. (1982), *The Theory of Natural Monopoly.* Cambridge: Cambridge University Press.

Sharkey, W.W., and **Sibley, D.S.** (1991), 'Optimal Non-Linear Pricing with Regulatory Preference over Customer Types', Bellcore Economics Discussion Paper, Bell Communications Research.

Sheshinski, E. (1976), 'Price, Quality and Quantity Regulation in Monopoly Situations', *Economica* 43: 127–37.

Sheshinski, E., and **Weiss, Y.** (1977), 'Inflation and Costs of Price Adjustment', *Review of Economic Studies* 44: 287–303. Reprinted in E. Sheshinski and Y. Weiss (eds.) (1993), *Optimal Pricing, Inflation, and the Cost of Price Adjustment.* Cambridge, Mass.: MIT Press, 117–41.

Sheshinski, E., and **Weiss, Y.** (1983), 'Optimum Pricing Policy Under Stochastic Inflation', *Review of Economic Studies* 50: 513–29. Reprinted in E. Sheshinski and Y. Weiss (eds.) (1993), *Optimal Pricing, Inflation, and the Cost of Price Adjustment.* Cambridge, Mass.: MIT Press, 143–67.

Sheshinski, E., and **Weiss, Y.** (1989), 'Staggered and Synchronized Price Policies Under Inflation: The Multiproduct Monopoly Case', *Review of Economic Studies* 59: 331–59. Reprinted in E. Sheshinski and Y. Weiss (eds.) (1993), *Optimal Pricing, Inflation, and the Cost of Price Adjustment.* Cambridge, Mass.: MIT Press, 169–213.

Shleifer, A. (1985), 'A Theory of Yardstick Competition', *Rand Journal of Economics* 16: 319–27.

Sinn, G., and **Sinn, H.-W.** (1992), *Jumpstart: The Economic Unification of Germany.* Cambridge, Mass.: MIT Press (Translation of *Kaltstart: Volkswirtschaftliche Aspekte der deutschen Vereinigung* (1991). Tübingen: Mohr (Siebeck)).

Smekal, C. (1963), *Die verstaatlichte Industrie in der Marktwirtschaft. Das österreichische Beispiel.* Cologne: Heymanns.

Smith, A. (1983), 'Tax Reform and Temporary Inefficiency', *Journal of Public Economics* 20: 265–70.

Spann, R.M. (1977), 'Public versus Private Provision of Governmental Services', in T. E. Borcherding (ed.), *Budgets and Bureaucrats: The Sources of Government Growth.* Durham, NC: Duke University Press, 71–89.

Spence, M. (1975), 'Monopoly, Quality, and Regulation', *Bell Journal of Economics* 6: 417–29.

Spence, M. (1977), 'Nonlinear Prices and Welfare', *Journal of Public Economics* 8: 1–18.

Spremann, K. (1978), 'On Welfare Implications and Efficiency of Entrance Fee Pricing', *Zeitschrift für Nationalökonomie/Journal of Economics* 38: 231–52.

Steiner, P.O. (1957), 'Peak Loads and Efficient Pricing', *Quarterly Journal of Economics* 71: 585–610.

Stevens, B. (1992), 'Prospects for Privatisation in OECD Countries', *National Westminister Bank Quarterly Review*, London.

Stiglitz, J.E. (1974), 'Incentives and Risk Sharing in Sharecropping', *Review of Economic Studies* 41: 219–55.

Sudit, E.F. (1979), 'Automatic Rate Adjustments Based on Total Factor Productivity Performance in Public Utility Regulation', in M.A. Crew (ed.), *Problems in Public Utility Economics and Regulation.* Lexington, Mass.: Heath, 55–71.

Telson, M.L. (1975), 'The Economics of Alternative Levels of Reliability for Electric Power Generation Systems', *Bell Journal of Economics* 6: 679–94.

Thiemeyer, T. (1964), *Grenzkostenpreise bei öffentlichen Unternehmen.* Cologne: Westdeutscher Verlag.

Tillmann, G. (1981), 'Efficiency in Economies With Increasing Returns', mimeo, Institute of Economics, University of Bonn.

Timmer, C.P. (1981), 'Is there 'Curvature' in the Slutsky Matrix?', *Review of Economics and Statistics* 63: 395–402.

Tinbergen, J. (1967), *Economic Policy: Principles and Design.* 4th edn. Amsterdam: North-Holland.

Tirole, J. (1988), *The Theory of Industrial Organization.* Cambridge, Mass.: MIT Press.

Tivey, L. (1966), *Nationalization in British Industry.* London: Jonathan Cape.

Tollison, R.D. (1982), 'Rent-Seeking: A Survey', *Kyklos* 35: 575–602.

Train, K.E. (1991), *Optimal Regulation. The Economic Theory of Natural Monopoly.* Cambridge, Mass.: MIT Press.

Tulkens, H. (1986a), 'The Performance Approach in Public Enterprise Economics: An Introduction and an Example', *Annals of Public and Co-operative Economy* 74: 429–43.

Tulkens, H. (1986b), 'La Performance Productive d'un Service Public: Définitions, Méthodes de Mesure et Application à la Régie des Postes en Belgique, l'Actualité Economie', *Revue d'Analyse Economique* 62: 306–35.

Tulkens, H. (1990), 'Non-Parametric Efficiency Analyses in Four Service Activities: Retail Banking, Municipalities, Courts and Urban Transit', mimeo CORE, Louvain-la-Neuve.

Tullock, G. (1967), 'The Welfare Costs of Tariffs, Monopolies, and Theft', *Western Economic Journal* 5: 224–32.

Turvey, R. (1968), *Optimal Pricing and Investment in Electricity Supply.* London: Allen & Unwin.

Turvey, R. (1971), *Economic Analysis and Public Enterprises.* London: Allen & Unwin.

Turvey, R., and **Anderson, D.** (1977), *Electricity Economics.* Baltimore, ML: Johns Hopkins University Press.

Ungern-Sternberg, T.R. von (1983), 'A Model of the Political Process with Party Loyalty', *Journal of Public Economics* 21: 389–96.

Usher, D. (1977), 'The Welfare Economics of the Socialization of Commodities', *Journal of Public Economics* 8: 151–68.

Varian, H.R. (1992), *Microeconomic Analysis.* 3rd edition. New York: Norton.

Vickers, J. (1987), 'A Note on Privatisation and Economic Efficiency', mimeo, Nuffield College, Oxford.

Vickers, J., and **Yarrow, G.** (1988), *Privatization: An Economic Analysis.* Cambridge, Mass.: MIT Press.

Vickers, J., and **Yarrow, G.** (1991), 'The British Electricity Experiment', *Economic Policy* 6 (issue 12): 187–232.

Vining, A.R., and **Boardman, A.E.** (1992), 'Ownership Versus Competition: Efficiency in Public Enterprise', *Public Choice* 73: 205–39.

Visscher, M.L. (1973), 'Welfare-Maximizing Price and Output with Stochastic Demand: Comment', *American Economic Review* 63: 224–9.

Vogelsang, I. (1988), 'Deregulation and Privatization in Germany', *Journal of Public Policy* 8: 195–212.

Vogelsang, I. (1989), 'Price Cap Regulation of Telecommunications Services: A Long-Run Approach', in M. Crew (ed.), *Deregulation and Diversification of Utilities.* Boston–Dordrecht: Kluwer, 21–42.

Vogelsang, I., and **Finsinger, J.** (1979), 'A Regulatory Adjustment Process for Optimal Pricing by Multiproduct Monopoly Firms', *Bell Journal of Economics,* 10: 157–71.

Wahlroos, B. (1984/5), 'Monopoly Welfare Losses under Uncertainty', *Southern Economic Journal* 51: 429–42.

Ware, R. (1986), 'A Model of Public Enterprise with Entry', *Canadian Journal of Economics* 19: 642–55.

Watzke, R. (1982), 'The Peak-Load Problem', mimeo, Institute of Economics, University of Bonn.

Weiss, Y. (1993): 'Inflation and Price Adjustment: A Survey of Findings from Micro-Data', in E. Sheshinski and Y. Weiss (eds.), *Optimal Pricing, Inflation, and the Cost of Price Adjustment.* Cambridge, Mass.: MIT Press, 3–17.

Weiss, L.W., and **Klass, M.W.** (1986), *Regulatory Reform – What Actually Happened.* Boston – Toronto: Little, Brown & Co.

Weyman-Jones, Th.G. (1992): 'Regulating the UK Electricity Utilities: The Issue of Economic Efficiency', mimeo, University of Bradford.

Weymark, J.A. (1979), 'A Reconciliation of Recent Results in Optimal Taxation Theory', *Journal of Public Economics* 12: 171–89.

Whitehead, C. (1988), *Introduction, Theory and Practice*, in C. Whitehead (ed.), *Reshaping the Nationalized Industries.* New Brunswick, NJ: Transaction Books, 1–21.

White Paper (1967), 'Nationalised Industries: A Review of Economic and Financial Objectives', Cmnd 3437, Her Majesty's Stationery Office, London.

White Paper (1978), 'The Nationalised Industries', Cmnd 7131, Her Majesty's Stationery Office, London.

Wiegard, W. (1978), *Optimale Schattenpreise und Produktionsprogramme für öffentliche Unternehmen.* Berne: Lang.

Wiegard, W. (1979), 'Optimale Preise für öffentliche Güter bei gegebenen Preisstrukturen in der privaten Wirtschaft', *Finanzarchiv* N.F. 37: 270–92.

Wiegard, W. (1980), 'Theoretische Überlegungen zu einer schrittweisen Reform der indirekten Steuern', *Jahrbuch für Sozialwissenschaft* 31: 1–20.

Williamson, O.E. (1966), 'Peak Load Pricing and Optimal Capacity Under Indivisibility Constraints', *American Economic Review* 56: 810–27.

Willig, R.D. (1978), 'Pareto-Superior Nonlinear Outlay Schedules', *Bell Journal of Economics* 9: 56–69.

Wilson, L.S., and **Katz, M.L.** (1983), 'The Socialization of Commodities', *Journal of Public Economics* 20: 347–56.

Wilson, R. (1993), *Nonlinear Pricing.* Oxford: Oxford University Press.

Windisch, R. (1987), 'Privatisierung natürlicher Monopole: Theoretische Grundlagen und Kriterien', in R. Windisch (ed.), *Privatisierung natürlicher Monopole im Bereich von Bahn, Post und Telekommunikation.* Tübingen: Mohr (Siebeck), 1–146.

Wintrobe, R. (1987), 'The Market for Corporate Control and the Market for Political Control', *Journal of Law, Economics and Organization* 3 (Fall): 435–48.

Worcester, D.A. Jr. (1973), 'New Estimates of the Welfare Loss to Monopoly, United States: 1956–69', *Southern Economic Journal* 40: 234–46.

Yarrow, G. (1985), 'Welfare Losses in Oligopoly and Monopolistic Competition', *The Journal of Industrial Economics* 33: 515–29.

Yarrow, G. (1986), 'Privatization in Theory and Practice', *Economic Policy* 1: 324–77.

Yarrow, G. (1993), 'Privatization in the UK' in V.V. Ramanadham (ed.), *Constraints and Impacts of Privatization*. London and New York: Routledge, 64–80.

Author Index

Acton, J.P. 186, 428

Aharoni, Y. 9, 413

Allen, K. 14, 431

Anderson, D. 186, 434

Armstrong, M. 287, 289, 413

Arrow, K.J. 196, 286, 413

Atkinson, A.B. 41, 78, 413

Attali, J. 15, 17, 413

Auerbach, A.J. 353, 413

Aumann, R.J. 135, 242, 245, 246, 413

Averch, H. 269, 270, 275, 278, 413

Backhaus, J. 15, 429

Báger, G. 32, 413

Bailey, E.E. 5, 69, 264, 269, 271, 275, 276, 413, 414

Baron, D.P. 51, 183, 306, 413

Barten, A.P. 356, 414

Baumol, W.J. 5, 16, 121, 232, 250, 264, 276, 414

Bawa, V.S. 275, 276, 414

Beato, P. 122, 387, 390, 414

Beesley, M.E. 414

Berg, S.V. 270, 414

Bergson, A. 60, 61, 83, 154, 414

Bertrand J. 397

Billera, L.J. 138, 242, 414, 415

Bizaguet, A. 400–3

Blanchard, O. 33, 415

Boardman, A.E. 35, 54, 55, 415, 434

Böhm, V. 356, 414

Boiteux, M. *v*, 1, 37, 63, 67, 71, 73, 74, 79, 81, 85, 91, 92, 94, 119, 120, 121, 122, 127, 137, 141, 144, 146–50, 152, 153, 167, 176, 186, 187, 191, 252, 269, 270, 272, 280, 301, 313, 317, 326, 329, 332, 341, 346, 355, 357, 415

Bolton, P. 33, 415

Borcherding, T.E. 53, 56, 415

Borensztein, E. 33, 415

Bös, D. *v*, *vii–viii*, 18, 25, 29, 32, 33, 34, 50, 51, 54, 56, 68, 85, 86, 124, 134, 143, 147, 148, 199, 217, 221, 224, 225, 231, 242, 245, 262, 279, 284, 286, 287, 292, 293, 294, 300, 302, 308, 318, 322, 370, 371, 389, 390, 395, 396, 415, 416

Bös, J. 20, 416

Bouin, O. 33, 417

Boyd, C.W. 53, 417

Bradford, D.F. 414

Bradley, I. 287, 417

Braeutigam, R.R. 278, 417

Brander, J.A. 353, 417

Brennan, T.J. 268, 288, 417

Brown, D.J. 123, 417

Brown, G. jr. 188, 417

Brown, S.J. 134, 354, 417

Buccola, S.T. 46, 417

Bumpass, D.L. 60, 429

Cabral, L.M.B. 286, 417

Subject Index